Understanding Social Work Research

Understanding Social Work Research

Betty G. Dawson
Memphis State University

Morris D. Klass
Memphis State University

Rebecca F. Guy
Memphis State University

Charles K. Edgley
Oklahoma State University

Allyn and Bacon

Boston   London   Toronto   Sydney   Tokyo   Singapore

Series Editor: Karen Hanson
Series Editorial Assistant: Laurie Frankenthaler
Production Administrator: Annette Joseph
Production Coordinator: Holly Crawford
Editorial-Production Service: Linda Zuk, WordCrafters Editorial Services, Inc.
Manufacturing Buyer: Megan Cochran
Cover Administrator: Linda K. Dickinson
Cover Designer: Suzanne Harbison

This textbook is printed on recycled, acid-free paper.

Library of Congress Cataloging-in-Publication Data
Understanding social work research / Betty Dawson ... [et al.].
    p.   cm.
    Includes bibliographical references and index.
    ISBN 0-205-12814-9
    1. Social service—Research.   I. Dawson, Betty.
    HV11.U38   1991
    361.3'2'072—dc20   90-48437
                                                              CIP

Printed in the United States of America

10 9 8 7 6 5 4 3 2 1   96 95 94 93 92 91

Acknowledgments

pp. 68, 69, 70, 71, 74, 75, 76, 77, 78, 80, and 82 reprinted with permission of The Free Press, a Division of Macmillan, Inc. from *Social Work Treatment: Interlocking Theoretical Approaches*, 3rd ed., Francis J. Turner, Editor. Copyright © 1986 by The Free Press.

Text pages 63, 64, 73, 246, and Table 12.1 from *Social Service Review* 62 (March 1988), by Peile, published by The University of Chicago. © 1988 by The University of Chicago.

pp. 254, 264–65, 267, and 270–72 from *Research in Education: A Conceptual Introduction*, 2nd ed. by

James H. McMillan and Sally Schumacher. Copyright © 1984 by James H. McMillan and Sally Schumacher. Reprinted by permission of Scott, Foresman and Company.

pp. 4–5, 64, 73, and 262 from Bradford W. Sheafor, Charles R. Horejsi, and Gloria A. Horejsi, *Techniques and Guidelines for Social Work Practice*. Copyright © 1988 by Allyn and Bacon. Reprinted with permission.

Credits continued on page 446, which constitutes an extension of the copyright page.

Contents

Preface   xi

I   Formulating Research Questions

1   Research: The Link in Professional Social Work Education   1

Why Research Is Relevant, 1
Social Work Research in Perspective, 8
References, 10

2   What Is Research and Why Do We Do It?   11

The Nature of the Research Process, 11
The Scientific Attitude: Myths and Realities, 19
References, 31

3   Choosing and Formulating a Research Question   32

Defining Terms, 33
The Role of Values in Choosing and Formulating Research Questions, 34
Factors Influencing the Choice of a Research Question, 35
Formulating a Research Question, 37
Evaluating a Research Question, 58
References, 62

4   The Role of Theory in Social Work   63

Science and Social Work, 63
The Relationship between Theory and Practice, 65
The Development of Social Work Theory, 68
What Is a Theory?, 70
Paradigms, 72
Dominant Models of Practice, 73

Conclusion, 82
References, 83

5   The Ethics of Social Work Research   86

Ethics as an Urgent Issue, 86
Current Ethical Considerations, 88
Social Work and Social Science Research, 89
Federal Influences on Research Ethics, 90
Common Ethical Issues, 91
Toward a Resolution, 96
References, 97

6   Choosing a Research Design   99

Research Design Defined, 100
The Relation of Theory to the Research Design, 101
The Importance of the Research Design, 101
Factors to Consider in Choosing a Research Design, 102
General Considerations, 118
The Research Design and Data Collection, 119
References, 120

7   Hypotheses and Evidence   122

Hypotheses Defined, 123
Hypothesis Construction as It Relates to Theory, 124
Hypotheses Testing Typology, 126
Characteristics of Hypotheses, 127
Testing Hypotheses, 131
Triangulation, 132
Use of Evidence in Hypothesis Testing, 133
The Hypothesis Cycle, 136
References, 139

II   Measurement, Data Collection, and Analysis

8   The Process of Measurement   140

The Meaning of Measurement, 141
Why Measure?, 141
Levels of Measurement, 143
Single Indicators as Measures, 146
Scales as Measures, 147
Comparison of Scaling Techniques, 159
Nonreactive Measures, 159
The Theory of Measurement, 161

Types of Errors, 162
Sources of Measurement Error, 163
Evaluating the Adequacy of a Measure, 166
References, 170

9   Sampling   172

Some Basic Definitions, 172
Why Sample?, 173
The Representativeness of a Sample, 174
Sampling Theory: How It Works, 177
Sampling Plans, 182
What Size Sample?, 189
References, 194

10   The Experiment   195

"Deviance in the Dark," 196
Creating Equal Groups, 198
Technical Considerations Concerning the Independent Variable, 200
Two Experimental Designs, 202
Laboratory versus Field Experiment, 204
Field Experiment, 205
Internal Validity, 207
External Validity, 210
True Experiment versus Quasi-Experiment, 211
Quasi-Experiment, 211
References, 212

11   The Survey   213

The Survey Defined, 214
Planning Your Survey Design, 218
Constructing a Questionnaire, 222
Self-Administered Questionnaires, 233
The Mailed Questionnaire, 234
Face-to-Face Interviews, 235
Telephone Interviews, 238
The Interview versus the Self-Administered Questionnaire, 239
Strengths and Weaknesses of Survey Research, 239
Using Secondary Data to Supplement Interview Data, 240
References, 242

12   Qualitative Research   243

Introduction, 243
Historical Perspective, 245
Similarities and Differences, 247

Field Research, 251
Historical Research, 253
Content Analysis, 260
Comparative Analysis, 263
Single-Subject Design, 264
Program Evaluation, 268
References, 272

13   Data Reduction and Organization   275

The Meaning of Datum/Data, 276
Why We Organize and Reduce Data, 276
The Role of the Computer in Data Reduction, 277
An Introduction to the Computer, 280
Preparing the Data for Computer Input, 282
Formatting the Data for Computer Input, 285
Keypunching the Data, 288
Editing the Data for Errors, 291
Storing the Data, 293

III   Using Data to Answer Research Questions

14   Analyzing Data: Descriptive Statistics   295

The Role of Statistical Methods in the Research Process, 296
Discrete and Continuous Data, 297
Discrete Frequency Distributions, 298
Continuous Frequency Distribution, 302
Descriptive Summary Measures, 306

15   Analyzing Data: Inferential Statistics   316

The Normal Curve, 317
The Standard Normal Curve, 319
The Standard Normal Curve as a Probability Distribution, 320
The t Test for Two Independent Samples, 324
The F Test for Three or More Independent Samples, 325
Correlation and Regression, 328

16   The Interpretation and Consequences of Research Data   345

Back to Paradigms, 346
The Consequences of Research, 352
Inductive and Deductive Interpretations, 355
References, 358

17 Writing the Research Report 359

Why Write a Research Report?, 359
Factors to Consider When Writing, 360
Characteristics of Scientific Writing, 361
Organization of the Research Report, 362
Rewriting the Research Report, 381
References, 382

Appendix A Using SPSS X and SPSS PC+ 383

Appendix B Tables 417

Glossary 430

Index 439

Preface

This text on social work research is written specifically for students at either the undergraduate or graduate level who are beginning the journey toward an understanding of social work research. We have found that many texts on research are difficult to read, abstract to the point of being far removed from a social worker's day-to-day practice, and sometimes lacking in a step-by-step approach to research considerations. The four authors, combining areas of expertise from years of teaching, research, agency-based experience, clinical practice, and administration, have written this text to address the need for a straightforward, easy-to-read text that does not sacrifice the integrity of the research process by oversimplification. Likewise, through examples and illustrations, we seek to remain close to the social worker's reality in daily experience in social service agencies and programs. Through references and studies from social work literature, as well as from classical and representative studies from sociology, social psychology, and anthropology, we attempt to illustrate the nature and usefulness of various research approaches. Examples and illustrations from areas and issues clearly pertinent to current social work practice help students make connections between theory and practice. These areas include aging, women's issues, diverse sexual orientation, homelessness, problem pregnancy, marriage and divorce, and child welfare.

Particularly noteworthy is the organization of this book in a manner that walks the student through the systematic processes of addressing the question of the value of research for social workers, consideration and development of the research question, ethical issues related to the use of human subjects, design issues that emanate from the purpose and focus of the research question, the varieties of data collection methods, data analysis and interpretation procedures, and the importance of report writing.

Specifically, Chapters 1 and 2 center on why social workers need to develop knowledge and skills that enable them to understand the research produced by others, and to undertake research activities within the agencies and programs in which they are employed. Upon this foundation, Chapters 3 and 4 focus on the nature of problem solving and decision making in selecting and refining a research question. Chapter 3 emphasizes how to conduct a review of relevant literature. Chapter 4 is distinctive in its discussion of the major paradigms and paradigm variations (i.e., schools of social work practice) that have characterized our profession since its inception. Efforts are made to show how theory and research design interface at this point. Chapter 5 gives prominent consideration to the importance of professional social work ethics and values inherent in the development of any research project. A discussion of the concept of informed consent, and of the potential abuses for clients involved in research, is included. Additionally, the text draws from the standards and functions of two national professional social work organizations—the National Association of Social Workers and the Council on Social Work Education—as guides for ethical decision-making.

Chapter 6 takes the student through the process of choosing a research design appropriate for the purpose of answering the research question, and gives an overview of both quantitative and qualitative designs, with their advantages and disadvantages. The importance of hypothesis formulation and the hypothesis "cycle" form the thrust of Chapter 7. Chapters 8 through 11 look at the essential features of measurement. Levels of measurement, various scales, and types of errors are discussed in Chapter 8. Chapter 9 provides a thorough discussion of sampling theory and techniques. The various types of experimental designs are the focus in Chapter 10, and an overview of the survey method is provided in Chapter 11. Chapter 12 presents an overview of the uses and methods of qualitative research designs; their growing importance in social work research endeavors is highlighted. To complete the research process, Chapters 13 through 17 provide a comprehensive and detailed discussion of data reduction and organization, analysis of data through descriptive statistics and inferential statistics, formulation of the interpretation of research findings, and finally, the writing of the research report.

Mary Belenky et al. have written that "all knowledge is constructed, and the knower is an intimate part of the known." As students study the research process, are informed from the findings of scholarly journals, texts, and reports, and initiate and finalize their own research endeavors, they are, in the final analysis, learning about their world, about others, and about themselves. It is at this point of interface that social work practice and research processes find their commonality, and meaning is created, and it is to this end that this text is offered.

The authors gratefully acknowledge the kind patience and supportive encouragement of Karen Hanson and Laurie Frankenthaler, of the editorial department at Allyn and Bacon. Their help has been invaluable in the process of completing this text. The authors are grateful to the Literary Executor of the late Sir Ronald A. Fisher, F.R.S., to Dr. Frank Yates, F.R.S., and to the Longman Group Ltd., London, for permission to reprint Appendix Tables 3, 4, and 5 from their book *Statistical Tables for Biological, Agricultural and Medical Research* (6th Edition, 1974).

**Understanding
Social Work
Research**

Chapter 1

Research: The Link in Professional Social Work Education

Why research is relevant
   Social workers as "doers"
   Social workers as "learners"
   Social workers as "helpers"

Social work research in
   perspective

No profession can afford any equivocation on the importance of research.
—DAVID FANSHEL

Why Research Is Relevant

"All I want to do is to learn how to help people. Why do I have to study research?" This clear, simple, and logical inquiry is often one of the first discussion items in a beginning social work research course. With or without this question, research faculty tend to present some form of an answer to it in their introductory lectures. In fact, such concern has been clearly articulated in two recent articles: "Pedagogy of the Perturbed: Teaching Research to the Reluctant" [1], and "Why Are They Different? Background, Occupational Choice, Institutional Selection and Attitudes of Social Work Students" [2].

    So you see, the answer to this initial question is considered to be of vital importance. The process of appreciating the essential nature of scientific inquiry, and the practical uses and applications of the research process, are quite a challenge for anyone. But for the social worker, there needs to be an understanding of how research is related to, and lends support to, what we actually do with clients in our everyday practice.

Obviously, you have already begun to form a picture of what social work is all about. You have drawn some conclusions about how one prepares to become a knowledgeable and skilled helper of people. But whether you recognize it or not, learning about people and helping them with their problems and needs requires a knowledge of social research methods and skills.

As a student of social work, you will be expected to form some understanding of the critical interface between scientific inquiry and social work practice. In addition, you will be expected to develop some degree of skill in analyzing and utilizing research findings (i.e., be a "consumer" of research) and in evaluating and assessing your own practice using some of these skills.

When assessing the question of why social workers need to study research, we notice immediately a meaningful pattern in the use of three action phrases that appear to give direction to professional goals: (1) to do, (2) to learn, and (3) to help. A careful scrutiny of these three aspects will provide us with some information with which to understand this vital interface.

Social Workers as "Doers"

Social work, as all professions such as law, medicine, and teaching, is a direct service activity that responds to people seeking some form of assistance. It should be noted that this professional social work orientation is in sharp contrast with the *academic study* of theoretical abstractions such as social relationships and patterns of societal interactions which are the focus of interest for the social science student.

Social work is an action-oriented, people-centered "profession," not a social science, although it does utilize a social science foundation. **Social work practitioners influence, enable, or facilitate change processes which empower vulnerable and at-risk individuals, groups, or communities to actualize their potentials.** Social workers serve real people and respond to the whole person as a living system. These service interventions are not carried out for the purpose of analyzing or organizing theoretical and abstract formulations. The direct service goals of social workers are designed to engage internal and external human resources in working with individuals, families, groups, organizations, and communities in planned change processes. Social service interventions address such quality-of-life issues as enabling single parents to obtain appropriate day care for their children so that they can participate in employment training opportunities; influencing drug-abusing teenagers to enter mental health counseling; initiating group support for persons with AIDS; or organizing public-housing residents to participate in activities to improve their homes. These actions are direct social services, the social work *doing*. The social worker, as a doer, makes planned, conscious, and disciplined use of self as a change agent who interacts with a variety of human systems [3].

Let's take a closer look at how the creative use of the social worker's personal self, professional education, and research knowledge interrelate. This professional use of self is complemented by the social worker's scientific orientation as described by William Reid [4], who notes that while social work practice is clearly an art, scientific orientations are drawn upon by the practitioner. This includes systematic and planful use of terms and concepts as well as appropriate collection of data, use of inferences, alternative explanations, and other applications of research-based knowledge with which to evaluate practice outcomes.

The provision of social services, the *art of doing*, is neither casual nor by chance for the professionally trained social worker. While good intentions and a caring concern are important, they are insufficient for providing competent social services. Social work practice requires careful assessment and selective use of empirically based information generated by research. This means that *doing* social work is a methodical and systematically structured endeavor using appropriate knowledge, skills, and prescribed guidelines for value-based ethical behavior.

Understanding the *doing* of social work also meshes with the on-the-job performance standards expected for professional social workers. This is a paramount issue for those in our profession. The specific organization that addresses this basic area of accountability is the National Association of Social Workers. The NASW sets forth a written Code of Ethics that defines appropriate ethical behavior for its members. In regard to maintaining professional competence, and the utilization of research methods and findings, the Code specifies:

> Development of Knowledge—The social worker should take responsibility for identifying, developing, and fully utilizing knowledge for professional practice.
>
> 1. The social worker should base practice upon recognized knowledge relevant to social work.
> 2. The social worker should critically examine, and keep current with emerging knowledge .... [5]

Thus, the Code of Ethics recognizes the need for members of the profession to be actively involved in contributing to the body of knowledge from which service interventions are designed and implemented.

Social Workers as "Learners"

The educational program that prepares you for professional social work practice has been continually evolving since the early 1900s. This evolution has been in response to diverse stimuli within the profession, as well as to changes in society in the form of new information, and political, economic, and social realities. The way professional groups ensure orderly and systematic changes in those educational processes that prepare future members to deal with these diverse changes is through *accreditation bodies*. The Council on Social Work Education, the national accrediting body for social work education, is organized to give leadership and service to social work education through such activities as standard-setting procedures, site visits, consultation, conferences, workshops, research, and special projects. Thus, the Council oversees and monitors social work education at all levels to achieve a continuous updating of relevant content [6]. The Council has responsibility for, and is concerned with both quality and quantity issues at undergraduate and graduate levels, as well as the profession's continued relevance to society [7]. This requires CSWE to study and evaluate systematically, in relation to defined educational standards, all college and university programs that have undergraduate and graduate social work programs. These standards address five content areas—human behavior in the social environment, practice skills, research methods, field work practicum, and social policy. Both the "doing" and the "learning" components of professional social work can be attributed to one or some combination of these five categories of social work curricular content. Additionally, research is often designed to concentrate on developing knowledge related to one of the five curricular areas. Thus, you see there are specific kinds of social work knowledge to learn and to apply in professional practice.

Particularly important is the strong emphasis on values and ethics in providing social services [8]. Interestingly, the basic principles of social science relating to the involvement of human subjects in research projects incorporate *ethical standards*. These principles stress protection for human participants that parallels social work values, including specification of methods to assure confidentiality, clear descriptions of possible negative effects, and informed consent forms signed by those involved. The dignity and worth of human beings, a primary value-set for social workers, has been a primary evolving concern of scientists undertaking medical and social research. More about this important aspect of research endeavors will be discussed in Chapter 5.

This concern for human subjects on the part of researchers was in reaction to Nazi experiments and holocaust atrocities documented in the war crimes trials of 1946 which led to the Nuremberg Code, "... the first internationally recognized code for research" [9]. Social science researchers, out of concern for safeguarding the rights and well-being of individuals who volunteer to be subjects of behavioral or biomedical research, have developed comprehensive programs to protect human beings. Historical events in both social work and social science sectors, as expressed through their respective ethical codes, have served to influence "principles of respect, beneficence, and justice" [10]. Throughout this text a number of linkages between social work problem solving and scientific methodology will be emphasized to illustrate examples of shared values and principles of working with people.

Social work students must also give particular attention to another component of professional learning that emphasizes the creative and focused use of what is known as **practice wisdom.** This kind of knowledge represents service information and professional behavior which has been accumulating over the years. It has been *experientially* "tested" and handed down by social work practitioners to each new generation of social workers. The learning of practice wisdom is also required of you as a student majoring in social work. It is a part of becoming "socialized" into the profession. However, you will discover that much of practice wisdom has not been validated through the use of objective and carefully formulated research designs. A word of caution is urged by Sheafor and his co-authors:

Inherent in professional socialization is pressure to perform in particular ways. It moves members of a profession toward a sameness that, although desirable in many respects, must be weighted against the importance of preserving one's uniqueness. [11]

A complex and challenging aspect of practice wisdom is the reality that one must become familiar with this kind of information while simultaneously maintaining an awareness of its limitations as expressed by Reid and Smith:

> We have reference to statements that would be useful, if true, but their truth is not apparent and substantiating evidence is lacking …. Some assertions may be backed by a considerable amount of carefully evaluated evidence sifted from practice experience; others may be based on biased impressions of unrepresentative examples. [12]

To illustrate, practice wisdom has stressed, from early in our historical development, the importance of the social worker demonstrating a nonjudgmental, accepting attitude. The social worker activates this principle through verbal and nonverbal behavior, affirming the dignity and worth of each individual served. Such behavior is seen as desirable because it is believed to be an effective way of building rapport and facilitating appropriate change. Subsequent research has borne this out until it is no longer questioned. On the other hand, until recently, practice wisdom concerning alternative sexual lifestyles tended to label nonconforming behavior as inevitably deviant, dysfunctional, marginal, and/or sick. However, research findings generated by social workers, psychologists, and psychiatrists provide strong evidence that currently indicates that sexual orientation, in and of itself, is unrelated to mental disorder. In other words, research findings served to offset long-held practice wisdom beliefs which now have been shown to be inaccurate or biased [13].

Social Workers as "Helpers"

Social work is recognized as the cornerstone of the helping professionals in the welfare field. Social work students are interested in direct and personal interactions with consumers of social services [14]. You care about, and have empathy for, vulnerable and at-risk individuals. You see social work as a profession with skills to help change barriers that deny qualitative living and opportunity for self-actualization [15]. Wanting to help people is a laudable and altruistic wish.

How is research connected to this praiseworthy stance? Scientific methods may seem too far removed from people-to-people interactions. Human warmth, caring, common sense, and good intuition feel much more like the activity that can make a difference in relating to troubled and stressed human beings. What on earth can dry, cold statistics and wordy, difficult-to-read research reports possibly add to people-helping interventions? As a student of social work these are appropriate issues for you to raise.

There are some effective, informative examples with which to demonstrate the usefulness of understanding research methods and skills. One component of the response requires us to look at established societal norms concerning the service-providing professions. As discussed earlier, social workers intervene in problematic situations using appropriate knowledge, practice skills, values, and ethical guidelines. Under these circumstances, society has demanded increasing accountability for qualitative performances by the individual practitioner, as well as from institutions such as schools, hospitals, and social agencies [16]. There is a national movement for professional social workers to obtain state licensure as an effective way of ensuring competent practice.

Additionally, provisions of the NASW Code of Ethics reflect a standard of practice that requires continual updating of practitioner knowledge and skills. Resources for achieving greater professional competence are proliferating in both regional and national organizations offering annual conferences, workshops, seminars, and specialized training. Over thirty professional journals with varying thematic and theoretical content are published to serve the social work community. The articles presented in the publications listed in Figure 1.1 focus directly on social work practice and research. From Figure 1.1, you can see how research findings are pertinent, essential resources for the practice of professional social work at all educational levels and in a variety of fields of practice.

FIGURE 1.1   Journals Publishing Social Work Research

General Subjects

Journal of Sociology and Social Welfare
New England Journal of Human Services
Social Service Review
Social Thought
Social Work

Field of Practice

Child Welfare
Children and Youth Services
Health and Social Work
Human Services in a Rural Environment
Journal of Gerontological Social Work
Journal of Social Work and Human Sexuality
Law and Social Work Quarterly
Public Welfare
School Social Work Quarterly
Social Work in Education
Social Work in Health Care
Women in Social Work

International and Foreign

British Journal of Social Work
Canadian Journal of Social Work Education
Canadian Welfare
Indian Journal of Social Work
International Child Welfare
International Social Work
Journal of International and Comparative Social Welfare
Social Work Today
Social Worker–Travailleur Social

Methods of Practice

Administration in Mental Health
Administration in Social Work
Clinical Social Work Journal
Clinical Supervisor
Journal for Specialists in Groupwork
Journal of Social Science Research
Journal of Social Work Supervision
Social Casework
Social Work Research and Abstracts
Social Work with Groups

Social Work Education and
School of Social Work Journals

Areté (University of South Carolina)
Iowa Journal of Social Work (University of Iowa)
Journal of Applied Social Sciences (Case Western Reserve University)
Journal of Continuing Social Work Education
Journal of Social Service Research (Washington University, St. Louis)
Journal of Social Work Education
Journal of Teaching in Social Work
Smith College Studies in Social Work (Smith College)
Social Development Issues (University of Iowa)
Social Group Work Practice (University of Connecticut)
Tulane Studies in Social Welfare (Tulane University)

Source: Bradford W. Sheafor, Charles R. Horejsi, and Gloria A. Horejsi, *Techniques and Guidelines for Social Work Practice* (Boston: Allyn and Bacon, 1988), pp. 161–3.

Optimally, *helping* is logically and necessarily linked with knowing and understanding research methods. Thus, the helping process requires not only a giving, personal involvement from the professional social worker, but also a commitment to increasing knowledge through the use of professional literature. This is intrinsic to one's professional development, and is, as our discussion suggests, a more complex and challenging task than it might at first appear.

Research findings, in the context of professional practice, also provide information for the formulation of new social service policies. For example, research reveals that thousands of children are trapped in foster care arrangements that systematically deprive them of their basic needs for a permanent and stable family environment. A consequence of these findings led to the development of *permanency planning services* wherein progress toward appropriate planning for, and placement of abused and neglected children in adoptive homes is monitored by the courts. In short, the practice wisdom of exclusively using foster home care as the best solution to child-care problems was modified by the validated knowledge derived from social work research findings [17]. As Brigham noted, "uncritical transmission of what *is* is not neutral, nor is it objective; it supports the status quo. Essentially it does not help develop change ..." [18]. Obviously, *caring* alone is a necessary but insufficient condition in planning social services for children who are without families and need permanent homes. Knowledgeable and planful use of research findings can best serve the needs of children who require much more stability and nurturing than that provided by transitory, nonpermanent foster home placements.

Witkin and Gottschalt have commented on the major tasks associated with evaluating research theory in social work:

> The development of a meaningful scientific framework for social work research requires an approach that reflects contemporary understandings of social scientific thought and is consistent with the values of the profession ... a perspective that (1) neither limits science to a narrowly defined empiricism nor leads to epistemological anarchy (i.e., "anything goes"), and (2) can accommodate the distinctive nature and mission of social work. [19]

Therefore, within the context of the foregoing discussion, we return to our original premise—social workers as *doers, learners,* and *helpers.* Hopefully, you now have some perspective in regard to the essential role that research methods must play in contributing to a well-rounded education for social work students. Under societal conditions of rapidly accelerating technological change, the professional social worker has increasingly complex assignments to fulfill. Information generated by research will take on greater significance in the professional's effort to stay abreast of the latest developments regarding service consumers, as well as planning and service options for responding to rapidly changing groups [20]. The social worker, when creatively approaching the absence of society's resources or the presence of social barriers, utilizes valid and reliable research findings. Furthermore, professionals will have opportunities during their careers to participate in studies of social service effectiveness and efficiency undertaken by social work agencies and other social scientists. Both public and private social services must systematically document their activities and provide evidence of evaluation efforts in order to be accountable to funding sources. Complementing these activities, the entry-level social worker is expected to be a skilled consumer of research reports and studies presented in the professional literature or at educational conferences and workshops.

As noted earlier, practice wisdom and long-cherished social work beliefs, theories, concepts, and principles are continuously being tested using the scientific methodologies of research investigation. For example, earlier social work intervention models, which assumed the universality of a nuclear family of mother, father, and children, have had to yield to the new realities of the growing number of one-parent households. Also, the practice of using fixed intervention patterns has dramatically shifted to using culturally and ethnically relevant helping alternatives [21]. Social work's use of "normalization" goals with developmentally delayed and retarded children has gained practice ascendency over more nonspecific service activities. The profession also now provides authentic acceptance and support for clients with nontraditional lifestyles, including the homeless, gays and lesbians, the physically handicapped, and others previously isolated or depreciated as recipients of social services. These are illustrations of specific ways in which research studies have influenced important new directions in social work practice.

So far, we have tried to assemble evidence to provide answers to the question of why the study of research methods is required for social work students. Answering this question is a multifaceted task because social work is a multidimensional and evolving profession. As a learned discipline, it must continually define and transmit to new generations of practitioners an updated, relevant body of knowledge. Social work does not have a single theory, but draws upon a number of theoretical domains (see Chapter 4). These theories include biological, psychological, sociological, economic, and political science bases of knowledge synthesized from fundamental research findings. Social work practice, education, and research is continually attempting to incorporate new social science findings at the interface of these endeavors.

This text is organized to provide clear, simple, and logical information about research methods. It is oriented to the student with a minimal social science research background. The content is designed to provide illustrative material specifically linked to entry-level social work practice. Later chapters will move you directly into an examination of the research process and an in-depth discussion of why and how it is operationalized. The nature of the research process is defined in relation to social work practice knowledge, and vocabulary that may be new to the student is introduced along with pertinent research terms. It is important to note at this point that social work research must always conform to the same standards of methodological rigor and interpretation as that strived for in the social sciences; therefore, the principles inherent in the attitude of scientific inquiry are incorporated throughout the text.

Social Work Research in Perspective

The social work orientation to research requires consideration of the profession as an emerging discipline that is responsive to both internal and external stimuli. This has led to changes, transitions, and adaptations. The structures and functions of the National Association of Social Workers and the Council on Social Work Education have continuously used research surveys to identify various needs and problems of practitioners, as well as recipients of services and members of other disciplines:

> Researchers and practitioners need to cooperate in order to marshall the facts and figures which will move the policymakers and legislators—numbers talk! Doctors, teachers, mental health professionals, lawyers, judges and social workers need to speak the same language so they can work as a team to help families they are concerned about. [22]

Over a decade ago, the Council on Social Work Education, with a keen awareness of the social work student's confusion about studying research methods, resolutely acted to address this thorny educational issue. The CSWE established a project on Research Utilization in Social Work Education and held a conference for practitioners and researchers from both academic and practice settings. "The general purpose of the conference was to review the state of the art on research utilization in social work education and to suggest directions for the future ..." [23]. This historic event included representatives from both NASW and the federal government.

The outcomes of this conference formally focused on several significant issues, but informally provided stimulus for research spin-offs which continue to the present time in both social work education and practice settings. For our purposes, it is informative to look at the consensus themes that emerged at this conference. The participants agreed upon the following principles:

1. There is a need to formulate empirically based practice models for social work in which research occupies an integral, essential role.

2. Social work research should be directed to finding solutions for the problems encountered by practitioners, with special emphasis on *developmental* research.

3. Social work students should be prepared for active participation in the research process, not only to be passive consumers of research.

4. The development of a new breed of practitioner–scientist should be cultivated and encouraged [24].

In the intervening years since this milestone conference, important dimensions of these four principles have taken shape. There has been the proliferation of more than thirty professional journals devoted specifically to the publication of social work research. Educational standards for over 400 undergraduate and more than 95 graduate programs have vigorously supported the integration of research findings and methodologies into every component of the CSWE standards for curriculum. Furthermore, both CSWE and NASW annually sponsor regional and national conferences on a variety of themes that consistently emphasize practice-oriented research reports. Research textbooks specifically designed for social work students have begun to emerge to meet a constantly expanding demand by social work educators and practitioners. These are strong indicators that reinforce the likelihood that the stage is set for the year 2000 to be a threshold for the development of a substantial cadre of the new breed of social workers as *practitioner–scientists*. It is our hope that your adventure in learning with this text will contribute to your interest in this exciting new direction!

References

1. Irwin Epstein, "Pedagogy of the Perturbed: Teaching Research to the Reluctant," *Journal of Teaching in Social Work*, Spring/Summer 1987.
2. Yael Enoch, "Why Are They Different? Background, Occupational Choice, Institutional Selection and Attitudes of Social Work Students," *Social Service Review*, Spring/Summer 1988.
3. Carel B. Germain, "An Ecological Perspective on Social Work in the Schools," in *School Social Work: Practice and Research Perspectives*, Robert T. Constable and John P. Flynn, eds. (Homewood, IL: Dorsey Press, 1982), pp. 3–5.
4. William J. Reid, "Research in Social Work," in *Encyclopedia of Social Work*, 18th ed., Anne Minahan, ed. (Silver Spring, MD: National Association of Social Workers, 1987), p. 474.
5. National Association of Social Workers Code of Ethics. Adopted by the 1979 Delegate Assembly of the National Association of Social Workers, effective July 1, 1980.
6. L. Diane Bernard, "Professional Associations: Council on Social Work Education," in *Encyclopedia of Social Work*, 18th ed., Anne Minahan, ed. (Silver Spring, MD: National Association of Social Workers, 1987), p. 330.
7. Bernard, *Encyclopedia of Social Work*, p. 331.
8. Martha W. Elliott, compiled by, *Ethical Issues in Social Work, An Annotated Bibliography* (New York: Council on Social Work Education, 1984), pp. v–vii.
9. *Evolving Concern: Protection for Human Subjects*, Videotape. Office for Protection from Research Risks, National Institutes of Health, Bethesda, MD 20892.
10. *Evolving Concern: Protection for Human Subjects*.
11. Bradford W. Sheafor, Charles R. Horejsi, and Gloria Horejsi, *Techniques and Guidelines for Social Work Practice* (Boston: Allyn and Bacon, 1988), p. 27.
12. William J. Reid and Audrey D. Smith, *Research in Social Work* (New York: Columbia University Press, 1981), pp. 26–27.
13. Hilda Hidalgo, Travis L. Peterson, and Natalie Jane Woodman, eds., *Lesbian and Gay Issues: A Resource Manual for Social Workers* (Silver Spring, MD: National Association of Social Workers, 1985), pp. 1–6.
14. Michael J. Austin, Judy Kopp, and Philip L. Smith, *Delivering Human Services: A Self-Instructional Approach*, 2nd ed. (New York: Longmans, 1986), pp. 44–45.
15. John S. McNeil and Roosevelt Wright, "Special Populations: Black, Hispanic, and Native American," in *Social Work and Mental Health*, James W. Callicut and Pedro J. Lecca, eds. (New York: Free Press, 1983), pp. 175–6.
16. Stephen Magura and Beth Silverman Moses, *Outcome Measures for Child Welfare Services: Theory and Applications* (Washington, DC: Child Welfare League of America, 1986), p. 1–2.
17. Erva Zucherman, *Child Welfare* (New York: Free Press, 1983), pp. 24–25.
18. Marian R. Pena, "Social Research: Transformative Agent or Keeper of the Status Quo?" *Cause and Function*, Richard Bell, Lynda Frank, Kris Perry, and Amy Siegel, eds. (San Francisco: School of Social Work Education, San Francisco State University, Spring 1988), p. 57.
19. Stanley L. Witkin and Shimon Gottschalt, "Alternative Criteria for Theory Evaluation," *Social Service Review*, June 1988, p. 211.
20. Betsy Ledbetter Hancock, *Social Work with Older People* (Englewood Cliffs, NJ: Prentice-Hall, 1987), pp. vi–viii.
21. Barbara Bryant Solomon, "How Do We Really Empower Families? New Strategies for Social Work Practitioners," in *Viewpoint* (Family Resource Coalition, FRC Report, 1985), p. 2.
22. Marcia Culver, "Special Conference Report: Empowering Families: A Celebration of Family Based Services," in *Prevention Report*, Marcia Culver, ed. (Iowa City, IA: National Resource Center on Family Based Services, The University of Iowa School of Social Work, Winter 1987/88), p. 2.
23. Allen Rubin and Aaron Rosenblatt, eds., *Sourcebook on Research Utilization* (New York: Council on Social Work Education, 1977), p. v.
24. Rubin and Rosenblatt, *Sourcebook on Research Utilization*, p. vi.

Chapter 2

What Is Research and Why Do We Do It?

The nature of the research process
  Research as human activity
  Some everyday sources of
    knowledge
  Puzzles and solutions
  Practice reflects shared beliefs
  The ongoing relationship
    between theory and
    research

A definition of methodology
  The need to study methodology
The scientific attitude: myths and
    realities
Traditional models of science
The practice of science
The promise and limitations of
    science

The next best thing to knowing something is knowing how to find it.
                                                    —SAMUEL JOHNSON

The Nature of the Research Process

This book, more than you might believe at the beginning, is about everyday things. For even though we are writing about the seemingly technical, often mysterious, and sometimes feared process of doing social work research, the procedures and issues we will be discussing are really a part of everyday activities. You have done the things between the covers of this book many times, even though you may have rarely thought about them in exactly the same way we will be talking about them here. So, in a very real sense, this book is about a topic you already know much about as well as use daily. And since you already know and have done many of the things described here, grasping them in the slightly different vocabulary of social science will not be as difficult as you may think.

One of our objectives in writing this book, then, is to help you think about social work research methods without losing sight of the fact that the research process is basically a systematized version of a set of activities experienced by almost everybody by virtue of the fact that they are curious, thinking, problem-solving creatures who live in the twentieth century, when social work research, its problems, and its products abound.

Research as Human Activity

If the purpose of research is to discover answers to questions by applying systematic procedures [1], then it can be said that some variety of research is common to all people everywhere. Curiosity has apparently led people for centuries to search for answers to the questions of how and why the world works as it does. Primitive people knew (sometimes far better than modern people do) the relationships among the stars, the tides, the seasons, and the occurrence of weather. Closer to home, the observation of patterns has sometimes led people to quite accurate predictions of weather just by watching the behavior of animals. An instructive test of such weather-predicting ability came a couple of years ago when an Iowa farmer challenged the local weather bureau to a contest. The farmer claimed that he could predict both short- and long-term weather changes more accurately by watching his goats and sheep than the weather bureau could with all of its sophisticated scientific instruments. The arrogant weather bureau took on the challenge, and careful records were kept over the course of a year. It was, as you may have guessed, no contest: the farmer and his goats won hands down.

Now, the Iowa farmer might not have been able to tell you in scientifically accurate terms exactly what his research procedure was, but he had one and it worked. In this sense, both the farmer and his animals were researchers, even though we are hardly recommending their methods as systematic research procedures. We can't do that, for part of good research is to be able to communicate one's procedures to others, and the farmer was not able to do that very well.

Nevertheless, the basic processes of social work research are *human processes*. They exist not simply in the world of nature, but in the natural world of human beings. We learn from patterns, and we are curious about the world around us. We recognize that one thing often does follow another, that prediction is possible, at least enough to make it a practical necessity for dealing with life. Not only do we predict, but we want to generalize from our own experiences and from the experiences of others. We hear a story about a man and we conclude, "Men are like that." We know that life is not just a random throw of the dice, that it involves pattern and regularity, and that despite the generally good advice that we treat everyone as individuals, nobody could really deal with anyone else without making inferences and using generalities, and making predictions based on what one has seen and understands about behavior, sex, race, education, money, culture, language, situations—the list is endless.

Some Everyday Sources of Knowledge

People everywhere have a store of knowledge. It is impossible to live in the world without using some kind of knowledge, even if it is sketchy, inaccurate, or just plain wrong. To examine how people obtain their information, then, is both useful and itself predictive, for if we know the sources of knowledge, we will be in a position to assess how much faith to place in them. There are three common sources of information that deserve mention: common sense, tradition, and authority.

Common Sense

We are told approvingly that a person has a large measure of common sense, or disapprovingly that another has a lot of book learning but no common sense. Common sense is, simply, what "everybody knows." Unfortunately, as a guide to reliable knowledge, common sense leaves much to be desired. Indeed, for years common sense told some people that the world was flat, that blacks were biologically inferior to whites, that if you made a lot of money it was proof that God was smiling on you, and that if you jumped out of an airplane with a parachute on you would suffocate before you touched the ground. Bergen Evans wrote a book entitled *The Natural History of Nonsense* [2], in which he cataloged a few of the more notorious fictions that for eons (and even to this day among some people in some places) passed themselves off as common sense. For example (p. 19):

1. Thunder sours milk.
2. Lightning never strikes twice in the same place.
3. Undertows and quicksand produce an irresistible suction that drags people down to their deaths.
4. Tornadoes have a dead center in which the law of gravity is inoperative.

As another example of the unreliability of common sense as a guide to knowledge, we might note all the commonsense phrases that are contradicted by other, equally commonsensical phrases. For example:

1. a. Look before you leap.
   b. He who hesitates is lost.
2. a. Repeat a lie often enough and people will believe it.
   b. Truth will prevail.
3. a. Out of sight, out of mind.
   b. Absence makes the heart grow fonder.
4. a. Opposites attract.
   b. Birds of a feather flock together.

Of course, there is at least a grain of truth in each of the preceding statements, and if they were subjected to proper research procedures, we could verify the grain of truth that is in them and also find out how they are *not* true as well as why they were so widely believed.

For example, there *is* a certain empirical truth to the idea that the earth is flat. The human being relying on his or her own senses and, without the perception afforded by advanced instruments and the abstractions of astronomy, concludes experientially that the world is flat. From the standpoint of everyday life, it is difficult to believe that an invisible force called gravity could keep us all from falling off an elliptical ball.

Similarly, the famous sucking force attributed to quicksand is probably a misunderstanding created by the fact that the bog makes a sucking sound when a large object is pulled out of it. But the suction is in the puller, not in the mire. Quicksand is about twice as buoyant as water, and if a person did not struggle and become fatigued, he would sink no higher than his armpits [3]. On the other hand, careful research would probably also show that people *do* struggle when in quicksand, and as a result sometimes go under. Most people's conception of quicksand probably comes from such reliable sources as old Tarzan movies.

As for lightning, it is far more likely to strike twice in the same place than not. The reason is that lightning passes through conductors, whose total surface constitutes only a very small part of the earth's surface. Evans reports that in the first ten years following its construction, the mast on top of the Empire State Building was struck by lightning some sixty-eight times. And people who have been struck by lightning are more likely to be struck again than people who have never had such a misfortune [4].

The notion that thunder sours milk is very simply a confusion between the thunder itself and the humid, stagnant air in which thunderstorms are most likely to occur. Souring is the result of bacterial action, and the bacteria are most likely to multiply in warm, moist air.

So, while common sense is not a very reliable guide to knowledge, the way in which common sense is arrived at is a legitimate concern of social science, and it has a profound effect on the way people behave. A theoretical point of view called ethnomethodology makes much of common sense, and we will discuss how it does this a bit later.

These examples all show the validity of Bertrand Russell's assertion that if an idea is part of common sense, there is at least as much chance that it is common nonsense as common sense.

Tradition

Another source of knowledge is tradition, and although it is similar to common sense in some respects, in other ways it is different. Common sense is always a part of tradition, but what is traditional is not always common sense. People everywhere have a knowledge base simply by virtue of the heritage that has been passed along to them by their culture. Previously obtained knowledge (including some gotten from scientific research) becomes the authority for new generations. None of the readers of this book figured out on his or her own that $E = mc^2$ or even exactly why 2 plus 2 equals 4. We come to accept these bits of knowledge along with millions of other bits because they are part of the conventional knowledge of the culture and the groups to which we belong. They "work" in our lives, largely because they *are* conventional. No one could possibly start from scratch and come anywhere close to knowing what modern men and women know. Knowledge is cumulative, and we are constantly building on the taken-for-granted knowledge of past generations. In this sense, the school system teaches not the truth—or even knowledge in the absolute sense of that word—but rather whatever is passing for it at a conventional moment in history. Although none of us could build very much knowledge on our own, the fact that much knowledge is simply traditional is often a stumbling block to further systematic inquiry. What do you do when you discover that you have learned something that completely refutes what has always been regarded as true? How do changes in knowledge occur, especially when the change is radical rather than trivial? The fact is, it *is* difficult to get a new idea across when it conflicts with what has traditionally been known.

Knowledge is not a static thing, but a continual process. Thus, anything held to be the case, no matter how compelling the research on which it is based, must be looked upon as tentative knowledge, based on the best possible research we have at the time. But few responsible researchers would claim that further research could not wash even the most cherished knowledge away.

Authority

Another common source of knowledge is authority. For generations, people have taken things to be true because of the authority of the church, the state, their mother or father, a close friend, or experts. In other words, something is true because of who said it. The last category deserves some special mention, because while many people can accept the notion that an idea is not necessarily so because the Pope says it is, these same people sometimes have difficulty applying that principle to those ideas supported by an expert in some particular field. In logic, this is technically known as an *ad hominem* fallacy—an argument that something is true or false because of who said it. And the fallacy is as mistaken when applied to researchers as when applied to popes.

On the other hand, like the previous sources of knowledge we have mentioned, the existence of authority as a source of truth is not without reason. It is usually impossible to track down information fully and to inform ourselves completely on our own when we make decisions. Therefore, part of the process of behaving as human beings in association with others is to rely on those who are presumably "in the know." When the runner Bill Rodgers wins the Boston Marathon, people might be more likely to believe him if he says that eating lots of yogurt is the secret to running twenty-six miles. They are less likely to accept the nutritional advice of even the most intelligent thinker on the subject who has never run farther than the refrigerator to grab another beer. In an age of degrees, certifications, celebrity status, and Nobel prizes, it is hard for us to understand that knowledge really respects none of this and that statements finally stand or fall on their own merits regardless of the authority of those who make them.

Puzzles and Solutions

The student of social work research methods might best understand the topic by thinking of it as a series of puzzles. One traditional way of seeing methods is simply as the vehicles in which we travel from a puzzle to its solution. We say *simply* because it has become increasingly apparent in recent years that the relationship between puzzles and solutions, between questions and answers, is much more complicated than we originally thought. Obviously, social work researchers conduct studies to find out as much as they can about a given problem in social service delivery. Are BSW social workers more likely to continue employment in the public welfare departments than MSW workers? What is the current attitude among members of the National Association of Social Workers toward AIDS? How well informed are child welfare workers regarding the guidelines for permanency planning for children in foster care? These are but a few of the thousands of questions that we have sought answers to with social work research over the years. But how is a problem derived? How do social workers know what to study? How do we know when we have found something meaningful for the practice of social work?

Our ways of thinking about these questions have undergone continuing change as social work research has gained increasing importance in the last two decades. As the various social sciences have evolved, social work researchers have drawn upon different frameworks. An important influence was the publication of a book in 1962 by Thomas Kuhn entitled *The Structure of Scientific Revolutions* [5]. Kuhn is a natural scientist who came to question the traditional scientific explanation of how research develops and how answers are found. Kuhn's work had a profound impact on the way we think about natural science, but if anything, its influence on social science methods used by researchers was even greater [6, 7].

The essence of Kuhn's book is the way in which changes in knowledge come about in science. According to the traditional view, presented in almost all introductory research methods books, science grows and changes in a progressive manner, with each advance building on those that preceded it. This building-block theory of knowledge conceives of science as a series of blocks, one carefully placed on top of the other, so that we slowly and incrementally move toward greater and greater levels of knowledge. Changes in scientific truths thus come slowly in a step-by-step fashion. Kuhn believes that this view of science is false. He asserts instead that this conception of the history of science is largely an illusion, created by the fact that each generation of scientists rewrites its textbooks to give the impression that the current stage of knowledge is the apex of what has been accumulated. In place of this incremental conception of science Kuhn advances the thesis that revolution marks the important changes in science. Truly major changes come about as a result of revolutions in the basic paradigms, or systems, of science.

Practice Reflects Shared Beliefs

Kuhn says that science takes the particular shape it does from the application of shared paradigms. More about the dominant paradigms in social work will be discussed in Chapter 4, but for the purposes of this discussion, a **paradigm** can be defined in its simplest form as **"the entire constellation of beliefs, values, techniques, and theories shared by the members of a scientific community"** [8]. These shared beliefs are strongly and directly operationalized into social work practice. For exam-

ple, many years ago in the social work practice field of adoptions, it was accepted as •
a basic "truth" that when placing a child with an adoptive family it was necessary to
maintain secrecy in order that the child and the adoptive parents would never know
the identity of the natural parents. Research evidence, as well as an increase in the
number of adopted children who were older and remembered their natural parents,
contributed to an empirically tested change in this shared belief. What was considered to be in the best interests of all parties began to change.

Over the years research studies accumulated. Typical of these studies is Depp's
work [9] which has focused on the reunion of adoptive children with their natural
parent(s). It concludes that (1) adoptees are more vulnerable than nonadoptees to
identity conflicts, (2) adoptive parents are capable of coming to appreciate the
adoptee's need for a reunion, and (3) regardless of whether positive or negative relationships existed between the adoptees and their adoptive parents prior to the reunion experience, it enhanced the adoptive relationship in one way or another.

Changes in the prevailing paradigms come about because no paradigm can
handle all of the possible questions the human mind is capable of asking or all of the
complexities of the human condition. New paradigms arise to handle these problems, and when a researcher gives up an old paradigm and embraces a new one, he
or she undergoes a kind of conversion experience, for such a decision can only be
made on faith [10].

The Ongoing Relationship between Theory and Research

Our discussion of paradigms has suggested the fact that we cannot really separate
theory from method, paradigm from procedure, assumptions from conclusions.
While social work research methods are an honest attempt to hold up a camera and
not a mirror to the world around us, we never really succeed, for every time we
click the shutter, we see part of ourselves in the picture. Does this mean that scientific research is impossible? Of course not, but it does mean that there is an ongoing relationship between our puzzles and our solutions, and it demonstrates that more
than lip service must be given to the role of theory in the research process. One of
the most deplorable situations in research methods courses is that they are typically
taught separately from theory courses; the two are seen essentially as distant enterprises that have only a peripheral bearing on each other. Although the professors
who teach them know better, students often see methods courses as "cooking
schools" in which one finds out how to mix up a research project. Ask most students
when they finish a project how their solutions related to their puzzles, and what
new puzzles were generated by their research, and they look bewildered. Cook-
books don't usually supply that kind of information.

Research methods are really part of larger paradigms that include theory, assumptions, goals, and perspectives, as well as techniques. To illustrate briefly some
of these connections, we can see what has been taking place in traditional social science and social work research. Stereotypical thinking and institutional sexism can
permeate the research process, affecting how the research questions are formulated,
how concepts are defined and variables operationalized, and how samples are se-

lected and findings are interpreted. Newton-Smith reminds us of this process by emphasizing:

> When social science includes women, minorities, and other underrepresented groups in the research agenda, they appear in skewed ways. They show up in studies of special populations, gendered arenas, or social problems. Women are found (and overrepresented) in studies of the family and children, of depression and occupations. Poor women are studied as welfare recipients, criminals, and prostitutes. Such boundaries isolate their subjects, focus on weakness rather than strengths, and risk perpetuating gender, race, and class stereotypes. [11]

As we proceed with this book, we want you to understand just how all of these and other things relate to the social work research process.

A Definition of Methodology

What, then, does the term *methodology* encompass? We have found no better definition than that offered by Bogdan and Taylor:

> **The term methodology in a broad sense refers to the processes, principles, and procedures by which we approach problems and seek answers.** In the social sciences the term applies to how one conducts research. As in everything else we do, our assumptions, interests, and goals greatly influence which methodological procedures we choose. When stripped to their essentials, most debates over methods are debates over assumptions and goals, over theory and perspective. [12]

Note the elements of this definition. Research methods are ways in which we (1) approach problems and (2) conduct research; (3) assumptions, interests, theories, and goals are intimately tied to which methods we choose; and (4) debates over methods are really debates over theory and assumptions. Such a definition, without explicitly saying so, underscores Kuhn's notion of the paradigm. In this book, we will try not to study methods without being mindful of the paradigms of which they are a part. We will discuss this matter in greater detail in Chapter 4.

The Need to Study Methodology

We live in a research-saturated environment. Research is used not only to learn things, but to promote, sell, and justify things. The graphs, charts, language, and logic of research can be found in everything from governmental actions to spray deodorants. To sift through this research and find what is consumable is no easy task. Students reading this book will range all the way from budding professional social work researchers who will not only need to know what is in this text, but will require years of future study as well—to those persons who will never read another book on research methodology, but will continue to consume its products (both voluntarily and involuntarily) for the rest of their lives. In short, anyone who buys things, sells things, reads, watches television, votes, tries to persuade others, and is persuaded by others needs to know something about research methods. We can think of no topic that holds more relevance for people in modern society, and we will try to reflect this personal connection you have with the subject as we continue through this book.

The profession of social work, in contrast with the scientific day and age in which it has matured, has a somewhat limited track record in research achievements. This is because of its practice orientation. Unlike medicine and many of the physical sciences, social work practice has tended to outdistance its knowledge base. Innovative practice patterns in social work have moved into usage more rapidly than the research that would have been relevant to inform them.

Although social work pioneers had called for appropriate research and scientific knowledge for the profession, this base of insight lagged far behind in its development. Currently, however, there appears to be a fuller appreciation of the importance of research-based knowledge to be organized from the growing networks of information in order to conceptually validate social work practice [13].

The Scientific Attitude: Myths and Realities

Traditional Models of Science

The word *science* has become one of the preeminent buzzwords of our century. As God and Heaven were to the nineteenth century, science is to the twentieth. In the modern world, to label something as "nonscientific" has virtually become like saying in past times that something was "of the devil." Nonscience is for many people the same as superstition. The social sciences, being somewhat younger and in more need of justification than the natural sciences, have been particularly wearisome about the use of the term "science." Indeed, the amount of writing produced by social scientists and social work researchers to justify why our work is scientific is so great that Samuel Stouffer once suggested that we "declare a moratorium on the use of the word 'science' in order to avoid all of those acrimonious (and generally profitless) debates over whether a given piece of work is or is not 'scientific'" [14].

Much of this murky passion about science could be cleared away if we think of *science as an attitude surrounded by a set of activities designed to make sense out of the world in which we live.* From this point of view, we can say that science holds no monopoly on truth, but competes (sometimes fairly and sometimes unfairly) in the marketplace of ideas. None of us, including scientists, act our lives out in a fully scientific way. Scientists, too, have emotions and sentiments, biases and passions. What, then, are the elements that compose the attitude of science? And what are the realities that both facilitate and interfere with this attitude? Traditionally, the attitude of science has been characterized by the following elements.

Science Is Empirical

By *empirical* we mean simply that science rests on sense data. Science is interested (as science) only in what can be seen, touched, tasted, heard, and smelled. The scientific attitude, for better or for worse, excludes from consideration all of those important notions in human affairs that do not have this property. Whether or not God exists is not a scientific question, but what people believe about God can be determined empirically. We can ask people about their concepts of God, and see their actions related to this important belief. This simple idea distinguishes science from many other human pursuits that seek to acquire knowledge. An empirical scientist who wanted to know how many teeth a horse has would not sit at a desk and logically try to figure out the answer to the question. Nor would the scientist waste time on the question of how many teeth a horse ought to have, or what people have traditionally believed about the matter (although that could be an interesting scientific question in its own right), or what the Bible has to say about the subject. The scientist would simply go find a bunch of horses and start counting teeth. In this sense, empirical science is an attitude that places the eyes, ears, nose, and other sensing devices of the human being as the ultimate arbiters of questions. What cannot be determined empirically may still be important, but stands outside the realm of science.

Science Is Logical

Science believes (although it cannot prove) that there is some ultimate link between logical thinking and empirical facts. The attitude of science is that objective reality not only exists, but is essentially in one piece, so that there should be no disparity between what is logical and what is empirical. Thus, logic is simply the rules by which inferences are made and constitutes the structure of scientific debate.

Science Is Generalizing

This is one of the characteristics of science that people find frustrating, even though as human beings we use it all the time. Science has no inherent interest in individual cases, for *the goal of science is to produce meaningful generalizations.* In an age of radical individualism, this seems perverse if not downright anti-American. Social work practitioners have always been interested in the individual and small group, as well as in societal perspectives. Nevertheless, science seeks general principles and is not in the business of trying to characterize individual situations or events. One way of understanding this idea is to contrast sociology and history. History is not really a science (although it does at points use scientific techniques) because its main concern is with giving complete and comprehensive descriptions of particular events. There was only one World War II, and a complete description of it would show the differences between it and every other armed conflict that has been waged on this planet. Sociology, on the other hand, is generalizing, and to the extent that it uses scientific techniques, it does so in an effort to reach general principles. World War II, to carry out our example, has no special fascination for sociologists, but is one case in a host of cases that together might lead them to meaningful generalizations about war as a form of organized conflict [15].

By contrast, social work's relationship to the generalizing nature of science has evolved out of its contacts with specific individuals, families, groups, and communities. This practice focus has created the desire to develop more effective practice interventions to address the human condition. For the pragmatic social worker, science needs to have meaning for helping people.

The emergence of graduate schools of social work provided a significant change for the social work research activity. Early in this century the individuals undertaking research were trained in the social sciences and had an interest in the study of social work services. Over time, graduate social work training provided the profession with a cadre of researchers able to meld a knowledge of social work and research methods. Thus, contemporary social work research has a core of studies undertaken by social workers, and incorporates the work of social scientists from allied fields who work within social work oriented settings [16].

Looking for meaningful generalizations usually involves two processes well known to both scientists and everyday people. These two processes are known as *induction* and *deduction*. **Induction is moving from the specific to the general** —from individual cases to general principles. If we study 150 cases of spouse abuse and try to figure out from these individual cases what is common to all of them, the statements we make about spouse abuse in general were produced by the process of induction. We used inductive reasoning because we moved from specific cases to general principles. On the other hand, sometimes we may generalize deductively. **In deductive reasoning we move from the general to the specific.** To use our previous example, on the basis of whatever general principles of spouse abuse we have arrived at, we might hazard an explanation of why a particular couple becomes involved in abusive behavior. Both induction and deduction are used by the scientist. Induction is the essential method of scientists in the effort to create general principles. And the goal of reaching generalizations is that we might better understand and explain the occurrence of particular events.

General principles, whether derived from scientific work or from everyday knowledge, common sense, authority, or some other source, can then be translated into *hypotheses*, which we can check against further experience, thereby verifying or modifying the general principles. Science is an ongoing, cyclical process of induction, deduction, modification, refinement, further testing, further induction, and further deduction. Scientific knowledge is never fixed; it is always tentative and always subject to further refinements.

Science Is Abstract

Many people want science to be concrete, and social science, especially, to solve the problems of the world. But science is not interested in concrete things, just as it is not interested in particular ones. Instead, the researcher is interested in making propositional statements that move increasingly up what is called the *ladder of abstraction*. This means that if we want to understand the world around us, it is necessary to abstract, or progressively leave things out of our descriptions in order to move from a low-level, concrete form of understanding to more complex and meaningful ones. Hayakawa [17] gives us a good example in thinking about a cow (see Figure 2.1).

When we abstract, then, we progressively leave out more and more characteristics for the sake of a more generalized understanding of something. In the process of social work research we almost always are looking for ways of combining characteristics of data to seek the most general understanding of a phenomenon that we can.

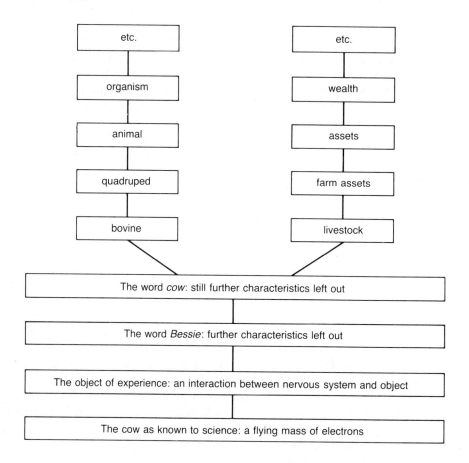

FIGURE 2.1   The Abstraction Ladder of Bessie the Cow.*

*Read from the bottom up.

Science Is Public, Not Private

Science is part of a public universe of discourse, and this is one of the major reasons for studying research methods. By using a common method, scientists are able to communicate their findings to one another in a common language. Methods constitute this language, and presumably, if everything were to work perfectly, the individual scientist's motivations, biases, personal opinions, values, ideologies, and so on, would be excluded from scientific conclusions because the common language of method would distill these contaminating factors out. Scientist A working on a common problem with scientist B and using the same methods ought to achieve the same results. (This almost never happens in the social sciences, but more on that later.)

The Practice of Science

The preceding characteristics of science may be looked at as an ideal, rarely achieved but nevertheless at least partially desirable. To understand and appreciate fully the scientific attitude, we must also investigate how science falls short of its goal, for in so doing we can know the pitfalls as well as the promises of science. Only by understanding both the ideal and the reality of science can we fully understand what we are doing when we try to carry out a research project. An analogy might be what medicine claims to be (see the Hippocratic oath or other such lofty statements) versus how doctors actually practice in the real world of money, power, law, and interpersonal relationships [18]. In other words, we might research science itself to see if it is what it claims to be in the same way that social science has investigated other institutions and human activities.

Kuhn's ideal of the paradigm, of course, is a starting point for seeing science as it is and not as we wish it were. A paradigm, by definition, includes a lot of nonrational elements and human frailties. Science, as we indicated at the beginning, is a human enterprise, and none of its methods is really capable of insulating it from this fact. The best single example we have of this, and a perfect case for understanding how scientists actually operate, is the case of moon rocks.

Moon Rocks and the Scientists

When Apollo 11 set down on the surface of the moon in July of 1969, a series of events were set into motion that have come to tell us a great deal about the realities of science. For as long as scientists (and humanity in general) have observed the moon, competing theories have emerged about the origins of the moon, its relationship to Earth, the beginnings of the solar system, and so forth. All of these hoary problems that led scientists into a number of different theoretical camps were thought to be due to the fact that we had no real physical evidence from the moon itself. Apollo 11 would lead us to a resolution of these scientific problems by providing us with the first sack of moon rocks—real, tangible, physical evidence that could be subjected to close observation, reliable tests, and the like. At last, we would know the answer to these age-old questions. Those scientists who were correct in their theories would be proven so, and those who chased error all these years would be revealed too.

The case led a social scientist named Ian Mitroff to see all of this as a revolutionary chapter in scientific history, one that could tell us far more about the nature of science, perhaps, than even the rocks themselves. The beginnings of his investigation are described as follows:

> The Apollo moon scientists were chosen for study for various reasons. A major initial premise, later confirmed, was that the Apollo program would be an excellent contemporary setting in which to study the nature and function of the commitment of scientists to their pet hypotheses in the face of possibly disconfirming evidence. A review of the scientific and popular literature before the landing of Apollo 11 found that various scientists had

strongly committed themselves in print as to what they thought the moon would be like, and in a few cases, what they ardently hoped the moon would be like. [19]

Mitroff commenced a study of over forty of the most eminent scientists who studied the moon rocks. Each scientist was interviewed four times over a period of three years. The interviews ranged from open-ended discussions in the first round to written questionnaires in subsequent rounds. The results showed that the sack of moon rocks did nothing to resolve competing theories about the nature of the universe. Instead, each camp of scientists, no matter how far they were away from each other in their astronomical theories, interpreted the evidence of the rocks themselves as substantiating their particular theory. Furthermore, closer examination of the scientists' attitude toward the traditional view of the scientist as a disinterested, dispassionate, objective observer indicated that they themselves viewed this conception of science as a fairy tale. Most surprising of all, the scientists not only rejected the notion of the disinterested scientist as an accurate descriptive account of the workings of science, but even rejected it as a desired *ideal* or *standard:*

> What was even more surprising was that the scientists rejected the notion of the "emotionally disinterested scientist" as a prescriptive ideal or standard. Strong reasons were evinced why a good scientist *ought* to be highly committed to a point of view. Ideally, they argued, scientists ought not to be without strong, prior commitments. Even though the general behavior and personality of their more extremely committed colleagues infuriated them, as a rule they still came out in favor of scientists having strong commitments. [20]

Mitroff concludes his interesting study by claiming that far from the traditional ideas of science, the most creative scientists are intensely aggressive and fiercely passionate about the ideas they hold and the research they conduct.

Now, none of this is to say that these same scientists did not use the traditional methods of science and do their work as honestly as possible. They were also zealous in applying healthy scientific skepticism to the work of their colleagues in competing camps. The real significance of Mitroff's work is that the process of doing scientific research is much more complicated and filled with subjective and even irrational elements than we have usually acknowledged, and certainly more than we have ever studied in much detail.

Apparently, strong commitment and bias on the part of the scientist is one of the strongest sustaining forces in the doing of research. Far from being dispassionate, creative scientists care about the world around them and care about the ideas they themselves are working with. Despite all of this, Mitroff winds up his study with a strong endorsement of scientific methods:

> If scientific knowledge were the product of uncommitted or weakly committed observers, its understanding would be trivial. Given the presumption of untainted, unbiased observers, it is a trivial matter to explain how objectivity results. It is also a trivial matter to justify the concept of objectivity as knowledge independent of the feelings or opinions of the person making them.

The problem is how objective knowledge results in science not despite bias and commitment, but because of them. [21]

The Real World

Just what *does* get in the way of the traditional ideals of the scientific method? First, researchers are human beings. They are motivated by the same emotions, anxieties, personal goals, and sense of value as the rest of us [22]. What researchers study, what they deem important, and what they exclude from consideration as a worthy topic of investigation often depend on criteria that may at best be described as whimsical. Given the cost of conducting much research, the needs of the sponsoring agencies are often the determinant of what kinds of research are done, not criteria that are intrinsic to science itself.

Furthermore, what research is published is often the result of the Byzantine politics of the scientific community and its journals. Personality conflicts, jealousies, petty but accepted lines of inquiry, and even the credentials of the researcher or the university he or she works for often become the criteria of publication, and not the intrinsic merits of the research itself. Social work journal editors, for example, have a great deal of power as gatekeepers to let in and keep out what research is reported to other social workers and to the public. The space requirements of the journals are fed not so much by the clear-cut scientific demands for quality research, but by the rat race of academia, which makes publication mandatory for faculty and researchers lest they forgo promotion or tenure, or even lose their jobs altogether. Such a circumstance often leads to research being cranked out as if on an assembly line, with additions to the researcher's résumé being the goal and no valid, scientifically sound criteria. Indeed, the idea that research proceeds in carefully selected steps (the building-block theory) is an illusion that can be seen clearly once we understand the ordinary contingencies of money, power, and personalities that circumscribe scientific work.

The matters we have just mentioned might be classified as the social, psychological, economic, and political contexts of research. But scientific work itself is also a compromise between what is and what could have been. The notion that research runs through a clearly defined cycle consisting of the formulation of a question, the development of hypotheses, the operationalization of concepts, the collection and analysis of data, conclusions, and the reformulation of theory is an idea reminiscent of the organizational chart of a corporation: everyone who works there can tell you that the place is not exactly what it says it is on the chart.

Instead of this careful, step-by-step process, in the real world of research, things are much more haphazard. Research questions, as we have mentioned, often reflect researchers' ulterior motives, while the rest of the process is frequently an uncertain and tentative set of activities, filled with unexpected results that sometimes modify original conceptions and sometimes do not. We virtually never *prove* a theory to be correct, especially in social work and the social sciences, nor do we ever fully invalidate existing ideas no matter how wrongheaded they are suspected to be. The idea that research is exciting work with never a dull moment also can be shown to be a myth, probably on a par with people's conceptions of flight attendants leading enchanting lives in the skies. Research, like delivering trays of sandwiches at 40,000 feet, can be dull, boring, onerous work. Sometimes a person works for days, weeks, months, or even years on a project, only to see nothing come of it. With contracted and externally funded work, as the deadline for completion approaches, creative fiction often gets produced in an effort to meet the external requirements imposed by the funding agency.

Lest the student doubt that research is as human an enterprise as the portrait painted here, a look at any number of memoirs of research activity will validate the general claim. James Watson's account of the discovery of the DNA molecule has been published in a book entitled *The Double Helix* [23]. The competition between scientists working toward the same goal, the personal animosities, the blind alleys, frustrations, and departures from the traditional scientific norms are well documented in this intensely human portrait of researchers at work. Similarly, Abraham Maslow has done an analysis of the scientist as human being in his book *The Psychology of Science* [24]. In the social sciences, there is still no better "inside" look at the real-work practice of social research than Phillip Hammond's *Sociologists at Work* [25].

These accounts of scientists at work sometimes give the cynical observer a jaundiced view of the whole enterprise. This is certainly not our intention here, and the student should not conclude that because science and scientists have feet of clay, their work is irrelevant. Instead, the ideals of science should be looked upon as a goal to achieve, a set of norms that guide research but neither should nor always do determine what is done in the name of science. The conclusion to be drawn from this real-world glimpse of science in practice is that research is both a human enterprise and in many ways an art. The art of science is as crucial to understanding research activities as the science of science. This is not to suggest that the beginning student break the rules; in fact, you can't really break them until you know what they are. Being apprised of the actual practice of research in addition to the norms of scientific research can only serve to give you a better appreciation of the complexity of scientific research work. This is our goal.

The Language and Rhetoric of Science

Learning to use the language of research without being used by it is one of the main tasks you will have as a student of research methodology. Like all disciplined lines of inquiry, research methods are as much mastering a body of language and symbols as a series of techniques. In this section, we want to mention a few of the major concepts, but in many ways the entire book will be an attempt to introduce you to the rhetoric of scientific method used in social work research.

Operational Definitions   Norman J. Smith has given us a good example of operational definitions in research:

> *Social workers (concept 1) are professionals (concept 2) who work (concept 3) in the area of human relations (concept 4).*

We may operationally define social workers as:

All people who hold an MSW degree from an accredited graduate school of social work who have been employed on a full-time basis for the last twenty-four months within Agency A.

The second definition is fairly straightforward and eliminates much, but not all, of the ambiguity that we present in the first statement. There are, however, many other operational definitions which we could have selected. Why did we operationally define social workers as people holding an MSW degree? Why not include BA, BSW, DSW, or Ph.D. degrees? Why did we not include people working on a part-time basis? Why only Agency A and not Agency B or C? Why did the social workers have to graduate from an accredited graduate school of social work? How about those who graduated with a counseling psychology degree from an accredited graduate school of psychology? [26]

The language of research is very tuned to operational definitions, that is, definitions that specify the exact procedure for identifying or generating the definition. We can never be confident of the conclusions we reach unless we are confident of the methodological procedures used to arrive at those conclusions. The idea of *operationalization* was first proposed by Percy Bridgeman in 1927 [27]. By 1939, George Lundberg had applied it to the social sciences and had made it the cornerstone in his scientific conceptions of social research. The high abstractions of social theory are meaningless, said Lundberg, unless and until these are brought down to the empirical world by the technique of operationalization. If we are going to use theoretical concepts, we should know the exact methodological procedures used to define them. Otherwise, our theories remain pure speculation.

In short, the operational definition of a dish is its recipe [28]. If someone were to ask you how much you were worth, your answer would be an operational definition because it would specify assets you could get your hands on. To say that you are worth a million dollars because that is how much you will someday earn is not nearly so precise as saying you are worth a million dollars because that is how much you have in your checking account. The latter is an operational definition of wealth, while the former is pie in the sky.

Now, pie in the sky is also important to research, and the emphasis upon the operationalization of concepts in no way suggests that theory is unimportant. Theory guides our operationalizations, and every good research project begins with a body of good theory. But theory is not enough—we must also know how to translate the language of theory into the language of methods so that we have a way of checking to see if our conceptualizations are correct. This is exactly what operationalization does.

On the other hand, just because we have operationalized a concept does not mean that we have captured all of it. It simply means that we have translated part of it into terms we can measure and employ in a specific context. We could define love in terms of the number of times people kiss, and it would work as an operational definition for certain narrow purposes. But very few people would be satisfied that such a definition really encompassed the concept of love.

Some researchers commit the "nothing-but" fallacy when they do research. That is, they confuse their own operational definitions with reality. Therefore, some of them become ensnared in the fallacy that reality is nothing but what they are measuring. Love is nothing but a bunch of hormones calling out to themselves. Social class is nothing but income, occupation, education, house type, dwelling area, and whatever else has gone into the operational definition. Behavior is nothing but the interaction of all previous episodes of conditioning. Such a doctrinaire stance is an easy one to fall into when a researcher operationally defines a concept and then starts to believe his or her own definitions. But it is important to know that operationalization is merely a technique, and that for any concept you can think of, there are virtually an infinite number of operationalizations that could be given for it, all of which would lead to a different conclusion about the nature of the reality under investigation. While the language of science is important and we could not get along without it, language never says all there is to say about any given concept. It is not reality itself, merely a procedure with which to assess it. But if there are *no* ways to get at a concept, then operationally the concept must simply collapse insofar as *empirical investigation* of it is concerned.

Validity and Reliability   These are important words in research, and it will be important to define them now while we are talking about the language of science. In the lexicon of research they are used over and over again. As we have already learned, every research project is an attempt to answer a question. The answer is provided by theory and the research is undertaken in order to test the answer. Validity and reliability are simple ways of determining how good the answer is.

In a general sense, **validity means that a particular research measure measures what it is supposed to measure.** If we can show that a piece of research is really getting at something other than what it says it is getting at, we have poked a large hole in its claim to be valid. More specifically, there are many different types of validity, and there are very few pieces of research that can claim to measure up to all of them. The following are only a few of the many kinds of validity used in social research.

First there is *pragmatic validity.* In essence, this is an answer to the question of whether or not the answer obtained by one's research "works." Are we better off with the answer than we were without it? Does it tell us anything we didn't already know?

There is also *predictive validity.* Does the research enable us to predict cases in the future? Much research in social work is *ex post facto* or *retrospective* research. It tells us a great deal about something that has already come to pass, but very little about what will likely happen in the future. Social work researchers, like other social scientists, are often quite concerned with the predictive validity of a piece of research.

Another type of validity is *internal validity.* Some types of research are invalid because the procedures used in doing the research were themselves invalid. We can hardly claim that our research as a whole is valid if the elements that make it up are not. For example, when researchers study any particular group in an experimental setting, their research can be shown to be invalid unless they carefully match the results of that group with a *control group*. Otherwise, we have no way of knowing whether the experimental manipulations are really the cause of the outcome of the study.

There is also *construct validity*, sometimes called *external validity*. This applies to the research as a whole. No matter how carefully the internal procedures are performed, no matter how accurate the individual techniques employed can be shown to be, the entire research project might be completely irrelevant to the question under investigation. A study of intellectual achievement, based on the result of IQ tests, no matter how carefully done and error-free, might turn out to be completely invalid when applied to people from different cultural backgrounds. This systematic bias in IQ tests can render all such measures meaningless. In fact, a large amount of research has been done in the last ten years on this very problem [29]. Construct validity deals, then, with the entire project and the theory that underlies it, and not simply with the particular elements of it.

A concept that is often confused with validity is that of reliability. In ordinary discourse, the word *genuineness* (validity, the real thing) is often used synonymously with the term *reliability*, but in social research we mean something quite different. **Reliability, in social research, refers to whether a piece of research can be replicated**—that is, whether a different investigator can achieve the same results using the same methods. Does a definition or measure of a particular idea always lead to the same result? Does a measure have the property of "same input, same output"? *Consistency* and *repeatability* have about the same meaning as *reliability* [30].

When we go to the grocery store, we are concerned with the reliability of the butcher's scale. Does it weigh a pound of meat the same way each time, or are there variations from time to time? Operational definitions need to be reliable. That is, does applying the same definition (methodologically operationalized) produce the same results every time? If not, it is not very reliable. Using our previous examples of IQ testing, a test would be reliable (all other things being equal) if it produced exactly the same score more than once for the same individual.

As you can see, reliability, while earnestly sought, is not very often achieved in social work research or in the social sciences. Very few pieces of research are replicated. There are good reasons for this, besides the inaccuracy of methods, and we will address ourselves to that question a bit later.

The Promise and Limitations of Science

In the last one hundred years, science, its language, and its promises, both explicit and implicit, have become prominent features of the world in which we live. Products are increasingly sold in the name of science, and political decisions are based on so-called scientific research. A large chemical company promises "better living through chemistry," teams of survey researchers canvass the land to find out everything they can about us from the kinds of shoes we wear to the most intimate details of our sex lives. A portion of this scientific quest is motivated by the pure desire to know, and science has certainly been one of the strongest advocates of knowledge purely for the sake of knowledge. But increasingly we have also wanted science to solve a whole range of human problems, and the natural physical sciences, as well as the social sciences and social work, have been caught up in the demand for the application of scientific research.

Not surprisingly, all of this scientific activity and its applications have generated a good deal of skepticism, for they have created a climate in which promises have been made or implied that science, in reality, cannot deliver. The promise that science might one day solve most, if not all, of our problems has created difficulties not only for the consumers of science, but also for researchers, who often know the impossibility of such a task. Furthermore, as increasing numbers of voices are telling us, science is itself creating certain social problems [31]. Skeptics of science and research now abound, and we may well be approaching the point where the baby will be thrown out with the bathwater.

Actually, the separation between intellectual questions (pure research) and practical questions (applied research) has never been as great as has been the tendency to claim. They are often discussed as though they were somehow opposed or even mutually exclusive [32], and frequently as if one (usually the one favored by the prejudices of the writer) were better than the other. A close look at the history of science, however, will dispel any such simplistic notions. We have never been satisfied with simply knowing for the sake of knowing, and social work research, in particular, has repeatedly and continuously been called upon to demonstrate its responsibility to the larger community by contributing something to the resolution of that community's practical concerns.

Nevertheless, as a practical matter, there is frequently a tension between these two objectives of science. Sometimes the desire to know can be totally subverted by the single-minded concerns of those who want simple, painless, and quick solutions to complex problems. But, by the same token, when researchers are building a body of knowledge, it is easy to lose sight of the problems of the everyday human being as they work in the solitary atmosphere of the laboratory. This tension has never been more eloquently stated than in quotations from two eminent scholars, Morris Cohen and Robert Lynd. Cohen, arguing the case for an unfettered pure science, once observed that purely theoretical contributions to astronomy and mathematics, by increasing the precision of navigation, have saved more lives at sea than any possible improvements in the carpentry of lifeboats. But Lynd, impatient with knowledge for the sake of knowledge, tells us that we are in acute danger of being caught, in the words of one of W. H. Auden's poems, "lecturing on Navigation while the ship is going down."

William Reid [33] aptly describes this tension from the viewpoint of the social worker by referring to two philosophic approaches to knowledge, the "tough-minded" and the "tender-minded," made by William James. He observes that this issue is rooted in differences that can never be completely resolved. It is an issue not only for social work researchers but also for direct practitioners. The so-called "tough-minded" seek evidence derived from quantitative and objective data with careful control for alternative explanations. The "tender-minded" are open to considering as true the unverified observations of a systematic study, particularly when it appears to represent more complex interrelationships of a given situation under study. These differences in social work tend to parallel a philosophical debate that is deeply imbedded in the traditions of science [33].

As in most endeavors, the only reasonable advice that can be given is an appeal to balance and perspective—to strive for keeping research and its products in some proper relationship to the demands of everyday life. Certainly, an understanding of the limitations of science, which we have attempted to point out, should help keep such problems in perspective.

References

1. Claire Selltiz, L. S. Wrightsman, and Stuart Cook, *Research Methods in Social Relations* (New York: Holt, Rinehart, and Winston, 1976).
2. Bergen Evans, *The Natural History of Nonsense* (New York: Anchor Paperbacks, 1958).
3. Evans, *The Natural History of Nonsense*, p. 20.
4. Evans, *The Natural History of Nonsense*, p. 21.
5. T. S. Kuhn, *The Structure of Scientific Revolutions* (Chicago: University of Chicago Press, 1962).
6. G. Ritzer, *Sociology: A Multiple Paradigm Science* (Boston: Allyn and Bacon, 1975).
7. R. W. Frederichs, *A Sociology of Sociology* (New York: Free Press, 1970).
8. Kuhn, *The Structure of Scientific Revolutions*, p. 175.
9. Carole Hope Depp, "After Reunion: Perceptions of Adult Adoptees, Adoptive Parents, and Birth Parents," *Child Welfare*, February 1982, p. 118.
10. D. Phillips, *Abandoning Method* (San Francisco: Jossey-Bass, 1973).
11. W. H. Newton-Smith, *The Rationality of Science* (Boston: Routledge and Kegan Paul, 1981).
12. R. Bogdan and S. J. Taylor, *Introduction to Qualitative Research Methods: A Phenomenological Approach to the Social Sciences* (San Francisco: Jossey-Bass, 1975), p. 1.
13. William J. Reid, "Research in Social Work," in *Encyclopedia of Social Work*, 18th ed. (Silver Spring, MD: National Association of Social Workers, 1987), p. 476.
14. Samuel Stouffer, "Sociology and Sampling," in *The Fields and Methods of Sociology*, L. L. Bernard, ed. (New York: Long and Smith, 1934), pp. 486–7.
15. R. Bierstedt, *The Social Order* (New York: McGraw-Hill, 1970), p. 14.
16. Reid, "Research in Social Work," pp. 476–7.
17. S. I. Hayakawa, *Language in Action* (New York: Harcourt, Brace, Jovanovich, 1940), p. 126.
18. I. Illich, *Medical Nemesis* (New York: Pantheon Books, 1974).
19. I. Mitroff, "Norms and Counter-norms in a Select Group of the Apollo Moon Scientists: A Case Study of the Ambivalence of Scientists," *American Sociological Review* 39 (1974): 581.
20. I. Mitroff, "Norms and Counter-norms in a Select Group of the Apollo Moon Scientists," p. 588.
21. I. Mitroff, "Norms and Counter-norms in a Select Group of the Apollo Moon Scientists," p. 591.
22. Abraham Maslow, *The Psychology of Science* (New York: Harper and Row, 1966).
23. James D. Watson, *The Double Helix: A Personal Account of the Discovery of the Structure of DNA* (New York: Atheneum, 1968).
24. Maslow, *The Psychology of Science*.
25. Phillip Hammond, *Sociologists at Work* (New York: Basic Books, 1968).
26. Richard M. Grinnell, Jr., *Social Work Research and Evaluation*, 3rd ed. (Itasca, IL: Peacock, 1988), p. 96.
27. G. Zito, *Methodologies and Meaning* (New York: Praeger, 1975).
28. J. L. Simon, *Basic Research Methods in Social Sciences* (New York: Random House, 1978).
29. Selltiz et al., *Research Methods in Social Relations*.
30. Simon, *Basic Research Methods in Social Sciences*, p. 21.
31. J. Ravetz, *Scientific Knowledge and Its Social Problems* (New York: Oxford University Press, 1971).
32. Selltiz et al., *Research Methods in Social Relations*, p. 4.
33. Reid, "Research in Social Work," p. 480.

Chapter 3

Choosing and Formulating a Research Question

Defining terms
The role of values in choosing
    and formulating
    research questions
Factors influencing the choice of a
    research question
  Personal interests
  Social concerns
  Chance
  Epilogue

Formulating a research question
  Learning about the subject:
    searching the literature
  Identifying the research
    impetus: reviewing the
    literature
Evaluating a research question
  Is it worthwhile?
  Is it feasible?
  Is it ethical?

A prudent question is one-half of wisdom.—FRANCIS BACON

One of the most difficult aspects of an endeavor is to *begin*, and research is no exception. The process by which a research problem is selected is, by its very nature, a creative process. It involves thinking about various ideas and issues, asking questions about them, and considering whether possible answers to these questions even exist. For most of us, it would be easier and certainly less painful if we could bypass this step and simply have someone tell us what to study. Creative thinking is hard work! However, this creative, largely intuitive searching process is a necessary and important first step in any research endeavor, and one with which you need to be familiar.

The importance of studying this aspect of the research process is heightened by the fact that it is one of the least obvious steps in the research endeavor. As you begin to read published research, you will notice that almost all research endeavors begin with the research question. Just how this research question was chosen or formulated is seldom discussed. Thus, the reader is not given access to the creative processes that give rise to a particular question being asked in the first place. In fact, you may find already published research an inadequate model for helping you choose and formulate your own research question, for as we shall see, most published research does not guide you through the process of choice and formulation. And your own efforts to engage in its creative process may be infused with confusion and uncertainty. You may, for example, question whether you are going about the process correctly. Accordingly, this chapter is about choosing and formulating research questions. Our task is to introduce you to the factors that can influence problem selection and formulation and to make this step in the research process more visible.

Defining Terms

Before examining this selection and formulation process, it will be helpful to define what we mean by a research question and a research subject. The **research question** is just what it suggests: **a question that can be answered by using the research process.** It is important to note that not all questions capable of being devised by the human mind are answerable by scientific research. Questions of whether or not God exists, what the purpose of life is, how a person seeks the good, and other such broad philosophical questions are not answerable by scientific research. However, each of these questions might be translated into a question that would be answerable by the research process if we asked it in terms of what people think about the issues, how they act in relation to them, and so forth. In other words, questions about the existence of things that lie in the nonempirical world are outside the realm of science, but questions about people's opinions, attitudes, and actions toward these matters most definitely are within its province. It is difficult to know exactly what death is scientifically, but we can ask if and how attitudes toward life influence attitudes toward death.

Research questions are usually specific and encompass only a few variables. In contrast, a *research subject* is quite broad and general. Research subjects include mental health, AIDS, child abuse, welfare reform, empowerment, and aging, just to name a few. There are many research questions that could be formulated on each of these research subjects. In general, we begin by identifying a research subject and then choosing and formulating a research question within that subject area. This process of choosing and formulating a research question within a research subject area is a filtering process that involves moving from the general to the specific.

The Role of Values in Choosing and Formulating
Research Questions

We begin our discussion of this selection process with a controversial but important issue—the role of values in choosing and formulating research questions. The issue of value-free research in the social sciences is almost as old as the social sciences themselves. To illustrate, it might be helpful to look at the beginnings of just one social science—sociology. Sociology emerged from the widespread changes that the industrial revolution brought to Europe. Before the industrial revolution, societies could be characterized as tranquil and stable. But the industrial revolution threw societies into turmoil. Cities were growing very rapidly. This rapid growth was followed by an increase in crime. Social problems were becoming more prevalent. As a result, people were anxious for a way to explain and deal with these rapid changes. Sociology was the discipline that emerged to study and explain these social phenomena. We might say, then, that sociology's beginnings were not value-free, but arose in a context of societal problems and difficulties seeking solutions.

In turn, these circumstances contributed to the development of the new profession of social work to address complex problems faced by individuals, families, groups, organizations, and communities.

We take the position that value-free social science for that matter, is fiction, not fact. The commandment "Thou shalt not commit a value judgment" is simply not tenable. It has been said that what a physiologist sees when he or she studies the brain is part of his or her own brain. If we recall Ian Mitroff's study of the moon rock scientists in Chapter 2, we realize that our values *do* influence what we research and how we go about researching. As you will learn, within any discipline there are generally several paradigms, or ways of looking at the reality being studied. There are different values for different paradigms, and the researcher's choice of paradigms is most likely influenced by his or her own values, background, and experiences, to say nothing of the restraints created by the fact that research is often performed by teams and with other people's money.

As social scientists we cannot disrobe ourselves of our personhood or selfhood. We cannot remove the cloak of culture when we enter the research setting. To even suggest that we can be value-free researchers in all phases of the research process is unrealistic. In truth, value-free research is impossible—so why pretend? Our fallacy as social work researchers, though, is not that we are unable to isolate ourselves from our values. Rather, it lies in trying to fool ourselves into believing that we can accomplish or have accomplished this end. If, as social scientists, we recognize that values are an integral part of who we are, both as persons and researchers, and if we recognize what these values are, we are better prepared to see how they influence our choice of a research question and the way we choose to study that question. If we can see, for example, that our values are directing us toward a particular paradigm, we may not hold so tenaciously to the paradigm if research consistently fails to support it. In effect, recognizing our values places us in a more objective position. *Value-free research cannot be our goal; value-aware research can.* It is toward this end that we should strive. This is highly consistent with our identity as professional social workers active in a discipline permeated by human and social values.

Factors Influencing the Choice of a Research Question

Personal Interests

The role of values in the research process becomes even more apparent when we consider the single most important factor influencing the choice of a research question—personal interests. In general, social scientists conduct research on questions that interest them. Certainly it is easier to endure the long research process if we are investigating a question that we personally like. Scientists who seek to uncover evidence of life after death, for example, most likely are personally fascinated by the subject. There is an old cliché in psychology that "researchers study their own hang-ups." And such personal interest generally stems from either personal experience or reading and other intellectual pursuits in a particular subject area.

Personal Experience

Much of what interests us evolves out of events that have happened to us. Robin Lakoff's research [1] on language and women's place, for example, was born out of her own experiences and observations that language is sexist. As a result, she began to look at ways in which males and females use language in an effort to determine whether differences really did exist.

Phillip Goldberg's classic study [2] on women's prejudices against women was also born out of his own personal experiences. Goldberg writes that in teaching his classes, he noticed marked differences between the males and the females. The women were bright, able, and hard-working, but they generally lacked intellectual aggressiveness. In contrast, the males were aggressive and quite willing to participate in classroom discussions. In Goldberg's words, "The girls could be counted on to do the work, the guys could be counted on to do the talking" [3]. Goldberg's evaluation of this situation was that women did not value themselves as they should. They were, he concluded, prejudiced against themselves—against women. As a result of this experience, Goldberg decided to devise an experiment that would allow him to test the hypothesis that women were prejudiced against women. Goldberg's thinking was confirmed.

Reading and Intellectual Pursuits

There are many social phenomena that interest each of us but for which we have no direct experiences. We do not, for example, have to commit a criminal act to be interested in a specific type of criminal behavior. Sometimes our interests grow and develop out of our reading, studying, or various other intellectual pursuits (such as brainstorming). But that we would even choose to read or study in a certain subject area generally suggests an interest. And that interest will either blossom or wilt as we continue to read. If the interest grows, it is probably safe to assume that our curiosity has been further aroused and that we now have more questions than before. The more we read, the more we realize we do not know, and the more curious we become. As you read in any subject area, it is a good idea to keep a file of questions that come to mind. Many of these questions will be researchable and could provide a basis for future research. If you are faithful in recording such "meteoric moments of mental magic," reading can be a valuable avenue for identifying new research questions.

Social Concerns

Still another factor affecting the choice of a research question is the social concerns of the day. There are those social scientists who prefer to do research in areas that demonstrate immediate social applicability. The issues must be socially and politically relevant. The last decade, for example, has witnessed an influx of research in the area of aging. This wave of interest has been due in large part to the increased attention the government has given to the elderly as a group. With both the birth and death rates dropping, the average age in the United States has been steadily increasing. Today, the elderly comprise a large segment of our population. In recognition of this segment, a great deal of research has been aimed at understanding this aspect of the life cycle.

Chance

One additional factor that can influence the choice of a research question deserves mention—*chance.* Sometimes we just happen to be in the right place at the right time. Many students, for example, find themselves doing research in a particular area because they happened to be paired with a particular professor. You may find yourselves doing research in a subject area because you just happened to get into a particular section of a methods class. If chance is the overriding factor in your choice of a research question, perhaps your interest in the question will be stimulated as you steadfastly pursue knowledge.

Epilogue

It is interesting to notice that spontaneity plays an important role with each of these selection factors. Quite often the research question does not evolve through our concerted efforts to be creative. Creativity is difficult to force. Rather, it emerges quite unexpectedly through the avenues of personal interests, personal experiences, intellectual exercises, social concerns, or chance. You should not construe this to mean that you could not sit down and derive a research question through creative processes. You probably could. But when research questions can emerge so naturally, you only need to be aware of these creative moments and take note. Most likely some of your best research questions will just come to you when you least expect it. Don't fight it; try to capitalize on it by maximizing the chances for such moments.

Formulating a Research Question

Learning about the Subject: Searching the Literature

Let's assume that you now have decided on a research subject and that you are ready to choose and formulate a research question. It perhaps goes without saying that you will not be able to manage an entire research subject. As we have already learned, research subjects are generally quite broad and seldom sharply defined. To say, for example, that you are interested in doing research on "marriage" is much too broad. Even to say that you wish to do research on "marital happiness" is too broad, but it provides a better starting point than just marriage. In effect, it becomes necessary to focus on some small aspect or at least some manageable aspect of the research subject. For example, you might elect to examine the effect of children on parent mental health, or the relationship between retirement and mental health. As we have indicated, this process of moving from research subject to research question is a filtering process. This process of sifting and fine-tuning must result in a research question that is both narrow and concrete.

This filtering process, though, is not automatic. Even though you may be able to identify a subject (e.g., marital happiness) that you would like to research, you are probably not knowledgeable about the research that has already been conducted on this subject. Consequently, you may be at a loss to initiate this filtering process. You may have some difficulty narrowing down the research subject to a specific research question. To be able to formulate a research question, then, you need to make some discoveries. You must first discover what research has already been done (research) and then use this information as a basis for deciding exactly what you want to do. We call this process of "discovering" a *search of the literature*. Primarily, this search of the literature generally requires the use of several types of reference materials including standard references, books, scholarly journals, government documents, and any other relevant sources.

Standard References

Encyclopedia of Social Work   As a social work student, you have available a valuable resource in the *Encyclopedia of Social Work* [4], which is published by the National Association of Social Workers. You will find an extensive compendium of social work subjects as the encyclopedia provides information on current, as well as historical, social service developments. In this publication you will also find biographies of leaders who have served the social work profession. The purpose of this publication is to present a thoughtful picture of the profession of social work from its origins in the United States. It systematically discusses social service provision, contemporary issues and problems, the art and science of social work, and how the profession perceives the future directions in education and practice [5]. Editorial decisions about which topics and themes to include were influenced by their implications for social work practice, including those for ethnic, racial, and cultural minorities, and women. A complete listing of entries in the 1987 *Encyclopedia of Social Work* is presented in Table 3.1.

NASW also published *Face the Nation 1987: A Statistical Supplement to the 18th Edition of the Encyclopedia of Social Work* [6]. These data are drawn from three principal sources: (1) official government agencies that gather, analyze, and disseminate data; (2) groups that advocate for the welfare of particular populations; and (3) research organizations. Note the breadth of content in this statistical supplement as presented in Table 3.2. It provides social welfare data and selected patterns of social services that represent mainstream social work practice patterns from the 1970s into the 1980s.

Social Work Dictionary   In 1987, NASW also began the publication of the *Social Work Dictionary* [7] in which over 3,000 terms from the profession of social work are defined. In the foreword, its purpose is explained.

> One of the characteristics of a profession is that it develops its own distinctive vocabulary. In describing their activities, members of a profession coin new words and develop new meanings for existing terms. The extensive history of the social work profession and the variety of approaches used by its practitioners indicated a compelling need for a comprehensive dictionary of social work terms. [8]

This work represents another step in establishing the unique characteristics of social work as a learned discipline. The author of the dictionary worked with a panel of social work experts who served as an editorial review board to represent all aspects of the social work profession. The goal was to provide a useful tool for social workers, to help them achieve clear communications and better common professional understanding. Terms are expressed in ways most commonly used, and are listed alphabetically. Cross-referencing is possible in that italicized words in the text are defined elsewhere in the dictionary [9].

In your efforts to pinpoint a research problem, it is important that key variables, concepts, and technical terms be precisely stated and carefully defined. Thus, the *Social Work Dictionary* is an especially helpful resource for you to use in providing accurate and clear information with which to focus the social work problem or issue in which you are interested.

Books

Often, students prefer to begin their search of the literature by looking for books related to their research subject. No doubt, this is partly because books are so familiar to us. As a child, you probably made frequent trips to the public library. As a college student, you have probably used the books in your library in writing English term papers.

A list of the books in any library can be found in the library's card catalog. *Card catalogs are organized in three ways: (1) by subject, (2) by author, and (3) by title.* If you know very little about a research subject and are seeking to make discoveries,

TABLE 3.1   List of Entries in Encyclopedia of Social Work

The following list contains the titles of the articles in this encyclopedia. It shows the precise form of the titles and the order of entries. By consulting this list, the reader may quickly gain an overview of the contents of the new edition.

Abortion
Administration: Environmental Aspects
Administration: Interpersonal Aspects
Administration in Social Welfare
Adolescent Pregnancy
Adolescents
Adoption
Adulthood
Advocacy
Aged
Aged: Services
Aid to Families with Dependent Children
Alcohol Use and Addiction
American Indians and Alaska Natives
Archives of Social Welfare
Asian Americans
Assessment in Direct Practice

Behavioral Approach
Blacks
Boards of Directors

Case Management
Child Abuse and Neglect
Child Care Services
Children
Child Sexual Abuse
Child Support
Child Welfare Services
Citizen Participation
Civil Rights
Cognitive Therapy
Community-Based Social Action
Community Development
Community Theory and Research
Computer Utilization
Consultation
Continuing Education
Contracting and Engagement in Direct Practice
Corporate Social Responsibility
Corrections System: Adult
Crisis Intervention

Day Centers: Adult
Deinstitutionalization
Developmental Approach to Research
Diagnostic and Statistical Manual (DSM)
Direct Practice: Trends and Issues
Direct Practice Effectiveness
Direct Practice in Social Work: Overview
Disabilities: Developmental
Disabilities: Physical
Disasters and Disaster Aid
Divorce and Separation
Domestic Violence
Drug Use and Abuse

Ecological Perspective
Emergency Health Services
Ethical Issues in Research
Ethnic-Sensitive Practice
Existential Approach

Family: Contemporary Patterns
Family: Multigenerational
Family: Nuclear
Family: One Parent
Family: Stepfamilies
Family and Population Planning
Family Life Education
Family Practice
Family Services
Federal Social Legislation Since 1961
Female Offenders
Feminist Social Work
Financial Management
Food Stamp Program
Foster Care for Adults
Foster Care for Children
Foundations and Social Welfare

General and Emergency Assistance
Generalist Perspective
Gestalt Therapy
Group Care for Children
Group Theory and Research

Health Care Financing
Health Care Specializations
Health Planning
Health Service System
Hispanics
History and Evolution of Social Work Practice
History of Social Welfare
History of Social Work and Social Welfare: Significant Dates
Homelessness
Homosexuality: Gay Men
Homosexuality: Lesbian Women
Hospice
Hospital Social Work
Housing
Human Development: Biological Perspective
Human Development: Sociocultural Perspective
Hunger and Malnutrition

Immigrants and Undocumented Aliens
Income Distribution
Income Maintenance System
Industrial Social Work (Occupational Social Work)
Infertility Services
Information and Referral Services
Information Systems: Agency
Information Systems: Client Data
Information Utilization for Management Decision Making
Intergroup Relations
International Social Welfare: Comparative Systems
International Social Welfare Organizations and Services
International Social Work Education
Interviewing

Juvenile Courts, Probation and Parole
Juvenile Justice System

(Continued)

TABLE 3.1   *(Continued)*

Juvenile Offender Diversion and Community-Based Services
Juvenile Offender Institutions
Juvenile Offenders and Delinquency

Legal Issues and Legal Services
Legislative Advocacy
Licensing and Regulation of Social Work Services
Linkage in Direct Practice
Literacy
Long-Term Care
Loss and Bereavement

Macro Practice: Current Trends and Issues
Mass Media
Men
Mental Health and Illness
Mental Health and Illness in Children
Mental Health Services
Mexican Americans
Migrant and Seasonal Farm Workers
Military Social Work
Minorities of Color
Mutual Help Groups

Natural Helping Networks
Neighborhoods
Nuclear War and Disarmament

Organizations: Context for Social Service Delivery
Organizations: Impact on Employees and Community

Parent Training
Patients' Rights
Personnel Management
Planning and Management Professions
Police Social Work
Policy Analysis: Methods and Techniques
Political Action in Social Work
Poverty
Prevention
Preventive Health Care and Wellness

Primary Health Care
Private and Proprietary Services
Professional Associations: Council on Social Work Education
Professional Associations: National Association of Social Workers
Professional Associations: Special Interest
Professional Liability and Malpractice
Profession of Social Work: Contemporary Characteristics
Program Evaluation
Prostitution
Protective Services for Children
Protective Services for the Aged
Psychosocial Approach
Psychotropic Medications
Public Health Services
Public Social Services
Puerto Ricans
Purchasing Social Services

Quality Assurance
Quality Control in Income Maintenance

Racial Discrimination and Inequality
Radical Social Work
Recording in Direct Practice
Refugees
Research in Social Work
Research Measures and Indices in Direct Practice
Resource Development and Service Provision
Resource Mobilization and Coordination
Retirement and Pension Programs
Runaways
Rural Social Work

School Social Work
Sectarian Agencies
Settlements and Neighborhood Centers
Sex Discrimination and Inequality
Sexual Assault Services

Sexual Dysfunction
Sexuality
Single Subject Research Designs
Social Planning
Social Planning and Community Organization
Social Planning in the Public Sector
Social Planning in the Voluntary Sector
Social Problems and Issues: Theories and Definitions
Social Security
Social Skills Training
Social Welfare Financing
Social Welfare Policy: Trends and Issues
Social Work and the Human Services
Social Work Education
Social Work in the Pacific Territories
Social Work in the U.S. Territories and Commonwealth
Social Work Practice with Groups
Staff-Initiated Organizational Change
Suicide
Supervision in Social Work

Task-Centered Approach
Termination in Direct Practice
Transactional Analysis

Unemployment and Underemployment
Unemployment Compensation and Workers' Compensation Programs
Unions: Social Work

Values and Ethics
Veterans and Veterans' Services
Victimization Programs and Victims of Crime
Vocational Rehabilitation
Voluntary Agencies
Volunteers
Voter Registration

White Ethnic Groups
White House Conferences
Women
Women in Macro Practice

TABLE 3.1 *(Continued)*

Work Experience Programs
Workfare
Youth Service Agencies
Appendix 1: NASW Code of
Ethics

Appendix 2: Curriculum Poli-
cy for the Master's Degree
and Baccalaureate Degree
Programs in Social Work
Education
Appendix 3: NASW Stan-

dards for the Practice of
Clinical Social Work
Appendix 4: Guide to Sources
of Information on Social
Welfare Agencies

BIOGRAPHIES

Abbott, Edith
Abbott, Grace
Addams, Jane
Altmeyer, Arthur J.

Barrett, Janie Porter
Barton, Clarissa (Clara)
    Harlowe
Beers, Clifford Whittingham
Bethune, Mary McLeod
Brace, Charles Loring
Breckinridge, Sophonisba
    Preston
Brockway, Zebulon Reed
Bruno, Frank John
Buell, Bradley
Burns, Eveline Mabel

Cabot, Richard Clarke
Cannon, Ida Maud
Cannon, Mary Antoinette
Coyle, Grace Longwell

Day, Dorothy
De Forest, Robert Weeks
Devine, Edward Thomas
Dix, Dorothea Lynde
DuBois, William Edward
    Burghardt
Dunham, Arthur

Eliot, Martha May
Epstein, Abraham

Fauri, Fedele Frederick
Fernandis, Sarah A. Collins
Flexner, Abraham
Follett, Mary Parker
Frankel, Lee Kaufer
Frazier, Edward Franklin

Gallaudet, Edward Miner
Gallaudet, Thomas
Gallaudet, Thomas Hopkins

Garrett, Annette Marie
Gonzalez Molina de la Caro,
    Dolores
Granger, Lester Blackwell

Hamilton, George
Haynes, Elizabeth Ross
Haynes, George Edmund
Hearn, Gordon
Hoey, Jane M.
Hopkins, Harry Lloyd
Howard, Donald S.
Howe, Samuel Gridley

Jarrett, Mary Cromwell
Johnson, Campbell
    Carrington

Kelley, Florence
Kellogg, Paul Underwood

Lassalle, Beatriz
Lathrop, Julia Clifford
Lee, Porter Raymond
Lenroot, Katharine Fredrica
Lindeman, Eduard Christian
Lindsay, Inabel Burns
Lodge, Richard
Lowell, Josephine Shaw
Lurie, Harry Lawrence

Manning, Leah Katherine
    Hicks
Matthews, Victoria Earle

Newstetter, Wilber I.

Pagan de Colon,
    Petroamerica
Perkins, Frances
Pray, Kenneth

Rapoport, Lydia
Reynolds, Bertha Capen

Richmond, Mary Ellen
Riis, Jacob August
Rivera de Alvarado, Carmen
Robison, Sophie Moses
Rodriguez Pastor, Soledad
Rubinow, Isaac Max
Rush, Benjamin

Schwartz, William
Seton, Elizabeth Ann Bayley
    (Mother Seton)
Simkhovitch, Mary
    Kingsbury
Smith, Zilpha Drew
Spellman, Dorothea C.
Switzer, Mary Elizabeth

Taft, Julia Jessie
Taylor, Graham
Terrell, Mary Eliza Church
Thomas, Jesse O.
Titmuss, Richard Morris
Towle, Charlotte
Truth, Sojourner
Tubman, Harriet

Wald, Lillian
Washington, Booker
    Taliaferro
Washington, Forrester
    Blanchard
Wells-Barnett, Ida Bell
White, Eartha Mary
    Magdalene
Wiley, George
Wilkins, Roy
Williams, Anita Rose
Witte, Ernest Frederic

Young, Whitney Moore, Jr.
Youngdahl, Benjamin
    Emanuel
Younghusband, Dame Eileen

Source: Anne Minahan, ed. "List of Entries," in *Encyclopedia of Social Work,* 18th ed. (Silver Spring, MD: National Association of Social Workers, 1987). Reprinted with permission from the *Encyclopedia of Social Work* Contents. Copyright 1987, National Association of Social Workers, Inc.

TABLE 3.2 Contents: Face the Nation 1987

1. U.S. Demographic Characteristics
2. The Economy, Wealth, and Income
3. Employment, Unemployment, and Underemployment
4. Government Revenues and Expenditures
5. Social Welfare Expenditures, Programs, and Recipients
6. Social Indicators
7. Health Status and Medical Care
8. Mental Health and Illness
9. Child Welfare
10. International Comparative Data
11. Social Work Education

Source: S. M. Rosen, D. Fanshel, and M. E. Lutz, eds. *Face the Nation 1987: Statistical Supplement to the 18th Edition to the Encyclopedia of Social Work* (Silver Spring, MD: National Association of Social Workers, 1987). Reprinted with permission from *Face the Nation 1987*, Contents. Copyright 1987, National Association of Social Workers, Inc.

the most useful of these indexes will be the subject index. (See Figure 3.1.) The subject index provides a listing of all books organized by subject headings. For example, if you were interested in the subject marital happiness, this might be one subject heading in the subject index. Using the subject index, though, can be just like using the Yellow Pages—frustrating! No single subject heading will provide all relevant references. You will need to make a list of related subject headings and look for each of them. With respect to marital happiness, for example, you might also look under the subject headings marriage, family relationships, and divorce. Also, individual references will sometimes provide you with additional subject headings. In fact, most of the time, when additional subject headings are appropriate, they are listed on the card catalog.

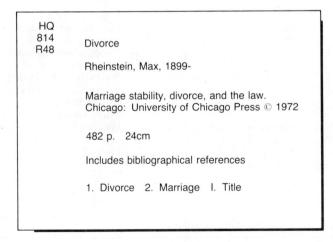

FIGURE 3.1 Catalog Card Indexed by Subject

The remaining two card catalogs differ only in that the organizing information is either the author's name or the title of the book. If you discover, for example, that a particular author has written one book related to your research subject, you may wish to check the author index to see if he or she has written any other related books.

Evaluating the Reference   As you locate the catalog cards for books that are subject-appropriate, you will have to decide which references to retain and which to eliminate. This is particularly so if you have retrieved an overabundance of book references. Carol Williams and Gary Wolfe [10] list seven factors to consider when deciding on whether to retain or reject a reference. Most of the time the card catalog will provide you with enough information to evaluate these factors.

1. *The book is out of date.* Generally speaking, five years ages a reference. And unless the work either is considered a "classic" in the area or stands as the only research in the area, more current references should be sought.

2. *The book is too elementary.* Most of the time, for example, you would not use introductory texts as main sources.

3. *The book is too advanced or technical.* If you found a book that described the marriage relationship in mathematical terms, you might decide to skip the reference. You might choose, though, to consult this reference at some later point when you have done more reading.

4. *The book treats an aspect of the subject you do not wish to cover.* A book on long-distance marriages—in which the two partners' careers force them to live in separate cities—would probably be discarded unless you were researching the influence of this factor on marital happiness.

5. *The author and publisher information suggests that the book may not be sufficiently authoritative.* Greater familiarity with the subject may be required to make this judgment.

6. *You have already consulted the book.*

7. *The book contains information you already have from other sources.*

Recording Adequate Information   If, after considering each of these factors, you believe that the reference can be useful to you, you will need to make out a bibliography card. (See Figure 3.2.) In making out this card, be sure to include all information that would be required to find this book later in your library: (1) call numbers, (2) author(s), (3) title, and (4) date of publication. In addition, you should record any other information that would be required for footnotes or bibliographical references in your paper—most notably the publisher and the place of publication.

Social Work Journals

As we have stated earlier in Chapter 1, social work and social service articles are published in over thirty journals. (See Figure 1.1 for a review of these journals.) In this discussion of social work journals, for illustrative purposes, emphasis will be given to those published by the National Association of Social Work. Each journal has a separate and unique focus. The articles published in a given issue will often

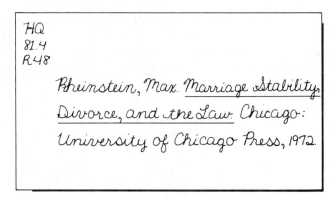

FIGURE 3.2   Bibliography Card

focus on a specific theme, such as social welfare, social insurance, gerontology, child abuse, a particular conceptual framework, social security, and so on.

In searching for published articles on an individual subject or by a particular author, you will be pleased to note that each journal prints an annual index of titles and authors for each year of publication. For example, one major professional journal, *Social Work*, prints its indexes in the November–December issue. Thus, when searching, you do not have to check each individual issue published that year. If you are interested in a particular subject, you just need to scan the annual index for pertinent titles and/or authors, and be directed to the specific issue.

In addition to *Social Work*, other scholarly journals published by NASW include *Social Work Research and Abstracts*, which contains original research pieces as well as abstracts of recent works from social work and related journals. Journals that focus on specialized fields of practice are also popular, including *Health and Social Work* and *Social Work in Education*.

Other Scholarly Journals

Although the card catalog is often the first place students turn in trying to make discoveries about their research subject, it is not usually the most productive source. Quite frequently, the greatest amount of information is obtained from reading the scholarly journals. But herein lies a problem. There are hundreds of scholarly journals. Each is generally published several (two to six or even twelve) times per year, and each issue contains several articles. Consequently, when we talk of scholarly articles, we are talking about thousands of articles per year. If we went to the library with the intention of perusing these journal articles to find those that are related to our research subject area, it would take forever—and we would probably overlook many. Fortunately, much of the guesswork and legwork has been taken out of this search. Just as the card catalog provides us with an indexing of published books, there are catalog-type sources that provide us with an indexing of the scholarly articles.

Sources that will be of substantial benefit to you in your search include the various *abstracts*. Abstracts are brief summaries of the major points of articles, usually written by the authors of the articles. Most likely, a search of the abstracts will be helpful to you regardless of the number of published articles on a subject. If there are very few articles on a particular subject, without the abstracts you may have trouble locating them. If there are many articles, you will need the abstracts to help you eliminate those that are not relevant. Two of the most used abstracts in the social sciences include the *Sociological Abstracts* and the *Psychological Abstracts*. Additional sources worth examining are various *indexes*. Indexes differ from abstracts in that they provide only bibliographical information—no brief summary. Two of the most used indexes include *Social Science Index* and *Social Science Citation Index*. Let's take a brief look at each of these abstracts and indexes. (See Figure 3.3 for sample entries.)

Sociological Abstracts   The *Sociological Abstracts* are a collection of nonevaluative abstracts which reflect the world's serial literature in sociology and related disciplines. Each issue contains the following:

Table of contents
The citations and abstracts themselves
Supplements
     A. IRPS (The International Review of Publications in Sociology)
        i. Book abstracts
        ii. Bibliography of reviews
     B. Abstracts of papers presented at major sociological association meetings
Indexes
     A. Author
     B. Source
     C. Subject

In addition, some issues contain abstracts of conference papers.

Sociological Abstracts assigns each article a four-digit code that serves to classify it. There are thirty-three major classifications into which articles may be coded. And for each major classification, there are subcategories that provide even further refinement. These major classifications are listed in Table 3.3. An article is classified in the section of *Sociological Abstracts* to which it is viewed as being most relevant. If two sections seem equally relevant, it is placed in the section where it will be most noticed.

Sociological Abstracts provides three indexes of articles: subject, author, and source. The subject index is a listing of assigned article codes organized by subject headings. The author index is a listing of authors and accession numbers by titles. As an additional aid, a cumulative index (of subjects, authors, and sources) is published at the end of each year. The subject index of this cumulative volume is composed of approximately five thousand key terms that appear in boldface type. Each entry appears with an informative or descriptive phrase to give the reader some idea of the article's content.

Let's suppose that you wished to locate the published research on marital happiness. You might begin by examining the listings in each issue classified under

FIGURE 3.3   Samples of Entries from Abstracts and Indexes

Excerpted entries from Social Science Citation Index, 1985.

The Family & Socialization

This entry was taken from "The Family and Socialization" section of one of the five issues of *Sociological Abstracts*. This is the only entry of this article that provides bibliographical information and an abstract. The author, source, and subject indexes found in this same issue will refer to this article by its accession number which is in the upper-left corner.

85O7129
Demaris, Alfred (Auburn U, AL 36849), A Comparison of Remarriages with First Marriages on Satisfaction in Marriage and Its Relationship to Prior Cohabitation, UM *Family Relations*, 1984, 33, 3, July, 443–449.
¶ Marital satisfaction of 122 remarried vs 187 first-married white couples aged 20–45 living in Gainesville, Fla, was examined & compared on the basis of questionnaire responses. Additionally, remarriers were compared to first marriers with respect to cohabitation before marriage & its effect on current marital satisfaction. No significant differences were found between first-married & remarried individuals in either marital satisfaction or the propensity to cohabit before marriage. Cohabitation was associated with significantly lower satisfaction among individuals in first marriages, while, among remarried persons, cohabitation made no difference in current marital satisfaction. 3 Tables, 20 References. Modified HA

Subject Index

This entry was taken from the subject index of the cumulative index volume. Notice that the accession number matches the code of the above entry. In order to obtain the bibliographical information for this article, the above abstract would have to be located in one of the five yearly issues.

Marriage/Marriages/Marital
major depression, middle-aged women; social setting/income/marital status/employment/adversity/religiosity; community survey; depressed/normal women, Sweden; O7271
marital breakdown; childlessness, birth timing; General Household Survey data, divorce records; married females, GB; O7021
marital mobility/homogamy, Spain; spouse's parents' education/occupation; questionnaire survey; Madrid & Guadalajara 1975/76; O6662
marital satisfaction, Moscow, USSR; self-diagnostic questionnaire tested; O7150
[marital satisfaction; remarriage vs first marriage, prior cohabitation; questionnaires; white couples, aged 20–45; O7129]
marriage alliance, kinship; literacy; ethnographic data; Angkola Batak, Sumatra, Indonesia; O6307

FIGURE 3.3   *(Continued)*

Developmental Psychology

This entry was taken from the "Developmental Psychology" section of one of the issues. This is the only entry of this article providing bibliographical information and an abstract. The author and subject indexes will list this article by its assigned code only.

840 Perlman, Daniel; Gerson, Ann C. & Spinner, Barry. (U Manitoba, Winnipeg, Canada) Loneliness among senior citizens: An empirical report. *Essence*, 1978, Vol 2(4), 239–248.—Reports an empirical study of loneliness among 158 senior citizens (average age 70 yrs) in Canada, each of whom completed a self-administered questionnaire. Greater loneliness was associated with less friendship contact, fewer close friends, social anxiety, ineffectiveness in influencing others, low marital satisfaction, and low life satisfaction. Lonely respondents watched more TV, would have liked more planned activities, and had difficulty getting transportation to places where they wanted to go. Furthermore, loneliness was linked with poor hearing ability, poor health, and having a lower income. Finally, being lonely was correlated with a variety of recently experienced emotions (e.g, feeling restless, bored, and angry). (French summary) (14 ref)—*Journal abstract.*

Subject Index

This is an entry taken from the subject index of the three-year cumulative index volume. Notice that the assigned code matches the number of the above entry. In order to get the bibliographical information for this article, the above entry would have to be located.

Marital Problems [See Marital Relations]
Marital Relations [See Also Marital Conflict]
analysis of Catholic family triads with 14–17 yr old daughters, application of circumplex model of family & marital systems, 7841
attitudes toward change in marital relationships, permanence of relationships, counseling implications, 8442
bases of power & communication processes, family planning & birth control decision making, husbands & wives, 12388

    .
    .
    .

family systems approach to marital & family conflict, reduction of extreme itching, 16 yr old female and her parents, 12935
females as perpetrators & victims of domestic & other violence, 10623
friendship contact & number of friends & social anxiety & ineffectiveness in influencing others & marital & life satisfaction, loneliness & amount of TV watching, aged, 840
high achievement in late adolescent task development, subsequent marital adjustment, married college students & student spouses, implications for developmental counseling model, 883

(continued)

FIGURE 3.3   *(Continued)*

Social Sciences Index

Excerpted entries from *Social Sci-ences Index.*

Marini, Margaret Mooney
Age and sequencing norms in the transition to adulthood. bibl *Soc Forces* 63:228–44 S '84
Women's educational attainment and the timing of entry into parent-hood. bibl *Am Sociol Rev* 49:491–511 Ag '84

Marital Age
Age at marriage, role enactment, role consensus, and marital satis-faction. S. J. Bahr and others. bibl *J Marriage Fam* 45:795–803 N '83; Discussion. 46:985–8 N '84
Early marriage as a career contingency: the prediction of educational attainment. G. D. Lowe and D. D. Witt. bibl *J Marriage Fam* 46:689–98 Ag '84
Out of sequence: the timing of marriage following a premarital birth. J. D. Teachman and K. A. Polonko. bibl *Soc Forces* 63:245–60 S '84
Professional women and marriage. S. M. Allen and R. A. Kalish. bibl *J Marriage Fam* 46:375–82 My '84
The social and demographic correlates of divorce and separation in the United States: an update and reconsideration. N. D. Glenn and M. Supancic. bibl *J Marriage Fam* 46:563–75 Ag '84

Marital instability. See Divorce

Marital satisfaction
See also
Kansas marital satisfaction scale
Age at marriage, role enactment, role consensus, and marital satis-faction. S. J. Bahr and others. bibl *J Marriage Fam* 45:795–803 N '83; Discussion. 46:985–8 N '84
Agreement, understanding, realization, and feeling understood as predictors of communicative satisfaction in marital dyads. A. Allen and T. Thompson. bibl *J Marriage Fam* 46:915–21 N '84

Excerpted entries from *Social Sci-ence Citation Index®*. (Copied with the permission of the Insti-tute for Scientific Information, © 1985.)

ARMSTRONG D			VOL	PG	YR
WEINMAN J	MED EDUC		18	164	84
80 MED ED PRIMARY HLTH					
ATKINSON P	SOCIAL SC M		19	949	84
82 ANN NEUROL	12 169				
SEE SCI FOR 1 ADDITIONAL CITATION					
ATKINSON JB	ARCH PATH L		106	341	84
82 RISE INT ORG SHORT H					
BAER GW	AM HIST REV	B	88	1250	83
83 MAY INT PERS MAN ASS					
BURKE MJ	J APPL PSYC		69	482	84
83 POLITICAL ANATOMY BO					
BELLABY P	SOCIOL REV	B	32	433	84
CHALFANT HP	SOCIAL FORC	B	63	610	84
MAGNER LN	AM SCIENT	B	72	218	84
SOFFER RN	AM HIST REV	B	89	445	84
WARREN CAB	CONT SOCIOL	B	13	622	84
83 POLITICAL ANATOMY BO		CH 3			
ARMSTRON D	SOCIAL SC M		18	737	84
84 ACQUIRED IMMUNE DEFI					
WEBER J	LANCET	B	1	714	84

TABLE 3.3   Classifications for Sociological Abstracts and Psychological Abstracts

Sociological Abstracts	*Psychological Abstracts*
methodology and research technology	general psychology
sociology: history and theory	psychometrics
social psychology	experimental psychology (human)
group interactions	experimental psychology (animal)
culture and social structure	physiological psychology
complex organizations (management)	physiological intervention
social change and economic development	communication systems
mass phenomena	developmental psychology
political interactions	social processes and social issues
social differentiation	experimental social psychology
rural sociology and agricultural economics	personality
urban structures and ecology	physical and psychological disorders
sociology of the arts	treatment and prevention
sociology of education	professional personnel and professional issues
sociology of religion	educational psychology
social control	applied psychology
sociology of science	
demography and human biology	
the family and socialization	
sociology of health and medicine	
social problems and social welfare	
sociology of knowledge	
community development	
policy, planning, forecasting, and speculation	
radical sociology	
environmental interactions	
studies in poverty	
studies in violence	
feminist studies	
Marxist sociology	
clinical sociology	
sociology of business	
visual sociology	

"The Family and Socialization." Following this search, you might use the subject index in the cumulative index volume to make sure that you didn't miss any references. If a particular journal seems appropriate (e.g., *Journal of Marriage and the Family*), you might check the source index for a listing of the articles in that journal.

If, from reading the brief summaries of these articles, you feel that an article is relevant, you should make a bibliography card. Information recorded should include author, title of article, journal name, volume number, date, and pages. On each bibliography card, be sure to record the code assigned to the article by *Sociological Abstracts*. As you move from each of the five yearly issues of *Sociological Abstracts* to the cumulative index for that year, some repetition of references is inevitable. If you have recorded the assigned codes, you may find that you have already examined many of these references, and you will not lose time looking them up again.

Psychological Abstracts *Psychological Abstracts* are similar to *Sociological Abstracts,* providing brief summaries for the articles published in some 950 journals that are international in scope. Each issue is divided into sixteen major classifications, each of which is further subdivided for finer distinctions. These sixteen classifications are listed in Table 3.3. Additionally, an index volume is published every six months and a cumulative index volume every three years. These index issues provide both subject and author listings. The subject listings are similar to those in *Sociological Abstracts* and are identified by boldface type. As in *Sociological Abstracts,* the index volume provides only a brief description of the study along with the code assigned by *Psychological Abstracts.* Again, if you think that the reference can be useful, you should record the necessary information on a bibliography card.

Social Science Index *Social Science Index* is an index to 263 social science periodicals. This index first appeared in June 1974 and is published four times a year. *Social Science Index* continues the indexing of seventy-seven periodicals previously covered by the *Social Science and Humanities Index,* which is no longer published. This index consists of author and subject entries in one alphabetical list. Book reviews are organized separately. Both the author and subject entries appear in boldface type.

Social Science Citation Index One additional index to the scholarly journals that can be quite beneficial deserves our attention, as it is somewhat different from the previously cited sources. The brochure of the *Social Science Citation Index* (*SSCI*) reports that it "indexes every article and every significant editorial item from every issue of over 1000 of the world's most important social science journals. In addition, *SSCI* selectively covers another 2200 journals indexing only those articles perceived as relevant to the social sciences." *SSCI* provides two indexing schemes: citation index and permuterm.

Citation indexing is based on the premise that an author's references (citations) to previously published material indicate a subject relationship between his or her current article and the older publications. In effect, articles that cite the same references usually have subject relationships with each other. Using this basic assumption, *SSCI* groups together all newly published articles that have cited the same earlier publication. Thus, the basis for organizing references is the author's own use of references.

Permuterm indexing uses the descriptors provided by the authors in the titles of their articles. The author's titles are taken just as they are published, and every significant term is used as a retrieval term. Every term in the title is paired (permuted) with every other term in that title to create a series of two-level indexing terms for each article. Thus, this procedure, like the other, indexes the articles just as they are described by their authors.

Although *SSCI* is complete and comprehensive, you should not use it to the exclusion of *Sociological Abstracts, Psychological Abstracts, Social Science Index,* or other relevant sources. Cataloging references around citations and title key words is certainly not foolproof. These techniques will not always uncover all relevant research. Consequently, other sources need to be examined. In fact, if there are relevant older references that several articles keep citing, you will probably not know this until you begin to read the literature. Thus, *SSCI* will likely be more useful after you have gained some degree of familiarity with the literature.

Government Documents

Most libraries reserve an area for government documents, which might include U.S. Census reports, the findings of studies commissioned by various government agencies, statistics published by various government offices, and the like. Some of these documents might be useful for your research. For example, if you were researching some aspect of marital happiness, you might wish to have the latest statistics on the percentage of the U.S. adult population who are married, divorced, and single. Certainly, you should consider using this section of your library.

Computer Search

If, by now, you have the idea that a search of the literature is no small job, you are right. If this search is done thoroughly and correctly, you may have to spend several days or even weeks in the library. But some of this time can be saved by an innovation of today's modern technology. If you do not wish to conduct a self-search of the published literature, you may conduct a computer search. Computer searches generally identify relevant references by using key terms from the articles' titles and abstracts (brief summaries). The databases for these computer searches are the abstracts and indexes we have already discussed (*Sociological Abstracts, Psychological Abstracts, Social Science Index, Social Science Citation Index,* etc.). The information in these sources has simply been stored in computer memory. Retrieved references can be sorted alphabetically by author or chronologically by year. The fee for such searches can range from $10.00 to possibly $500.00 or even more. Most institutions that perform such searches will ask the requester to place a price ceiling on the search. Most large university libraries are generally equipped to perform such searches. In addition, the indexing publications (*Sociological Abstracts, Psychological Abstracts*) perform such searches, and information on how to obtain such a search through these publishing organizations can be found in most issues of these publications.

Identifying the Research Impetus: Reviewing the Literature

The filtering process has begun. In searching the various indexes (card catalog, abstracts, etc.) for research related to your research project, you have retained some references and rejected others. This filtering process has allowed you to narrow the research subject. You may, for example, have retained those references relating marital happiness and retirement but discarded those references concerned with the effect of children on marital happiness. In effect, filtering has allowed you to eliminate certain aspects of the research subject. But you are not yet ready to formulate the research question. In order to accomplish this task, you need to know more than just what research has been done. You need to be familiar with the knowledge communicated through this body of research. In other words, you now need to read or review this literature. Reviewing the literature will help you to identify the established findings on your chosen research subject. Understanding and organizing these findings will help to provide the impetus for your own research question.

By research impetus we mean the motivating forces or factors that lead to a specific research question. One purpose of research is to further knowledge, and your research should be no exception. No single research endeavor stands alone. In the social sciences, it has become customary to begin research by citing previous research. To this extent, the impetus for all research is some previous research. As you review the research literature, you should read with the idea of linking your research to previous research. This linking will help to provide the impetus for your research and thus lead to the formulation of your research question.

There is no single research impetus that adequately accounts for the bulk of research questions formulated in any research subject area. Rather, there are several motivating factors out of which research questions are formulated, and each is important in its own right. Selltiz, Wrightsman, and Cook [11] have identified several such factors, including (1) testing theory, (2) using theory to understand a research question, (3) challenging prior research, (4) clarifying an underlying process, (5) attempting to account for unexpected findings, (6) replication, and (7) seeing if research in one area extends to another. Let's see how each of these factors can provide the impetus for a specific research question.

Testing Theory

Sometimes the primary impetus for a specific research question is to test theory. We will talk about theory in detail in Chapter 4. At this point, it might be helpful to think of theory as a set of postulates, logically linked to provide a plausible explanation of some social phenomenon. Let us illustrate with an interesting study. In late September in the early 1950s, a newspaper carried the following headlines on a back page: "Prophecy from Planet. Clarion Call to City. Flee that Flood. It'll Swamp Us on Dec. 21, Outer Space Tells Suburbanite." The story followed:

> Lake City will be destroyed by a flood from Great Lake just before dawn, December 21, according to a suburban housewife. Mrs. Marian Keech of 847 West School Street says the prophecy is not her own. It is the purport of many messages she has received by automatic writing. The messages, according to Mrs. Keech, are sent to her by superior beings from a planet called "Clarion." These beings have been visiting the earth, she says, in what we call flying saucers. During their visits, she says, they have observed fault lines in the earth's crust that foretoken the deluge. Mrs. Keech reports that she was told the flood will spread to form an inland sea stretching from the Arctic Circle to the Gulf of Mexico. [12]

This newspaper account was read by Leon Festinger, a psychologist, who thought that Mrs. Keech and her followers would provide an interesting study on attitude change. Festinger had been working on a theory of attitude formation and change that he labeled cognitive dissonance theory. Cognitive dissonance theory suggests that when individuals are faced with two or more obverse facts (one fact does not follow from the other), either the facts must be made to agree or attitude change will occur. Festinger viewed Mrs. Keech and her followers as an ideal group for testing his theory. If the flying saucer was to land on a designated date as Mrs. Keech predicted and yet it did not land, cognitive dissonance should result, according to Festinger. And the group could resolve this dissonance by either changing the facts or by changing their attitudes and beliefs. By concocting stories of communication with extraterrestrial beings, two of Festinger's graduate assistants were able to join the group. (We will reserve judgment about the ethics of this project until later.) As participants, they were able to observe the natural behaviors of all group members and to record the changes that group members underwent as they waited for the flying saucer. Their observations and written accounts provided substantial support for Festinger's theory of cognitive dissonance.

Festinger's theory of cognitive dissonance has been repeatedly tested since its inception in 1957. Festinger and Carlsmith [13] devised an ingenious laboratory test of this theory. Students participated in an experiment requiring them to work on a boring task. Upon completion of the task, each student was asked to inform the incoming student that the task was pleasant and even exciting. For communicating this information, some students were paid $1.00 and others were paid $20.00. Festinger and Carlsmith reasoned that the students paid $1.00 should experience greater cognitive dissonance, as $1.00 was not sufficient reward to justify the bold lie. The experimental findings confirmed the hypothesis and thus provided a test of the theory. In any field, when theory is constructed, one must test it by means of numerous research endeavors. Such research is essential if we are to know the extent to which the theory is supported.

Using Theory to Understand a Research Question

Sometimes the impetus of research is not to test theory per se, but simply to use theory as an aid in understanding and answering a research question. In effect, it provides a perspective through which the research question can be viewed. To illustrate, in the late 1950s and early 1960s, Thiabaut and Kelley [14] and Homans [15] independently formulated theories on interpersonal attraction. Both theories explain interpersonal attraction in terms of the rewards exchanged and the costs incurred. Specifically, a person (P) is attracted to other (O) when, in the course of interacting, O offers P more rewards than costs. When a person's profits (rewards minus costs) are directly proportional to investments, the result is distributive justice, a concept discussed by George Homans.

Out of this research on distributive justice grew equity theory, which suggests that individuals compare their inputs to their outcomes and expect to get as much as they give. If the outcome is not proportional to the input, dissatisfaction results. Shafer and Keith [16] have conducted an interesting study in which they use equity theory as a basis for understanding depression among married couples. Specifically, they have applied equity principles to the study of performance in certain marital roles or tasks. In marriage, they reason, there generally exists a division of labor that provides role expectations for both husband and wife. These expectations include not only role performance but also the quality of that performance. Shafer and Keith suggest that both husband and wife make determinations about the fairness of their own and their partner's role performances. They propose that marriage partners who perceive inequity in the performance of marital roles will feel more psychological distress than partners who perceive equity. They further propose that marriage partners who perceive that they are overbenefited will feel less psychological distress than partners who perceive that they are underbenefited. Their findings support the first proposition and are in the stated direction of the second. Thus, they conclude that equity theory is helpful in understanding depression among married couples.

Challenging Prior Research

Frequently the impetus of research is simply to challenge some previous research. Recognized research seldom goes unchallenged. As we have already discovered, social scientists are different enough that they quite often see things differently. When this is the case, research often serves to challenge. Research, for example, has clearly demonstrated sex differences in nonverbal communication. That is, males and females have been shown to use nonverbal clues differently [17]. These sex-specific models of nonverbal behavior have been labeled *genderlects*. Lamb [18] has challenged such research, suggesting that though a few forms of nonverbal behavior may be sex-specific, "in general, they reflect patterns of power and control between the sexes, which are found in all human groups regardless of sex composition" [19]. Consequently, Lamb believes that these modes of nonverbal cues are perhaps more appropriately labeled *powerlects*. Lamb believed if he could demonstrate these patterns of nonverbal behavior in same-sex groups, he would have evidence of powerlects instead of genderlects. His findings show that females are just as consistent as males in using these forms of control with members of their own sex, suggesting that power rather than sex is the important factor in these nonverbal and paraverbal modes of communication.

Clarifying an Underlying Process

Sometimes, independent research endeavors that test similar hypotheses produce inconsistent and even contradictory findings. Since there is usually any number of logical and plausible explanations for these differences, research is often undertaken in an effort to clarify. Self-disclosure research provides an excellent example of such research inconsistencies. Self-disclosure can be described as the communication of intimacy or the act of revealing personal information to others. Research on self-disclosure has generally assumed self-disclosure to be a reward or positive outcome. This assumption would suggest a positive relationship between self-disclosure and attraction. That is, the more revealing the self-disclosure, the greater the attraction between the people concerned. However, existing research on self-disclosure and attraction is actually inconsistent. Although several studies demonstrate a positive relationship between self-disclosure and attraction, there are other studies that suggest a negligible or nonsignificant relationship and still others that indicate a negative relationship between these two variables.

Gilbert and Horenstein [20] designed a study aimed at clarifying these inconsistencies. Their insight into the inconsistencies was derived from an earlier study by Gilbert [21] in which a negative relationship between self-disclosure and attraction had been demonstrated. That is, subjects were found to be more attracted to a person (a confederate) who disclosed him- or herself less. Gilbert noted, though, that the low disclosure consisted of mild positive content (a woman's feelings about her brother who was getting married), while the high disclosure consisted of negative content (a woman's negative feelings about her mother and herself). Drawing from this observation, Gilbert and Horenstein suggested that perhaps the inconsistencies in the research on self-disclosure and attraction might be due to previous studies' failure to distinguish between the degree of intimacy (high or low) and the valence (positive or negativeness) of self-disclosure and their relationship to interpersonal attraction. With this in mind, a total of eighty males and females were assigned to one of four experimental conditions: (1) high positive, (2) low positive, (3) high negative, and (4) low negative. Their findings showed that subjects demonstrated the greatest degree of attraction when the disclosure content was positive, regardless of the degree of intimacy of the disclosure.

Attempting to Account for Unexpected Findings

Sometimes research efforts produce the unexpected. The patterns that emerge from the data are unforeseen. When such findings emerge, we label them **serendipitous** (unexpected, unanticipated). But it is not enough to just note the occurrence of serendipitous findings. Further research is often undertaken to determine whether or not these findings will reoccur. In 1976, Inbar and Adler published an article entitled "The Vulnerable Age Phenomenon: A Serendipitous Finding." The "vulnerable age phenomenon" refers to the finding that "children in about the 6- to 11-year-old bracket may be more vulnerable to crises in their environment than either younger or older youths" [22]. This finding surfaced in a cross-cultural study of immigrants. The impetus to search for this finding was a case study by Martan [23] investigating the school achievements of children as a function of the impact of the Israeli educational system on youths. Martan expected to find a negative relationship between age of children and successful schooling (measured as the percentage having attended college). That is, a greater percentage of the younger children as compared with the older children would be more likely to attend college. This expectation was based on the notions that younger children learn a new language faster than older youths and that language problems for adolescents translated into school failures. Contrary to expectation, a positive relationship was found between age of children at immigration and chances of attending college. Specifically, younger children were less likely to attend college than older youths.

Martan's serendipitous finding served as a starting point for Inbar and Adler. Since Inbar and Adler were already planning a cross-cultural study of immigrants, they decided to look for the vulnerable age phenomenon. And, in fact, their study also demonstrated this phenomenon. Following this study, Inbar sought even further evidence of the vulnerable age phenomenon in two additional studies. In both studies the phenomenon was again documented. Inbar and Alder [24] explain this phenomenon as a function of stress resulting from school transfers. While older children can articulate their problems, younger children sometimes have difficulty. Thus, the problems encountered by grade-school children often go unnoticed. When serendipitous findings occur, new research is needed. Without new research, we cannot know if the finding is reliable (will occur again) or is simply one of chance.

Replication

If the social sciences are to establish a rigorous body of knowledge, research must be replicated. It is simply not enough to say that one study produces fact. Any study has its limitations—of time, places, people. We might ask, for example, for any study, "Would the findings hold for another group of people? For another place? For another time?" Inbar attempted to replicate the vulnerable age phenomenon to see it if would hold for another group, in another place, at another time.

In the social sciences, as we have learned, replication is generally the exception, not the rule. However, there have been some studies where the research impetus was to replicate the findings of an earlier study. In 1933, for example, Katz and Braly [25] conducted what is now a classic study on stereotypes. The subjects for this study were one hundred Princeton students. Each student was given a list of ten ethnic groups and forty-eight traits and was asked to check those traits that seemed typical for each group. In addition, they were asked to choose for each group the five traits that seemed most typical. If students' selection of traits had been completely random, each trait would have been selected only 6 percent of the time. However, many of the traits that were chosen more often yielded stereotypic views of the different ethnic groups. Moreover, the same traits were not selected for each group. Hence, Katz and Braly conclude that stereotypic images do exist.

The Katz and Braly study was replicated in 1951 by Gilbert [26] and again in 1969 by Karlins, Coffman, and Walters [29]. Both replications also used Princeton University students. Most apparent from these replications were the changes in stereotypes over this thirty-five-year period. The stereotypic image of Americans became less positive while the stereotypic image of blacks and Jews became more positive. (See Table 3.4.) In fact, Karlins, Coffman, and Walters argue that stereotypic images are fading. While these studies were aimed at replicating the Katz and Braly findings, Kutner [28] conducted a study aimed at replicating the Katz and Braly methodology. Kutner's study is also one of challenge. Primarily, Kutner suggests that if replications of ethnic stereotypes are to be conducted, an updating of the adjective checklist is needed. Replicating the methodology of Katz and Braly, she produced an updated list of traits. Kutner's research produced nineteen new descriptive traits, and of these, thirteen subsequently appeared among the five traits most frequently mentioned as typical of the ethnic group under study. Thus, Kutner concludes that perhaps stereotypes are not fading as much as previously thought. Rather, the Katz and Braly checklist is not meaningful to today's images.

Seeing if a Relationship in One Area Extends to Another

Often, our knowledge base is expanded by attempting to see if a relationship observed in one area can also be observed in another. Piaget's research on the cognitive

TABLE 3.4   Percentage of Princeton College Students Assigning Traits to Ethnic Groups

		% checking trait					% checking trait		
	N:	100	333	150		N:	100	333	150
Trait	Year:	1932	1950	1967	Trait	Year:	1932	1950	1967
AMERICANS					ITALIANS				
Industrious		48	30	23	Artistic		53	28	30
Intelligent		47	32	20	Impulsive		44	19	28
Materialistic		33	37	67	Passionate		37	25	44
Ambitious		33	21	42	Quick-tempered		35	15	28
Progressive		27	5	17	Musical		32	22	9
CHINESE					JAPANESE				
Superstitious		34	18	8	Intelligent		45	11	20
Sly		29	4	6	Industrious		43	12	57
Conservative		29	14	15	Progressive		24	2	17
Loyal to family ties		22	35	50	Shrewd		22	13	7
Industrious		18	18	23	Sly		20	21	3
ENGLISH					JEWS				
Sportsmanlike		53	21	22	Shrewd		79	47	30
Intelligent		46	29	23	Mercenary		49	28	15
Conventional		34	25	19	Industrious		48	29	33
Tradition-loving		31	42	21	Grasping		34	17	17
Conservative		30	22	52	Intelligent		29	37	37
GERMANS					NEGROES				
Scientifically minded		78	62	47	Superstitious		84	41	13
Industrious		65	50	59	Lazy		75	21	36
Stolid		44	10	9	Happy-go-lucky		38	17	27
Intelligent		32	32	19	Ignorant		38	24	11
Methodical		31	20	21	Musical		26	33	47
IRISH					TURKS				
Pugnacious		45	24	13	Cruel		47	12	9
Quick-tempered		39	35	43	Very religious		26	6	7
Witty		38	16	7	Treacherous		21	3	12
Honest		32	11	17	Sensual		20	4	9
Very religious		29	30	27	Ignorant		15	7	13

Source: M. Karlins, T. Coffman, & G. Walters, "On the Fading of Social Stereotypes: Three Generations of College Students," *Journal of Personality & Social Psychology*, 1969, Vol. 13: 1–16. Copyright 1969 by the American Psychological Association. Reprinted by permission.

development of children contributes very importantly to the social work human behavior knowledge base, and therefore serves as an excellent example. Piaget argued that cognitive processes in children develop in stages. This stage theory of cognitive development suggests that children and adults organize their world differently. This differential organization has been demonstrated, for example, through conservation experiments. For example, in a conservation-of-volume experiment, a child is first shown two identically shaped beakers filled with water to an identical level. The water in one of the beakers is then poured into a third beaker, which is narrower and taller. Naturally, the water level in the third beaker is higher than in the original beaker. The child is then asked, "Which beaker holds more water, or do they hold the same amount of water?" Whereas adults and older children recognize and respond that they both hold the same, preoperational children (under age seven) identify the narrow cylinder as holding more water.

With these conservation experiments in mind, Acker and Tiemens [29] performed an ingenious experiment by making an analogy to television. The appearance of an object on television is changed by zooming in or cutting to a close-up without changing the actual size of the object. Adults recognize a zoom or a cut as simply a change in camera perspective. However, given the findings of Piaget's and others' research, we might suspect that preoperational children perceive the transformation as representing a change in the object itself. In effect, this was the proposition set forth and tested by Acker and Tiemens. In addition to the conservation of television images, they used traditional conservation tasks. Their findings showed that when a zoom is used, children more readily perceive the object as growing large. Can you imagine the implications for advertising, especially for toys?

If you think of the research impetus as the motivating factor or force leading you to a specific research question and if you review the literature with this in mind, the task of formulating a research question will become easier. Remember, reading is a creative endeavor. Ask questions as you read. You cannot play a passive role even in this phase of research.

Evaluating a Research Question

Let's assume that you now have formulated a research question. At times this process has been frustrating and tedious. You are probably quite relieved to have progressed to this point. But wait! The process is not yet complete. We must now evaluate this question in an effort to determine whether it is both reasonable and desirable to pursue. To make this evaluation, we need to ask and answer several questions.

Is It Worthwhile?

This first question is not really a new one. We have considered it, at least indirectly, throughout this chapter. As you identified and read the relevant research literature, you were trying to formulate a research question, which, when answered, would make a contribution to knowledge. The potential contribution of any research question is not always obvious. Consequently, you should not make this decision hastily. If you bounce your research question off another person, don't be too discouraged or even necessarily swayed by such comments as, "Oh, everybody knows the answer to that. It s just common sense." As we have seen in Chapter 2, common sense is not always a reliable teacher. It does not always guide us either wisely or correctly. As a general rule of thumb, if you are convinced that knowledge in the field will be furthered by answering a particular research question, it is most likely worthwhile.

Is It Feasible?

The issue of feasibility is a broad one and can only be dealt with by asking and answering several further questions. Consider the following:

What Is the Scope of the Study?

We have tried to stress that the process of choosing and formulating a research question is a filtering process. We begin with a research subject. We end with a research question. The broad and general nature of a research subject encompasses too many issues and too many concepts. It is simply not realistic to think that we could manage all of these issues and concepts in a single research endeavor. Take, for example, the research subject of factors influencing intelligence. It would be ambitious of us to assume that we could identify most of the important factors and examine them in a single project. Inconsistent and contradictory findings on this research subject have resulted in research introducing several factors: (1) sibship size, (2) birth order, (3) physiological condition of mother, (4) treatment of children by parents, (5) social class, (6) race, and (7) marital disruption, just to name a few. To consider all of these variables would be demanding for the research novice. Even the experienced researcher would be facing quite a challenge. In effect, the scope must be narrow enough that the research is manageable. Generally, a research question that considers no more than three or four concepts should be sufficient. This does not necessarily mean you will only collect data on these three or four concepts. You may collect data on several other concepts for answering a second or even third research question. If you use a questionnaire, for example, it may be constructed to answer several research questions. But for any specific research question, you certainly do not have to use every question on the questionnaire. Once again, the key is manageability.

How Much Time Is Required?

Reading the research literature does not always give you an adequate appreciation of the time required to do research. When you read a study that prints into seven or eight pages, you may think, "Oh, I'll bet that didn't take very long." But the natural flow of the published research narrative can be quite deceptive. Almost everything takes more time than we think. In Chapter 5 we refer to Humphreys's research on impersonal sex in public places. In discussing his research, Humphreys [30] notes that the time investment for this study was approximately three and one-half years. The observation of impersonal sex acts (conducted part-time, as he was also a graduate student) took two years. Another six months of full-time work was invested in administering interview schedules to over one hundred respondents. And still another year went into data analysis. Carefully planned research takes time. The several steps in the total research process cannot be passed over lightly. It takes time to:

1. Identify the relevant literature on a research subject
2. Read this relevant literature

3. Formulate the research question
4. Locate measures for the concepts to be studied
5. Locate the groups to be studied
6. Collect the data
7. Code all of the data if stored in a computer
8. Analyze the data
9. Write the research report

These are just a few of the more obvious tasks to be performed. If you can establish even an approximate time schedule, you can pace your progress. Don't be disappointed if you find you cannot follow it to the letter. Such a schedule is only meant to provide guidelines and to give you some idea of the time required.

How Much Money Is Required?

Research can be quite costly, and for most researchers, the sky is not the limit! Consider the following possible expenditures:

Photocopying articles when reviewing the literature

Requesting articles from other libraries when your library does not carry the reference

Purchasing or renting equipment (e.g., a tape recorder)

Paying subjects

Having a questionnaire or interview schedule typed or copied

Purchasing computer time for data storage and analysis

These are only some of the costs that might be incurred. There may be many others. When Festinger was studying the doomsday group, for example, he had to fly two of his graduate assistants to the group's meetings. Costs are very real and the researcher needs to examine this factor before beginning any research endeavor.

Are Subjects Available?

If subjects are not available, nothing else really matters: the research cannot be done. There are research questions that require unique groups of individuals. If you wanted to study "swinging" activity among adults, you would have to locate a group of swingers. If such a group could not be found, you would have to choose another research question. If you were interested in studying "long-distance marriages," you would probably have to exert a great deal of energy and ingenuity to locate the appropriate couples. For most research questions, subjects can be found, although the search may be time-consuming and even costly. But if you are sufficiently interested in the research question and have the time and resources to locate individuals, subject availability should not be an insurmountable problem. If you find that subjects are not readily available and the time and resources required to locate subjects are not realistic, you will probably want to consider another research question.

Will Subjects Cooperate?

If you find that subjects are available, you will next need to determine whether you can obtain their cooperation in your research endeavor. Suppose you learn, for example, that a "swinging" group does exist in your area. However, after contacting several group members, you realize that you will not be able to gain their cooperation. You might then decide to abandon the research question and choose another. Sometimes institutional officers deny a researcher permission to question or interview students, employees, or others whom they presume to control. In many cases, the official may have exceeded his or her actual authority. One researcher, for example, was denied permission to interview black students at a state university campus. The researcher simply ignored the officer, went to the campus, and interviewed the required informants at the student center. Quite honestly, the university had no right to deny the researcher normal access to the public facilities of that institution. In some instances, administrative authority cannot be countered. It is sometimes difficult to gain entrance into public schools. And if the research question deals with a hypersensitive issue (such as sex education), entrance is doubly difficult, if not impossible. In effect, if the cooperation of those in authority cannot be gained, the researcher may need to redirect his or her research.

Are the Necessary Equipment and Facilities Available?

The testing of some research questions requires sophisticated equipment that can be quite expensive. For example, if the test of your research question requires conducting an experiment, you will need a laboratory facility and possibly a tape recorder, television, public address system, and other items. If such facilities and equipment are not available, the research question may have to be abandoned.

Is It Ethical?

We cannot leave the area of evaluation without addressing the issue of ethics. Specifically, is the test of the research question ethical? Is the researcher being honest with his or her subjects, or does he or she intentionally deceive them? If deception is used, could it potentially harm the subjects? Does the treatment of subjects in any way harmfully alter their perceptions of self? Are their personal rights violated? The researcher should exercise a sense of responsibility toward his or her subjects. In fact, a principle of "reciprocal responsibility" should be operating. An individual who agrees to participate in any research endeavor is placing trust in the researcher. The researcher, in turn, should not violate that trust. The reader is referred to Chapter 5 for a more extensive look at important issues surrounding the practice of ethics-based social work research.

References

1. Robin Lakoff, *Language and Woman's Place* (New York: Harper and Row, 1975).
2. Phillip A. Goldberg, "A Personal Journal," in *The Research Act*, M. Patricia Golden, ed. (Itasca, IL: Peacock, 1976).
3. Goldberg, "A Personal Journal," p. 55.
4. Anne Minahan, ed., *Encyclopedia of Social Work*, 18th ed. (Silver Spring, MD: National Association of Social Workers, 1987).
5. Minahan, "Preface to the 18th Edition," *Encyclopedia of Social Work*, p. v.
6. Sumner M. Rosen, David Fanshel, and Mary E. Lutz, eds., *Face the Nation 1987: Statistical Supplement to the 18th Edition of the Encyclopedia of Social Work* (Silver Spring, MD: National Association of Social Workers, 1987).
7. Robert L. Barker, *Social Work Dictionary* (Silver Spring, MD: National Association of Social Workers, 1987).
8. Barker, "Foreword," *Social Work Dictionary*, p. vii.
9. Barker, "Preface," *Social Work Dictionary*, p. xi.
10. Carol T. Williams and Gary K. Wolfe, *Elements of Research: A Guide for Writers* (Sherman Oaks, CA: Alfred Publishing, 1979).
11. Claire Selltiz, L. S. Wrightsman, and Stuart W. Cook, *Research Methods in Social Relations* (New York: Holt, Rinehart and Winston, 1976).
12. L. Festiger, G. W. Reicken, and S. Schachter, *When Prophecy Fails* (Minneapolis: University of Minnesota Press, 1956), p. 30.
13. L. Festiger and J. M. Carlsmith, "Cognitive Consequences of Forced Compliance," *Journal of Abnormal and Social Psychology* 58 (1959): 203–10.
14. J. W. Thiabaut and H. H. Kelley, *The Social Psychology of Groups* (New York: Wiley, 1959).
15. G. C. Homans, *Social Behavior: Its Elementary Forms* (New York: Harcourt, Brace, Jovanovich, 1961).
16. R. Shafer and P. Keith, "Equity and Depression among Married Couples," *Social Psychology* 43 (1980): 430–5.
17. N. M. Henley, *Body Politics* (Englewood Cliffs, NJ: Prentice-Hall, 1977).
18. T. Lamb, "Nonverbal and Paraverbal Control in Dyads and Triads: Sex or Power," *Social Psychology Quarterly* 33 (1981): 49–53.
19. Lamb, "Nonverbal and Paraverbal Control in Dyads and Triads," p. 43.
20. S. J. Gilbert and D. Horenstein, "The Communication of Self-Disclosure: Level versus Valence," *Human Communication Research* 1 (1975): 316–22.
21. S. J. Gilbert, "A Study for the Effects of Self-Disclosure on Interpersonal Attraction," Unpublished doctoral dissertation (University of Kansas, 1972).
22. M. Inbar, *The Vulnerable Age Phenomenon* (New York: Russell Sage, 1976), p. 5.
23. M. Martan, "Comparative Study of Communities of Yad Rambam in Israel," Paper presented at the World Congress of North African Jews (Jerusalem, Israel: 1972).
24. M. Inbar and C. Adler, "The Vulnerable Age Phenomenon: A Serendipitous Finding," *Sociology of Education* 49 (1976): 193–200.
25. D. Katz and K. W. Braly, "Racial Stereotypes of 100 College Students," *Journal of Abnormal and Social Psychology* 28 (1933): 175–93.
26. G. M. Gilbert, "Stereotype Persistence and Change among College Students," *Journal of Abnormal and Social Psychology* 46 (1951): 245–54.
27. N. Carlins, T. L. Coffman, and G. Walters, "On the Fading of Social Stereotypes," *Journal of Personality and Social Psychology* 13 (1969): 2–32.
28. N. Kutner, "Use of an Updated Adjective Checklist in Research on Ethnic Stereotypes," *Social Science Quarterly* 54 (1973): 639–47.
29. S. R. Acker and R. K. Tremens, "Children's Perceptions of Changes in Size of Televised Images," *Human Communication Research* 7 (1981): 340–6.
30. L. Humphreys, *Tearoom Trade: Impersonal Sex in Public Places* (Chicago: Aldine, 1970).

Chapter 4

The Role of Theory in Social Work

Science and social work
The relationship between theory
    and practice
    Theory leads the process
        of research
    Theory is modified from
        research findings
The development of social work
    theory
What is a theory?
    Definitions
    Hypotheses

Paradigms
Dominant models of practice
    Psychosocial approach
    Functionalist approach
    Problem-solving approach
    Behavioral approach
    Crisis intervention approach
    Task-centered approach
Conclusion

Science is a graveyard of theories. —GREGORY STONE

Science and Social Work

Social work has been referred to as both an art and a science. Roberts and Nee [1] describe the discipline by noting that intuitive insights and spontaneity "... are combined with continuous effort to develop and systematize knowledge and understanding of objective truths about [people] and [their] social expressions, relationships, and organizations." The term *science* has been widely misunderstood, but one faction of the scientific community would argue that the only knowledge that is valid and "scientific" is that which can be isolated, quantified, controlled, tested, examined, and replicated. Such an approach to knowledge acquisition is sometimes referred to as "the scientific method," "empirical research," "positivism," or "hard science," and is common in fields such as chemistry, physics, and biology [2].

The scientific perspective can become problematic in social work practice as pointed out by Sheafor, Horejsi, and Horejsi [3]:

> The application of the scientific method is very difficult in the social and behavioral sciences; perhaps this is why they are termed the "soft" sciences. Social problems cannot easily be quantified and are frequently of such a nature (e.g., child abuse or spouse battering) that it would not be appropriate to initiate problem situations for experimental purposes. In addition, human subjects are often not available for controlled study, and sufficient identical items do not exist to accumulate adequate samples for scientific testing.
>
> This scientific component of social work affects the client through the decisions and behaviors of the social worker. These actions are guided by theories and concepts drawn from disciplines such as psychology, sociology, philosophy, economics, and political science and by the theoretical formulations, conceptual frameworks, and practice models that have been developed within the social work profession. However, the new social worker often finds it difficult to sort through the available science to determine what is helpful for several reasons: (1) social work deals with such a wide variety of human situations; (2) it draws much of its knowledge from related disciplines; and (3) its own knowledge is scattered unevenly through the literature.
>
> It is useful to recognize that knowledge can take several forms. On a continuum, the science can range from individual intuition, to hunches or wisdom that develop through experience, to concepts of ideas about a particular phenomenon or activity, to a collection of concepts that constitute a model or theory of practice, to rigorously tested and validated laws or axioms. The forms of knowledge at the less rigorously tested end of the continuum (i.e., intuition, hunches, practice wisdom) represent valuable knowledge that a social worker brings to his or her practice. In their zeal to become more "professional," social workers should not forget that these forms of knowledge represent a substantial part of the social worker's knowledge base. Practice effectiveness can be improved by consciously recognizing that this type of knowledge is being utilized, examining it for its appropriateness to the practice situation, and searching for more conceptual or validated knowledge that might be applied.

Peile [4] notes that the debate between the "empirical" (i.e, "hard science") approach and the "normative" (i.e., "soft science") approach in social work is not a new development, but one that has confronted social workers for a very long time, and has characterized the question of whether social work is an art or a science. This debate comes sharply into focus in social work research activities. The empirical and the normative are not simply points of difference, "… but are cast as opposites, or as direct contradictions." Peile proposes the "creative paradigm" approach which adopts a holistic view of reality in which parts are not separable, but where both empirical and normative approaches are synthesized. Neither approach is seen as better than the other, but both are seen as contributing significantly to theory-building.

The Relationship between Theory and Practice

Theory is to practice what a road map is to driving. Without it, all roads look the same, you can never tell for sure where you are, you waste a lot of time making wrong turns and getting lost, and when you get where you're going, you may not know it. These same problems plague the research process, and the answer is almost as simple as it is in driving. Theory is the practitioner's road map, and it is indispensable.

In this chapter we will look at the inseparable aspects of theory and the practitioner's research activities. Astonishingly, not nearly enough attention is ordinarily given to the role of theory in guiding and directing research. We frequently give lip service to theory and then forget it in our day-to-day difficulties in operationalizing a research project. It is our perspective, however, that the two are by nature and function joined. To try to separate theory from research endeavors is like trying to decide which side of your hand to put into your pocket first.

Many social workers pride themselves in being common-sense thinkers and regard themselves as practical people who are not interested in what they consider to be the rarefied atmosphere of theory. As "nuts and bolts" people, we prefer dealing with the everyday challenges of each new and different client problem situation, preferring not to risk getting lost in the morass of theoretical intricacies. The realities of human suffering encountered in the social worker's work-a-day world seem sufficient to demand all our attention and energy. A pregnant teenager is in need of prenatal care. The homeless wanderer is in need of shelter and food on a winter night. The baby with AIDS has been abandoned in the hospital. These are strong pulls away from the ivory tower of theory and into the trenches of practicality.

In reality, all practical acts, all commonsense notions about how human beings behave and what they need, and of how society should be structured to address these issues, are laden with theoretical propositions. Someone has said that the person who takes pride in being atheoretical is probably the slave of some long-dead theories. A clear-cut societal example of this point occurred on January 17, 1977. On that date a firing squad in the state of Utah executed Gary Gilmore, a convicted murderer. It seemed like common sense to many people that executing a murderer is a regrettable but nonetheless necessary and effective way of dealing with violent crime. It appears to be a practical answer, apart from theory. In actual fact, however, execution is far from an atheoretical act. The theory informing capital punishment is almost 300 years old and goes something like this: Human beings are rational creatures who weigh their acts in terms of a calculus of pleasure and pain. They attempt to maximize pleasure and minimize pain. In weighing the costs of an act, they will refrain from doing something they know will cost them their lives, and so capital punishment obviously must act as a deterrent to the commission of capital crimes. This so-called common-sense formulation, believed fervently by any number of people, is actually a reformulation of a theory that is at least 400 years old and has been shown to be correct only in highly restricted circumstances, certainly not the ones that pertain in the commission of capital crimes. Most murders are emotionally charged crimes of passion in which there is little if any rational weighing of factors of pleasure or pain. Furthermore, given the typical time lag between crimes and punishment, whatever chance this theory has of being true is typically destroyed by circumstances that are built into the U.S. criminal justice system.

By the same token, many people who pride themselves on being practical thinkers feel that it only makes sense that if you give people long terms on the rock pile they will think twice before doing whatever it is that got them there in the first place. However, such a practical and workable plan is not atheoretical either. Not only does it suffer from many of the theoretical assumptions that rational thinkers have built into arguments favoring capital punishment, but it is also hampered by the deficiencies in learning theory. One would think that if people are treated harshly and punitively, they would indeed think twice before acting that way again. The evidence, however, is not overwhelming, for it seems that for every person who is taught a lesson by harsh treatment, there are many more who are hardened, embittered, and made even worse by the same treatment.

Likewise, the "progressive" and "enlightened" thinker about crime and punishment is often the slave of bankrupt theories too. It was once fashionable to prove one's reputation as a clear thinker by advocating rehabilitation. The criminal is obviously a victim of society, and with proper programs, virtually all criminals can be salvaged, shown the error of their ways, and brought back into the fold of reasonable human beings. This idea, no matter how humane and decently motivated, is not atheoretical either, and the theory that underlies it is equally suspect. The theory that supports rehabilitation is the very old notion (at least since Rousseau) that holds that human beings are pure and innocent, and it is society and its demeaning evils that corrupt them. Treated right, people will act right. Treated wrong, they will act wrong. No matter how much we might wish to believe this idea, research has simply not shown an enormous array of support for that theoretical proposition.

Our point in this short excursion into the emotionally charged issue of crime and punishment is simply this: the business of theory cannot be avoided in favor of "practical" approaches to the problems of life any more than the laws of economics can be avoided by taking a vow of poverty. Social workers, even while decrying theory as impractical and of little value in their daily case management activities, are acting out of certain sets of systematic assumptions that they use to give direction and place value upon what they do.

Since theoretical propositions underlie everything we do, certainly everything that we think, they must be faced rather than avoided. Our goal as professional social workers is to recognize where and when certain theories have value, and to use them to quicken our understanding of how best to help clients. Some other professionals have many tools and instruments to bring to bear on their helping. For example, medical personnel have laboratory tests, x-rays, and cat scans, and so on. Psychologists have their psychometric instruments. Social workers, however, have only themselves and what they carry within as the instrument for delivering services—our value base, knowledge base, and skill base. Theory is an integral part of that knowledge base, giving coherence to the value base and providing the rationale for the use of differential skills.

Theory Leads the Process of Research

Theory, then, leads the process of research by setting forth a logically coherent series of interrelated propositions that might account for some phenomenon in which a social worker is interested. For example, let us suppose that as a result of a course in human behavior, you have become interested in why there is so much divorce in the United States these days. Perhaps you yourself came from a broken home and feel that, at least in your case, your father's drinking was responsible for the breakup of your parents' marriage. You want to know, then, whether the general theory that alcoholism causes broken homes is true or not. You have not yet generated a theory but simply have an idea about the issue. What do you do next? A search of the literature might reveal that quite a bit has been written about these marriage relationships and that the issues are a lot more complicated than you thought. Other variables are suddenly brought to your attention that might have some effect on what you are now beginning to see as a very complex marital relationship. Psychoanalytic theory, communication theory, family systems theory, ego psychology theory, and codependence theory may offer ideas worthy of consideration. Out of this plethora of theoretical material, you can then begin to develop a specific hypothesis that may be tested by appropriate methodological techniques.

Theory Is Modified from Research Findings

The whole idea of research is to find out the solutions to puzzles; that is, answers to questions our minds and our experiences inevitably pose about our social work practice, and specifically certain client situations, treatment considerations, and intervention strategies. These questions, if they are worth asking, don't usually have simple answers. We began this chapter by quoting Greg Stone's observation that science is a graveyard of theories. He means that there is no theory capable of answering all the questions the human mind is capable of devising. Theories come and go; questions persist. Theories are "built" upon the findings of previous research, and they accumulate over time. They are also discarded sometimes, when the weight of findings so indicates. Nothing is more useful than a good theory, but reality is an infinitely flexible and elusive process for which no single explanation is ordinarily satisfactory, and which will change over time anyway. This means that the process of building an edifice of theory, although necessary, is never complete. What we find modifies what we thought was the case. We must necessarily begin with a theory, for how else will we know what to make of the facts we uncover during the research process? But those very facts, informed and directed by theory, usually lead to the modification of the theory. To use our earlier analogy of theory as road map, it seems that while we must have a road map to guide us through research, we don't assume that our road map is accurate. Rather, we must be ready to modify it as we discover new territory not on the map. If we find that someone has cut a new road, that doesn't necessarily mean the map was wrong—just that it wasn't complete or as up to date as we would like our maps to be. As it turns out, the analogy was not too far off after all, for maps (theories) must constantly be updated by what we find—not that they are useless or that we would want to start our journey without one.

The Development of Social Work Theory

In the first chapter of his edited work on social work theory entitled *Social Work Treatment: Interlocking Theoretical Approaches*, Frances J. Turner [5] describes two principal themes: (1) there is an assumption in the social work profession about the "… expected relationship between theory and practice," and that (2) "… the interest in the wide range of theories, models, and systems of practice … is an important and underattended reality." He develops an intriguing, essentially chronological, scenario of the theory-building process in the social work profession by looking at the nature and character of the literature that has brought theory to us. He maintains that fourteen different approaches to theory can be identified [6]:

1. *Pretheory.* Turner defines "pretheory" as the first formal attempts to record social work theory. Cited as examples of this phase are Mary Richmond's *Social Diagnosis* [7] and Gordon Hamilton's *Theory and Practice of Social Casework* [8].

2. *A cluster of writings based on a framework accepted as a theory.* Psychodynamic theories played an important role in early social work, and authors speculated on the implications of these approaches for social work practice in articles, monographs, and books. Cited as examples are Howard Parad's two books, *Crisis Intervention: Selected Readings* [9] and *Ego-Oriented Casework,* co-authored with Roger Miller [10].

3. *Authors who drew on their practice experience and presented a particular stance or conceptual approach that represented their own thinking.* Helen Harris Perlman's *Social Casework: A Problem-Solving Process* [11] represents certain applications of John Dewey's problem-solving theory to social work in the form of principles or axioms, while Florence Hollis's "psychosocial system" [12] draws heavily on psychodynamic theories.

4. *Literature organized around three distinct segments of clinical practice: casework, group work, and family therapy.* Rather than focusing on the commonalities between these methodologies, the differences in the conceptual underpinnings were emphasized.

5. *Broadening of the conceptual bases.* During the 1950s and 1960s, interest in a broader range of theories developed. Perlman published a book on social role theory [13], Parad edited two books based on ego psychology [14, 15], Jehu wrote from a learning theory perspective [16], Werner dealt with cognitive theory [17], and Lutz [18] and Hearn [19] published in the area of systems theory.

6. *Recognition of the connectedness among theories.* The next phase of writings attempted to draw comparisons and distinctions between this breadth of important theories. Among the writers contributing in this area are Stein [20], who studied

family theory, and Roberts and Nee [21], who surveyed the various schools of practice.

7. *Rapid proliferation of theories applied in social work practice.* Once it had become acceptable to look far afield for meaningful theories to use in practice, there was a virtual explosion of these that social workers were willing to consider, including gestalt, transactional analysis, task-centered, life model, and others, taking us beyond the six basic approaches noted by Roberts and Nee. Turner's edited volume is representative of this phase by its inclusion of more than twenty theoretical approaches.

8. *Writings describing the nature of theory itself and the theory-building process.* These writings did not look at specific theories themselves, but urged us to "... look at the process in the abstract ...." This strategy was considered most carefully by Lutz and Hearn (see references 18 and 19), both of whom, interestingly, then moved into the specific applications of theory concepts in a systems orientation [22].

9. *Literature based on research activities.* Turner notes that this process has been greatly neglected in social work practice. Here, various concepts related to our field are operationally defined and tested through the formulation of hypotheses and the examination of resultant data. Examples cited of important work done are Ripple, Alexander, and Polemis's [23] studies on aspects of the problem-solving approach, Reid and Shyne's [24] work on short-term therapy, and Fischer's [25] work in the area of cognitive and behavioral principles.

10. *Authors describe and apply theories to their particular orientation to treatment.* Turner says this approach is represented by his volume of theories. Similar to approach 7, he points out that his work develops a "... two-way analysis of theory and methods ...."

11. *Eclecticism.* In this approach to theory building, selected concepts are extracted from a variety of theories and synthesized into a single practice approach. Two forms of this are noted: (1) the practitioner picks those concepts that have appeal based on value perspectives and personal affinity, or (2) those aspects that research has shown to be more effective.

12. *Applications of highly specific components of discrete theories.* This more recent trend is apparent in two ways: (1) authors are making a specific application of a thought system (e.g., the use of crisis theory in a classroom setting), or (2) making an application of a discrete concept from a thought system into practice (e.g., the concept of "homeostasis" applied in marital therapy).

13. *The wedding of theory and practice.* This approach is as much a prediction as an observation. Turner thinks that social workers are beginning to understand the importance of lessening the existing dichotomy and bringing together academic research and direct practice.

14. *Theory as antithetical to treatment.* This last point is one which has obviously been present all along in the development of theory, and has been noted earlier in this chapter; and that is, that there have always been social workers who view theory as "... unimportant and indeed counterproductive to good practice ...."

We have examined some of the issues and questions surrounding the often uneasy relationship between social work practice and scientific inquiry. In addition, we have examined how theory has been finding a meaningful place for itself over time within the profession. We can now examine more closely specific definitions of theory, and look at important terms and concepts necessary to understanding the "wedding" of theory with practice.

What Is a Theory

A lot of confusion surrounds the seemingly simple question "What is a theory?" Although there is what Wittgenstein called a family resemblance among most definitions of theory, the definitions themselves differ rather widely. For us, the term *theory* is most often confused with a variety of related terms such as *concept, typology, model, proposition, assumption, hypothesis, paradigm,* and so forth.

Let's begin by stating what theories are *for,* and in doing so we will begin to get at what they *are.* **The primary purpose of a theory is to account for or explain a particular phenomenon.** It is this *explanatory function* that distinguishes a theory from other related concepts. Without theory we would have no way of even beginning to know the meaning of what we have found in our research. This function of theory, then, is to account for or to explain the findings of research. With that function as background, here are a few definitions of what a theory is from various social science scholars and social workers who have written about it:

> There is a general agreement that a theory is a set of propositions or theoretical statements. [26]

> A theory ought to create the capacity to invent explanations. [27]

> A theory is an integrated set of relationships with a certain level of validity. [28]

> theory emerges through the process of ordering facts in a meaningful way, … theory builds a series of propositions about reality; that is, it provides us with models of reality and helps us to understand what is possible and how we attain it. [29]

These differing definitions all have in common the idea that theories state, in as logical terms as possible, a set of general statements that explain or account for some phenomenon the social worker is interested in.

Turner has further defined four terms that are essential to theory: concepts, facts, hypotheses, and principles. **Concepts are symbols, labels, or agreed-upon terms that describe a phenomenon.** Easily confused with a reality, a concept is not concrete, but an abstraction. A few commonly used concepts in social work practice are "relationship, identity, treatment, empathy."

Using methods of scientific inquiry, **facts can be empirically verified** and supported as having value. As more and more facts are thereby verified, they can be ordered in meaningful ways, and theory begins to emerge as new relationships between facts are recognized. This process of identifying new relationships between facts first begins by the researcher predicting a given relationship in a statement known as a *hypothesis.* As the process of hypothesis testing continues over time, some of the predictive statements are recognized as being dependable and consistently useful in describing some aspect of reality, and thus principles are developed [30].

Theories are usually stated in the form of propositions and are worded in terms of concepts. A concept usually begins as a kind of mental image. Hugh Prather [31] says that a concept is "… always a partial perception. A 'good' concept simply allows me to see more than before. It will soon be replaced by other words, if words are what is needed, that allow my mind an even greater scope." We have an idea we are curious about, but in order to articulate it enough to begin the research process, we must translate this idea into a concept or a series of concepts. Let's say that we want to study the relationship between child abuse and poverty. We all have heard about child abuse, and have read about child abusers in the newspapers. And we surely know what poverty is. Or do we? Just what do we mean by such terms? To think about any relationship between child abuse and poverty, we have to translate general ideas into specific concepts, and then define these concepts for the purposes of research. We do this carefully and consistently, so that we will not be measuring apples and oranges.

In everyday life, concepts are important, but precision in their use is not always necessary. If someone says, "It's cloudy outside," we don't generally ask, "What do you mean by cloudy?" But the researcher is in roughly the same situation as the weather bureau. Their work (like ours) necessitates a rather precise definition about such nonspecific terms as *cloudy*. For example, pilots need to know exactly what the weather is, and vague concepts just will not do. What kinds of clouds are we talking about? Cirrus clouds? Cumulus clouds? Stratus clouds? Cumulonimbus clouds? Just knowing that it's "cloudy" without knowing what kinds of clouds can be very important if you are thinking about flying through them.

By the same token, our research endeavors are going to depend considerably on how well we are able to define our concepts. The process of *conceptualization,* then, is central to precise research, and going through this process will help to stimulate additional thinking that will clarify just what the researcher wishes to find out. We know that two people have a legal contract between them called "marriage." But just knowing they are married may not be precise enough for some research projects. Does that automatically mean that the couple is living together under the same roof? Does it mean they are both monogamous? Does it mean they share financial responsibilities? Since there are many different ways to "do" marriage in our society, these differences can make a crucial difference in the way a research project is designed and executed. For some studies, the splitting of conceptual hairs is irrelevant, for others it is essential. Turning the vagueness of a concept into an operationalized definition with sharpness is an important part of the conceptualization process which can make or break a research project.

Definitions

Concepts involve definitions, but definitions are even more precise than concepts. Suppose we want to evaluate a rehabilitation program. We have a pretty good idea of what we want to get at, but we have to define our basic terms carefully. If we are looking at the amount of services delivered to a certain disabled population, how do we define "disabled"? Totally disabled—meaning bedridden? Or partially disabled—using wheelchair, crutches, and/or walker? Or are we looking at the question from a standpoint of *type* of disability? Mental, visual, neurological? There also may be a difference between a social definition of disability and a medical one. Someone can be considered disabled by a large number in society and not be considered so by medical definition, and vice versa. Problems of definition are exactly why the data from one study seem to contradict, or at least not support, those from another study. There is nothing inherently wrong with different research about the same phenomenon coming up with different results. However, we will always want to be clear about just what definition we are using and, even more important, why we are using it.

Hypotheses

We have devoted an entire chapter to hypotheses because they are so important to the research process. It will be enough here to define them and show their relationship to theory. Ideas, in the form of defined concepts, must be arranged for research purposes into hypotheses we can test. Hypotheses are always derived from theory. Technically, a **hypothesis** is an expectation about the nature of things according to theory. **It is a statement of what we ought to find if our theory is correct.** To use a grim example, from racist theories we might derive the hypothesis that blacks, being intellectually inferior to whites, will perform badly on intelligence tests. Of course, the aforementioned problem of concept and definition will come into play in building such a hypothesis because we must carefully define what we mean by *intelligence* and *intelligence test* and also deal with the theoretical problem of whether performance on an intelligence test is actually a measure of intelligence. Actually, emotional theories like those about racial inferiority are rarely tested fairly because the authors of such theories usually seek to prove their theories and assume that any data that do not fit them must be wrong. This problem occurs in other theories too, with many value-laden issues in our society such as homosexuality, child abuse, abortion, or religion. We must always guard against using research as an ideological tool to prove pet theories. Theory is the good-faith, intellectually honest enterprise of keeping an open mind but not an empty one. We must not become so enamored with a theory that we will do anything to prove its correctness. This is intellectually dishonest. A good hypothesis is both carefully stated and tough–minded in the sense that ideally we want the hypothesis to be a fair and rigorous test of theory. Done well, good hypotheses enable us to ask further questions (rather than close the door) and to modify theory as we mentioned in our previous discussion.

Paradigms

T. S. Kuhn [32] helps us to understand the definition and function of a paradigm. He says that a paradigm can be defined, in its simplest form, as "… the entire constellation of beliefs, values, techniques, and theories shared by the members of a scientific community." In other words, for the social worker, **a paradigm is a fundamental image held by members of a professional community about the subject matter of their practice.** Kuhn further states that there is no such thing as independent facts or other factors or standards that are independently true. The idea of what constitutes a fact is, instead, paradigm-dependent, or a judgment rendered by practitioners who apply one system or another.

Since social work is an "applied" profession, our paradigms (or systems of shared beliefs) are not only thought systems, but also activity endeavors sometimes referred to as "schools of practice," or "models of practice." This will be discussed in more detail later in this chapter, but suffice it to say at this point that each school or model of practice is usually based on a synthesis of two or more "theories," and from that synthesis a methodology of practice, or an expectable set of intervention skills, is developed. As Sheafor, Horejsi and Horejsi [33] express it,

> A model is a form of theory that often develops through the process of making analogies from one situation to others. They may help to formulate particular practice questions, suggest means of perceiving practice situations, or offer guidance for the selection of intervention approaches.

Peile [34] points out that the choice between empirical and normative research "… approaches should be based on the compatibility of the research method with the researcher's own preferred paradigmatic assumptions or worldview …." In all of science, paradigms function to set the stage for questions to be asked and, at the same time, set the framework for their answers. The facts to be explained as well as the very idea of an explanation are paradigm-dependent.

Scientific activity varies in its use of paradigms. Some sciences or professional disciplines use a single paradigm that is dominant and holds a broad consensus among scholars and practitioners in the field. Such was the case with the psychoanalytic, or psychosocial, paradigm in social work history. For many years it was so widely held that some critics lament that we tried to cure poverty with it! At other times in our history, a number of paradigms or paradigm variations have competed for attention and following, among the more notable are the problem-solving, functional, behavioral, crisis intervention, and task-centered schools. Masterman [35] has pointed out that when no dominant paradigm exists, practitioners spend a great deal of time defending their own favorite paradigm against attack. Social work certainly has not been exempt from this experience of infighting and disagreement, as we shall see.

Dominant Models of Practice

Psychosocial Approach

This model of intervention began developing as a powerful theoretical framework in the fledgling social work profession in the early 1930s. The term *psychosocial*, originally intended as a bridging concept between the disciplines of psychology and sociology, found meaning in social work as it developed into a distinct approach for helping. Early systematic developers of the model were Gordon Hamilton, Betsy Libby, Bertha Reynolds, and more recently Florence Hollis [36, 37]. Because of the heavy influence of Freudian theory, which was finding wide acceptance in the United States at that time, this school was also known as the "Freudian school," the "diagnostic school," or the "psychoanalytic school." Adopting the psychiatric/medical model of treatment, social work practitioners began to more away from the earlier settlement house, community-based emphases of the late 1800s and early 1900s, and began to focus on treatment through individual interviews, usually held at regular intervals, in the practitioner's office. They were concerned both with the inner psychological realities of the client and the social context in which he or she lived. Thus the well-used term *person-in-situation* came to be a central focus. Gaining ascendancy during the Child Guidance Movement in this country, a strong emphasis on family relationships and child development emerged. Use of this model in group settings also emerged. Treatment was seen as lasting over a period of months or even years. This model was particularly suited to working with middle-class and upper-class clients with high educational levels. The chief ingredient of treatment was seen as the "helping relationship" formed between the worker and client. "Diagnosis," in the psychiatric sense, was widely utilized, and ego functioning was assessed as part of this diagnosis. Emphasis was placed on obtaining a lengthy and detailed social history. In fact, this model of practice was largely responsible for developing the skill of history-taking to a fine art. Chronology, developmental milestones, family interactions, as well as societal influences were considered of great importance in formulating the diagnosis.

In more recent years those who practice from this perspective have been incorporating more recent concepts from learning theory, family systems theory, role theory, crisis theory, and gestalt theory. Also, consideration is now given to race, class, ethnicity, religion, and other cultural factors that influence a client's level of ego functioning, making it more flexible than some of its critics would acknowledge [38]. The primary focus remains, however, on the intrapsychic functionings of the individual.

Hollis [39], in her discussion of psychosocial practice, lists the following values that give shape and character to this paradigm:

1. The social worker must accept the client by having a commitment to the client's welfare, exhibiting care and respect.
2. The relationship must be "other-oriented," with the worker giving precedence to the client's needs.
3. Insofar as possible the social worker must understand the client with scientific objectivity, removing personal bias in evaluation and response. (The influence of the "hard sciences" can be seen here.)
4. The worker must recognize the client's right to make his or her own decisions and the value of encouraging this self–directedness.
5. The worker must recognize the interdependence of the client with others and realize that there may be times when the client's self-direction may need to be limited to protect others or self from harm.

In summary, we can say that this paradigm, or practice model, is distinguished by assessment of intrapsychic functioning of the individual or group members, an emphasis on past adjustments, understanding of person-in-situation, detailed social history gathering, diagnosis in the psychiatric or Freudian tradition, treatment delivered through regular therapy sessions in the clinician's office, and treatment perhaps continuing for many months or years.

Practitioners wishing to develop a research activity based on this paradigm would want to look into issues that are emphasized in this practice model. For example, one might compare the progress made by clients treated by two or more different therapists using this model, or seek to find how many regularly scheduled sessions seem to create the most improvement, or what co-factors in the clients' environment seem best to support adjustment. Additionally, one might be curious about the role of various family members as it relates to improvement, or look from the perspective of various diagnostic categories of clients to determine if one treatment technique is superior to another.

Functionalist Approach

The functionalist approach began to develop at the School of Social Work, University of Pennsylvania, in the late 1930s. The leading theorists were faculty members Jessie Taft and Virginia Robinson. This school of thought, in stark contrast to the diagnostic school, developed with quite different assumptions and goals. The conflicts between the two schools generated considerable debate and controversy during the years between the late 1930s and the 1950s. According to Yelaja [40], they differed in three essential areas: (1) their underlying assumptions about human growth and development, (2) the nature of the client–worker relationship, and (3) the purpose of social work.

In understanding the nature of humankind, functionalists were strongly influenced, not only by Herbert Mead and John Dewey, but especially by Otto Rank and his "psychology of growth." The functionalists considered the psychosocial school to be pessimistic in that it considered humans to be prey to the dark forces of the unconscious, and driven by the influences of the restrictive internalized parent. They were also critical of the concept of "illness" applied to clients through the influence of the medical model.

The concept that came to give direction to functionalism, and gave it a name, was the term *the use of agency function,* coined by Jessie Taft. The *social agency* was seen as the focal point of client helping. The programs, services, and resources provided by the agency were the key ingredients. Rank's contributions included the importance of *relationship* with the client and the significance of *time* in the helping process. In fact, this approach used the term "helping" rather than "treatment" which was so popular with the Freudians. So in functionalist practice, social work is seen primarily as being "institutionalized" through the agency's administration of social services rather than through the individual tasks and efforts of the social worker [41].

Later writings by Ruth Smalley [42, 43] contributed greatly to the clarification of this approach and the systematization of its theoretical underpinnings. Yelaja [44] paraphrases the five generic principles of functionalist practice, which are applicable not only to casework, but to group work and community organization interventions as well.

1. Diagnosis should be related to the use of services, should be developed as services are given, should be changed as the phenomenon changes, and should be shared with the client.

2. Time phases in the social work process (beginnings, middles, and endings) should be fully exploited for the use of the client.

3. The use of agency function gives focus, content, and direction to social work processes, assures accountability to society, and engages the client in the process characterized by partialization, concreteness, and differentiation.

4. Conscious use of structure, related to function and process, introduces form into the relationship between client and worker.

5. All social work processes involve a relationship in which choices or decisions are made by the person being helped, and the relationship must be of such a character as to further the making of purposive choices and decisions.

Social workers who would use this model as a theoretical paradigm to guide their research activities would naturally look to some aspect of the agency around which to develop a design. Possibilities are practically limitless, including a study to evaluate the effectiveness of a particular agency program as compared to another, a cost-effectiveness study of a given program, a longitudinal study to learn about the changes in client demographics over time, some comparison of casework and group work services, a client survey to evaluate clients' perceptions of the quality of services, or an opinion survey of referring agencies in the community.

Problem-Solving Approach

Emerging out of the 1950s, and branching off from the psychosocial school, the problem-solving approach was conceptualized by Helen Harris Perlman. By her own word we understand it to be "eclectic" in its theoretical foundations. Growing out of her discomfort with the "iron determinism of the person's past" touted by the Freudians, and their lack of awareness of the "moving forces in current life experiences," Perlman formulated her model. It drew heavily upon ego psychology theory, philosophic views of existentialism, social learning theory, and social psychology concepts about the development of the social self through social role transactions [45]. Perlman also credits the foundational work of Gordon Hamilton, especially her ideas of "person-in-situation" and her view that "… casework lies midway between therapy and education." Other useful ideas which she gleaned from the functionalists were [46]:

1. A *focus* on the "here and now."
2. The reality of the impact for the client of *the agency itself.*
3. The use of *relationship*, with its tremendous powers for motivation or deterrence.

4. The *importance of time,* with its beginnings, middles, and endings.
5. The skill of *partialization,* that is, the cutting down of a complex problem into specific and manageable parts.

From John Dewey she caught the vision that "... if a person's motivation and abilities are to be engaged in learning, he [or she] must *feel* and *see* that there is a problem to be solved ...," and that "... the problem in some way involves him [or her]."

In 1957, Perlman published her landmark work presenting her ideas, entitled *Social Casework: A Problem-Solving Process* [47]. The basic assumption from the problem-solving perspective is that the inability to cope on the part of a client is due to some lack of motivation, capacity, or opportunity to work on, solve, or mitigate the problem in appropriate ways. Thus, the M-C-O acronym formed the cornerstone of diagnosis, or "assessment" in this model of practice. The person's *workability* was thus determined and casework interventions were planned based on the interaction of what came to be known as the "4 *P's*" (Person, Problem, Place, Process). The *person,* whether individual client or group, is held to be in the process of becoming [48], signifying the reality of expectable personality change; the *problem* is that which is defined by client and social worker together; the *place* refers to the social agency with its services, programs and resources; and the *process* refers to the dynamic interactional capacities of worker and client as they enter into intervention activities through the helping relationship. (Her students humorously refer to these as "four peas in a pod.") Perlman notes that she would now add two more *P's* to the pod—*professional,* the representative of the place with his or her self-management in the interest of the client, and *provisions,* to identify those "opportunities" or resources to meet the material and relational needs of clients [49].

So we can see how important was the synthesis of some aspects of the theories, concepts, and ideas of psychodynamic thought, functionalism, learning theory, and problem-solving to Perlman's seminal work. Several other widely known models of practice, or what we might call "paradigm variations," were influenced by the problem-solving model, including crisis intervention and the task-centered approach, to be considered later in this chapter.

Social workers who are interested in conducting research activities using this model as the guiding paradigm might be designing studies that look at motivational levels of clients measured by available standardized instruments, or at specific relationship components in the process, such as empathy, support, trust, and so forth. Additionally, one could look at utilization rates of various types of resources as compared to identified client problems, or, using a single-subject design, measure pretest to posttest change of a client on any number of variables.

Behavioral Approach

Whether they work with clients as individuals, groups, or communities, social workers are often involved in the process of seeking the alteration or stabilization of behaviors. The behavioral approach offered practitioners a theoretical framework in which to assess behaviors, and a variety of techniques for assessment and modification. According to Thomas [50], there are certain common assumptions underlying all behavioral techniques:

1. The focus is on *observable* behaviors. Although behaviorists do not deny the operation of intrapsychic factors in the personality, they focus on the external manifestations of these in the form of behaviors that can be made objective through scientific measurement.

2. Behaviors can be divided into two basic categories or "fundamental classes." *Operant* behaviors are those that are voluntary, such as walking, talking, and much of what is termed "thinking." *Respondent* behaviors are essentially involuntary, such as anxiety reactions and/or phobias.

3. No underlying "psychic disease" is assumed, but rather these symptoms are seen as manifestations of behavior. (It is at this point that behavioralists are the most divergent from those of the psychosocial school.)

4. The focus of intervention is primarily aimed at the immediate *antecedents* or the *consequences* of the dysfunctional behavior. Strong emphasis is also placed on the role of sustaining conditions in the environment or within the interactions of people in the environment.

Although felt more strongly in the development of the disciplines of psychiatry and psychology, behavioral approaches in social work have had a considerable impact. According to O'Leary [51], the behavioral paradigm has clearly emerged as "one of the top three ranked orientations." Beginning to emerge as a system of thought and an object of research in the 1950s, B. F. Skinner's work, *Science and Human Behavior* [52] presented "… one of the most empirically based theories of human behavior and set the foundation for contemporary behavior therapy" [53]. Other important contributors were Thorndike, Watson, Hull, and Pavlov. These researchers contributed most directly to the *conditioning theory* which is at the heart of behavioralism. Skinner, on the other hand, contributed the concept of *reinforcement* which maintained that:

> Operant behavior (voluntary behavior) emitted by an individual could be increased in frequency of occurrence if such behavior was positively or negatively reinforced. Alternatively, the frequency of occurrence of the behavior could be decreased by either administering punishment or withholding reinforcement; this latter process being referred to as extinction. In other words, the essence of the Skinnerian or operant model of conceptualizing human behavior relied heavily upon an understanding of the environmental (behavioral) events that preceded and/or followed the behavior(s) under scrutiny. [54]

Joseph Wolpe's [55] research activities in the area of *systematic desensitization* have contributed the foundation for this widely used intervention technique in behavioral practice. Frequently aimed at the reduction of a client's debilitating anxiety or phobic reaction, systematic desensitization techniques seek to teach new responses. Subsequently, relaxation techniques such as deep muscle relaxation and/or mental imagery are incorporated into the intervention process.

Essentially, social work practice based on the behavioral paradigm will focus for analysis and intervention on three major elements of the client's observable behavior, the *antecedent events,* the *behavior itself,* and the *consequences* of the behavior, thus the acronym A-B-C becomes a way of distinguishing this model. Simplistically stated, once a dysfunctional "target" behavior is identified, the chain of events or interpersonal interactions that precede it are analyzed. Also, the expectable behavioral consequences (or rewards) are determined. Intervention is structured so as to break the patterned chain of events that lead to the behavior and/or to alter the patterned results in order to make the targeted behavior unnecessary. In addition to the preceding techniques, others mentioned in the literature are covert sensitization, implosive therapy, flooding, behavioral rehearsal (role playing), exchange systems, modeling, "fading," and rule making [56].

Since Skinner originally conceptualized behavioralism as a model that emanated from empirical or "hard science" investigation, the use of a variety of measurement tools or instruments is common; such as frequency charts, forms, checklists, time tables, and other measures conducive to self-report. Electrical and mechanical devices are also widely used; such as stopwatches, ordinary timepieces, tape recorders, and counters. The purpose is to objectify and quantify the data in such a way as to make them readily amenable to methods of empirical measurement.

Social workers attempting to evaluate practice through research activities based on this paradigm would note that these approaches have been used widely and quite successfully with children. A study comparing its effectiveness between children and adults might be of interest. A qualitative study of a group of children in a residential facility might focus on the levels of involvement of the children's parents in each child's treatment program, looking at parental factors that increase or decrease likelihood of successful behavioral change outcomes for the children. Other research designs might draw on two paradigms in order to study the usefulness of differential behavioral techniques with various categories of dysfunctional behavior in children (i.e., children previously diagnosed as schizophrenic as opposed to those previously diagnosed as mentally retarded).

Crisis Intervention Approach

Earlier in our look at the problem-solving approach, we noted that Perlman said that the crisis intervention model, sometimes referred to as short-term treatment, developed as a variation of the problem-solving school. Lydia Rapoport [57] specifically refers to Perlman's concept of "focus" as a major contribution to practice in crisis settings.

Parad [58] observes that this model lacks the characteristic of possessing a theory that has the formal attribute of systematic validation. Naomi Golan [59] agrees that

> the parameters are probably too broad and too amorphous to grant it recognition as a systematic theory in the sense of its being an internally con-

sistent body of verified hypotheses .... Nevertheless, enough generalizations and conclusions have coalesced to recognize the emergence of a discernible framework within which to examine stressful situations, to offer a body of guidelines and techniques for intervention at such times, and to distinguish between crises and other forms of stress.

A prolific body of literature has developed, including studies conducted by Lindemann, Caplan, Rapoport, Parad, Kaplan, Jacobson, Golan, Taplin, and others. Erik Erikson contributed the concept of life-cycle stages, separated by what he terms "transitions," or "psychological crises." Studies emanating from stress situations created by natural disasters such as floods, fires, and earthquakes, as well as not-so-natural disasters such as war and terrorism, generated a wealth of valuable insights into what came to be recognized as the "crisis sequence."

Golan [60] outlines the major principles of this approach in the following manner:

1. An individual [or family, group, or community] is subjected to periods of increased internal and external stress throughout the normal life span that disturbs the customary state of equilibrium with his or her surrounding environment. The event may be a single catastrophic occurrence or a series of lesser mishaps that have a cumulative effect.

2. The impact of the hazardous event disturbs the individual's homeostatic balance and puts him or her into a vulnerable state, marked by heightened tension and anxiety. To regain equilibrium, the person goes through a series of predictable phases.

3. At this point, a precipitating factor can bring about a turning point, and the individual enters a state of active crisis.

4. As the crisis situation develops, the individual may perceive the initial and subsequent stressful events primarily as a *threat*; as a *loss* of a person, status, role, or capacity; or as a *challenge* to survival, growth, or mastery.

5. Each of these perceptions calls forth a characteristic emotional reaction that reflects the subjective meaning of the event to the individual.

6. Although a crisis situation is neither an illness nor a pathological experience, it may become linked with earlier unresolved or partially resolved conflicts.

7. The total length of time between the initial blow and final resolution of the crisis situation varies widely. The active state of disequilibrium, however, is time-limited, usually lasting four to six weeks.

8. Each particular class of crisis situation seems to follow a specific sequence of stages that can be predicted and mapped out. Emotional reaction and behavioral responses at each phase can often be anticipated.

9. During the unraveling of the crisis situation, the individual tends to be particularly amenable to help. [It can be the "teachable moment" that Havighurst refers to.]

10. During the reintegration phase, new ego sets may emerge and new adaptive styles may evolve, enabling the person to cope more effectively with other situations in the future.

One international organization that is readily present in times of disaster is the International Red Cross. Local chapters respond immediately to catastrophes such as fires, floods, and earthquakes. Studying affected groups or entire communities, Red Cross social workers might be interested in conducting research activities based on variant emotional responses to the various types of disasters, or studies looking at the duration of incapacitation following a disaster. Another study may try to distinguish between the multiple coping mechanisms that victims of disasters exhibit. Emergency room social workers who are involved in helping victims of spouse abuse would be interested in the results of research projects that would indicate effective ways to help these clients through the crisis period. These kinds of studies can continue the theory-building process and contribute to the future effectiveness of social workers practicing in crisis settings.

Task-Centered Approach

The task-centered approach can be seen as another paradigm variation. William Reid [61] describes this approach as a "… system of brief, time-limited practice that emphasizes helping clients with specific problems of their own choosing through discrete client and practitioner actions or tasks." It developed out of the privately funded Task-Centered Project, at the School of Social Service Administration, University of Chicago. Research on the model was conducted by William Reid and Laura Epstein [62] between 1970 and 1978. As such, it may be one of the most extensively researched models in social work practice.

By design, task-centered practice has a systematic and sequential way of unfolding. Usually no more than two problems are addressed at one time, and these are to be clearly identified within the first one or two interviews between client and social worker. A preferably written, but sometimes oral, *contract* is then developed which will specify in detail a time period to work on the problems, or a number of scheduled interviews that will be necessary. The worker's responsibility is to create a favorable climate for task performance, reviewing progress on problem alleviation, and arranging for termination, extension, or follow-up of the original contract.

The contract, and its formulation, are of major importance. Rothery [63] notes that the advantages of contracts include: (1) the opportunity to dispel unrealistic expectations by keeping the client fully informed of what is possible and reasonable, (2) involving clients more fully in their change process by basing goals and activities directly upon the targeted problem(s) as specified by the client, and (3) protecting the client from being dealt with "behind his or her back"; all of which creates the possibility for more positive outcomes. Other advantages pointed out by Epstein [64] are that the model can be used with a variety of personal, interpersonal, and situational problems, with many different types of clients and settings, with families and groups, "… with difficult cases, easy cases, and all cases that fall between."

Although "diagnosis" in the psychiatric sense is sometimes incorporated into the assessment process, this is certainly not a requirement for work in this modality. Lengthy history taking is also given little emphasis, because this theory does not attempt to deal with remote or historical origins of a problem but rather with current obstacles that may be blocking the resolution or with resources that may facilitate it ... the person is seen as less a prisoner of unconscious drives than in the theories of the psychoanalyst and less a prisoner of environmental contingencies than in the views of the behavioralist. [65]

Perhaps because the tasks involved in the unfolding of task-centered practice are usually quite behaviorally specific, and designed to be measurable, Perlman has noted that today's task-centered practice is more closely allied with behavioral theory than with problem-solving theory [66].

The types of research studies generated by this paradigm have been extensive, as mentioned earlier. Treatment-of-choice studies have been done comparing task-centered with other approaches [67]. Practitioners may wish to determine model effectiveness with groups of foster children by designing a study to measure the improvement in their academic achievement, using a control group that has worked out a contract together versus a matched group that has no such contract. Additionally, a social worker affiliated with a special project aimed at reducing the number of single mothers on public assistance may look at the social and environmental factors of the people in his or her caseload and the impact these factors have on task accomplishment.

Conclusion

In this chapter we have examined the relationship between science and social work, discussed how theory guides the process of research, and how theory is, in turn, modified from research findings. We have also seen how theory has developed in the social work profession through time. We have defined certain concepts and terms essential to the research process and presented an overview of the major paradigms or models of practice that have shaped social work practice. Additionally, we have presented a few ideas or examples of the kinds of research studies that might be designed using each paradigm.

There seem to have been three "watershed" paradigms that have set the historical parameters of social work theory—psychosocial, functional, and behavioral. From these, three additional significant approaches have evolved—problem-solving, crisis intervention, and task-centered. Each has brought forward certain characteristic concepts from its parent paradigm, and each has developed significant differences and unique characteristics that delineate it from its predecessors. Figure 4.1 schematically demonstrates this process.

When we begin to look at the theory-building process in the social work profession and review the practice models that have developed, it quickly becomes obvious that theory and practice are realistically inseparable for the social worker. Practical, common-sense approaches (or "practice widsom" as defined earlier) lead to questioning what we as social workers do for and with our clients. Research ac-

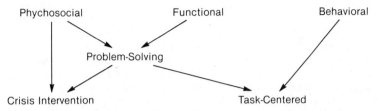

FIGURE 4.1   Major Paradigms and Paradigm Variations

tivities that are designed to seek answers to those questions contribute to theory. Theories, synthesized over time, develop into paradigms or widely accepted schools of practice. These, in turn, contribute intervention strategies for helping. As these are incorporated into practical, everyday activities, the cycle continues.

References

1. Robert W. Roberts and Robert H. Nee, *Theories of Social Casework* (Chicago: The University of Chicago Press, 1970).
2. Colin Peile, "Research Paradigms in Social Work: from Stalemate to Creative Synthesis," *Social Service Review,* March 1988.
3. Bradford W. Sheafor, Charles R. Horejsi, and Gloria A. Horejsi, *Techniques and Guidelines for Social Work Practice* (Boston: Allyn and Bacon, 1988), pp. 29–30.
4. Peile, "Research Paradigms in Social Work," pp. 5, 12.
5. Francis J. Turner, "Theory in Social Work Practice," in *Social Work Treatment: Interlocking Theoretical Approaches,* 3rd ed., Francis J. Turner, ed. (New York: The Free Press, 1986), pp. 1–2.
6. Turner, "Theory in Social Work Practice," pp. 6–10.
7. Mary Richmond, *Social Diagnosis* (New York: Russell Sage, 1917).
8. Gordon Hamilton, *Theory and Practice of Social Casework,* rev. ed. (New York: Columbia University Press, 1958).
9. Howard J. Parad, ed., *Crisis Intervention: Selected Readings* (New York: Family Service Association of America, 1958).
10. Howard J. Parad and Roger Miller, eds., *Ego-Oriented Casework: Problems and Perspectives* (New York: Family Service Association of America, 1963).
11. Helen Harris Perlman, *Social Casework: A Problem-Solving Process* (Chicago: University of Chicago Press, 1957).
12. Florence Hollis, *Casework, A Psychosocial Therapy,* 3rd ed. (New York: Random House, 1981).
13. Helen Harris Perlman, *Persona: Social Role and Responsibility* (Chicago: University of Chicago Press, 1968).
14. Parad and Miller, *Ego-Oriented Casework.*
15. Howard J. Parad, *Ego Psychology and Dynamic Casework* (New York: Family Service Association of America, 1958).
16. Derek Jehu, *Learning Theory and Social Work* (London: Routledge, 1967).
17. Harold D. Werner, *A Rational Approach to Social Casework* (New York: Association Press, 1965).
18. Werner Lutz, *Concepts and Principles Underlying Casework Practice* (Washington, DC: National Association of Social Workers, 1956).
19. Gordon Hearn, *Theory Building in Social Work* (Toronto: University of Toronto Press, 1958).
20. Joan W. Stein, *The Family as a Unit of Study and Treatment* (Seattle: Regional Rehabilitation Research Institute, University of Washington, School of Social Work, 1969).
21. Roberts and Nee, *Theories of Social Casework.*
22. Turner, "Theory in Social Work Practice," p. 9.
23. Lillian Ripple, Earnestina Alexander, and Ber-

nice Polemis, *Motivation, Capacity, and Opportunity: Social Service Monographs* (Chicago: University of Chicago Press, 1964).

24. William J. Reid and Ann W. Shyne, *Brief and Extended Casework* (New York: Columbia University Press, 1969).

25. Joel Fischer, *Effective Casework Practice: An Eclectic Approach* (New York: McGraw-Hill, 1978).

26. J. Hage, *Techniques and Problems of Theory Construction in Sociology* (New York: Wiley, 1972).

27. A. L. Stinchcombe, *Constructing Social Theory* (New York: Harcourt, Brace, Jovanovich, 1968).

28. D. Willer, *Scientific Sociology: Theory and Method* (Englewood Cliffs, NJ: Prentice-Hall, 1967).

29. Turner, "Theory in Social Work Practice," pp. 2, 13.

30. Turner, "Theory in Social Work Practice," pp. 3–4.

31. Hugh Prather, *There Is a Place Where You Are Not Alone* (New York: Doubleday, 1980), p. 17.

32. T. S. Kuhn, *The Structure of Scientific Revolutions* (Chicago: University of Chicago Press, 1962).

33. Sheafor, Horejsi, and Horejsi, *Techniques and Guidelines for Social Work Practice*, p. 32.

34. Peile, "Research Paradigms in Social Work," p. 8.

35. M. Masterman, "The Nature of a Paradigm," in *Criticism and Growth of Knowledge*, I. Lakatos and A. Musgrave, eds. (Cambridge, MA: Harvard University Press, 1970).

36. Francis J. Turner, "Psychosocial Theory," in *Social Work Treatment: Interlocking Theoretical Approaches*, 3rd ed., Francis J. Turner, ed. (New York: The Free Press, 1986), p. 485.

37. Florence Hollis, "Social Casework: The Psychosocial Approach," in *Encyclopedia of Social Work*, 16th ed., Robert E. Morris, ed. (Washington, DC, National Association of Social Workers, 1973), pp. 1217–26.

38. Turner, "Psychosocial Theory," p. 487.

39. Florence Hollis, "The Psychosocial Approach to the Practice of Casework," in *Theories of Social Casework*, Robert W. Roberts and Robert H. Nee, eds. (Chicago: The University of Chicago Press, 1970), pp. 37–38.

40. Shankar A. Yelaja, "Functional Theory for Social Work Practice," in *Social Work Treatment: Interlocking Theoretical Approaches*, 3rd ed., Francis J. Turner, ed. (New York: The Free Press, 1986), p. 46.

41. Ruth Smalley, "Social Casework: The Functional Approach," in *Encyclopedia of Social*

Work, 16th ed., Robert E. Morris, ed. (Washington, DC: National Association of Social Workers, 1973), p. 1197.

42. Ruth Smalley, *Theory for Social Work Practice* (New York: Columbia University Press, 1967).

43. Smalley, "Social Casework," pp. 1195–1206.

44. Yelaja, "Functional Theory for Social Work Practice," p. 53.

45. Helen Harris Perlman, "Social Casework: The Problem-Solving Approach," in *Encyclopedia of Social Work*, 16th ed., Robert E. Morris, ed. (Washington, DC: National Association of Social Workers, 1973), pp. 1206–16.

46. Helen Harris Perlman, "The Problem-Solving Model," in *Social Work Treatment: Interlocking Theoretical Approaches*, Francis J. Turner, ed. (New York: The Free Press, 1986), pp. 247–51.

47. Perlman, *Social Casework*.

48. Perlman, "Social Casework," p. 1208.

49. Perlman, "The Problem–Solving Model," p. 254.

50. Edwin J. Thomas, "Social Casework and Social Group Work: The Behavioral Approach," in *Encyclopedia of Social Work*, 16th ed., Robert E. Morris, ed. (Washington, DC: National Association of Social Workers, 1973), pp. 1226–7.

51. K. O'Leary, "The Image of Behavior Therapy: It Is Time to Take a Stand," *Behavior Therapy* 15 (1984): 219–33.

52. B. F. Skinner, *Science and Human Behavior* (New York: Macmillan, 1953).

53. Ray J. Thomlinson, "Behavior Therapy in Social Work Practice," in *Social Work Treatment: Interlocking Theoretical Approaches*, 3rd ed., Francis J. Turner, ed. (New York: The Free Press, 1986).

54. Thomlinson, "Behavior Therapy in Social Work Practice," p. 133.

55. Joseph Wolpe, *The Practice of Behavior Therapy* (New York: Pergamon, 1969, 1984).

56. Thomas, "Social Casework and Social Group Work," pp. 1229–32.

57. Lydia Rapoport, "Crisis Intervention as a Mode of Treatment," in *Theories of Social Casework*, Robert W. Roberts and Robert H. Nee, eds. (Chicago: University of Chicago Press, 1970), p. 270.

58. Howard J. Parad, "Crisis Intervention," in *Encyclopedia of Social Work*, 16th ed., Robert E. Morris, ed. (Washington, DC: National Association of Social Workers, 1973), p. 197.

59. Naomi Golan, "Crisis Theory," in *Social Work Treatment: Interlocking Theoretical Approaches*, 3rd ed., Francis J. Turner, ed. (New York: The Free Press, 1986), p. 296.

60. Golan, "Crisis Theory," pp. 296–8.

61. William Reid, "Task-Centered Social Work," in *Social Work Treatment: Interlocking Theoretical Approaches*, 3rd ed., Francis J. Turner, ed. (New York: The Free Press, 1986), p. 290.

62. Laura Epstein, *Helping People: The Task-Centered Approach*, 2nd ed. (Columbus, OH: Merrill, 1988). pp. i, 11.

63. Michael A. Rothery, "Contracts and Contracting," *Clinical Social Work Journal* 8, No. 3 (1980).

64. Epstein, *Helping People*, pp. 8–9.

65. Reid, "Task-Centered Social Work," p. 270.

66. Perlman, "The Problem-Solving Model," p. 259.

67. William J. Reid, "Treatment of Choice or Choice of Treatments: An Essay Review," *Social Work* (January 1984): 33–8.

Chapter 5

The Ethics of Social Work Research

Ethics as an urgent issue
Current ethical considerations
Social work and social science
    research
Federal influences on research
    ethics

Common ethical issues
    Deception
    Manipulation
    Project selection
Toward a resolution

Ethical issues in research are grounded in conflicts among values. —DAVID GILLESPIE

Ethics as an Urgent Issue

The issue of ethics has persisted throughout the twentieth century as an area of critical concern in the development of both professional social work practice and research. Late in the nineteenth century and early in this century, professional leaders called for a "scientific philanthropy" while debating the most ethical approach. In contention were such issues as "uplifting" and "rehabilitating the poor" versus the position of emphasizing political activism and "tax-supported relief" [1]. As the twentieth century draws to a close, residuals of these earlier ethical issues continue to be a part of public debates on program options for "truly needy," dependent, and at-risk populations. Social work research informs the advocates of these various options.

    For our purposes in exploring the role of ethics in research, it is meaningful to note that the early leaders in professional social work called for more scientific study in their work, but overlooked client rights and needs. For example, Mary Richmond advocated for "technical competence in the provision of social services" [2], but did not deal with protecting clients from harm or safeguarding their vulnerabilities as human beings. Specifically missing was any attention given to the issue of confidentiality. Richmond saw the ideal social work agent as a "detective."

> Hence she never saw the contradiction of proceeding with an investigation without the client's awareness or informed consent of the steps being taken. This has contributed to the public's perception of social workers as being agents of social control. More specifically, social workers have been accused of having hidden agendas or of being outright unethical in their pursuit of the facts about the client's situation. [3]

Thus, social work began as a professional activity stressing the importance of systematic and standardized study processes with a strong call for improved scientific approaches. However, this point of beginning was rife with moral and ethical conflicts regarding what constituted responsible social service practice as well as scientific investigative processes.

A more appropriate and balanced understanding of how to protect the interests and well-being of clients involved in social work research tended to evolve in a pattern parallel with social science research.

> Scientific research has produced substantial social benefits. It has also posed some troubling ethical questions by reported abuses of human subjects in biomedical experiments, especially during the Second World War. During the Nuremberg War Crimes Trials, the Nuremberg Code was drafted as a set of standards for judging physicians and scientists who had conducted biomedical experiments on concentration camp prisoners. This code became the prototype of many later codes intended to assure that research involving human subjects would be carried out in an ethical manner. [4]

In the United States an "ethical primer," entitled *The Belmont Report: Ethical Principles and Guidelines for the Protection of Human Subjects of Research* [5], was developed to guide both biomedical and behavioral research.

This has become a statement of principles and methodologies held in high regard by social work researchers and social scientists. It was issued by the National Commission for the Protection of Human Subjects of Biomedical and Behavioral Research in 1978.

The Belmont Report identifies three principles or general prescriptive judgments to guide researchers in protecting participants:

1. *Respect for persons.* Human subjects should be treated as autonomous agents, and persons with diminished autonomy are entitled to protection [6].

2. *Beneficence.* Research participants "are treated in an ethical manner not only by respecting their decisions and protecting them from harm, but also making efforts to secure their well-being" [7].

3. *Justice.* Attention should be given to just ways of distributing burdens and benefits of the research process. Examples of injustices include the exploitation of

"... unwilling prisoners as research subjects in Nazi concentration camps as a particularly flagrant injustice" [8], or in the United States in the 1940s, "... the Tuskagee syphilis study used disadvantaged, rural black men to study the untreated course of a disease that is by no means confined to that population. These subjects were deprived of demonstrably effective treatment in order not to interrupt the project, long after such treatment became generally available" [9].

In discussing applications of these principles, the Belmont Report specified three requirements for ethical research processes:

1. *Informed consent.* Research participants must be given clear and adequate information of what their involvement will entail and "... to the degree that they are capable, be given the opportunity to choose what shall or shall not happen to them," and the "voluntariness" of their participation must be specified [10].

2. *Assessment of risks and benefits.* The participant shall have "... an opportunity and a responsibility to gather systematic and comprehensive information about the proposed research" [11]. The human subject must be fully informed about the personal advantages or disadvantages.

3. *Selection of subjects.* The application of the principle of justice requires that there be fair procedures and outcomes in the selection of research subjects. These principles and their application require considerably more than a superficial and simplistic attention by the social work researcher or social science investigator. This is a complex social issue and researchers must be aware of social accountability expectations under which they function in our society.

Current Ethical Considerations

In recent years, the ethics of social work and social science investigators has become a crucial issue as we have discovered, under the prodding of laypersons as well as sensitive researchers themselves, the moral dilemmas posed by some of our research techniques, uses, and applications. As we have seen, social science researchers did their work without much concern about whether the rights of subjects were being violated, the motives of funding agencies were sullied, or the ways the findings would be used.

Part of this lack of concern for ethical issues in social science research can be traced to the fact that the objectives of scientific inquiry are neither moral nor immoral—they are *amoral*. An atomic reaction is a natural process, and the fact that people may get in the way of such reactions (to say nothing of instigating them) has not been seen as ultimately the responsibility of the investigator. By modeling themselves after natural sciences, the social sciences have often argued for the same kind of immunity from ethical concerns. Indeed, a long-held stance of the scientist has been that of ethical neutrality, or *value-free* inquiry, the idea that if we are to attain objectivity in our investigations, we must not take an ethical position with regard to our subject matter or the findings of our research.

This strict scientism, as our earlier discussion of moon rocks in Chapter 2 pointed out, has not stood the test of close scrutiny. If a purely scientific investigation in theoretical physics like the government-sponsored Manhattan Project, which led to the development of the world's first atomic bomb, can cause the deaths of 250,000 people in a second, the project can hardly be exempted from ethical concerns, even though the atomic reaction itself was quite amoral. To control the circumstances of the release of such forces is, of course, to bring ethics into the picture if for no other reason than the fact that we can elect *not* to set such forces into motion. As our capability of controlling more and more of nature has increased, the question of ethics has similarly become more pressing, if only because the option of control leads to the option of no control, and this choice is the basis for all ethical questions. The reason nature itself is not concerned with ethics is that nature has no choice. The reason human beings are always concerned about ethics is that we do.

Social Work and Social Science Research

Professional social work is a learned discipline with a human-centered value base. This frame of reference permeates all activities undertaken by social workers. For example, these values are translated into a professional Code of Ethics formulated by the National Association of Social Workers. It applies to all acts undertaken by members of NASW. Furthermore, the code specifically identifies *scholarly inquiry* as an activity to which it is to be applied.

Scholarship and Research—The social worker engaged in study and research should be guided by the conventions of scholarly inquiry.

1. The social worker engaged in research should consider carefully its possible consequences for human beings.
2. The social worker engaged in research should ascertain that the consent of participants is voluntary and informed, without any implied deprivation or penalty for refusal to participate, and with due regard for participants' privacy and dignity.
3. The social worker engaged in research should protect participants from unwarranted physical or mental discomfort, distress, harm, danger, or deprivation.
4. The social worker who engages in the evaluation of services or cases should discuss them only for professional purposes and only with persons directly and professionally concerned with them.
5. Information obtained about participants in research should be treated as confidential.
6. The social worker should take credit only for work actually done in connection with scholarly and research endeavors and credit contributions made by others. [12]

Additionally, these ethical guides are reflective of basic social work values that pervade the curriculum of social work education programs accredited by the Council on Social Work Education at both the undergraduate and graduate levels. Increasingly, required courses for a BA, MSW, DSW, or PhD degree in social work are grounded in content developed from social work and social science research data [13].

Also in the social sciences, because the objects of inquiry are really subjects (human beings and their activities), the concern over ethics is particularly well placed. The phenomena we study may not be of any ethical concern, but the study of them always is. This distinction between phenomena and inquiry into phenomena forms the basis of a consideration of ethics.

Methodology, at its most simplistic level, is about *techniques* of inquiry. Ethics, at its most simplistic level, is about *good* and *bad*. Obviously, a methodological technique may be either good or bad, not only technically, in terms of its effectiveness as a research instrument, but also in terms of its consequences for the people being researched and the society at large. Inquiry always has consequences: some obvious, some subtle, some long-term, some short-term, some good or bad from someone's point of view. A correlation between two social factors is without moral meaning, but the act of running the correlation, publishing the findings, acting on those findings, and so forth, does have moral consequences, and thus the study can be said to participate in this universe as well as in the objective realm of scientific phenomena. In his book on ethics and values, Kimmel describes this challenges when he says:

> The ethical issues encountered in applied social research are subtle and complex, raising difficult moral dilemmas that, at least on a superficial level, appear unresolvable. These dilemmas often require the researcher to strike a delicate balance between the scientific requirements of methodology and the human rights and values potentially threatened by the research. As such, the underlying guiding research principle is to proceed both ethically and without threatening the validity of the research endeavor insofar as possible. It thus is essential that investigators continually ask how they can conduct themselves ethically and still make progress through sound and generalizable research. [14]

The ethical challenges for the social work practitioner are no less critical for the social work researcher. Such issues as abortion, interethnic adoptions, or gay foster parents present value questions that arise in formulating underlying assumptions in designing a research proposal and selecting methodology to operationalize a study. So much of social work research is grounded in the realities of agencies and practitioner-oriented problems.

Federal Influences on Research Ethics

A particularly significant aspect of ethics in social science research is the role of the federal government in this nation's academic environment. Every campus receiving federal funding for a research or demonstration project involving human subjects is required to maintain an *Institutional Review Board*. This committee process must systematically examine and judge each research proposal involving human subjects in order to submit a *certification*. This statement is a notification to the appropriate governmental department that "… the risks of harm anticipated in the proposed research are not greater, considering probability and magnitude, than those ordinarily encountered in daily life or during the performance or routine physical or psychological examinations or tests" [15]. It incorporates a validation that the other principles specified in the Belmont Report are clearly and effectively dealt with in the research proposal. The monitoring of ethics in research by the government requires maintenance of records associated with the work of the Institutional Review Board.

> (a) An institution, or where appropriate an IRB, shall prepare and maintain adequate documentation of IRB activities, including the following:
>> (1) Copies of all research proposals reviewed, scientific evaluations, if any, that accompany the proposals, approved sample consent documents, progress reports submitted by investigators, and reports of injuries to subjects. [16]

Why is the role of governmental involvement of any consequence? The answer to this question is readily obvious when we examine this factor in light of the past several decades of social science research. Governmental participation in social and applied research has had, and continues to have, an impact on a number of disciplines. The federal government, responding to public concern about inhumane manipulation of human subjects, has used its funding resources to influence ethical procedures.

> The history of Federal support for the behavioral and social sciences shows the Federal Government has played a major role in shaping these fields of science via funding and through the creation of institutions to support basic and applied research, train students, and *regulate some research procedures.* [Authors' italics]
>> Over the last forty years, the bulk of Federal support has gone to *applied,* not to basic behavioral and social science, and for social sciences, as opposed to behavioral sciences (psychology). The major social science disciplines supported have been economics and sociology. [17]

This pattern of governmental stimuli to achieve high standards in social science research appears to have had productive results. However, due to the multitude of governmental bureaucracies and differing interpretations of guidelines, in a time of rapid technosocial change, ethics in social science research will continue to require careful monitoring by the public and scientific community. In this discussion, it is important to mention some of the more prevalent ethical problems facing social work researchers and to show how social science professionals have tried to systematize basic principles with which to handle them.

Common Ethical Issues

Deception

A major issue in social research is the question of deception. Moral codes for centuries have condemned the practice of lying, and yet social scientists have been doing it for years [18]. Strategies range from outright lies, in which experimental subjects are given false information, to the use of confederates as part of the group of subjects. A classic example is a study in social psychology by Rosenthal and Jacobson. In order to find out how much teacher expectations affect student performance, the researchers deceived a number of elementary-school teachers. They told them that certain children in their classes would do well academically and that others probably would not. They said these predictions were based on a test of "intellectual blooming." In fact, there were no significant academic differences in the children. At the end of the school year, the two researchers found what they had predicted: the children who were expected to achieve did so, and those who were not expected to do well did not. They called this result the *Pygmalion effect*, and it has been repeated since in over 200 separate studies, all of which have used essentially the same deceptive methodology.

Studies based on deception are very difficult to give up. For one thing, they have a dramatic effect and receive widespread publicity when reported. In addition, many researchers do not feel that valid information about various kinds of behavior can be obtained if subjects know the purpose of the experiment. In other words, a Pygmalion effect exists in human affairs. If people know the purpose of an experiment, they are likely to play to it or try to subvert it. In either case the validity of the research is destroyed.

> There is no rigorously gathered information to demonstrate that the unethical use of these practices is widespread. Abuse appears to occur in all scientific disciplines involving human subjects, and may stem, in part, from competition to publish and establish a reputation, in order to obtain increasingly scarce Federal research dollars. In order to minimize the negative impacts of these practices, professional societies, "… have proposed ethical guidelines for policy-related social research that requires that the relevant data be immediately available for re-analysis by other social scientists." [19]

The ethical dilemmas posed by deceptive research can be obvious or quite subtle. In the case of the Rosenthal and Jacobson study, we can see the problems at a glance. Parents were furious when they discovered that their children had been used as guinea pigs without their knowledge or permission. Moreover, to create the possibilities for such failure and to cost a child a whole year in school for the benefit of proving something seems clearly wrong. On the other hand, the research was unethical to the very extent that it proved to be correct. Had there *not* been a Pygmalion effect, had the research not discovered the predicted relationship, the ethical dilemma posed would not have been nearly so great. The defense given by the researchers in this case is also compelling. They argued that the discovery of the Pygmalion effect has had a profound impact on teaching and that many children who might previously have been impaired by teacher expectations are now more likely to be taught by teachers who are aware of the problem and take steps to do something about it. In other words, we are on balance better for having done the study, even though some might have been hurt in the original doing of it.

Sometimes the deception is more subtle. All that Laud Humphreys [20] did in researching his classic book *Tearoom Trade* was to observe a particular kind of homosexual behavior occurring in public restrooms, often called *tearooms* in the language of the gay community. In order to obtain information about those who frequented tearooms, Humphreys himself posed as a so-called "watch queen." He observed impersonal sex acts between consenting homosexuals while at the same time faithfully signaling the participants if police or "straights" were about to enter the restroom.

Later, Humphreys engaged in a more serious form of deception by following up with a survey of the participants. Having obtained their license-plate numbers while serving as watch queen, he went to their homes posing as a market researcher in order actually to collect social and demographic data about them. He did not tell them that he was doing a study of homosexual behavior, of course, nor did he reveal that he knew they were homosexuals, and he maintained their anonymity by never revealing who they were. By doing his work in a public place, Humphreys minimized the deception to a certain extent. He also was a valid participant as well as an observer in the sense that he performed the role of watch queen competently. However, had his research interests been revealed, his work would have been much more difficult. And, although he was clearly sympathetic to the situation of the homosexuals, he still deceived them.

Humphreys's work set off a hailstorm of criticism and debate, both within the ranks of social scientists and from without. In a celebrated exchange between defenders and opponents, Horowitz and Rainwater defended Humphreys, while newspaper columnist Nicholas Von Hoffman castigated his work as an example of the bad ethics rampant in the field.

Horowitz and Rainwater [21] defended Humphreys on two grounds. First, they said, he was sympathetic toward the plight of homosexuals and used his research in an effort to show that their behavior was harmless and did not warrant the police-state tactics being used to stop them. Second, such a strategy provided intimate knowledge of the homosexual community that social scientists did not previously have. Von Hoffman [22] countered by saying that lofty ends do not justify snooping into the private lives of people and deceiving them by social scientists any more than by the CIA or the FBI.

A further perspective on the unethical research cited previously can be found in the following statement of Nancy Humphreys, NASW president, 1979–81:

> Knowledge and a sensitivity to gay and lesbian issues are a necessary part of the social worker's practice repertoire for at least three good reasons. First, gays and lesbians who receive social services from social workers are becoming an increasingly large constituent group of the profession. Second, many social workers are gay or lesbian, some of whom still choose to hide themselves in order to evade the stigma society attaches to the gay person. Third, and perhaps most importantly, gay and lesbian people represent an oppressed population, the protection of whose rights, as those of all oppressed populations, should be of primary concern to the profession of social work. [23]

These values are also articulated in the Council on Social Work Education's curriculum policies in terms of required content on minority groups subject to "social, economic and legal bias or oppression" [24]. Social work research, therefore, would be expected to be guided by clearly different principles than those that influenced social investigators in the early 1970s.

Manipulation

Sometimes subjects are not only deceived but manipulated in ethically questionable ways. This type of methodology is most often employed in laboratory studies. In one of the most famous laboratory studies of our time, *Obedience to Authority*, Milgram [25] used confederates who faked receiving an electric shock. His aim was to test whether ordinary citizens would engage in behavior that they believed was injuring someone if they were told that some high authority approved it.

A naive experimental subject is told that he or she is taking part in a study of learning with another subject (who is secretly a confederate of the researcher). The two draw to see who is the teacher, but the drawing is rigged so that the experimental subject will be the teacher and the confederate the learner. The subject watches as electrodes are pasted to the confederate's arm. The confederate says he or she is not sure about this procedure because of an earlier heart condition, but the experimenter assures the confederate that everything is all right—the experiment might be painful but not harmful. All of this is enacted for the benefit of the experimental subject, who now understands that his or her supposed partner has a heart condition and will suffer some pain. The subject is then given a series of word pairs such as *nice–day* and *fat–neck* to read to the confederate. The list is then repeated, with the subject reading the first word and the confederate—who is now behind a partition—choosing the second from a list of four multiple-choice options. The learner pushes a button. If the answer is correct, the experimental subject goes on. If the answer is wrong, the subject pushes a switch that buzzes and supposedly gives the learner an electric shock.

The experiment begins with what the subject thinks is a 15-volt shock, and the voltage is then increased with every wrong answer. The control board goes from 15 to 450 volts, and also has verbal descriptions of the shock levels, ranging from "slight shock" to "danger: severe shock." If at any point the subject hesitates to push the button, the experimenter calmly tells him or her to go on. The idea of the study is to find the shock level beyond which the subject will refuse to push the button. A recording coming from behind the partition simulates the resistance from the confederate. The objections start with a grunt at 75 volts and build up to a "Hey, that really hurts" at 125 volts. The voice becomes desperate with "I can't stand the pain, don't do that!" at 180 volts, complains of heart trouble at 195, gives an agonized scream at 285, refuses to answer at 315, and then is silent.

The results were devastating. Believing at first that few people would go all the way through the board to the dangerous levels, Milgram found that virtually all subjects would, especially if they were encouraged by the authority of the experimenter. On the basis of these studies, Milgram concluded a number of important things about obedience to authority. Among them was his idea that, if Nazi-like extermination camps were set up around the country, there would be little difficulty in recruiting ordinary citizens to staff them.

This is perhaps the most ingenious scheme of manipulative deception ever devised by a social science researcher, and Milgram has established a high academic reputation on the basis of it. The justification for it is the same: in the name of science, such manipulation is justified because it helps us understand more about human behavior.

Project Selection

In a perceptive section of their book on research methodology, Sjoberg and Nett [26] point out that every research project holds the potential for changing the subjects under investigation if they know they are being researched either before the project or afterward. If the subject is an organization such as a corporation, business enterprise, or academic institution, a research project can have devastating consequences by pointing up the discrepancies between what the organization claims to be and what it actually turns out to be, given the findings of the research study. The political nature of this dilemma interposes with the ethical one. Conservatives tend to be cautious about upsetting the moral order and might find research to be a threat to what is already established. Political liberals often see themselves as having no vested interest in the prevailing order and wish to carry out research even if the results make it extremely difficult for the organization to continue as before. Both stances pose serious ethical dilemmas, as Sjoberg and Nett point out:

> Because the more conservative social scientist seeks to avoid controversy, and because social research by its very nature involves a degree of exposure, and therefore controversy, the conservative's action may contravene some of the ideas of science, particularly that calling for freedom of inquiry. Moreover, the mere acceptance of the broader society's definition of what is right may lead one to support and advance policies that are fundamentally at odds with "man's welfare." Thus, many German scientists, who passively accepted the goals and norms of Naziism, were instrumental in aiding and abetting, through their work, the destruction of millions of Jews. On the other hand, the more liberally inclined may find themselves challenging through their research and analysis their own associational structure—the very system that underwrites and supports the scientific method. The liberal scientist may unwittingly collect data that could be used to question or challenge the democratic political system, some form of which is essential for sustaining social research. [27]

All of this is made even more confusing by the fact that so much of social research is funded by agencies that almost always have a vested interest in what is found out. Governments fund studies of social control; funeral directors fund studies to find out whether funerals are valuable; any number of groups fund evaluation research to find out if their programs are successful. Obviously, money has a way of getting in the way of objectivity, perhaps in subtle ways unrecognized even by the person doing the research.

Toward a Resolution

There can be no easy solution to the ethical dilemmas posed by social work and social science research. Several possibilities have been offered, all of which have both benefits and liabilities. Jung [28] has suggested a time-consuming and expensive procedure in which a representative sample of a group about to be studied would be contacted to review the experimental procedures and to indicate what they consider to be the major ethical problems associated with them. The American Psychological Association advocates the use of a risk–benefit analysis to see whether the potential benefits of a study outweigh its drawbacks. Such a judgment is left to the individual investigator, who, of course, is likely to see the benefits more than the risks, as we have already seen in the examples described.

Babbie [29] has suggested a number of principles to guide us ethically in our research but concedes that any or all of them may need to be violated in order to obtain valid information in a research project. His principles include voluntary participation of subjects, no harm to the people being studied, respect for anonymity or confidentiality of sources, and honesty in the analysis and reporting of research data findings. These principles are not always easily realized. For example, do we always know just how voluntary the participation of our subjects was? Even when a subject says that, yes, he or she will participate in a research project, we don't always know what kind of hidden agenda has gone into that decision. Perhaps the subject harbors a secret fear of harm if he or she doesn't cooperate. But whatever the reasons for volunteering, we cannot always be sure that it was a fully uncoerced act.

The idea that harm should not be done to the people studied is obvious, but this too, may be difficult to carry out in practice. First, we can never know positively that people will not be hurt as a result of our research, because very few researchers fully control the uses to which their data are put. Furthermore, if we add to that the fact that subjects may be psychologically affected in a negative way by their participation in a research project, we can see that it becomes almost impossible to say that our research harmed no one. We can only guess what kind of psychological harm might have come to the subjects in Stanley Milgram's *Obedience to Authority* study.

Protecting the confidentiality of respondents is relatively easy to do, although it may require some extra work. If a researcher were studying deviant behavior, for example, he might have to hide identified interview schedules or questionnaires and even be prepared to go to jail were the police to subpoena such records in an effort to enforce existing laws against the people he was studying. One way around the problem is to ensure the anonymity of a respondent by designing the project so that even the researcher does not know the identity of the subjects. For some types of projects that require only statistical information, this is reasonable. But for others, where the respondent is to be interviewed, it is obviously impossible.

In the analysis and reporting of the data from social research, there are so many ways to be dishonest that we could write a whole book about this topic alone. After having waded around in data, and having been party to the many difficulties that confront a researcher in the course of doing a project, the author of the report often knows full well the inadequacies of the research, and the moral dilemma often posed is, "Shall I relay the inadequacies to the reader or keep them to myself?" Theoretically, honesty is the best policy, but there is an area where all sorts of practical considerations can emerge that interfere with the workings of this norm. In no other single area of research does the reader rely so much on the integrity of the author of a research report.

This discussion of ethics may make it seem that producing honest, morally sound, and at the same time scientifically valid research is virtually impossible. And while ethics and good science sometimes conflict, it must also be pointed out that often they do not. Erikson has put it best: "It seems to me that any attempt to use masquerades in social research betrays an extraordinary disrespect for the complexities of human interaction, and for this reason can only lead to bad science" [30].

References

1. Donna L. Franklin, "Mary Richmond and Jane Addams: From Moral Certainty to Rational Inquiry in Social Work Practice," *Social Service Review* (December 1986): 504–10.

2. Franklin, "Mary Richmond and Jane Addams," p. 519.

3. Franklin, "Mary Richmond and Jane Addams," p. 519–20.

4. *The Belmont Report: Ethical Principles and Guidelines for the Protection of Human Subjects of Research*, U.S. Department of Health, Education, and Welfare Publication (OS)78-0012, 1978, p. 1.

5. *The Belmont Report.*

6. *The Belmont Report*, pp. 4–6.

7. *The Belmont Report*, pp. 5–8.

8. *The Belmont Report*, pp. 8–10.

9. *The Belmont Report*, pp. 10–14.

10. *The Belmont Report*, pp. 14–18.

11. *The Belmont Report*, pp. 18–20.

12. *Code of Ethics of the National Association of Social Workers* (Silver Spring, MD: National Association of Social Workers, Inc., July 1980), p. 4.

13. *Handbook of Accreditation Standards and Procedures* (New York: Council on Social Work Education, Revised July 1984), Section 7.7, unpaginated.

14. Allan J. Kimmel, *Ethics and Values in Applied Social Research* (Beverly Hills, CA: Sage, 1988), p. 9.

15. *Code of Federal Regulations, Public Welfare*, 45, Parts 1 to 199 (Office of the Federal Register, National Archives and Records Administration, Revised as of October 1, 1988), p. 143.

16. *Code of Federal Regulations, Public Welfare*, 45, p. 143.

17. Science Policy Study Background Report 6: Research Policies for the Social and Behavioral Sciences (Washington, DC: U.S. Government Printing Office, September 1986), p. 223.

18. D. Warwick, "Social Scientists Ought to Stop Lying," *Psychiatry Today* (February 1975): 249–60.

19. Science Policy Study, p. 194.

20. L. Humphreys, *Tearoom Trade: Impersonal Sex in Public Places* (Chicago: Aldine, 1970).

21. I. Horowitz and L. Rainwater, "On Journalistic Moralizers," *Trans-Action* (1970): 7.

22. N. Von Hoffman, "Sociological Snoopers," *Washington Post*, January 30, 1970.

23. N. Humphreys, "From the President," *NASW News* 26 (May 1981): 2.

24. "Curriculum Policy for the Master's Degree and Baccalaureate Degree Programs in Social Work Education" (New York: Council on Social Work Education, 1982), unpaginated.

25. S. Milgram, *Obedience to Authority* (New York: Harper and Row, 1974).

26. G. Sjoberg and R. A. Nett, *A Methodology for Social Research* (New York: Harper and Row, 1978).

27. Sjoberg and Nett, *A Methodology for Social Research*, pp. 122–23.

28. J. Jung, "Snoopology," *Human Behavior* (October 1975): 6–8.

29. E. Babbie, *The Practice of Social Research* (Belmont, CA: Wadsworth, 1975).

30. K. A. Erikson, "A Comment on Disguised Observation in Sociology," *Social Problems* (1967): 366–73.

Chapter 6

Choosing a Research Design

Research design defined
The relation of theory to the
    research design
The importance of the research
    design
Factors to consider in choosing a
    research design
  Who or what? (unit of analysis)
  When? (research time frame)
Where? (research setting)
Why? (research purpose)
Judging the adequacy of the
    design
Research designs
General considerations
The research design and data
    collection

If you is goin' anywhere in particular
Up here, ud'd better figger fust
How ta git thar
Cuz by jest goin'
Afore ya know where yere goin'
Ya might not wanta be. —ANONYMOUS

Let's begin by reviewing your progress. You have selected a subject area in which you wish to do research. You have spent time studying library materials to identify what has already been accomplished and to help in narrowing down the research subject to a research question. You have also used this relevant body of literature to formulate a plausible answer to the research question. This plausible answer consti- tutes your theory. Specifically, it determines the relationships you anticipate among the phenomena under study.

But theory is still theory. It remains a speculative or conjectural view of the way things work; it is not a fact. And though logic and previously established fact may have been used to define the anticipated relationships, "the relations of logic are not necessarily the relationships of man" [1]. The use of logic to formulate theory, then, is only a tool. Science insists that the knowledge derived through the use of this tool be tested in the real world. But you have already discovered that theory is not directly testable. The abstract nature of stated relationships among concepts make such relationships and concepts vulnerable to multiple definitions (i.e., operationalization can take many forms). In fact, the more general the concepts, the more meanings and definitions there are to choose from. Thus, the researcher must devise a strategy whereby the theory can be, at least indirectly, tested. *Research design* is the name we give to this strategy.

There is increasing involvement at all levels of social work practice in research planning, participation, and utilization. Professionals are expected to be informed and to incorporate new knowledge in responding to their social service clientele's needs and problems. Also there are expectations that social workers in direct practice learn to use simple research designs to improve their specific skills and effectiveness [2]. They learn to planfully assess their work by monitoring and evaluating practice interventions in a way that provides feedback about the reliability and objectivity of judgments made. It also provides a basis for determining, for both social worker and client, how the presenting problem is or is not changing.

Research Design Defined

By research design we mean the plan of procedures for data collection and analysis that are undertaken to evaluate a particular theoretical perspective. The research design involves the entire process of planning and carrying out a research study [4]. It is all the procedures or steps undertaken to ensure an objective test of the theory under investigation.

If you were presented with the pieces to a jigsaw puzzle and challenged to fit the pieces together, most likely your strategy for accomplishing this task would be something other than haphazard. Suppose the scene on the puzzle box were a red barn set in a wheat field under a blue sky. You might begin by sorting the pieces according to the major colors: blue, yellow-gold, and red. Or you might begin by identifying those pieces with a straight edge that provide the border for the picture. Such procedures suggest an organized approach to the puzzle's solution. Likewise, in attempting to evaluate a proposed answer to a research question, you should employ an organized approach. Before beginning you should outline the steps required to test the theory. These steps become your "blueprint," which serves to guide you in this test.

The principles of research design are those factors that influence the choice of a research design. Active researchers are frequently called on to make design decisions, and the factors that influence their choice of design are not always apparent. You can think of the principles or factors influencing design choice as different-colored puzzle pieces. As you consider the factors by answering certain relevant questions, your search for an answer to the research question will begin to take on some order. This order ensures a more objective approach to the research question. In addition to considering the factors that influence design choice, we will also relate these factors to the various research designs. This particular task can be somewhat tricky, though, since social researchers do not always agree on the labels they give to the various design alternatives. For this book, we have chosen to use the commonly applied labels: experiment, survey, field research, historical research, content analysis, comparative analysis, and single-subject design. This chapter will not describe in detail these basic designs; that task will be saved for Chapters 10, 11, and 12. Primarily, this chapter is designed to help you think logically through a series of factors and to relate these factors to the design alternatives in such a way that you can make a reasonable and adequate design decision. The presentation of these factors is based on the premise that there are certain questions that can be asked, and, when answered, offer concrete guidance in choosing the most adequate design. These factors also provide us with a basis for making comparisons between research designs.

The Relation of Theory to the Research Design

The relation of theory to the research design, although basically quite simple, is of tremendous importance and deserves special comment. We have already established that theory is not directly testable. The concepts and the stated relationships among concepts must be reworked into variables (measurement of characteristics on which people differ) and stated relationships among variables (hypotheses) if they are to be tested. In effect, the research design provides us with a plan whereby these transformations can take place. Whereas theory guides our answer to the research question, the research design guides our test of this answer. Thus, theory is instrumental in guiding our choice of a research design by identifying who or what is to be observed, how it is to be observed, and how these observations are to be interpreted. In fact, we must constantly be concerned with whether or not the research design fits the theory in order that our research will lead us to the relevant facts [5]. The researcher simply must not get this process backward.

The Importance of the Research Design

To ensure the elimination of bias (the detection and correction of errors) as much as possible, science, as a way of knowing, requires a plan—a research design. Although a research design cannot guarantee reliable knowledge, it does provide an organized and stable approach to this mission in several ways. First, the use of a research design ensures that we are striving toward *objectivity*. Selective perception is not permitted. The researcher is obligated to examine a variety of cases, including cases that can disconfirm as well as confirm the theory being tested. Lombroso [6], in his classic study of physical characteristics and criminal tendencies, did not do this. Lombroso believed that criminal behavior was inborn. To determine whether this position represented "truth," he developed a number of tests to measure the physical characteristics of convicted criminals. And true to his position, he found a number of recurring characteristics in criminals: shifty eyes, strong jaw, wispy beard, and receding hairline. However, Lombroso's fatal flaw was selective perception—that is, his failure to look for these same physical characteristics in the noncriminal population. Consequently, he did not really establish that these characteristics occurred more frequently in the criminal population—only that they did occur in the criminal population.

Second, the use of a research design ensures that our approach to knowledge is *systematic*. The researcher proceeds methodically, delineating in detail each step to be taken. Who or what is to be sampled? What is to be measured? How is measurement to be accomplished? How is measurement to be obtained? How is analysis to be done? And though no research design is a guarantee that the research process will be smooth, it is certain that it will be smoother.

Such a systematic approach suggests a third function of the research design. A research design ensures that the knowledge can be *replicated*. As we have already discovered, replication in the social sciences is not the rule. We might even say that it is the exception. That is, social work studies and those in the social sciences are seldom replicated. But the knowledge that the findings of a study can be checked and even rechecked is an essential characteristic. Having a research design makes this possible. The importance of a research design lies in the fact that it provides a means by which we are able to adhere to the scientific method in our quest for reliable knowledge. Without a research design, it is easier for our personal biases to get in the way in this search for knowledge. Thus, you might say that we employ a research design to keep from "straying off the straight and narrow."

Factors to Consider in Choosing a Research Design

We are finally ready to proceed from the realm of abstract ideas (theory) to concrete instances (research design). Many researchers feel uncomfortable with this transition, for they are more comfortable when ordering abstract ideas (formulating theory). However, there comes a time when we must choose a concrete version of an abstract question. Broadly speaking, the researcher has two broad categories of designs from which to choose: qualitative or quantitative. In deciding which of these designs to use, several factors must be considered, including the following: *Who* or *what* will we study? *When* will we study them? *Where* will we study them? *Why* (for what purpose) will we be studying them? *What* is the most crucial criterion for judging the adequacy of the design? As you read about these factors and become familiar with the issues of concern, please remember that the answers to these questions will not dictate your choice of a research design. They will only provide concrete guidelines that aid in your choice.

Who or What? (Unit of Analysis)

As you have already seen, the social work researcher is interested in the social phenomena of relationship, condition, or change. More specifically, social workers are interested in evaluating practice and related issues through research designs. These concepts are quite broad and as such offer researchers tremendous latitude in who or what they can study. **The unit of analysis chosen for study can be defined as the concrete research case used to address the research question.** Basically, we can distinguish between four levels of the unit of analysis: (1) individuals, (2) groups, (3) organizations, and (4) social artifacts. Certainly, of these four, individuals most frequently serve as units of analysis. In other words, we usually describe social phenomena by studying the individuals who are a part of them. The *individual* as the unit of analysis can be characterized in many ways: student, client, supervisor, worker, friend, spouse, parent, and so forth. Suppose, for example, you were interested in young people's attitudes toward teen pregnancy. The individual would be the unit of analysis. If you were interested in whether males and females differed in their perceptions of leadership styles in psychotherapy groups, the individual would, again, be the unit of analysis.

It is worth noting, at this point, that although the individual serves as the unit of analysis, the write-up of analysis is not on this individual level. We are often not interested in any given individual's attitudes or behaviors. We are interested in the attitudes and behaviors of an aggregate of individuals. Recall that one of the characteristics of science is that it is generalizing. We talk to people, but we are interested in them as social beings who interact with others. Thus, we tend to describe and explain phenomena by grouping and summarizing the descriptions of individuals. This is generally true in both experimental and qualitative designs. However, in the case of single-subject designs, one individual may be the focus of the study and therefore the write-up of the analysis (see Chapter 12).

The *social group* may also serve as the unit of analysis in the study of social phenomena. Groups that might be studied, for example, include families, parenting groups, AA groups, assertiveness groups, and support groups of various kinds. When the group is used as the unit of analysis, the group's characteristics are usually derived from the characteristics of its individual members. Hoffman and Maier [7], for example, were interested in studying how heterogeneous and homogeneous groups differ in their approaches to solving problems. In order to define heterogeneity or homogeneity of group membership, these researchers evaluated the degree of dissimilarity of the personality profiles of individual members. The characteristics of the individual members were then used to derive the characteristics of the group.

Organizations can also be treated as the unit of analysis. We may wish to study, for example, such organizations as private, sectarian child welfare agencies. We might, for example, be interested in the degree of bureaucratic structure within these agencies. In this instance, the unit of analysis would be the various agencies as classified by type (i.e., residential, outpatient, foster care, emergency shelter, etc.). When the organization is the unit of analysis, it is defined in terms of its organizational characteristics.

Finally, the unit of analysis does not always have to be human; it may instead be a *social artifact*. Such units of analysis are sometimes called nonreactive measures, as they require neither participation in the world under investigation nor manipulation of that world. People leave evidence of their presence, and researchers can use this evidence to find out various things about them. One interesting example occurred when Chicago's Museum of Science and Industry was interested in learning which museum display was the most popular. The unit of analysis used to make this discovery was not human. Instead of questioning people directly about their favorite displays, the researchers discovered that the tiles around the exhibit containing living, hatching chicks had to be replaced approximately every six weeks. Tiles in other areas of the museum lasted for years without replacement [8].

Probably the most popular nonreactive measure used is content analysis, in which words, sentences, or topics frequently serve as the unit of analysis. Book content has been analyzed, for example, to understand sex-role stereotyping in U.S. society. Content analysis performed on grade-school readers (the classic Dick and Jane books) have shown a bias for placing women in domestic roles and men in career roles, thus helping to establish these stereotypic images in children's minds [9]. Content analysis of the group therapy clients' verbalizations can be an example of a good source of data for research. Social artifacts, as the unit of analysis, can sometimes provide a data source not available through any other means.

Whatever the unit of analysis, there are primarily three ways in which this unit can be grouped: (1) real groups, (2) treatment groups, and (3) statistical groups. A *real group* is one that has an ongoing life of its own apart from the research setting. Such groups are formed by members' awareness of and involvement with one another, especially in a natural setting. The family is a good example of a real group. If you were interested in studying decision-making processes within the family, you would not think of randomly pairing a male, a female, and one or more children. The natural processes that function to create a family or any real group are germane to the issue.

In sharp contrast, the *treatment group* is an artificial group. It is one constructed by the researcher for a specific purpose. Individuals grouped in this way may have no relationship to one another outside the research situation. In fact, membership within a treatment group is often determined by the toss of a coin. Aronson and Mills's classic study [10] of the effect of severity of initiation on liking for a group is an excellent example of treatment groups. Their study employed sixty-three college women who were randomly assigned to one of three groups: (1) severe initiation group, (2) mild initiation group, and (3) control group (no initiation). The women participating in the study were told that they were going to join a discussion group on sex, but in order to join, they were required to pass an initiation. In the severe initiation group, subjects were asked to read some very embarrassing material before joining the group discussion. In the mild initiation group, the material read was not very embarrassing. And in the control group, no reading was required. These three groups constituted the artificial or treatment groups. Membership was determined by the toss of a coin. As we shall see, such groups give the research tremendous power over the research situation and are of particular interest to the researcher using the *experimental design*.

The third unit of analysis is the statistical group. In this type of group, the units need not be located in the same place or even be aware of each other. Statistical grouping results from all units possessing some characteristic central to the research question. Suppose, for example, we were interested in studying the differences in self-concept among adopted and nonadopted adolescents [11]. The two statistical groups would be adopted adolescents and nonadopted adolescents. Comparisons of

males and females, blacks and whites, marrieds and singles are all examples of statistical groups. The individuals composing these groups probably would not know
each other or even be aware of each other. A subject's placement in one group or the
other would be totally contingent upon possessing the defining characteristic. The
more information obtained from each unit studied, the greater the possibilities for
creating statistical groups. Primarily, the *survey design* uses this type of grouping.

When? (Research Time Frame)

Human behavior takes place in time and through time. Time is an important element for at least two reasons and as such should be considered in your choice of a
research design: (1) Time helps in ordering the sequence of behavior and is an important determinant of causation; (2) Time positions behavior at some point along a
continuum and thus raises the issues of generalizability for other positions along the
continuum.

   The study of social phenomena is conducted either at a single point in time or
at several (two or more) points in time. Studies that examine social phenomena by
obtaining data at a single point in time are called **cross-sectional.** Such studies portray events at a moment in time, as in a snapshot [12]. Such static studies are useful
in defining the state of things as they are. Also they serve as important benchmarks
for subsequent studies of process and change.

   Studies that examine social phenomena by obtaining data at two or more
points in time are called **longitudinal studies.** Political scientists who study the voting patterns of U.S. citizens over a five- or ten-year period are conducting longitudinal research. Economists who study change in spending and lending patterns in the
United States over time are engaged in longitudinal research. Longitudinal and
cross-sectional studies will be discussed at greater length in Chapters 10, 11, and 12.
Right now, our concern is with understanding the role of time in the choice of a research design. Generally speaking, field studies are longitudinal in nature. The researcher is interested in observing natural groups over a period of time. The survey
design can either be longitudinal or cross-sectional. Most experiments have a longitudinal quality in that data are collected at two points in time. But the period of time
between the two data collections is usually short. Single-subject designs are also by
nature longitudinal to some extent.

Where? (Research Setting)

Since human behavior also takes place in a particular setting, the research design
must also take the setting into account. Every piece of research takes place in a setting that is unique with respect to time and space. Very simply put, the choice of setting reduces to two: the natural or the artificial, depending upon whether the research takes place in a real or contrived setting.

   Although the choice of a research setting seems quite simple and even obvious, it should be given careful thought and consideration. In truth, a number of factors need to be considered when choosing a research setting. Four of these are wor-

thy of mentioning: (1) the nature of the research question, (2) the types of variables being studied, (3) the form of the hypothesized relationships among variables, and (4) the nature of rival hypotheses and the degree of control desired.

One factor affecting the choice of a research setting is the nature of the research question. Some research questions, for example, imply a definite concrete setting. If your research were concerned with trials, mental patients, or prisoners, you would probably go to a courtroom, a mental hospital, or a prison. Other research questions are less definite with respect to setting. If you were interested in studying homelessness, spouse abuse, or teen pregnancy, your choice of setting would be much more varied.

A second factor is the types of variables being studied. Zeroing in on the independent variable, Ellsworth has written, "If the question or hypothesis concerns powerful or highly arousing events or strong feelings, the laboratory is usually not the most appropriate place to test it" [13]. For example, if you were interested in fear, grief, or love, the laboratory would probably not be the most appropriate setting since the response range of these variables would be restricted to fairly low levels. In general, laboratory variables are weak and the more variables you try to control (manipulate), the weaker they are [14]. Consequently, when control is more important than intensity, the laboratory is probably the preferred setting. When intensity is more important, a natural setting is probably preferable. As for the dependent variable, the problem in the laboratory is one of subjects trying to "look good." Subjects know they are being studied and they want to look their best. Thus, they often respond in ways that they perceive to be appropriate and acceptable. Studies that involve socially undesirable behavior may often be better tested outside of the laboratory even in a situation where subjects do not know they are being observed. (We must be careful here, however. The ethics of such a procedure must be thought about carefully. We address this question in other sections of this book.)

A third factor to consider when choosing a research setting is the form of the hypothesized relationship among variables. "In general, laboratory studies are limited to studying immediately reactive variables such as self-esteem, liking, or commitment. Chronic self-esteem, lasting friendship, or long-term commitment may have quite different effects from their reactive counterparts. For long-term effects or the study of processes over time, a natural setting is certainly desirable" [15]. Suppose, for example, you were interested in studying interpersonal attraction between clients and social workers. You constructed an experiment in which paired individuals were asked to talk for fifteen minutes. One of the pair is always a member of the research team (worker), the other is the true subject (client). In the course of a fifteen-minute conversation, the worker has been instructed to offer fifteen comments providing reinforcement for the subject ("You're so right." "That's very perceptive." "I fully agree."). Following the fifteen-minute conversation, the subject is asked to fill out a brief questionnaire which, among other things, questions him on his feelings toward his conversational partner. Research similar to this design has generally suggested that these studies deal with first impressions rather than with long-term relationships and with interpersonal attraction as a one-time event rather than as a continuous process. Since important factors in a relationship differ from time to time, the natural setting to study the career (development over time) of a relationship is important.

A fourth factor to consider is the nature of rival hypotheses and the degree of control desired. No hypothesis stands alone as the sole explanation of some social phenomenon. Alternative plausible explanations are the "stuff" of hypotheses. Certainly, it is in the researcher's best interest to eliminate as many of these rival hypotheses as possible in order to lend credibility to his or her hypothesis [16]. Suppose, for example, your reading in methodology led you to this methodological research issue: the usefulness of a neutral point on a five-point response scale. Assume that the response alternatives on a five-point scale are (1) strongly agree, (2) agree, (3) neutral, (4) disagree, and (5) strongly disagree. Such a scale, as we shall see, is called a *Likert scale* (see Chapter 8). But for the moment, interest is in whether the presence or absence of a neutral position on the scale significantly affects an individual's score.

To test this hypothesis, you might consider having your subjects respond to the scale items twice: first with the alternatives strongly agree, agree, neutral, disagree, and strongly disagree. If you assigned weights to these response alternatives and then summed the weights to get each subject's two scores, you could compare the scores to determine if they were *significantly different* (statistical jargon). If different, your inference would be that the difference was due to the presence or absence of the neutral point. But there is another possibility: a rival hypothesis. The difference might be due to simply having taken the same test twice. To control for this rival hypothesis, you might decide to use two different tests whose content is similar. Although this eliminates the problem of taking the same test twice, it does not eliminate the problem of taking two tests. So there is still the possibility of a testing effect—that is, the difference observed between a subject's two scores is a function of testing (i.e., taking two tests) and not the presence or absence of a neutral point. Your choice of a research design would have to consider this rival hypothesis and maybe others and attempt to eliminate them [17]. In general, then, we start with the relationship of interest and then scan the logical rivals to see which are plausible rivals in the particular instance; then we choose our research setting in such a way as to control for or measure the strongest contenders.

Why? (Research Purpose)

Once the researcher has answered the questions of who or what, when, and where (though not necessarily in this order), the important question of *why* must be dealt with. The question of why is concerned with the research purpose. But before considering specific research purposes, there are two frequently held misconceptions concerning purpose that need to be mentioned. First, it is an overgeneralization to assume that each researcher approaches a research question with a single purpose in mind. Although there may be only one purpose, it is not inconceivable or even improbable that the researcher would have two purposes in mind. Second, research purpose is not synonymous with research design. Although a certain purpose may seem more suitable and more frequently used with one design over another, purpose does not dictate design.

There are three general research purposes that seem applicable to the study of most social phenomena: explanation, description, and exploration.

Explanation

Explanation as a research purpose is concerned with why things are the way they are. We have named explanation first as it is the most advanced of scientific purposes. Many think it is the purpose toward which all scientific research should strive. To do research with this purpose in mind requires greater knowledge of the research question. Ultimately, the ability to explain gives one the ability to predict. And such predictive power assumes the ability to establish cause–effect relationships among variables. Killeffer [18] says, "Basic to the scientific method is the fundamental axiom that the physical universe is a rational, ordered one in which cause and effect are inevitably linked and where events fit together in logical patterns." In other words, we accept as self-evident that events are causally related and that we can discover the cause or causes of any event. In research, the variable said to be the "cause" is called the *independent variable*. The variable said to be the "effect" is called the *dependent variable*.

At this point, we might recall that strictly speaking, causal arguments cannot be verified empirically. Causal inferences are not on the operational level; they are on the theoretical level. They involve purely hypothetical if–then statements that are inherently untestable [19]. To put it even more bluntly, "There is no direct way to demonstrate that a relationship is causal. Nothing we can see, smell, or perceive in any way 'proves' that one thing caused another" [20]. Thus, we cannot establish beyond absolute doubt that the independent variable caused change in the dependent variable. We can only establish beyond *probable* doubt that the independent variable caused change in the dependent variable.

To establish beyond probable doubt that a cause–effect relationship exists, three essential criteria must be met. *First, there must be a relationship between two variables.* In particular, the two variables must covary (change together), and unless two variables do covary, we cannot infer that one is the cause of the other. *Second, there must also be a time order to the variables.* That which is cause must precede that which is effect in time. The third and final criterion is that *we must be able to eliminate all plausible alternative explanations* (rival hypotheses). Events are not such that a single cause produces a single effect. Probably any number of causes could produce a particular effect. In the example of the neutral position on a five-point scale, we identified two possible reasons for a particular effect. In theory, the number of possible causes is infinite. In practice, though, the most plausible causes can probably be identified. Consequently, if the research purpose is one of explanation (cause–effect), we must choose a research design that will allow us to make the best possible indirect test of cause and effect.

We will want to remember here our discussion in Chapter 4. *Cause* and *effect* are terms that stem from one particular theoretical model (the empirical or positivistic one), and so if we search for causes methodologically, we will want to do so only because we are working with a theory that uses this idea. To the extent that cause is tied to explanation, it is also theory-derived, and theory-dependent. If the researcher is using other theoretical paradigms (such as symbolic interactionism) cause and effect are not a part of the search and analytical description becomes the appropriate methodological technique.

Description

Studies whose primary purpose is one of description have one or two goals:

1. To portray accurately the characteristics of a particular individual, group, organization, or institution.
2. To determine the frequency with which something occurs or is associated with something else.

Description, as a research purpose, is concerned with delineating the way things are. Although the social researcher might like to be in a position to explain social phenomena, this is not always possible. Sometimes the present state of knowledge in an area makes explanation impossible. Hence, an enormous amount of social research is conducted for the purpose of describing. Descriptive research concentrates on accuracy and completeness. In fact, studies having a descriptive purpose are typically more accurate and precise than studies having a causal and predictive purpose.

A familiar example of research with a descriptive purpose is the taking of the U.S. census. A U.S. census describes the people who live in the United States: the number of males and females, whites and non-whites, marrieds, singles, widowed, and divorced. Such an endeavor is primarily concerned with precision and completeness. Marketing researchers study people to learn what kinds of products they will buy. New products are not usually placed on the market blindly (and neither are commercials on television). Before a company invests a sizable sum of money in a new product, they want to make certain it will sell. Consequently, they first poll the targeted population at which the product is aimed.

Exploration

Exploration, as a research purpose, is concerned with uncovering the way things are. Exploratory studies are undertaken primarily for four reasons:

1. To satisfy the researcher's curiosity and desire for a better understanding.
2. To test the feasibility of undertaking a more comprehensive study.
3. To develop methods to be used in a more comprehensive study.
4. To formulate a problem for more precise investigation or for developing hypotheses.

Social scientists sometimes display a tendency to underestimate the value of exploratory studies and to assume that such studies are not scientific. This is a gross inaccuracy and does injustice to exploration as a major research purpose. Granted, when exploration is the purpose, the level of scientific knowledge is usually not as advanced. However,

> The relative youth of social science and the scarcity of social science research make it inevitable that much of this research, for a time to come, will be of a pioneering character. Few well-trodden paths exist for the investigator of so-

cial relations to follow; theory is often either too general or too specific to provide clear guidance for empirical research. In these circumstances, exploratory research is necessary to obtain the experience that will be helpful in formulating relevant hypotheses for more definitive investigation. [21]

Agreeing with this position, Hoover writes, "We have barely figured out how to lay the foundation for a structure of theory to explain social behavior. People have muddled around for centuries trying to sort through significant connections" [22]. Science is a "slightly elevated form of muddling" by which these connections are often tried and tested and exploration is often a necessary first step.

Judging the Adequacy of the Design

It should be apparent by now that research design decisions are influenced by whom or what we study, when we study them, where we study them, and why we are studying them. But even given answers to these questions, three additional criteria remain that can help us in making our research design decision: (1) control, (2) representativeness, and (3) naturalness.

Control

When the researcher's primary concern is to establish unambiguously a causal link between two variables (as when explanation is the purpose), control is the most crucial criterion for judging the adequacy of the research design. *By control, we mean the researcher's ability to manipulate all independent variables that could influence (causally connect to) the dependent variable.* This would mean not only those independent variables which are central to the study but also those which are unknown or unobserved.

With the experiment, such control is established by making comparisons between a minimum of two groups that are initially "alike" in all ways but one—the independent variable. If these two groups are found to be different on the dependent variable, then the targeted independent variable is said to be the reason (cause). But how is such "alikeness" accomplished? One way is through matching the characteristics of subjects, which results in all such variables being *held constant* (i.e., such characteristics do not vary). Such a procedure, though, has distinct advantages. Consider this excellent example offered by Orenstein and Phillips:

> Imagine that we have a thousand potential subjects. Little Patricia is among them: She is black, highly intelligent, hates mathematics, is the first born child in her family, from a lower-middle-class home, and a girl.
>
> Each of these characteristics may influence the dependent variable. Therefore, we must find another subject who is exactly the same on all six variables. Without an exact match, we cannot use Patricia as a subject. To find pairs of children who are matched on one or two variables is easy. To find pairs who are alike on many variables would require many more potential subjects than we normally have available. [23]

And it goes without saying that we could not match on every possible variable (e.g., number of brothers and sisters, religious background, parents' educational levels). Thus, many variables would remain uncontrolled. Just how these unmatched (uncontrolled) independent variables influence the dependent variable would not be known or even measurable. In effect, we could never really be sure we had eliminated all possible rival hypotheses. Because of these problems, another method of creating alikeness (equal groups) is needed. There is another method—*random assignment of subjects to groups.* In other words, a subject's membership in one group as opposed to another is determined by flipping a coin, just as in Aronson and Mills's study of mild and severe initiation. While random assignment of subjects to groups does not guarantee equivalent groups, it does make equivalence more likely. Campbell and Stanley [24] concede that though randomization may be a less than perfect way of establishing initial equivalence between groups, it is nonetheless the most accurate way. Control through randomization is a frequent technique used in the experiment, and we will have more to say about this later.

Sometimes the nature of the research problem requires the use of independent variables that cannot be manipulated during data collection. If you were interested in whether males and females differed in leadership abilities, you would not flip a coin to decide a subject's sex: heads you're female and tails you're male. *When control cannot be introduced at the point of data collection because of the nature of the independent variable, it is generally introduced at the point of data analysis.* Such statistical control is quite frequent in survey research that seeks to explain since quite often the variables of interest in such studies cannot be manipulated during data collection (i.e., sex, race, marital status, social class, etc.).

Representativeness

When the researcher's primary concern is the accurate portrayal of characteristics or relations within a particular population, representativeness becomes the most crucial criterion in the choice of a research design. When this is the primary goal, the researcher must be able to identify the target population. He or she will then need to select a sample from that population whose characteristics mirror those of the population. Generally speaking, this means the use of probability sampling procedures (discussed in Chapter 9). *Representativeness implies generalizability; that is, the ability to make inferences about the population from knowledge about the sample.* Survey research whose primary purpose is to characterize accurately a population is generally most often concerned with representativeness.

Naturalness

When a researcher's primary concern is to understand the underlying processes of a particular social phenomenon or event, naturalness becomes the most crucial criterion in the choice of a research design. Generally speaking, it is the qualitative study that is most concerned with the quality of naturalness. Here the researcher's concern is that behavior be uncontaminated by whatever sources: the researcher's presence, the subject's awareness of his or her subject status. *There is no effort on the part of the researcher to manipulate or control subjects' behavior.* Behavior is allowed to flow in natural sequence. For example, recall Festinger's field research [25] on the doomsday group (Chapter 3). Group members' unawareness of the identity of the graduate students allowed for the natural flow of behavior. Festinger's students were able to record behavior and events unobtrusively. Thus, events occurred in their natural sequence, uncontaminated by the subjects' knowledge of being researched. In the case of the doomsday group, this would not have been possible had the graduate students' true identity been revealed. And this would certainly be the case for many research endeavors.

Research Designs

Now that we have examined the factors that affect our choice of research designs, let's look at the two broad categories of research designs: quantitative and qualitative. Each of these categories will be dealt with in greater detail in Chapters 10, 11, and 12. Here our intent is simply to relate the designs to the five factors affecting our choice of design discussed earlier.

Quantitative

Experiment   Delbert Miller writes, "Experiments have always been associated with science and have been considered the most powerful tools" [26]. The experiment is often held up as the standard for science—that is, the standard of what research *should* be like. This is not too surprising when we realize that the experiment provides a very convincing argument in the establishment of cause–effect relationships, and thus paradigms that use cause find it appealing. As Doby [27] notes, the logic of causation and the logic of the experiment are the same. And as we have tried to demonstrate, this sameness serves to distinguish relationships that can be called *associational* from those that can be called *causal*. Ultimately, *the experiment's strength in dealing with cause–effect relationships lies in the high degree of control* (manipulation of independent variables) that can usually be achieved with this design. (See Figure 6.1.)

Experiments are sometimes labeled according to their setting: laboratory experiments and field experiments. In the laboratory the researcher has the greatest potential to manipulate independent variables and thereby control. But this gain in control costs the researcher in terms of naturalness. At some point, he or she must deal with the artificiality of the setting. "If theory is to eventually explain behavior in spite of all extraneous variations of real life, then some research must take place in that complex real world" [28]. Decreasing artificiality, though, will mean a loss of control over many extraneous variables (noise, weather, etc.). We can summarize the two experimental designs as they relate to the various design factors:

Laboratory Experiments use treatment groups in contrived settings; they are strong on control, weak on naturalness and representativeness; they are most likely to be used in causal research. Although data are usually collected at two points in time, the time span between these points is relatively short.

Field Experiments use treatment groups in natural settings; they

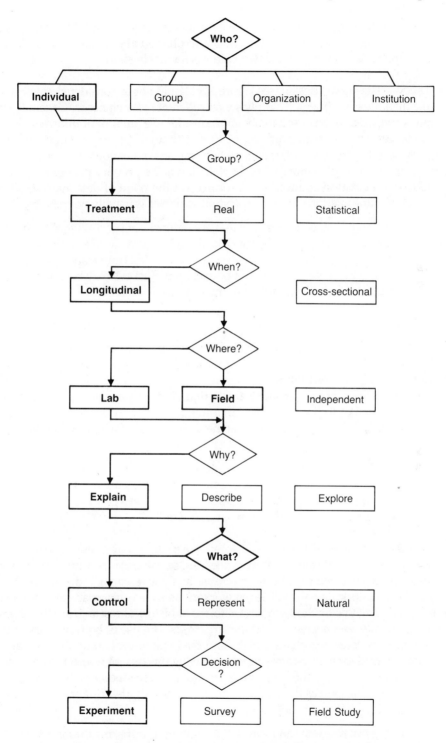

FIGURE 6.1   Flowchart of the Decision-Making Process for Experimental Design

achieve some control and some naturalness; they are most likely to be used for causal research. Although data are collected at two points in time, the time span between these two points is relatively short.

Survey   The survey design (see Figure 6.2) should not be considered any less scientific than the experiment. It simply serves different research needs. Generally speaking, survey research is used to obtain a considerable amount of information which can be generalized to an entire population. Although the survey can accommodate any research purpose (exploration, description, or explanation), it is usually used for description or explanation. When explanation is the primary purpose (causal connections), statistical controls are introduced at the point of data analysis since researcher manipulation of the independent variables is usually not possible.

> Surveys use statistical groups that are independent of setting; they are especially strong on representativeness, though control and naturalness are not entirely sacrificed. While surveys are usually descriptive and causal, exploratory purposes should not be excluded. Surveys may be either cross-sectional or longitudinal, although most are cross-sectional.

Qualitative

Field Research   The field study comes close to approximating real life. (See Figure 6.3.) Here the researcher is primarily concerned with natural patterns of interaction and therefore does not attempt to exercise researcher control. The primary objective of such studies is not to generalize but to find fresh insights into the nature of a particular system or to find new ideas that might later be subjected to more rigorous testing. Such a design offers the researcher a great deal of freedom. Consequently, it is often used for purposes of exploration or description.

> Field studies use real groups in natural settings; they are strong on naturalness, weak on control and representativeness; they are most likely to be used in exploratory or descriptive research. Such studies generally take place through time and are therefore longitudinal.

Historical Research   In historical research we try to discover and interpret the wisdom of the past, and thereby learn something of value for the future. Historical research is also referred to in the literature as "analytic research," "documentary analysis," or "historical analysis." Social workers, as well as historians and other social scientists, use this method. Important forms of historical research are the *biography*, the *case study*, and *analysis of evolutionary trends*. The use of both primary and secondary data sources is characteristic, and the issue of evaluating the accuracy and reliability of sources is paramount to conducting this type of research. This decision-making process constitutes a primary control in these studies, and representativeness of the data sources must be considered. Obviously, description and exploration are the primary foci of historical research.

> Historical research can focus on individuals, groups, institutions, movements, or concepts. There has been wide usage of this method in social work literature. With it, we can gain an understanding of change processes, deter-

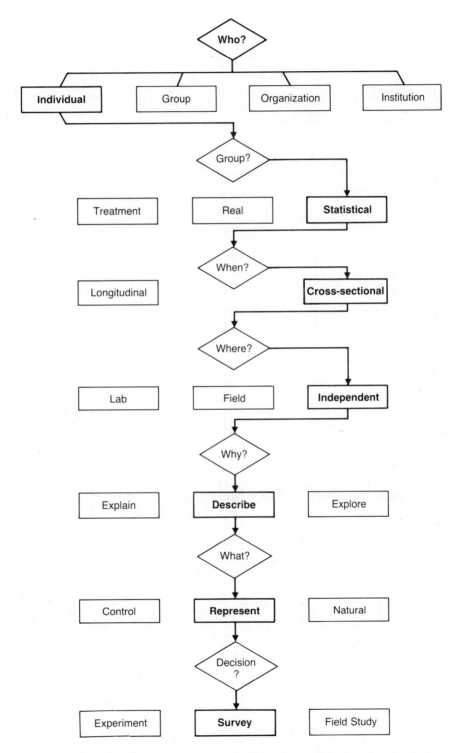

FIGURE 6.2 Flowchart of the Decision-Making Process for Survey Design

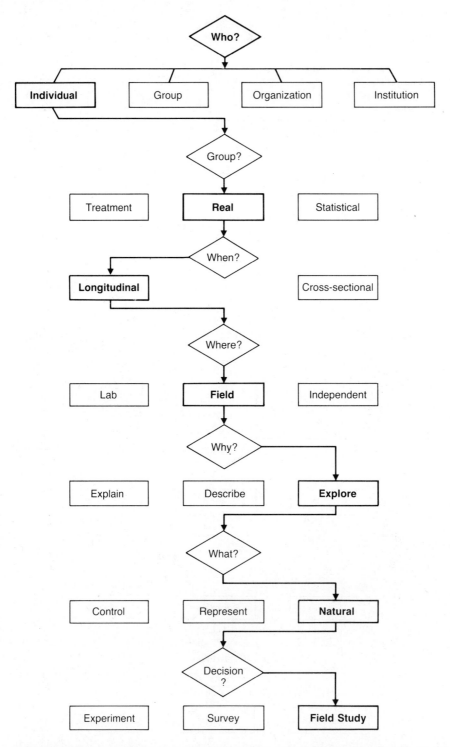

FIGURE 6.3 Flowchart of the Decision-Making Process for Field Study Design

mine the relative success or failure of social welfare programs and provisions, and deepen and broaden our insight into the lives and struggles of social work pioneers.

Content Analysis   Content analysis can be used as a contributing method to experimental studies as well as to qualitative designs, and has been widely used in social work research. The analysis of the content of many forms of "communication," including verbal, written, various media forms, patterns of behavior, and so on, can have great use for the researcher. The unit of analysis, whether a specific phrase, behavior, attitude, or value must be *systematically* and *objectively* coded. Many times this calls for extensive training to be provided for the raters as a control effort. Naturalness is enhanced because there are no efforts made to influence the subject as in the experimental setting. In the case of the analysis of documents, naturalness is inherent. This method can contribute greatly to description and/or exploration of the research subject. Representativeness may be weak, depending on subject selection procedures, and generalizability is obviously limited.

> "Content analysis is a research technique for the objective, systematic, and quantitative description of the manifest content of communication" [29].

Comparative Analysis   Comparative analysis is often of two types—historical or cross-cultural. Whereas historical research, as discussed previously, would show developments of themes or practices *through* time, comparative historical research would seek parallelism and/or contrast between two or more entirely separated cross-sections of time. Cross-cultural comparative studies focus on variables that are consistent across two or more cultures. The methods used can be similar to those used in other studies, including ethnographic field work, surveys, aggregate data analysis, experiments, or content analysis. In studies of this design, the representativeness of the sample and the standardization of controls across cultures become a real challenge for the researcher.

> Comparative Analysis can focus on comparing historical phenomena at two or more points in time or studying certain topics from a cross-cultural perspective.

Single-Subject Design

Single-subject research came into prominence in the social service community in the 1970s, having been adapted from the medical arena. It is called single-system research when the case is a family, group, or organization. Its usefulness to the profession is enhanced because this kind of design can be used in the everyday activities of practitioners, and it gives indication of a client's progress or change *during* treatment rather than waiting until after. Another benefit that accrues is that needed adjustments to treatment can be made more promptly. Also, the variables and measures can be better tailored to the individual. There are several variations on the single-subject design (discussed in Chapter 12), and these are designated with the use of letters: AB, B, ABA, ABAB, ABC, ABCD, ABACA, and so forth. The letter A always represents the baseline condition, and the other letters represent different treatment procedures. *Successive treatment designs* and *multiple baseline designs* are more sophisticated variations. Control of variables is possible and description or explanation is customary.

> Single-Subject Design is the examination of the planned change processes of one client, usually involving the establishment of a baseline condition and making comparison to it using one or more controlled treatment procedures.

General Considerations

In choosing a research design, apart from the five factors already discussed, some additional practical guides should be mentioned. Doby [30] has identified five general considerations that need to be kept in mind when thinking about a research design. In Lewis's [31] terms, "Different strokes for different folks." *Most researchers have their favorite methods, which they will use over and over.* Some researchers, for example, feel most comfortable with the experiment. Others prefer the survey or the single-subject approach. Obviously, one's feelings of expertise will play a role in design choice. *Second, no set of factors points to a single correct research design.* Any choice of design will represent a compromise dictated by the many practical considerations that go into social research. We all operate on limited time and money. Additionally, we must be concerned with the availability of subjects and the ethical appropriateness of how we study them. In effect, the best approach to a particular research question may not be possible.

Suppose, for example, you were interested in the effects of social isolation on the socialization of a child. You would not raise some children in isolation and others among people to answer this research question. But sometimes life's circumstances provide us with data on such research questions, as in the cases of Anna and Isabelle [32, 33]. Anna and Isabelle were raised for the first six and one-half years of their lives in isolation. For a researcher to set about creating such data would be ethically reprehensible. When such data exist, though, we do make use of them. *Third, no research design is a rigid blueprint to be followed without deviation.* When the research is finished, it will be the rare researcher who can look back and say he or she followed the design to the letter. The research design is a series of guideposts to keep you headed in the right direction. You must always be flexible, as any research design will involve some "on-the-spot decision making," just as in putting together the pieces of a puzzle. *Fourth, the research design does not guarantee definitive proof of your hypothesis.* As you have already learned, in most cases multiple explanations will be plausible. Demonstrating your hypothesis does not rule out the alternative hypotheses, and vice versa. The best you can do is make your own hypothesis look more or less plausible. *Fifth, it is meaningless to argue whether or not a certain design is scientific.* The question is not one of being scientific or not scientific but rather one of effectiveness of design. In fact, it may be preferable to sacrifice some science in favor of a more widely used procedure for the purpose of comparability to past research. This may be essential if the subdisciplines in the social sciences are to ever blend their knowledge [34].

The Research Design and Data Collection

Whatever the research design, there are only a few basic ways to collect data, and the most widely used techniques are observing behavior and asking questions. In addition to these firsthand data collection procedures, the researcher may use other alternatives: secondary sources, client or agency records, and archival sources. Each of these data collection procedures will be discussed in detail in Chapters 10, 11, and 12.

Data collection is the tool or vehicle through which measurement is actualized. You have transformed concepts into variables since theory is not directly testable. But the creation of a variable is not the final step. Measurement is only realized through data collection. You may say, for example, that you wish to measure alienation with five statements. But then these statements become part of either a self-administered questionnaire or an interview schedule. You may wish to define leadership within a group as a function of the amount of talking one does, but then you must observe and record the amount of talking for each group member. Or you may decide to evaluate sexism in grade-school readers, but then you must use content analysis to determine the frequency of occurrence of traditional versus nontraditional sex roles for men and women.

Certainly the research design does not dictate the data collection procedures. *But it is true that certain data collection techniques are more commonly used with certain designs.* Field studies, for example, are more likely to use observational techniques and archival data, whereas surveys are more likely to use interviews or self-administered questionnaires. Experiments, in contrast, are more likely to use structured observations and self-administered questionnaires.

It is important to remember that no design requires that data collection be reduced to a single method. In fact, too much social science research has relied on a single collection method. Both Webb et al. [35] and Denzin [36] advocate the use of more than one method of data collection in any given research endeavor. This use of more than one method in data collection is known as *triangulation*.

The term *triangulation* comes from surveying practices on topographic maps. The surveyor, wanting to locate a new object on a map, sets the map up at three known points on the ground, orients the map to coincide with the north direction, and sights on the new object. The surveyor draws a line along the sighting on the map from the known point toward the new object, then moves to the other two known points, again orients the map to the north direction, and draws two more sighting lines from the known point on the ground toward the new object. Usually, the three sighting lines will intersect with a small triangle called the *triangle of error*. The best estimate of the true location of the new object on the map is the center of the triangle, assuming that the three lines are about equal in error. This process is called locating the point by triangulation. Two sighting lines would intersect at one point, but this point is probably somewhat off. The third line permits a more accurate estimate.

In social science research this concept is applied by using a set of three different types of data collection techniques for a single research question. For example, suppose you were interested in high school students' attitudes and social priorities. Coleman [37], in researching this issue, used three different data collection techniques. He combined (1) questionnaires on preferences and attitudes, (2) sociometric tests for identification of friendship groups, and (3) interviews of school personnel. The three kinds of information helped to reinforce and focus his conclusions: Athletics and social activities rank far higher both in the students' value systems and in the attention they receive from school authorities than does academic performance. The picture was much more complete and the findings were more convincing because of the three-pronged attack on the problem [38]. The use of triangulation in data gathering can serve to strengthen the overall research design.

References

1. P. Sean, *Social Science and Its Methods* (Boston: Holbrook, 1971), p. 23.
2. Walter W. Hudson and Bruce A. Thyer, "Research Measurements and Indices in Direct Practice," in *Encyclopedia of Social Work*, 18th ed., Anne Minahan, ed. (Silver Spring, MD: National Association of Social Workers, 1987), p. 487.
3. Hudson and Thyer, "Research Measurements and Indices in Direct Practice," p. 487.
4. D. Miller, *Handbook of Research Design and Social Measurement* (New York: David McKay, 1975).
5. M. Riley, *Sociological Research* (New York: Harcourt, Brace, Jovanovich, 1963).
6. C. Lombroso, *Crime, Its Causes and Remedies* (Boston: Little, Brown, 1912).
7. L. R. Hoffman and N. R. Maier, "Valence in the Adoption of Solutions by Problem-Solving Groups: Concept, Method, and Results," *Journal of Abnormal and Social Psychology* 69 (1964): 264–71.
8. E. Webb, et al., *Non-Reactive Measures in the Social Sciences* (Boston: Houghton Mifflin, 1981) pp. 7–38.
9. "Women on Words and Images," *Dick and Jane as Victims: Sex Stereotyping in Children's Readers* (Princeton, NJ: Princeton University Press, 1972).
10. E. Aronson and J. Mills, "The Effect of Severity of Initiation on Liking for a Group," *Journal of Abnormal and Social Psychology* 59 (1959): 177–81.
11. M. J. Norvell and R. F. Guy, "A Comparison of Self-Concept in Adopted and Non-adopted Adolescents," *Adolescence* 12 (1977): 443–48.
12. Riley, *Sociological Research.*
13. P. Ellsworth, "From Abstract Ideas to Concrete Instances: Some Guidelines for Using Natural Research Settings," *American Psychologist* 32 (1977): 604–15.
14. G. H. Lewis, *Fist Fights in the Kitchen* (Pacific Palisades, CA: Goodyear, 1975).
15. Ellsworth, "From Abstract Ideas to Concrete Instances," p. 607.
16. H. L. Manheim, *Sociological Review* (Georgetown, Ontario: Dorset, 1977).
17. R. F. Guy and M. J. Norvell, "The Neutral Point on a Likert Scale," *Journal of Psychology* 95 (1977): 199–204.
18. D. H. Killeffer, *How Did You Think of That? An Introduction to the Scientific Method* (Garden City, NY: Anchor Books, 1976), p. 21.
19. H. M. Blalock and A. Blalock, *A Methodology in Social Research* (New York: McGraw-Hill, 1968).
20. A. Orenstein and W. R. Phillips, *Understanding Social Research: An Introduction* (Boston: Allyn and Bacon, 1978), p. 129.
21. C. Selltiz, L. S. Wrightsman, and S. Cook, *Research Methods in Social Relations* (New York: Holt, Rinehart and Winston, 1976), p. 91.
22. K. Hoover, *The Elements of Social Science Thinking* (New York: St. Martin's, 1976), p. 25.
23. Orenstein and Phillips, *Understanding Social Research*, p. 6.
24. D. T. Campbell and J. Stanley, *Experimental and Quasi-Experimental Designs for Research* (Chicago: Rand McNally, 1963).
25. L. Festinger, H. W. Reicken, and S. Schachter, *When Prophecy Fails* (Minneapolis: University of Minnesota Press, 1956).
26. Miller, *Handbook of Research Design and Social Measurement*, p. 22.
27. J. T. Doby, *An Introduction to Social Research* (New York: Appleton-Century-Crofts, 1967).
28. R. K. Liek, *Methods, Logic, and Research in Sociology* (Indianapolis: Bobbs-Merrill, 1972), p. 12.
29. Bernard Berelson, *Content Analysis in Communication Research* (New York: Hafner, 1952, 1971), p. 18.

30. Doby, *An Introduction to Social Research.*
31. Lewis, *Fist Fights in the Kitchen.*
32. K. Davis, "Extreme Social Isolation of a Child," *American Journal of Sociology*, n.v. (1940).
33. K. Davis, "Final Note on a Case of Extreme Isolation," *American Journal of Sociology* 52 (1947): 232–47.
34. Hoover, *The Elements of Social Science Thinking,* p. 25.
35. Webb, et al., *Non-Reactive Measures in the Social Sciences.*
36. N. K. Denzin, *Sociological Methods: A Sourcebook* (Chicago: Aldine, 1970).
37. J. S. Coleman, *The Adolescent Society: The Social Life of the Teen-Ager and Its Impact on Education* (New York: The Free Press, 1961).
38. Webb, et al., *Non-Reactive Measures in the Social Sciences.*

Chapter 7.

Hypotheses and Evidence

Hypotheses defined
Hypothesis construction as it
    relates to theory
    Hypotheses constructed from
        classical theory
    Hypotheses constructed from
        grounded theory
Hypotheses testing typology
    Research hypotheses
    Null hypotheses
Characteristics of hypotheses
    Hypotheses should be
        objectively worded
    Hypotheses must be specific
        and precise
    Hypotheses must be testable
    Hypotheses should provide
        an answer to the
        research question
Testing hypotheses

Triangulation
Use of evidence in hypothesis
        testing
    The persuasive power of
        evidence
    The effect of data sources on
        evidence
    The effect of the research design
        on evidence
    Replication in scientific research
The hypothesis cycle
    Hypothetical statements of
        relationship
    The test of a hypothetical
        relation
    Conclusion that affirms or
        disaffirms the hypothesis
    Start of a new hypothesis
    Serendipity in research
        outcomes

Truth can be defined as the working hypothesis best suited to open the way to the next better one. —KONRAD LORENZ

Hypotheses Defined

The word *hypothesis* defines itself when we recognize its two major parts. *Thesis* means a proposition or statement that can be supported by argument and evidence. In higher education, for example, we require graduate students working on a master's or doctoral degree to make a statement about a research question and then to support it with evidence well enough to remove or at least reduce reasonable doubt. The Greek prefix *Hypo*, means "beneath" or "underlying."

A hypothesis, then, is a nonobvious statement that makes an assertion. The assertion may simply describe some phenomenon or specify a relationship between two or more phenomena. Such a statement becomes the basis for research that is designed to prove the truth of the statement. However, *hypothesis* implies that the true statement is not certainly known, or is hidden beneath appearances. The aim of a hypothesis, then, is to establish a testable base about a doubtful or unknown statement. A test of this statement discloses whether the hypothesis is tenable. As we have already learned, final proof is not possible, but successful research reduces doubt enough to convince other researchers.

William Stephens has described a hypothesis as the smallest possible unit of description:

> It presumes to describe just one "fact," one thing. It can usually be stated in a single sentence. Those "descriptions" which take up entire paragraphs, pages, books—for example, theories, arguments, narratives, ramified explanations—are compounded of many hypotheses. The hypothesis is the essential unit, or building block, out of which the more complicated descriptions are made. [1]

Stephens offers the following examples of hypotheses:

1. Slums breed crime.
2. It is a cold day.
3. Economic development facilitates democratic government.
4. The older you are when you marry, the better your chances of making a go of it.
5. The earth is flat.

Stephens also offers an example of a statement packed with eight hypotheses:

> Women, as compared with men, are more active in church but less active in politics; mature earlier; live longer; drive fewer miles and have fewer accidents; threaten suicide more often but actually commit suicide less often. [2]

By now it should be fairly obvious that a hypothesis is a statement. But it is not just any kind of statement. **It must be a statement that can be tested.** It must be worded in such a way that it can be either rejected or not rejected, depending on the outcome of the test. Things are simple with hypotheses; you either have the evidence to support them or you don't.

The hypothesis stage of the research process, like all stages, is extremely important. Recall that to this point, we have chosen a research question and we have examined theory relevant to answering this question. We have given some thought to how we might test this answer by looking at alternative research designs. But even with all of this, the research process is far from complete. Theory is not directly testable, and although the research design provides us with a blueprint for testing, the theory must be reworded for such a test. We might say, then, that hypotheses are theories or parts of theories reworded into testable form. In this chapter, we will introduce you to the hypothesis stage of the research process. We will acquaint you with the different approaches to hypothesis construction, different types of hypotheses, and characteristics of hypotheses. Finally, we will examine the hypothesis-testing process and some important factors to consider when testing hypotheses.

Hypothesis Construction as It Relates to Theory

Like all phases of the research process, hypothesis construction is not haphazard. Hypotheses must be carefully thought out and carefully derived. Generally speaking, this construction process will take one of two directions. Hypotheses may be constructed from classical theory or from grounded theory.

Hypotheses Constructed from Classical Theory

The ideal form of a scientific hypothesis is derived from formal or classical theory. Classical theory, as we have already learned, is stated logically. It is also based on extensive knowledge of the entire class of phenomena under study. But recall from our earlier discussion that formal theory cannot be directly tested. It is constructed with concepts that are abstract and operationally inexact. To remove the haze and render precision, we transform the concepts into variables. This transformation process is called measurement (discussed in Chapter 8). Hypotheses provide a means by which we can indirectly test formal theory. Thus, with this approach, *the theory precedes the hypotheses.* And this jump from theory to hypotheses is in many ways a leap of faith. Though the test of the hypotheses is said to be a test of the theory, we cannot know for certain how well we have tested the theory. Hence, it becomes imperative that we take painstaking care in constructing and testing hypotheses.

One highly respected formal theory in sociology from which hypotheses have been so derived is Max Weber's 1904 study of the relationship between the Protestant work ethic and the development of modern capitalism. Weber theorized that the developing capitalism of the European West was made possible through the influence of the Protestant work ethic [3]. As a leading authority on comparative religion, Weber noted that Protestantism in the Calvinist tradition supported a work ethic that stressed full dedication to any kind of productive work through body or mind, coupled with self-denial in the form of thrift and saving for ideal future goals. The combination of maximizing production and minimizing consumption produced a substantial surplus for reinvestment in productive enterprises. This encouraged capital formation and supported an expansion of industry, commerce, and economic growth.

One hypothesis that has been derived from Weber's theory is that in societies where the Protestant ethic is dominant, capitalism is encouraged and sustained. To test this hypothesis, we might compare predominantly Catholic countries such as Spain, Greece, Ireland, czarist Russia, and the countries of South America with Protestant countries like England, Germany, France, Sweden, and the United States. And for the early industrial period from 1750 to 1900, this hypothesis seems to be supported. Since 1900, though, some major industrial societies have developed without the direct influence of a Protestant work ethic, including the Soviet Union, Japan, the Republic of Korea, and the Republic of China (Taiwan). Thus, for this later period of time, the hypothesis does not seem to be supported.

Hypotheses Constructed from Grounded Theory

Grounded theory is theory discovered directly from data as they are systematically obtained and analyzed in social research [4]. We must stress two factors here. First, unlike classical theory, which must precede and imply the research hypothesis, the researcher does not develop grounded theory until after the data become organized sufficiently to suggest hypotheses. Thus, with this approach, *the hypotheses precede the theory.* Moreover, theory that is grounded in newly assembled or newly assessed data continues to evolve as the researcher is able to identify new hypotheses.

Although classical theory is abstractly formulated in a more or less elaborate logical system and classical hypotheses are logically derived from theory, only the hypotheses are tested with empirical data. In contrast, grounded theory and hypotheses are both implicit in the empirical data. And grounded theory continues to be modified step by step throughout the research process through the testing of various trial hypotheses as theoretical implications occur to the researcher. In many ways grounded theory is closer to the world of social interaction than is classical theory. Remember, hypotheses, by definition, are statements concerning nonobvious processes and relations. In a research quest where the primary elements are obscure or poorly defined, the researcher is generally less informed. The rapid evolution of grounded theory in the data analysis phase, from the first uncertain hunches to the more adequately supported theoretical explanations, is often a useful approach to hypothesis construction.

The Swedish sociologist Gunnar Myrdal applied the principles of grounded theory in his massive study of race relations in the United States in the 1940s. Starting with the general hypothesis that there was a profound contradiction between the exalted ideals of liberty, equality, and justice for all in the U.S. political tradition and the stark reality of systematic oppression of millions of black Americans, Myrdal employed a team of anthropologists, psychologists, sociologists, economists, political scientists, and professional educators to study the relationship between white and black Americans. These professional social scientists carried out careful separate studies of personal, social, institutional, judicial, and political systems in which this nation dominated by whites systematically excluded black Americans from equal participation in national, regional, and local affairs.

As the study progressed and the data were accumulated over several years,

Myrdal developed and supported the hypotheses that white Americans (1) were uncomfortable about the unfair and oppressive treatment of black Americans, (2) could acknowledge the objective studies, and (3) were willing to make corrections in the system. Out of this information he also discovered a previously unrecognized agreement between what the white community was most ready to provide and what the black community was ready to receive. That was economic opportunity through education, training, and employment on equal terms at all social levels. Myrdal's hypotheses, grounded in practical affairs, such as black Americans' need for access to public and commercial facilities and to economic opportunities, were readily understood in all intellectual and professional circles. His voluminous book *An American Dilemma* [5] was influential in legal, industrial, political, and religious circles, far beyond the impact of most publications in the social sciences.

Myrdal's evidence was thoroughly convincing because it covered the whole complex picture, and did so in meticulous objective detail and in clear, nontechnical language. This work was an important step in justifying the U.S. Supreme Court decision outlawing segregation in educational institutions in 1954, and for the civil rights acts that followed a decade later.

Hypotheses Testing Typology

Whether hypotheses are constructed from grounded theory or classical theory, generally speaking, they are classified as one of two types: research or null.

Research Hypotheses

The research hypothesis is a statement that describes or specifies a relationship between two or more variables. Stephens's hypotheses given earlier are examples of research hypotheses. Homans's well-known hypothesis on interaction and liking is also an example of a research hypothesis. This hypothesis asserts that an increase in interaction between individuals is positively associated with an increase in liking [6]. Interaction is measured by reported frequency of contact by pairs of individuals in an interactive group. The degree of liking is measured by each individual's report of a degree of liking for the other individuals in the same group. And this hypothesis is generally supported by empirical research.

After long and detailed study of suicide rates, Durkheim demonstrated that the individual's social position affects vulnerability to suicide. As an underlying principle, he tested the hypothesis that there is an inverse relationship between the suicide rate and the individual's integration into society. Specifically, those less fully engaged with social ties have a higher suicide rate. Although suicide occurs with only 10 to 30 persons per 100,000 population per year, the rate tends to be higher with unmarried adults than with married adults of the same age. The suicide rate is higher with childless men than with married fathers. The suicide rate is also higher with Protestant individuals who bear greater individual responsibility in their lives than with Catholic communicants who get more personal support from the agencies of the Catholic church. Durkheim called this type of suicide "anomic suicide," indicating an effect of reduced social guidance.

Null Hypotheses

The null hypothesis is written in a form that negates or nullifies the descriptions or relations specified in the research hypothesis. We could, for example, transform Stephens's research hypothesis into null hypotheses:

1. Slums do not breed crime.
2. It is not a cold day.
3. Economic development does not facilitate democratic government.
4. Age does not influence one's chances of making a successful marriage.
5. The earth is not flat.

In Homans's research, the null hypothesis would be that there is no relationship between the extent of interaction and degree of liking. With Durkheim's research, the null hypothesis would be that there is no relationship between suicide rate and an individual's integration into a society. In other words, the null hypothesis negates the assertion or suggests that two variables do not vary together in any observable pattern.

Statisticians Neyman and Pearson [7] have suggested that researchers should always begin with the null hypothesis. The reasons for this are largely a function of the nature and limitations of statistical procedures used to test hypotheses. When we test a hypothesis, *one* case can make it false and so we would reject it. In contrast, even if we identify millions of cases that would make a hypothesis true, we can never really accept it since we can't be 100 percent certain of the next case. The very next case could make the hypothesis false, and then we would have to reject it. If we test the null hypothesis and are able to reject it, though, the rejection points us in the direction of the research hypothesis. That is, *rejecting the null hypothesis lends support to the research hypothesis.*

Characteristics of Hypotheses

We have said that a hypothesis is a nonobvious statement describing or specifying a relation among objects. And it should be stated as simply as possible since a primary purpose of a hypothesis is to find the most direct and most basic relation between objects. The Thomas theorem—"If men define situations as real, they are real in their consequences"—can even operate as a hypothesis [8]. In the social sciences, mental constructs do serve as objects. A belief in human love, or faith in a social institution, for example, has observable consequences for the way men and women treat each other—for example, the transactions that people execute through banks each month in paying periodic bills. Hypotheses, when properly constructed, should have certain characteristics. Let's take a look at some of these important characteristics.

Hypotheses Should Be Objectively Worded

In the social sciences, a hypothesis might encompass social values concerning property, money, security, social prestige, and other concepts, but the researcher should constantly strive to exclude personal values, hopes, and wishes from the wording of hypotheses. As we have already indicated, research is not value-free. Since researchers are ordinary human beings, their values follow them into any research endeavor. **Since we cannot divorce ourselves from our values, our goal must be value-aware research.** If we are aware of our values, we will be sensitive to their potential influence on our research. And one way of controlling this influence is to strive for objectively worded hypotheses. The following hypothesis, for example, is value-laden: "The more deserving employees receive the higher incomes." This hypothesis, if supported by evidence, might be used to justify an existing wage scale in a large bureaucracy. But the word *deserving* is a value word that may be arbitrarily applied by the sponsor based on the race and sex of the employee. A more applicable hypothesis in this case might be, "Individuals whom the employer favors receive higher incomes, regardless of their production on the job."

Consider the following hypothesis: "Social adjustment is improved in retirement communities if there are good facilities for sports." This hypothesis suggests that men and women in their seventies have the same social values of competition and performance expertise that are common in the researcher's own age group and social class. Older people may prefer a slow pace and may even be satisfied with a lower level of performance than is assumed for younger energetic professionals. The hypothesis betrays the personal values and biases of the researcher. Consider one last example. Suppose you were to hypothesize that people's interest in the town where they lived would be reflected in their knowledge of the names of the town's officeholders, including the auditor, surveyor, city engineer, chief of police, and others. Again, the hypothesis betrays the researcher's personal bias suggesting that interest in a town is accurately reflected through political knowledge and awareness. People may love their town and yet know little about its politics. Their love for the town may be demonstrated in other ways.

Hypotheses Must Be Specific and Precise

The elements in a research hypothesis should be as exact as possible. That is, **each must have a single unambiguous meaning.** A long-time subscriber to the British humor magazine *Punch* once wrote to the editor stating, "*Punch* is not as funny as it used to be." The editor responded with: "It never was!" This critic's hypothesis is simply not precise enough. It could be the isolated judgment of one reader. Moreover, the time frame is unspecified. At what earlier time was *Punch* funnier? Is "funny" an objective quality or a subjective quality? Subjective internal feelings are not comparable. However, *Punch* is designed to amuse, and it might be possible to establish an ordinal scale of the degree of amusement. Did the reader laugh more loudly or more heartily or more quickly at earlier issues? This also would be difficult to test since the humor of *Punch* often hinges on awareness of current events and fashions. A joke or cartoon that was amusing ten years ago might not have any meaning for a contemporary trying to evaluate old issues. Specificity and precision in hypotheses are important. A loose hypothesis—even though it may be supported by data—is both meaningless and inaccurate.

The hypothesis "Education is positively related to income" is simple, and we might agree that the terms *education* and *income* are readily understood. However, gross bias against employing certain minorities or the convention of withholding young married women from the work force makes this hypothesis inapplicable to a large segment of the population where no income is earned. A better form of this hypothesis would be, "For employed persons, education is positively related to income." And even this hypothesis would prove rather poor if a third of the work force, such as all working women, was generally confined to low-paying and low-skill jobs. The women would tend to be held in a narrow range of income variation so that regardless of variation in education, women employees tended to remain at a fairly uniform income. In effect, the hypothesis would not be supported. With so many irregularities in the distribution of income, particularly as it relates to years of formal education, the serious researcher would be wise to avoid such a loose and imprecise hypothesis. Educational patterns by sex and ethnic identification and by type of occupation would be more productive when relating education to income.

Hypotheses Must Be Testable

As a researcher, you cannot test what you cannot see, hear, touch, taste, or smell. You cannot test the existence of God, heaven, or hell. You cannot prove beyond reasonable doubt the existence of angels or the devil. **Scientific hypotheses, to be tested, require sense data.** In constructing a puzzle, when you pick up a puzzle piece and attempt to fit it in a particular position, you are testing the hypothesis that the piece fits in an identified location. Every attempt to position a piece of the puzzle is a test of a hypothesis. And notice that each test requires the use of sense data. When you attempt to fit the puzzle piece in a particular location, you observe visually whether or not it belongs there. If the piece does not fit, you reject the hypothesis. If it does fit, you do not reject the hypothesis.

Recent research efforts have begun to toy with the idea of testing hypotheses that have been heretofore untestable. The hypothesis "There is life after death" would seem to be untestable by our previously established criteria. However, several individuals have attempted to test this hypothesis by recording accounts of individuals who have been declared clinically dead and then revived. Work done by Elizabeth Kubler-Ross [9, 10, 11, 12, 13] over the years has pioneered in this area. Verbatim accounts of such experiences have shown common threads running through them. Although such evidence does not remove all doubt (for example, the question of whether clinical death is "really" death or merely "close to death"), it has been interpreted by some as supportive of this hypothesis.

Even if sense data are available, a particular hypothesis may not be testable if you can-

not find ways to measure accurately the variables to be included. Changing times, for example, often impose difficult restrictions on research unless the researcher establishes comparable records for a well-distributed series of time intervals. Davies and
Kandel [14] faced such time restrictions in their research on the influence of parents
and peers on adolescents' education plans but were able to overcome them. These
researchers used questionnaire data from a linked triad of respondents made up of
an adolescent, one of the adolescent's parents, and the adolescent's closest school
friend. The adolescent indicated her or his own educational aspirations and his perception of the parent's educational aspirations for him. The parent indicated her or
his educational aspirations for the child. The best friend indicated her or his own educational aspirations. With a sample of more than 700 triads, the researchers demonstrated that parental influence was much stronger than peer influence. In fact, for
boys, peer influence was insignificant. This research also demonstrated that the
parental influence was greater than assumed by the child's perception of the parent's aspirations for her or him. This hypothesis was testable because the researchers
found stable ways to measure the variables and to demonstrate the hypothesized relationship.

Hypotheses Should Provide an Answer to the Research Question

The test of a hypothesis should provide a direct answer to the research question.
This does not mean that the hypothesis is supported. A direct answer may deny the
research hypothesis and suggest alternative answers. But in any case, the research
question is not left unanswered. In a research study comparing offense rates of
delinquent and nondelinquent boys, it was hypothesized that the rates of law violation would be lower for church-attending boys when compared with non-church-at-
tending boys based on the positive moral influence of church attendance. The evidence was clearly in the opposite direction. Church-attending boys reported
significantly higher rates of law violation [15]. Though the answer suggested was
not supported, the hypothesis did provide an answer. Rejection of the suggested answer compelled—as it often does—consideration of alternative hypotheses for later
study. One alternative hypothesis consistent with this finding is that church-attending boys have additional opportunities through group associations to develop anti-
establishment norms and behaviors as a kind of extension of the adolescent's resistance to parental authority. This hypothesis, too, provides an answer, although it
may not be supported when tested.

Bridges tested a set of hypotheses derived from a theory that marginal industries employ more women while the more productive wealthier core industries employ more men. Using U. S. Census data from 1970 through 1976, he found strong
support for only one of his six hypotheses: "Women are less likely to be employed in
primary and secondary industries with high levels of fixed assets per worker" [16].
Bridges found only slight support for a second hypothesis, that women were under-
represented in industries providing higher wages to male workers. There was no
support for four other hypotheses that were relevant to and implicit in the theory

linking marginal industries with female employment. While the hypothesis does not have to be supported, it must provide an answer—whether that answer be one of support or denial.

Testing Hypotheses

The primary reason for testing a research hypothesis is to minimize doubt about assertions or stated relationships. And the test of a hypothesis is said to succeed if and only if it is objective. That is, the variables and the process by which they are related are based on concrete observable events that are stable and can be consistently measured by a fixed standard.

If you see a social researcher working at a computer terminal and you ask her what she is dong, she might respond, "Massaging the data." We have also heard social scientists jokingly claim, "If at first you don't succeed, massage again." While a scientist may "work" the data to *avoid* drawing erroneous conclusions, she would not "work on" the data to *aid* her in drawing such conclusions. While all scientists dabble in data, it is not their intent to dabble in deception. Suppose, for example, you were interested in establishing the extent to which students at City University take math courses. If you position yourself outside the math building and survey as many students as you can flag down, you will probably conclude that students at City U take a lot of math. If you position yourself outside the history building and ask the same question, you may reach an entirely different conclusion. Both procedures lack objectivity.

Testing a hypothesis objectively means looking at *all* evidence—both positive and negative—weighing the positive and negative evidence, and then making a decision. It does not mean looking at *some* of the evidence and then making a decision. If we could be so selective when testing hypotheses, we would never state an incorrect hypothesis. We would confirm everything we set out to confirm!

Any successful test of a research hypothesis must provide a clearly positive or negative result. If the result is inconclusive, the test fails, though the hypothesis is not affected. Suppose we hypothesized that years of education beyond high school is positively related to a rise in social class. But we only recognized two social class levels: lower and upper. The hypothesis could be supported only for cases where years of education coincided with a shift across the boundary from lower class to upper class. If the upper class is defined by wealth and income, and is confined to less than 3 percent of the population, such shifts would be quite rare and the measure would ignore substantial improvements within the very broad lower class associated with higher education.

If a hypothesis is stated in universal terms, a single conclusively established negative case can disprove it. It was popular in the early years of the present century to say that there was no social class structure in the United States. Lloyd Warner conducted a long and meticulous study of a single small town in New England where he clearly identified three major social class divisions, each of which could be subdivided into lower and upper parts [17]. The researchers interviewed extensively at all social levels in the community and verified social standing and resources in public records in the community. The respondents recognized and affirmed their own and others' social class position with sufficient consistency to support the hypothesis of a recognized social class structure. Recognized membership in the upper class was based on "old money" and social position inherited from earlier generations. The lower-upper class depended on substantial "new money" earned from business enterprise and investment by people in the current generation. At least in terms of specific urban communities, it seems that there is a recognized social class structure in the United States within the limits of definition and respondent perceptions. These findings were confirmed in several other communities.

In an absolute sense, no hypothesis is conclusively supported because new theoretical developments or new instruments may bring the conclusion into question and plausible alternative test results may have the same effect.

Triangulation

Recall from Chapter 6 that *triangulation means going at a problem from several methodological directions at the same time.* By combining several approaches to data collection, it provides a more conclusive test of the hypothesis. If a researcher has three measures of perceived interpersonal communication between husband and wife, based on careful analytic interviews with the husband, the wife, and their marriage counselor, the data would be useful for testing hypotheses on variable consensus levels in relation to other variables. Such variables include length of marriage, personal satisfaction with the relationship, and orientation to other family members. School performance could be measured from the student's self-report, the school records, and the teacher's evaluation. The degree of agreement of the three sources could be related to the student's self-concept, socialization level, and patterns of interpersonal relations with peers.

Kinsey used the triangulation principle to support his working hypothesis that sensitive data could be secured. In taking the self-reported histories of sexual behavior of thousands of men and women, he wanted to assure that these personal data could not be linked to any individuals who gave them. He developed a three-phase system to separate the respondents' identity from their history of sexual behavior. First, Kinsey developed an elaborate code of special symbols for the different forms of sexual behavior in which the symbols had no apparent relation to the act reported. The histories were recorded in these codes, known only to the interviewers. Second, the respondents were assigned unique numerical codes that were stored separately from their names. Only the code numbers were tied to the encoded histories. Third, Kinsey kept all records in heavy metal safety file cabinets with three-combination locks. Finally, the materials were kept separately for each interviewer so that only one member of the research team could establish the identity of the source of her or his own protocols. Kinsey's hypothesis of complete security of the identity of his informants would have been disconfirmed if any identity had been revealed. But over the several years of the study, there was never a case in which these intimate and potentially embarrassing details were disclosed.

Use of Evidence in Hypothesis Testing

The Persuasive Power of Evidence

The ultimate test of any scientific hypothesis is that the evidence must be totally convincing to people who are both judicious and well informed. An ideal example of this quality of evidence is the proof of Leverrier's hypothesis that there was an eighth planet in our solar system. Leverrier's hypothesis was based on the analysis of irregularities in the motion of the seventh planet, Uranus, which far exceeded the limits of measurement error in astronomic observations. Given such irregularities, Leverrier predicted the approximate position of the new planet and requested a search for it in September 1846. Observations at the Berlin Observatory taken twenty-four hours apart disclosed a twenty-one-inch angular movement in a faint object previously listed as an eighth-magnitude star. This hard evidence settled the question forever. We can now predict the position of the eighth planet, Neptune, at a given time as it advances a little over two angular degrees per Earth-year in its orbit around the sun.

The power of evidence in the area of medical sociology is demonstrated in the discovery of the cause of the highly infectious and often fatal puerperal fever. A young German physician, Semmelweiss, was concerned about the high morbidity and equally high mortality resulting from "childbed fever" in the obstetrics ward of the Vienna Hospital. Keeping detailed and meticulous records, he was able to determine that the infection rate was highest among mothers attended by doctors or medical students who came directly from the room where they had been dissecting cadavers. Semmelweiss met resentment and resistance from physicians senior to him who were professionally offended that a junior colleague should accuse them of infecting their own patients. Semmelweiss persevered and was able to demonstrate a reduced rate of infection in maternal deliveries attended by doctors or internists who thoroughly scrubbed their hands and arms with strong soap between the dissecting room and the obstetrics ward. Such evidence gradually persuaded obstetricians and surgeons to scrub their hands and arms thoroughly and to boil their instruments before touching the insides of their patients.

The Effect of Data Sources on Evidence

In social research, the source data requirements vary enormously with the scope of the research objectives. If the research concerns a widespread social characteristic, such as U.S. culture, it becomes apparent that culture includes social institutions, social identity, local, regional, and national history, and many well-differentiated kinds of technologies, social systems, and specialized communication systems. Source data regarding popular culture in the United States would require a good representative sample from the entire country. When such a sample is not available, researchers should carefully limit their claims to the population actually represented in their sample and search for any corroborating data developed by other researchers. Studies of the characteristics of criminals, which are commonly based on samples of prisoners in penal institutions, fall far short of the study of crime in general. Prison populations are largely made up of working-class offenders who have very limited social or financial resources. The more skilled, more resourceful, and wealthier law violators are not likely to be found in prison populations and therefore would not be included in any study of patterns of criminal involvement or patterns of criminal careers based on observations of prison records and interviews with prison inmates.

If a social phenomenon is thought to be fairly uniform in a society, a dense, well-controlled sample from a limited area may be very convincing because of the power of the evidence. Farnworth and Horan [18] wanted to evaluate the effect of race on treatment in the criminal justice system, based on the dynamics of such treatment in the court process of case handling. Their sample included 12,454 non-traffic violations in eighty-three counties tried in the North Carolina court system from January 1967 to April 1969. The hypothesis was: "Extensive authority vested in social control institutions creates an unequal distribution of power conducive to exploitation of society. Least powerful groups are most subject to that authority. Low social power is characteristic of minority racial groups, females, and the young." A second hypothesis was: "Those with high resources are more likely than those with low resources to avoid and to resist negative labeling." The researchers found that for white defendants the private attorney avoids conviction much more successfully than the court-appointed attorney. In contrast, the private attorney does not help the case of the black defendant as compared with the court-appointed attorney for the black defendant.

The severity of the offense has a negative effect on the probability of conviction, and the negative effect is significantly greater for white than for black defendants. The occupational level negatively affects probability of conviction for white but not for black defendants. Prior court involvement increases probability of conviction for black but not for white defendants. At every step in the legal process, the lower-class person is more likely to feel the sting of the law enforcement process [19]. The great strength of this evidence derives from a combination of a large number of cases, the large number of political units, the extended block of time, and the authenticity of the court records. The primary hypothesis, that social groups low in power are less able to escape conviction and imprisonment, is consistent with the overrepresentation of black inmates in state prisons.

The Effect of the Research Design on Evidence

Research designs vary greatly from simple to complex. A simple research design is demonstrated in a study of differential attitude change comparing medical and surgical students at a three-year interval at the University of Pennsylvania teaching hospital [20]. An eight-item questionnaire was given in July 1977 to sixteen medical and eighteen surgical students in the first year of training, and again to twenty-three medical and twelve surgical students at the end of the third year of training. The questions were Likert-scaled on five points: strongly agree, agree, undecided, disagree, and strongly disagree. Two questions were scored on each of four substrate variables: (1) confidence in subordinates' capacity; (2) information exchange; (3) allowing subordinates to share in decision making; (4) ability of subordinates to be responsible for their own actions. The nonparametric Mann–Whitney ranks test indicated that on all four dependent variables, the surgical students were similar to the medical students on the first test but had shifted significantly toward authoritarian attitudes on the second test. This design is too simple to provide strong evidence on medical and surgical students' attitudes: (1) only a single class-year of students was tested; (2) these respondents could not be independent of each other in attitude formation; (3) the real difference developed from score ranks could be in doubt because of the very narrow range of variability for a set of two attitude designs.

An example of a more elaborate design concerns the hypothesis that family size influences asset accumulation [21]. The data came from a three-year longitudinal data file of 494 families from 1967 to 1970. This analysis showed that in the early years of marriage, changes in the husband's income produced large changes in family consumption, a negligible effect on savings, and a partly compensatory decrease in the wife's work effort and income. The young worker receiving a big pay increase revises standards upward, increases consumption, and reduces savings. In contrast, pay raises for the more mature worker result in a savings increase. Young families pressed harder by a poor capital market adjust by the wife's working more and by reducing consumption. The pressure of children keeps family consumption stable or reduced, owing to reallocation of the parents' time. The mechanism of more children is to reduce both the hours worked by the wife and family consumption, with a net reduction in savings. Only if the husband gets a higher wage rate does the family consume more. For example, in the research period (1967–1970), a child in the first year of marriage reduced savings by $1,181.00 and family consumption declined by $414.00. But by the ninth year of marriage, children have a positive effect on savings because of a smaller decline in female earnings and working hours. In this study, the elaborateness of the research design permitted more detailed data analysis and thus a better grade of scientific evidence.

Replication in Scientific Research

If a researcher confirms a hypothesis of a close relationship between two variables, other researchers should be able to repeat the research under similar conditions and obtain similar results. Sherif's hypothesis on the formation of group norms [22] was replicated in his own research many times. He was able to show that verbally announced judgments of the amount of movement of a point of light in a completely dark room varied from person to person in a group of observers, but that the judgments over a large number of observers were normally distributed. Individuals with extreme judgments of movement above or below the group mean would tend to reduce these judgments toward the group mean on hearing others' judgments in later experimental sessions. Other researchers have repeated these experiments under similar conditions, and the hypothesized process of norm formation in small groups is well established among social workers, social psychologists, and other social scientists.

Replication is used both to confirm or to reject hypotheses. Durkheim reclassified his data on suicide statistics many many times in his search for a convincing explanation of the social principles affecting suicide. He could exclude poverty as an explanation for suicide in several different tests by showing low suicide rates in areas where income was the lowest. He rejected the hypothesis that increased geographic north latitude increases the suicide rate by a number of comparisons showing that suicide did not consistently vary in cities of similar size at different north latitudes. He excluded the effect of cities by measuring suicide rates at increasing distances from the city center and found no uniform effect. When he tried a series of tests on the effect of social involvement, he did find consistent differences in which persons less bound to others in social and relational ties had higher suicide rates. Durkheim's conclusions have been subject to extensive reanalysis and criticism, but they stand as a major landmark in the development of social science precisely because of his careful and exhaustive replications of many plausible hypotheses. Replication is essential to the hypothesis-testing process, as it provides a means of increasing the body of evidence.

The Hypothesis Cycle

Hypothetical Statements of Relationship

The hypothesis cycle starts with a proposition in verbal or mathematical form that makes an assertion or describes a relationship among variables. The hypothesis often applies a new approach to answering a question that the scientist believes could give a more adequate understanding to the research question. The Western Electric studies began with the hypothesis that there was some optimal level of illumination that would be associated with maximum output by workers repeating the assembly of telephone relays from a set of simple parts. The hypothesis implied that insufficient illumination would cause a reduction of daily output per worker and that illumination exceeding the optimum level would waste electrical power and fixtures. The hypothetical form is: "The graduated change in level of illumination, if recorded in relation to daily output per worker for one week, will demonstrate the degree of change in output related to a measured change in illumination." Similar hypotheses were ready for research regarding the effect of graduated changes in room temperature and humidity.

The Test of a Hypothetical Relation

As a part of the experimental control to test the hypothesis of the effect of illumination on worker productivity, a group of workers had to be separated from workers in the rest of the large factory. They were placed temporarily under the control of the researchers. The workers were told that these researchers would be making various changes to determine the best conditions for work and that they should cooperate to the best of their ability. When more lights were installed in the initial test, there was an increase in worker output over a one-week period. The hypothesis was confirmed. Illumination was again increased, and again production increased. The replication was confirmed.

If the hypothesis of a direct correlation between light level and output were correct, production should be lower if the illumination was reduced. Consequently, the researchers reduced the light level for the next week, but instead of decreasing, production increased again. The hypothesis was now clearly in doubt. The researchers reduced illumination to the original level, and again production increased for the week. Then they reduced illumination to a level where it was actually difficult to see. Production declined under these adverse conditions, but was still above the original level before the tests started.

Conclusion that Affirms or Disaffirms the Hypothesis

From the carefully recorded results of the experiment with the light level, the researchers began to realize that within rather wide limits, workers can adjust to variation in light level and vary their output independently. It was clear that setting the illumination level in itself had no fixed effect on worker output. And they assumed that the same would be true if room temperature or humidity were similarly varied.

Start of a New Hypothesis

The testing of a research hypothesis can have three outcomes. First, it may be *confirmed*. If it is, the test conditions can be tightened to establish whether it will still be confirmed under more rigorous conditions. The researcher can try to find the limits of applicability of the hypothesis. Second, the hypothesis may be *contradicted*. If so, the researcher needs to reexamine the theory and the assumptions from which the hypothesis was derived. The contradiction of the hypothesis throws new light on the theory and on the system of elements included in the theory. Third, the outcome of the test may be *ambiguous*, giving only partial or weak confirmation or denial of the hypothesis. In this case, the researcher should improve the testing conditions or attempt to improve the power of the test instrument. The outcome of the initial test of a new hypothesis is often confounded by misconceptions of the researcher that can be identified and corrected only by reordering concepts, definitions, focus, and method, until more definitive and useful results are obtained.

In the Western Electric studies, when the manipulation of light levels gave contradictory results, the researchers reexamined their test situation to see what other factor could account for the improved production levels in the telephone relay assembly room. They saw that the only other change in the work setting was the substitution of the researchers for the regular bosses. The regular bosses had been rather formal, distant, and demanding in relation to the workers. They would reprimand or discharge a worker who showed a poor attitude or lacked regularity or sustained working speed. In marked contrast, the researchers had a very different relation to the workers. It was much more friendly and permissive since they had to persuade the workers to cooperate with the test conditions. The workers responded by trying hard to do what the researchers seemed to want them to do. In addition, the workers in the relay assembly room gained a special status in relation to the other workers in the factory because they were privileged to work under less stringent supervision and were indeed getting extra work breaks of varying lengths. The factory was known as the Hawthorne Plant, and the positive response patterns of the experimental group have become known as the *Hawthorne effect*, or alternatively as the guinea pig effect, which is less fitting since guinea pigs are not particularly responsive to the personal influence of the researcher.

The researchers at the Western Electric plant went on to test a series of hypotheses. They supported the hypothesis that the workers' group was the primary influence in establishing and enforcing work production norms. These worker-derived norms were in contravention of company policy and a contradiction to the employer's assumption that company rules and close supervision were the primary causal factors in motivating and controlling worker productivity.

Serendipity in Research Outcomes

Recall from Chapter 3 that *serendipity* is a specialized term used in the description of scientific research procedures to note the unexpected discoveries that researchers often uncover in their attempt to find something else. Often the original planned research goal is based on faulty theory, and the misdirected search turns up something far better by accident. The practical value of this effect for the researcher is to encourage the development of theory in spite of inadequate prior information, and the development of a research design in spite of doubt about instruments and direction. An element of profound doubt shrouds all scientific research precisely because the operation of the target system is not known. Researchers, working in partial or total ignorance, will certainly stumble and fall in much of their research efforts.

Resourceful researchers combine background knowledge, imaginative theorizing, and inventive research techniques and instrumentation to resolve major problems. In some cases the researcher must develop or adapt new instruments as demanded by the nature of the problem. The serendipitous clue usually comes from close observation or seeming irregularities in the data, combined with a willingness to be flexible in both thought and action. The researcher must be willing to modify assumptions, theory, and technology to incorporate new and seemingly radical hypotheses to see the implications of the new and unorthodox information.

The most dramatic examples of serendipitous research events occur in the exact sciences. The Curies stumbled on the phenomenon of radioactivity in matter when they discovered that samples of pitchblende ore bearing radium caused action on unexposed photographic film. The ore samples were on top of an iron door key, on top of the box of new film in a desk drawer. When they developed the film, the outline of the iron key appeared on the negative. They immediately realized that the energy source was something from the pitchblende, which led to intensive research into the atomic energy field. Quasars or radio stars invisible to optical telescopes were discovered from unexpected small squiggles in the traces of longer-wavelength radio emissions from optically visible stars in radio telescopes.

There have also been examples of serendipity from research efforts in the social sciences. Merton [23] realized that he was on the wrong track in trying to estimate the influence of a national news magazine on the general public through the influence of high-value readers. When he reorganized his research approach, he was able to show that the influence in social communities comes from persons specializing in specific topics and that media sources exercised their influence indirectly through opinion leaders widely dispersed through all levels and regions of the community. As researchers we need to be open both to seeking and to establishing new knowledge.

References

1. W. N. Stephens, *Hypotheses and Evidence* (New York: Thomas Y. Crowell, 1968), p. 1.
2. Stephens, *Hypotheses and Evidence*, p. 1.
3. M. Weber, *The Protestant Ethic and the Spirit of Capitalism* (New York: Scribner's, 1958).
4. B. Glaser and A. Strauss, *The Discovery of Grounded Theory* (Chicago: Aldine, 1967), p. 1.
5. Gunnar Myrdal, *An American Dilemma* (New York: Harper and Row, 1958).
6. G. C. Homans, *Social Behavior: Its Elementary Forms* (New York: Harcourt, Brace and World, 1961), p. 64.
7. J. Neyman and E. S. Pearson, *Joint Statistical Papers* (Berkeley: University of California Press, 1967).
8. W. I. Thomas, "The Relation of Research to the Social Processes," in *Essays on Research in the Social Sciences*, W. I. Thomas, ed. (Washington, DC: Brookings Institute, 1931), p. 572.
9. Elizabeth Kubler-Ross, *On Death and Dying* (New York: Macmillan, 1969, 1970).
10. Elizabeth Kubler-Ross, *Questions and Answers on Death and Dying* (New York: Macmillan, 1974).
11. Elizabeth Kubler-Ross, *Death: The Final Stage of Growth* (Englewood Cliffs, NJ: Prentice-Hall, 1975).
12. Elizabeth Kubler-Ross, *To Live Until We Say Goodbye* (Englewood Cliffs, NJ: Prentice-Hall, 1978).
13. Elizabeth Kubler-Ross, *Living with Death and Dying* (New York: Macmillan, 1981).
14. M. Davies and D. B. Kandel, "Parental and Peer Influence on Adolescents' Educational Plans: Some Further Evidence," *American Journal of Sociology* 87 (1981): 363–87.
15. H. Sandhu and D. E. Allen, "A Comparative Study of Delinquents and Nondelinquents: Family Affect, Religion, and Personal Income," *Social Forces* 46 (1976): 263–9.
16. W. P. Bridges, "Industry, Marginality, and Female Employment: A New Appraisal," *American Sociological Review* 45 (1980): 73.
17. W. L. Warner and P. S. Lunt, *The Social Life of a Modern Community* (New Haven, CT: Yale University Press, 1941).
18. M. Farnworth and P. M. Horan, "Separate Justice—An Analysis of Race Differences in Court Processes," *Social Science Research* 9 (1980): 381-99.
19. Farnworth and Horan, "Separate Justice—An Analysis of Race Differences in Court Processes," p. 385.
20. J. M. Eisenberg, D. S. Kitz, and R. A. Webber, "Development of Attitudes about Sharing Decision-Making: A Comparison of Medical and Surgical Students," *Journal of Health and Social Behavior* 24 (1983): 85–90.
21. J. P. Smith and M. P. Ward, "Asset Accumulation and Family Demography," *Demography* 17 (1980): 243–60.
22. M. Sherif, *The Psychology of Social Norms* (New York: Harper and Row, 1948).
23. R. K. Merton, *Social Theory and Social Structure* (New York: The Free Press, 1949).

Chapter 8

The Process of Measurement

The meaning of measurement
Why measure?
    To describe properties
    To determine relationships
        among properties
Levels of measurement
    Nominal level of measurement
    Ordinal level of measurement
    Interval level of measurement
    Ratio level of measurement
Single indicators as measures
Scales as measures
    Rating scales
    Questionnaire-based scales
Comparison of scaling techniques
Nonreactive measures
    Physical traces
    Historical and public records
    Content analysis
The theory of measurement
    The true quantity
    The measured quantity

Types of errors
    Systematic error
    Random error
Sources of measurement error
    Instability in the property
    Instability in measuring
        instruments
    Transient personal factors
    Situational factors
    Variation in administering
        research instruments
    Item sampling error
    Clouded instruments
    Mechanical and processing
        errors
Evaluating the adequacy of a
        measure
    Validity
    Reliability
    The relation between validity
        and reliability

Aristotle could have avoided the mistake of thinking that women have fewer teeth than men by the simple device of asking Mrs. Aristotle to open her mouth.

—BERTRAND RUSSELL

Given a research question, a theory that provides a plausible answer to the question, and a chosen research design, we are now ready to begin thinking about measurement. You will recall that theory is composed of concepts that are logically linked. Since theory is not directly testable, these concepts must be transformed into variables. Measurement is the process by which this transformation takes place. But alas, here lies one of the true challenges for social research. Some of the concepts that interest social researchers are relatively easy to measure because there is broad consensus on how to evaluate their underlying properties. For example, age of individuals, education, and income are concepts that are relatively simple to measure since the properties are concrete and easy to assess. But social workers are also interested in many other concepts whose properties are more difficult to evaluate. Improvements in social functioning, group cohesion, social relationships and support networks, various aspects of the effectiveness of social service delivery systems, and client treatment modalities are but a few of the many concepts that social workers have attempted to measure and with only varying degrees of success. Consider, for example, the concept of "clinical improvement"—a difficult concept to measure. But the issue of how much a client participates in clinical activities is much easier and tells us something about the first concept too.

In this chapter we will introduce you to measurement—the process by which concepts are transformed into variables. We will identify various types of measuring techniques, alert you to various sources of measurement error, and familiarize you with methods for evaluating the effectiveness of your measures.

The Meaning of Measurement

We will accept S. S. Stevens's definition of measurement: "Measurement is the assignment of numerals to objects according to a rule" [1, 2, 3]. If you have ever visited a large hotel, you know that for the management to assign numbers to rooms in some fixed order is easier for everyone than to assign numbers at random regardless of floor or order. The same type of reasoning applies to the assignment of numbers for measures. Social researchers usually try to express their measurements in terms of numbers to remove as much confusion and ambiguity as possible. The necessity of using numbers in research is also because much research is concerned with comparison of quantities, and for this, the mapping of properties in terms of some kind of number sequence is indispensable. This process is referred to as *quantitative* research. Another type of research referred to as *qualitative* will be discussed in Chapter 12.

Why Measure?

Why do we want to measure social phenomena? What value is there in trying to transform concepts into variables? These are important questions, and we will try to answer them by mentioning two primary objectives of the measurement process.

To Describe Properties

In the study of social relationships, many of the concepts we deal with can be described in purely verbal terms without the use of more systematic measurements. We might say, for example, that more recently developed methods of social intervention seem to be more effective than earlier ones. But such statements can be better focused and better used as a basis for decision, if more exact measures are included. Similarly, we can be much more informative in describing a city if we use such measured properties as the approximate population for a given year, the distribution of population by age and sex, the number of vehicles, and the number of industries. Other descriptive measures for quantification might include the literacy level, the extent of health and leisure facilities, increases or decreases in education, public services, and the city's requirements for water, energy, and other resources. Numerical representations of level of employment, personal and corporate income, and the level of development of public institutions for education, finance, and communication media permit a much better and more specific description of a city, a nation, or a region [4].

Social scientists also devise measures to describe the properties of social events. The idea of social class, for example, can be studied more effectively if we can determine an ordered hierarchy of social class based on measures of income, education, lifestyle, and patterns of consumption. In fact, many of the most socially significant properties of our lives are conceived mainly in terms of an arbitrary system of measurement. Consider, for example, the importance of a paper-and-pencil test of perhaps 150 questions including factual statements, and logical and number problems scored according to the proportion of correct answers. The score may be converted into an intelligence quotient (IQ) equaling 100 if the score is average for persons of the same age, or below 100 if the score is under average and above 100 if the score is higher than average for the standard of a given age group. Now we can give an operational definition of intelligence: "Intelligence is whatever it may be that the intelligence test measures" [5]. The measure of IQ, in other words (or any concept for that matter), depends entirely on social acceptance and researchers' willingness to use it. *The measured property is "real" because we act as if it is real.* As you proceed in this chapter, try to be aware of the implications of this simple notion, as they are profound and far-reaching.

To Determine Relationships among Properties

Measurement also permits comparisons, determinations of change, and decision making in research. Do husbands and wives see social roles in their own family in the same way? A well-designed measure of male and female roles given to both spouses can demonstrate the degree to which they share perceptions. Do blacks and whites with equal qualifications have equal opportunity for promotion in industry and government? Do men and women of equal qualifications get equal career opportunities? Careful measurement of level of qualification in relation to the attained position in pay and status permits us to answer this question [6].

Levels of Measurement

Now that we have established what measurement is and that it is essential in social research, we are ready to examine different measurement techniques. But before doing that, it is important that we be familiar with the classification of measurement. A widely accepted classification has been constructed by Stevens [7] in which he identifies four levels: nominal, ordinal, interval, and ratio. The use of the word *levels* is both intentional and appropriate. As we shall see, Stevens's classification describes measures in terms of basic mathematical properties, and the properties are cumulative as we move from one level to the next.

Nominal Level of Measurement

The nominal level of measurement is primarily a classification system. Quite simply, it is **the assignment of names or numbers to categories, the names or numbers having no mathematical meaning.** Many of the properties that will interest us are of this type. Sex, race, marital status, political preference, and religious preference are excellent examples. Sex, of course, has two categories, to which we assign the labels *male* and *female*. But there is no underlying mathematical meaning imputed to these categories. We cannot order them nor can we add them together in the same way we can add a quarter and a nickel. Even if we assigned numbers to these categories (males = 1; females = 2), adding these assigned numbers together to get 3 makes no sense.

There are two criteria that the categories in any nominal set must meet. First, they must be *mutually exclusive* so that each case is counted in only one category. Second, they must be *logically exhaustive* so that every case does belong in one of the categories of the set.

The fact that nominal-level measures have no mathematical properties does not mean that mathematical operations are inappropriate. We may not be able to order or average the categories, but mathematical functions can be performed with a category and used to compare across categories. The most frequent mathematical operations used on nominal-level measures are the calculation of frequencies (e.g., number of males = 15; number of females = 10); simple proportions (males = 15/25 or 0.60; females = 10/25 or 0.40), and percentages (males: 0.60 = 60%; females: 0.40 = 40%).

Ordinal Level of Measurement

Unlike nominal-level measures, ordinal-level measures are characterized with the most basic of mathematical properties. Ordinal scales incorporate a rising order of inequality between categories or scale points. (See Figure 8.1.) This inequality feature means more of something, comparing any higher-scale point with a lower-scale point. However, the distance between scale values is of unspecified size. Thus, we can talk in terms of "greater than" or "less than," but we do not know how much

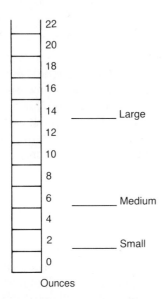

Ounces

FIGURE 8.1 The Difference between Large and Medium Is Not Necessarily Equal to the Difference between Medium and Small

greater or how much less. To illustrate, if soap bars are sold in small, medium, and large sizes, we know that the large bar is larger than the medium bar and that the medium bar is larger than the small bar. But we do not know how much larger, and the difference between small and medium and between medium and large may not be the same. We know nothing about the exact size of any of these bars, only their relative rank in terms of size. *All ordinal-level measures incorporate the mathematical property of order or rank.* Here are three examples of ordinal measures, each with five ranks:

Weight	*Military Rank*	*Education*
5 very fat	5 general	5 masters or higher
4 fat	4 colonel	4 college graduate
3 average	3 major	3 some college
2 thin	2 captain	2 high school
1 very thin	1 lieutenant	1 grade school

For such measures, the ranks are assigned (1) according to the number of categories (in each of these examples, five categories), and (2) in ordered sequence (from less to more of a property).

Interval Level of Measurement

In addition to the mathematical property of order, interval scales assume an equal distance between points representing order. **In an interval scale the distance between the points of a measuring instrument is known and this distance between points is equal.** On a Fahrenheit scale, the distance between a reading of 50 and 51 degrees is the same as the distance between a reading of 51 and 52. This is because, as with all interval scales, each unit is exactly equal to every other unit, regardless of position in the series. However, we cannot say that 100 degrees Fahrenheit is twice as hot as 50 degrees Fahrenheit since an interval scale does not have an absolute or real zero position. *The placement of zero on this scale is arbitrary since the best we can do is operationally define the absence of the property being measured.* On a centigrade scale, for example, zero, the absence of heat, is operationally defined as the temperature at which water freezes. Thus, 0 on a centigrade scale is equivalent to 32 on a Fahrenheit scale since this is the Fahrenheit temperature at which water freezes.

Many of the measures constructed by social scientists are interval measures. Scales constructed to measure feelings, beliefs, and behaviors generally have arbitrary zeroes. In the measurement of attitudes toward adoption, for example, we may assume that the difference between a score of 2 and 3 is the same as the difference between a score of 6 and 7. However, the absence of attitude or neutrality still requires an arbitrary placement of 0.

Ratio Level of Measurement

Ratio measures incorporate both of the mathematical properties already mentioned (order and equal intervals) and one additional property: the presence of a natural or absolute zero. The ratio level of measurement is based on an ordered series of equal intervals, beginning with an absolute or natural zero. Since the zero on a ratio scale is absolute, it always means absence (none) of the property being measured. A checking account at the bank, for example, has a natural origin of zero. A deposit of $25.00 makes the balance $0.00 plus $25.00, or $25.00. A second deposit of $75.00 makes the balance $100.00 (assuming no checks have been written and no withdrawals made). Now the balance is four times as much as it was following the first deposit. Notice with an absolute zero, the numbers on the scale indicate the actual amount of the property being measured, and this makes possible mathematical operations with ratios. The ratio of 100.00 to 25.00 is 100/25, or 4/1. Thus, we can say $100.00 is four times as much as $25.00. Age is a ratio-level measure, as the moment of birth represents a natural zero. Thus, when a person is sixty years old, we can say she has lived twice as many years as a person who is thirty.

Our measurement of concepts will include all four of these levels. For most concepts, there is no single correct measure. In fact, most concepts can be transformed into variables in many different ways. And the different measures of a given concept may even be at different levels. The measure chosen for any given concept will depend in large part on (1) what measures are currently available, (2) what has been used in past research, and (3) what has been proved adequate. Several measurement techniques have been introduced to help us construct adequate measures. These include single measure indicators and scales.

Single Indicators as Measures

Some of the most widely used measurements in social research are indicators that yield indirect measures of some property. The best common example is a clock. A direct measure of time depends on the apparent movement of the sun from the eastern horizon to the north–south meridian, directly overhead. A division of the angle of the sun's movement into sixths would correspond to the hours from sunrise to noon, and in similar measure from noon to sunset. The clock is designed to coincide exactly with the Earth's daily rotation, driving the hour hand around the dial twice each day. Once the clock is set, it continues to synchronize or keep time with the Earth's rotation, and the rotation of the hand indicates the rotation of the Earth.

We could put together a clock to measure anything indirectly. The Bureau of the Census in Washington, D.C., maintains a population clock, which indicates the estimated population of the United States moment by moment. With 0.5 percent natural increase, and more than 240 million people, the United States increases one unit of population (excess of births over deaths) about every thirty seconds. Visitors can see the population grow by three to four persons while they watch for just two minutes.

A single measure indicator can be constructed in just two steps: (1) a decision on what observations are used to measure a concept and (2) a procedure for combining these observations operationally [8]. The number of law violations reported to the police can provide an approximate indicator of the annual crime rate. It is limited as an indicator, though, since as many as half of the violations against persons are not reported, and an unknown number of paper violations, such as underreporting income on taxes and falsifying financial records, are never exposed. Entertainers use decibel meters to record the loudness of and timing of applause as an indicator of overall appreciation of a show.

Many different kinds of figures can serve as indicators if we know how to interpret them. For example, U.S. railroads reported about 2,500 derailments per year in the late 1970s. Since nearly all rail movements are of freight, these accidents typically were of little concern to the public, except when dangerous chemicals and fuels were released. However, they may be regarded as an indicator of the condition of the roadbeds and of the relative condition of the U.S. railroad industry. Many large rail lines have gone into bankruptcy, and most are in severe financial difficulties. These facts, taken together, provide a single measure indicator that is significant for employment, public safety, and sectors of the national economy, including farms, factories, and certain elements of national defense, all of which depend on rail service for their operations.

There is currently some interest in establishing dependable single measure indicators of U.S. society to help identify changes, trends, and problem areas. The Senate passed the Full Opportunity and Social Accounting Act of 1967, which responded to a need for a concise picture of conditions in health, education, housing and vocational opportunity, arts, humanities, and other areas of life [9]. As indicators of social change, a series of surveys has already been conducted to measure such concepts as life-cycle fertility, duration of marriage, prestige of public employment, political participation, alienation and discontent, schooling, income, and attitudes [10]. Such single measure indicators are one means of transforming concepts into variables.

Scales as Measures

The term *scale* refers to a special type of measurement in which numbers are assigned to positions, the assignment indicating varying degrees of the property under consideration. We can think of a scale as a standard measurement procedure providing the basis for agreement among social scientists that assessment of a property is appropriate [11]. When a concept is measured using a scale, the result is usually a single score for an individual. The score represents the degree to which an individual possesses the property being measured. There are many different types of scales in social research. In the following pages, we will present some of the more frequently used including rating scales and questionnaire-based scales.

Rating Scales

Generally speaking, rating scales all have one feature in common. **The person or object being rated is placed in one of an ordered set of categories where numerical values are assigned to categories.** Rating scales can be used to secure individuals' ratings of themselves or someone else's ratings of them. For the most part, self-rating is more accurate, as most individuals are in a better position to evaluate their own feelings, behaviors, and skills. However, this assumption is only true if individuals are aware of their own feelings and behaviors and are willing to reveal them. Three of the more commonly used rating scales are the graphic rating scale, itemized rating scale, and comparative rating scale.

Graphic Rating Scales

Graphic rating scales are those constructed with (1) a designated number of ordered scale points and (2) a written description for every or every other scale point. It may help to think of a graphic rating scale as analogous to a ruler. The points are positioned at equal intervals, and a written description is supplied for most or all points. The rater is instructed to select the one written description (and hence the corresponding scale point) that most closely approximates his or her position. Miller [12] has devised a battery of twenty graphic rating scales for evaluating important norms and patterns within national cultures. All of his graphic rating scales have six positions ranging between two contrasting poles. (See Figure 8.2.)

3. Concern for and trust of others

1	2	3	4	5	6

High concern for others. Respect for the motives and integrity of others. Mutual trust prevails.	Moderate or uneven pattern of concern for and trust of others.	Lack of concern for others and lack of trust.

4. Confidence in personal security and protection of property

1	2	3	4	5	6

High confidence in personal security. Free movement night and day, for both sexes. High sense of security of property. Locking of homes is optional.	Moderate confidence in personal security. Confidence of men is high in personal security but women are warned to take precautions. Movements of women restricted to daytime. Simple property precautions essential.	Low confidence in both personal security and protection of property. Men and women restrict all movement at night to predetermined precautions. Many property precautions obligatory. Extensive use of locks, dogs, and guards.

5. Family solidarity

1	2	3	4	5	6

High solidarity with many obligations of kinship relations within large, extended family system.	Relations of solidarity within a limited kinship circle with specified obligations only.	Small, loosely integrated, independent family with highly specific individual relations.

6. Independence of the child

1	2	3	4	5	6

Child is raised to be self-reliant and independent in both thought and action.	Child is given specified areas of independence only.	Child is raised to be highly dependent and docile.

FIGURE 8.2   Graphic Rating Scale

Source: D. Miller, Graphic Rating Scale, Handbook of Research Design and Social Measurement (New York: David McKay, 1975). Reprinted by permission.

Itemized Rating Scales

Itemized rating scales are composed of a series of ordered statements to which point values have been assigned. Although raters may read through the statements and check all of those with which they agree, generally they are instructed to check only one statement. The statements vary in terms of *intensity,* the middle statement expressing a relatively neutral position. The statements may also vary in *length* from one sentence to several sentences including illustrations. The clearer the distinctions among statements (and therefore scale positions), the more reliable the scale. The Survey Research Center at the University of Michigan frequently uses itemized rating scales when conducting national surveys. Since these surveys generally cover a broad range of topics, it is not feasible to measure all concepts with a battery of statements, each of which requires a response, as the questionnaire would become much too long. The 1968 survey, for example, included the following itemized scale [13]. Respondents were asked to choose the statement closest to their own views.

1. The Bible is God's word and all it says is true.
2. The Bible was written by men inspired by God but it contains some human errors.
3. The Bible is a good book because it was written by wise men but God had nothing to do with it.
4. The Bible was written by men who lived so long ago that it is worth very little today.

Comparative Rating Scales

Comparative rating scales are those that ask the rater to position self or other on a scale where the position is judged relative to some other individual or group. This type of scale differs from an itemized scale in that an itemized scale does not require that the rating be made in direct reference to someone else. The position assigned by the rater is based on his or her knowledge of the referent. For example, when a professor is asked to evaluate a student seeking admission to graduate school, there is frequently a question requesting a rating of the student's ability to do graduate work:

Of the students you have known, is this student in the top:

1. 5%
2. 10%
3. 25%
4. 50%

To make this evaluation, a teacher must have a clear picture of this student in relation to other students she or he has worked with.

Ziller [14] has developed a comparative scale for measuring social self-esteem where social self-esteem is conceptualized as relative to the social reality of the individual. (See Figure 8.3.) The self-esteem measure consists of six circles displayed horizontally, followed by a list of "people" such as (1) doctor, (2) father, (3) friend, (4) nurse, (5) self, and (6) someone you know who is unsuccessful. There are six such lists, all including self. Respondents are asked to place each person in a circle. The further to the left one places self, the higher one's self-esteem.

Precautions That Should Be Taken with Rating Scales

Some precautions should be taken when using rating scales because there is potential for systematic error (error that occurs over and over) whether the rating is made by self or other. Potential errors include (1) halo effect, (2) generosity error, and (3) contrast error. *Halo effect* refers to the tendency to create a generalized impression of a person and to carry this impression over from one rating to the next. If, for example, a rater evaluates a person as aggressive and believes that aggressive people are dominant, independent, and assertive, this person would also get high marks on these characteristics. Thus, the halo effect introduces high association among rated traits. The *generosity* error refers to the rater's tendency to overestimate the positive

Directions: The circles stand for people. Mark each circle with the letter standing for one of the people in the list. Do this any way you like, but use each person once and do not omit anyone.

List for student form of the measure:

F− someone flunking;

K− someone you know who is kind

H− happiest person you know

S− yourself

Su− a successful person you know

St − strongest person you know

Five sets of social objects in the **student form** of the instrument:

a) doctor, father, friend, mother, yourself, teacher;

b) someone you know who is a good athlete, a good dancer, someone who is funny, someone who gets good grades, yourself, someone who is unhappy;

c) an actor, your brother or most like a brother, your best friend, yourself, a salesman;

d) someone you know who is cruel, a judge, grandmother, a housewife, a police officer, yourself, your sister or most like a sister;

e) doctor, father, nurse, yourself, someone you know who is unsuccessful.

FIGURE 8.3 A Measure of Self-Esteem

Source: Robert C. Ziller, Joan Hagey, Mary Dell Smith, Barbara Long, 1969 "Self-Esteem: A Self-Social Construct." Journal of Consulting & Clinical Psychology Vol. 33 No. 1 pp. 84–95. Extract from Col. 2, p. 85. Copyright 1969 by the American Psychological Association. Reprinted by permission of the publisher and author.

traits of those persons he or she likes. *Contrast error* is a tendency for raters to see those rated as opposite self.

The halo effect can be controlled by using more than one rater. If raters independently make evaluations, their evaluations can be compared and the average or middle rating might be used. The generosity error and the contrast error can be controlled by avoiding extreme scale point descriptions or extreme statements. One additional means of controlling for these types of errors is to use a different type of scale—a questionnaire-based scale.

Questionnaire-Based Scales

By questionnaire-based scales, we simply mean the use of multiple statements that are tallied so as to create a single composite score. The use of the phrase *questionnaire-based* is not meant to imply that rating scales are not included on questionnaires. This phrase is only meant to suggest that questionnaire-based scales are formatted much like questionnaires in that multiple statements are used. With questionnaire-based scales, respondents are asked to respond to every statement. By using a battery of statements to create a composite score, the researcher is also in a better position to avoid the errors noted with rating scales. Several questionnaire-based scales have received wide acceptance in social research, including Thurstone, Likert, Guttman, and semantic-differential.

Thurstone Scales

Of the questionnaire-based scales, the Thurstone scaling technique is the most elaborate. (See Figure 8.4.) To construct a Thurstone scale, a set of statements is arranged along a continuum where the scale points vary from 1 to 11. The location of each

Attitude toward the Church

This is a study of attitudes toward the church. Below are twenty-four statements expressing different attitudes toward the church. Put a check mark (✓) if you agree with the statement. Put a cross (×) if you disagree with the statement. If you cannot decide about a statement, you may mark it with a question mark. This is not an examination. People differ in their opinions about what is right and wrong on this question. Please indicate *your own attitude* by a check mark when you agree and by an "x" when you disagree.

Scale Value		
3.3	1	I enjoy my church because there is a spirit of friendliness there.
5.1	2	I like the ceremonies of my church but do not miss them much when I stay away.
8.8	3	I respect any church-member's beliefs but I think it is all "bunk."
6.1	4	I feel the need for religion but do not find what I want in any one church.
8.3	5	I think the teaching of the church is altogether too superficial to have much social significance.
11.0	6	I think the church is a parasite on society.
6.7	7	I believe in sincerity and goodness without any church ceremonies.
3.1	8	I do not understand the dogmas or creeds of the church but I find that the church helps me to be more honest and creditable.
9.6	9	I think the church is a hindrance to religion for it still depends upon magic, superstition, and myth.
9.2	10	I think the church seeks to impose a lot of worn-out dogmas and medieval superstitions.
4.0	11	When I go to church I enjoy a fine ritual service with good music.
0.8	12	I feel the church perpetuates the values which man puts highest in his philosophy of life.
5.6	13	Sometimes I feel that the church and religion are necessary and sometimes I doubt it.
7.5	14	I think too much money is being spent on the church for the benefit that is being derived.
10.7	15	I think the organized church is an enemy of science and truth.
2.2	16	I like to go to church for I get something worthwhile to think about and it keeps my mind filled with right thoughts.
1.2	17	I believe the church is a powerful agency for promoting both individual and social righteousness.
7.2	18	I believe the churches are too much divided by factions and denominations to be a strong force for righteousness.
4.5	19	I believe in what the church teaches but with mental reservations.
0.2	20	I believe the church is the greatest institution in America today.
4.7	21	I am careless about religion and church relationships but I would not like to see my attitude become general.
10.4	22	The church represents shallowness, hypocrisy, and prejudice.
1.7	23	I feel the church services give me inspiration and help me to live up to my best during the following week.
2.6	24	I think the church keeps business and politics up to a higher standard than they would otherwise tend to maintain.

FIGURE 8.4   Thurstone Scale

Source: L. L. Thurstone and E. J. Chane, The Measurement of Attitude (Chicago: University of Chicago Press, 1929). Reprinted in Marvin F. Shaw and Jack M. Wright, Scales for the Measurement of Attitudes (New York: McGraw-Hill, 1967), pp. 545–546.

statement along the continuum is achieved by asking a panel of judges to evaluate the statements along that continuum. We should stress that judges are responding to the statements, not on the basis of their own feelings, but rather on the basis of the statements' meaning. The final scale consists of some two dozen statements (approximately two statements for each scale position) whose positions on the scale have been agreed upon by the judges. We have summarized the steps that must be followed to create this type of scale:

1. You must first choose the concept you wish to measure. You might be interested, for example, in measuring attitudes toward women's rights issues, such as the Equal Rights Amendment, wife abuse, or women in ministry. If so, the concept selected is ready to be transformed into the variable (measurement).

2. Once the concept has been selected, you must construct or collect a wide variety of statements about the concept. These statements may be collected from newspapers, magazines, books, individuals, or self. The statements should represent a wide variety of opinions since the end result is to identify statements that can be positioned at each of the eleven scale positions.

3. Approximately 100 statements are assembled on file cards. Only one statement should be placed on each card, as the identification process to follow is made easier by this procedure.

4. A panel of 200–300 judges is solicited to sort these cards into eleven piles. The eleven piles are labeled A through K, with A representing the most negative statements, K the most positive, and F neutral. The statements placed in each pile are assumed to be an equal distance from statements placed in the other piles as estimated by the judges. In other words, those statements placed in pile A are assumed to be an equal distance from those statements placed in pile B, which are assumed to be an equal distance from those statements in pile C, and so on.

5. Judges who performed their task carelessly are eliminated together with those statements that received widely different ratings from the 200–300 judges.

6. The scale values for each statement are then calculated by computing the median scale values. The spread of judgments about the median is also computed. Some researchers prefer using the mean and the spread of scores about the mean. Use of the mean or median will depend on the size of the panel of judges. If a large panel is used, the two measures should give approximately equivalent results. If the panel is small, the median will probably be more appropriate. Calculation of either the mean or the median assumes conversion of the scale to a number continuum where A = 1, B = 2, C = 3, and so on.

7. Final selection for the scale is made from those statements that have a small spread and are equally spaced along the scale. Equal representation should be given to each of the intervals. With two statements per interval, the final scale would contain twenty-two statements. If there are many statements from which to choose, clarity and brevity of wording may serve as additional criteria for selection.

8. The scale is administered by having respondents check only those statements with which they agree, and a respondent's score is the mean scale value for all the statements he or she has endorsed.

Likert Scales

Shortly after the development of the Thurstone scale, Rensis Likert [15] offered an alternative to it. (See Figure 8.5.) Basically, there are three differences between Thurstone and Likert scales, and we will look at each. *The first difference is in the statement format and the instructions given to the respondents.* With the Thurstone scale, no scale weights are given with the statements and respondents are asked to check only those statements with which they agree. With the Likert scale, respondents are asked to indicate the degree of agreement or disagreement for all statements on the instrument using a five-point scale. In other words, five response categories are provided for each statement; strongly agree, agree, neutral, disagree, strongly disagree. On an a priori basis, the researcher must determine the direction (positive or negative) of each statement. Each of the five alternatives is assigned a weight from 1 to 5

Death Attitude Scale

DIRECTIONS: This form measures your attitudes on a number of important issues. Each item is a statement of belief or attitude. At the right of each statement is a place for you to indicate your feeling. Please circle the symbols that best express your point of view. Please respond in terms of how you feel, not how you think others feel or what society wants you to feel.
WORK QUICKLY AND PLEASE RESPOND TO EVERY ITEM.

SA—Strongly Agree
 A—Agree
  ?—Neutral, don't know
 D—Disagree
SD—Strongly Disagree

  4   In many instances, married couples should be encouraged to use birth control devices.

             †SA   A   ?   D   SD

  7   Mercy-killing, assuming proper precautions are taken, will benefit people on the whole.
 *9   Preventing conception by mechanical birth control devices is as wrong or almost as wrong as taking a human life after birth.
*10   Laws which provide the death penalty for crimes are morally wrong.
*11   Although my definition of God may differ from that of others, I believe there is a God.
*14   Physical or mental illness, no matter how severe or hopeless, should never be the basis for taking the life of the involved person.
*16   Killing during war is just as indefensible as any other sort of killing.
 18   As unfortunate as it is, killing during wartime may be justifiable.
 19   The possibility that God exists today seems very unlikely.
 23   If a mother's life is seriously endangered, forced abortion of the fetus may be necessary.
 26   Life after death seems an improbable occurrence.
*27   I find the prospect of my eventual death disturbing.
 29   There is some sort of existence after our present life ends.
*30   Forced abortion of the fetus is wrong, regardless of the health of the mother or the social conditions involved.

*The items are negative and their weights must be reversed for purposes of scoring.
†The same response alternatives are used with all items.

FIGURE 8.5 Likert Scale

Source: L. A. Kalish, "Scale of Attitudes Toward Death," *Journal of Social Psychology* 59:137–45 (1963). Reprinted with permission of the Helen Dwight Reid Educational Foundation. Published by Heldref Publications, 4000 Albemarle Street, N.W., Washington, D.C. 20016. Copyright © 1963.

such that agreement with favorable statements will be treated equivalent to disagreement with unfavorable statements:

	SA	A	N	D	SD
Favorable statement	1	2	3	4	5
Unfavorable statement	5	4	3	2	1

It is a good idea to have both positively and negatively worded statements. Sometimes when all of the statements are worded in only one direction, a response set develops. By response set we simply mean a tendency to answer all statements the same. If all the statements were positively worded, a respondent might pencil in *agree* for each statement without reading any of the statements carefully.

A second difference between Likert and Thurstone scales is in the scoring. Whereas Thurstone scales are scored by computing the mean (or median) value of those statements endorsed, Likert scales are scored by simply summing the weights for all statements. With a twenty-statement Likert scale, for example, we would expect a minimum score of 20 and a maximum score of 100. Both of these values assume that all twenty statements are answered.

A third difference between Thurstone and Likert scales is in the method used to choose the statements. With Thurstone scales, this is determined through a panel of judges. With Likert scales, no panel of judges is needed. Instead, a large number of statements (approximately 100) are administered to a group of respondents who are assumed to be representative of those for whom the scale is being constructed. Responses are analyzed to determine which statements best differentiate between the low- and high-scoring individuals. And the best statements are those that differentiate between high and low scorers. Those statements for which high and low scorers respond similarly are eliminated.

Likert also specifies that an objective check of each statement can be obtained by correlating each statement with the total cumulative score. This check will serve not only to determine whether the statements are discriminating between low and high scorers but also to determine whether the numerical values are properly assigned. A negative correlation indicates that the numerical values are not properly assigned and that the 1 and 5 ends of the scale should be reversed. If a zero or near-zero correlation results, the statement does not differentiate between low and high scorers. Likert [16] gives four reasons for why a statement may prove undifferentiating:

1. The statement may involve a different issue from the one involved in the rest of the statements; that is, it relates to a different concept.
2. The statement may be responded to in the same way by practically the entire group. [E.g., Likert found that some two thousand students responded to the following statement in practically the same way: "Should the United States repeal the Japanese Exclusion Act?"]
3. The statement may be so expressed that it is misunderstood by members of the group. This may be due to its being poorly stated, phrased in unfamiliar words, or worded in the form of a double-barreled statement [e.g., "I feel my age, but it does not bother me"].

TABLE 8.1 Assessment of Terms of Agreement and Disagreement

Agreement	*Disagreement*
Absolutely Agree	Absolutely Disagree
Totally Agree	Totally Disagree
Agree Unconditionally	Disagree Unconditionally
Extremely Agree	Extremely Disagree
Intensely Agree	Intensely Disagree
Agree Strongly	Disagree Strongly
Agree Utterly	Disagree Utterly
Agree Greatly	Disagree Greatly
Agree Very Much	Disagree Very Much
Agree a Great Deal	Disagree a Great Deal
Agree	Disagree
Mostly Agree	Mostly Disagree
Do Not Agree	Do Not Disagree
Tend to Agree	Tend to Disagree
Agree Somewhat	Disagree Somewhat
Agree Slightly	Disagree Slightly

Adapted from: G. Rotter, "Attitudinal Points of Agreement and Disagreement," *Journal of Social Psychology* 86 (1972): 211–18.

4. It may be a statement of fact which individuals who fall at different points on the continuum will be equally likely to accept or reject [e.g., "Everyone dies, including me"].

Since the development of the Likert scale in 1932, the basic scoring procedure has remained the same. However, for reasons not always specified, researchers have often found it desirable to modify the number of response alternatives accompanying each statement and to change the wording used to describe these alternatives. In general, the number of response alternatives has ranged from 2 to 7. But the wording used to describe these alternatives has experienced greater change. Rotter [17] has attempted to shed light on these various alternatives by determining the extent of agreement connoted by the various descriptions. (See Table 8.1.) He also (1) identified descriptions representing equivalent counterpoints of agreement and disagreement and (2) selected end points of the scale that approached totality or the entire range of agreement–disagreement. Rotter recommends seven response alternatives for use with Likert scales:

Totally Agree	+3
Agree Very Much	+2
Tend to Agree	+1
Neutral or Don't Know	0
Tend to Disagree	–1
Disagree Very Much	–2
Totally Disagree	–3

These seven-scale points were selected for three reasons:

1. These end points best anchored the range of agree–disagree.
2. The parallel counterpoints best represented equivalent distances from the neutral position.
3. The numerical values approximated an equal interval scale.

Although Rotter's research will probably not squelch the use of various response alternatives and arbitrary weights, it is an empirical effort to identify appropriate response alternatives and meaningful weights.

Guttman Scales

A third prominent measurement technique, developed and introduced in the 1940s, is referred to as Guttman scaling [18]. Guttman scaling is a scoring technique that assumes an underlying cumulative continuum. In other words, knowledge of a total score allows us to predict perfectly a subject's responses to each individual statement. The statements assume an a priori order such that agreement with any particular statement assumes agreement with the statements preceding it. Let's take, for example, a series of simple mathematical equations:

(1) $1 + 1 = 2$
(2) $2 \times 3 = 6$
(3) $48/12 = 4$
(4) $\sqrt{25} = 5$

For these four equations, we are assuming an a priori order. Of all mathematical processes (except counting), addition is considered to be the simplest and is usually the first learned. Multiplication is considered more difficult than addition; division more difficult than multiplication; and square root more difficult than division. If these four problems were administered to a subject and one point was scored for each correct answer, a maximum score would be 4. Similarly, if a subject could answer none of these four, a minimum score of 0 would be obtained. With a minimum score of 0 and a maximum score of 4, perfect prediction is possible, as it is readily apparent that either none or all of the problems were answered correctly. With a score of 1, 2, or 3, though, if prediction is to be consistently accurate, it must be founded upon some sound assumptions. The ability to predict accurately lies in the assumed cumulative character of the items. If the solutions to problems 2, 3, and 4 assume prior learning (problem 1), it is reasonable to predict that a subject who receives a score of 1 answered correctly only the first problem. Likewise, if a subject receives a score of 2, we would predict that he or she answered problems 1 and 2.

Because the reliability of the scale depends on our ability to reproduce perfectly statement responses, a method of checking the degree of reliability is needed. Guttman has worked out such a method. It is accomplished with the *coefficient of reproducibility (r)*. Mathematically the formula can be represented as follows.

$r = 1 - e/nk$

Where: e = number of errors in predicting

n = number of subjects
k = number of statements on the scale

For example, with a four-statement scale, the following predictions would be made for scores of 4, 3, 2, 1, and 0.

Score	Statement Responses
4	+ + + +
3	+ + + −
2	+ + − −
1	+ − − −
0	− − − −

Any other series of plusses and minuses for a subject would constitute an error. If a subject with a score of 3 had scored + + − + our prediction would have created an error, as we would have predicted the preceding order (+ + + −) for a score of 3. The coefficient of reproducibility ranges between 0 and 1.00, where 0 indicates no predictability and 1.00 indicates perfect predictability. *Scalability is said to exist if the coefficient of reproducibility is equal to or greater than 0.9.* If the coefficient of reproducibility does not reach 0.9, the scale is questionable and we should reexamine the order of the statements. However, reordering the statements is not always the answer. A low coefficient of reproducibility may not necessarily be the result of faulty ordering but rather may be the result of a multidimensional set of statements (i.e., more than one concept being measured with the set of items) [19]. With a low coefficient of reproducibility, it is sometimes difficult to determine whether the set of statements was actually multidimensional or whether irrelevant statements were included in the pool.

Paul Wallin [20] has developed a Guttman scale for measuring women's neighborliness. (See Figure 8.6.) The scale consists of twelve statements and can be scored by counting each GN (greater neighborliness) answer as 1 and each LN (lesser neighborliness) as 0. The coefficient of reproducibility of the scale from two samples of women was 0.920 and 0.924. The scale is included in its entirety on the next page.

Semantic-Differential Scales

The semantic-differential scaling system, one of the oldest measuring devices, depends on a collection of opposite-pair adjectives with 7 to 11 scale points related to a specific concept [21]. The opposite-pair adjectives are selected to gauge three aspects of the concept being measured: *evaluation, potency,* and *activity.* The instrument may include up to nine such semantic-differential scales for each of these dimensions, and each scale is marked from 1 to 7 or 1 to 11. Statements may also be reversed to avoid response sets. For instance, on the question "How do you view football?," the following adjective pairs might be used:

EVALUATION Dimension
Bad   Good
Boring   Interesting
Harmful   Beneficial

A Guttman Scale for Measuring Women's Neighborliness

Variable Measured: The neighborliness of women under sixty years of age.

Description: This instrument is a unidimensional Guttman scale consisting of twelve items. The scale items can be simply scored for any sample by counting each GN (greater neighborliness) answer as 1 and each LN (lesser neighborliness) as 0. The possible range of scores is 12 to 0.

Where Published: Paul Wallin, "A Guttman Scale for Measuring Women's Neighborliness," *The American Journal of Sociology* 59 (1953): 243–46. Copyright 1953 by the University of Chicago.

Reliability: The coefficient of reproducibility of the scale from two samples of women was .920 and .924.

Validity: Face validity.

1. How many of your best friends who live in your neighborhood did you get to know since you or they moved into the neighborhood? Two or more (*GN*); one or none (*LN*).
2. Do you and any of your neighbors go to movies, picnics, or other things like that together? Often or sometimes (*GN*); rarely or never (*LN*).
3. Do you and your neighbors entertain one another? Often or sometimes (*GN*); rarely or never (*LN*).
4. If you were holding a party or tea for an out-of-town visitor, how many of your neighbors would you invite? Two or more (*GN*); one or none (*LN*).
5. How many of your neighbors have ever talked to you about their problems when they were worried or asked you for advice or help? One or more (*GN*); none (*LN*).
6. How many of your neighbors' homes have you ever been in? Four or more (*GN*); three or less (*LN*).
7. Do you and your neighbors exchange or borrow things from one another such as books, magazines, dishes, tools, recipes, preserves, or garden vegetables? Often, sometimes, or rarely (*GN*); none (*LN*).
8. About how many of the people in your neighborhood would you recognize by sight if you saw them in a large crowd? About half or more (*GN*); a few or none (*LN*).
9. With how many of your neighbors do you have a friendly talk fairly frequently? Two or more (*GN*); one or none (*LN*).
10. About how many of the people in your neighborhood do you say "Hello" or "Good morning" to when you meet them on the street? Six or more (*GN*); five or less (*LN*).
11. How many of the names of the families in your neighborhood do you know? Four or more (2); one to three (1); none (0).
12. How often do you have a talk with any of your neighbors? Often or sometimes (*GN*); rarely or never (*LN*).

FIGURE 8.6   Guttman Scale

Source: P. Wallin, "A Guttman Scale for Measuring Women's Neighborliness," The American Journal of Sociology 59 (1953): 243–45. Reprinted by permission of the University of Chicago Press.

POTENCY Dimension

Weak	Strong
Cheap	Expensive
Unimportant	Important

ACTIVITY Dimension

Slow	Fast
Quiet	Loud
Simple	Complex

The semantic-differential scale correlates well with other scales and appears somewhat more straightforward and direct in its approach to the rating problem. There is greater flexibility in the selection of opposite adjective pairs. As with other scale techniques, a semantic-differential scale should be pretested in a pilot group to assess the validity of terms and the need for change.

Comparison of Scaling Techniques

With the proliferation of scaling techniques for measurement, you might begin to question the relationship of one scaling technique to another. Do the different scaling techniques yield similar results? Veevers [22] attempted to answer this question by investigating drinking attitudes and drinking behavior using Thurstone scales, Likert scales, itemized rating scales, and graphic self-rating. One hundred thirty-three items were developed from the literature on alcohol use, and sixty-seven judges from diverse backgrounds were asked to evaluate the statements. Twenty-one statements were selected and split into two equivalent scales, with one statement common to both scales. The graphic self-rating was determined by having subjects indicate a position by circling a number on a continuum. The subject's own drinking behavior was measured by the Alberta Quantity Frequency Index (AFQ Index) developed by Maxwell [23]. Respondents were categorized into six groups ranging from abstainers to heavy drinkers. Veevers concludes that with the exception of the graphic self-rating, all of these scaling techniques yield essentially the same results.

Nonreactive Measures

By now you may have the impression that the researcher conventionally applies a scale of some sort to individuals or groups in order to measure. Certainly, such measures have drawbacks. Respondents, for example, may counterfeit their true response patterns to fit the researchers' expectations, or answer when they may not know or care. Or the researcher may distort the world in terms of personal biases. Researchers do use other measures to help circumvent such problems. Nonreactive measures permit the world to speak for itself in its own way. Such measures are called *nonreactive* because *the source of inquiry is operating on its own environment without being changed or affected by the researcher's act of measurement.* Although mentioned here in our discussion of quantitative research, these three measures are also widely used in qualitative research (see Chapter 12).

Physical Traces

An unannounced head count of those attending religious services at a large sample of churches would give a better estimate of church attendance than members' estimates and reports of their own attendance in response to an interview. Photographs taken from the air provide evidence for counting and estimating crowd size, and this kind of evidence is sometimes more trustworthy than official reports. For example, the reported size of crowds turning out for public celebrations varies by a factor of ten between police, news reporters, and the organizers' estimates. The historical shifts in patterns of consumption and evidence of change in cultural interest are reflected in the trash dumps of some cities. Many of the discarded items are dated, and the chronology is suggested by their depth in the layers of refuse.

Historical and Public Records

The vast array of historical records, both recent and ancient, is an almost infinite source for productive research. Durkheim [24], almost a century ago, used contemporary newspaper and government records from many counties and cities to compare suicide rates by marital status, by occupation, by religion, and by time of year to show that the rate of suicide is partly a negative function of people's involvement in society. Rogoff [25] used the occupations entered in marriage license applications by grooms for themselves and their fathers as evidence in intergenerational occupational mobility. Newspapers often maintain complete files of all past issues of the newspaper for the researcher who wants to find detailed information on the records of local athletic teams, the quality and amount of reported social activities, labor and commercial activities, changes in process and product emphasis, from one decade to the next. To find a sample of firstborn six-year-olds, a researcher checked birth announcements in the local paper files six years earlier, noting the sex of the child and the names of parents. Checking these with current telephone listings indicated which children were still in town, and a telephone call determined whether the child was firstborn.

Many kinds of social processes demand a span of time such as two, three, or four decades or in some cases a century for proper measurement. For example, suppose we wanted to examine the changes in the intergenerational rate of reproduction. Birth registration has been fairly complete and constant in certain cities. What has been the trend, comparing 1920, 1940, 1960, and 1980 for the age of the mother at first and last birth? What has been the trend in homelessness, changes in funding of public and private social service programs, and the pattern and frequency of health care programs for teenage mothers? What are the primary trends in government service, influence, and intervention, comparing local, state, and national levels? These kinds of questions can be approached through the use of a variety of public and private records.

Content Analysis

Content analysis is a form of measurement applied to text of various kinds. Such text may be anything in written form, such as personal letters, newspaper reports, government documents, advertising, transcriptions of recorded conversations, movie scripts, children's essays, period literature, technical journals, plays, song lyrics, magazines, and sacred writings. And the possible kinds of measurements that can be achieved with content analysis are just as diverse. Item counts include the number of reports published in a given time period on political, military, social, or economic events [26]. Quantity may be given by estimates of word count. In analyzing factors stressed in newspapers, the number of column inches may indicate relative importance of subject matter. This may be weighted by prominence of display on the early pages of the newspaper or as a lead article in a journal.

Topical analysis combines an identified range of topics with a frequency count, but the primary aim is usually to make inferences about the culture. Thomas and Znaniecki [27] collected several hundred personal letters between Polish immigrants in Chicago and their relatives in Poland. Znaniecki translated these from Polish into English. Their content analysis demonstrated the kind of family ties and the unaccustomed personal problems the immigrants had in making the transition from the highly supportive culture of the rural Polish village to the impersonal and nonsupportive culture of Chicago. The letters also demonstrated explicit pressures on relatives still in Poland to come to the United States to reunite the families. Support of this cultural transplant is still evident in Chicago and other cities where Polish workers were so eagerly sought by U.S. industrialists.

The Theory of Measurement

Like other processes in social work research, the measurement processes we have been discussing are guided by theory. The theory and set of assumptions underlying measurement are always open to question, but in plain honesty, we must state what they are and then allow you, the reader, to draw your own conclusions about how plausible the theory really is. The following discussion concerns the theory underlying measurement.

The True Quantity

Quantitative research always aims at the actual, real, or true dimensions of the concept being studied. In other words, it assumes an empirical paradigm (see the discussion of paradigms in Chapter 4). A city has an actual population at any given moment in time. It is this actual population that a demographer considers in making projections about increases or decreases in the future size of the city. Presumably, but more problematically, a marriage can be assessed at any given time as to its relative strength. Such elements as the degree of commitment of each spouse to the other and to the family, the support and influence of close relatives, the pressures of work and community, and the resources of each spouse to meet the varying demands of the marriage could all be brought together in an instrument that would give at least a rudimentary measure of how strong the marriage actually is. The size of a city may be easier to measure than the strength of a marriage, but similar, if not identical, principles go into both.

To evaluate or measure the true properties of a concept, we work from sense data that have exact quantities. For this, four things are required: (1) a conceptual model that defines the case, (2) an empirical definition of its properties, (3) actual cases that fit the concept, and (4) a recognition of what the indicators will tell us when we have seen them [28]. It is important that the language used in assigning numbers to properties be consistent and applied under a set of rules [29]. However, despite our efforts, we can never be sure the measurement we make is the measure of the true quantity.

The Measured Quantity

Basically, a measure of some concept is a logical construct that can only approximately map reality. For example, the smaller a set of numbers, the more accurate a count is likely to be. If we say there are three boys "out there," or seven horses, the accuracy of these statements is pretty good. *But as the count increases, the true quantity is more open to doubt.* When frequency counts are in the thousands, we find real difficulty in verifying their accuracy. In counts of millions, we are taking things very much on faith. When it comes to ratios and proportions, the numbering system becomes quite inexact. One divided by three, seven, and nine cannot be exactly expressed in decimals. Generally, then, the use of numbers to represent a measure is an approximation. "The notion that any correction beyond what we have the instruments and art to make is a mere fiction of the mind, useless and incomprehensible," said Hume 200 years ago, and his statement is as reasonable today as it was then.

Types of Errors

Given that measurement can only approximate reality, there is likely some difference between the true quantity and the measured quantity. In effect, error is virtually inevitable. "Everyone makes mistakes." This old saying should be forever chiseled into the front of our minds when we seek to measure. However, knowing what kinds of mistakes are most likely to be made is going a long way in reducing them.

Error tends to balloon and magnify in the successive steps of the research process and quickly invalidates any evidence the scientist may claim to find. **The most important and immediate task of the serious researcher is to control and reduce measurement error to a practical minimum.**

Systematic Error

Systematic error is a form of bias in the measurement process that usually distorts the data in one direction. In other words, *systematic error will result in respondents' scores being consistently too high or consistently too low.* A weighing scale misadjusted by two pounds when nothing is on the platform systematically makes all weighings two pounds too heavy. Systematic error may be induced with human subjects by cues from the researcher or by the makeup of the research instrument. A researcher who, for example, is attempting to prove a hypothesis may faithfully record favorable results while sometimes neglecting to record unfavorable results. This would result in systematic error favorable to the researcher's hypothesis. Systematic error will also result from respondents' either knowing or guessing the desired outcome. Whenever there is a choice, the respondents will often select the choice believed to be the most favorable or most popular. The respondent easily controls the impressions given, and most respondents make the impression positive [30]. In fact, many respondents exaggerate their position on a question beyond what is habitual for them when they know they are under observation.

Random Error

Random error is a form of bias in which distortions in the measurement process result in fluctuations on either side of the true quantity. A large volume of small random errors tends to balance out in positive and negative fluctuations around the true values. If the random errors are very large, they may make the whole research project useless because they conceal the central tendency with a very wide margin of error. If there are only one or two pieces of data, random errors on each may completely distort the facts. Increasing the number of items helps to distribute such errors more uniformly on both sides of the true average.

Suppose we measured the social activity of college students at a university by recording the number of persons each individual talked with in the course of a regular weekday at school. A sample of 300 students is randomly selected from the total of those attending the university. The total population of 15,000 students would report some exact number of conversation partners, and this population average would probably be slightly higher or lower than that reported by the 300 students actually sampled. The difference in the count recorded of an unbiased sample and the count that would come from the population is random error resulting from the sampling selection process. A relatively small random sample cannot exactly match the exact distribution of the whole population.

Sources of Measurement Error

There are several common sources of measurement error, whether they are systematic or random. An awareness and understanding of these error sources can help you to avoid these pitfalls.

Instability in the Property

Measurement processes are degraded by a broad variety of factors, including instability in the property being measured [31, 32]. In other words, many of the social properties we might wish to measure are inherently fluctuating. An individual varies considerably from day to day and from hour to hour. Response to any standard stimuli will lag more or less in time and will fluctuate in intensity or depth of response. The researcher can measure several times, hopefully at representative levels of the intensity cycle, but the respondent's constant shifting makes the evaluation irregular and masks the "true quantity." Social phenomena with rather long time cycles (e.g., the effects of divorce on children over their lifetimes) challenge the skill of the researcher to keep track of all the relevant variables.

Instability in Measuring Instruments

In all research, the measuring instrument contributes systematic error to all measurements. It is the researcher's duty to check and recheck the instruments whenever they are used, to guard against contamination of the data. Electrical and electronic circuits fail without any external indication of change. Settings and control switches are bumped into the wrong position. A researcher unknowingly administers the wrong form of a survey instrument, and the respondents are unaware. Questionnaires can easily become outmoded in three to five years so that the responses to items on racial attitudes, sexual behavior, or political concerns are not at all comparable to those of the earlier studies or to the intent of the researcher.

A researcher who uses the same instrument over several years is likely to undergo basic changes in orientation and judgmental standards. The instruments become too familiar, and the researcher may skip rapidly over detail that received more meticulous attention in the earlier phase of the research. Control of measurement error demands that the researcher guard against such lapses and gradual changes. This problem is partially resolved by keeping organized notes and records of all events in the research process, and through frequent review of definitions, rules, and conventions of research, plus conferences with colleagues and assistants to revalidate the primary measures.

Transient Personal Factors

Errors of the personal type result when respondents are careless in reading and responding to questions. Carelessness may be attributed to such factors as fatigue, hunger, or general bad mood. When such personal factors are present, the result will be wide differences in the quality of responses. The responsible researcher will try to verify the appropriateness of each respondent's answers.

Situational Factors

In everyday activities, temporary but major events may be significant for the researcher. Among many that we could consider is *noise*. An interview can succeed well only in a fairly private environment. The researcher must provide suitable accommodations or check to be sure that the interviewee's situation provides such a place. For example, empty classrooms and main offices in public schools are poor places to interview teachers or students. But the school authorities usually know of a more adequate place if the interviewer explains the need. Other situational factors might include a poorly heated or cooled facility, inadequate lighting, uncomfortable desks, and interruptions.

Variation in Administering Research Instruments

Measurement can easily be flawed by careless administration of the instrument. Researchers have been known to leave a set of questionnaires for supervisors to administer without clear instructions, and the supervisors may then turn them over to an assistant who merely lets anyone who wishes fill one in. Each copy of a questionnaire should carry sufficient instructions, including specification of those for whom the instrument is intended. For instruments given to groups, the researcher should have a well-prepared paragraph explaining the project at least enough to orient and motivate the respondents. This should be read exactly the same way to each group. The researcher should remain available to answer any question that might arise. He or she should take notes on the apparent mood and spirit of the respondents. The date, time, and place should also be recorded, and note should be made of any comments about the research. The researchers should review the instruments as they are turned in for omitted items and should correct oversights where possible.

Item Sampling Error

Any measurement assumes a sampling of items randomly drawn from the universe of possible items. If we are interested, for example, in measuring self-esteem, we know that the items chosen to measure this concept are not the *only* items that could have been used. Had other items been chosen, our measurement would probably be somewhat different. With Thurstone scales, for example, we begin with one hundred statements. The final scale, though, has only twenty or so statements. If we had selected a different set of twenty from the original hundred, no doubt our measurement would be somewhat different. Or if we had started with a different set of one hundred statements, our measurement would be different. This difference is labeled item sampling error.

Clouded Instruments

Instrument error is a prime source of difficulty in developing convincing evidence on a social property. Exact measurements of temperature are slightly affected by the temperature of the thermometer. A cool thermometer slightly cools the mouth of the patient and slightly reduces the temperature reading from the correct value. A dipstick inserted in a container of fluid to measure the depth itself displaces fluid and falsifies the reading to varying degrees. This error would be small using a large stick in a ten-liter pot, and it would be large in a teacup of fluid. The precision possible in all measuring instruments is limited, and this is particularly true of instruments used in the social sciences [33, 34].

The basic requirement for an instrument applied in scientific research is that it permit clear, consistent, and relatively invariant values of a particular property when applied in the same way to the same object. Therefore, the instrument should be stable and inelastic when operated on the property it is designed to measure.

Mechanical and Processing Errors

In every phase of data processing, there is a constant threat of errors, large and small. Duplicated data cards are unintentionally retained in the deck. In very large decks of data cards, it is easily possible to leave out a large number of cards unless there is constant verification and rechecking to control against such an omission. In typing, transforming, and reproducing data, there is a human tendency to transpose numbers, decimal points, and letters unawares. One of the more humorous cases of data processing error was reported for the 1950 Census of Population:

> Our first clue was the discovery in the 1950 Census of Population of the United States of startling figures about the marital status of teenagers. There we found a surprising number of widowed 14-year-old boys and, equally surprising, a decrease in the number of widowed teen-age males at older ages. The numbers listed by the Census were 1670 at age 14; 1475 at age 15; 1175 at 16; 810 at 17; 905 at 18; and 630 at age 19. Not until age 22 does the listed number of widows surpass those at 14. Male divorces also decrease in number as age increases, from 1320 at age 14 to 575 at age 17. Smaller numbers of young female widows and divorcees are listed—565 widows and 215 divorcees at age 14. [35]

After some careful searching and some shrewd detective work, it was finally determined that a shift in columns during keypunching was the source of the error. And although the proportion of error was small, it was sizable enough to be detected.

The more transformation and recordings, the greater the potential for error through oversight, transposing, and mishandling. Most calculations should be performed twice to guard against such errors. Coded data should be thoroughly verified, code by code, against source documents. Careful editing and proofreading are mandatory, as the data and derived measures move step by step through the research process. The best that can be hoped is that through thorough and continued verification the total amount of error will be reduced to 1 percent. Whether it is, in most cases, will never really be known. The error problem is particularly serious when data are transformed to ratio form because small errors, both random and systematic, can be seriously magnified in ratio transformations.

Evaluating the Adequacy of a Measure

Validity

The validity of a measure refers to whether or not a measurement actually measures what it purports to measure. Does a certain scale, for example, really measure attitudes toward death? Is the wearing away of tiles on a floor really a measure of the popularity of a museum display? We have indicated throughout this chapter that measurement is the process whereby concepts are transformed into variables. Concepts, we know, exist on an abstract level; variables exist on a concrete level. And the gap between concept and variable may be quite large. What we are really concerned with is whether the concept and variable are synonymous. *A measure is said to be valid if the true quantity (concept) and the measured quantity (variable) are one and the same.* Although we know, in theory, that there is a true quantity for any concept, we also know, in reality, that this true quantity cannot be identified. If validity is the degree to which the true quantity and the measured quantity match and if the true quantity cannot be identified, then validity cannot be directly tested. *There is, in fact, no direct test of validity.* Hence, we do the next best thing; we establish validity through indirect tests. There are several techniques that can be employed to establish validity, and these result in different types of validity. Some of the more frequently used include face, content, concurrent, predictive, construct, and discriminant validity.

Face Validity

Face validity refers to the apparent reasonableness of the measure. A medicine flask with a false bottom would have face validity, even if the buyer had no idea how much fluid should be contained in a four-ounce flask that it resembles. A measure with face validity has no obvious characteristics that make it appear incorrect for the property it is to measure. A twenty-dollar bill in U.S. currency bearing Lincoln's picture lacks face validity as a measure of dollars because Jackson's face belongs on the twenty-dollar bill. If a counterfeit twenty-dollar bill bore Jackson's face, and was generally true to the engraving and printing standards of regular currency, it would have face validity. An instrument is said to have face validity if, *on the face of it*, it appears to measure what it purports to measure. This technique is primarily an "eyeballing" technique and does not require stringent statistical procedures.

Content Validity

Content validity indicates that the measuring device does incorporate the essence of the property it purports to measure. Tape measures, when stretched taut, have the property of linearity on a relatively inelastic line. Color samples of paint may incorporate rectangles of the actual paint, in which case they have high content validity in "measuring" color intensity and hue to be found in the actual commercial paint. But if the colors were printed in printer's ink to resemble the actual colors in the bulk paint, they would probably fall short of content validity. A questionnaire aiming to measure interpersonal adjustment in family relations would have content validity it if stuck realistically to questions relating to interpersonal adjustment. Content validity would be reduced if extraneous, unrelated questions were included [36].

Concurrent Validity

Concurrent validity has to do with existing conditions and existing relationships. *If a measure agrees with what we already know, it would be trustworthy in testing other populations* [37]. If a measure of alienation consistently identifies criminal offenders and psychiatric patients already known to be highly alienated against individuals and society, then the measure has concurrent validity. If a measure of mechanical aptitude were given to an appropriate sample of high school students and it failed to identify those who actually had high mechanical aptitude by other good criteria, and indicated high aptitude for those who had none, it would lack concurrent validity.

Predictive Validity

Predictive validity is established for a measure when it consistently predicts correctly the quality or property that it is constructed to measure. Many social work graduate schools consider applicants for advanced standing partly on the basis of their scores on a standardized test. The test incorporates the kinds of questions and problems used in social work, social welfare systems, and intervention strategies. If results on this test consistently identify those who later succeed well as social work students, then it has predictive validity. Generally, we are well satisfied with a measure that has predictive validity.

Construct Validity

A construct is an idea developed in the social scientist's mind that is used to define and identify objects and events. Constructs help to organize thinking and promote understanding on an abstract level. "Social cohesion" is a construct defining the force that binds individual members to a group. Cohesion is presumed to increase as members devote more time, energy, and resources to cooperating with others to achieve group goals. *A measure would have construct validity if, at the real-world level, it varied with other measures in ways suggested by the theory.* For example, if our measure of social cohesion varied with measures of members' time, energy, and resources in the presumed ways, we would say our measure had construct validity.

Many widely used constructs in social work and the social sciences are of doubtful construct validity. One such construct is the causal effect of the broken home on juvenile delinquency. Extensive research on this connection indicates that the broken home as such need not lead to delinquency since many delinquents come from intact homes, and the proportion of delinquent children among all children from broken homes is not consistently high. In short, the broken home as a construct to measure delinquency has rather low validity [38].

Discriminant Validity

A measure is said to have discriminant validity if the measure consistently identifies or differentiates the construct being measured from other constructs. If a measure correlates too highly with other measures from which it is supposed to differ, the measure is lacking in discriminant validity. We would not, for example, expect to find a strong relationship between education and social isolation. Dean [39], in seeking validation of his alienation scale, found a correlation of –0.07 (0.00 is no correlation at all) between social isolation and education, which is evidence of discriminant validity.

Reliability

Reliability in a measure means consistency of measurement. That is, **a measuring device is said to be reliable if it gives the same or almost exactly the same results on repeated measures of the same object, assuming that the object itself is stable.** A linear measuring tape that shrinks and expands both with temperature changes and with the strength of the pull on the tape would be unreliable. A questionnaire containing indecisive questions to which the same subject would answer differently depending on his mood at the time would also be unreliable because of the inconsistency of response. An interviewer who varied the depth and wording of questions depending on the widely variant quality of his or her own reaction to the respondent would be unreliable as a measuring instrument since the measures would indicate the interviewer's unique pattern of personal preferences more than the objective characteristics of the respondents. It is not uncommon for measures to reveal more of the character and preferences of the researcher than of the objects of research [40]. Several techniques for establishing reliability have received wide use. Three of the most frequently used are test–retest, split-half, and internal consistency.

Test–Retest Reliability

One technique for assessing reliability is to make repeated measures of the same object, perhaps with different testers. If the differences are very slight (usually determined through correlation techniques), the instrument is considered reliable. If the differences are relatively large, the instrument is considered unreliable. In the case of questionnaires, the test–retest application permits comparison of results if the researcher can assume that there was no marked learning between the repeated measures. Test–retest also assumes stability in the property tested, and when the subjects are human beings, they may be much more or much less responsible if they completed the questionnaire at different times in the week [41].

Split-Half Reliability

If the measurement is relatively long and the items are well mixed in sequence, *the items may be divided into two halves and the responses comprising each half may also be used to give a measure of reliability.* Frequently these two halves are created by assigning the odd-numbered items to one half and the even-numbered items to the other. It is not a good idea to assign the first 50 percent of questionnaire items to one half and the second 50 percent to the other. Transient personal factors and item difficulty might influence the reliability coefficient. If the correlation between pairs of subscores for the split-half is large, the test is judged reliable. If the results are highly varied, the correlation coefficient will be low (i.e., close to zero) and the measure is judged unreliable [42].

Internal Consistency: Cronbach's Alpha

A questionnaire-based scale can be tested for internal consistency by *comparing the variation for any single item with the variation of the entire set of questions.* This measure, called Cronbach's alpha, ranges from a maximum value of 1.00 to 0.00. An alpha value of less than 0.25 shows very little consistency for a single item to vary in the same way as the total set of questions of which the item is a part. There should be at least five questions in the set to make this measure meaningful. An alpha value of 0.8 would show a relatively high consistency or internal agreement between an item and the set. The alpha coefficient is defined as follows:

$$\alpha = \frac{n}{n-1} \left[1 - \frac{\Sigma S_i^2}{S_x^2} \right]$$

Where: n = the number of questions in the set
S_i^2 = the variance of a single item
S_x^2 = the variance of the total set

If an item has a low alpha value, it should be dropped out of the set, and the alpha, when recomputed with the reduced set, will be higher. In addition, the instrument will measure more effectively.

The Relation between Validity and Reliability

Before leaving validity and reliability, a word must be said about the relationship between these two. Quite obviously, validity and reliability are not the same thing. **Whereas validity is concerned with whether or not we are measuring what we say we are measuring, reliability is concerned with the stability of a measure from one measurement to the next.** If the measured quantity matches the true quantity, we know we have achieved validity. If a measure is consistent from one measurement to the next, we know we have achieved reliability. *Validity, though, is not directly testable.* We cannot know for certain that the true quantity matches the measured quantity. On the other hand, *reliability is directly testable.* We can determine the degree to which a measure is consistent from one measurement to the next. Unfortunately, in social research, we usually demonstrate the tendency to reason, "If a measure is reliable, that is enough." We frequently attempt to establish reliability—but seldom validity. Hence, many of the measurements used in social research must rest on face validity. Our failure to establish validity probably stems in part from the fact that it cannot be directly tested, whereas reliability can be directly tested. Quite honestly, though, this is a mistake. If a measure is valid (if the measured quantity represents well the true quantity), we will get the same results from one measurement to the next. In essence, *a measure that is valid will also be reliable.* However, the reverse is not always true. *A measure that is reliable is not necessarily valid.* Bathroom scales that are set at two pounds instead of zero will consistently weigh everything two pounds too heavy. The measurement is not valid, but from one weighing to the next, the weight registered will be consistent. Consequently, it is reliable. As social work researchers, we need to expend greater energy establishing the validity of our measures. Reliability will be a natural consequence.

References

1. S. S. Stevens, "On the Theory of Scales and Measurements," *Science* (1946): 684, 677–80.
2. C. Lachenmeyer, *Essence of Social Research* (New York: The Free Press, 1973).
3. F. N. Kerlinger, *Foundations of Behavioral Research* (New York: Holt, Rinehart and Winston, 1979).
4. A. L. Stinchcombe and J. Wendt, "Theoretical Domains and Measurement in Social Indicator Analysis," in *Social Indicator Models*, K. Land and S. Spilerman, eds. (New York: Sage, 1975), p. 37.
5. H. M. Blalock and A. Blalock, *Methodology in*
   Social Research (New York: McGraw-Hill, 1968), p. 8.
6. W. S. Torgerson, *Theory and Methods of Scaling* (New York: Wiley, 1958), p. 10.
7. Stevens, "On the Theory of Scales and Measurements."
8. J. S. Coleman, *Introduction to Mathematical Sociology* (New York: Holt, Rinehart and Winston, 1964), p. 77.
9. K. C. Land and S. Spilerman, *Social Indicator Models: An Overview* (New York: Sage, 1975), p. 9.
10. O. D. Duncan, *Measuring Social Change via*

Replication Surveys (New York: Sage, 1975), p. 111.

11. J. C. Nunnally and W. H. Wilson, *Method and Theory for Developing Measures in Evaluation Research* (Beverly Hills, CA: Sage, 1975).

12. D. Miller, *Handbook of Research Design and Social Measurement* (New York: David McKay, 1975).

13. Survey Center Research, *General Social Science Survey Codebook* (Ann Arbor, MI: Institute of Social Research, University of Michigan, 1973), p. 540.

14. R. Ziller, J. Hagey, M. Smith, and B. Long, "Self-Esteem: A Self-Social Construct," *Journal of Consulting and Clinical Psychology* 33 (1946): 84–95.

15. Rensis Likert, "A Technique for the Measurement of Attitudes," *Archives of Psychology* 1932, No. 14.

16. Likert, "A Technique for the Measurement of Attitudes," p. 46.

17. G. Rotter, Attitudinal Points of Agreement and Disagreement," *Journal of Social Psychology* 86 (1972): 211–8.

18. L. Guttman, "The Basis for Scalogram Analysis," in *Measurement and Prediction*, S. A. Stouffer, ed. (Princeton, NJ: Princeton University Press, 1950).

19. Guttman, "The Basis for Scalogram Analysis."

20. Paul Wallin, "A Guttman Scale for Measuring Women's Neighborliness," *American Journal of Sociology* 59 (1953): 243–6.

21. J. G. Snider and C. E. Osgood, *Semantic Differential Technique: A Sourcebook* (Chicago: Aldine, 1969).

22. J. E. Veevers, "Drinking Attitude and Drinking Behavior: An Exploratory Study," *Journal of Social Psychology* 85 (1971): 103–9.

23. M. A. Maxwell, "A Quantity-Frequency Analysis of Drinking Behavior in the State of Washington," *Northwest Science* 32 (1958): 57–67.

24. E. Durkheim, *Suicide,* Translated by J. A. Spaulding and G. Simpson, G. Simpson, ed. (New York: The Free Press, 1964).

25. N. Rogoff, *Recent Trends in Occupational Mobility* (Glencoe, IL: The Free Press, 1953).

26. B. Berelson, *Content Analysis in Communication Research* (New York: Hafner, 1982).

27. W. I. Thomas and F. Znaniecki, *The Polish Peasant in Europe and America* (Chicago: University of Chicago Press, 1918).

28. M. Riley, *Sociological Research* (New York: Harcourt, Brace, Jovanovich, 1963), p. 328.

29. A. V. Cicourel, *Method and Measurement in Sociology* (Glencoe, IL: The Free Press, 1964), p. 15.

30. D. Phillips, *Abandoning Method* (San Francisco: Jossey-Bass, 1973), p. 42.

31. C. Selltiz, L. S. Wrightsman, and S. Cook, *Research Methods in Social Relations* (New York: Holt, Rinehart and Winston, 1976).

32. Miller, *Handbook of Research Design and Social Measurement.*

33. A. Kaplan, *Conduct of Inquiry* (San Francisco: Chandler, 1964).

34. Lachenmeyer, *Essence of Social Research.*

35. A. J. Coale and F. F. Stephan, "The Case of the Indians and the Teen-Age Widows," *Journal of the American Statistical Association* 57 (1962): 338.

36. Nunnally and Wilson, *Method and Theory for Developing Measures in Evaluation Research.*

37. J. B. Williamson, D. A. Karp, and J. R. Dalphin, *The Research Craft: An Introduction to Research Methods* (Boston: Little, Brown, 1977).

38. Nunnally and Wilson, *Method and Theory for Developing Measures in Evaluation Research.*

39. D. Dean, "Alienation: Its Meaning and Measurement," *American Sociological Review* 25 (1961): 753–8.

40. T. Hirschi and H. C. Selvin, *Delinquency Research: An Appraisal of Analytical Methods* (New York: The Free Press, 1967).

41. Lachenmeyer, *Essence of Social Research.*

42. Williamson, et al., *The Research Craft.*

Chapter 9

Sampling

Some basic definitions
Why sample?
The representativeness of a sample
    The 1936 election
    The 1948 election
    The 1968 election
    The 1976 election
Sampling theory: how it works
    The population distribution
    The sample distribution
    The sampling distribution of
        sample means

Sampling plans
    Probability samples
    Nonprobability samples
    Combining probability and
        nonprobability sampling
        techniques
What size sample?
    z-score transformation
    Confidence interval estimates
    Determining sample size

By a small sample we may judge the whole piece. —CERVANTES

Some Basic Definitions

Sampling is a method of selecting some part of a group to represent the total [1]. In research, the total group is called the *population*, while that part of the total that is selected is called the *sample*. Sampling in social research can take place at several different stages of the process, including (1) the selection of research units, (2) the selection of research sites, and (3) the choice of indicators by which the researcher wishes to measure the theoretical concepts. Choosing the population (whether it be sites, individuals, groups, institutions, or indicators) and the method of sampling this population are very important steps in research. In this chapter, we examine the sampling process closely.

Why Sample?

The objective of sampling is to estimate population values from information contained in a sample. Suppose, for example, we wanted to know what proportion of people in the United States are happily married. We would probably select a sample of married Americans from the population and identify the proportion in the sample that report happy marriages. We might then reason that the proportion for the population is the same as that calculated for the sample. At first glance, such a procedure might seem careless. After all, if we really want to know something about a particular group, why not study everybody? But research would be tedious and often impossible if it always required that we study an entire population. It is also not very practical. Populations are usually too large, too obscure, or too inaccessible to study in their entirety. In our study of married Americans, for example, think of the hurdles we would encounter in trying to get information from all married couples. And if we were interested in studying some topics, such as prostitution or "swinging," the population would probably be both obscure and inaccessible. Thus, to facilitate our research efforts, we study samples and generalize to the total population. Sampling is a definite plus in our research endeavors and for several important reasons. Let's look at some of the reasons.

1. *Sampling reduces the length of time needed to finish a study.* If we were to conduct research using an entire population, the larger the population, the more time we would need to finish the study. Data collection takes time. And once collected, the data must be analyzed. Consider the Population Census Survey, which is conducted once every ten years. Data collection for the population of U.S. households takes approximately two months. But even more time-consuming are data coding and analysis. Some of the data collected from the 1990 census, for example, will not even be available until 1993.

2. *Sampling helps cut research costs and thus permits more diligent follow-up.* Generally speaking, the more people included in a study, the greater the cost. Every unit studied adds some cost to research, whether in data collection or data analysis, or both. And if that population is also geographically dispersed, there are even more costs. Consider the costs incurred by the federal government for the 1980 census—one billion dollars! By sampling from the population, one can reduce the cost of research substantially. In addition, more time can be devoted to locating and collecting data from all those units selected for the sample.

3. *Sampling allows for better supervision, record keeping, and training of researchers.* With fewer people to be studied, there is more time to invest in other phases of the research process. There is more time to train and supervise researchers. Such training, as we have already discovered, is important to the total research endeavor—especially if we are paying close attention to being as objective as possible in the collecting and coding of data.

4. *Sampling is almost as accurate as studying the entire population, and sometimes even more so.* It seems reasonable that studying an entire population would be more accurate than studying only a part of it. And although it may seem logical that studying a part of something could be about as accurate as studying the total, it seems absurd that it could be *more* accurate. Yet errors can spring from several sources. We may choose to study an entire population and then find ourselves scurrying with insufficient time for training, supervision, and record keeping. The resulting errors may be greater than the errors we would have sustained had we studied a sample. Recognizing this potential problem, the Bureau of the Census follows its decennial (every ten years) census with a sample survey for purposes of evaluating the data collected from the total population.

Without a doubt, sampling procedures have aided scientific research. Most likely, a considerable amount of research is conducted that would otherwise be impossible. But obviously not just any sample will do. If we estimate the proportion of happily married Americans by sampling only friends and acquaintances, for example, the estimate will probably be wrong. Using a sample value to estimate a population value is useful only if we can estimate correctly.

The Representativeness of a Sample

The best way to ensure that sample values correctly estimate population values is to select a *representative* sample. The results obtained from such a sample are what we would have found had we studied the entire population. Thus, **representativeness ensures the generalizability of the research conclusions** [2]. Establishing the representativeness of a sample can be tricky; ideally, we would need to compare our sample characteristics with the population characteristics. But when the population characteristics are difficult or impossible to obtain, this is not practical. In fact, a sample is sometimes selected and an estimate computed because a population characteristic is not known and cannot be determined. Consequently, the representativeness of a sample is often assumed rather than proved. We can strengthen the integrity of the assumption of representativeness, though, by considering two important factors.

The first factor is *the degree of precision with which the population is specified*. Confidence in representativeness increases if the population is well defined. The empirically defined population from which the sample is taken is called the *sampling frame*. We might, for example, be interested in studying all individuals currently enrolled in at least one credit hour in a U.S. college or university. Although this population might be difficult to access, it is defined. By the same token, if we wanted to study potential buyers of microcomputers, the population is less well defined. When a sample is selected from an unknown population or a poorly defined population (i.e., sampling frame), it is labeled biased. Usually such samples are controlled by unconscious selection procedures. Though such procedures may be thought of as "random," they probably are not. Smith, in his discussion of this problem, writes, "There are studies showing that if subjects are asked to sample 'randomly' from a universe of pebbles, they will unconsciously make biased selections—some will tend to pick smoother pebbles, others tend to pick larger pebbles, and some choose particularly colored pebbles" [3]. This tendency for people to have unconscious response biases is so well known to professional sampling experts that most respectable research organizations will not allow their interviewers to make any sampling decisions. Sometimes interviewers make the mistake of drawing a sample from a working population without having clearly identified the theoretical population to which they wish to generalize. The resulting bias is usually unmeasurable (we have no way of knowing how much), and our ability to generalize from sample to population becomes questionable.

The second important factor is *the heterogeneity or homogeneity of the population* —that is, how similar (homogeneous) or dissimilar (heterogeneous) population units are. The more alike the units of a population, the smaller the sample can be and still be representative. But remember, to identify the degree to which the population units are the same or different, the population must still be well defined.

An analysis of public opinion surveys is helpful in understanding the extent to which samples can represent populations. This is no easy task since changes in public opinion are largely unpredictable—responsive to external forces that are themselves unpredictable. Widely held general opinions, such as "Females are weak and need male protection," are not likely to change very rapidly. But opinions on specific topics and persons, such as presidential election polls, can shift dramatically from week to week in response to current events, and selecting a representative sample becomes a challenge. Because political polling was so instrumental in developing the art and science of sampling, a comparison of the political polls predicting the presidential elections in 1936, 1948, 1968, and 1976 is informative in understanding how sampling evolved.

The 1936 Election

In 1936, *Literary Digest* made a prediction that left its editors with egg on their faces. They predicted that Alfred M. Landon would win the presidency over Franklin D. Roosevelt by a landslide—in fact, by nearly 15 percentage points! Needless to say, *Literary Digest* was wrong even though they polled nearly 2 *million* voters. (As we said, the size of a sample may have little to do with its accuracy.) *Literary Digest*'s fatal mistake resulted from its definition of the population. Its sample was selected from a population defined with telephone directories and automobile registration records instead of from a listing of all registered voters in the United States. And while this sampling frame might have been sufficiently workable in the 1920–1932 elections, it was not workable in 1936. In the midst of the Great Depression, there was an unprecedented number of poor voting citizens who could not afford automobiles or telephones in their homes. Thus, they were not represented in the polls and the sample did not provide a representative cross section of U.S. voters.

Apparently, a majority of the poorer people (who were not included in the sample) voted for Roosevelt, while a majority of the richer people (who were included in the sample) voted for Landon as *Literary Digest* predicted. The sample was representative of rich voters, but it was not representative of all voters, rich and poor alike. A second survey was conducted in the same year by George Gallup, who correctly predicted that Roosevelt would win the election. Gallup succeeded where *Literary Digest* failed because his sample better ensured that all U.S. voters, both rich and poor, were represented in the poll.

The 1948 Election

Even though Gallup was very successful in predicting the 1936 election, he and most other political pollsters failed to predict the victory of Harry Truman over Thomas Dewey in the 1948 election. A combination of factors was responsible for this fiasco. First, regardless of the fact that public opinion steadily shifted toward Truman over the course of the campaign, most pollsters ended their polling too soon. Second and perhaps more important, the 1948 polls exposed the serious shortcoming of nonprobability sampling techniques. We will discuss this topic later in the chapter.

The 1968 Election

The 1948 election prompted a number of academic researchers to experiment with probability sampling techniques, and their findings showed such samples to be amazingly accurate. In the 1968 election, for example, the Gallup poll predicted that Richard Nixon would receive 43 percent of the vote and the Harris poll predicted 41 percent. Nixon's actual vote was 42.9 percent. Furthermore, both of these predictions were made using a sample of only 2,000 of the approximately 73 million voters from the population. Contrast this to the sample of 2 million voters used by *Literary Digest* to make an incorrect prediction in the 1936 election. Good sampling, at least on such discrete matters as for whom a person is going to vote, does work!

The 1976 Election

The results of the 1976 election polls seem to have rectified whatever harm the history of political polling brought to sampling. In the 1976 presidential election, Gerald Ford received 48.9 percent of the two-party vote, while Jimmy Carter received 51.1 percent. The week before the election, George Gallup, Louis Harris, Burus Roper, and the *New York Times* in collaboration with CBS conducted national polls. Regardless of the respondents who were undecided during the polling, the poll estimates were accurate. Discounting the "undecideds," the *Times*–CBS polls predicted 48.9 percent for Ford and 51.1 percent for Carter. The other three polls deviated from the actual vote by 0.6 to 1.6 percentage points. And again, approximately 2,000 voters were found to be representative of the nearly 80 million citizens voting. (Of course, polling companies are only one election away from disaster at any time, so they must be very careful in order to keep public confidence.)

The conclusion to be drawn here is that studying a sample can be as accurate as studying an entire population. In fact, despite early difficulties, public opinion polls have actually compiled a very good track record. The obvious question here then is, How is this possible? How can a sample provide us with as much or almost as much accuracy as the population? Let's take a look at how this works.

Sampling Theory: How It Works

If all members of a population had the same characteristics and were the same in every way, there would be no need for sampling. One unit would represent the entire population. But human beings, at least, are heterogeneous—different from each other in many ways. Any given human population, then, is composed of varied individuals. And any sample drawn from that population must contain essentially the same variations that characterize the entire population if we are to infer that the sample is representative of the population. To make such an inference, as we have already indicated, theoretically, we would have to compare the sample value to the population value to determine how similar they are. But most of the time the population value is neither known nor obtainable. Thus, we are left in the position of trying to determine whether a sample value is representative of an unknown population value. To overcome this obstacle, we employ statistical inference. **Statistical inference describes the process of inferring a population characteristic from a sample characteristic.** The use of statistical inference requires the consideration of three different and distinct distributions: the population distribution, the sample distribution, and the sampling distribution of sample means.

The Population Distribution

The population distribution is a map or plot of all of the unique values for the variable under study and the frequency of occurrence of each value. If we are studying many variables, we have many populations—in fact, one for each variable. For example, if we were studying housing sales in a large metropolitan area for 1978, we might be interested in (1) selling price, (2) mortgage price, (3) square footage, and (4) number of rooms. For each of these variables, there is a population distribution, and each has its own unique shape. Given every member of a population and a value for the variable being considered, the exact shape of each population can be determined by plotting all unique values and the frequency of occurrence of each. The shape of the population distribution for the variable "number of rooms," for example, might appear as we have pictured it in Figure 9.1. From this population distribution, we can see that there are a few houses selling that have only three rooms and a few houses selling that have eleven rooms, but most houses selling have six rooms. The population distribution for the variable "selling price" might appear as it is pictured in Figure 9.2. From this distribution we can see that there are a few houses selling for $10,000 and a few houses selling for $120,000 but most houses are priced between $30,000 and $40,000. Most of the time, though, we do not deal directly with populations since most are so large and/or obscure that it is impossible to evaluate every unit.

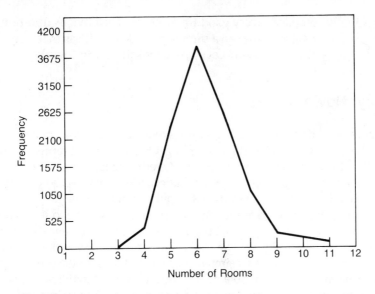

FIGURE 9.1   Population Distribution for "Number of Rooms"

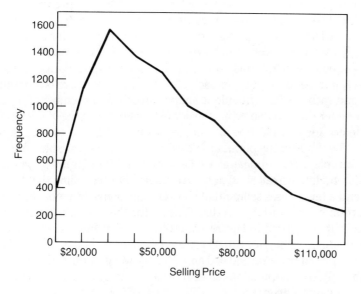

FIGURE 9.2   Population Distribution for "Selling Price"

The Sample Distribution

The sample distribution is the distribution that we deal with directly. **The sample distribution refers to the way in which the variable as measured is distributed in the sample.** We have reproduced in Figure 9.3 the sample distribution for the variable "number of rooms" for a sample of size 100. If the sample is representative of the population, the two distributions should be similar in shape and, theoretically, the sample distribution and the population distribution should have the same mean and the same standard deviation. *The difference between the population distribution and the sample distribution is that the population distribution is a mapping or plotting of all units or members, whereas the sample distribution is a mapping of only a part of the population.* Notice, for example, that Figure 9.3 has the same approximate shape as Figure 9.1. Similarly, Figure 9.4 has the same approximate shape as Figure 9.2. But although they are similar, they are not exact. And unless they are exact, there is sampling error. Regardless of how careful we are, errors in sampling will always result just from the "luck of the draw." Suppose, for example, we selected three samples from our population of housing sales in a large metropolitan area. The variable of interest is "selling price." Let's assume that the population of housing sales in this area for 1978 is 10,000, with a mean selling price of $36,762.67 and a standard deviation of 15,078.88. Each of the three samples drawn includes 100 sales records. We calculate the mean selling price of a house for each of these three samples:

Sample 1: $36,133.19
Sample 2: $38,268.22
Sample 3: $35,159.56

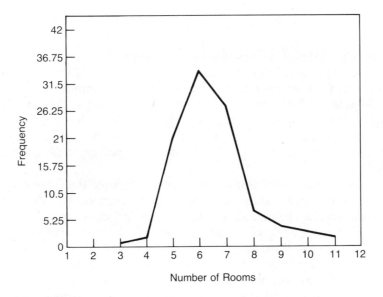

FIGURE 9.3   Sample Distribution for "Number of Rooms"

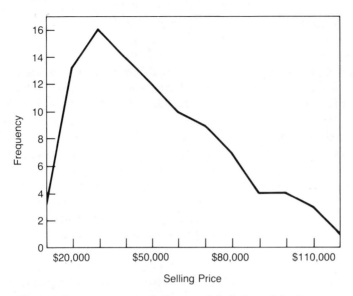

FIGURE 9.4 Sample Distribution for "Selling Price"

Notice the error encountered by sampling. *The magnitude of the error can be computed as the difference between the population mean and a sample mean.* And this error cannot be completely eliminated because the luck of the draw will always result in some differences from one sample to the next, regardless of how many samples we draw.

The Sampling Distribution of Sample Means

One way of tackling sampling error is to (1) select several samples, (2) calculate the mean for each sample, and (3) average these sample means. In other words, **we calculate the mean of the sample means as an estimate of the population mean.** This procedure helps to eliminate variability associated with the luck of the draw. For our three samples, if we average the means, we get $36,520.32, which *is* closer to the true population mean (i.e., there is less error). Theoretically, the more sample means we have to include in this averaging process, the closer we will get to the true population mean.

If we were to draw many, many samples of a designated size (in our case, size 100) from this population and calculate the mean for each sample, these sample means could themselves be treated as a distribution. In fact, we could draw every possible sample of some designated size (e.g., 100), calculate the mean for each sample, and then map or plot these means. Such a plot even has a special name: *the sampling distribution of sample means.* And any sampling distribution of sample means will always have three important characteristics (Figure 9.5).

1. *This distribution will take the form of a normal distribution regardless of the shape*

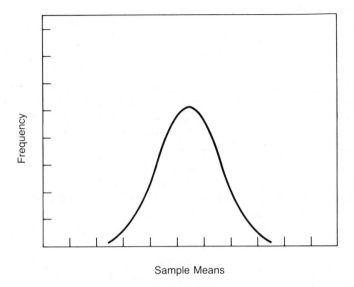

FIGURE 9.5 Sampling Distribution of Sample Means

of the population distribution.[1] Even if the variable in the population is distributed in a nonnormal fashion (as is selling price), the distribution of sample means will be normal. A note of caution here, though: the more the population distribution deviates from normal, the larger the samples must be in order to produce a distribution of sample means that is normally distributed.

2. *The mean of the sampling distribution will equal the mean of the population from which the samples were drawn.* Recall from our earlier example that when we averaged our three sample means, the average was closer to the true population mean than any single sample estimate. And if we were to draw every sample of size 100 from this population, calculate the mean for each, and average these estimates, this average would not only be closer, it would be *equal* to the population mean.

3. The third characteristic has to do with the standard deviation or spread among the sample means comprising this distribution. *The standard deviation of the sampling distribution of sample means will equal the standard deviation of the population divided by the square root of the sample size:*

$$\sigma_{\bar{x}} = \sigma / \sqrt{n}$$

Notice from this formula that unless we draw samples of size 1, the standard deviation of the sampling distribution will be less than the standard deviation of the

---

[1]By normal we mean a symmetrical bell-shaped curve. All normal distributions have four properties: (1) They are symmetrical. (2) The curve never touches the base line since theoretically scores could extend in either direction to infinity. (3) The scores tend to cluster toward the center. (4) The mean, median, and mode are all equal and all in the center of the curve.

population. In effect, the plot of sample means forms a closer-knit distribution than the population distribution. This is because when we increase the number of population members that comprise a sample, we also decrease the likelihood of drawing a sample with a mean extremely different from the population mean. In our three samples, while there was variation between sample means, no single sample mean was really extreme. Restated, *as we increase sample size, we can expect less variation from one sample mean to the next.* In fact, if every sample included every population unit, there would be *no* variation between sample means; they would all be the same.

It is generally costly in both time and resources to draw just one sample, let alone many samples. And drawing all samples to create the sampling distribution of sample means is simply not practical. Thus, in any research endeavor, we usually select only one sample from the population. But we also know that our sample is just one of many, many (in fact an infinite number) samples of this size that could be selected from the population. For example, when we draw one sample of 100 housing sales records from the population of 10,000 sales records, we know that in the population there are many, many more samples of size 100 that could be drawn. In short, the real importance of the sampling distribution of sample means lies in the fact that it can be used to determine the probability of likelihood of drawing just one sample with a particular sample mean from the population. (For more on the sampling distribution of sample means, see Chapter 15.)

Sampling Plans

In modern sampling theory, a basic distinction is made between probability and nonprobability samples. **The distinguishing characteristic of probability samples is that the researcher can specify for each unit in the population the likelihood that it will be included in the sample.** In the simplest case, each unit of the population has the same chance of being included in the sample. It is because of this known probability of inclusion that we can determine sampling error—or variability associated with the luck of the draw. **In contrast, with nonprobability samples, there are population units that have no chance or that have an unknown chance of being included in the sample.** In other words, a restriction on the definition of the population is implied. If a complete listing of the population is not possible, then we cannot specify the population, and the concept of sampling error or variability associated with the luck of the draw is not meaningful.

Suppose, for example, in our study of housing sales, we had decided to make our sample all those houses that sold in the month of January. Certainly, with this procedure, not all housing sales have a known chance of being included in the sample. And because they don't, we cannot identify the probability of any single housing sale being included. The difference between the population mean and the sample mean is no longer just a function of sampling error or variation associated with the luck of the draw. Now we have introduced a selection bias (month of January) as well. And we do not know to what extent the difference in the population mean and the sample mean is a function of one or the other. If we calculate what we think is the sampling error, as we would with a probability sample, these two types of error will be entangled. They simply cannot be separated, and thus the concept of sampling error no longer makes sense. In other words, *for nonprobability samples, we cannot determine our sampling error.* Although this limitation might be troublesome, it is not fatal. In fact, there are a number of research situations in which nonprobability samples are really more practical and more useful.

Probability Samples

Simple Random Samples

Simple random sampling is the basic probability sampling design, and it is incorporated in all of the more elaborate designs. **A simple random sample is defined as a sample in which every member of the population has an equal and independent chance of being selected.** If, for example, in our population of 10,000 housing sales records, a simple random sample of 100 is to be selected, the probability of any population unit's being included in the sample is 100/10,000, or .01. Randomness in the sample selection process can be accomplished with one of two methods: *lottery* or *a table of random numbers.* Both methods require a listing of the population units. With the lottery method, every member of the population is represented on a piece of paper and dropped into a lottery cylinder. The pieces of paper are mixed well and the sample is drawn. With a table of random numbers (see Appendix B), we begin by assigning all population units a unique number (0 to N). Our starting point in the sample selection process is a random number (i.e., one that is randomly selected from a table of random numbers). Numbers from a table of random numbers are read in order (up, down, or sideways—the direction is not important as long as we are consistent). When a number that appears in the table corresponds to a number on the population list, that unit is included in the sample. This procedure is continued until the desired sample size is reached. Notice that with either of these methods, the selection of any given unit does not restrict the selection of other units.

Systematic Random Samples

A systematic sample is one that approximates a simple random sample. To obtain a systematic sample, we begin with a listing of all elements in the designated population. We then determine the desired sample size and divide it into the population size to give us our increment value, labeled N. **The sample selected is composed of every Nth element from the population.** If, for example, we wanted a sample of 100 housing sales and if the number of units in the population equaled 10,000, we would divide 10,000 by 100. In effect, every 100th element in the population would be selected for the sample. But in order to ensure randomness, the first selection must be determined by some random process such as a table of random numbers or lottery. A word of caution here: it is a good idea to begin with a randomly ordered population list. Consider, for example, what might happen if we ordered the sales by month of sale. If a disproportionate number of sales occurred in the months of June to August as compared with March to May, our listing of the population would ensure the inclusion of a larger number of sales for the summer months. The ordering itself would introduce a selection bias such that every sale would not have an equal chance of being included. Those homes selling in the June-to-August period would have a greater chance of being included than those selling in the March-to-May period. This selection bias can be eliminated by beginning with a population list that is randomly ordered. All in all, systematic random sampling is much easier than simple random sampling, even though many researchers treat systematic and simple random samples as one and the same [4]. Grinnell also points out that systematic sampling is obviously easier to use when the size of the *sampling frame* (a list of the population) is large or lengthy. It is also often used as one phase of a sampling design, in combination with two or more sampling procedures [5].

Stratified Random Samples

The stratified sample is still another modification of a simple random sample. But with stratified samples, **the population is divided into layers, or strata.** Stratification is especially useful when a population is characterized as heterogeneous but consists of a number of homogeneous subpopulations or strata. When a population is homogeneous, little or no benefit is obtained from stratification. Suppose, for example, we wished to study a large urban public assistance agency employing workers from different ethnic backgrounds: black, white, Asian, and Hispanic. We decide to study a sample of 80 workers. If we want each ethnic group to be represented in the sample, we might divide the workers into strata according to their ethnic classifications and select from each stratum. Basically, there are two ways to determine the number of elements being sampled from each stratum: proportional and disproportional.

Proportional Stratified Samples   Of the stratified samples, proportional stratified samples are perhaps more frequently used by researchers. With this procedure, **the number of items selected from each stratum will be proportional to the size of the stratum within the population.** In our example of public assistance workers, if the black workers comprise 30 percent of the population of workers, they should also comprise 30 percent of the population of the sample. The following simple equation can be used to identify the number of elements to be selected for each stratum in the sample.

$$n(E) = N(E)/(N)(n)$$

Where $n(E)$ = the size of the ethnic stratum in the sample
n = the desired sample size
$N(E)$ = the size of the ethnic stratum in the population
N = the population size

If we were to apply this formula to our example, the number of workers in each ethnic group to be included in the sample would be as follows (with rounding to the nearest whole number):

Black workers   = 120/(400)(80) = 24
White workers   = 160/(400)(80) = 32

Asian workers   = 56/(400)(80) = 11
Hispanic workers = 64/(400)(80) = 13
Total sample size = 24 + 32 + 11 + 13 = 80

This type of sampling design assures representativeness with respect to the property forming the strata and decreases the chances of excluding members of the population because of the classification process. However, it requires accurate information on population proportions for each stratum. And if stratified lists are not available, it may simply be too costly to prepare them [6].

Disproportionate Stratified Samples   With disproportionate stratified samples, *the sample size of each stratum is not proportional to the size of each stratum within the population.* The size of each stratum is based on analytic considerations or convenience. One simple and practical approach is to select an equal number of items or respondents from each stratum regardless of size, cost, or variability. In our sample of 80 public assistance workers, for example, 20 workers would be selected from each of the four strata.

This method is a more efficient and better predictor than the proportional stratified sampling technique for comparison of strata. But it is less efficient for determining population characteristics. Grinnell provides some clear guidelines for making the decision to use stratified random sampling.

> The decision to utilize stratified random sampling is determined by several factors. The first is whether the data necessary for stratification are available for the population prior to our research study. If they are not, stratification is impossible unless the necessary data are gathered, and this would add to the cost and time requirements for the study.
>
> A second factor is the relative homogeneity of the strata. If the stratification process does not result in reasonably homogeneous strata, there is little to be gained by creating strata at all. Third, stratification should result in gains of sampling efficiency through reduced sample size and a related reduction in data collection costs. We must take care that these savings are not offset by the costs of developing the stratification data base for the sampling frame. Finally, if we are looking at more than one variable, it is difficult to create strata which are homogeneous with respect to all the variables. [7]

Cluster Samples

Cluster sampling is still another form of simple random sampling. Like stratified sampling, it requires the grouping of population units. Unlike stratified sampling, the **units are grouped by clusters instead of homogeneous strata within the population.** Using our example of the public assistance workers, we might choose a sample that included all workers (regardless of ethnic background) in the Foster Care Division of the agency. Rather than selecting individuals, we are randomly selecting divisions.

Cluster sampling is not costly if the clusters are geographically defined. It requires listing only the selected clusters. The characteristics of the clusters as well as those of the population can be estimated, and the same clusters can be used for subsequent samples since clusters, not individuals, are selected. On the other hand, cluster sampling yields larger errors for a comparable sample size than other probability sampling techniques, and it requires that each member of the population be uniquely assigned to one and only one cluster. The inability to do this may result in the duplication or omission of individuals. In other words, in our example, if several Foster Care workers are also assigned to work part of their time in the Adoptions Division, this can cause problems in using cluster sampling.

Multistage Sampling

The four probability sampling designs discussed thus far provide the fundamental selection techniques for the multistage sample system—so called because **the selection process takes place in a series of stages.** A form of random sampling is used in each of the sampling stages, and in some cases, sampling units are selected with probabilities proportionate to their size in the population. The Bureau of the Census, for example, uses multistage sampling in conducting the surveys that it prepares before and after the census in some areas in the United States. For such surveys, the sampling stages might look as follows:

Stage 1: Random selection of regions
Stage 2: Random selection of neighborhoods within regions
Stage 3: Random selection of households within neighborhoods

Each stage of the multistage procedure may involve any of the possible sample designs already discussed. This method of sampling has a wide range of applications, but in general it is most useful in sampling a large number of units, especially when cost saving is important [8]. If the units are geographically defined, travel and field research costs will be lowered. On the other hand, sampling errors are likely to be larger than the sampling errors with simple or systematic random samples of the same size.

In sum, probability sampling can be quite simple or extremely complex. It can be time-consuming or time-saving. It can be expensive or inexpensive. Whatever the situation, however, it remains the most effective method for selecting population units because it avoids conscious or unconscious biases in the sample selection process and thus permits the estimation of sampling error.

Nonprobability Samples

In general, **nonprobability samples are used for those research situations in which probability samples would be extremely expensive and/or when precise representativeness is not essential.** Furthermore, if a population cannot be defined because no listing of the population is available, the researcher will be forced to use a nonprobability sample [9]. With nonprobability sampling techniques, though, we will never be able to specify the probability of each population unit's being included in the sample, and thus we have no assurance that every unit does, in fact, have some chance of being selected. The major problem with nonprobability samples, then, is that there is no formal procedure for generalizing from sample to population since sampling error cannot be determined. And since generalizability is so important, researchers are often advised to use nonprobability samples with caution and primarily when probability methods are not feasible [10, 11]. Nonprobability sampling techniques include convenience, purposive (judgmental), snowball, and quota.

Convenience Samples

A convenience sample, sometimes referred to as an "availability" or "accidental" sample [12], is one in which **the researcher selects those respondents who are "close at hand."** Using a convenience sample saves time, money, and effort. Thus, what is lost in accuracy is gained in efficiency. A common example of a convenience sample is data collected in a classroom setting. Only those students enrolled in the selected classrooms have any chance of being included.

Haphazard or volunteer subjects samples, such as those used by archaeologists or historians, are also convenience or accidental samples. When news reporters conduct street surveys, they are using convenience samples. In effect, they simply talk to whoever is available. Researchers who use such samples draw conclusions from whatever units are available. But since generalizability is questionable, caution should be exercised in drawing conclusions from such samples.

Purposive or Judgmental Samples

Sometimes **a researcher selects a subgroup that, on the basis of available information, can be judged to be representative of the total population.** Choosing the first three days of the month as typical days for auditing ledgers or picking a typical village to represent a national rural population is an example of a purposive sample. Purposive or judgmental samples are used by researchers because they reduce the cost of preparing the sample since ultimately units can be selected so that they are close together. However, again, variability and sampling error cannot be measured or controlled. Hence, such samples require strong assumptions or considerable knowledge of the population and the subgroup being selected [13].

Snowball Samples

The use of snowball samples has actually snowballed in recent years as more researchers are making use of this technique. The term is taken from the analogy of a snowball, which begins small but becomes bigger and bigger as it rolls downhill. In the first stage of sampling, only a few respondents are identified as having the required characteristics and are interviewed by the researchers. But these **respondents are used as informants to identify others** who also qualify for inclusion in the sample. The second stage is interviewing these new persons, and so on. This sampling technique is particularly useful in observational research and in community studies. Snowball sampling is also useful for the study of obscure or hidden populations. Studies of prostitution, abortion, or homosexuality, for example, often fare better with this sampling technique.

Quota Samples

A quota sample is a nonprobability sample similar to a stratified sample. **Quota sampling generally requires that each stratum be represented in the sample in the same proportion as in the total population** [14]. In the United States, for example, when the government wants to admit immigrants from different countries, it stipulates that the number of immigrants from a specific country should be proportional to the number of U.S. Americans originating from that country. This method of sampling is not costly and introduces some stratification effect. On the other hand, it also introduces observer bias in the classification of subjects and nonrandom selection within classes [15]. Quota samples are most successful in controlling for objective variables whose measurement depends on the judgments of the interviewers.

Combining Probability and Nonprobability Sampling Techniques

It is possible to combine probability and nonprobability sampling techniques in the same design if sampling is done in a series of stages. One or more of the stages are accomplished using the principles of probability sampling, while other stages are accomplished by using the principles of nonprobability sampling [16]. Let's examine how this might work. Suppose we wanted to study unemployment rates in different regions of the United States. We could use a multistage probability sampling technique to choose the counties in each state and the neighborhoods within each county. For the final stage of choosing respondents within each neighborhood, though, we could use a nonprobability quota sample controlling for, say, ethnicity and race.

Such a design is relatively inexpensive, especially with the use of a quota sample in the final stage. On the other hand, we benefit from probability sampling at least in the earlier stages of sampling areas and neighborhoods. Using probability samples at the earlier stages gives the researcher added security at relatively little cost.

A second example of combining both probability and nonprobability samples demonstrates how these two broad types of sampling techniques can be combined yet a little differently. Suppose we were to select different regions of the United States for the study of unemployment rates and then draw a probability sample of respondents from within these regions. The purposive sample of regions might be based on the knowledge that for a long period of time some regions were considered prosperous with a low rate of unemployment, while other regions were considered poor. Within each of these regions, we might use a probability sampling technique to choose neighborhoods and respondents within each neighborhood.

One way of looking at this type of design is to think of the typical regions as defining a population. If a probability sample of this population were taken, the mathematical theory of probability sampling would be completely applicable, and we could measure our sampling error. We could then generalize the inferences regarding this restricted population to the national population, subject to the assumption that the typical regions were still typical of their respective states. So long as this assumption was valid, it seems likely that such a sampling plan would produce the most dependable sampling results at a low cost.

What Size Sample?

Beginning students of social work research are often stumped when it comes to determining sample size. Students generally suspect that there is some minimum sample size needed to represent the population from which they are sampling in order to generalize findings. And by the same token, they realize there is some maximum sample size beyond which additional sampling does not improve generalizability. Thus, the question becomes: Just how small is minimum and how large is maximum? A sample may be one population unit, all but one unit, or any number in between. And since most samples will probably be some number in between, guidelines are needed to aid in this decision-making process. Let's take a look at what goes into this decision.

z-Score Transformation

Recall from our earlier discussion of sampling theory that we were interested in establishing the representativeness of our particular sample mean. To establish representativeness, we must be able to locate the position of our sample mean on the curve of sample means. In short, we are primarily concerned with the position of our sample mean relative to the population mean and the likelihood of drawing a sample (of a designated size) from the population whose mean is a certain value. To locate our sample mean on this curve (sampling distribution of sample means), though, we must transform the mean to a z score. In other words, we must transform the mean to a score that represents the number of standard deviation units it is from the population mean. And this transformation requires that we know the mean and standard deviation of the sampling distribution of sample means. This transformation score is computed as follows:

$$z = \frac{\bar{X} - \mu}{\sigma / \sqrt{n}}$$

Again, our primary concern is with whether or not the z-score transformation of our sample is less than or greater than ±1.96 since ±1.96 represents the scores bounding off 95 percent of the area under the curve (see Figure 9.6). If our mean is located within this 95 percent area, we will reason that the difference between our sample mean and the population mean is just chance fluctuation resulting from the luck of the draw. Therefore, the sample mean is viewed as representative of the population mean and the sample representative of the population. If our sample mean is located outside of this 95 percent area, we will reason that the observed difference is not likely to be chance fluctuation since the luck of the draw doesn't often result in a sample with so *extreme* a mean. Therefore, we will conclude that the sample mean is not representative of the population mean and the sample is not representative of the population.

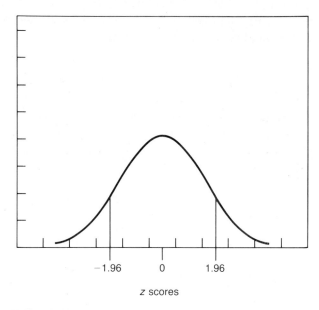

z scores

FIGURE 9.6 Standard Normal Curve

Confidence Interval Estimates

By rearranging this formula, we can also compute something known as a confidence interval estimate. When a sample value is computed to represent a population value, it is called a *point estimate*. Our sample mean, for example, is a point estimate of the population mean. A confidence interval estimate is a probabilistically constructed range about a point estimate that provides an interval estimate of a population value (in our case, the population mean). The probability associated with this estimate indicates the likelihood that the statement concerning the population value is true [17]. Suppose, for example, a sewing machine company stated in its pamphlets that it was 95 percent confident that the average life of the company's machine is between 3 and 5 years under heavy usage. Restated, the true population value (i.e., life of the sewing machine) should be between 3 and 5 years for 95 out of every 100 of the company's sewing machines. This probability of 95 percent is derived by bounding off 95 percent of the area under the curve from the other 5 percent. As we have already indicated, for the standard normal curve, the scores establishing the 95 percent level of confidence will always be ±**1.96** since the curve is fixed. If we want to be more certain, say 99 percent, the boundaries become ±**2.58** since these are the scores that bound off 99 percent of the area from the other 1 percent. Notice that to be this confident, the interval is widened to include more values. The interval itself is either right or wrong.

The confidence interval pictured in Figure 9.6 indicates that we are 95 percent confident the true population mean is within this interval since 95 out of every 100 samples of some designated size drawn from the population will have a mean with-

We begin with:

$$z = \frac{\bar{X} - \mu}{\sigma/\sqrt{n}}$$

By substitution:
(*e* is the maximum error we are
willing to tolerate in prediction)

$$e = \bar{X} - \mu$$

Thus:

$$z = \frac{e}{\sigma/\sqrt{n}}$$

Solving for *n*:

$$n = \frac{z^2\sigma^2}{e^2}$$

FIGURE 9.7 Determining Sample Size

in this range. We computed these lower and upper values by establishing the two scores located approximately two standard deviations below and above the mean. We chose two standard deviations below and above since ±1.96 (approximately 2.0) is the standard score providing the boundaries setting off 95 percent of the area under the curve:

$$\bar{X} - 1.96\sigma/\sqrt{n} < \mu < \bar{X} + 1.96\sigma/\sqrt{n}$$

If you look closely at this rearranged formula, you might notice that given a fixed level of confidence (95 percent or 99 percent) and a fixed standard deviation (*s*), there is only one way we can improve our precision in estimating the population value from the sample value (i.e., narrow our interval estimate), and that is by increasing our sample size. If, in our housing sales example, we increase our sample size from 100 to 1,000, notice what happens to the confidence interval when it is computed: 35,828.07–37,697.27. And if we increase our sample size to 5,000, notice what happens to the interval: 36,344.71–37,180.64. In fact, with a second rearrangement of this formula, we can solve for *n* (sample size). (See Figure 9.7.)

Determining Sample Size

Suppose we decided in advance of conducting our study just how much precision we desired. That is, we decided what size interval we would be willing to tolerate around the population mean. We will call this *e* (for *error*). If we also knew or could estimate the population standard deviation and we decided on a level of confidence (e.g., 95 or 99 percent), we could determine the sample size needed to obtain the specified precision at the desired level of confidence since the formula for determining sample size is just another rearrangement of the z-score formula (see Figure 9.7).

For example, to estimate the population mean within $1,000 (±$500) at the 95 percent level of confidence, we would have computed the sample size as follows:

$$n = \frac{(1.96^2)(15,078.88^2)}{1,000^2}$$

$$= 874$$

To be within \$500 (±\$250 on either side) of the population mean at the 95 percent confidence level, we would need a sample of size 3,494. Notice that the sample size must be quadrupled just to narrow the interval width by \$500. Thus, with a sample of 874, we can be 95 percent confident that the sample value is within \$1,000 (±\$500) of the population value. But with a sample of 3,494, we can be 95 percent confident that the sample value is within \$500 (±\$250) of the population value. As a researcher you would have to decide whether the increased precision is worth the additional time and cost required to collect the sample.

Although this formula provides us with a quick and simple answer to "What size sample?," there still remain several issues and questions to be considered. First of all, the designated sample size suggested by this formula is based on a single variable. And even the simplest of research projects makes use of more than one variable. Usually we want to estimate several characteristics from the same sample, and the sample size needed to achieve the desired precision for one population characteristic may be smaller or larger than the size needed to achieve the desired precision for others. But this problem can ordinarily be solved by selecting a sample large enough that each of the most important characteristics is estimated with sufficient precision at the desired level of confidence. Suppose, for example, we conducted a survey collecting 100 variables. We could conceivably identify 100 potential sample sizes—one for each of the 100 variables. Using this approach, our final decision on sample size would equal the largest estimate. Such an approach would be conservative in that we would be collecting a sample size that for most variables was even larger than that required for the designated precision and level of confidence. However, computing 100 potential sample sizes is not very practical. A more practical approach would be to identify those variables central to the study and compute estimates of sample size based only on those. We would then collect a sample whose size equaled the largest estimate.

A second issue and unanswered question that remains is, What if all the important variables are not variables for which we can compute means and standard deviations? What if, for example, we are concerned with such variables as sex (male, female) or marital status (single, married, widowed, divorced)? For these variables, mean and standard deviation make no sense. In such cases as these, we employ a variation of the z-score formula that uses the standard deviation of the distribution representing a plot of such discrete or categorical responses. Such distributions require that we consider dichotomized categorical responses. With a variable like marital status, for example, we would need to identify four population distributions: (1) married versus not married, (2) single versus not single, (3) widowed versus not widowed and (4) divorced versus not divorced. For such variables, the most conservative estimate (i.e., the largest sample size needed for any such categorical responses) will be computed when the proportions associated with each of the two categories are $p = (1 - p) = 0.5$. This is because the maximum value for population variance will be reached at these values since the product of p and $(1 - p)$ is a maximum value: $(0.5)(0.5) = 0.25$; $(0.6)(0.4) = 0.24$; $(0.7)(0.3) = 0.21$; and so on. Consequently, for any and all categorical variables, we can always estimate the maximum sample size needed by assuming equal proportions (i.e., 0.5) for variables with dichotomized categorical responses. While we will sometimes wind up with a sample larger than necessary, it will never be too small—given a designated level of confidence and a desired range of precision.

A third issue and unanswered question is, Doesn't this formula for determining sample size consider sampling error? The answer is yes. In fact, when we establish the degree of precision desired (i.e., the interval around the population value), we are actually specifying how much sampling error we are willing to tolerate. This is an extremely important point given our earlier discussion of sampling error. In effect, since sampling error can be computed for probability samples, we can readily use this procedure to determine sample size. However, with nonprobability samples, since it is not possible to determine sampling error, this formula is simply not meaningful. In fact, with nonprobability samples, there are no quick and easy formulas for determining sample size. Thus, with nonprobability samples, a decision on sample size must be based on other considerations.

One of the primary considerations when nonprobability samples are used is, How are the results to be analyzed? It is important to estimate how many times the sample may have to be subdivided during data analysis and to ensure an adequate sample size for each subdivision. Generally speaking, the minimum sample size should equal ten times the maximum number of subdivisions. Beyond data analysis the primary considerations become cost and time. Researchers are always cautioned to select an adequate sample that will be cost- and time-efficient.

A sound rule taught to beginning students of research is "Use as large a sample as possible." The smaller the sample, the larger the error, and the larger the sample, the smaller the error. But large samples are not championed because large numbers are good in and of themselves. They are championed to give the principles of randomization a chance to work [18]. To some extent, sample size does depend on population size. Some populations are quite small—for example, all Catholic Popes in the Vatican. For such studies the entire population is fewer than fifty and we would probably study the entire population. Other populations are quite large—for example, all voting U.S. citizens—and a sample of 2,000 or 3,000 would be necessary.

Because it is not always possible to determine the exact sample size needed, a researcher will sometimes fall back on the experience of others.

> If the topic of research or the population being sampled is of great interest and if it has not been studied before, it is quite possible that even a study based on a small sample (and consequently of relatively low accuracy) will be of general interest. On the other hand, if the topic is one that has been repeatedly studied using large national samples, it is quite possible that there will be little interest in the proposed study unless it too is based on a large national study. [19]

Grinnell offers another insight on the subject of sample size. Since the standard deviations of the population variables are usually unknown, and are usually estimated from the sample data,

> they cannot be determined until the samples have been drawn and the data collected and analyzed. For this reason, a convention on sample size has been adopted; in most instances, a sample of one-tenth (1/10) the size of the

population will give reasonable control over sampling error. This proportion also applies in various categories of the population: one-tenth of each category can be sampled. [20]

But regardless of the sampling technique used, sampling bias is not affected by sample size. Certainly *Literary Digest* was not saved by having used a large sample in its election poll. Generally speaking, for most research endeavors, samples will be adequate if within the limits of 30 and 500. Samples of less than 30 are usually too small, while samples of greater than 500 are seldom necessary.

References

1. D. Warwick and S. Oshersen, *Comparative Research Methods* (Englewood Cliffs, NJ: Prentice-Hall, 1973), p. 33.
2. L. H. Kidder, *Selltiz, Wrightsman, and Cook's Research Methods in Social Relations* (New York: Holt, Rinehart and Winston, 1981), p. 78.
3. H. W. Smith, *Strategies of Social Research: The Methodological Imagination* (Englewood Cliffs, NJ: Prentice-Hall, 1981), p. 269.
4. M. Walizer and P. Weiner, *Research Methods and Analysis: Searching for Relationships* (New York: Harper and Row, 1978), pp. 435–6.
5. Richard M. Grinnell, Jr., *Social Work Research and Evaluation*, 3rd ed. (Itasca, IL: Peacock, 1988), pp. 244–7.
6. D. Miller, *Handbook of Research Design and Social Measurement* (New York: David McKay, 1975), p. 57.
7. Grinnell, *Social Work Research and Evaluation*, pp. 249–50.
8. V. Cangelosi, T. Phillip, and R. Phillippe, *Basic Statistics* (New York: West Publishing, 1979), p. 235.
9. D. Nachmias and C. Nachmias, *Research Methods in the Social Sciences* (New York: St. Martin's, 1976), p. 430.
10. Walizer and Weiner, *Research Methods and Analysis*, p. 437.
11. L. Kish, *Survey Sampling* (New York: Wiley, 1965), p. 19.
12. Grinnell, *Social Work Research and Evaluation*, p. 251.
13. Miller, *Handbook of Research Design and Social Measurement*.
14. K. Bailey, *Methods of Social Research* (New York: The Free Press, 1978), p. 81.
15. Miller, *Handbook of Research Design and Social Measurement*, p. 58.
16. Kidder, *Selltiz, Wrightsman, and Cook's Research Methods in Social Relations*, pp. 438–9.
17. Cangelosi, Phillip, and Phillippe, *Basic Statistics*, pp. 156–7.
18. F. N. Kerlinger, *Foundations of Behavioral Research* (New York: Holt, Rinehart and Winston, 1979).
19. J. Williamson, D. Karp, J. Dalphin, and P. Gray, *The Research Craft: An Introduction to Social Research Methods*, 2nd ed. (Boston: Little, Brown, 1982), pp. 114–5.
20. Grinnell, *Social Work Research and Evaluation*, pp. 196–7.

Chapter 10

The Experiment

"Deviance in the dark"
Creating equal groups
  Matching as a means of creating
      equal groups
  Random assignment of subjects
      to groups
  Matching versus random
      assignment
Technical considerations
      concerning the
      independent variable
  Manipulating the independent
      variable
  Preventing unintended
      differences in treatment
  Criteria for causality revisited
Two experimental designs
  Pretest/posttest control group
      design
  An important note

Posttest-only control group
      design
Laboratory versus field
      experiment
Field experiment
  "From Jerusalem to Jericho"
  Control in the field experiment
  Control in evaluation research
Internal validity
  History
  Maturation
  Testing
  Instrumentation
  Regression effect
  Experimental mortality
External validity
True experiment versus
      quasi-experiment
Quasi-experiment

No amount of experimentation can ever prove me right; but a single experiment can prove me wrong. —ALBERT EINSTEIN

"Deviance in the Dark"

The setting is a college classroom building. The event is a student casually perusing a cluttered bulletin board. After a few minutes of careful reading, she spots a notice seeking students' participation in a research study. The notice includes a telephone number for interested students to call. Upon calling, our student is told that the study in question is on "environmental psychology." She is given an address to go to and a time for her participation. Upon arrival, a man ushers her into an empty room and asks her to fill out a series of written forms. Twenty minutes later, he returns and takes her to a totally dark chamber. The chamber or room is approximately ten by twelve feet. Both the walls and floor are padded, and the ceiling is out of reach. The only light in the room is a pinpoint of red light over the door for emergency exiting.

Our student is told that she will be left in the room, along with seven other students, for approximately one hour. She is told that there are no rules as to what to do. She is also told that at the end of the hour she will be escorted from the room alone, hence providing no opportunity to meet face-to-face with the other participants. The student slips off her shoes, empties her pockets, and enters the room.

The research question addressed by Kenneth and Mary Gergen and William Barton in their study "Deviance in the Dark" began just this way. Their question: "What do people do under conditions of extreme anonymity?" [1]. In other words, what do people do with each other when the normal sanctions that govern their behaviors are severed? Will they willingly forsake these sanctions for alternate ways of interacting? Or will they continue to behave in normative ways despite the knowledge that there is no way to reward or punish subjects appropriately for their behavior? With this question in mind, Gergen and his colleagues hypothesized that extreme anonymity would free subjects of the routinized behavior we have come to expect in today's society and thus enable them to act in any way deemed mutually acceptable.

Approximately fifty individuals participated in the Gergen et al. study. Subjects were primarily students between the ages of eighteen and twenty-five. Participants were divided into groups of eight, half males and half females. All voice communications were tape-recorded during the one-hour sessions. The pinpoint of red light above the emergency exit was enough to videotape all movement using infrared cameras.

In addition to the dark chamber condition, Gergen et al. created a second condition. Some groups of subjects spent one hour in the chamber with the lights left on. In both conditions, each subject was asked to write down his or her impressions of the experience after being removed from the chamber.

The data collected in this study confirm the researchers' hypothesis. In fact, the differences between students in the dark-room condition versus the lighted-room condition proved to be quite enlightening. First, subjects in the lighted room kept a continuous stream of conversation going from the start to the finish of the session. In the dark room, talk slacked off dramatically after the first thirty minutes. Second, subjects in the lighted room quickly found a place to sit (seldom closer than three feet to any other subject) and remained seated in the same position for the entire hour. In fact, the research team wrote that they could predict with 90 percent accuracy within the first five minutes where a subject would be seated in the last five minutes of the session. In contrast, subjects in the dark room moved about fluidly, making it impossible to predict with greater than 50 percent accuracy where a subject would be from one five-minute period to the next.

All dark-room participants accidentally touched one another, while less than 5 percent of the lighted-room participants did. Approximately 50 percent of the dark-room subjects reported that they hugged one another, and 80 percent stated that they felt sexual excitement. In marked contrast, none of the lighted-room subjects hugged each other, and only 30 percent acknowledged being sexually aroused.

The written impressions of the dark-room subjects only serve to confirm even more the lack of normative structure under a condition of extreme anonymity. One student wrote:

> As I was sitting Beth came up and we started to play touchy face and touchy body and started to neck. We expressed it as showing "love" to each other. Shortly before I was taken out, we decided to pass our "love" on, to share it with other people. So we split up and Laurie took her place. We had just started touchy face and touchy body and kissed a few times before I was tapped to leave.

In contrast, the subjects in the lighted room were less likely to explore the chamber and more likely to report boredom.

From the data collected in this study, Gergen et al. conclude that intimacy is quite natural, at least for people aged eighteen to twenty-six. When freed from the normative constraints of everyday life, people in this age group developed very immediate and close relationships.

What we have just described is an experiment. As we learned in Chapter 6, the experiment is a research design that uses at least two groups in either a contrived or a natural setting, and it is a design that is higher on control than representativeness. We shall discuss each of these points later in the chapter.

The experiment can be thought of as the one research design that epitomizes the standard of science. As we indicated in Chapter 6, this is largely because the logic of causation and the logic of the experiment are one and the same. The goal of an experiment is to determine whether two or more variables are *causally connected*. Recall from Chapter 6 that a variable is any characteristic on which individuals or groups differ. In the experiment just described, for example, the researchers were interested in whether the condition of extreme anonymity would cause changes in behavior typically governed by norms. In this experiment, *extreme anonymity* is the *independent variable*—the *presumed cause*, while *behavior* is the *dependent variable*—the *presumed effect*.

In addition to labeling the variables in an experiment, we also label the groups. The group receiving some treatment is the *experimental group*. The comparison group is the *control group*. In the experiment just described, the group spending one hour in the dark chamber is the experimental group, while the group spending one hour in the lighted chamber is the control or comparison group.

As you begin to reflect on the experiment just narrated, several questions will probably come to mind. How did the researchers decide who would be in the experimental group versus the control group? How could the experimenters be sure that the observed behavior differences between the two groups were really a function of extreme anonymity? Is this experiment truly characteristic of real life? Can these kinds of research findings be generalized to the larger population? In our discussion of the experimental design, we shall attempt to answer each of these questions, and we hope our answers will begin to broaden your understanding of this design.

Creating Equal Groups

The logic of the experimental design requires that all groups must be initially equal. In short, this means that if 50 percent of group 1 is male, then 50 percent of group 2 should also be male. If 85 percent of group 1 is single, then 85 percent of group 2 should also be single. If the average age of group 1 is twenty, then the average age of group 2 should also be twenty. As we shall see, if we cannot assume equal groups before the experiment begins, we cannot establish beyond a probable doubt that any observed differences between groups are a function of the independent variable.

Suppose, for example, in the "Deviance in the Dark" experiment, that the researchers had not bothered to establish equal groups. Now the *cause* of the observed difference in behavior between groups would be in question. Would the difference between groups be a function of the independent variable (light versus dark) or a function of one or more of the differences that existed initially between these two groups? Unfortunately, there would be no way of knowing, and under such conditions the experimental data would not provide us with many (if any) answers.

Matching as a Means of Creating Equal Groups

One method of creating equal groups is through matching—a process of identifying two similar subjects who are alike on a number of measured characteristics and placing these subjects in separate groups. If, for example, we selected a student who is single, female, twenty-two, black, and a psychology major with a 3.6 grade-point average to go in group 1, we would need to find another student matching on all of these same characteristics to go in group 2. Although it may be relatively easy to find pairs of subjects matching on one or two characteristics, it becomes next to impossible to create such matches on a half-dozen or more variables.

Matching creates an exact equivalence only on the measured and matched variables. Regardless of how careful we are to match on every conceivable variable that may be causally connected to the dependent variable, there remain unmeasured and uncontrolled variables whose influence may be crucial. Suppose, for example, five years after the "Deviance in the Dark" experiment, someone discovered that eating chocolate significantly affected behavior. Suppose chocolate was shown to lift people's inhibitions. If we were reflecting back on the "Deviance" experiment, we might now begin to wonder whether group 1 had eaten more chocolate one hour before the experiment. Perhaps group 1's more liberal behavior was actually a function of all subjects ingesting chocolate before participating in the experiment. Although this hypothesis may seem somewhat preposterous, the fact remains that without measuring this variable and controlling for it, we would have no way of knowing the extent to which chocolate was responsible for the observed difference between groups. In short, the problems inherent in the matching process suggest that there must be a more efficient way to establish equality.

Random Assignment of Subjects to Groups

A second means of establishing equal groups is through random assignment. *The random assignment of subjects into groups means that the placement of each subject in a group is based on chance.* In other words, the decision to place a subject in group 1 versus group 2 is based on, for example, the flip of a coin—heads you are in group 1; tails you are in group 2. By using such a method, every subject has an equal chance of being in any given group, and the process is not based on human decision. Also, by using this process, we can safely assume that our groups are approximately equal. In other words, when we identify the proportion of males in group 1, it should be approximately the same for group 2. When we identify the proportion of singles for group 1, it should be approximately the same for group 2. When we compute the average age for group 1, it should be approximately the same for group 2.

We don't want to leave you with the impression that randomization is the panacea for all experiments. Certainly, there are risks. With chance operating, we could conceivably end up with all the singles in one group and marrieds in another. Or we could end up with all the older subjects in one group and the younger subjects in another. Although the probability of this happening is pretty remote, we must recognize that it could happen.

To safeguard against such a problem, our best strategy is to measure our subjects on a number of easily obtained variables that could prove influential. If our groups do not differ markedly on these variables, they probably do not differ markedly on others.

Matching versus Random Assignment

While matching creates an *exact equivalence,* randomization creates an *approximate equivalence.* However, the exact equivalence created with matching is only with respect to the set of measured variables used in the matching process. In contrast, the approximate equivalence created with random assignment is in reference to *all* variables—those identified and measured and those unidentified and unmeasured. If two years after the "Deviance in the Dark" experiment chocolate was discovered to be causally linked to behavior, the "Deviance" findings would not be affected. Even without knowledge of this variable, the random assignment of subjects to groups suggests that the average number of ounces of chocolate ingested by group 1 the hour before the experiment was approximately the same as for group 2. Trading an exact equivalence for an approximate equivalence may seem unreasonable, but it is a good trade when we realize that the equivalence applies to all variables—those unidentified and out of sight as well as those identified and measured.

Technical Considerations Concerning the Independent Variable

Once subjects have been assigned to either the experimental or the control group, we can turn our attention to the treatment—the manipulated independent variable. The second step in an experiment is applying different treatments to the various groups. In the ideal experiment, the treatment to which subjects are exposed should differ in only one way, although in reality this is not always the case. Let's see how this works.

Manipulating the Independent Variable

As we have already indicated, the experiment begins with at least two groups that are alike in every way. Once equality is established, the researcher is in a position to decide what each subject will experience next. In the "Deviance in the Dark" experiment, for example, the researchers decided which subjects would experience the dark room and which subjects would experience the lighted room. The research team did not ask each subject which setting they preferred. Subjects were given no choice in the matter. In fact, they were not even aware that any other condition existed. And in making this decision, the researchers actually manipulated the *independent* variable.

Manipulation of the independent variable has the effect of giving the researcher total control over the research setting. With this kind of control, the researcher can be reasonably certain that the only difference between the two groups is the difference he or she introduces (i.e., the independent variable). (Obviously the control of every single possible variable is impossible, as we will show in a moment.)

It perhaps goes without saying that some variables cannot be manipulated. If, for example, you wanted to know whether or not males and females react differently to a particular type of film presentation, you cannot randomly assign sex. Sex is a more or less permanent attribute that does not lend itself to this kind of manipulation. There are actually a number of such nonmanipulative variables used by researchers—marital status, age, race, and occupation, just to name a few. These variables are not easily manipulated in a laboratory setting. And this is no doubt a factor contributing to the low usage of the experimental design within social work and the social sciences.

Preventing Unintended Differences in Treatment

Total control over the research setting does not guarantee identical experiences for all persons involved. Each subject enters the research setting cloaked in personal experiences, and these experiences will no doubt contribute to what he or she sees. To illustrate, a subject who is afraid of the dark will probably not have exactly the same experience as a subject who loves the dark. However, this is not a major methodological flaw. In fact, it is usually not even a problem. It is not really necessary that all subjects have exactly the same experiences. As long as subjects' *differences in experiences* are not systematically related to whether they are a part of one group versus another, the difference is inconsequential. Restated, the differences between individuals' experiences must not be systematically related to the independent variable. Unsystematic differences are nothing to worry about. In fact, we expect subjects' individual experiences to be somewhat different.

Criteria for Causality Revisited

As we have already noted, while the experiment does a good job of testing cause–effect models, this test is not direct. In effect, we are able to *infer* a cause–effect link from three essential pieces of information: time order, relationship between variables, and rival hypotheses.

Time Order

First, there must be a time order to the variables. Specifically, this means that *the independent variable must precede the dependent variable in time.* In the "Deviance in the Dark" study, the independent variable (lighted room versus dark room) preceded in time the dependent variable (behavior). Time order is crucial if we are to say that one thing caused another. Something that occurs later in time cannot be the cause of something that occurred earlier. By manipulating the independent variable, we can ensure that the time order to the variables is correct.

Relationship between Variables

A second essential piece of information needed to infer cause–effect relationships is establishing a relationship between the independent and the dependent variable. *If one variable is to be considered the cause of the other, then these two variables must vary together in some kind of pattern.* As one goes from the lighted chamber to the dark chamber, for example, behavior becomes more diverse.

Rival Hypotheses

In the "Deviance in the Dark" experiment, Gergen et al. begin with the notion that extreme anonymity has some influence on behavior. In fact, they suggest that it can alter behavior significantly. But you and I know—or at least suspect—that other things can also alter behavior. Perhaps intelligence is an important variable. If so, we might hypothesize that people with high IQs are more likely to experiment with alternative behaviors, normative or otherwise. To eliminate this hypothesis, we must select students whose IQs are the same. A second plausible alternative hypothesis might suggest that religiosity influences the extent to which people are willing to experiment with alternative behaviors. To eliminate this alternative, we would have to select students with similar levels of religiosity. As we have already noted, we can accomplish this through matching or through random assignment.

The logic of eliminating these alternative hypotheses is extremely important to the experiment. It is, in fact, this elimination process that makes cause–effect statements possible. To begin with, Gergen et al. cannot definitely show (beyond absolute doubt) that extreme anonymity causes behavioral changes in participating students. As we learned in Chapter 6, cause–effect models are actually theoretical. Because cause–effect links exist only in theory, there is no *direct* test of such models. Hence, we must test cause–effect models indirectly. This indirect test is really a process of eliminating rival hypotheses. The more rival hypotheses we can eliminate—with our hypotheses still in the running—the more confident we can be that a causal link exists. In fact, the more alternatives we can eliminate, the better our hypothesis looks.

Two Experimental Designs

To introduce you more fully to the experimental design, let us now examine two simple but frequently used experimental designs.

Pretest/Posttest Control Group Design

R Y1 X Y2
R Y3   Y4

In this experimental design, two groups are created and each is tested twice. *The R's in this model indicate that subjects have been randomly assigned to groups.* By randomly assigning subjects to the two groups, we can assume that these two groups are initially equal in every respect. And although we cannot test for this equality on an infinite number of variables, we do establish it for the dependent variable. *The Y represents our observed measurement of groups 1 and 2 on the dependent variable.* Once measured, the researcher introduces a difference between the two groups. This is accomplished by manipulating the independent variable. The X in the preceding model represents the treatment or the independent variable introduced to group 1. Notice that no treatment is given to group 2. It is the introduction of this treatment to one group and not to the other that results in creating a difference between the two groups, which were initially equal. Finally, we take a second measurement of the dependent variable for both groups. If a comparison of the groups on this second measurement now demonstrates a difference between the two groups, we can reason that the difference is due to the one difference we introduced—the independent variable.

Let's now examine these rather abstract procedures within the context of a real example. Suppose, as a researcher, you were interested in the extent to which microcomputers aided in the learning of interviewing skills in undergraduate social work. You gain permission from the responsible administrative person, and you are ready to begin the design of your experiment. First, you realize that you will need two undergraduate groups—those who will be using micros and those who will not. Second, you realize you must make these two groups initially equal. You do this by randomly assigning the social work students to one of the two groups—heads you're in the computer group; tails you're in the noncomputer group.

Once our two groups have been established, we test these groups on their interviewing skills. Random assignment suggests that this test should demonstrate no differences between the mean scores of these two groups. This testing represents our pretest—our first measurement of the dependent variable. Now we introduce the treatment. One group learns course content with the aid of micros; the other learns the same content without the aid of micros. At the end of the semester, we test our groups again on the dependent variable. This testing represents our posttest—our second measurement of the dependent variable. Since an entire semester has passed for both groups, we expect both groups to change some (more about this later). However, if our treatment is effective, we are expecting a greater change from the experimental group over the control group. If the group using micros scores considerably higher than the other group on the skill test, we can conclude that the measured difference is a function of using micros in the curriculum design.

An Important Note

As we have already noted, although random assignment ensures equality between groups, there may be other subtle differences. What about differences introduced by the teacher, the course content, or the time of day? We might want to ensure that both groups take the interviewing class at the same time of day, and we will probably want to use the same book in both classes. We will also want to instruct both teachers as to how they should behave toward students. However, as you can see, students' experiences are not always going to be the same. And, as indicated earlier, it doesn't really matter. As long as the differences in students' experiences are not systematically related to whether they are a part of one group versus the other, there is no real problem with different experiences.

Posttest-Only Control Group Design

R X Y1
R   Y2

In the posttest-only control group design, as in the previous design, two groups are created and subjects are randomly assigned to one of these two groups. However, unlike the previous design, no pretest is run. The random assignment of subjects to groups allows us to assume equality between groups, and no pretest is run to confirm it. As in the previous design, the researcher manipulates the independent variable and thereby introduces a difference between groups. Following manipulation of the independent variable, both groups are measured on the dependent variable. If a difference can be established, this difference is attributed to the independent variable.

By now you may have realized that the "Deviance in the Dark" experiment is a posttest-only control group design. Recall that in this experiment the researchers randomly assigned subjects to one of two groups—the dark chamber or the lighted chamber. No measure of conformity to normative behavior was taken prior to the manipulation of the independent variable (such a measure would probably be difficult!). Instead, once the dark-room or lighted-room condition was established, behavior was observed. In effect, the researchers created a posttest-only control group design.

Laboratory versus Field Experiment

So far, our discussion of the experimental design has focused on what we might label laboratory experiments. The researcher creates an environment in which he or she has virtually total control. And in so doing, he or she has created what Orenstein and Phillips [2] label the laboratory drama. This drama, if staged well, has all the properties of a well-rehearsed play.

But a drama is not real, and neither is a laboratory experiment. This fact has made the laboratory experiment fall prey to heavy criticism. Are laboratory experiments realistic and, if so, how realistic? Just how realistic, for example, is the extreme anonymity condition created by Gergen et al.? Is the laboratory drama generalizable? Can we correctly generalize that under conditions of extreme anonymity in a real-world setting, individuals would behave similarly to the subjects in this drama?

To answer these questions, we must take a closer look at the concept of realism as it is used in social research. Laboratory experiments do not need to seem "real" in the conventional sense. That is, it is not necessary for laboratory situations to parallel exactly situations as they are found in the real world. To understand why this is so, let's take a look at the now-classic experiment of Solomon Asch.

Three decades ago Asch [3] devised an experiment whereby a real subject and a number of stooges (confederates who were members of the research team) are asked to judge which of three lines most closely matches a reference line in length. The task was not designed to be tricky. Over repeated trials, the correct answer was actually quite obvious, and without others present, subjects almost always guessed correctly. However, in the laboratory setting, with the stooges, the real subject gives his or her answer only after all of the stooges have given their incorrect answers. Will the real subject over repeated trials give the obvious and correct answer, or will he or she conform to the unanimous but incorrect response of the stooges?

Aronson and Carlsmith [4] note that the Asch study involves little down-to-earth realism since situations similar to this are not likely to occur in the real world: "In everyday life, it is rare to find oneself in a situation where the direct and unambiguous evidence of one's senses is contradicted by the unanimous judgment of other persons." In addition, the task itself is rather trivial—one that is not likely to occur outside of the laboratory. Nevertheless, Aronson and Carlsmith argue that the Asch experiment does demonstrate considerable realism. The subjects are involved in the laboratory situation, and they do take the task seriously. Subjects sweat and squirm. They appear troubled and anxious. The situation is real for them. In short, the contrived situation poses a real choice of conforming or not conforming.

Field Experiment

One way of increasing mundane realism in the experiment is to take it out of the laboratory and into a natural setting. Let's illustrate with an example.

"From Jerusalem to Jericho"

In Darley and Batson's study "From Jerusalem to Jericho" [5], they note that "Helping other people in distress is, among other things, an ethical act." We learn very early in life that one should help others who are in distress. And as these authors note, the classic story on helping appears in the New Testament:

> "And who is my neighbor?" Jesus replied, "A man was going down from Jerusalem to Jericho, and he fell among robbers, who stripped him and beat him, and departed, leaving him half dead. Now by chance a priest was going down the road; and when he saw him he passed by on the other side. So likewise a Levite, when he came to the place and saw him, passed by on the other side. But a Samaritan, as he journeyed, came to where he was; and when he saw him, he had compassion, and went to him and bound his wounds, pouring on oil and wine; then he set him on his own beast and brought him to an inn, and took care of him. And the next day he took out two denarii and gave them to the innkeeper, saying, 'Take care of him; and whatever more you spend, I will repay you when I come back.' Which of these three, do you think, proved neighbor to him who fell among the robbers?" He said, "The one who showed mercy on him." And Jesus said to him, "Go and do likewise." (Luke 10:29–37 RSV)

After reading this story carefully, Darley and Batson began to reflect on the types of persons the priest, the Levite, and the Samaritan were. After some consideration, Darley and Batson came up with a list of characteristics out of which three hypotheses were derived:

1. People who encounter a situation possibly calling for a helping response while thinking religious and ethical thoughts will be no more likely to offer aid than those persons thinking about something else.
2. Persons encountering a possible helping situation when they are in a hurry will be less likely to offer aid than persons not in a hurry.
3. People who are religious for intrinsic reasons or whose religion emerges out of questioning the meaning of their everyday lives will be more likely to stop to offer help to the victim.

To test these hypotheses, seminary students were asked to participate in a study on religious education and vocations. During the first testing session, personality questionnaires measuring types of religiosity were administered. In a second, individual session, each subject began his participation in one building and was asked to report to another building for his final participation. While in transit, each subject passed a slumped "victim" planted in an alleyway.

The dependent variable for this study was whether and how each subject would help the victim. The independent variables for this study were (1) the degree to which each subject was told to hurry to the other building and (2) the talk he was to give when he arrived. Some subjects were instructed to talk on jobs in which seminary students would be most effective. Others were instructed to talk on the parable of the Good Samaritan.

Control in the Field Experiment

There is a price to be paid for increased mundane realism, and that price is researcher control. (Another price is an ethical one. See Chapter 5.) In the Good Samaritan study, for example, of the forty-seven subjects scheduled to participate, seven were eliminated and three of these seven because of contamination. (Contamination refers to unexpected events over which the researcher has no control, which can alter the ways in which the dependent variable behaves.) What brought about the uncontrollable problems resulting in contamination? In the researchers' own words:

> we found the spot. A short dead-end alley ran between the building which housed the psychology department and a partially condemned old building in which some members of the sociology department had their offices.... We asked the faculty members to help us by taking a longer route to their office which avoided the alley. They graciously complied. ... Service traffic was harder to control because it was sporadic. One morning about ten minutes before the first subject was to be sent through the alley, we found a telephone truck sitting squarely in the middle of the alley, with no phone men in sight. A frantic search produced one of the service men, who rather quizzically but amiably moved his truck out of sight. The janitor also presented a problem. On the second day of running, just as the subject entered the alley, he came out of a side door and cheerily called over to our "victim" huddled ready and waiting, "Feeling better today?" One subject's data, $2.50, and over an hour of experimenter time evaporated. [6]

In a field experiment, the setting is not usually under the complete control of the experimenter. And this lack of complete control can be crucial to inferring cause–effect links. In short, while we have increased mundane realism, we have probably sacrificed some degree of control.

Control in Evaluation Research

The problem of control so evident in the field experiment also finds its way into the area of evaluation research. **The term** *evaluation research* **is used to refer to a whole range of studies conducted to test whether or not a particular "program" is having the desired effect.** (See Chapter 12.)

As Orenstein and Phillips note, government reports provide some of the best evidence of the difficulties of the field experiment.

Between 1962 and 1972, according to its own estimate, the Federal government spent 179.4 million dollars on experimental job training programs for the poor. A major goal of these projects was to find out if people who are retrained earn more money and are raised above the poverty line. The results of the many studies done were summarized for the Joint Economic Committee of Congress. The report concludes that most of the studies were so ill-conceived that they can support few reliable conclusions; in other words, we have not learned much about the question that prompted the research. [7]

The most frequent methodological blunder in these government-financed evaluation studies was failure to use a control group. Instead of randomly assigning welfare recipients to either a training or a no-training group, the researchers used no control group. And without a control group, very little, if anything, can be concluded. Even if a difference is observed for a single group from one time period to another, we have no way of knowing if the difference is any less than or greater than what might have been observed in a control group. Without a comparison group, the findings are meaningless.

Another methodological flaw in these government-financed studies noted by Orenstein and Phillips was the failure to follow subjects for a long enough time. Benefits from training may not be so noticeable in a period as short as six months or even a year. It may take several years for a person to move up and stabilize in an occupational slot. If long-term differences are to be observed, subjects must be followed for a longer period of time.

Internal Validity

In their classic book *Experimental and Quasi-Experimental Designs for Research*, Campbell and Stanley write that "Internal validity is the basic minimum without which any experiment is uninterpretable" [8]. *Internal validity* **refers to whether or not we can appropriately draw the inference that the independent variable has caused some change in the dependent variable.** (See Figure 10.1.) Presumably, such a causal inference is possible because we have established initial equality between groups (i.e., matching or random assignment) and thereby eliminated any plausible alternative explanations. However, no matter how careful we are, certain subtle but uncontrolled variables creep in, serving to threaten internal validity. This threat essentially suggests that plausible alternative hypotheses or competing explanations may be responsible for any observed difference between groups.

Campbell and Stanley [9] have identified a number of threats to internal validity, and we will discuss six of them here: history, maturation, testing, instrumentation, regression effect, and experimental mortality.

History

History refers *to the specific events occurring between the first and second measurement of the dependent variable in addition to the manipulated independent variable.* If events occur

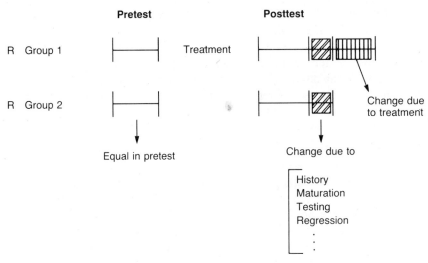

FIGURE 10.1   Internal Validity

that could potentially alter the second measurement of the dependent variable, we would have no way of knowing how much of the observed change is a function of the independent variable versus these specific events.

Let's suppose that you wish to conduct a study to evaluate the influence of a media message on voluntary charitable contributions. You design an experiment with three experimental groups and one control group. In the three experimental groups, you vary the intensity of the media message. Your experiment will involve the collection of data over a six-month period. In the fourth month of your experiment, the governor of the state vetoes a highly publicized piece of welfare legislation. Your experimental findings are now potentially contaminated with this specific event. In short, you have no way of determining the extent to which this event is influencing your measurement on the dependent variable. However, if subjects have been randomly assigned to groups, you can safely assume that the effect of this specific event is the *same* for all groups. In other words, this specific event would alter all groups' scores in the same way, so that even though the scores might be different from the pretest, they would still be the same. Hence any observed difference between groups can be interpreted as a function of the treatment.

Maturation

Maturation refers to *the process within respondents operating as a function of the passage of time* per se—for example, growing hungrier or growing older. In our hypothetical study on the effect of computer-aided instruction on the interviewing skills of undergraduate social work students, maturation could certainly be at work. During the course of the semester, each student—most of whom may be late adolescents —was getting older. With increases in physical age, we can usually expect an increase in mental skill. This factor would increase in importance, especially with even younger respondents. With maturation at work, we may not be able to determine whether the observed differences in interviewing skill are a function of age or a function of computer-aided instruction. If, however, subjects are randomly assigned to groups, we can expect any age effect to be the same for both classes. In other words, while maturation only would change both classes' scores, the classes would still be equal. Hence, any observed difference between classes can be attributed to the manipulated independent variable (computers versus no computers).

Testing

Testing refers to *the effects of pretest scores on posttest scores.* If subjects are taking a test for the second time (or an alternative form of a previously taken test), will they do better than subjects taking the test for the first time? The answer to this question is yes, they probably will, and hence this influence serves as a potential source of contamination on the second measure. In short, we may not know whether scores on the second measurement are being influenced by what subjects remember about the first measurement. If subjects have been randomly assigned to groups, any testing effect is neutralized since we would expect it to be the same for each group. Any observed difference can be viewed as a function of the independent variable.

Instrumentation

By instrumentation we mean that *changes in the calibration of a measuring instrument or changes in the observers or scorers used may produce changes in the obtained measurements.* In other words, the instrument may not be measuring what you intend it to measure, or a second group of observers recording measures may not be using the same criteria for making judgments as the first group.

Suppose you are doing an experiment on dieting and your experimental design calls for weighing your subjects. If your scales are faulty, weighing all subjects five pounds too heavy, you have introduced a potential contaminating effect resulting from instrumentation. As with previous threats to internal validity, though, the effect of instrumentation is neutralized if you have randomly assigned subjects to groups.

Regression Effect

By regression effect (or "regression toward the mean") we mean *the tendency for people who score at the extremes on a first test to move toward a middle position of a second test.* Suppose, in our hypothetical study on computer-aided interviewing instruction for students, we had chosen to create our two classes on the basis of math performance on the pretest. Since we have reason to believe that computers will aid greatly in interviewing skill, we decide to place our poorest students in the computer class. At the end of the semester, our posttest demonstrates a reduced difference between the groups. Can we conclude that computers greatly aided the poorer students in their learning of these skills? The answer is no.

People who score very well on a test usually do so because they know the material and because there is a little bit of good luck involved. People who perform very poorly on a test usually do so because they do not know as many answers and because there is a little bad luck involved. On a second testing, the law of averages suggests that the good scorers will not score quite as good and the poor scorers will not score quite as bad. In other words, both groups should move toward some middle ground. If we had divided the students on the basis of pretest performance, we would not be able to separate regression effects from the effects of the treatment. However, if we randomly assign subjects to groups, the regression effect should be the same for each group. Hence, any observed difference can be attributed to the independent variable—in this case, microcomputers versus no microcomputers.

Experimental Mortality

Mortality refers to *the dropout rate in a study*. Subjects can drop out of an experiment for a number of reasons—people get sick, move, or even die. If subjects have been randomly assigned to groups, we can generally assume that the mortality rate for all groups will be roughly the same. Hence, any observed difference can be attributed to the independent variable.

External Validity

External validity refers to the generalizability of the study—the ability to generalize the findings of a single study to the larger population. High external validity requires that subjects be randomly selected from the larger population. Recall from Chapter 9 that a random sample ensures the representativeness of a sample. Since random samples are rarely used in experiments, external validity is rarely high in experiments. In most experiments, the sample of subjects is composed of volunteers, and it seems unlikely that these volunteers are representative of the larger target population. In fact, given the nonrandom nature of the sample, it is usually not possible to establish representativeness.

Failure to draw a random sample of subjects from the target population and hence ensure external validity is certainly not fatal in the case of the experiment, particularly when we remind ourselves of what the experiment is trying to accomplish. *The experiment is a test of causal models.* This is an important step in theory development and one that needs to come before generalizability. Often, in designing research, we labor under the false impression that external validity (generalizability) is perhaps even more important than internal validity. In reality, *internal validity must come before external validity.* Without internal validity, we cannot establish the causal link we are trying to test. Without the ability to establish this causal link, we are only generalizing contaminated findings. Even without generalizability, the experiment is making an important and significant contribution to our understanding of social work phenomena.

True Experiment versus Quasi-Experiment

Generally speaking, there are two basic forms of experiment—the true experiment and the quasi-experiment. As we have already seen, in every true experiment, three elements must be present. First, there must be at least two groups (one experimental, one control). Second, there must be an intentional manipulation of the independent variable. Third, subjects must be randomly assigned to groups. In the quasi-experimental design, the researcher cannot directly manipulate the independent variable and subjects are not randomly assigned to groups. Hence, comparisons are established by *ex-post facto* means.

Because of our inability to use random assignment in quasi-experimental groups, internal validity poses quite a threat. If we cannot find some means of establishing initial equality, we have no way of separating the effects of the manipulated independent variable from these contaminating sources. Hence, cause–effect statements become more difficult to make, but they can be made.

Quasi-Experiment

The strict requirements of experimental designs in laboratory and natural settings are so difficult to achieve at times that other possibilities must be entertained if the researcher wishes to complete a project at all. For this reason, a quasi-experiment is sometimes called for. **A quasi-experiment differs from a true experiment primarily because it lacks the randomness and control characteristic of a true experiment.** Remember that in a true experiment it is essential that subjects be assigned to groups in a random fashion. But when this is impossible, we may be able to salvage the situation after all by using an experiment-like procedure.

Quasi-experiments are also sometimes called *ex-post facto* experiments, and their most important distinguishing characteristic is that some force *clearly unrelated to the independent variable* causes the change in the dependent variable.

The multitude of research studies on smoking and health offers an example of both the uses and the deficiencies of quasi-experiments. Ideally, if we wanted to experiment with the effects of smoking, we would get a group of nonsmokers, randomly assign them to smoking and nonsmoking status, and then watch to see who developed health problems and who did not. Obviously, we can't do that (forcing people to take up smoking is not only ethically reprehensible but probably impossible!). In other words, people have already chosen to smoke or not to smoke, so we can't randomly assign the independent variable to our experiment. Therefore, we have to go at this in another way and put up with the less-than-perfect results of our choice.

We could forgo studying people at all and do studies on rats and mice—after all, you can force *them* to smoke, with few problems. (Note that we said *few*, not none.) But, of course, the problem there is that conclusions about people drawn from animal experiments are always suspect.

What we can do to overcome some of these obstacles is to find a group of smokers and a group of nonsmokers, and then assign them to our experimental and control groups not randomly, but selectively by attempting to match them on the basis of every single variable we think might have something to do with health problems *except smoking* and hope that the careful matching cancels out the effects of those variables. Then we can see whether or not the smoking group had more incidence of health problems. This is not perfect and is not a true experiment, but it does help us study something that otherwise would be difficult to study.

Another way to go after this quasi-experiment would be to find a culture in which smoking had been recently introduced after a long period of not smoking and see whether health records could be compared. In other words, the quasi-experiment seeks to match the experiment for groups that are, in effect, self-selected. The results are not perfect, but they can help us understand some things that would be difficult to study with a true experiment.

References

1. Kenneth J. Gergen, Mary M. Gergen, and W. H. Barton, "Deviance in the Dark," *Psychology Today* 75 (1973): 129–30.
2. A. Orenstein and W. R. Phillips, *Understanding Social Research: An Introduction* (Boston: Allyn and Bacon, 1978).
3. S. E. Asch, *Social Psychology* (Englewood Cliffs, NJ: Prentice-Hall, 1952).
4. E. Aronson and J. M. Carlsmith, "Experimentation in Social Psychology," in *The Handbook of Social Psychology,* G. Lindzey and E. Aronson, eds. (Reading, MA: Addison-Wesley, 1968).
5. J. M. Darley and C. D. Batson, "From Jerusalem to Jericho: A Study of Situational and Dispositional Variables in Helping Behavior," *Journal of Personality and Social Psychology* 27 (1973): 100–8.
6. Darley and Batson, "From Jerusalem to Jericho," p. 209.
7. Orenstein and Phillips, *Understanding Social Research,* p. 53.
8. D. T. Campbell and J. Stanley, *Experimental and Quasi-Experimental Designs for Research* (Chicago: Rand McNally, 1963).
9. Campbell and Stanley, *Experimental and Quasi-Experimental Designs for Research.*

Chapter 11

The Survey

The survey defined
  The United States Census
  Public opinion polling
  Marketing surveys
  Survey research in social work
Planning your survey design
  Define your research objectives
  Identify the unit to be
    researched
  Sample the population
  Choose an appropriate setting
  Choose the time frame for your
    research
Constructing a questionnaire
  Describe the information you
    seek
  Decide on the type of questions
    you will need
  Create a first draft

Review and revise your
    questionnaire
Write a cover letter and
    introduction
Pretest your instrument
  An illustration
Self-administered questionnaires
The mailed questionnaire
Face-to-face interviews
  Effects of interviewer
    characteristics
  Tips for interviewing
Telephone interviews
The interview versus the self-
    administered questionnaire
Strengths and weaknesses of
    survey research
Using secondary data to
    supplement interview data

Do you ever get the feeling that the only reason we have elections is to find out if the polls were right? —ROBERT ORBEN

The Survey Defined

Have you ever been asked to evaluate a course and its teacher at the end of a school semester? If you agreed to such a request, you were probably given an evaluation form to fill out. If you completed this form, you have participated in a *survey*. You should recall from Chapter 6 a list of factors that characterize the survey design. *First, surveys use statistical groups that are "independent of settings."* In a course evaluation survey, for example, it doesn't really matter where the survey form is filled out, although the classroom is usually the designated place. And the data generated by these forms are usually analyzed (grouped statistically) by such characteristics as classification, grade-point average, and expected course grade.

Second, surveys are especially strong on representativeness, though control and naturalness are not entirely sacrificed. While course evaluation surveys, for example, usually aim to look at a total population (in our example, a class of students), such ambitious surveys are the exception rather than the rule. The popularity of the survey rests largely with its potential for representativeness—that is, its ability to evaluate large populations using relatively small samples. With the survey it is possible to examine a small segment of society (a research sample) and from that small segment make certain inferences about the population from which the sample was originally taken. In short, if a survey is carefully designed and executed, the results yielded from a sample can be an amazingly accurate portrayal of the original population, although we can never totally rule out the possibility of misleading or inaccurate findings.

Third, while surveys are usually descriptive or causal, exploratory purposes should not be ruled out. Surveys can be used to collect data that explore, describe, or explain some social phenomenon. Demographic information that might be collected for any one of these purposes includes sex, marital status, education level, income, political preference, and religious preference. Surveys can be used to explore, describe, or explain respondents' knowledge about a particular subject, their past or current behavior, or their attitudes and beliefs concerning a particular subject. Legislative assistants, for example, gathering information on proposed legislation aimed at raising the national drinking age, might wish to probe into respondents' previous knowledge of the drinking age controversy. In effect, the survey technique has been used to research a wide variety of topics including attitudes toward criminal offenders, political orientation, knowledge of taxation laws, consumer trends, and NFL teams that might make it to next year's Super Bowl.

Finally, *surveys may be either cross sectional or longitudinal,* although most are cross sectional. With cross-sectional surveys, data are collected at one point in time. With longitudinal surveys, data are collected at several (at least two) points in time. We will have more to say about this a little later.

In this chapter, we will examine the survey design and its many variations. We will take a look at the steps involved in designing a survey and in constructing a questionnaire. We will also look at the primary methods used to collect questionnaire data and compare their relative advantages and disadvantages. Finally, we will look at secondary data as an additional or alternate source of survey data. Let's begin, though, by looking at four rather different examples of the survey: the U.S. Census, public opinion polling, market surveys, and a survey of social workers.

The United States Census

Once every ten years, the United States Bureau of the Census conducts a special survey aimed at collecting demographic data on *all* persons within this country. From these data emerge demographic statistics—descriptive statistics that deal with the quantitative aspects of a population, including such characteristics as sex, age, and racial/ethnic background, economic and health characteristics, and geographic distribution. The U.S. Census is the largest survey attempt conducted in the United States, and it has been required by law since the writing of the Constitution in 1790.

The main purpose of this decennial survey is to gather data essential to the functioning of our government. (Technically, and constitutionally, the main purpose of the U.S. Census is to allow for apportionment of the House of Representatives. All other uses are ancillary to this.) Federal funds, for example, are often distributed according to census counts—those areas having high population counts (as tabulated by the census) will receive more funds than those areas having low population counts. Other uses the federal government has for census data include calculating economic indicators, projecting the future of agencies such as Social Security, and formulating domestic policies such as federal housing legislation.

The usefulness of the census data is not limited to the federal government. Numerous researchers have also found them to be extremely valuable to their work. However, using the entire body of census data can be quite cumbersome and certainly cost-prohibitive. Hence, the Census Bureau also prepares samples of the original (nationwide) population data. These samples range from 25 percent of the total population (one out of every four Americans) to a mere 0.04 percent (one out of every 10,000 Americans). These samples are recorded on magnetic computer tapes and are made available to anyone wishing to use them.

Since the Census Bureau's basic questionnaire is relatively short (twelve demographic questions and eight housing questions) and hence does not allow for collecting extensive information, the bureau has also developed a more extensive questionnaire, which is distributed to every twentieth person. In other words, selected persons (one out of every twenty Americans) representing a cross-sectional sample of the entire population are asked to fill out a longer form (twenty additional demographic questions and twenty additional housing questions). Since the cost of collecting census data by the government restrains the number of questions that can be asked of the population, this carefully selected sample allows the Census Bureau to collect a greater variety of information that can be viewed as representative of the total population.

Although this massive decennial survey is an admirable task, it is not without problems. As you might suspect, data collected once every ten years soon becomes outdated in a rapidly changing society. Since data collection is really needed more frequently than once every ten years, a multistage sampling design is also used to conduct a monthly Current Population Survey. (See Chapter 9 for a discussion of multistage sampling.) And the sampling methodology used for this survey is even more rigorous than for the decennial census [1]. First, interviewers are selected and trained more carefully than for the decennial census. Additionally, the interviewers gain a greater level of expertise since they work over extended periods of time. What's more, the data generated by the Current Population Survey is usually more up to date than that collected in the decennial survey. However, since the current population survey is generated using a sample, we cannot be certain that it is as accurate as the decennial population survey, which uses the total population.

Public Opinion Polling

We have become quite accustomed to the idea of public opinion polling through the works of such well-known polls as Gallup, Harris, and Roper. But unlike the U.S. Census, polls rarely (if ever) make use of a total population. Instead, opinion pollsters attempt to select a sample of interviewees who seem to be typical of the overall population with respect to identified social and economic characteristics. This need to obtain a sample that is typical of the total population makes random sampling an important and compelling consideration. Whenever possible, opinion polling should include some form of random sampling. *With random sampling each member of the population is assured a known chance of being included in the sample* (see Chapter 9). Hence, this form of sampling gives the best assurance that the sample will be characteristic of the entire population [2].

But not all opinion polls use random samples. In fact, nonrandom samples are quite frequently found in opinion polling. One *nonrandom* sampling technique frequently used in public opinion polls involves the *selection of natural cases occurring so rarely that a random sample simply would not be feasible.* Examples of such nonrandom samples might include mothers of quintuplets or impeached politicians. A second type of nonrandom sample used in public opinion polls involves the collection of data from available or willing participants. Examples of such *haphazard samples,* as they are often called, include customers in a restaurant or students hanging out in the student center. A third nonrandom sample that is often used as a quick check of rapidly changing data by public opinion pollsters is *quota sampling*—the establishment of quotas within a sample that are based on the population proportions for relevant characteristics [3]. When it is necessary to use nonrandom samples, it is essential that checks and controls be used since nonrandom sampling techniques often result in bias.

We do not want to leave you with the impression that bias is limited to nonrandom samples. This is certainly not the case. As we stressed in Chapter 9, bias can occur even when random samples have been selected if you are not careful. Recall from Chapter 9 our discussion of the *Literary Digest* presidential poll of 1936. *Literary Digest* pollsters were guilty of failing to draw a random sample. They did in fact select a *random* sample through telephone directories and automobile registration records. Based on the responses obtained, the magazine predicted a clear victory for the Republican candidate Alf Landon, although Franklin Roosevelt won by a whopping majority. The *Literary Digest* sample failed because it excluded millions of the poor and unemployed during the Great Depression who could not afford either telephones or automobiles. In short, the *Literary Digest* sample proved to have a built-in bias despite the random selection process because the sample was selected from a base that excluded a large proportion of the population—primarily the Democratic voters.

Marketing Surveys

Have you ever wondered how manufacturers decide which products to market and which to scrap? How do manufacturers know, for example, that cheese grits will sell or that flavored potato chips will be a family favorite? How do they know that perfume will be more appealing if packaged in container A instead of B, or that two-ply toilet paper will be more marketable than single-ply paper? Before manufacturers put a new product on the market, they want and need to know how consumers will react to that product. Marketing research is conducted with the goal of predicting such consumer reactions. To identify these reactions, though, marketing researchers almost always use nonrandom samples. Have you ever been stopped while shopping and asked to answer a few questions or to take a "taste test"? Such haphazard or convenience samples provide a quick and inexpensive way of gathering product-evaluation data.

Until recently, marketing researchers have shown little interest in the theory and testing of social science hypotheses. Their primary interest has been limited to predicting the marketing future of specific products. However, in this day of rapidly expanding private sector social services—especially in the health-related fields (i.e., home health care, mental health, and substance abuse treatment centers)—marketing surveys are being utilized more frequently. Although marketing researchers are often accused of studying superficial problems to the neglect of theory and hypothesis testing, market surveyors have been able to provide those who make marketing decisions with accurate and reliable predictions.

Survey Research in Social Work

In social work practice surveys can be used quite productively to gather data on a wide range of subjects of interest. To give you one example, we will look briefly at a study by Sze and Ivker [4]. These researchers used the survey method to study the impact of work setting and role on stress and strain of social workers. Random sampling was obtained by using the then-latest issue of *NASW Professional Social Work Directory* [5]. The researchers chose the Nth, N10th, and N20th names, or 5.25 percent of the persons listed in the directory.

Each social worker was then sent a questionnaire with a cover letter to explain the project, and each one was asked to provide specific personal and social data, educational and work history, work-related data, and stress-related symptoms and behaviors. A checklist of twenty stress-related symptoms was developed to determine if there had been an increase in any of these in the previous two years. After discarding returns that were incomplete or did not meet other preestablished criteria, 686 returns formed the basis for data analysis.

This study revealed many interesting findings. Most responses to job-related conditions were rather positive. "A majority of respondents felt that they were able to make their own decisions and that their roles were clearly defined .... Fewer than 50 percent of the respondents, however, gave favorable responses to questions of salary adequacy, efficient running of the agency, encouragement for career advancement, high morale for fellow workers, a job matching training level, social contact with colleagues, and opportunity for advancement within the agency" [6]. It is interesting to note that 83.2 percent indicated a desire to change agencies and this, coupled with a lack of opportunity to advance within their agency, appeared to be the major factors in job satisfaction and stress. Almost 60 percent perceived an increase in stress-related symptoms during the previous two years, with hospital social workers and university social work teachers ranking as the two groups most affected.

Planning Your Survey Design

Define Your Research Objectives

Now that we have examined the survey through several concrete examples, let's look specifically at the steps you must take when designing your own survey. When beginning any type of survey, **the first step is to define clearly your research objective(s).** What do you want to know by administering this survey and why do you want to know? Surprisingly, this is often the single most difficult step in the research process for most researchers and particularly beginning researchers. One thing that may help in this definition process is the formulation of a *thesis statement*. This thesis statement should have several important characteristics. First, it should generally be one sentence in length. Second, it should contain a subject and a verb and should not be written as a fragmented or run-on sentence. Third, this statement should define the objective of the survey. If, for example, the purpose of your survey is to describe the attitudes of social work students under age twenty-one toward the Equal Rights Amendment, then the thesis statement should state this purpose. If the purpose of your survey is to determine how students who support the ERA differ from those who do not, then the thesis statement should state this purpose. If your purpose is to investigate the relationship between students' ages and their opinions on the ERA, then this purpose should be stated in the thesis statement. The thesis statement is invaluable insofar as it provides a means of precisely defining your research subject, and you should give considerable thought to its development. Some examples of thesis statements for survey research follow.

1. This study has two major objectives—(1) to examine determinants of attitudes toward the Equal Rights Amendment and (2) to examine the role of education in explaining the attitudes of social work students toward the ERA.
2. In this study we focus on the effects of class size on social work students' achievement in social research.
3. In this study we will investigate whether the trend of the 1960s and 1970s toward more egalitarian sex-role attitudes continued into the late 1970s despite a general conservative drift in social and political sentiment.

As you can see, the research objective can be very clearly defined in one complete sentence. Once you have constructed your thesis statement, your research should have clear direction, and your project should then flow from this statement in a logical and coherent fashion.

Identify the Unit to Be Researched

The second step in planning a survey design is to identify the units that comprise the population you are researching. The unit for analysis for survey research can range from individuals, such as the social workers randomly selected from the *NASW Professional Social Work Directory* as in the earlier example, to entire segments of the nation's population, such as all recipients of food stamps. Each respondent is one case in your data set. As a researcher, you must become familiar with the range of units available (see Chapter 6) before deciding which to use in your own survey.

Sample the Population

The third step in planning a survey is to sample from the population with an eye to representativeness. As we have already noted, the popularity of the survey rests largely with its potential for representativeness. When careful probability (random) samples are selected, the sample characteristics can be generalized to the larger population. For a full discussion on sampling, see Chapter 9.

Choose an Appropriate Setting

The fourth step in planning your survey design is choosing an appropriate research setting. Generally speaking, the survey design is independent of setting. That is, the setting is usually unimportant to the data collection process. Self-administered questionnaires, for example, may be filled out individually in any quiet place or in large groups in a classroom or auditorium setting. Similarly, mailed questionnaires can be filled out almost anywhere. However, you may wish to create a standard environment. If you are conducting interviews, for example, you may ask respondents to come to one central location. In any case, a decision on setting must be made.

Choose the Time Frame for Your Research

The fifth step in planning a survey design is to choose the time frame for your research. In short, you must decide whether the data for the survey can be collected at one point in time using a cross-sectional design, or whether it should be collected at different points in time using a longitudinal design.

Cross-Sectional Studies

In a cross-sectional survey, data are collected from a chosen sample at a single point in time. *A cross-sectional survey is a single, unrepeated survey that produces prompt results and can be completed in a relatively short time.* As we indicated in Chapter 6, such a survey is analogous to a still snapshot taken by a camera. While it does provide you with a good picture of the population at one point in time, it does not reveal any movement or change over time. The census, for example, gives us an instantaneous picture of the U.S. population at one point in time—really no more and no less. Without a doubt, cross-sectional surveys are the most frequently used in social work research primarily because of their low costs and their quick results.

Longitudinal Studies

Some topics of interest to social workers are dynamic processes that are not static in time but tend to develop over extended periods. Research studies designed to measure events over a span of time are called longitudinal studies. *With longitudinal studies, data are collected at several points in time during the survey period.* Such research is analogous to a motion picture camera, which portrays an event in motion over a period of time. In short, longitudinal studies provide the researcher with data that can be analyzed in terms of change. Three common types of longitudinal designs are used by social researchers: trend studies, cohort studies, and panel studies. Let's take a brief look at each of these.

Trend Studies   A trend study is actually *several cross-sectional studies conducted successively over some designated period of time.* Each survey is *administered to a different sample of respondents* but under similar conditions and using a similar survey instrument. These surveys are then analyzed to measure change over time. Many public opinion polls are administered repeatedly to determine changes in the opinions of the U.S. public. In an election year, for example, public opinion polls are constantly assessing the public's voting preferences. Such polls are conducted periodically up to the time of an election and change in public opinion is assessed and reported to the public.

If you choose to use a trend study, it is essential that you remember to standardize your variables since measures taken at one point in time are not necessarily compatible with measures taken at another point in time. If, for example, you were to compare the cost of providing housing for a homeless family in 1978 with the cost of providing the same housing in 1988, the comparison would be meaningless unless you standardize (control) for several important factors. Specifically, without standardization, you would not be able to differentiate between changes caused by internal factors or processes (e.g., the number of members in the family's household) from changes caused by external processes (e.g., the rate of inflation).

Another important factor to consider in trend studies is the extent to which the time periods included in the study seriously affect the outcome. Short-run attitudes on matters of high but temporary interest (such as the outcome of an election) must be studied over a period of weeks. Other types of changes, such as changes in the attitudes of college students, must be studied over a period of years. The time frame to be analyzed should match the tempo of change over time in the subjects being surveyed.

One of the major advantages of trend studies is that they permit us to view changes or developing trends that occur within a given population. In addition, they allow for intelligent speculation about the reasons for trend shifts. The disadvantages of trend studies include the long period of time needed to complete the study and the unknown reliability and validity resulting from different samples and several researchers collecting data. Hence, when changes are documented by such surveys, it is sometimes impossible to pinpoint the source of change. The changes identified by trend studies may be real changes reflected in the population over time, or they may be spurious changes resulting from the research methods used (e.g., different subjects at each time interval). Consequently, in reporting results from trend studies, we do run the risk of misrepresenting the trend.

One variation of the trend study that helps to overcome this problem is the *retrospective* time series technique. With this technique a group of respondents are asked questions about specific events, experiences, or opinions that are now a part of their past. The biggest danger in this form of survey is memory distortion; one's recollection of the past is almost always tainted by the present. One means of overcoming this problem is the panel study.

Panel Studies *A panel study is a specific type of trend study that requires repeated interviewing with the same sample (panel, or group of subjects) over an extended period of time.* Like the trend study, its purpose is to measure change in attitudes or behavior over time. In many cases, the panel is given the same set of questions at regular time intervals over a specified time period. A panel, for example, might be given the same questionnaire asking about attitudes toward the death penalty at six-month intervals for three successive years in an attempt to analyze the stability of attitudes toward this controversial issue.

The primary advantage of panel studies is that they do indeed tend to show the amount, direction, and timing of shifts in opinions or behaviors [7]. However, while the panel study can be quite effective in many cases, it does have its disadvantages. First, the costs of a panel study are much higher than the costs of other types of studies. This is largely because the researcher must maintain contact with the same group of respondents. Second, more time is consumed in this type of research since maintaining contact with the same group of individuals over several years requires a great deal of time as well as money. Third, cooperation of respondents on a repetitive basis is often difficult to obtain. While most people will agree to participate in a study one time, fewer people are willing to participate several times over an extended period. Thus, when conducting a panel study, you can bet that your original panel size will probably be much larger than your final panel size. Fourth, respondents can be lost because of changing residences, job changes, vacations, and the like. And with both of these latter disadvantages, results may become biased.

Cohort Analysis *Cohort analysis is a method of analyzing the experiences of cohorts throughout their lives for some specific period of time.* Such studies begin with a cohort—a group of persons who share some common characteristic. Examples of cohorts might include all persons using a particular agency service during 1986, or all persons who were foster parents during 1987. Data collection for such studies would generally require measuring attitudes, behaviors, opportunities, and so forth, for a sample of members of this cohort group over an extended period of time.

Cohort analysis is a very good method for exposing long-term trends. We could, for example, examine the opportunities open to women with PhDs by identifying female doctoral candidates from selected universities during the five-year interval 1971–1975 and comparing their professional experiences with those of women graduating in the later intervals of 1976–1980 and 1981–1985. A longitudinal study of different cohorts would allow us to compare age-specific patterns of behavior and achievement for successive groups.

Cohort analysis is frequently used in demographic research. It permits prediction of changes within a population and allows the development of rather precise estimates of longevity for successive age cohorts.

Constructing a Questionnaire

Once the survey has been planned, you are ready to identify the data needed to accomplish your research objective. **A questionnaire is a data collection instrument containing a select group of questions chosen because of their relevance, carefully worded for clarity, and carefully formatted for printed copy.** A questionnaire is essential to the collection of survey data. When constructing your questionnaire, you should always seek to reach two specific goals. First, the questions you ask should produce the data you need to gather. This task seldom proves to be as easy as it sounds. Second, to be reliable, the questions you ask must tap the same type of information in each person participating. Like the first goal, this is also easier said than done. Meeting both of these goals will require a great deal of effort on your part. However, the task will become easier if you will follow these six essential steps in questionnaire construction:

1. Describe the information that you are seeking.
2. Decide on the type of questions needed.
3. Write a first draft of the questions to be asked.
4. Review and revise the questions.
5. Document the procedures for using the questionnaire.
6. Whenever possible, pretest the questionnaire in a pilot study.

Let's take a quick look at each of these steps.

Describe the Information You Seek

The first step in questionnaire construction, describing the information that you seek, is probably the single most important step in developing your survey instrument. By adequately describing the data you seek, you have provided a starting point for planning the organization and composition of the questions to be included. Such a description of the data, particularly if you are a beginning researcher, will help you to exclude any irrelevant questions and will prevent you from omitting data that are essential for your research.

Decide on the Type of Questions You Will Need

The second step in questionnaire construction is deciding on the type of questions you will need to reach your research objective. In determining the type of questions to ask, you should consider the educational and social levels of your respondents and your plans for data analysis. In general, your questions will be either open- or closed-ended.

Open-Ended Questions

The open-ended question requires respondents to answer in their own words. If, for example, you were to ask some college students their ideas about why some teenage girls experience early pregnancies, they might respond with a variety of answers such as, "… they lack adequate information about birth control methods," "they have no access to birth control," "they want a baby," "too much peer pressure toward early sexual activity," or a "lack of parental supervision," and so forth. In short, respondents answer the questions in their own words, and sometime later these responses are categorized. This process of categorization serves to organize the responses into coded data for analysis and interpretation. But these categories are not presumed before starting the research.

In general, open-ended questions are most useful when you expect an issue to provoke a wide range of responses or when responses are likely to be very detailed and you do not wish to limit the possible range. However, open-ended questions should not be mistaken or substituted for the kind of involved exploration and probing that characterizes intensive interviews—a whole different research method. Nor should they be expected to produce revealing or provocative in-depth responses. In fact, the heavy use of open-ended questions can lead to disappointment if your respondents neglect to respond or give only brief, superficial answers.

As you might have already suspected, coding open-ended questions can present a unique set of problems, particularly if two or more persons are involved in coding these responses. Simply put, coders must be well trained to code responses in a consistent manner. If two coders categorize the same response in two different categories, the data analysis becomes meaningless. In short, reliability of the research results demands agreement among all coders as to the categorization of responses. Therefore, it is advantageous to review the coding of open-ended responses with the coders prior to data analysis. We shall have more to say about this in Chapter 13.

Closed-Ended Questions

Closed-ended questions are structured to offer a list of acceptable answers from which respondents may choose. This list of answers should cover all significant alternatives without any overlap between categories, and may include a catch-all category for respondents whose answers are not provided among the choices. While this catch-all category may change with the nature of the question, it usually takes the form of "other" or "don't know." The wording of closed-ended questions should also be clear, definite, and impartial.

The biggest advantage of closed-ended questions is the relative ease of coding and analyzing data. Because each categorical response can usually be given a numeric code, the data can quickly be entered into a computer. The major disadvantage of such questions is that the categories typically do not contain all possible responses, and you therefore run the risk of forcing your respondents to fit (though somewhat incorrectly) into predesigned categories.

Create a First Draft

The third step in questionnaire construction is to create a first draft of your questions, giving special attention to both content and format (question layout). Since both of these issues are very important to your finished product (the questionnaire), let's take a brief look at each.

Questionnaire Content

Relevance is the key word in questionnaire content, and considerable thought needs to be channeled into your content. Your questionnaire content will be determined in part by the theory from which the survey springs, in part by your research objective (the task described in your thesis statement), and in part by the requirements of the statistical procedure(s) to be used. The questions you choose to include must satisfy both the requirements of your study and the limitations of your respondents. Last but not least, the questions you choose must measure the concepts they are designed to measure. Issues related to questionnaire content include the (1) structure of questions, (2) number of questions, and (3) order of questions.

Structure of Questions   All questions must be relevant, clear, and to the point. In some cases, the educational level of most of your respondents will not be as high as yours. Consequently, your respondents will probably not share your professional vocabularies. In short, the vocabulary used in the questionnaire must be understandable and recognizable to your respondents. Professionals, for example, may use the term "delinquent," whereas teenagers talk about "being in trouble." Similarly, "higher education" may mean high school to a respondent and the completion of an undergraduate degree to a researcher. It is a good idea to contact someone familiar with your target population to inquire about the best terminology to use.

A good question is emotionally neutral, leaving the choice to the respondent. A biased question is emotionally colored, leaving little or no choice to the respondent. A biased question might be, "Don't you feel that temporary foster home arrangements are better for dependent children than group residential arrangements?" A much better (and neutral) question would be:

> Comparing temporary foster home care arrangements for dependent children with group residential care arrangements, which do you think usually benefits a child most?
> a. Temporary foster home care
> b. Group residential care
> c. They are equally beneficial
> d. Don't know

The more sensitive the issue, the more care you should put in the composition of the question. Questions dealing with issues such as deviant behavior, political issues, and personal relations can be particularly sensitive. In short, questions should be worded to minimize respondents' negative reactions.

Number of Questionnaire Items   A good questionnaire is limited to the minimum number of items needed to satisfy the research requirements. You must consider the amount of time respondents will need to complete your survey. If participation is voluntary and the survey is quite long, many respondents will not complete the form. As a general rule of thumb, you should make a rather lengthy list of potential questions and then carefully trim down the list. Pilot studies are good indicators of which questions can be dropped from the questionnaire and which should be left in. When conducting a pilot study, it is a good idea to include more questions than you intend to ask and then let the results of the pilot study assist you in further reducing your questionnaire. We will have more to say about pilot studies a little later.

Ordering the Questions   The order in which the questions appear on the questionnaire is also extremely important in questionnaire construction. The questions should appear in some logical pattern, and transitions should appear in cases where the logical flow is interrupted. The first (lead) question should be both interesting and noncontroversial to your respondents. Additionally, this first question should make your readers want to continue. More difficult or sensitive questions should appear toward the end of the survey, to be encountered by respondents after sufficient interest and trust have been developed.

Often, beginning researchers have a tendency to unknowingly group two questions into a single question. For instance, consider the question "Does your employer have lower salary categories for racial minorities and women?" A respondent might answer "yes" if lower salary categories apply for women but not minorities, or "yes" if lower salary categories apply for minorities but not women, or "yes" if lower salary categories apply for both minorities and women. In the first two conditions stated previously, it is equally conceivable that a respondent would answer "no" to the question if the lower salary categories did not apply to both groups. In effect, two questions are being asked, and two questions should be written.

Question Format

You may think that talking about questionnaire format is rather silly and even wasteful of space in this book. However, we believe that once you start your own questionnaire construction, you will see things a little differently. The format of your questionnaire is extremely important because it invariably helps to set each respondent's mood. If the questionnaire appears disorganized, your respondents will become confused and their motivation to complete the questionnaire will be dampened. Among important issues related to questionnaire format are (1) spacing, (2) boxes for response alternatives, (3) handling contingency questions, and (4) matrix questions. Let's take a brief look at each of these.

Spacing   One way to communicate an air of order and organization is by spreading the questionnaire out and allowing some white spaces to slip in. If the questions are crammed together, your respondents may accidentally skip one or more questions or become confused by the clutter. Attractive spacing of questions will make your instrument easier to read.

Using Boxes for Recording Responses   For closed-ended questions, it is a good idea to use some kind of box for response alternatives. These boxes can best be created with parentheses or brackets. If, for example, you ask your respondents to indicate their sex, each response alternative, male and female, should be listed with a box. The use of boxes gives respondents a very clear idea of where they are to record their responses. Without a box, respondents may not know where you want them to put their answers.

Contingency Questions   Sometimes there are questions whose relevancy depends on a respondent's answer to a previous question. Such questions are called contingency questions and must be carefully formatted on your questionnaire. Suppose, for example, you are doing research to determine client satisfaction with your agency's emergency food program. One question you might ask is:

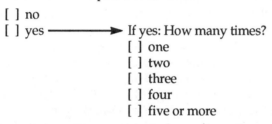

> Have you received an emergency food order from the Metropolitan Food Bank within the past six months?
>
> [ ] no
> [ ] yes ──────────▶ If yes: How many times?
>   [ ] one
>   [ ] two
>   [ ] three
>   [ ] four
>   [ ] five or more

Contingency questions must be formatted in such a way that your respondents will know to answer them only if their answer to a previous question warrants it. Again, the important thing is that you do not confuse your subjects. If necessary, add arrows and additional instructions before such questions to ensure clarity.

Matrix Questions   Sometimes you will have a series of questions whose response alternatives are all the same. For example, if you were assessing students' attitudes toward social statistics, you might have a series of statements whose response alternatives are in Likert format (see Chapter 8). In such cases, it is useful to construct a matrix of questions. This matrix format is illustrated in Figure 11.1.

The matrix format has several distinct advantages. First, it is *space efficient*. It allows the placement of similar questions in a relatively small amount of space. Second, it is *time-efficient*. Generally, respondents will be able to answer questions put in this format in a reasonable amount of time. Third, it *allows for direct comparisons of answers across questions*. As respondents answer each question, they can look back to see how they have answered previous questions. This ability to examine previous answers, though, does have its disadvantages. In short, this kind of comparison can lead to a response set. If subjects agree with the first statement in the matrix, they may check "agree" for all similar statements without really reading the questions or without giving the questions much thought. When using matrix questions, you will need to check for response sets.

For each of the following statements, choose the response alternative that best describes your feelings. Response alternatives are STRONGLY AGREE (SA), AGREE (A), UNDECIDED (U), DISAGREE (D), and STRONGLY DISAGREE (SD).

	SA	A	U	D	SD
1. Statistics should NOT be a part of the social work curriculum.	[ ]	[ ]	[ ]	[ ]	[ ]
2. I would take this course even if it were not required.	[ ]	[ ]	[ ]	[ ]	[ ]
3. It is very difficult to pass statistics the first time.	[ ]	[ ]	[ ]	[ ]	[ ]
4. Statistics frightens me.	[ ]	[ ]	[ ]	[ ]	[ ]
5. Statistics is similar to other courses in the social work curriculum.	[ ]	[ ]	[ ]	[ ]	[ ]
6. I find math challenging and therefore am excited by the prospects of such a course.	[ ]	[ ]	[ ]	[ ]	[ ]
7. Statistics is irrelevant to the profession of social work.	[ ]	[ ]	[ ]	[ ]	[ ]
8. What I have heard about this course from others has primarily discouraged me.	[ ]	[ ]	[ ]	[ ]	[ ]
9. Statistics can be learned if I am willing to work.	[ ]	[ ]	[ ]	[ ]	[ ]
10. Statistics is a valuable skill to the social worker.	[ ]	[ ]	[ ]	[ ]	[ ]

FIGURE 11.1   Example of Matrix Questions

Review and Revise Your Questionnaire

The fourth step in questionnaire construction is reviewing and revising your questions. One misgiving that beginning researchers often have is that once the questions have been committed to paper, they need not be altered. This is simply not so. Generally speaking, questions will need to be revised—that is, refined for clarity, depth, and lack of ambiguity—again and again. As we have already stressed, you should seek comments from individuals who have had experience dealing with persons similar to your targeted population. If, for example, your targeted population is Vietnam veterans, it would be advantageous to have a Vietnam veteran review your questionnaire. Look for technical defects at this step and be sensitive to redundant questions. In addition, look for formatting problems that might result in confusion.

Write a Cover Letter and Introduction

The fifth step in questionnaire construction is writing an introduction to the questionnaire and, in the case of a questionnaire that is to be mailed, a cover letter. The primary purpose of a cover letter is to introduce the questionnaire to respondents and to explain what your research is all about. Additionally, the cover letter serves to legitimize the questionnaire in the eyes of your respondents. Your cover letter should strive to convey to each respondent the importance of his or her responses in the research endeavor and to emphasize the need for truthful and accurate answers. Your letter should also point out that there are no right or wrong answers and that all information given will be kept confidential.

Instructions for filling out a questionnaire usually appear before each new section. In general, the instructions explain how the questionnaire is to be filled out. Like the cover letter, the instructions should emphasize the need for honest answers and ensure respondents their anonymity. If only one choice is allowed for each question, the instructions should also make this clear. If any of the terms used in the construction of questions holds a special meaning or tends to be ambiguous, it needs to be clearly defined in the instructions.

Most problems can be avoided if the instructions are prepared carefully. In short, the instructions should be prepared well enough to meet the needs of your least sophisticated respondent. At the same time, you should keep instructions brief and to the point.

Pretest Your Instrument

The sixth step in questionnaire construction involves pretesting the questionnaire through a pilot study, which gives you the opportunity to discover unforeseen problems of administration, coding, and analysis. **A pilot study is essentially a pretest of the survey instrument.** It is conducted to test the instrument for ambiguous or misleading questions and to offer you the opportunity to evaluate the performance of the survey instrument prior to its general distribution. Often, the pilot study indicates that a question on the survey is not tapping the desired information. At other times, the pilot study will forewarn you that your instrument is too long or too complex for the average respondent to complete. The pilot study also provides an opportunity for you to test the statistical methodology of your survey and to determine if reorganization is needed. Finally, information yielded from the pilot study may suggest new channels of inquiry and inspire ideas about additional questions that can enrich your research.

An Illustration

To help you see all of the steps come together into a concrete product, we have included a composite illustration of a questionnaire. The questionnaire presented here was constructed by an undergraduate student for a senior research project. If you were a social worker employed in a probation office or a criminal diversion program, the findings of this kind of questionnaire could be helpful in determining community attitudes toward your clientele.

We have not selected this questionnaire because we think it is perfect. On the contrary, we know there are some problems with the instrument. Carefully examine the questions and take time to read the notes that we have provided as a partial critique of the instrument. A careful study of this questionnaire and the accompanying notes should help you with your questionnaire construction.

Dear Respondent:

You have been selected to participate in a study concerned with people's perceptions of criminal offenders. There are no right or wrong answers to these questions. We would simply like to know how you feel about the situations and issues described in this survey.

Please take some time to fill out the accompanying form. Do not put your name on the survey form. There will be no attempt to identify any respondents.

Thank you for your cooperation.

Sincerely,

Questionnaire

Listed below are twelve criminal cases brought to trial. You are to assume the guilt of the persons involved. The "criminals" mentioned in these descriptions are not real persons, and any similarity in names or circumstances to any real persons is merely coincidental.[1] Two questions follow each brief description. You are asked to check one and only one answer for each question. Remember, there are no right or wrong answers to these questions.

FOR QUESTION NUMBER 1: You are to imagine that you are the judge in the courtroom. Each person described has been found guilty, and you must pronounce sentence.

FOR QUESTION NUMBER 2: You are to imagine that you are each person's neighbor. You know what he or she has done. How would you treat him or her, knowing the misdeed.

CASE NO. 1
Jones Meat Packing Company has engaged itself in a price-rigging scheme with Brown Meat Packers, Inc. Since these two companies together control a large segment of the meat-packing industry in central Louisiana, their actions have driven up the prices of meat considerably in the area. They have been found guilty of price-rigging.

    1. Would you sentence them to[2]:
        [ ] a prison term of one year or greater
        [ ] a jail term of less than one year or probation[3]
        [ ] other treatment or no sentence
        [ ] can't say

    2. In interacting with Jones and Brown, would you[4]:
        [ ] avoid associating with them
        [ ] continue to associate with them but with reservation
        [ ] continue the relationship as though nothing had happened
        [ ] can't say

CASE NO. 2
Michael Reed, a 20-year-old male, had been dating Karla, a 16-year-old female. On a date to Chaplin's Lake, Michael and Karla willingly and eagerly engaged in sexual intercourse. Karla's parents found out and were enraged, and they charged Michael with statutory rape.

    1. Would you sentence him to:
        [ ] a prison term of one year or greater
        [ ] a jail term of less than one year or probation
        [ ] other treatment or no sentence
        [ ] can't say

    2. In interacting with Michael Reed, would you:
        [ ] avoid associating with him
        [ ] continue to associate with him but with reservation
        [ ] continue the relationship as though nothing had happened
        [ ] can't say

CASE NO. 3
Debbie Carloss, a junkie, was picked up on skid row for possession of heroin. Although this was her first time for possession, she did have a couple of petty thefts on her record.

    1. Would you sentence her to:
        [ ] a prison term of one year or greater
        [ ] a jail term of less than one year or probation
        [ ] other treatment or no sentence
        [ ] can't say

2. In interacting with Debbie Carloss, would you:
   [ ] avoid associating with her
   [ ] continue to associate with her but with reservation
   [ ] continue the relationship as though nothing had happened
   [ ] can't say

CASE NO. 4
Tom Grest, a 31-year-old male, was arrested after an attack where a good deal of force was used in the sexual assault of a 21-year-old female. Grest was found guilty of rape.[5]

1. Would you sentence him to:
   [ ] a prison term of one year or greater
   [ ] a jail term of less than one year or probation
   [ ] other treatment or no sentence
   [ ] can't say

2. In interacting with Tom Grest, would you:
   [ ] avoid associating with him
   [ ] continue to associate with him but with reservation
   [ ] continue the relationship as though nothing had happened
   [ ] can't say

CASE NO. 5
Patrick Dowen was drunk when he strangled his girlfriend at the culmination of an argument. Dowen was found guilty of second-degree murder.

1. Would you sentence him to:
   [ ] a prison term of one year or greater
   [ ] a jail term of less than one year or probation
   [ ] other treatment or no sentence
   [ ] can't say

2. In interacting with Patrick Dowen, would you:
   [ ] avoid associating with him
   [ ] continue to associate with him but with reservation
   [ ] continue the relationship as though nothing had happened
   [ ] can't say

CASE NO. 6
Paul Hill met Ray Boulder in a public restroom where the two men engaged in a voluntary homosexual act. They were found guilty of homosexuality.

1. Would you sentence Paul Hill and Ray Boulder to:
   [ ] a prison term of one year or greater
   [ ] a jail term of less than one year or probation
   [ ] other treatment or no sentence
   [ ] can't say

2. In interacting with Paul Hill and Ray Boulder, would you:
   [ ] avoid associating with them
   [ ] continue to associate with them but with reservation
   [ ] continue the relationship as though nothing had happened
   [ ] can't say

CASE NO. 7
Keven Cross was picked up for robbery after he held up a liquor store, threatening the proprietor with a Saturday night special.[6]

1. Would you sentence him to:
   [ ] a prison term of one year or greater
   [ ] a jail term of less than one year or probation
   [ ] other treatment or no sentence
   [ ] can't say

2. In interacting with Keven Cross, would you:
   [ ] avoid associating with him
   [ ] continue to associate with him but with reservation
   [ ] continue the relationship as though nothing had happened
   [ ] can't say

CASE NO. 8

Harold Pitt is a local business executive arrested by police for drunk driving after a New Year's Eve party.

1. Would you sentence him to:
   [ ] a prison term of one year or greater
   [ ] a jail term of less than one year or probation
   [ ] other treatment or no sentence
   [ ] can't say

2. In interacting with Harold Pitt, would you:
   [ ] avoid associating with him
   [ ] continue to associate with him but with reservation
   [ ] continue the relationship as though nothing had happened
   [ ] can't say

CASE NO. 9

Ralph Dorn is a 29-year-old male who exposed himself to several coeds walking on campus during the day. He was charged with exhibitionism.[7]

1. Would you sentence him to:
   [ ] a prison term of one year or greater
   [ ] a jail term of less than one year or probation
   [ ] other treatment or no sentence
   [ ] can't say

2. In interacting with Ralph Dorn, would you:
   [ ] avoid associating with him
   [ ] continue to associate with him but with reservation
   [ ] continue the relationship as though nothing had happened
   [ ] can't say

CASE NO. 10

Ann Greene was picked up in her car for possession of an ounce of marijuana. It was her first offense.

1. Would you sentence her to:
   [ ] a prison term of one year or greater
   [ ] a jail term of less than one year or probation
   [ ] other treatment or no sentence
   [ ] can't say

2. In interacting with Ann Greene, would you:
   [ ] avoid associating with her
   [ ] continue to associate with her but with reservation
   [ ] continue the relationship as though nothing had happened
   [ ] can't say

CASE NO. 11

William Tracy was a bookkeeper for the First National Bank in Summerville. In an ingenious scheme, Tracy manipulated the books in such a manner that he was able to borrow over $15,000 from the bank over a three-year period. Tracy was found guilty of embezzlement.

1. Would you sentence him to:
   [ ] a prison term of one year or greater
   [ ] a jail term of less than one year or probation
   [ ] other treatment or no sentence
   [ ] can't say

2. In interacting with William Tracy, would you:
   [ ] avoid associating with him
   [ ] continue to associate with him but with reservation
   [ ] continue the relationship as though nothing had happened
   [ ] can't say

CASE NO. 12
Mary Ross passed a bum check while she was mildly under the influence of alcohol.

1. Would you sentence her to:
   [ ] a prison term of one year or greater
   [ ] a jail term of less than one year or probation
   [ ] other treatment or no sentence
   [ ] can't say

2. In interacting with Mary Ross, would you:
   [ ] avoid associating with her
   [ ] continue to associate with her but with reservation
   [ ] continue the relationship as though nothing had happened
   [ ] can't say

For each of the following statements, choose the response alternative which best describes your feelings. Response alternatives are STRONGLY AGREE (SA), AGREE (A), UNDECIDED (U), DISAGREE (D), and STRONGLY DISAGREE (SD).

	SA	A	U	D	SD
1. The courts mollycoddle criminals.	[ ]	[ ]	[ ]	[ ]	[ ]
2. All persons are treated equal under the law.	[ ]	[ ]	[ ]	[ ]	[ ]
3. Rehabilitation should be the goal of our criminal justice system.	[ ]	[ ]	[ ]	[ ]	[ ]
4. The answer to the rising crime rate is to build more prisons.	[ ]	[ ]	[ ]	[ ]	[ ]
5. A defendant who can hire a good defense lawyer will get off easier than someone who cannot afford such a lawyer.	[ ]	[ ]	[ ]	[ ]	[ ]
6. Most adult criminals cannot be rehabilitated.	[ ]	[ ]	[ ]	[ ]	[ ]
7. If a person with a past criminal record were to move next door to me, I would not want to know about it.	[ ]	[ ]	[ ]	[ ]	[ ]
8. If I were on a jury, I would consider sentencing a defendant to death if he/she were convicted of first degree murder.	[ ]	[ ]	[ ]	[ ]	[ ]
9. Alternatives to a prison term should be considered when the defendant is a first offender.	[ ]	[ ]	[ ]	[ ]	[ ]
10. A person should always obey the law, even if the law is not a good one.	[ ]	[ ]	[ ]	[ ]	[ ]

PLEASE GIVE THE FOLLOWING BACKGROUND INFORMATION ON YOURSELF. THESE DATA WILL BE USED FOR STATISTICAL PURPOSES ONLY.

Sex: [ ] male   [ ] female

Age: _____ (in years)

Marital status: [ ] single
                   [ ] married
                   [ ] divorced, separated, or widowed

Number of children: _____

Religious affiliation: _____

Education level   [ ] never completed high school
                   [ ] graduated from high school

[ ] some college
[ ] graduated from college
[ ] graduate degree

Are you currently employed?
[ ] no
[ ] yes

    If yes: What is your current position? _____

Notes

1. Including a disclaimer in a questionnaire concerning names and real-life circumstances is a good thing to do—especially for circumstances such as described here.
2. When constructing a questionnaire such as this, there is a risk that respondents' answer to the first question related to each case will affect their answer to the second question. If you have questions such as this, you should make it a point to check for response sets.
3. Two of these response alternatives reflect two real alternatives: a jail term of less than a year or probation and other treatment or no sentence. Because these four alternatives have been combined into two, some information is lost and some ambiguity is introduced. If, for example, a respondent checks the third alternative, you have no way of knowing if he or she prefers "other treatment" or "no sentence."
4. Case No. 1 refers to "them," but it is unclear as to who "them" really is. It may be Mr. Jones and Mr. Brown or it may be both the Jones and Brown Corporations. To make things clearer, it would be better to ask "Would you sentence Mr. Jones and Mr. Brown ...?"
5. The rape described in Case No. 4 is more stereotypical in its description than it is typical of the rape cases that generally come before the courts. When this survey was administered, this case received the strongest formal and informal sanctions by respondents. If the question had portrayed a more typical rape case, the responses might not have been so strong.
6. This question presumes the respondent knows what a "Saturday night special" is. It might have been better to have replaced "Saturday night special" with "a hand gun."
7. Case No. 9 assumes that everyone will know what "exposed" himself means. But in constructing a questionnaire, it is best to be as simple as possible. We might want to use a more descriptive term like "took down his pants in front of several women." Try very hard not to use language that some strata of society will not understand.

Self-Administered Questionnaires

By definition, a self-administered questionnaire is one given to respondents with the assumption that each respondent can read the questions, has the knowledge and interest to answer them, and has a pencil, a place, and time to complete the instrument. Respondents may complete such a questionnaire in a group or individually.

If you are dealing with respondents in a public setting where all can be presumed to be aware of and concerned about a problem, a convenience sample can often be used. In such instances, a questionnaire is distributed in random locations and at times when typical members are passing by. As part of an aroused group, they may have higher than usual motivation to answer. Some examples might include students on a university campus concerned about an unexpectedly large increase in tuition or fees, or people in an area devastated by a windstorm. If the questionnaire is distributed at a group meeting, such as a school class or public assembly, respondents may be encouraged to answer more frankly because of group support than they would if they were alone.

The Mailed Questionnaire

Mailed questionnaires are used extensively in social work research because they are capable of reaching sample respondents living in widely dispersed geographic areas at relatively low costs. With the mailed questionnaire, respondents answer and return the questionnaire only if they are motivated to do so. Therefore, it is especially important that a persuasive cover letter be enclosed with each questionnaire. The word processor is a powerful tool in creating personal letters, and you should consider using one if it is available to you. You should also make responding to your questionnaire as easy as possible by minimizing the costs in both time and money for your respondents. Using a short questionnaire and a self-addressed return envelope, for example, will tend to increase your response rates.

With the mailed questionnaire, one of your prime concerns will be maximizing your response rates. Response rates may be well below 50 percent for a mailed survey.   However, this return rate can definitely be increased with follow-ups. Professional researchers often use up to four mailings (i.e., follow-ups) to increase their return rate. If you plan to use the mail-back procedure, it is imperative that you develop a method for checking the address of each respondent returning the questionnaire. Without such a code, you will not be able to determine who has returned the questionnaire and who has not. One method that you might use is to print a number on the questionnaire or envelope so that you are able to match up the return numbers with those on the original mail-out list. Often a blank questionnaire is mailed out along with the reminders, just in case the first questionnaire has already been "filed." Besides serving as a reminder to fill out the questionnaire, the repeated mail-back procedure demonstrates to your respondents how much you value their responses. Repeated appeals to answer the survey can also serve to persuade initially reluctant respondents to fill out the questionnaire.

Mailed questionnaires have several advantages. First, they are *less costly to conduct.* Since there is no difference in the cost of collecting data within your own city or across the nation, mailed questionnaires are frequently used to collect data from across the United States. Second, there is little personal bias involved with the mailed questionnaire because respondents are able to answer the questionnaire by themselves and at their own convenience. Hence, they have no one to influence them and more time to consider their answers. Third, there is a standardization of the questions asked in the mailed survey since all respondents are given the same printed questions. Since there is no personal meeting with a researcher, respondents cannot be influenced by face-to-face interaction. Fourth, training requirements for assistants are minimal since there is little or no researcher–respondent interaction.

Several disadvantages are associated with mailed questionnaires. First, *you can never really know for certain who filled in the questionnaire.* Was it the person to whom it was sent, or was it a friend or a relative? Second, out-of-date mailing lists may result in questionnaires that cannot be delivered, forcing you to make special provisions when this occurs. One way of handling this problem economically is to arrange with the post office for return-postage-guaranteed envelopes. When this type of arrangement is made with the post office, return postage is paid only on those envelopes actually returned.

With mailed questionnaires, every return must be scrutinized to ensure that it was not falsely or frivolously filled in. It is your responsibility as researcher to do everything possible to remove contaminated and spoiled returns.

Face-to-Face Interviews

In a face-to-face interview, a researcher (or research assistant) contacts respondents personally to answer the research questions. Questions are asked orally by the researcher—although charts, cards, or other visual aids are sometimes used during the interview process—and they are answered orally by the respondents.

Face-to-face interviews have several distinct advantages, and knowing these may help you decide whether this procedure is best for your study. First, in a face-to-face interview, the interviewer can clarify questions that seem confusing or that are misinterpreted by respondents. If a respondent clearly misunderstands a question, such clarifications are essential or data may be lost. When confusing or misinterpreted questions call for clarification, it is important that clarifying remarks be standardized. Without such control, you can never be sure whether your respondents are responding to the question or the clarifying remarks. Second, the interview typically produces a higher response rate than does the mailed questionnaire. This is most likely because it is a lot more difficult to turn someone down face-to-face than to turn someone down by throwing away a printed questionnaire. Third, the presence of an interviewer usually serves to decrease the number of "don't know" and "no answer" responses. With the interview, you can gently probe respondents for a position. Fourth, in addition to asking questions, the interviewer can observe. These observations may include general reactions to the respondents' dress, grooming, and mannerisms as well as the physical surroundings.

Although the advantages of interviewing will probably outweigh any disadvantages, several *disadvantages* should be mentioned. First, interviews are very time-consuming. Interviewers must be trained, and this training must make use of the final interview schedule to ensure that the intent and spirit of the research project are being positively served. The success of the interview ultimately depends on the interviewer's skill, persuasiveness, and persistence. Second, interviews are costly in time and resources. While the per-case collection cost in a mailed questionnaire is about equal to five first-class postage stamps ($1.25 in 1990), or about a third of an hour's labor at minimum wage rates, each interview is likely to cost an average of three hours' labor at minimum wage rates. This includes time in contacting and scheduling and rescheduling interviews, travel time to the interview location, and an hour or more to complete the interview. In general, a brisk, short, well-planned interview has a better chance of succeeding than a long, rambling one does. The latter is prone to interruption, and if it is interrupted, the spirit of the interview may be difficult (even impossible) to recover. Sometimes funded researchers find it advantageous to pay interviewees to come to a central site for interviews. Although this procedure may reduce net costs somewhat for the interviewer, it frequently raises the cost for the interviewee and hence the rate of refusals.

In sum, the interview is superior for gaining extensive information, verified by extended discussion and probing in problem areas. If the interviewer is well matched to the respondent for sex, age, background, and interests, the flow of information is usually enhanced. For many respondents, the research interview is rewarding in itself. For most of us, personal contact is inherently rewarding if the partner is pleasant, responsive, and considerate.

Effects of Interviewer Characteristics

Untrained, inept, or insensitive interviewers can easily defeat the objectives of data collection by scheduled interview. Thus, the interview method is more risky than the questionnaire method unless you give serious attention to your choice of interviewers. Dress, appearance, and social background are very important, and generally should be similar to that of your respondents. Perceived common background and interests will usually put respondents at ease. In doing research on working women's attitudes toward feminism, for example, it would be a mistake to send a strong-willed traditional male to do the interviewing. And in doing research on the fertility rate in inner-city black neighborhoods, black female interviewers would probably be more successful.

Interviewers should be well rehearsed on the basic research objectives and knowledgeable in the practical aspects of the research subject. Training sufficient to assure self-control and resilience in the give and take of interviewing is essential. Interviewers must also have good conversational skills and good social skills to deal smoothly and pleasantly with a wide variety of respondents. Finally, interviewers must be skilled in turning the conversation in the right direction, shifting to the next subject when one subject has been satisfied, and terminating the interview gracefully.

Tips for Interviewing

Interviewing for research purposes, as differentiated from the more accustomed social worker–client helping interview, presents some distinctive characteristics. First, research interviews are very highly focused information-gathering situations. The interviewer is not interested in the wide range of topics of importance to the client, but purposefully seeks to limit input to those areas and topics identified by the research design. Second, in other client contacts the social worker always seeks to individualize the client and interact with him or her in a deferential manner, recognizing the personal and situational uniqueness. In the research interview the interviewer seeks to standardize as much as possible the required interaction with the respondent to avoid creating any unnecessary assumptions or ideas that will affect or "lead" the respondent. Third, the primary purpose of most social worker–client interactions is for assessing need and providing some form of intervention or "help" to the client. In the research interview this is not the case. In fact, in one sense the respondent is helping the researcher. In a broader sense, however, research interviews can, and often do, contribute to findings that may alter social policy, the kinds of services offered by an agency, or the manner in which services are delivered. It is hoped that this process will improve circumstances for future clients and provide greater support for social work activities.

We would like to share with you a few tips that we believe can prevent problems.

- o Try to establish a friendly relationship with the respondent, who is usually greatly affected by the interviewer's presence. As the interviewer, you should create a comfortable atmosphere for the respondent by being pleasant, courteous, well groomed, neat, and low-keyed. In addition, giving some interesting information on the research project can help to set the tone of the interview.
- o Conduct the interview in a comfortable, private place to avoid distraction from other activity and interruptions from callers. A private office is preferred over a home since interviews often encounter intrusive family activity.
- o Keep the interview on the subject as required by the interview schedule. Avoid any discussion of the respondent's personal affairs or concerns with politics, religion, or any extraneous matters. If such subjects are introduced by the respondent, show polite interest, then get back to the interview question or go on to the next question. The main flow of information should be from the respondent to the interviewer. A good interviewer does very little talking but stimulates relevant conversation from the respondent.
- o Especially sensitive issues should be introduced late in the interview, after the respondent has developed a rhythm of communication and has become accustomed to the interviewer's style and manner. Lead up to sensitive matters by asking routine questions. Sensitive issues might include death of family or friends, sexual and criminal behavior, and close personal matters such as health, career security, and past failures. Always show sympathetic interest and understanding. With proper attention from the interviewer, the respondent may feel relief at being able to talk about traumatic personal matters.
- o Avoid giving the respondent the idea that you can help to solve any personal problems. You are only there in the capacity of an interviewer engaged in data gathering. (This is very difficult for most social workers!)
- o Avoid making any suggestions to the respondent except those implied by the interview schedule and the research objectives. As interviewer, you should repeatedly review these objectives, making sure that all are included when there is opportunity.
- o If the research objective requires discussion of family relationships, income, and age, you should anticipate that such issues may be difficult for the respondent to discuss. Here, the "universalizing" technique may be helpful, such as the statement that all families have problems to varying degrees, with relations between spouses, and between parents and children, and the elderly. This provides an opening and a little bit of planning time for the respondent to discuss family matters.
- o If it becomes apparent that the respondent is lying or concealing or falsifying facts, do not worsen the situation with hard or incisive questions. Be tactful in moving on to other subjects without harming the interview relationship.

- o It is permissible to accept minor hospitality such as an offer of coffee, tea, or a soft drink. In such cases, consume the drink discreetly and without much delay in order to proceed with the interview.
- o Recording the interview must be limited to what is agreeable to the respondent. A common method is the tape recorder, and it is soon forgotten once the interview is under way, provided the respondent is willing. If a tape recorder is permissible, use a sensitive microphone incorporated in the recorder and keep the machine to one side or out of sight. It is usually too distracting for the interviewer to take notes during the interview, so cultivate the skill of remembering necessary details and outline them completely as soon as the interview is ended. A concise and well-organized interview schedule will help keep the interview on track and will help reduce the volume of unnecessary information. If the interviewee asks you not to include or use some information from the interview, you should cooperate and honor the request since the interview is voluntary.
- o End the interview with some light, routine questions and with a pleasant comment that is appropriate to the situation and the time.
- o At the end of the interview, thank the respondent for donating time and effort to your research project. It is appropriate at this time to ask if the respondent is interested in seeing a copy of the research report. Some respondents will greatly appreciate such an offer.

Telephone Interviews

One alternative to the face-to-face interview is the telephone interview, which can greatly reduce the cost and inconvenience of reaching and personally interviewing respondents. Such interviews can cover a wide geographic area at relatively low costs, even when compared with local travel costs. With telephone interviews, there is also less need to match the characteristics of interviewer and respondent. And in fact, rather extensive information can be obtained, though the contact is less close and less intense than the direct personal interview. As with the face-to-face interview, interviewers should rehearse with the actual research interview schedule. A thorough critique of each interviewer's approach, explanation of the project, plea for cooperation, and skill in following the schedule are very helpful in improving the quality and success of telephone interviews. It is estimated that telephone interviewing is about 43 percent as costly as face-to-face interviewing [8].

The telephone interview should include only brief, simple questions, with fewer questions than the direct interview schedule, and far fewer than the self-administered questionnaire. While you might think that direct personal interviews are more reliable, surveys using the same items by telephone and by direct personal interview have yielded very similar results, suggesting that randomly selected telephone numbers is a cost-effective alternative to the direct interview. As in any data collection procedure, some telephone interviews are lost because of interruptions on the respondent's end, and some are lost because of respondents' reluctance to discuss sensitive issues by telephone. In these contemporary times, with news reports and rumors of so much crime, such as sophisticated swindles, burglary setups, or high-pressure sales tactics from unreputable marketing groups, many individuals are understandably reluctant to give any information to strangers over the telephone. This should be considered when deciding upon the method of data gathering.

The Interview versus the Self-Administered Questionnaire

Both questionnaires and interviews rely on the validity of verbal reports, but there are important differences between these two procedures. Information obtained from questionnaires is limited to the respondents' written answers to a prearranged printed set of questions that are given directly to respondents or sent to them by mail. In the interview, the interviewer and respondent are in direct contact during the time of the information exchange. In the face-to-face interview, the interviewer can observe the respondent's reaction to questions and to the surrounding situation. In short, the interview requires more skill in sustaining personal relations and in eliciting information. And while it also takes far more time and money, the quality of information just may compensate for the added expense.

Strengths and Weaknesses of Survey Research

Although we have discussed the strengths and weaknesses of the questionnaire and the interview schedule, we believe it would be very worthwhile to look at the strengths and weaknesses of the survey in general. Like all research designs, the survey is not perfect. Although it does have its strengths, it also has its weaknesses. Some of its *strengths* are as follows:

1. *The survey is particularly useful for describing the characteristics of a large population.* A carefully developed questionnaire administered to a random sample allows us the opportunity to describe the population from which the sample was taken.

2. *Large samples are feasible, especially when the survey is self-administered.* Large surveys are really not unusual, and when the questionnaire has a sizable number of items, the sample must be large for purposes of statistical analysis.

3. *Surveys permit standardization of measurements.* Once questions are worded, this wording becomes a standard in that every respondent is exposed to it. In essence, exactly the same wording of questions is presented to all subjects.

Survey research also has a number of *weaknesses.*

1. *Surveys frequently rely on respondents' memories, which may make relevant data less assessable by the researcher.* When memory is a factor, the data are only as good as the respondents' memories.

2. *Respondents' motivations and abilities vary widely, and this variation can affect results.* With survey data and especially the self-administered questionnaire, motivation is a key factor in getting all questions answered. Since this answering process requires substantial energy on the part of the subjects, motivational levels must be kept high.

3. *Survey research is weak on validity and strong on reliability.* Surveys are poor approximations of direct observations. Hence, our measures are not always good indicators of what they are supposed to measure. On the other hand, they are strong on reliability in that the measures used tend to produce the same results over repeated measures. However, validity is also essential and needs to be examined more often than it is.

Using Secondary Data to Supplement Interview Data

Secondary data is an inclusive term that refers to documents, records, reports, and books from a variety of sources that are already in existence, as well as the use of existing data sets from previous surveys that can be used for other purposes. Major surveys take a considerable amount of time and money to do right, and as a result, many researchers have neither the time nor the money to construct their own data set from scratch. Using secondary data, the researcher can acquire a set of data collected from some other survey and, by careful analysis, often use the responses to that survey to figure out a population's response toward other questions. This has led Phillips to define secondary data analysis as "the analysis of available data with a framework that differs from that used in the original study" [9].

An enormous amount of such material exists, including government documents at the national, state, and local level, reports by consumer groups and professional organizations, and reports by individual researchers working for a wide variety of social agencies and programs. Other sources include professional journals, national conference proceedings, seminars, and plenary sessions. Much data are available in major libraries and can be obtained at a fraction of the cost of a new survey.

One of the major sources of secondary data is the census. As indicated earlier, the census is taken completely every ten years with a variety of smaller studies done between periods. It asks a variety of questions, which can then be used for other kinds of purposes. Questions asked of households concerning the number of persons living there, whether they are headed by a male or a female, whether or not the members are married to each other, and so forth, can tell us a considerable amount about changes in the U.S. family.

Similarly, every four years the national election sends forth a host of survey researchers armed with questionnaires, asking the populace questions aimed at uncovering attitudes perceived as affecting voting behavior. Secondarily, however, these same studies can be used to construct creatively a wide variety of studies of things that have virtually nothing to do with voting behavior. Because surveys have become big business in politics, these data sets are often quite sophisticated in their sampling techniques, reliability coefficients, and so on, and offer the limited-budget researcher an enormously appealing source of information to be used for other research purposes. In fact, Daniel Yankelovitch [10], a political pollster of some talent, secondarily analyzed much of his previous work on political attitudes in order to come up with an entire book, *New Rules,* which is not about politics at all but about larger changes that have taken place in American values. One might say that secondary data analysis is a way by which the researcher "spins off" new uses for research data in the same way that technological spinoffs occur everyday (we got nonstick cookware as a by-product of the space program, for example).

Every single day researchers across the land are punching computer cards, administering questionnaires, conducting interviews, and engaging in other research projects for countless purposes. The trick is to get these researchers to let you use their data for your purposes. It can be expensive or cheap (it can even be free), and the cooperative spirit in research can be appealed to in such a way that researchers can even trade data sets so that each can get more than he or she could acting alone. Given the expense of conducting research from the ground up, it is not at all surprising that secondary data analysis has become such an important subject in contemporary research.

Secondary analysis of the data is not without pitfalls, however. When using resources that were collected for some purpose other than what you are interested in, you must take time to evaluate the validity and applicability of such existing sources. There is nearly always some relevant published information to relate to these new research projects. Generally, the value of new research is to demonstrate the nature and extent of changes since the publication of earlier data. For example, comparison with earlier data on the extent of state support for welfare programs is useful in analyzing changes in that population. Ongoing problems such as the spread of AIDS among the heterosexual population would benefit from analysis over time.

Our preoccupation in this book with connecting theory and research, however, also calls for a special set of cautions the researcher needs to take when subjecting data to secondary analysis. *Secondary data rarely afford a perfect match to the research design requirements of the new study.* Research projects are always constructed according to some theoretical notions of the researcher, and questions are constructed accordingly. This is because words are never neutral; some theoretical biases are always embedded into the very nature of the questions that are asked. (This is why smart respondents sometimes respond to a question by asking back, "Why do you want to know?") Therefore, it will be of prime importance for the researcher to know what kinds of theoretical underpinnings guided and directed a particular research project. Why did the researcher ask the particular questions he or she asked? How were the questions asked? What did the researcher want to know? These questions help establish the theoretical direction and assumptions of the research and let you know whether or not the answers are consistent with the research you are doing.

When a researcher uses secondary data, he or she is still responsible for the methodological inadequacies of those data. This is a crucial ethical problem because the tendency is either not to know how the original data were collected or, since there is nothing you can do about it after the fact, use it as though it were valid. Time is a crucial variable, too, for a significant change often occurs in terminology and cultural values if several years have intervened between the time of the earlier material and the current research. Such differences must be identified and adjusted if the secondary data are to be applied correctly.

Some researchers rely on the legitimacy of official sources of data, when in fact every data source, including highly placed ones, often has serious shortcomings. For example, material from the U.S. Department of Labor is sometimes regarded as highly reliable. However, a close check on the quality and method of the original data gathering and analysis may show serious deficiencies. Again, it is the responsibility of the researchers to defend the data they are using secondarily, just as if it were being collected and used for the first time. If, as will be frequently the case, the validity and reliability of the data cannot be determined, the conscientious researcher will candidly note that the data are subject to limitations of method and standards prevailing at the time they were produced.

References

1. M. Spiegelman, *Introduction to Demography* (Cambridge, MA: Harvard University Press, 1968), p. 22.
2. H. Weisberg and B. Bowen, *An Introduction to Survey Research and Data Analysis* (San Francisco: W. H. Freeman, 1977), p. 19.
3. D. Bogue, "Against Adjustment," *Society 18,* (18) (1981): 85.
4. William C. Sze and Barry Ivker, "Stress in Social Workers: The Impact of Setting and Role," *Social Casework* (March 1986).
5. National Association of Social Workers, *NASW Professional Social Work Directory 1978* (Washington, DC: National Association of Social Workers, 1978).
6. NASW, *NASW Professional Social Work Directory 1978,* pp. 144–5.
7. H. W. Smith, *Strategies of Social Research: The Methodological Imagination* (Englewood Cliffs, NJ: Prentice-Hall, 1981), p. 410.
8. H. J. Rubin, *Applied Social Research* (Columbus, OH: Merrill, 1983), p. 267.
9. B. Phillips, *Social Research Methods: An Introduction* (Homewood, IL: Dorsey, 1985), p. 260.
10. Daniel Yankelovitch, *New Rules* (New York: Random House, 1981).

Chapter 12

Qualitative Research

Introduction
Historical perspective
Similarities and differences
  Epistemology
  Attitude of the researcher
  Inductive and deductive
    reasoning
  Hypothesis development
  Numbers versus human
    situations
Field research
  Participant observation
Historical research
  The process of historical
    research
  Primary and secondary sources

Locating sources and retrieving
  information
Synthesizing information
Report writing
Content analysis
Comparative analysis
Single-subject design
  Characteristics of single-subject
    designs
  Types of single-subject designs
Program evaluation
  Uses of program evaluation
  Quality assurance
  Approaches to program
    evaluation

Life can only be understood backwards, but it must be lived forwards.
—SOREN KIERKEGAARD

Introduction

Most of our preconceptions about research are probably of the kind we speak of as *quantitative,* also referred to in the literature as "empirical," "logical positivistic," or "reductionistic." **Quantitative research** is often, incorrectly we believe, associated exclusively with the scientific method. It **attempts to make generalizations based**

on precisely measured quantities. The question that informs quantitative research is "How much?" Many of the chapters in this book address themselves to quantitative research, and for many research problems such an approach is indispensable. On the other hand, quantitative research is not suitable for all types of problems. The techniques used for "knowing about" are not the same techniques we would use for "knowing."

Just as the word quantity asks the question "How much?," the word quality asks the question "What kind?" *Qualitative research* seeks to discover what kinds of things people are doing, what kinds of processes are at work, what kinds of meanings are being constructed, what kinds of purposes and goals inform the participants' acts, and what kinds of problems, constraints, and contingencies they see in the worlds they occupy. Other terms used in the literature to refer to qualitative research processes are "normative," "naturalism," "naturalistic inquiry," or "inductive." Bogdan and Taylor define qualitative research this way:

> Qualitative methodologies refer to research procedures which produce descriptive data: people's own written or spoken words and observations. This approach directs itself at settings and the individuals within those settings holistically; that is, the subject of the study, be it an organization or an individual, is not reduced to an isolated variable or to an hypothesis, but is viewed instead as part of a whole. [1]

In other words, as Epstein defines it, **qualitative research tries to fully describe and comprehend the subjective meanings of events to individuals and groups** [2].

Rodwell further explains the naturalistic approach in relation to the profession of social work by saying that it

> provides a different construction of expectations for the profession. These expectations rest on multiple points of view and the uniqueness of the individual in his or her own context .... Naturalism allows the acceptance of multiple rationales, conflicting value systems, and separate realities. The naturalistic paradigm provides different assumptions, different expectations, and supports the profession's value-based behaviors. [3]

While one often encounters the view that qualitative and quantitative are not opposing ways of doing research, it must be stated in all candor that they do represent different ways of approaching a research project. Therefore, we will want to be especially cautious about the assumptions made in the theories we are using, for some types of theories demand quantitative data, while others insist that only qualitative data will be suitable. Those who caution us not to see these types of strategies as opposing are correct when they point out that the two can be, and often are, combined in various research projects. **Quasi-experimental designs are a form of research that makes use of aspects from both quantitative and qualitative research.** The example study discussed in Chapter 17, *Assessing Growth in Undergraduate Field Education,* is of this type. There is in this design the absence of a control group, which is necessary for an *experimental* study. Instead, the subjects under study are evaluated in terms of their change over time, from a starting point (i.e., pretest) continuing through to an ending point (i.e., posttest). The *change scores* between the pre-

and posttests become the focus of interest. As can be seen in the example, the use of selected statistical operations are a substantive part of the analysis. But also notice that the use of descriptions of group characteristics, as well as demographics such as age, race, and income, become very important to the study.

Quantitative data can lead us to a field for further qualitative study, as when we encounter statistics about the divorce rate and decide to do a qualitative study of a divorced men's self-help group in order to understand the experience of divorce. Or we may become interested the other way around, as when we first do a descriptive, qualitative study of children of divorce and then later firm up the research with some quantitative data on numbers, demographic characteristics, and so forth.

Researchers have questioned the use of logical positivistic approaches in social work research on several grounds [4, 5]. Pieper says that (1) controlled experiments have little resemblance to actual social work practice, (2) no observations are truly free from bias because it is not possible for practitioners to be neutral, (3) the client's perceptions are often useful for understanding both the problem and the intervention, (4) trying to reduce very complex, messy, and interactive problems to simple variables or sets of variables moves the practitioner further away from, rather than closer to, desired solutions, (5) in helping clients, situational knowledge seems more productive than do universal laws, (6) no statistical technique or research design can obviate the need for, or replace the informed judgment of, the researcher, and (7) no value-free observations or data exist in reality.

Historical Perspective

The dissent within the social sciences between the advocates of the two approaches has gone on for a very long time and has given rise to debates of whether social work is to be defined as an art or a science. Historically, it would appear that social work became linked with the empiricists' research methodologies through the influences of the Settlement House Movement in the early 1900s. Concern for broad societal problems affecting the laboring and immigrant classes, such as child labor abuses, poverty, unfit living and working conditions, and so on, cried out for an understanding of these issues from broad-based perspectives. Settlement leaders turned to any available knowledge that had been developed in the sociological, anthropological, economic, and political arenas to shed light on and bring direction to their efforts. The methodologies used by sociology and other disciplines to develop this knowledge base became vitally important in establishing a framework for social work interventions through settlement house programs and legislative efforts [6].

Glaser and Strauss describe this process of the historical development of empirical research methods as follows:

> beginning in the 1930's and especially after World War II, quantitative researchers made great strides both in producing accurate evidence and in translating theoretical concepts into research operations. The result was an ability to begin the challenge of testing theory rigorously.

Thus, advances in quantitative methods initiated the zeal to test unconfirmed theories with the "facts." Qualitative research, because of its poor showing in producing the scientifically reproducible fact, and its sensitivity in picking up everyday facts about social structures and social systems, was relegated ... to preliminary, exploratory, groundbreaking work for getting surveys started. Qualitative research was to provide quantitative research with a few substantive categories and hypotheses. Then, of course, quantitative research would take over, explore further, discover facts and test current theory.

The strength of this position, which soon swept over American sociology, was based on the emerging systematic canons and rules of evidence of quantitative analysis: on such issues as sampling, coding, reliability, validity, indicators, construction, and parsimonious presentation of evidence. The methods of qualitative researchers on these issues had not been developed to the point where they offered any assurance of their ability to assemble accurate evidence and to test hypotheses. [7]

One of the earliest methodological emphases of this period was the survey (see Chapter 11). Sociologists, and later social workers, used the survey to gather data in order to publicize the needs of communities and to unify the populace into taking remedial action. A word of caution, as well as an indication of the importance of this method is noted by Reid [8], who pointed out that the advocates of the survey movement tended to oversell the survey method as an instrument of social reform. However, he states that it did serve to focus attention on the problems of urbanization, and became the predecessor of the "needs assessment."

At the 1915 National Conference of Charities and Corrections, Abraham Flexner challenged the fledgling social work profession by declaring that it could not become a profession because it lacked a distinctive professional method. Pioneer social work educator Mary Richmond picked up the gauntlet and rallied others to the task of method development, including techniques of analysis, synthesis, assessment, and intervention planning [9]. The early product of her work was the classic text entitled *Social Diagnosis* published in 1917 [10]. In their efforts to meet this challenge, social work researchers throughout the next decades adopted notions of linear causality and aligned themselves with the "... scientific revolution and to the consequent assumption that experimental science produces the only legitimate knowledge" [11].

Peile [12] did a review of the literature for the past five years as it appears in four major social work journals and affirms that even today the debate between the factions continues. He points out that their separate characteristics are not simply points of difference, but that the acceptance of a characteristic from one side requires the denial of its opposite and suggests that the normative and empirical approaches are in a relationship of antagonistic contradiction. (See Table 12.1.)

In his article in the eighteenth edition of the *Encyclopedia of Social Work*, William Reid [13] presents a rather thorough review of recent social work research literature with the intent of demonstrating what types of studies have been done in the profession. He makes the following assertions:

1. The major strategy of social work research is the study of phenomena by naturalistic methods—that is, without experimental manipulation.

TABLE 12.1   Characteristics of Alternatives to Empiricism

Empirical Alternative	*Normative Alternative*
Prediction	Explanation
Bias limitation (value-free)	Bias incorporation (value-laden)
Separation of knowledge	Integration of knowledge and values
Observation	Understanding
Quantitative	Qualitative
Measurement and testing	Insight and intuition
Objective	Subjective
Detachment	Involvement
Certain knowable world absolutism	Relativism—multiperspectives
Focus on content	Focus on process
Aim for certainty	Reliance on faith

Source: Colin Peile, "Research Paradigms in Social Work: From Stalemate to Creative Synthesis," *Social Service Review* 62 (March 1988): 4. Copyright © 1987 by The University of Chicago.

2. Descriptive or correlational studies—using interviews, standardized instruments, questionnaires or available data, and nonrepresentative samples—are dominant in the research on the characteristics of client populations, practitioners, programs, and communities.

3. Evaluation research usually makes use of "before and after" or, more commonly, "after-only" studies of change associated with social work programs.

4. Experimental designs in which interventions or other inputs are withheld, delayed, or systematically compared account for only a small portion of social work research—probably less than 5 percent of published studies.

5. Controlled experimental tests of direct social work practice approaches have been reported in the literature at a rate of about two or three a year.

Similarities and Differences

Let's turn our attention now to highlighting some of the aspects that may be considered as similarities and differences between quantitative and qualitative research processes.

Epistemology

Epistemology refers to the ways in which we come to "know" something and accept it as true; in other words, our theory of how knowledge is derived. *Logical positivism* is an epistemological stance that maintains that a proposition is acceptable *only* if there is a quantitative research method for measuring and verifying it to be true or false [14]. The empirical approach accepts logical positivism as its basic premise and has borrowed methodologies from the physical sciences (i.e., experimental designs, objective measurement, statistical analysis, etc.), applying them to social phenomena. The emphasis placed on this approach allows for the replication of studies and findings, further providing evidence of the credibility of a particular finding. Qualitative researchers, on the other hand, "... assume that the subjective dimensions of human experience are continuously changing and cannot be studied using the principles of quantitative methodologies" [15]. One of the very important issues for social workers in their selection of a research paradigm is its congruence with the values and techniques of practice. According to Reid [16], the ultimate goal of qualitative research in social work is not the generation of knowledge, but the building of intervention technologies. To state it another way, *knowledge not only for knowledge's sake, but for use in practice.* Rodwell supports this position when she asserts that

> following the assumptions favoring the existence of a single reality is the very thing that inhibits what is best in social work practice, that is, understanding the unique experience of the individual in context. Recognizing the ill-defined, complex problems to which practitioners must respond, (the naturalistic position) roughly translates to "it is better to achieve approximate answers to right questions than exact answers to wrong questions." [17]

Attitude of the Researcher

Since empirical researchers place great emphasis on *objectivity* and *neutrality,* this attitude is an assumed prerequisite for experimental research. Great effort is made to introduce "controls" into a research design through sampling techniques, standardized application of any manipulated variables, and training of research assistants. The naturalistic approach, however, "... does not assume the separation between the observer and the observed, nor does it contain the conviction that the final, true explanation of the world can be found" [18].

The emphasis on "value-free" attitudes is perhaps commendable, but according to qualitative researchers, impossible to attain. Qualitative researchers approach the business of values in a somewhat different way. In any professional social work activity, whether research or client-related interventions, *acceptance* and *respect for individuality* are essential. Acceptance requires an understanding of the subject's viewpoint. It does not require, however, agreement with that viewpoint. But it does require some empathy with it. Our acceptance of the reality that all activities of life are value-bound can help us attain an attitude of *humility* as we approach research endeavors (see Chapter 3 for further discussion of this topic).

Inductive and Deductive Reasoning

Another way of comparing the two approaches is by looking at their respective processes of reasoning. Epstein describes this difference between quantitative and qualitative logic very aptly when she says that

> quantitative methods tend to rely on deductive logic (i.e., applying the so-

cial science theory to the social reality under investigation). Generally, qualitative methods are being used inductively (i.e., deriving concepts and theory from the social reality being studied). This inductive strategy for theory development has been referred to as *grounded theory* and is more suited to the study of relatively uncharted social terrain. The quantitative approach is best suited to studying phenomena which have previously had a high degree of conceptual development, theory construction and hypothesis testing. [19]

The preceding quote uses the term **grounded theory.** This term is used in the literature to refer to **theory that is discovered from data** [20], in contrast to the logico-positivistic process that seeks to verify existing theory through data. Glaser and Strauss point out at least two important reasons why the grounded theory approach has value [21]: (1) "Theory based on data can usually not be completely refuted by more data or replaced by another theory" and (2) "... grounded theory can help to forestall the opportunistic use of theories that have dubious fit and working capacity." As Becker [22] has succinctly pointed out, grounded theory helps us "... avoid framing foolish hypotheses."

Hypothesis Development

Becker's comment leads us to point out briefly another possible difference between the two methods. Some quantitative approaches may assume that an already developed hypothesis is being tested, and the question is how can that hypothesis best be tested. "Such a presentation ... leaves out one crucial step in the development of any piece of research: the process by which we acquire the hypothesis to be tested" [23]. Many easily overlook the earlier role that qualitative methods have played in the development of the foundational information from which the hypothesis has been derived. To even subtly denigrate the qualitative process in the role of hypothesis development is to "deny the mother which bore the child," so to speak. Becker uses the illustration of someone buying a secondhand sailboat. He advises that one should never throw away any piece of junk found on the boat, whether a nail or a bit or wood or whatever, because it will undoubtedly turn out that it was there for a reason, that the former owner had used it for something important. Likewise with findings from qualitative research—"You dare not throw anything away until you know what jobs it was called on to do and devise another way to do those jobs" [24].

Numbers versus Human Situations

Another way of looking at the similarities and differences between quantitative and qualitative methods has already been suggested by earlier comments. Quantitative research relies heavily, and almost exclusively, on being able to reduce the phenomenon under investigation to numbers, which are then manipulated in a variety of ways through *statistical operations.* Some of the possible operations are described in detail in several other chapters in this book. On the other hand, qualitative procedures certainly may make use of numbers in many ways, depending on the subject matter, but will probably rely heavily on descriptions, comparison, observation, content analysis, historical review, and single-subject processes. It will use methods of inquiry that are extensions of normal human activities, such as looking, listening, speaking, and reading, because these expose the nature of the transaction between the investigator and respondent more accurately. The ultimate goal of empirical research is to present constructions in *nomothetical* fashion (i.e., as lawlike generalizations), while naturalistic inquiry interprets data *idiographically* (i.e., in terms of a particular case) [25]. Guba and Lincoln point out that the normative framework is "… extremely useful in understanding discrete phenomena, but the structure of naturalism is more attuned to investigating and portraying the realities of everyday life" [26].

Perhaps you can understand from the foregoing discussion that we support the appropriate use of both quantitative and qualitative methods in social work research activities. The choice of which approach to use, or the use of them in combination, is entirely dependent on the subject under study. Some investigations are more conducive to one or the other. We have also pointed out that the nature of social work, with its practice orientation, may find a natural affinity with qualitative methodologies [27]. Even though the philosophical tide in the social sciences has been strongly toward logical positivism, much social work research has made use of naturalistic methods. Perhaps this is true because our responsibility as practitioners as well as researchers calls for us to accept the responsibility to represent accurately our clients' experiences in order to be constantly improving our practice interventions.

Since this chapter tries to present primarily the philosophical bases, advantages, and uses of naturalistic inquiry, the following points made by Rodwell may provide a useful summary. She asserts that naturalism is based on the following five axioms [28].

1. *The nature of reality.* There are multiple constructed realities that can be studied only in their totalities.

2. *The relationship of knower to known.* The inquirer and the "object" of inquiry interact to influence one another. There can be no objective distance between knower and known.

3. *The impossibility of generalization.* The aim of inquiry is to develop a characteristic body of knowledge in the form of tentative suppositions that describe the individual case.

4. *The impossibility of causal linkages.* All entities are in a state of mutual influence and shaping so that it is impossible to distinguish causes from effects.

5. *The role of values in inquiry.* Inquiry is value-bound. The inquirer's values are expressed in the choice of a problem and in the framing, bounding, and focusing of that problem. Values influence the choice of the paradigm that guides the investigation into the problem. Values influence the choice of the theory utilized to guide the collection and analysis of data and in the interpretation of findings.

At this point, let's turn our attention to a brief discussion of several of the qualitative approaches that might be used in social work research studies.

Field Research

One important characteristic of the modern world is that we increasingly *know about* far more than we *know*. There is nothing intrinsically wrong with this; indeed there is much of the world that we could never do more than know about. Because of this distance between the researcher and his or her subject matter, what is known about is often a stereotype at worst or an oversimplification at best. **Field research is** an attempt to remedy this problem by **grounding our studies in the field of their natural occurrence.** Although there is a long-standing debate among researchers about whether this type of research is "scientific" or not, we can look upon it simply as a way of respecting the nature of a certain subject matter.

The concept of "field" is a bit cloudy, for people often use the term in different ways. When someone asks you what "field" you are studying, they probably mean your academic major; something quite different from what we mean when we talk about "field research." In social work we use the term "field" in a number of ways. When we speak of a "field of practice," we are referring to a broad set of concepts and strategies held in common by those who may deal with a certain type of client defined by age or type of problem, such as the broad areas of child welfare, mental health and retardation, aging, or family planning.

In social work education we refer to "field work," "field instruction," "field education," or "field practicum" rather interchangeably to refer to one of the five major curriculum components required by the Council on Social Work Education for all accredited social work programs (see the discussion in Chapter 1). Specifically, we are referring to the supervised experience or internship each social work student has in a social service agency or program.

On the other hand, the main component of the concept of "field" as the term is used by researchers is that it *locates* the research in a particular place—the place in which the phenomenon being investigated occurs. If we want to study the routines of eligibility workers in a public welfare office, we will have to go to the office. If we wish to investigate life in a nursing home, we will have to go there. If we want to study the world of probation officers, it will be necessary for us to gain access to the environments in which they live and work.

It is essential to note in this chapter that field research *not* be taken as the equivalent of laboratory research, merely conducted in a different place [29]. Experimental research, even when it is conducted in the "field," laboratory research, and even to some extent survey research are primarily interested in controlling variables as precisely as possible so that careful manipulations can be made to produce some kind of information. While the idea of control itself is open to some question, the kind of research we are discussing under this heading is simply not amenable to that kind of treatment. We will want to understand behavior *as it occurs.* In most instances the researcher will not try to control it because to do so would be to violate the naturalistic principle that governs this type of activity.

Participant Observation

Participant observation in social science research is probably the best-known technique of field research. There are actually several variations of participant observation, but the classical meaning of the term **participant observation refers to a researcher entering a setting he or she wants to study and actually participating in the very scene he or she is observing, analyzing, and writing about.** The researcher is at the same time actor and audience; player and spectator. The impetus for this approach to research occurred in the United States primarily around the turn of the century when the "Chicago School"—the sociology department at the University of Chicago, their students, and disciples—developed directional observational studies under the influence of Robert Park. Well-known examples in sociological literature include Howard Becker's study of jazz musicians [30]. Becker actually became a member of the jazz group he was studying. Festinger's research on the doomsday cult [31] was conducted by two graduate students who actually became members of a doomsday cult waiting for the destruction of the world and the arrival of the flying saucer that was to save the handful of believers. Humphreys's controversial work, *Tearoom Trade* [32], which investigates homosexual encounters in public restrooms, also employs the techniques of participant observer. The essence of participant observation, then, is to place oneself *within* the process of conduct without disrupting it and to take the perspective of the participants. By actually participating in the social worlds they are describing, the researchers not only observe events but also experience the emotions and concerns of the people they are trying to understand.

Complete Participant

There are at least four roles that the participant observer can take [33]. The complete participant is a *disguised observer.* He or she infiltrates the group under study, gains access to their world by posing as one of them, and then collects research information without telling them what he or she is really doing. Two potential problems with this approach are obvious—the ethical one of deceit and the problem of becoming so immersed in the role that the observer half of the role is lost. The complete observer must deceive the people he or she is studying by pretending to be only what he or she appears to be to them: namely, a colleague in the world. Instead of being him- or herself in the role, the complete participant is something other than that because of dual commitments and the perceived necessity of hiding the observer self from other participants in the scene. Not only might the complete participant suffer severe qualms about this activity, but he or she may become so immersed in the role that even writing a report may be troublesome.

Participant-as-Observer

In the participant-as-observer role, *both the researcher and the people under study are aware of the researcher's role.* This resolves the problem of deceit, but the difficulty of balancing the requirements of the two roles remains an important issue. The researcher tries to develop a certain intimacy with persons who are a part of the scene being studied in order to gain information from them; but the process of accomplishing that can jeopardize the research in one of two ways. First, the informant may become so identified with the field research that it becomes difficult to continue to function as an informant. To view oneself as being "studied" may change in some subtle ways the nature of one's own views and experiences. Second, in this role, as in the previous one, the researcher may "go native" and run the risk of losing the observer role. In other words, the problems of the known participant-as-observer have to do with the difficulties posed by trying to balance the requirements of two roles. None of this is to say that such a balance cannot be struck, but merely that it is difficult to do, and the researcher must be on guard constantly lest the balance fall too much one way or the other. Sensitive researchers, in fact, often do pull off the role of participant-as-observer and in the process produce fine studies.

Observer-as-Participant

The observer-as-participant role involves *the researcher's going to the scene of the study to collect information without in any way trying to carry off the pretense that he or she is a participant.* This role is usually taken on when the field researcher is studying a series of processes that require short interviews on the scene with persons in a position to know. One problem is that the advantages of acquiring knowledge from inside participation are lost, the informants may be more likely to misunderstand the researcher, and he or she is likely not to understand them as well.

Complete Observer

The role of complete observer is sometimes called "nonparticipant observation." Nonparticipant observation means *observing situations in terms of what can be understood purely from the outside.* The persons being observed usually do not know they are being watched. As an adjunct to complete-participant or participant-as-observer studies, this method is often employed in the initial phases to determine many of the practical elements of the setting, such as the time when events occur, the physical arrangements of places and things, and the appearance of participants.

It is impossible for us to say just what role a researcher ought to adopt in any particular instance. This is part of the art of methodology and will depend both on ethical and substantive questions and on a variety of contingencies involved in the project itself.

Historical Research

In historical research we try to discover and interpret the wisdom of the past, thereby learning something of value for the present. This method is also referred to in the literature as "documentary analysis" and "historical analysis." With the process of historical analysis, social science and social work researchers align themselves with historians and use methods prevalent in that discipline. McMillan and

Schumacher [34] group historical analysis along with social policy and legal analysis, under the broad heading of "analytic research." In this regard, they indicate that in doing this type of study the researcher

> approaches a research problem differently from the way researchers conducting quantitative studies approach it. The search for facts begins with the location of sources. While other researchers create the data, usually administering the instruments to a sample or population, the analyst is dependent on those sources that were preserved .... The search for facts requires locating both primary and secondary sources.

Historical research can focus on individuals, groups, institutions, movements, or concepts. This form of publication is found frequently in social work journals. Several of the studies cited in this chapter serve as examples. The uses of this approach and its value to the broad area of social work research are notable. First, as we become aware of the longitudinal view, we can gain understanding of the processes of change and can heighten our understanding of what has been successful and what has not worked in our attempts to bring about social change and improve societal conditions. Second, as we learn about specific social welfare programs and provisions through time, we can use this wisdom to avoid problems and pitfalls in future endeavors. In other words, maybe we will not find ourselves trying to reinvent the wheel. Additionally, historical study can deepen and broaden our insight into the lives and struggles of social work pioneers—those who have gone before and made contributions from which we benefit today.

One important form of historical research is the *biography*. Much of the historical writing in social work literature is biographical in nature [35]. Book-length biographical works like Trattner's *Biographical Dictionary of Social Welfare in America* [36] are a valuable resource in this regard. Another form is the *historical case study*. The emphasis of this form of research is "... on examining in detail one reasonably limited set of historical events" [37]. In this approach, as in other approaches, it is imperative that the researcher consider the "representativeness" of his or her case. Attention must be given to whether the case under study is a singular and isolated set of events or just one aspect of a much larger and more complex phenomenon. It is essential that rigorous analysis and critical review be applied to ascertain the quality of the sources used in this process.

A third form that historical research can take is the *analysis of evolutionary trends*, such as the long-term effects of the Social Security Act of 1935 on subsequent welfare legislation, or the reasons for the increase in the number of public welfare recipients in the 1960s, as studied by Piven and Cloward [37].

> In *Regulating the Poor* (1971), Frances Fox Piven and Richard Cloward also create a historical analysis of poverty .... Through a combination of history, political interpretation, and sociological analysis, they endeavored to explain the recent, rather dramatic increases in the number of people receiving public welfare. They made it plain at the outset, however, that their concern was not simply with describing the welfare system. Rather, they wished to see how the welfare institution in the United States has been linked to other major social institutions, how it functions today and has functioned in the

past to serve the larger political and economic order. Their historical analysis traced the welfare system in the United States from the Great Depression to the present, revealing a distinctive pattern of relief policy; at certain times relief policy has been quite liberal and at other times highly restrictive.

The major thesis, which is convincingly documented through their historical investigation, is that the welfare system has been used to control and regulate the poor. "Historical evidence suggests that relief arrangements are initiated or expanded during occasional outbreaks of civil disorder produced by mass employment, and are then abolished or contracted when political stability is returned" (Piven and Cloward, 1971, xiii). It is by examining the operation of the welfare system in historical perspective that we can comprehend the explosion of welfare programs following the civil disturbances of the early 1960's. [38]

The Process of Historical Research

A brief review of the process used to accomplish historical research is in order at this point. Stuart [39] has outlined this four-phase process as follows: (1) choosing a research question, (2) gathering evidence that bears on the research question, (3) determining what the evidence means (synthesis), and (4) writing the report. As Figure 12.1 indicates, each phase flows into the next and cannot really be seen as independent components. It is also noted that the process of hypothesis formulation is an ongoing operation throughout the endeavor, up to and including the analysis and conclusion phase. This, as you will remember, is one distinct difference, and possible advantage, that qualitative research has in comparison to quantitative research.

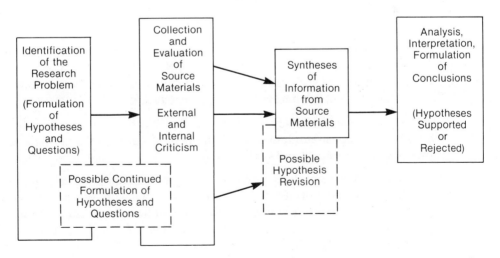

FIGURE 12.1   The Four Phases of Historical Research

Source: Reproduced by permission of the publisher, F. E. Peacock Publishers, Inc., Itasca, Illinois. From Paul Stuart, "Historical Research," in Social Work Research and Evaluation, 3rd ed., Richard M. Grinnell, Jr., ed., 1988 copyright, p. 345.

Primary and Secondary Sources

In considering what materials will become part of the historical analysis, one must give attention to the concepts of primary and secondary sources. Gottschalk [40] offers a rather definitive definition of a **primary source.**

> **the testimony of an eyewitness, or of a witness by any other of the senses, or of a mechanical device like the dictaphone—that is, of one who ... was present at the events of which he tells. A primary source must thus have been produced by a contemporary of the events it narrates.**

This type of source is considered to be the most accurate, and studies based upon primary sources are generally regarded more highly in the scholarly community. Obviously, the length of time between the historical event under study and the recording of it by the witness are important points of interest. The sooner it was recorded, the more accurate and complete it is likely to be. The researcher must continually be asking the question of how much faith to place in the source. "The evaluation of historical data, then, poses special problems of reliability and validity that do not normally confront the researcher who studies contemporary phenomena." [41]

By contrast, **a secondary source is one which offers indirect or hearsay evidence by other than eyewitnesses and is often an analysis and synthesis of primary sources.** These are valuable resources for any researcher, and it is not uncommon to find articles in social work journals which indicate that they are a "review of literature" or "secondary review" covering a certain topic or concept. Three examples are cited from *Social Work,* a journal published by the National Association of Social Workers. McMurtry's [24] article entitled "Secondary Prevention of Child Maltreatment: A Review" states in the abstract:

> Secondary prevention of child maltreatment involves identifying potential abusers and treating them before the abuse takes place. This article reviews research on attempts to screen parents to identify those who are at risk of maltreating their children. The author concludes that although accurate identification of such parents may eventually be possible, more research is needed to establish intervention to prevent abuse.

Another article by Rubin [43], entitled "Practice Effectiveness: More Grounds for Optimism," demonstrates how a certain number of studies done during a specific time-frame are examined and synthesized.

> Recent experiments have provided more grounds for optimism regarding the development of effective forms of direct social work practice. This review updates the field concerning experiments that have been conducted subsequent to prior reviews. Twelve research studies published between July 1, 1978, and June 30, 1983, are examined.

The third example, entitled "Trends in Research Publications: A Study of Social Work Journals from 1956 to 1980" [44], demonstrates an even broader analysis of historical sources.

The author analyzed the content of six social work journals—four of which could be described as general journals and two of which publish primarily research articles—to review research trends from 1956 to 1980. A typology of empirical and nonempirical research was used to classify the types of research published. Although the number of research articles rose over the 25-year period, no significant changes in the publication of research articles could be attributed to the appearance in 1977 of the specialty research journals.

In summary, although it can be said that it is usually preferable to use primary sources if they are available, secondary sources are a very important part of the historical research process and should be considered in light of any discernable bias of the witness, the rigor of this method, and the contributions they can make to the overall project.

Locating Sources and Retrieving Information

One of the major challenges of doing historical research is the discipline involved, not only in assessing sources, but in discovering them in the first place. The final product of research can be no better than the process of discovery in the collection and evaluation phase.

Cooper [45] indicates that there are at least four techniques that can be used to locate and retrieve information on a particular research problem.

1. *Invisible college approach.* This is the most informal approach and involves becoming aware of sources through contacts with colleagues and other persons or groups interested in the subject.

2. *Ancestry approach.* Here the pool of information is increased by "tracking" citations from one study to another. These studies have bibliographies that cite earlier, related research.

3. *Descendancy approach.* This approach involves using indexes, such as the *Social Science Citation Index,* to locate works that are central to a topic and then screen them for relevance.

4. *On-line computer search.* Since the time when computers became generally available, this approach has probably been the most widely used. Computers can scan vast amounts of material in abstracting services and citation indexes at rapid speeds and they eliminate much of the initial painstaking work previously done by hand.

Primary and secondary sources for historical research projects may come in many forms and derive from many places as noted previously. The synthesized information in Figure 12.2 should be useful in helping us to identify these sources [46, 47]. In addition, one of the social work areas in which historical research is often focused is in social policy development. The wealth of material available can be overwhelming to the researcher. A very helpful article by Mary R. Lewis [48] should be useful to one initiating a study of this type. The purpose of the article is to summarize the basic sources available for doing social policy research, and

FIGURE 12.2   Possible Sources for Historical Research

Documents	Letters	Budgets
	Diaries	Bills and receipts
	School records	Autobiographies
	Newspapers	Journals, magazines
	Bulletins	Catalogs
	Films	Personal records
	Voting records	Institutional records
	City directories	Committee minutes
	Tax records	Unemployment figures
	Graduation records	Government budget records
	Police arrest records	
Oral Testimonies	Participants in a historical event	
	Audio recordings	
	Video recordings	
	Personal interviews	
	Dictaphone recordings	
Relics	Textbooks	Buildings
	Maps	Equipment
	Samples of work	Furniture
	Teaching materials	

Source: J. M. McMillan and S. Schumacher, Research in Education (Boston: Little, Brown, 1984), p. 280; and J. B. Williamson et al., The Research Craft: An Introduction to Social Research Methods, 2nd ed. (Boston: Little, Brown, 1982) pp. 244–5. Reprinted by permission of Scott, Foresman and Company.

suggests ways of using original documents to acquire an overview of legislative, executive, and judicial action in relation to a specific policy which has been enacted. It also offers advice about following current legislative activity and presents a practical guide to the use of documents which are basic tools in social policy analysis.

Synthesizing Information

The process of synthesizing information is actually one that begins during the process of discovering sources. The researcher begins to make preliminary assessments of the worth of each source as soon as it is reviewed. Determining if the source is authentic, particularly in the case of personal records, is an important first step. If authentic, is it germane to the specific period of time or topic under study? If it is, does it substantiate other materials discovered, or does it contradict them? Does it enrich the subject, or does it add a new perspective previously not thought of? How much weight to give to any piece of material or source is entirely at the discretion of the researcher, and it is here that his or her expert knowledge, discipline, and professional integrity are the foundations upon which the scholarly research endeavor is based.

It is recognized that areas of interest that are substantiated by several pieces of information are generally regarded as more accurate than those with only one source. However, this does not mean that the one source you have found is inaccurate or should be discounted. Internal consistency among sources, however, does add credibility to the product of research.

As Reid and Smith [49] point out, the processes of data collection and analysis are not necessarily separate processes as they are in quantitative research. The activity of synthesizing materials obviously can send the researcher back to the search for additional sources. When an exciting new approach to the subject is perceived, the need to search further for sources to verify can be compelling. "At the simplest level one looks for commonalities or themes in the data," but the importance of the researcher's creativity in discovering themes and issues from the material and systematizing them in meaningful ways cannot be overemphasized. The following except succinctly outlines this activity.

> As data are collected, the researcher begins looking for patterns, themes, or organizing constructs. When these emerge, a tentative analytic framework is developed. The framework may involve the construction of categories or hypotheses or both. Further data collection is guided by this analytic framework, and the usefulness of the framework is ascertained. Categories are added or subtracted and hypotheses modified as the new data indicate. This process of sequential analysis and increasingly focused data collection continues until the researcher is satisfied with her understanding of the phenomenon. At this point she stops collecting data, engages in a final period of systematic thinking and reflection about all of her data, completes the analysis and interpretation, and writes her report. [50]

Report Writing

The next step is to present the results of the study in such a way that the study can take on meaning for others interested in the subject. The manner in which it is written and the quality of the organization and presentation take on great importance. The reader is referred to Chapter 17 for an extensive and detailed account of this report-writing activity. However, we have mentioned earlier in this chapter several distinctions of qualitative research as compared to quantitative research which will affect the way the report is written. The most obvious difference is in the use of numbers in reporting. Although numbers are used in both, descriptions and processes will be highlighted in qualitative reporting with numbers generally taking a secondary role. One may also find more frequent reliance on the use of illustrations, examples, and analogies in qualitative reports.

One of the first decisions to be made is what organization and presentation form is most conducive to the material. Generally the choice is between a *chronological* presentation or a *thematic* one [51]. The nature of the material itself will lead the researcher to the most appropriate selection. There are many historical studies found in the social work literature, but the two following will serve as examples of the two approaches. The first, entitled "The Problem of Duty: Family Desertion in the Progressive Era" [52], illustrates the use of a thematic outline. The article concerns the responses of social welfare activists to male desertion of dependent families between 1890 and 1920. The outline includes the following sections: Introduction, The Charitable Analysis of the Deserter, The Legal Treatment of Desertion, and Psychology and the Deserter. Through this historical analysis the author presents the attitude changes of charity workers and settlement workers and characterizes them as moving through the phases of family problem definition, punitive legalism, to an emphasis on the psychological inabilities of deserters.

The second example illustrates the chronological approach to report writing. It is entitled "Fallen Women, Federated Charities, and Maternity Homes, 1913–1973" [53]. Here, Morton traces the influence over time of a federated charity organization on the member maternity homes and looks at the decline of religious impulse in private social services and the concomitant rise of secular services. The sections are titled: Maternity Homes and Moral Rescue, 1869–1912; Federated Charities and Efficiency, 1881–1913; An Uneasy Consensus, 1913–1929; Heightened Differences, 1929–1936; New Directions in Social Policy, 1936–1960; The Homes' Responses, 1950–1960; Change and Conflict, 1960–1973; and Postscript, 1987.

In summary, a historical analysis report will generally include the following areas: (1) an explanation of the purpose of the review; (2) a summary of the methods used to locate the primary and secondary sources; (3) a description of the information retrieval techniques used; (4) an outline of the analytical methods used to draw inferences, conclusions, and recommendations; (5) a presentation of findings; and (6) suggestions for future studies.

Content Analysis

Although often singled out for discussion as a freestanding qualitative research technique, content analysis is actually a tool that can be used as well within other research approaches. Content analysis can be used as a contributing method to experimental studies as well as qualitative designs. As we proceed, it will become clear how content analysis is often a central technique used in historical research designs, as discussed earlier.

Being a versatile technique, content analysis has been used widely in social work research. Smith [54] points to three general areas where contributions have been made: (1) numerous valuable studies of the processes of clinical social work; (2) the investigation of trends in social work literature; and (3) the analysis of documents in historical, administrative, and policy studies.

Several definitions of this process can be found in the literature.

> Content analysis is a multipurpose research method developed specifically for investigating any problem in which the content of communication serves as the basis of inference. [55]

> **Content analysis is a research technique for the objective, systematic, and quantitative description of the manifest content of communication. [56]**

Practically speaking, for social work researchers, the essence of content analysis is generally the categorizing and coding of materials (either those that are available or those that are generated for study) to analyze the processes of communication. [57]

Bernard Berelson first wrote about this technique in his classic work in 1952, and his book has remained a standard on the subject. He notes the following uses that serve to give the reader an understanding of the breadth of possibilities for research usage:

o to describe trends in communication content
o to trace the development of scholarship
o to disclose international differences in communication content
o to compare media or "levels" of communication
o to audit communication content against objectives
o to reveal the focus of attention
o to describe attitudinal and behavioral responses to communications
o to construct and apply communication standards
o to aid in technical research operations (to code open-ended questions in survey interviews)
o to expose propaganda techniques
o to measure the "readability" of communication materials
o to discover stylistic features
o to identify the intentions and other characteristics of the communicators
o to determine the psychological state of persons or groups
o to detect the existence of propaganda (primarily for legal purposes)
o to secure political and military intelligence
o to reflect attitudes, interests, and values ("value patterns") of population groups [58]

In addition to the uses noted above, Smith [59] focuses on the use of content analysis for social work research on clinical intervention processes. The question addressed is "Do social workers do what they say they do?" This question of outcomes and skills becomes increasingly important as issues of licensure, certification, and competency testing gain significance in our profession.

As with any research technique, the use of content analysis to discover meanings must direct the researcher to attempt to answer three important questions—How objective is the process? How reliable is it? Can the findings be generalized? The issue of *objectivity* is addressed by the creation of explicit rules for classifying material. Painstaking effort must be made to develop the unique rules of analysis for each individual study, and these need to be finalized before the data can be categorized. Obviously, the nature of the rules will be determined by the purpose and focus of the study. Researchers and their assistants must follow the established rules regardless of their own personal values and biases. The *systematic* application of the rules of analysis serves to increase the reliability of the study. In other words, the categories of analysis remain the same across all of the elements studied, and items are systematically assigned to categories according to the rules. Although it is recognized that one can never quite eliminate all subjectivity, extensive periods of training are often needed for research assistants or "coders" to minimize this bias.

The concept of *generalizability* requires that the findings have theoretical relevance. "All content analysis is concerned with comparison, ... a datum about communication is meaningless until it is related to at least one other datum" [60]. Krippendorff argues that "... data should at least be reproducible by independent researchers, at different locations, and at different times, using the same instructions for coding the same set of data" [61, 62].

This leads us to look briefly at the process for identifying and determining relevant categories. Both Berelson [63] and Williamson [64] stress the importance of this phase. Berelson says that content analysis "... stands or falls by its categories," and indicates that the results of a study are no better than the system of categories, which should be specific and concrete in order to be meaningful. Williamson says that the categories must faithfully reflect the major theoretical concepts being studied. And if the categories are well laid out and unambiguous, the coding of the data will achieve a high degree of consistency or reliability.

Having designated the *unit of analysis* (i.e., a specific behavior, a phrase, an attitude, a value, a form or type of communication, etc.), which is derived from the purpose of the study, this process will usually suggest to the researcher the dimensions of importance. Creativity is a vital factor at this stage. Allowing data to "speak for themselves" is an intuitive skill that should be minimized.

Researchers will normally develop *coding categories* by making a list of all the possible phenomena under study. The training provided to the coders should give them very specific instructions on how to recognize, for example, certain adjectives, phrases, content of sentences, attitudes expressed, and so forth. Coding can be a very complicated process, and it is understood that interpretive judgments will have to be made. Hopefully, the coders will be prepared to make those based on a predetermined protocol.

"Coding reliability must be high if faith is to be placed in the accuracy of the final data tabulations" [65]. Williamson continues by offering several "rules of thumb" in this regard:

1. Categories need to be *exhaustive* so that every specimen of data or every case under investigation will fit into at least one of the categories developed.
2. The fewer the number of decisions, interpretations, or judgments coders must make as they classify data, the greater will be the overall reliability of the study.
3. As the number of categories increases allowing for more extensive analysis of the data, the more complicated the study becomes, and issues of reliability and accuracy increase.

One cannot speak about content analysis without dealing with the implications of sampling techniques used to create the data set under study. Figure 12.2 listed many of the types of sources from which researchers will draw their samples. For social work practitioners, it goes without saying that a very important source of data is agency files and records. The reader is directed to Chapter 9 for a more complete treatment of the subject of sampling.

Comparative Analysis

At this point, let's look briefly at the process of comparative analysis. It will be apparent to the reader that there can be much overlap with previously mentioned forms of research. Comparative research is often of two natures—historical or cross-cultural. It is similar to historical research in the instances when "comparisons" are being made between two distinct historical periods. Whereas historical research would show developments of themes or practices *through* time, as discussed earlier, comparative analysis would take the slightly different approach of **seeking parallelism and/or contrast between two entirely separated cross-sections of time.**

An example of this type of study is found in the following work by Dore, Young, and Pappenfort, entitled "Comparison of Basic Data for the National Survey of Residential Group Care Facilities: 1966–1982" [66]. The abstract states that

> Reported here is the summary of findings from the upcoming *National Survey of Residential Group Care Facilities for Children and Youth.* The authors analyze current data and compare them to data gathered for a similar survey in 1966. Important changes have taken place.

The results are reported by classification into four "streams." The *child welfare stream* showed a decrease in the number, by relative proportion, of residential group care facilities for neglected, abused, or dependent children. It also showed that this arena was clearly dominated by the private sector in 1981. In regard to facilities for *pregnant adolescents,* in spite of an increase in the number of births to this age group there was a distinct shift away from residential facilities as the preferred method of serving this group. In the *juvenile justice stream,* they found a rather staggering overall increase of 154 percent in the number of residential facilities and noted a substantial increase in private sector sponsorship. Four times as many facilities were found in the *mental health stream* in 1981 when compared to 1966. The study also showed the emergence of specialized residential treatment centers for alcohol and/or drug abuse among children and youth, representing a major change in the comparison. Again, this increase has been mainly under private auspices. The most striking overall change, however, was in the size of facility, with the overwhelming trend being toward housing much smaller residential populations.

Cross-cultural comparative studies offer us a unique insight into our world. Although this type of study is relatively rare in the literature, it is obvious that if variables are demonstrated to be consistent over cultures, then the generalizability of such findings is greatly enhanced. The methods used can be similar to those used in other studies, including ethnographic field work, survey research, aggregate data analysis, experimentation, content analysis, or historical research [67].

One study made some cross-cultural comparisons between femininity, masculinity, and sexual orientation across three countries, Australia (n =163), Sweden (n = 176), and Finland (n = 149). Ross [68] indicates that these samples were compared

> on the Bem Sex Role Inventory and on various measures of partner preference in order to establish the relationship between degree of homosexuality in terms of Kinsey Scale position and gender identity. Results suggest that

while there is no relationship between femininity and degree of homosexuality, masculinity is inversely related depending on the degree of sex role stereotyping and anti-homosexual attitudes of the society the subjects live in. Such findings suggest that deviant gender identity is a function not of homosexuality as such but of societal attitudes which may reinforce a homosexual role.

It is important to note in this study that the same instruments, including the Bem Sex Role Inventory [69], were used with each of the three samples, and the results were similarly compared against the same highly regarded theoretical background developed by Alfred Kinsey and his associates [70]. The careful selection of representative samples, as well as controlling for as many variables as possible, are both as important to the integrity of this type of study as is the standardization of the use of instruments.

Single-Subject Design

Single-subject designs came into the research repertoire of social work in the late 1960s primarily from the behavioralists. By definition, **single-subject or single-case designs refer to the examination of the planned change processes of one client.** The term *single-system design* is used when the subject is a family, group, or organization. Pressures toward accountability by human service agencies and programs created a need for ways to establish the efficacy of social work interventions, and this approach provided a useful set of tools. By the 1970s, many practitioners, looking for ways to verify the effectiveness of what they do with clients, began to discover and incorporate single-case approaches in their work. Social workers have found that the integration of this form of research with their everyday activities can yield continuous feedback about treatment issues *during* the treatment process rather than waiting until after. Additionally, the variables and measures chosen can be individually tailored to each client, thereby enhancing a response to the uniqueness of each one. Treatment methods may change in response to the more immediate feedback provided through this type of design. Nuehring and Pascone [71] point out that analysis of the data "... provides detailed information on the process of change, when change occurs, whether it occurs for all or just some of the problems being treated, and how long lasting the change is."

Characteristics of Single-Subject Designs

McMillan and Schumacher [72] have summarized five important characteristics of these designs:

1. *Reliable measurement.* Single-subject designs usually involve many observations of behavior as the technique for collecting data. It is important that the observation conditions, such as time of day and location, be standardized, that observers be well trained and checked for reliability and bias, and that the behavior observed be operationally defined. Consistency in measurement is especially important as the

study moves from one condition to another. Because accurate measurement is crucial to single-subject designs, the researcher typically reports all aspects of data collection so that any threat to validity can be reasonably ruled out.

2. *Repeated measurement.* A distinct characteristic of single-subject designs is that a single aspect of behavior is measured many times, in the same way, throughout the study. This is quite different from measurement in many group studies in which there is a single measure before or after the treatment. Repeated measurement controls for normal variation that would be expected within short time intervals, and provides a clear, reliable description of the behavior.

3. *Description of conditions.* A precise, detailed description of all conditions in which the behavior is observed should be provided. This description allows application of the study to other individuals in order to strengthen both internal and external validity.

4. *Baseline and treatment condition; duration and stability.* The usual procedure is for each condition to last about the same length of time and contain about the same number of observations. If either the length of time or number of observations varies, then time and number of observations become confounding variables that complicate the interpretation of the results and weaken internal validity. It is also important that the behavior be observed long enough for the establishment of a stable pattern. During the first phase of single-subject research *the target behavior is observed under natural conditions until stability is achieved.* This period of time is called the *baseline.* The treatment phase occurs with a change in conditions by the researcher and also must be long enough to achieve stability.

5. *Single-variable rule.* It is important to change only one variable during the treatment phase of single-subject research, and the variable that is changed should be described precisely. If two or more variables are changed simultaneously, the researcher cannot be sure which change, or changes, caused the results.

Types of Single-Subject Designs

Since there are several forms of research design available, it is often a chore for practitioners to decide which one is the most appropriate to use for the client or circumstance to be studied. Guidelines for choice must always be sensitive to individual situations. In designating the different forms of possible designs, letters are used to distinguish between them. The letter *A* is used to represent the baseline condition, or the state that exists *before* any intervention is introduced. In other words, this represents the "uncontrolled condition" where the subject is allowed to operate without any influence from the practitioner, agency, service, or intervention technique. The letters *B, C, D,* and so forth, represent distinct treatment interventions or "controlled" conditions introduced into the process. These are sometimes characterized as the "observational" condition versus the "treatment" condition [73].

B Design

This design is the crudest of these discussed and is simply the administration of a treatment when no baseline has been determined. This design is widely used because it is easy to administer and is hardly distinguishable from the traditional methods of assessment to which social workers are accustomed through their years of practice. Obviously, it is an attempt to monitor data, but *is essentially a trial-and-error approach that lacks control of any variables*. Although it may direct a practitioner to try other procedures until a desired effect is achieved, it does not promote the formulation of new hypotheses, it may lead to inaccurate inferences, and it does not provide any information about the variables that may be responsible for any change noted [74].

A-B Design

This design is slightly more sophisticated in that it allows for *the comparison between the baseline condition and a treatment condition*, and therefore adds some element of experimental control to the independent variable [75]. This approach is very useful because the effects of a particular intervention technique can be documented, and practitioners can begin to form a knowledge bank about what is effective with clients with similar problems [76].

A-B-A Designs

The A-B-A design is one in which *the baseline is reinstated after the treatment phase*. It is also known as the "reversal" or "withdrawal" design. The advantage of this design is that a stronger causal inference can be made if the behavior pattern returns to baseline once the treatment is removed because the researcher is able to demonstrate that the B condition was primarily responsible for the rate of change. Although there are problems with its use, in some cases the design is strengthened greatly by reinstituting the treatment condition, thus developing an A-B-A-B pattern. Browning and Stover caution that disadvantages to this design can include (1) the fact that it is sometimes impossible for the baseline to be reestablished, thus contaminating the later treatment condition; (2) the more successful the initial treatment program, the more difficult it is to return to a true baseline; and (3) successive replications may have the effect of training the subject to retrieve the undesired behavior more quickly [77].

A-B-C-D Designs

All one is doing in this design is *establishing a baseline, then instituting several different treatments successively* (not overlapping), to gain some indication of the value of each one for creating change in the target behavior. Obviously, this approach is weak in the area of controls, and the risk is that previous treatments are affecting subsequent ones. But it can give the practitioner some indication of treatment directions for the future.

A-B-A-C-A Design (Successive Treatments Design)

Obviously, the A-B-C-D design can be greatly enhanced by *reintroducing the baseline condition if one wishes to compare two or more intervention strategies*. It also demonstrates much more control over the independent variables.

Another form of successive treatment design is illustrated in the following schematic.

```
       B
       |
A—C—B or C or D
       |
       D
```

Browning and Stover [78] describe this schematic as follows:

> Symbol A represents a behavioral baseline, preferably obtained under uncontrolled conditions as previously described. B, C, and D in the vertical arrangement represent three treatment conditions, which ... [are] three social reinforcement contingencies for one behavior. The three conditions were administered simultaneously and successively by three groups in counterbalanced order .... The final period, symbolized as B, C, or D, indicated that the treatment condition effecting the most desired behavior changed was programmed for continued use with the [subject].

Multiple Baseline Designs

In this construct, although the A-B logic is employed (i.e., one subject, one target behavior), the researcher is looking at "... two or more actions, subjects, or situations, or some combination of actions, situation, and subjects" [79]. McMillan and Schumacher give us the following definitional explanations:

> *Multiple-Baseline across Behavior.* To provide a meaningful comparison it is necessary to begin the treatments at different times for each one. In this way, behavior remaining at the baseline condition provides control for that receiving the treatment condition. The most troublesome problem with this design is using two or more behaviors that are so similar that the first time the treatment is introduced, it affects both. This problem can be thought of as a threat to internal validity because of a diffusion of treatment.
>
> *Multiple-Baseline across Situations.* In this design a single type of target behavior of one individual is observed in two or more settings.
>
> *Multiple-Baseline across Individuals.* This design uses two or more individuals and holds the behavior and the situation constant. After a stable baseline is observed for one subject, the treatment is introduced for that subject only. After a given time interval, the second subject receives the treatment, and so forth. This design is effective as long as the subjects involved are uninfluenced by one another because one of them has received the treatment. [80]

Blythe and Briar [81] allude to several considerations that must be given to the use of the single-subject or single-system designs. Although an increasing number of designs are available to social work practitioners, *there are few guidelines for the selection of the most suitable design* for the research situation. As a general rule, the less rigorous designs tend to be the most easily applicable to clinical settings. Second, *inadequate control of variables*, which might influence the outcome in these types of designs, is an ever-present criticism. Third, since statistical analysis of single-case data is rare, the emphasis must fall on *competent description, explanation, and visual analysis.* And finally, *ethical considerations* are always a critical issue. Any time the removal of beneficial treatments is instituted with clients, the clients' well-being may be jeopardized, and the ethical responsibility of the practitioner is called into question.

Program Evaluation

Evaluation research can be applied to a wide variety of organizational endeavors, and at several levels, including administration, middle management, line staff; or to any segment, category, department, or program within an organization. The research skills discussed in this text are used to answer questions about the organization that may be posed by the community, the chief executive officer, the board of directors, external standard-setting agencies, funding sources, consumer groups, or professional groups.

Uses of Program Evaluation

This evaluation process, when applied to social service agencies and programs, is often referred to as program evaluation. A working definition for our purposes could be that **program evaluation is the application of one or more research skills and techniques to social service agencies, programs, or provisions to accomplish stated purposes.** The overriding purpose of these activities generally is to establish *accountability* measures that are used by boards of directors, administrators, and/or program supervisors to verify the effectiveness of their efforts, and/or to demonstrate the need for continuation, expansion, or increased funding for their work. These research means are also frequently used to verify for *external* accrediting bodies that their standards are being met by the program, department, or service. For example, the Council on Social Work Education is the national accrediting body for all undergraduate and graduate programs in social work. As they prepare their self-study materials for review by the council and prepare for the site visit by the accreditation team, it is common for program directors to use some of these research skills to add strength and clarity to their presentations.

Notwithstanding the importance of program evaluation to external bodies, it also has great *internal* value to social service agencies or programs. In these days of limited financial and staff resources, supervisors are under great pressure to use their resources most efficiently. The social work profession, as well as other disciplines, continue to experience these pressures toward accountability. The results of systematic program evaluation activities can aid greatly in decision-making processes.

Quality Assurance

It is common for larger public and private agencies to have systematic evaluation efforts incorporated through the establishment of quality assurance programs, which may be a separate department or office within the agency. In 1972 the Professional Standards Review Organization came into being. As a result, the Joint Commission on Accreditation of Hospitals developed standards to require that hospitals have quality assurance processes. Initially then, quality assurance was a medical care management tool for inpatient care, but it has quickly entered the broader human service arena [82]. Smaller agencies, on the other hand, which cannot afford a separate department with its own staff for these evaluation activities, can incorporate program evaluation through existing departments, groups, or even an individual staff member who is assigned the task of program evaluation.

Make no mistake about it, as we have discussed earlier about some other purposes for research endeavors, program evaluation exists to help an agency or program demonstrate how effective and necessary is its continuation—in other words, there is a built-in recognized bias. The rigor and systematic development of the design then becomes increasingly important to give the evaluation validity. On the other hand, program evaluation activities can also be misused by administrators, CEOs, or boards to intimidate or threaten the staff by putting unreasonable pressure on outcomes that are unattainable. Ethical considerations in program evaluation research activities are no less important than in any other research endeavor.

Nuehring and Pascone [83] set forth evaluation questions and assorted techniques associated with quality assurance as follows:

1. *Structural considerations*—such as appropriate qualification of and sufficient number of staff who deliver the direct service, adequacy of physical facilities, and other resources—are determined by various administrative audits.

2. *Care considerations*—such as the choice of appropriate treatment to fit the diagnosis, timeliness of treatment, avoidance of excessive retention in the program, and the program's capacity to make contact with the desired target population.

3. *Outcome or results of services*—approached through clinical chart audits to test recorded results against predetermined treatment goals, through follow-up studies of clients, through profile analyses of aggregate data at the agency level, and through clinical care evaluation studies.

4. *Questions of adequacy, appropriateness, and sufficiency of services*—approached through profile analysis (if an agency's statistics include units of service delivered). Whether services are being used by the neediest clients is tackled through utilization review, through comparing profiles of clients drawn from aggregate data.

Approaches to Program Evaluation

Let's now look at several approaches to program evaluation that can be used by the evaluator in deciding on specific research designs. McMillan and Schumacher [84] offer four approaches that can be readily adapted for use in social service settings.

Objective-Based Evaluation

In this approach the evaluation measures the outcomes of practice and the degree to which the objectives of an intervention have been met. Say, for example, that we want to evaluate an inpatient psychiatric unit. Each patient would have an individual treatment plan with objectives outlined which was developed upon admission. A *peer review* technique could be used to have a clinician from another area of the hospital review the progress of randomly drawn patient charts against the stated objectives of their treatment plan to measure to what degree the objectives have been, or are being, met.

Another technique would be the *continued stay utilization review*. These reviews are characteristically used to study cases in which extended treatment time is observed, and they are designed to determine if continued care is beneficial or necessary. Single-subject designs can be very useful for this process by showing client progress, the degree and stability of change, and the relationship between certain interventions and change, thereby clarifying and documenting the rationale for retaining certain cases in treatment [85]. These objectives are many times expressed as *behavioral* descriptions or as *performance objectives*. In other words, if the patient is demonstrating a certain unacceptable social behavior, the objective could be stated in terms of the cessation of that behavior. If the objective is stated that the patient needs to increase the use of a particular socially acceptable behavior, this performance objective can also be measured through a single-subject design.

An additional approach to objective-based evaluation is referred to as a *clinical care evaluation study*. It is a time-limited study of some subgroup of clients or particular problem area (e.g., mental patients with criminal records, behaviorally disturbed children with vision problems, probationers with physical disabilities), with the purpose of providing information to correct the problem or better manage the type of client. If samples of certain groups are large enough, the research could use aggregate data analysis. But if the samples are too small, single-subject designs can be used [86].

Profile analysis is another technique that can be used to evaluate objectives and outcomes. This typically involves "... study of the existing aggregate data of a program to examine patterns of service for the purpose of monitoring service delivery and identifying deviations from accepted and desirable practice." Patterns can be compared across clinicians, across groups of clients, or across time periods, depending on the area of interest [87].

Looking at aggregate data implies that the study is *ex post facto*, or "after the fact." In other words, the analysis is done on data that have been collected at a previous time, and perhaps even for purposes other than for evaluation. These studies involve no manipulation of variables, but may look for causal relationships between variables apparent in the data between two or more groups or conditions.

Systems and Cost Analysis

Levin outlines four modes of analyzing costs which can aid in policy choices and decisions: cost benefit, cost effectiveness, cost utility, and cost feasibility. Table 12.2 highlights and summarizes these modes.

TABLE 12.2   Modes of Cost Analysis

Type of Analysis	Distinguishing Feature	Strengths	Weaknesses
Cost–benefit (CB)	Outcomes measured in monetary values	Compares alternative within service Compares across services Results expressed as internal rate of return, net benefits, or cost–benefit ratios Replicable	Difficulty of converting all outcomes to monetary values
Cost-effective (CE)	Outcomes measured in units of effects	Outcomes can be measured as psychological or physical changes Replicable	Unit of effectiveness must be same among programs with same goals
Cost-utility (CU)	Outcomes measured by subjective judgments	Can integrate multiple outcomes into a single value	Measures are subjective Not replicable
Cost-feasibility (CF)	Estimate possibility of cost within fiscal constraint	Indicates if further consideration of alternative is feasible	Not deal with outcomes of alternative

Source: Adapted from H. M. Levin, "Cost Analysis," in *New Techniques for Evaluation,* N. L. Smith, ed. (Beverly Hills: Sage, 1981). Copyright 1981 by Sage Publications, Inc. Reprinted by permission of Sage Publications, Inc., and the author.

It is necessary for policymakers to consider systematically their choices in light of the financial impact. They need to be in a position to estimate costs between the various desired alternatives, comparing cost effectiveness and cost benefits, and to make enlightened estimates of differential costs. However, there are several possible limitations to the cost analysis approach: (1) those programs, activities, and so forth, being compared must have the same objectives and similar clients; (2) cost analysis can be expensive, particularly if agency records dealing with time and cost are not readily available; (3) indirect costs and spinoff costs are often impossible to identify; and (4) different measures of cost, such as cost per case, per client, per hour of service, may have different implications [88].

Decision-Oriented Evaluation

In this approach, also called *process analysis,* the evaluator takes an even broader perspective and looks at the ways decisions are made—the *processes* that go into decision making. Attempts are made to categorize the steps or elements of the process—such as selecting, collecting, analyzing, and reporting [89].

Agencies often need to reconsider how they go about making important policy, personnel, or intake decisions. An analysis of this nature can help policymakers systematically examine these issues and better understand where changes need to be made. An example might be that the board of directors of a residential treatment center wants to examine how intake decisions are made in day-to-day operations. Questions they would want to collect data on might include: Where do clients come from? Who refers them? What is their condition on arrival? Who interviews them first? How is intake information collected? Is it sufficient information? How long do they wait? What staff members have contact with them? Who actually makes the decision to admit or reject? What skills are required to make this decision? What role do family members or friends have? What complaints do residents have about the process? Examining the data collected around these kinds of questions can aid policymakers in deciding if one or more of the steps in the intake process needs to be changed, strengthened, or emphasized.

Responsive Evaluation

This mode of evaluation is used to research events that recur and is based on what people do naturally: observe and react [90]. Accuracy of communication is imperative, and the responsive evaluator has direct interaction with the audience, listening, negotiating, and asking questions. The evaluator uses several different audiences to test out the findings that surface. The evaluator recognizes the concerns of different audiences about a program and understands that these differences represent differing values and needs. An example of this form of research could take place at an after-school youth program in a specific lower-income neighborhood. The evaluator might set up open meetings with several identifiable components of the community (e.g., church groups, parents, business owners, etc.) to hear from each group what they see as the major problems facing their neighborhood youth and hear possible solutions they might propose. After listening, negotiating, asking questions, and sharing facts and figures, the evaluator draws up a report for the agency, analyzing the data and prioritizing the responses. He or she may also make recommendations in light of the findings for the agency board of directors to consider. Since the community must be involved and supportive of any actions, it would be professionally sound in this case to provide a copy of the report to each of the community groups involved, and the agency would hopefully consider its plans and negotiate with the community about what it would like to do in terms of programming.

References

1. R. Bogdan and S. J. Taylor, *Introduction to Qualitative Research Methods: A Phenomenological Approach to the Social Sciences* (San Francisco: Jossey-Bass, 1975), p. 4.
2. Irwin Epstein, "Quantitative and Qualitative Methods," in *Social Work Research and Evaluation,* 3rd ed., Richard M. Grinnell, Jr., ed. (Itsaca, IL: Peacock, 1988), p. 186.
3. Mary K. Rodwell, "Naturalistic Inquiry: An Alternative Model for Social Work Assessment," *Social Service Review* (June 1987): 241–6.
4. Martha H. Pieper, "The Future of Social Work Research," *Social Work Research and Abstracts* 21 (Winter 1985): 3–11.
5. Rodwell, "Naturalistic Inquiry," p. 237.

6. Rodwell, "Naturalistic Inquiry," p. 232.
7. Barney G. Glaser and Anselm L. Strauss, *The Discovery of Grounded Theory: Strategies for Qualitative Research* (Chicago: Aldine, 1967), p. 1.
8. William Reid, "Research in Social Work," in *Encyclopedia of Social Work*, 18th ed., Anne Minahan, ed. (Silver Spring, MD: National Association of Social Workers, 1987), p. 476.
9. Rodwell, "Naturalistic Inquiry," p. 233.
10. Mary Richmond, *Social Diagnosis* (New York: Russell Sage, 1917).
11. Rodwell, "Naturalistic Inquiry," pp. 242–3.
12. Colin Peile, "Research Paradigms in Social Work: From Statement to Creative Synthesis," *Social Service Review* 62 (March 1988): 1–19.
13. Reid, "Research in Social Work," pp. 478–9.
14. Epstein, "Quantitative and Qualitative Methods," p. 186.
15. Epstein, "Quantitative and Qualitative Methods," p. 186.
16. Reid, "Research in Social Work," p. 480.
17. Rodwell, "Naturalistic Inquiry," p. 237.
18. Peter Skagestad, "Hypothetical Realism," in *Scientific Inquiry and the Social Sciences*, Marilyn B. Brewer and Barry E. Collins, eds. (San Francisco: Jossey-Bass, 1981).
19. Epstein, "Quantitative and Qualitative Methods," p. 188.
20. Glaser and Strauss, *The Discovery of Grounded Theory*, p. 1.
21. Glaser and Strauss, *The Discovery of Grounded Theory*, p. 2.
22. Howard S. Becker, "On Methodology," *Sociological Work: Method and Substance* (Chicago: Aldine, 1970), p. 23.
23. Becker, "On Methodology," p. 21.
24. Becker, "On Methodology," p. 10.
25. Rodwell, "Naturalistic Inquiry," p. 239.
26. Egon Guba and Yvonna Lincoln, *Effective Evaluation* (San Francisco: Jossey-Bass, 1983).
27. J. B. Taylor, "Towards Alternative Forms of Social Work Research: The Case of Naturalistic Methods," *Journal of Social Welfare* 4 (1977): 119–26.
28. Rodwell, "Naturalistic Inquiry," pp. 238–9.
29. L. Schatzman and A. L. Strauss, *Field Research: Strategies for a Natural Sociology* (Englewood Cliffs, NJ: Prentice-Hall, 1973).
30. Howard Becker, *Outsiders: Studies in the Sociology of Deviance* (New York: The Free Press, 1963).
31. L. Festinger, H. W. Riecken, and S. Schachter, *When Prophecy Fails* (Minneapolis: University of Minnesota Press, 1956).
32. Laud Humphreys, *Tearoom Trade: Impersonal Sex in Public Places* (Chicago: Aldine, 1970).
33. R. L. Gold, "Roles in Sociological Field Observations," in *Issues in Participant Observation*, G. J. McCall and J. L. Simmons, eds. (Reading, MA: Addison-Wesley, 1969), pp. 30–39.
34. James H. McMillan and Sally Schumacher, *Research in Education* (Boston: Little, Brown, 1984), pp. 280–1.
35. Paul Stuart, "Historical Research," in *Social Work Research and Evaluation*, 3rd ed., Richard M. Grinnell, Jr., ed. (Itasca, IL: Peacock, 1988), p. 343.
36. William A. Trattner, ed., *Biographical Dictionary of Social Welfare in America* (Westport, CT: Greenwood, 1987).
37. Frances Piven and Richard Cloward, *Regulating the Poor: The Functions of Public Welfare* (New York: Random House, Vintage, 1971).
38. John B. Williamson, David A. Karp, John R. Dalphin, and Paul S. Gray, *The Research Craft: An Introduction to Social Research Methods*, 2nd ed. (Boston: Little, Brown, 1977), pp. 253–4.
39. Stuart, "Historical Research," pp. 344–58.
40. Louis Gottschalk, *Understanding History: A Primer of Historical Method* (New York: Knopf, 1950), p. 53.
41. Williamson et. al., *The Research Craft*, p. 243.
42. Steven McMurtry, "Secondary Prevention of Child Maltreatment: A Review," *Social Work* (January–February 1985).
43. Allen Rubin, "Practice Effectiveness: More Grounds for Optimism," *Social Work* 30 (November–December 1985).
44. Tony Tripodi, "Trends in Research Publications: A Study of Social Work Journals from 1956 to 1980," *Social Work* 29 (July–August 1984).
45. Harris M. Cooper, "Scientific Guidelines for Conducting Integrative Research Reviews," *Review of Educational Research* 52 (Summer 1982).
46. McMillan and Schumacher, *Research in Education*, p. 280.
47. Williamson et. al., *The Research Craft*, p. 252.
48. Mary R. Lewis, "Notes on Research," *Social Service Review* 50 (December 1976): 647–54.
49. William R. Reid and Audrey D. Smith, *Research in Social Work* (New York: Columbia University Press, 1981), p. 291.
50. Reid and Smith, *Research in Social Work*, pp. 289–90.
51. Stuart, "Historical Research," pp. 356–8.
52. Martha May, "The 'Problem of Duty': Family Desertion in the Progressive Era.," *Social Service Review* 62 (March 1988).
53. Marian J. Morton, "Fallen Women, Federated

Charities, and Maternity Homes, 1913–1973," *Social Service Review* 62 (March 1988).

54. Audrey D. Smith, "Another Look at Content Analysis: An Essay Review," *Social Work Research and Abstracts* 18 (Winter 1982): 5.

55. Ole R. Holsti, *Content Analysis for the Social Sciences and Humanities* (Reading, MA: Addison-Wesley, 1969), p. 2.

56. Bernard Berelson, *Content Analysis in Communication Research* (New York: Hafner, 1952, 1971), p. 18.

57. Smith, "Another Look at Content Analysis," p. 5.

58. Berelson, *Content Analysis in Communication Research*.

59. Smith, "Another Look at Content Analysis," p. 9.

60. Holsti, *Content Analysis for the Social Sciences and Humanities*, pp. 4–5.

61. Klaus Krippendorff, *Content Analysis: An Introduction to the Methodology* (Beverly Hills, CA: Sage, 1980), p. 132.

62. Smith, "Another Look at Content Analysis," p. 8.

63. Berelson, *Content Analysis in Communication Research*, p. 148.

64. Williamson et al., *The Research Craft*, p. 273.

65. Williamson et al., *The Research Craft*, pp. 274–5.

66. Martha M. Dore, Thomas M. Young, and Donnell M. Pappenfort, "Comparison of Basic Data for the National Survey of Residential Group Care Facilities: 1966–1982," *Child Welfare* 63 (November–December 1984): 485–95.

67. Williamson et al., *The Research Craft*, pp. 309–12.

68. Michael W. Ross, "Femininity, Masculinity, and Sexual Orientation: Some Cross-Cultural Comparisons," *Journal of Homosexuality* 9(1) (1963): 27–36.

69. Sandra L. Bem, "The Measurement of Psychological Androgyny," *Journal of Consulting and Clinical Psychology* 42 (1974): 155–62.

70. Alfred C. Kinsey, W. B. Pomeroy, and C. E. Martin, *Sexual Behavior in the Human Male* (Philadelphia: W. B. Saunders, 1948).

71. Elaine M. Nuehring and Anne B. Pascone, "Single-Subject Evaluation: A Tool for Quality Assurance," *Social Work* 31 (September–October 1986): 360.

72. McMillan and Schumacher, *Research in Education*, pp. 230–1.

73. Robert M. Browning and Donald O. Stover, "Same-Subject Experimental Designs," *Behavior Modification in Child Treatment* (Chicago, IL: Aldine-Atherton, 1971), p. 80.

74. Browning and Stover, "Same-Subject Experimental Designs," pp. 80–84.

75. Browning and Stover, "Same-Subject Experimental Designs," p. 89.

76. Betty Blythe and Scott Briar, "Developing Empirically Based Models of Practice," *Social Work* 6 (November–December 1985): 483.

77. Browning and Stover, "Same-Subject Experimental Designs," pp. 91–93.

78. Browning and Stover, "Same-Subject Experimental Designs," p. 105.

79. McMillan and Schumacher, *Research in Education*, p. 233.

80. McMillan and Schumacher, *Research in Education*, p. 234–7.

81. Blythe and Briar, "Developing Empirically Based Models of Practice," pp. 484–5.

82. Nuehring and Pascone, "Single-Subject Evaluation," p. 359.

83. Nuehring and Pascone, "Single-Subject Evaluation," p. 360.

84. McMillan and Schumacher, *Research in Education*, pp. 341–51.

85. Nuehring and Pascone, "Single-Subject Evaluation," p. 363.

86. Nuehring and Pascone, "Single-Subject Evaluation," p. 363.

87. Nuehring and Pascone, "Single-Subject Evaluation," p. 363.

88. Joseph P. Hornick and Barbara Burrows, "Program Evaluation," in *Social Work Research and Evaluation*, 3rd ed., Richard M. Grinnell, Jr., ed. (Itasca, IL: Peacock, 1988), p. 416.

89. M. C. Alkin, "Evaluation Theory Development," *Evaluation Comment* 2 (1969): 2.

90. McMillan and Schumacher, *Research in Education*, p. 349.

Chapter 13

Data Reduction and Organization

The meaning of datum/data
Why we organize and reduce data
The role of the computer in data
    reduction
An introduction to the computer
Preparing the data for computer
    input
    Coding the data
    Developing a codebook
    Coding nonstandard responses
    Checking for coder reliability
    Coding missing data and
        nonresponses

Formatting the data for computer
    input
Keypunching the data
    The transfer sheet
    Edge coding
    Optical scanning sheets
    Direct keyboard entry
Editing the data for errors
    Possible punch cleaning
    Contingency cleaning
Storing the data

Simplify, simplify. —HENRY DAVID THOREAU

Rhonda Reason is a junior social work major taking Methods of Social Work Research. Since course requirements include conducting a term research project, Rhonda has been keeping her eyes and ears peeled for a research question. After several weeks of looking, listening, reading, and thinking, Rhonda has become interested in whether or not males and females choose social work as a major for the same or different reasons. Rhonda begins by formulating her research question: "Are males' and females' reasons for majoring in social work the same or different?" Rhonda then goes to the library to do a more extensive search of existing literature. After several sessions with a variety of books and journals, Rhonda formulates a theoretical position and a hypothesis that suggests that males' and females' reasons for majoring in social work are not different. Now it is time to devise a test of this hypothesis. After careful and thoughtful evaluation, Rhonda decides to use the survey design. With decisions made on how to measure each variable, Rhonda constructs her questionnaire. The questionnaire covers a lot of territory: personal information (age, sex, race, marital status, father's occupation, mother's occupation, etc.); attitudes toward people, work, and social work; previous majors and double majors; and reasons for majoring in social work, to name just a few. In fact, Rhonda's questionnaire consists of exactly fifty questions. Now Rhonda must decide *whom* she will ask to fill out this questionnaire. Ideally, she would like to solicit the help of all undergraduate social work majors in her region. But with 875 majors among five state universities, this admirable plan would cost too much in time and money. So Rhonda decides to draw a random sample of 400 majors and mail each selected major a copy of her questionnaire along with explicit instructions on how to complete it. Although 400 may seem like a somewhat ambitious number, Rhonda knows about poor return rates from mail questionnaires. Even so, she is hoping for a 50 percent return on the 400 questionnaires mailed out. In due time (and after two follow-ups), Rhonda does receive 150 questionnaires—not as good as she had hoped, but typical of mail questionnaires!

The Meaning of Datum/Data

What Rhonda has stacked in front of her are known in the research world as *data*. In social work, we use the term *data* to refer to any observations or information collected during the research process. We should distinguish, at this point, between *datum* and *data*. *Datum* is the singular of *data*. The term *datum* is used to refer to any single observation of any single piece of information—a subject's age, a subject's sex. Generally speaking, we are concerned with many observations or many pieces of information. Hence, we generally use the term *data*. Rhonda, for example, has 150 questionnaires, each with 50 pieces of information. That multiplies out to 7,500 pieces of information. And these 7,500 pieces of information comprise Rhonda's data.

Why We Organize and Reduce Data

You may not have conducted a survey like Rhonda's, but if you have completed the data collection phase of a research project (whether survey, experiment, or field study), you also should have in your possession a collection of information, and this collection of information represents your data. And the imminent question now becomes, "What's next?" To answer this question for both you and Rhonda, let's take a look at some of the options available to Rhonda. She could begin by reading through the 150 returned questionnaires, and when she is finished, she will have read all 7,500 pieces of information. Though this option is admirable, if she were to choose it, what would she really know? How much of the information could we expect her to retain? Would she have a tendency to remember those pieces of information that support her hypothesis and forget those that do not? Perhaps it goes without saying that this is not the most plausible option for either Rhonda or you to adopt. Rhonda could also begin by grouping like pieces of information together. Of the 7,500 pieces of information, for example, 150 represent age. Another 150 (each) represent marital status, sex, race, and so on. If Rhonda were to organize her data by variables, she would be constructing a number of distributions—in fact, one for each variable. A *distribution* is simply a listing of all values for some designated variable. To illustrate, the distribution of ages would consist of the 150 values representing age—one for each subject unless, of course, someone did not answer this question. Since Rhonda has fifty variables, she also has fifty distinct distributions. But even with these kinds of groupings, there still remains more information than Rhonda can make sense of. And with fifty distinct groupings, Rhonda would lose the ability to examine two variables in relation to each other. While Rhonda could examine the distribution of ages and the distribution of males and females, for example, she could not examine the distribution of ages for males apart from the distribution of ages for females.

While it might be possible to identify some merit in both of the preceding methods, what Rhonda really needs is an even better method—one that will permit her to organize and reduce the data to a more meaningful and interpretable level. One plausible procedure for accomplishing the desired level of organization and reduction is to put some of the data in *matrix form*. Suppose, for example, Rhonda were to take a large piece of paper (about the size of poster board) and label fifty columns across the top, one for each variable. Then she numbers 150 rows, one for each subject. If she now copies her data from the questionnaires onto this piece of paper, she will have transformed her selected data to matrix form, where each row represents a subject and each column in that row represents a variable response belonging to that subject. The data might appear as in Figure 13.1. While Rhonda still has fifty distributions since each column (variable) is a distribution, she can also identify smaller distribution—the distribution of females' ages or the distribution of males' ages. By now you should begin to see that data organization and reduction is a method of transforming data in order to facilitate the search for meaningful patterns. Without data organization and reduction, data would remain an overwhelming and meaningless mass of information.

The Role of the Computer in Data Reduction

Let's consider for just a moment the steps that Rhonda might go through in order to compute the average age of her sample, using only her hands, eyes, and brain. Rhonda begins by reading the age on the first questionnaire (the questionnaire numbered 001) and remembering this numeric value. In other words, Rhonda *reads* this value and stores it in her *memory*. Now Rhonda reads the age written on the second questionnaire. But instead of storing this age in memory, Rhonda decides to add its

FIGURE 13.1 Rhonda's Data Matrix

?#	Age	Sex	MS	Father's Occ.	Mother's Occ.	Reasons/Major
001	21	F	S	history teacher	librarian	Like to work with people
002	18	M	S	carpenter	housewife	Because of interest in aging
003	19	M	M	minister	housewife	Complement psychology major
004	20	F	M	accountant	pharmacist	Not sure
005	20	F	S	professor	math teacher	Understand self better
006	21	M	S	lawyer	housewife	Like to work with people
007	18	F	M	doctor	doctor	Have an interest in marriage/family counseling
008	19	M	S	electrician	housewife	Want to go into counseling
009	20	M	S	lawyer	lawyer	Want to go into counseling
010	23	M	M	doctor	lawyer	Tried everything else
.						
.						
200	24	F	M	lawyer	professor	Like to work with people

value to the first age and store their sum. You see, Rhonda has already determined that she cannot quickly and efficiently memorize 150 ages and then add these ages together. So she begins with a sum of zero, reads into memory the first age, and adds that age to her initial sum (zero). The sum, at this point, is really just the first age (0 + first age = first age). This sum is then stored in memory, and Rhonda reads the second age. This second age is added to the sum, and the new sum is stored in memory. Now Rhonda reads the third age and adds its value to the current sum. Once all ages have been input, Rhonda divides the sum by 150 to obtain the average age, and this value is *output*—perhaps written down. This process has been diagramed for you in Figure 13.2.

Can you imagine what data organization and reduction would be like if the only tools at your disposal were your hands, eyes, and brain? Computing the average age for Rhonda's 150 respondents turned out to be quite a task. But suppose Rhonda now decides to compute the average age for males and then the average age for females. She would first have to sort the 150 ages into two distributions—ages belonging to males and ages belonging to females (a fairly simple task using her data matrix)—and then compute the average age of each distribution. Now let's further suppose that Rhonda needs to know the average age by marital status, race, and college classification. The sorting process must begin again for each of these variables before average age can be computed. The sorting possibilities for age alone are endless, not to mention the sorting process for other variables (average income, occupational prestige, and GPA by sex, marital status, college classification, etc.) with which we might do this very same thing.

In a nutshell, data organization and reduction with only our hands, eyes, and brain would be extremely time-consuming and laborious. In addition, human beings engaging in such tasks are highly susceptible to fatigue and boredom, and both of these factors are likely to result in increased errors. Rhonda can compute the average age of her sample by adding up all the ages and dividing the sum by 150. But the more averages Rhonda computes, the more likely she is to make a mistake. Even if Rhonda were to use a calculator to help her brain, the numbers would have to be

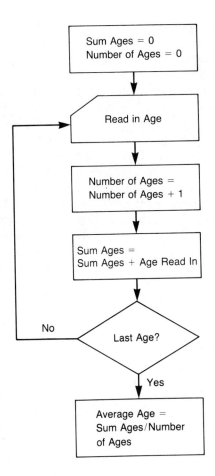

FIGURE 13.2   Diagram of Steps Needed to Compute an Average

entered into the calculator for each average computed. And with each value entered, the potential for error increases.

With the advent of the computer age, data analysis in research has taken on an entirely new meaning. Computers are very good at repetitive tasks like sorting and adding, the same tasks that cost you and me increasingly higher error with each repetition. What's more, computers can work at incredibly high speeds—speeds that no human can approach—and they can do this without sacrificing accuracy. To be more precise, computers can compute at speeds approaching one-fourth the speed of light! This speed is so incomprehensible to the human mind that someone has described it with this comparison: If you were interacting with a computer—you giving the computer data, the computer giving you data, back and forth—it would take you each time, in the computer's time frame, *eight years* to respond!

Despite the extraordinary nature of these marvelous machines, computers are not loved by all—not even by all social workers! There are some people who have always feared that computers would take over the world. Remember the movie

2001? The only villain was HAL the computer. While this early image still lingers with us, it is an image that needs to be dispelled. The fact is that a computer is not really a machine to be feared. In actuality, a computer is a very simple-minded machine. It knows only two things: yes and no. You see, a computer is just an intricate pattern of circuits that are either opened or closed, representing yes or no. Anything else a computer "knows" is the result of human programming. If you think you have caught the computer in an error, you probably need to think again. Since computers are programmed by humans, they do exactly what humans tell them to do.

To a social worker, the computer, with its ability to perform repetitive tasks at incredibly high speeds, can be an invaluable tool. Complex analyses of both large and small data sets that were heretofore impossible have now become run-of-the-mill. Complex analyses that might have taken months, even years, can now be done within minutes or hours. With the aid of the computer, researchers can examine their data more carefully and more thoroughly than ever before thought possible. In reality, the marvel of the computer lies not in any power it holds for itself but rather in the power it can give to those of us who are willing to use it in our research.

An Introduction to the Computer

Since computers are programmed by humans, it should come as no surprise to learn that they work very much like the human brain. Let's recall for a moment the steps that Rhonda went through in order to compute the average age of her sample. The ages were *input* one at a time into her *memory*. Once in memory, a *control center* triggered another part of her brain to do some *arithmetic*. Once the arithmetic was done, another age was read in. When all 150 ages had been read into memory, a control center triggered the final arithmetic operation, and the answer was *output*. The basic components of a computer are the same as those used by Rhonda's brain to compute average age: (1) memory, (2) control unit, (3) arithmetic–logic unit, and (4) input–output (i/o) unit. A diagram of these four components is given in Figure 13.3. It is these four components that communicate with one another to process data. Let's take a brief look at each.

The memory is that part of the computer where data are stored. Most memories contain thousands of locations that are capable of storing thousands of pieces of information. Generally speaking, two types of information are stored in a computer's memory. The first type of information you are already familiar with: it is the data (represented in matrix form) to be analyzed. The second type of information stored in a computer's memory is a set of instructions or codes that tell the computer what to do with the data. Instructions, for example, may tell the computer how to sort the data or how to compute an average (e.g., average age). When instructions tell the computer what to do with the data, they are labeled a *program*. In other words, **a program is a sequence of instructions that causes data to be processed in some unique way.** Both types of information (programs and data) are stored in the computer's memory.

The control unit is that part of a computer which is responsible for a program's being executed automatically without outside help. More specifically, the control unit sequentially examines the instructions in a program and issues signals

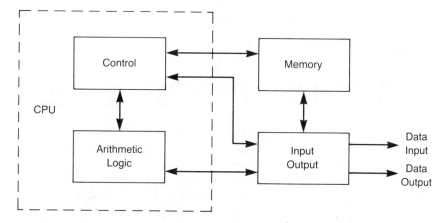

FIGURE 13.3   General Block Diagram of a Digital Computer

to other sections of the computer, which carry out the instructions. Each instruction is retrieved from memory by the control unit, interpreted, and then executed one at a time until the program is completed. As each instruction is examined or decoded, the control unit generates timing and control signals that tell other sections of the computer what to do to carry out the operation specified by the control unit.

The arithmetic–logic unit is that section of the computer that actually processes the data. Two main types of processing are carried out: arithmetic operations, such as addition and division, and logic operations, such as AND and OR. For example, if we wanted to identify married females, we would ask the computer to sort out those cases where sex equals female AND marital status equals married. If we also wanted to compute the average age of these respondents, we would store the appropriate "add" and "divide" instructions in memory. The control unit would then retrieve each instruction, interpret each, and send signals to the arithmetic–logic unit that would result in the ages being added together and their sum being subsequently divided by the number of ages. The control section and the arithmetic–logic unit are very closely related. They operate together and are often viewed as a single unit. When the control unit and the arithmetic–logic unit are thought of as one, we use the term *central processing unit* (CPU). In other words, the CPU is the control unit and the arithmetic–logic unit combined.

The input–output (i/o) section of a computer is the set of logic circuits that permits the central processing unit and the memory to communicate with the outside world. All information that transfers into and out of the computer must pass through the i/o section. The i/o acts as an interface between the computer and any device that permits input and/or output. And there are a wide variety of input and output devices. Data may be entered into the computer, for example, through a typewriterlike *keyboard*. Data can also be entered using *cards, disks,* and *magnetic tape.* Data can be output on a *cathode-ray tube* (CRT) or printed by a *typewriter.* Data can also be output to a high-speed *line printer, cards, disks,* or *magnetic tape.* You should note that input and output devices are not mutually exclusive. In fact, as you can see from this discussion, several devices can be used for both input and output.

Preparing the Data for Computer Input

Coding the Data

Whenever data are input into a computer for storage, analysis, and retrieval, they must be transformed into a highly condensed form in order to conserve space and simplify analysis. This transformation process is known as coding. **By "coding" we mean the assignment of numbers to all data** (pieces of information). If you reexamine Rhonda's data pictured in Figure 13.1, you will quickly notice that some variable responses are represented as numbers while others are represented as letters or phrases. When Rhonda recorded each respondent's age, for example, she used a number, since age is a number. On the other hand, when Rhonda recorded each respondent's sex, she used a letter, and when she recorded "primary reason for majoring in social work," she used a phrase. Rhonda's decision to use an M or F for sex and a phrase for "primary reason" was based upon the fact there is no clear-cut and universally understood number representation for these variables. Now, while Rhonda or you or I could look at her data matrix (Figure 13.1) and understand fully its contents, several response identifiers could be more efficiently represented. All primary reasons, for example, could have been coded as numbers, and these numbers could have been placed in the matrix to represent respondents' answers. This transformation of responses to numeric codes results in a highly condensed data form that conserves space and, as we shall see, simplifies data analysis. If Rhonda's data matrix were transformed to numeric form, it might appear as in Figure 13.4.

When such variables as sex, age, race, marital status, and college classification are to have some numeric representation, then we must assign it. A conventional procedure in the social sciences for coding sex, for example, is to code males as 1 and females as 2. Please notice that these numbers do not mean anything mathemat-

FIGURE 13.4 Rhonda's Data Matrix in Numeric Form

?#	Age	Sex	MS	Father's Occ.	Mother's Occ.	Reasons/Major
001	21	2	2	78	47	1
002	18	1	2	39	99	2
003	19	1	1	69	99	1
004	20	2	1	57	61	4
005	20	2	2	78	78	5
006	21	1	2	76	78	1
007	18	2	1	82	82	6
008	19	1	2	49	99	7
009	20	1	2	76	76	7
010	23	1	1	82	76	8
.						
.						
.						
.						
.						
200	24	2	1	76	78	1

ical. They are simply being used to identify or designate a person's sex. Now you might want to reason that using a one-digit number to code sex is really no more conservative or efficient than using M or F. While it is true that alphabetical codes are sometimes used to represent response alternatives, they are *not* recommended. When alpha (alphabetical) codes are used, they eventually have to be transformed to numeric codes for purposes of data analysis since most statistical software (i.e., statistical programs—instructions) has been written to expect numeric input. Hence, to eliminate one unnecessary step and thus simplify data analysis, it is preferable to code all data with numbers.

Developing a Codebook

Before coding any data, the trained researcher will begin by developing a codebook. **The codebook is an outline of what is to be coded and how it is to be coded.** It is a list of variables and the numeric values being used to represent each variable response. Let's face it, researchers are human and they do forget things. When 1 means 1 as in age, there is no problem with memory. But when 1 means "male" (as in sex) or "I like to work with people" (as in primary reason for major), there may be a memory problem. If you set your data aside for four weeks, will you remember that 1 represents "male" or that 1 represents "I like to work with people"? The codebook provides you with written instructions for transforming each variable response into a numeric value and serves as documentation for what you have done.

Deciding on Numeric Codes

How do you decide on the numeric codes to be used? First, you will probably look to convention and note how these same variables have been coded in past research. In addition, you should consider your own theory and hypotheses to be tested. As a general rule of thumb, it is preferable to code all variables at the highest level of measurement possible. If, in the process of data analysis, you find you need to regroup and recode a variable, it will be easy to do so. Suppose, for example, you are interested in studying some facet of social development throughout the various life stages—infancy, childhood, adolescence, young adulthood. Instead of coding actual age, you decide to code each subject into one of these life stages. In effect, you define an age range for each life stage and code your subjects on the basis of their ages. If, in the course of analyzing your data, you decided to alter the age ranges defining each life stage and thereby also alter the life stage into which some subjects fall, you would not be able to do it. If you had coded age initially, you could now play with the ranges as much as you liked. In other words, coding your data at the highest possible level of measurement will give you the greatest flexibility in your data analysis.

General Requirements

In developing the coding scheme for your set of variables, two general requirements must be met. *First, your coding categories must be mutually exclusive.* That is, there should be no values that could be coded in more than one category. *Second, your cod-*

ing categories must be logically exhaustive. That is, they should allow for classification of *all* categories or values that appear in the study. No category or value identified through the study should be omitted. Let's examine these characteristics more closely by again looking at Rhonda's data. Two of the questions on Rhonda's questionnaire are:

1. What is your sex?   (1) male   (2) female
2. What is your primary reason for majoring in social work?

If you look closely at these two questions, you will notice that they are really very different. Whereas the first question has two response alternatives from which each subject must choose, the second question has none. Recall from Chapter 11 that the first question is a closed-ended question; the second is an open-ended question. Closed-ended questions are *precoded*—that is, the response alternatives and their assigned numerical values are determined before the data are collected. Variables like sex, race, marital status, and education are usually precoded. Open-ended questions, on the other hand, are not often precoded primarily because we do not know what the range of response alternatives will be. Instead, open-ended questions are *postcoded*—that is, the response alternatives and their assigned numerical values are determined after the data are collected and after we have had a chance to view the response alternatives given. *Postcoding requires that you read through all answers received on an open-ended question and develop a categorical scheme for those answers.* Rhonda's question, for example, on "primary reason for majoring in social work" is going to require postcoding since there is really no way that Rhonda can determine prior to data collection all the various responses that will be given. Hence, this question and similar questions will require a close examination of the data once the data are collected.

Coding Nonstandard Responses

Despite the care and energy invested in developing the codebook and despite the type of questions asked (precoded or postcoded), there will probably be some respondents who give answers that seem to defy the categories and coding scheme. To standardize coding and reduce error associated with unexpected responses, it is a good idea to let one person (someone designated as *editor*) go through the questionnaires and edit the data—that is, make coding decisions on all nonstandard answers. If there is a great deal of data and it would be too time-consuming to have one individual examine each questionnaire, then the editor should be on hand as the questionnaires are coded to handle such situations as they arise. In effect, the editor's job is to ensure clarity so that coders have only to make standard decisions that can clearly be based on the codebook.

Checking for Coder Reliability

If working on a large research project where several people are working with the same large data set, checking the reliability of coders is also a vital part of the coding process. Just as one coder should always make the same decisions about how a question is to be coded each time he or she confronts it, so should different coders always code the same responses in the same way. To ensure a high level of coder reliability, the coding staff should be thoroughly trained on all coding procedures. This training process should include some testing to determine the extent to which coders agree on how a response should be coded. In addition, it is a good idea to monitor coders at all times. Preferably monitoring should be done by the editor. We stress again, the presence of an editor will help to ensure that nonstandard responses are treated the same by all coders.

Coding Missing Data and Nonresponses

No matter how carefully your questions are constructed or how hard you try to obtain complete data, there will probably be some questions left blank by some respondents. It is a good idea to assign a specific numeric code to nonresponses since no code is really a code—a blank—and can result in error and ambiguity. And when the computer reads blanks using the same instructions it uses to read numbers, the blanks become zeroes. In other words, blanks are read as zeros, and for those variables having a legitimate code of zero, nonresponses or missing data have been miscoded. Suppose, for example, one of the questions on Rhonda's questionnaire is "What is your annual income?" Since income is a sensitive question for many respondents, there will probably be several individuals who choose not to answer. There may be others who do choose to answer this question and whose income is zero dollars. If Rhonda does not code (i.e., leaves blank) nonresponses, they will be read as zeros. Hence, respondents not answering this question will appear to have an income of zero dollars, and it will be impossible to separate those individuals having no real income from those refusing to answer the question.

To avoid ambiguity and this unnecessary source of error, it is a good idea to identify some numeric value or values that will represent missing data. A conventional procedure in the social sciences is to assign a 9 or a group of 9's (e.g., 99, 999, 9999) to represent missing data. The number of 9's assigned is contingent upon the largest valid code for the specified variable. Suppose, for example, you are trying to determine your missing values coded for income. If the largest income reported by your respondents is $30,000, you would use 99999 to code missing data. On the other hand, if the largest income reported is $5,000, a code of 9999 would be sufficient. Each missing value code should be a number composed of 9's that is larger than the largest valid code for the specified variable.

Formatting the Data for Computer Input

Once each piece of information in the data matrix has been assigned a numeric code, we are now ready to consider our data format. **By data format we mean specification of the precise form the data will take for computer input.** And these specifications are an essential part of our codebook. Of the input devices available, the most frequently used by beginning researchers is the computer *card*. Hence, we will begin our discussion of data format by taking a brief look at the computer card's design.

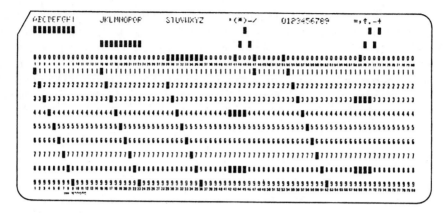

FIGURE 13.5   Computer Card

The computer card is a heavy piece of paper that forms a matrix of eighty columns and twelve rows. This card is pictured in Figure 13.5. While the number of columns on this card is easily identified, the number of rows is not quite so obvious. Ten of the rows on the card are marked with the numbers 0 through 9. There are two additional, unmarked rows just above the zero row.

When holes are punched in this special card (using a keypunch machine only), it becomes readable to a computer. Each column on this card is a card location, and only one character (i.e., single-digit number, alphabetical letter, or special character) can be punched per card column. For each single-digit number (0–9), alphabetical letter, and special character, there is a predefined pattern of holes. This predefined pattern allows for any character (single-digit number, alphabet letter, or special character) to be punched into one column using one or more of the twelve rows in that column to create the appropriate punch pattern. A numeric punch, for example, is a single-hole punch. This means that there will be only one hole punched in the column you designate to store a number 0 through 9. If you want to put a 0 in column 1, only the 0 will be punched out. Restated, any single-digit number will consist of only a single punch. An alpha character, on the other hand, is a two-hole punch in a single column. In other words, there will always be two holes punched in any column in which you store an alphabetical character. The pattern of these two-hole alpha punches is derived by dividing the alphabet into three sets. The first nine characters in the alphabet (A–I) are in the first set, the second nine characters (J–R) in the second set, and the last eight characters (S–Z) in the third set. A punch in one of the first three rows (of the designated column) indicates the alphabetical set. A second punch using rows 1 through 9 (of the designated column) indicates the alphabetical character in that set. If, for example, the letter A were punched in column 1, we should find punches in row 1 (unmarked row) and row 4 of that column. These two punches tell us that the character punched in column 1 is the first letter in the first alphabetical set—or the letter A. Figure 13.5 also shows the punch patterns for special characters. Interestingly enough, special characters can be anywhere from a one- to a three-hole punch in the designated column. In sum, any single digit or character (alpha or special) can be punched in a single column. The computer's representation of that character will be either a single- or multiple-hole punch. In either case, the character is housed in a single column.

Suppose, for example, you wanted to store "subject's sex" in column 1. If the subject is female and you are using the numeric codes of one equals male and two equals female, a hole would be keypunched in row 2 of column 1. Since you have twelve rows for each column to use in creating the appropriate punch pattern, you can punch any single-digit number, alphabet letter, or special character in any column. When variable response alternatives require more than one digit, they are coded onto computer cards by assigning a specific set of contiguous columns to a variable. A set of contiguous columns assigned to a variable is called a *field*. To keypunch an age of 37, for example, after punching the numeric code for sex in column 1, we would punch a 3 in column 2 and a 7 in column 3. Although fields may vary in width (number of columns), each must be large enough to allow one column per digit for the largest number to be coded in that field. Suppose, for example, we had one subject whose age was 102. In order to code *this* age we would need a field of three columns. This means we must reserve a specific field of three contiguous columns for age. For those subjects whose age is represented by two digits, the two digits must be *right-justified* in the field. Age 37, for example, becomes 037 or blank-37. If you fail to right-justify this age and keypunch 37-blank, the computer will read the blank as zero and you will have a respondent whose age appears to be 370!

Let's suppose you have conducted a short telephone survey, making 200 successful calls and collecting eight pieces of information per call:

1. Respondent number (questionnaire number)
2. Sex of respondent
3. Marital status
4. Age
5. Husband's education
6. Wife's education
7. TV on? (yes or no)
8. Channel

You now have in your possession 1,600 pieces of information, and in order to make some sense of these data, you must examine them for meaningful patterns. This will require data organization and reduction. Since you plan to input the data into the computer, you begin by developing a codebook. Your codebook for these variables might look like Figure 13.6. Your record length for these data is twenty-one since we have used twenty-one columns per card. Now suppose we were to keypunch all 200 surveys to computer cards and then spread these cards out as in Figure 13.7. You should notice that any given variable always occupies the same column or sequence of columns on each card. Questionnaire number, for example, is always in columns 1 to 3. Sex is always in column 5. Now, if you can imagine the card images disappearing, you are left with rows and columns of data. These rows and columns form our data matrix, where the columns identify all the variables and the rows identify

FIGURE 13.6 Codebook for Short Questionnaire

Variable Name	Values	Column(s)
Questionnaire ID #	0–200	1–3
Sex of Respondent	1 = male	5
	2 = female	
	9 = missing	
Marital Status	1 = single	7
	2 = married	
	3 = divorced	
	4 = widowed	
	5 = cohabit	
	9 = missing	
Age	18–78	9–10
	99 = missing	
Husband's Education	in years	12–13
	99 = missing	
Wife's Education	in years	15–16
	99 = missing	
TV on?	1 = no	18
	2 = yes	
	9 = missing	
Channel?	1–36	20–21
	99 = missing	

the subjects. If these same data were stored on magnetic tape or disk, we would have this same matrix. Each row or line of data (on tape or disk) is the equivalent of a card image. And the column representations for disk or tape are identical to the column representations for cards. In their card image form, the data are referred to as a *deck*. In their tape or disk form, the data are referred to as a *file*.

Keypunching the Data

With numeric codes assigned to all response alternatives and card space allocated, we are now ready to consider having the data keypunched. There are several ways to integrate the coding and keypunching procedures, including transfer sheets, edge coding, optical scanning sheets, direct keypunching, and direct keyboard entry.

The Transfer Sheet

The conventional method of data processing involves first writing the numeric codes on *transfer sheets (or code sheets)* and then having a keypunch operator keypunch from the transfer sheets. A transfer sheet is a sheet of paper that is ruled off in eighty columns of a computer card. Each line of a transfer sheet represents a computer card. This transfer sheet is pictured in Figure 13.8. To use a transfer sheet, you would simply write the numeric values to be keypunched onto the transfer sheet in

010	1	2	41	14	15	01
009	2	2	37	16	14	2	03
008	1	2	62	11	10	2	13
007	1	2	56	12	11	2	05
006	2	2	45	13	13	2	13
005	1	1	19	12		2	13
004	1	3	36	12		2	05
003	2	3	30		16	1
002	2	2	25	15	14	1
001	1	1	20	12		1	03

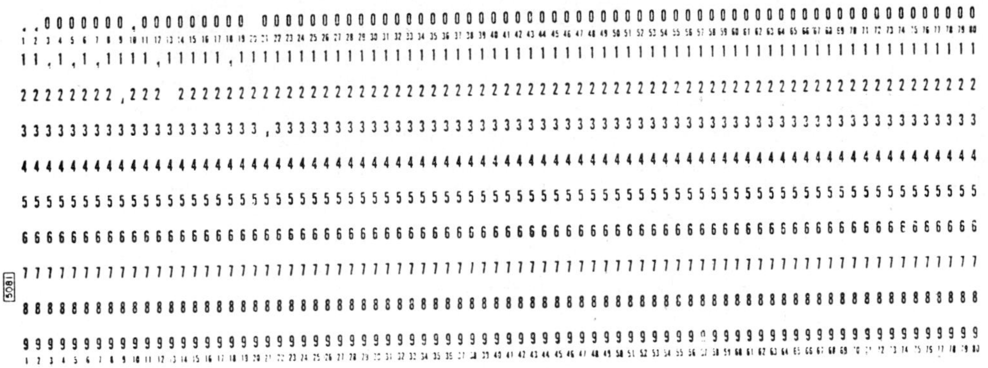

FIGURE 13.7   Data Matrix Created with Computer Cards

the appropriate columns. These sheets are then given to a keypunch operator, who will punch a card for each line of data on the sheet. If, for example, you give the keypunch operator five filled transfer sheets, he or she will return to you one hundred punched cards (twenty cards per sheet since each line is a card equivalent).

Once the cards are keypunched, they are run through a card verifier. Although a card-verifying machine looks very much like a keypunch machine, it performs a very different task. Whereas a keypunch machine punches holes in cards, a verifier reads the holes that have been punched. The verifier operator begins the verifying process by loading the punched deck (not blank cards) into the verifier, which then simulates the repunching of the cards from the transfer sheets. If the verifier operator types a number that does not match, a red light will illuminate and the machine will come to an abrupt halt. The operator will have two more tries to match the number. If he or she fails, the card is notched over the questionable punch. All notched cards must be repunched. When all corrections have been made, the cards are returned to the researcher.

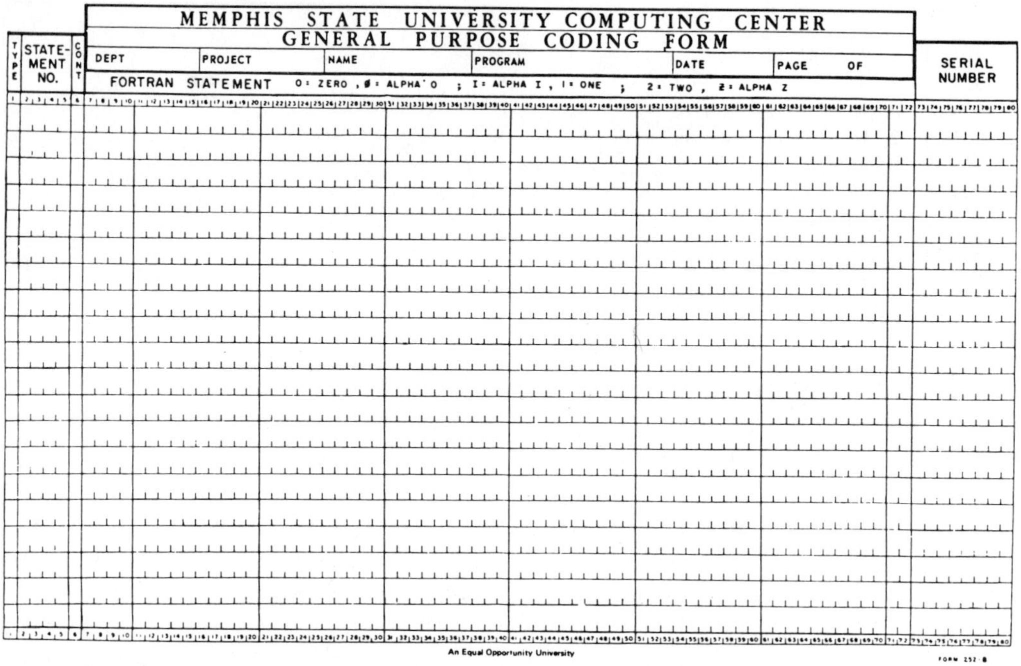
MEMPHIS STATE UNIVERSITY COMPUTING CENTER
GENERAL PURPOSE CODING FORM

TYPE | STATEMENT NO. | CONT | DEPT | PROJECT | NAME | PROGRAM | DATE | PAGE OF | SERIAL NUMBER

FORTRAN STATEMENT 0 = ZERO , Ø = ALPHA O ; I = ALPHA I , 1 = ONE ; 2 = TWO , Ƶ = ALPHA Z

An Equal Opportunity University

FIGURE 13.8 Transfer Sheet

Edge Coding

One coding technique that eliminates the need for transfer sheets is edge coding. With edge coding, the card column specification for each variable (i.e., 1–80) along with a blank line are written in the outside margin of each page. Once the data are collected, the numeric cards are transferred to these spaces and the cards are punched directly from these codes.

Optical Scanning Sheets

Sometimes it is possible to print a questionnaire on a specially formatted and specially prepared form known as an optical scanning sheet. When such sheets are used, the respondents read the questions and shade in a small area (representing their choice of answers) with a number 2 pencil. These sheets are then read through a machine (optical scanner), which reads these marks and produces a punched deck. Although the use of optical scanning sheets is faster and more accurate, an added cost for the special forms is required. In addition, shaded areas that are only partially filled in or lightly filled in are not likely to be read. And this is a problem you will detect only after you have begun your analysis with the punched cards.

Direct Keyboard Entry

An increasingly popular and seemingly more expeditious data entry technique is direct keyboard entry. With this technique, a coder sits before a video terminal displaying a coding form. The video screen displays case one, variable name one, and prompts the coder for the numeric code. The coder keys in the code, and the screen then prompts for the code for variable two of the same case. The terminal will prompt for each variable in order until all data on the questionnaire have been entered. Once all data for that questionnaire have been entered, the data will be stored to the data file and the computer begins again—prompting for variable one, case two.

In sum, the keypunching procedure that you choose to use should be based on your needs and resources. Not everyone, for example, will have access to optical scanning forms or to software that allows for direct keyboard entry. By assessing your needs and establishing the options available, you will be able to determine the most efficient keypunch procedure for your research.

Editing the Data for Errors

Although transferring your data from questionnaires to computer cards is a necessary and important step, it is not your last step in data organization and reduction. You are now ready to examine your data for errors. This process is known as *data cleaning*. Now, you might be thinking that this step is a duplication of effort—especially if an editor has been available to make decisions and nonstandard responses and if the computer cards have been verified. But no matter how carefully the data have been coded and keypunched, some errors are inevitable. Since we humans are not perfect, the coding and transfer process is not likely to be perfect.

Data cleaning can be accomplished with two procedures, both of which are essential to this process: possible punch cleaning and contingency cleaning.

Possible Punch Cleaning

Take a quick look at the codebook developed for our telephone survey, Figure 13.6. You will notice that for each variable listed, specific numeric codes are assigned. The variable sex, for example, has three legitimate codes: 1 for males, 2 for females, and 9 for missing data. If we were to find a case where sex has the code 6, we would know that an error had been made since 6 is not a legitimate code for this variable. On the other hand, the variable age has many more than three legitimate codes. In order to identify illegitimate codes, we must first have some knowledge of the youngest and oldest persons in the sample. The best way to detect errors of this nature is to use possible punch cleaning.

There are two methods that can be used to accomplish possible punch cleaning. First, there are computer programs that are designed specifically for this purpose. With such programs, you simply specify all possible punches that can be found in each card column and check for a legitimate punch. When illegal punches are found, the computer will let you know. To correct the punch, you will need to examine the original questionnaire. This document can be identified by matching the identification code on the card to the identification code on the questionnaire.

If a special program is not available for possible punch cleaning, an alternate procedure for accomplishing the same task is to create a frequency distribution for each variable being coded. A frequency distribution is simply a listing of all unique variable values and the number of times each value appears in the sample. If, for example, we wanted to examine our sex codes with a frequency distribution, we might have the following:

1	male	75
2	female	120
6		1
9	missing	4

This frequency distribution tells us that we have 75 males and 120 females in our sample. We also have three cases for which we have no information on sex. The one case having a code of six, though, we know is incorrect. Thus, while we have identified an incorrect punch on sex, we have not identified the case number. We will now need to go into the data file and locate the appropriate case before a correction can be made.

From a data cleaning standpoint, direct keyboard entry has the edge over the other keypunch techniques. When special programs are used in direct keyboard entry, the program will ask you to identify those codes considered appropriate for each variable. If you attempt to input a value that is incorrect, the computer will not accept it. Such programs provide greater assurance that the data will be coded and keyed correctly.

Contingency Cleaning

A second type of data cleaning that is more complex but often essential is contingency cleaning. This technique identifies the appropriate coded responses contingent or dependent on responses assigned on another variable. Recall, for example, the strange data produced in the 1950 census of the population (see Chapter 8). Two variables were involved: age and marital status. We expected some fourteen-year-olds, and we expected some married persons, but we didn't expect these characteristics to belong to the same persons. To our surprise, there were quite a few fourteen-year-old males and females who were married. What's more, the percentage of married males and females declined with age! This is not the pattern we would expect. In fact, it is just the opposite. These counts suggest to us that something is definitely wrong, as fourteen-year-olds are usually not married.

Contingency cleaning may be accomplished through computer programs designed especially for this purpose or through the use of the cross-tabulation procedure. By cross-tabulation we mean a cross-classification of two variables and a count of the number of observations in each cell. To discover the error in the 1950 census, for example, we might use a cross-tabulation like the one in Figure 13.9.

Age	S	M	D
14	1670		1320
15	1475		
16	1175		
17	810		575
18	905		
19	630		

FIGURE 13.9   Cross-Tabulation of the 1950 Census Data

It perhaps goes without saying that no data cleaning method will be 100 percent successful in identifying all errors. Even after both methods are used, errors may be later discovered. For example, you may discover that a male was coded as a female or that a twenty-seven-year-old was coded as 37. Possible punch cleaning and contingency cleaning can only identify those punches which are outside of some specified range. These techniques cannot detect wrong punches that fall within the specified range.

Storing the Data

Once the data have been keypunched, we must now concern ourselves with storage. This is a particularly important issue since data analysis is not a one-shot deal. In fact, the process of data analysis may take place over a period of weeks or possibly months.

When data are punched on cards, these cards may be used to process the data or they may be used to transfer the data to the medium of tape or disk. Regardless of the storage medium used, it is important to remember that storage is more than housing the numeric codes. It is also important to keep accurate written records of all variables, numeric codes for all variable response alternatives, and card and column locations. If data transformations are performed, this information should be written down and kept as part of data documentation.

As we have seen, one of the primary purposes of a computer card deck is to provide a medium whereby the data can be input into the computer's memory. The computer card deck also serves another very important function: it is a medium whereby the data can also be stored. Data stored on cards can also be transferred to magnetic tape or to disk for storage. Of these three, disks are the ideal form of storage, as they are quickly and easily accessed. Of the three mediums, though, disk is the most expensive. The most economical form for data storage is magnetic tape. Tapes are capable of storing thousands of pieces of information. If you choose cards as your medium for storing your data, you should keep your cards in a pressurized cabinet especially designed for computer cards. Such storage is both necessary and essential since computer cards, like any card made of paper, are highly susceptible to warpage. Once warped, the cards cannot be read through a card reader.

With our data in numeric and matrix form and prepared for computer input, we are now ready to consider how we will process the data—that is, what statistical procedures will we be running in order to ferret out any patterns in our data? We are now ready to look ahead to Chapter 14.

Analyzing Data: Descriptive Statistics

The role of statistical methods in the research process
Discrete and continuous data
Discrete frequency distributions
    Definition
    Handling missing data
    Graphing the discrete frequency distribution
    Grouping discrete data

Continuous frequency distribution
    Definition
    Graphing the continuous distribution
Descriptive summary measures
    Measures of central tendency
    Measures of variability

Two statisticians were drafted into the army and found themselves fighting on the front lines. Simultaneously spotting an enemy, both soldiers raised their rifles and fired. Statistician 1 fired a foot too far to the right. Statistician 2 fired a foot too far to the left. Turning to each other with pride and smiles plastered all over their faces, they shook hands and congratulated each other. On the Average, the Enemy Soldier Was Dead.
—RICHARD P. RUNYON

While every stage of the research process is fascinating, we think that you will find the data analysis stage to be especially so. Prior to this stage, the substance of your research has only been conjecture. You have identified a research question. You have tentatively answered this question by developing hypotheses within the framework of theory. And you have collected data to test these hypotheses. But as yet, you have no definitive answers. It is in the data analysis stage of your research that you gain such answers to your research question.

The basic intent of data analysis is to examine a body of data for the hypothesized relationships and to exhibit the results in a clear and understandable manner. This important and essential examination can take two general forms: qualitative analysis and quantitative analysis.

Heated debates comparing qualitative to quantitative methods have fueled the fires of social work research discussions for many, many decades. Despite often polarized views, we believe that these two broad categories represent different approaches to a research problem and are therefore both essential to the research process. As we learned in Chapter 12, the word *quantity* asks the question "How much?" while the word *quality* asks the question "What kind?" More to the point, some types of theories demand quantitative data while others insist that only qualitative data be used. Since theories are really answers we give to research questions, the type of data that will test these answers depends largely on the nature of the research question. Hence, if your research calls for qualitative data, we hope you will use that kind. If quantitative data seem more appropriate, then this should be your choice. And remember, there is nothing wrong with using both types of data. Since we have already taken a detailed look at qualitative methods of analysis in Chapter 12, we will not repeat our discussion here. Instead, we will begin our detailed examination of quantitative methods.

The Role of Statistical Methods in the Research Process

It is often acknowledged that numbers provide a level of precision that is unequaled by any descriptive vocabulary that we might choose to use. Suppose, for example, we were to describe a room as large. Such a description could certainly be labeled as vague because the descriptive adjective *large* is vulnerable to multiple interpretations, each influenced by individual perceptions of space. In other words, the descriptive adjective *large* is not precisely defined. If, on the other hand, we were to describe a room as eight by fifteen feet, there would be no misconception about the size of the room or its comparison with similar measures of space.

As a second example, suppose we wanted to study the effects of drug addiction on academic grades within college. If we chose to describe our research findings with definitive adjectives, we might have the following: "Drugs are bad." "Drugs are harmful to students' grades and general college performance." While such descriptions would tell our readers that we have identified a social problem, they would not provide a precise account of the problem. What's more, they would not give any accurate indication of the severity of the problem. On the other hand, if we were to collect data from students and then analyze these data *statistically*, we could present exact information on the number of students taking drugs, the amount of drugs being used, the frequency of use by age, sex, and ethnic background, and the grades of those taking drugs in each of the age, sex, and ethnic categories.

The simple little examples just given demonstrate clearly the importance of *statistical methods*—the methods used in collecting, presenting, and interpreting data. Such methods are absolutely essential if meaningful information is to be extracted from a *large* body of data. Two main approaches comprise the subject matter of statistics. One is **the descriptive approach—describing characteristics of a population or sample.** The other is the **inferential approach—generalizing sample characteristics to a total population.**

Quantitative research findings are normally presented in statistical form along with a discussion linking the reported findings to theory. To understand and fully evaluate the information provided by your data, you must have a good working knowledge of the various statistical procedures available to you. With your research objective in mind, you must decide whether your research is descriptive or inferential. From your reading of published research, you will find that most researchers use both types of procedures, beginning with a descriptive summary of characteristics and moving to inferential statistics for the test of hypotheses. Since both descriptive and inferential statistics are integral to the research process, we will devote a full chapter to each. In this chapter, we will address the subject of descriptive statistics. Chapter 15 is devoted to the issue of inferential statistics.

Discrete and Continuous Data

Recall from Chapter 13 that every set of data is comprised of *variables* and *variable values*. Each variable and its corresponding values constitute a *distribution*. Remember Rhonda's questionnaire, which included such variables such as age, sex, race, marital status, father's occupation, mother's occupation, attitudes toward people, work, and social work, previous majors, and reasons for majoring in social work? The collected values for each of these variables were described as a distribution. In fact, Rhonda had as many distributions as she had variables. Suppose Rhonda is ready to analyze her data. Before she can properly begin this process, she must identify each variable by *type*.

Each of Rhonda's variables (or all variables for that matter) can be classified as either discrete or continuous. **Discrete variables are those variables that can assume only a limited or finite number of values.** In Rhonda's data set, for example, sex, race, and marital status are discrete variables because each assumes a finite number of values (e.g., sex—male and female; marital status—single, married, widowed, divorced, separated). Although sex and marital status represent nominal-level variables (see Chapter 8), discrete variables may be measured at any level of measurement (nominal, ordinal, interval, ratio). Number of children in a family and number of sales in a company are also examples of discrete variables, but measured at the ratio level. In general, if it is possible to list or count every single value that a variable can assume, the variable is said to be discrete.

Sometimes, though, **the number of values a variable can assume is so great that it is impossible to even identify them all, much less list them.** Such variables are called **continuous variables.** Again, using Rhonda's data set, age can be viewed as a continuous variable. Other continuous variables include income, time, weight, and height, to name a few. In general, **if between any two values a variable assumes there are other values the variable can assume, the variable is said to be continuous.**

Discrete Frequency Distributions

Definition

The most common method for summarizing the values of a discrete variable is the frequency distribution. We will define **a frequency distribution as a listing of all variable values and a count of the number of times each value occurs.** Let's illustrate the discrete frequency distribution with a study on marital status data for the male and female clients of a very large social service agency. Our data are represented in Table 14.1. If you examine this table closely, you should notice three important things. First, all values for the variable marital status are represented. Second, the frequencies for each variable value (single, married, divorced, separated, and widowed) are listed. Third, the corresponding *percentage* for each frequency has been computed. Percentage transformations convert any set of frequencies to the standard base 100 by (1) adding all cases in the independent category (for example, males), (2) dividing that total into the frequency for each discrete variable value, and (3) multiplying the computed value by 100. This procedure gives the rate per 100 or, in the Latin form, percentum. To illustrate, for the 120 divorced males, for example, these computations would be as follows:

$$120/1000 = 0.12 * 100 = 12\%$$

By comparing the percentages of married males and married females, we can easily demonstrate that a higher percentage of females than males are married. Additionally, the percentage of separated males exceeds the percentage of separated females by a factor of 4 (i.e., 40 percent for males versus 10 percent for females). There is also a much higher percentage of single females (25 percent) than males (8 percent). These kinds of comparisons simply would not be apparent if we compared the frequencies because the two groups differ considerably in size. In short, *the conversion of frequencies to percentages applies the useful statistical technique of standardization, which makes data sets of different sizes directly comparable.*

TABLE 14.1 Frequency Distribution of Clients' Marital Status by Sex (without Missing Data)

	Males		Females	
	f	%	*f*	%
Single	80	8	125	25
Married	300	30	200	40
Divorced	120	12	100	20
Separated	400	40	50	10
Widowed	100	10	25	5
TOTAL	1,000	100%	500	100%

Handling Missing Data

As we have often indicated, the road to research is not paved with perfection, and you will frequently be reminded of this as you begin your data analysis. During data collection, for example, it is not uncommon for some respondents to skip one or more questions on the questionnaire. When this happens, you must have some method of dealing with this missing information. Assume, for example, that for the data just examined, there were actually 110 males and 41 females who did not answer the question on marital status. In other words, while each of these 151 subjects completed almost all of the questionnaire, they for some reason (inadvertently or intentionally) did not answer this question. Rather than lose these subjects entirely (and thus lose all of the data they have provided for all other questions), we can recompute our percentages to recognize missing data. Table 14.2 reflects an added column showing the *adjusted percentages*—computed from only those respondents answering the marital status question (i.e., adjusted for missing data). These percentages are identical to those presented in Table 14.1. In contrast, the *unadjusted percentages* are computed from a base of total respondents, including nonrespondents. In effect, nonrespondents comprise a residual category of unknown data that must be excluded from data analysis (but noted).

Graphing the Discrete Frequency Distribution

Bar Graph

Although the discrete frequency distribution provides a simple and meaningful picture of the data represented, it is not always easy to read and interpret. This is especially true when your reading audience has little statistical training. On such occa-

TABLE 14.2 Frequency Distribution of Clients' Marital Status by Sex (with Missing Data)

	Males			Females		
	f	*Unad. %*	*Ad. %*	*f*	*Unad. %*	*Ad. %*
Single	80	7	8	125	23	25
Married	300	27	30	200	37	40
Divorced	120	11	12	100	18	20
Separated	400	36	40	50	9	10
Widowed	100	9	10	25	5	5
MISSING	110	10	MISS	41	8	MISS
TOTAL	1,100	100%	100%	541	100%	100%

Unad. = unadjusted
Ad. = adjusted

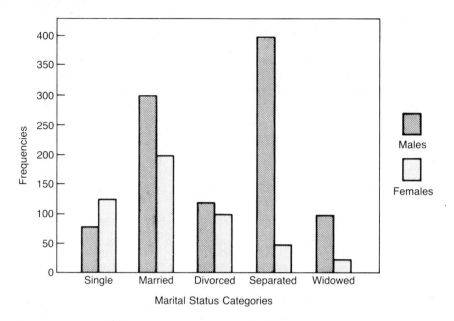

FIGURE 14.1   Bar Graph of Marital Status Distribution by Sex

sions, it is a good idea to use a graphic display because this kind of presentation increases readability and understanding. The bar graph is probably the most popular kind of graph used to depict the distribution of a discrete variable. *A bar graph, like all graphs, is a pictorial presentation of a discrete variable.* The specific characteristics of a bar graph will become apparent as we construct one.

The first step in creating a bar graph is computing the frequency distribution for the targeted variable. In our case, this has already been done for marital status. Second, we must create the vertical and horizontal coordinates of the graph. While not etched in stone, you will generally find that the frequency values are plotted along the vertical axis and the discrete variable values along the horizontal axis. Rectangular bars are then used to plot the frequency (represented as a height on the vertical axis) of each discrete variable value. A bar graph for the data in Table 14.1 is presented in Figure 14.1. One of the most distinguishing characteristics of a bar graph is the *obvious spaces separating the bars.* These spaces are intentional and designed to reflect the discrete (noncontinuous) nature of the discrete variable values being plotted.

Pie Chart

Our marital status distribution could also have been graphically displayed by the pie chart. The pie chart is a circular graph usually used to show the relative proportions of a conceptual whole. This chart is applied to nominal-level (discrete) variables so that there is no presumption of order—that is, greater than or less than. Figure 14.2 displays the marital status distribution for males using a pie chart.

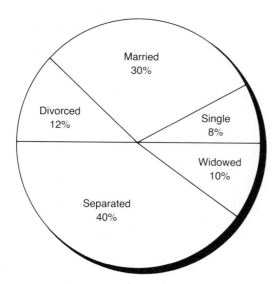

FIGURE 14.2   Pie Chart of Marital Status Distribution for Males

Grouping Discrete Data

As we have already indicated, discrete variables do not have to be nominal. They may be measured at any level of measurement. But if we were creating a frequency distribution for a discrete variable measured at the ordinal, interval, or ratio level, our procedure might need to be a little different from the one just described. Suppose, for example, we wanted to create a frequency distribution for number of children in a family. The raw values for this variable are listed in Figure 14.3. While we could list each unique value (just as they appear in Figure 14.3), such a listing could easily get out of hand with a large number of values. To overcome this problem, we might choose to group the variable values. If we choose this option, there are four essential steps that we must follow.

   1. *Compute the range*—the difference between the largest and smallest number of children in a family plus 1. For our example, the largest number of children in a family, 12, minus the smallest number of children in a family, 0, plus 1 produces a range of 13.

   2. *Divide the number of intervals desired into the range to obtain the interval width*—the number of unique scores in each interval. Using our example, the range, 13, is divided by 7, the desired number of intervals, to yield an interval width of 2 (some rounding may be necessary). Hence, our distribution of "number of children in family" is organized into 7 intervals of size 2.

   3. *Specify the end points of each interval.* For our first interval, the end points would be 0–1. For our second interval, they would be 2–3.

   4. *Tabulate the frequencies for each interval.*

The frequency distribution for these data is presented in Table 14.3. The bar graph giving a pictorial view of these data is presented in Figure 14.4.

FIGURE 14.3   Distribution of "Number of Children in Family" Variable

Unordered	Ordered
0	0
12	0
6	1
7	1
4	1
4	2
3	2
2	2
1	3
1	3
10	3
0	3
3	4
5	4
9	5
3	6
2	7
1	9
2	10
3	12

TABLE 14.3   Frequency Distribution for "Number of Children in Family" Variable

Interval	f
12–13	1
10–11	1
8–9	1
6–7	2
4–5	3
2–3	7
0–1	5

Continuous Frequency Distribution

Definition

Now suppose that we want to create a frequency distribution for the thirty-one ages listed in Figure 14.5. Since age is a continuous variable, our procedure again will need to be somewhat different from that used for discrete variables. As with discrete

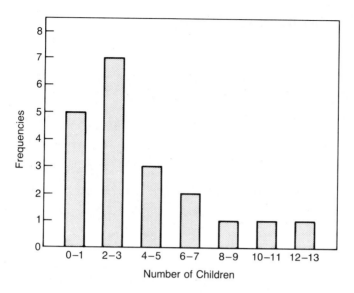

FIGURE 14.4   Bar Graph of "Number of Children in Family" Distribution

data (except nominal), we begin by finding the range. Second, we divide this range by the number of intervals desired, rounding any fraction upward to the nearest integer. This integer represents the *interval width* or *the number of unique values in each interval*. In our present example, the highest age, 31, minus the lowest age, 22, plus 1 gives a range of 10. If we choose to divide our age distribution into five intervals, we divide 10 by 5, yielding 2. Hence, for this distribution, we have chosen to use five two-year intervals. (If this division had produced a fraction, we would have rounded upward to the nearest integer.) Third, we specify the end points for each interval. Our age distribution organized into six two-year intervals is shown in Table 14.4. If you examine this distribution closely, you should notice at least one glaring problem. Since age is a continuous variable, there is really no interval for recording ages between 30 and 31, 40 and 41, 50 and 51, and so on. In our age distribution, for example, there are two ages that cannot be placed in any of these intervals: 21.25 and 30.75, and to place these variable values we had to round them off—21 and 31. In order to place every possible value (i.e., age) within one of these intervals, these so-called gaps must be eliminated. After all, this is a continuous variable! We eliminate these gaps by creating *upper* and *lower boundaries*. In effect, the upper boundary of one interval becomes the lower boundary of the interval just above it. Generally these boundaries are defined as halfway between two whole numbers. The frequency distribution for age has been re-created in Table 14.5, where we have computed the upper and lower boundaries for each interval. In addition, we have computed the midpoints of each interval. As we shall soon see, the *midpoint*, defined as *the average of the two boundaries*, can be used to graph a continuous frequency distribution.

FIGURE 14.5 Distribution of Ages

20
21.25
23
23
24
24
25
25
25
25
25
26
26
26
27
27
27
27
27
27
28
29
29
29
29
29
29
29
29
30.75
31

TABLE 14.4 Frequency Distribution of Ages
Organized into Six Two-Year Intervals

Intervals	f	%
30–31	2	6.4
28–29	9	29.0
26–27	9	29.0
24–25	7	23.0
22–23	2	6.4
20–21	2	6.4
TOTAL	31	100.0

Graphing the Continuous Distribution

The Histogram

The histogram represents a plot of continuous data. By using the vertical axis for frequencies and the horizontal axis for the interval boundaries, we can create a graphic display of our age distribution. For the histogram, like the bar graph, the frequencies

TABLE 14.5 Frequency Distribution of Ages with Boundaries and Midpoints

L.L.	Interval	U.L.	Midpoint	f	%
29.5	30–31	31.5	30.5	2	6.4
27.5	28–29	29.5	28.5	9	29.0
25.5	26–27	27.5	26.5	9	29.0
23.5	24–25	25.5	24.5	7	23.0
21.5	22–23	23.5	22.5	2	6.4
19.5	20–21	21.5	20.5	2	6.4

are represented with bars. However, for the histogram, the bars are plotted somewhat differently. Specifically, *the bars are plotted around the lower and upper boundaries of the interval.* Since the upper boundary of one interval is the lower boundary of the interval above it, *each interval shares one stern of the bar with another interval.* Figure 14.6 illustrates our age distribution graphed with a histogram. By removing the vertical lines separating the adjoining bars, the graph actually gives the appearance of a continuous variable. In this instance, the histogram presents an outline of the distribution of frequencies for each age interval.

The Polygon

The polygon is another means of graphing a continuous variable. Like the histogram, the polygon assumes a continuous variable plotted along the horizontal axis. Unlike the histogram, though, *the polygon graphs with points that are plotted above*

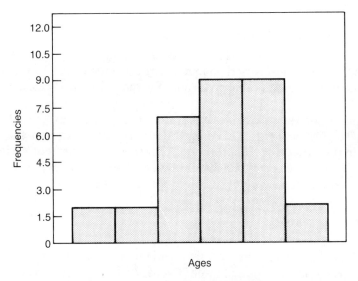

FIGURE 14.6 Histogram of Age Distribution

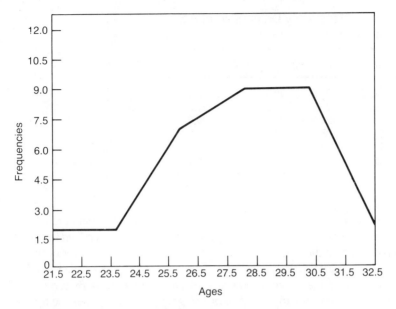

FIGURE 14.7   Polygon of Age Distribution

the midpoints of each interval, and these points are then connected with line segments. These points and lines together show the frequency distribution pattern. Figure 14.7 illustrates the age distribution graphed with a polygon. With a polygon, the connecting line is sometimes dropped to the base line at each end, presupposing the termination of the scale for this distribution.

Descriptive Summary Measures

Social workers use frequency distributions and graphic displays because they know that this kind of presentation will reduce misunderstanding and increase readability. In addition to these data summary techniques, there are some valid and viable alternatives that are more economical of space and, for analytical purposes, even more precise.

Two types of such summary measures can be used to describe the values in a distribution. The first, **measures of central tendency, indicates how the scores "bunch up" in the middle of a distribution.** The second, **measures of variability, indicates how widely the scores in a distribution vary above and below the center of the distribution.** Let's take a look at both types of measures.

Measures of Central Tendency

Three measures of central tendency are frequently used to describe the center of a distribution—the mode, median, and mean. The use of these measures can help you to convey an accurate and economical picture of any distribution. Let's begin our discussion of these three measures by defining each. To help clarify these definitions, we will illustrate each measure using the ages listed in Figure 14.5.

Defining the Mode, Median, and Mean

Mode   The mode is the most frequently occurring score in a distribution. This measure of central tendency is actually found by counting the number of occurrences for each unique variable value. In short, **the variable value with the highest count is the mode.** For our distribution pictured in Figure 14.5, the mode is 29, since 29 occurs more often than any other value (eight times).

You may be somewhat surprised to learn that the mode is not always located at the center of a distribution. In our distribution of ages, for example, the mode is at the high end of the age distribution, not in the center. What's more, a distribution may have more than one mode. If the frequency count for two or more scores in a distribution is the same, a distribution is described as either *bimodal* (two modes) or *multimodal* (many modes).

Median   **The median is the score that divides an ordered distribution into two equal halves.** Notice that this definition stipulates an ordered or ranked distribution. That is, before you can find the median, you must first order the scores from lowest to highest. For our distribution of ages (Figure 14.5), the median is 27. In this distribution the median is pretty easy to find because there is an odd number of scores (31). When there is an even number of scores in a distribution, the median is computed as the average of the middle two scores. If, for example, we were to add one age, 55, to our age distribution, the median would become the average of the two middle scores, which in this case would produce the same value: $(27 + 27)/2$ or 27.

Mean   The mean is the balance point of a distribution. It is the **arithmetic average or the value obtained by adding all the scores in a distribution and dividing the sum by the number of terms.** For our distribution of thirty-one ages, this means $20 + 21.25 + 23 + \cdots + 29 + 30.75 + 31 = 797/31 = 25.7$.

Comparing the Mode, Median, and Mean

Now that we have defined these three measures of central tendency, let's compare them. In general, we can say that the mode represents "most," the median represents "middle," and the mean represents "average." Of these three measures, *the mean is by far the most precise and the most sensitive*. In fact, the mean is so precise and so sensitive that it will change if only *one* value in a distribution is changed. Suppose, for example, we were to add 25 points to the largest term in our age distribution (Figure 14.5). Our new distribution appears in Figure 14.8.

As you can see, the mode is still 29 and the median is still 27. However, the mean has changed from 25.7 to 26.5. If you are paying close attention, you have probably realized that we could have altered a score, which would have changed the mode and median. We could, for example, have changed the 26's to 27's and the mode would be 27. Or we could have changed the 27's to 26's and the mode would be 26. In short, any single change in a distribution will change the mean, whereas

FIGURE 14.8   Distribution of Ages

```
20
21.25
23
23
24
24
25
25
25
25
25
25
26
26
26
27
27
27
27
27
27
28
29
29
29
29
29
29
29
29
30.75
56
```

only specific changes will alter the mode and median. Hence, the mean is viewed as the most sensitive of these three measures.

Applying the Mode, Median, and Mean

Although the mode is not used much in social work research, it does play an important role in other substantive areas. In fact, the mode is especially useful in marketing research. A shoe store owner, for example, might like to know the most popular (modal) sizes in women's shoes so she can order accordingly. A marketing research team might like to know people's favorite (modal) colors so they can advise their firm to package products accordingly. In marketing research, the mode seems to be synonymous with popular.

The fact that the median is not affected by the size of extreme values does make it a very useful measure of central tendency for some purposes. *The median is an especially important measure when there are a few extreme scores in a distribution.* Since extreme scores pull the mean in their direction, the mean of such a distribution is somewhat distorted. In such instances, the median is really more representative of the central tendency than the mean. The distribution of annual incomes in the United States is a good example of a distribution with extremes. While most Americans' earnings are on the lower end of the income continuum, a few Americans do earn millions of dollars. Since all incomes are used to compute the mean, the mean is pulled in the direction of these extreme incomes. Thus, the average income for American earners will appear larger than it really is. For such lopsided distributions, the median is a more representative measure of central tendency than is the mean.

Despite the uses for the mode and median, the mean remains the most important measure of central tendency. The sensitivity of the mean makes it a good indicator of the size of the terms in a distribution. In a very general sense, the higher the mean, the higher the terms in a distribution tend to run. The mean is also used to compare locations of distinctive groups on the same scale. When we say, for example, that the mean test score for females is larger than the mean test score for males, we are really saying that females did better on the test. In addition to these descriptive uses, you will soon discover (in Chapter 15) that the mean is a very useful measure in inferential statistics.

Measures of Variability

While measures of central tendency are concerned with how the scores in a distribution are grouped together, measures of variability are concerned with how the scores in a distribution are spread apart. Four measures of variability are frequently used in social research: range, semi-interquartile range, variance, and standard deviation. Of these four measures, we will find variance and standard deviation to be the most valuable. However, an understanding of range and semi-interquartile range will give us a greater appreciation of the more useful measures.

Defining Range and Semi-Interquartile Range

Range   The simplest measure of variability is the **range—the difference between the lowest and highest values in a distribution plus 1.** For the distribution of ages pictured in Figure 14.5 the range is 12 (30 – 21 plus 1) because there are twelve unique scores in this spread (i.e., 20, 21, 22, 23, 24, 25, 26, 27, 28, 29, 30, 31).

Although the range does convey some meaning concerning the spread of scores in a distribution, it is really a rather crude measure of variability and hence rather unstable. To illustrate, we have already noted that the distribution of ages pictured in Figure 14.5 has a range of 12. But when we added 25 points to the highest age (Figure 14.8), the range became 27—considerably larger. By changing one value, we actually doubled the range. In effect, we have identified the primary limitation of the range. This measure of spread is only sensitive to the highest and lowest values in a distribution. It is insensitive to any variation between these two extremes, making it rather unstable.

Semi-Interquartile Range   To overcome the instability of the range as a measure of variability, the semi-interquartile range may be used. This measure of variability is found by computing the difference between the score at the 75th percentile (labeled the third quartile) and the 25th percentile (labeled the first quartile) and then dividing this difference by two. **The semi-interquartile range includes only the two in-**

terior quartiles, or 50 percent of the total distribution. By excluding the two exterior quartiles, we do eliminate most extreme scores, but the measure remains somewhat crude. Like the range, it is still computed from only two scores in a distribution.

Defining the Variance and Standard Deviation

Given the insensitivity and instability of the range and the semi-interquartile range, we need to find a measure of variability that will overcome these limitations. If we were to identify the criteria or the conditions that would produce the ideal measure of variability, we might come up with the following list.

1. *It should be sensitive to every score in a distribution.* Unlike the range and the semi-interquartile range, which are affected by only two scores, we want a measure of variability that is affected by every score in a distribution. Ideally, our measure of variability should be so sensitive that a change in only one score would also result in a change in variability.

2. This ideal measure of spread *should produce a small value when the scores in a distribution are close together and a larger value when the scores are farther apart.* Consider, for example, the scores in the following distributions:

Distribution A	Distribution B
1	100
2	200
3	300
4	400
5	500

At a glance, you can quickly see that the scores in Distribution A are closer together than those in Distribution B. Hence, we would also like our measure of variability to reflect this obvious difference.

3. *It should be independent of the number of scores in a distribution.* In other words, our measure of variability should not be affected by the number of scores in a distribution. Consider the following distributions:

Distribution A	Distribution B
3	3
3	3
3	3
3	3
3	3
	3
	3
	3
	3
	3

Distribution B has ten scores, while Distribution A has only five. Yet, if you look at the scores comprising each of these distributions, it should be fairly obvious that their variability is the same. This sameness should be reflected in our measure of variability.

4. This ideal measure of variability *should be independent of the mean.* That is, it should not get smaller as the mean gets smaller and larger as the mean gets larger. Again, consider the following two distributions:

Distribution A	Distribution B
3	5
3	5
3	5
3	5
3	5

Quite obviously, Distribution A has a mean of 3 while Distribution B has a mean of 5. Despite this difference in the two means, it is also obvious that there is *no* variation in either distribution. Hence, both distributions should have the same variability. Put another way, Distribution B should not have a larger variability score merely because its mean is larger.

Given these four characteristics, what measures of variability can we identify that satisfy all? As it turns out, there are actually two measures of variability that satisfy all four conditions—the variance and the standard deviation.

Variance   The variance can be defined as the mean of the squared deviations from a distribution's mean. In other words, **it is the sum of the squared deviations from the mean divided by the number of squared deviations.** In formula form, the variance can be expressed as:

$$S^2 = \Sigma \frac{(X - \bar{X})^2}{N}$$

To gain a better understanding of this definition (and formula), let's compute the variance for the following three distributions:

Distribution 1	Distribution 2	Distribution 3
3	0	1
3	2	2
3	2	3
3	5	4
3	6	5
$\bar{X} = 3$	$\bar{X} = 3$	$\bar{X} = 3$

To compute the variance for any one of these three distributions, we must carry out the following steps:

1. *Compute the $\bar{X}$ for each distribution.* For our three distributions, the means are all the same—3.

2. *Subtract the $\bar{X}$ from every term in the distribution.* For our three distributions, we would have the following:

Distribution 1		Distribution 2		Distribution 3	
X	X − $\bar{X}$	X	X − $\bar{X}$	X	X − $\bar{X}$
3	0	0	−3	1	−2
3	0	2	−1	2	−1
3	0	2	−1	3	0
3	0	5	2	4	1
3	0	6	3	5	2

3. *Square each deviation from the mean, and then add up these squared deviations:*

X − $\bar{X}$	$(X − \bar{X})^2$	X − $\bar{X}$	$(X − \bar{X})^2$	X − $\bar{X}$	$(X − \bar{X})^2$
0	0	−3	9	−2	4
0	0	−1	1	−1	1
0	0	−1	1	0	0
0	0	2	4	1	1
0	0	3	9	2	4
0	0	0	24	0	10

4. *Divide the sum of the squared deviation by the number of terms in the distribution.* The obtained value is a mean. In fact, it is *the mean of the squared deviation from the mean—or variance.*

Distribution 1	Distribution 2	Distribution 3
0/5 = 0	24/5 = 4.8	10/5 = 2

If you study these three distributions and their variances, you will soon discover that this measure of variability meets our earlier stated criteria. It appears to be sensitive to all the scores in a distribution. The more "bunched up" the scores are, the smaller its value. The more "spread apart" the scores are, the larger its value. It is independent of the number of terms in a distribution and independent of a distribution's mean. How do we know all of this? Let's make some careful comparisons.

If you look again at the terms in each of these three distributions, you should easily see that the terms in Distribution 1 are closer together than those in Distributions 2 and 3. In fact, the terms comprising Distribution 1 are all identical. On the basis of our previously established criteria and this observation, we would expect Distribution 1 to have the smallest variance—and it does! Additionally, the variance appears to be independent of the number of terms in a distribution and independent of a distribution's mean. Again, a quick glance at our three distributions will confirm that all three distributions have the same number of observations and the same mean. If variance were affected by a distribution's size and mean, we would expect these three distributions to have the same variance. Since all three distributions have different variances, we can surmise that our measure is independent of these characteristics. If you are still not convinced of the validity of these criteria, you should create some distributions of your own and try computing their variances.

Standard Deviation   Before we impute meaning to this measure of variability, let's consider one additional measure of variability—standard deviation. **The standard deviation can be defined as the positive square root of the variance.** Using our three previously cited distributions:

Distribution 1	Distribution 2	Distribution 3
variance = 0	variance = 4.8	variance = 2.0
$SD = \sqrt{0}$	$SD = \sqrt{4.8}$	$SD = \sqrt{2}$
SD = 0	SD = 2.2	SD = 1.41

Since the standard deviation is derived from the variance, we can safely assume that this measure of variability also fulfills our earlier established criteria. In addition, the standard deviation has one advantage that the variance does not have. Unlike the value of variance, the value of the standard deviation has the same underlying scale as scores in the distribution. To understand why this is so, we must reconsider briefly our procedure for computing variance.

As you will recall, the second step in computing the variance requires that we subtract the mean from every term in a distribution. If you look closely at the three distributions of *deviations from the mean,* you should quickly discover that each of these distributions (of deviations) sums to zero. This is not just a coincidence. *For any distribution (regardless of size), the sum of the deviations from the mean is zero.* If you're not convinced, create some distributions of your own, calculate the mean of each, and sum the deviations from the mean. The sum of the deviations from the mean will always be zero.

Because the sum of the deviations from the mean is always zero, we cannot use this sum to compute the variance. In short, if we did use this sum, the variance would always be zero—sum of deviations/N. To circumvent this problem, the mean deviations must be altered. You will recall that we altered the mean deviations by squaring each of them. And except for those rare cases where all the terms in a distribution are the same (e.g., Distribution 1), the sum of the squared deviations is a positive number.

Although squaring the mean deviations does eliminate one problem (i.e., a sum of zero), it also creates another problem. Squaring these deviations inflates (increases) the value of each deviation. When the squared deviations are summed, the sum is also inflated, and when this sum is divided by the number of terms in the distribution, this value (variance) is also inflated. In short, the value of variance is not based on the same underlying scale as the scores comprising the distribution. To correct for this inflation, we use the mathematical procedure that represents the reverse of squaring—square rooting. By taking the square root of the variance we have the standard deviation—a measure of variability whose value can be interpreted within the context of the original distribution's scale.

Applying the Variance and the Standard Deviation

Imagine that you are in the library looking for research references that are relevant to your research topic, "Changing Attitudes toward Sexual Behavior: 1980 to the Present." As you begin to page through the *Journal of Sexual Facts,* you notice an article that appears to be pertinent. This article, you soon discover, is on the differences among age groups with respect to attitudes toward sexual behavior. You decide to read a little further. In the methods section of the paper, the authors indicate that they are using an attitude scale whose scores can vary between 10 and 50, where 10 represents a negative attitude and 50 a positive attitude. In the results section of the paper, the authors submit that sexual attitudes vary little if any across age groups. The data supporting this declaration are also presented in table form:

Age Intervals	Mean Attitude Score
50–59	23.93
40–49	24.26
30–39	25.00
20–29	24.51

You glance at this table and immediately see that the means are close together, giving some credence to the authors' conclusions. But you are still somewhat troubled. Something seems to be missing. Aha! Suddenly it comes to you like greased lightning! While you can survey the means for each age category, you cannot determine how representative these means are of their respective distributions. Without this information, you feel you really cannot evaluate the research findings.

Now suppose you actually had access to the raw attitude scores by age group and the distributions were as follows:

Ages 20–29	Ages 30–39	Ages 40–49	Ages 50–59
23	20	10	10
25	20	11	10
26	22	15	11
27	22	17	15
28	28	21	20
28	28	37	31
28	31	40	45
29	33	41	46
29	33	43	48
30	36	46	49

From a close examination of these scores, it is apparent to you that the means have been computed correctly. However, the distributions look different. In fact, the mean equivalences are clouded by the very obvious differences in the scores of the four distributions.

What's missing from the authors' presentation is the standard deviation for each of these distributions. Since the standard deviation is a measure of average distance from the mean of a distribution, we can use it to assess the representativeness of each mean. In fact, we could easily do without the distribution of raw scores if we had access to the standard deviation for each of these four distributions.

Computing the standard deviation for each of these distribution, we obtain:

Ages 20–29	Ages 30–39	Ages 40–49	Ages 50–59
$s = 2.0$	$s = 5.6$	$s = 14.0$	$s = 16.7$

From the standard deviations, it is apparent that the means of Distributions 1 and 2 are more representative of their respective distributions than are the means of Distributions 3 and 4 for theirs. In fact, the scores in Distributions 3 and 4 are so spread out that neither mean appears representative of the scores listed.

While the mean gives us some information about the center of a distribution, by itself it is not enough. Similarly, while the standard deviation gives us some information about the spread in a distribution, alone it is not complete. When taken together, the mean and the standard deviation, like love and marriage, render an unmatched union.

Variance and standard deviation, like the mean, are not limited to descriptive purposes. Both measures, as we shall soon see, are also an integral part of inferential statistics.

Chapter 15

Analyzing Data: Inferential Statistics

The normal curve
The standard normal curve
The standard normal curve as a
    probability distribution
The *t* test for two independent
    samples
The *F* test for three or more
    independent samples

Correlation and regression
    Simple correlation and
        regression
    Multiple correlation and
        regression analysis

*Then there is the man who drowned crossing a stream with an average depth of six
inches.* —W. I. E. GATES

Most students have difficulty with the inevitable chapter in methods books on
statistics, and unfortunately, this one may be no exception. Inferential statistics is not
a subject for the queasy, but neither is it an impossible task. We have assumed that
you have some familiarity with statistical procedures, and while this chapter is an
overview of how to analyze data using statistical inference, the student who has difficulty might wish to refer to an elementary statistics text for more basic information
than that which informs this chapter.

    In our discussion in Chapter 14 we focused on those quantitative measures
that are used to *describe* the characteristics of a sample. In short, we suggested that
this description would usually take the form of a frequency distribution, a measure
of central tendency, and/or a measure of variability. While such descriptive informa-

tion concerning one's sample is always useful, it is seldom enough by itself since such information applies only to the sample on which it is computed. In most research situations, the sample is not our main concern. Rather, our primary concern is for the population from which the sample has been drawn, and the sample is merely the vehicle for learning about the population.

Our concern for the population over the sample introduces an interesting and rather provocative dilemma. As we have already learned (see Chapter 9), in most research situations we do not have access to the total population. On the contrary, we usually have access to only a part of a population—a sample. If we do not have access to a total population, how, then, can we identify its characteristics? In effect, we cannot actually *identify* them. We can only *infer* them from our knowledge of the sample characteristics. **The term statistical inference is used to describe the process of inferring the characteristics of a population from the characteristics of a sample.** This process of statistical inference is made possible through the use of probability distributions.

A probability distribution is a list or map of all the possible outcomes that can occur for a designated phenomenon and the likelihood of occurrence for each outcome. Suppose, for example, that the total number of housing sales in Memphis, Tennessee, for 1978, was 10,000. This number represents the population of housing sales. Now suppose we were to draw a sample of 100 sales records from this population. Although we may compute the mean selling price for this sample, our real concern is for the population mean. Since we cannot actually identify the population mean, we would like to infer that its value is the same as the sample mean. To make this inference, we need to examine the probability distribution for this particular variable.

If we could draw an infinite number of samples of size 100 from this population, compute the mean of each sample, and plot these means, this plot of sample means would constitute a probability distribution. From this distribution, we could determine the likelihood of occurrence of our one sample mean. However, such a probability distribution would be almost impossible to compute since it would require extensive knowledge of the population. In fact, we might as well compute the population's characteristics as create this probability distribution! Fortunately, we have been saved from all of these computations. We can use a *theoretical distribution* (instead of a finite distribution) to map all possible outcomes. To understand fully how this is possible, let's first take a look at one theoretical distribution—the standard normal curve—and then examine how this curve can be used as a probability distribution.

The Normal Curve

In the eighteenth century, a Frenchman, Abraham de Moivre, presented a mathematical solution for mapping (plotting) an infinite number of outcomes. Moivre's formula actually computes the number of times (Y, defined by height of curve) a specific event (X) will occur. This calculation is based on two familiar characteristics of a distribution: the mean and the standard deviation. If Moivre's formula were used to calculate the Y's (the number of times each specific event occurs) for an in-

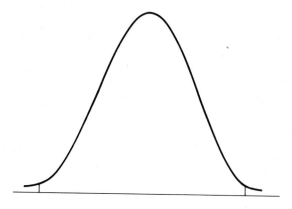

FIGURE 15.1   The Normal Curve

finite number of X's (all possible events), the line defining this shape would be a *curve*. And if the phenomenon represented by this curve is normally distributed, the figure produced is that of a normal curve. The normal curve is pictured in Figure 15.1. Every normal curve possesses the following characteristics:

1. It is *symmetrical*. The left half of the curve is a mirror image of the right half. If the curve were folded in the middle, one half would be identical to the other.

2. It is *bell-shaped*. This means that the scores tend to cluster about the center. And as we move away from the center, the frequency of scores decreases.

3. The *mean, median, and mode of the distribution are the same*. Restated, the point of balance for the distribution (mean) is also the point that divides the distribution into two equal halves (median) and the point at which the greatest number of scores occur (mode).

4. It is *asymptotic*. It is made up of an infinite number of scores on the X axis, each of which has a corresponding Y value that never touches the base line. As we move away from the mean in either direction, the frequency of Y values decreases and approaches zero. But zero is never reached, as there is always some likelihood that a value more extreme than the last one will occur.

5. *The total area encompassed by the curve is equal to 1.00.* Thus, the Y value for any given X divides the curve into two parts, with some portion of the area falling below that value and some portion falling above. For example, the mean divides the distribution into two equal parts, so we can say that 50 percent of the area lies below the mean and 50 percent of the area lies above it.

Given Moivre's formula for a normal curve and a set of X values, we could calculate the corresponding Y value for each X to derive the actual points on a curve. Once we had calculated these points, we could identify the frequency of occurrence of any given score within a distribution. However, our task would not be an easy one since these calculations would have to be redone for each set of X's as changes in the mean and standard deviation would alter the location and shape of the curve. Fortunately, these individual calculations can be avoided by transforming the original distribution of scores into *standard form*.

The Standard Normal Curve

The standard normal curve is based on a distribution of scores in z form. Any distribution that is converted to z-score form will have a mean of 0 and a standard deviation of 1.00. Although the z-score values theoretically extend to infinity in either direction, the majority of cases fall within the range of ±3. Any set of interval scores can be transformed to z-score form by the following formula. Figure 15.2 illustrates this transformation:

$$z = \frac{X - \bar{X}}{s} = \frac{x}{s}$$

Where: X = any individual score in a distribution
  $\bar{X}$ = the mean of the distribution
  s = the standard deviation of the distribution

You should notice that a z-score transformation is a linear transformation in that it does not change the relative position of any score. In short, all normal distributions converted to z-score form will be identical and have identical properties:

1. Their centers will all be located at the same point on the scale—0.
2. They will have the same spread since they all have the same standard deviation—1.00.

If Moivre's formula were used to calculate the Y values for a set of X's in z-score form, the result would be a standard normal curve. Since all distributions in standard normal form look the same, individual calculations are no longer necessary. And since the area associated with each z score never changes, tables have been prepared for us (see Appendix B).

The utility of converting observed scores to z-score form and the importance of a table describing the proportion of area under the curve associated with z scores rests on the assumption that the likelihood or probability of the occurrence of any given score can be established using such a theoretical distribution. In effect, the z-score transformation can be used to evaluate whether an outcome is usual or unusual—that is, likely or not likely to occur by chance. Let's turn our attention now to understanding how such a theoretical distribution can be used to establish probabilities.

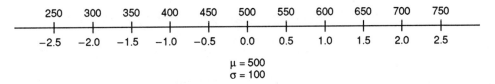

FIGURE 15.2   z-Score Transformation

The Standard Normal Curve as a Probability Distribution

If we knew the *frequency* associated with each unique sample mean that could be computed on samples of some fixed size drawn from a population, we could use this information to determine the *probability* (i.e., likelihood) of drawing a sample with a specific mean:

$$\text{PROBABILITY} = \frac{\text{number of successful events}}{\text{total number of events}}$$

$$\begin{array}{l} \text{RESTATED:} \\ \text{PROBABILITY} = \end{array} \frac{\begin{array}{c}\text{number of samples (size } n) \\ \text{with a particular mean}\end{array}}{\begin{array}{c}\text{total number of samples (size } n) \\ \text{with any mean}\end{array}}$$

However, just as a population is usually *infinite* in size, so is the number of samples of some fixed and designated size that can be drawn from a population. And given an infinite number of samples of some designated size, we can calculate neither the *absolute count of successful events* nor the *absolute count of total events*. To accommodate this limitation, we simply restructure our definition of probability within the framework of *proportions* instead of *absolute counts*. Probability, redefined, is *the proportion of successful events (e.g., proportion of samples with a certain mean) relative to the proportion representing the total number of events—samples with any mean (always 1.00).*

$$\text{PROBABILITY} = \frac{\text{proportion of events representing success}}{\text{total events expressed as a proportion}}$$

Restated, the area under the curve is simply read as a proportion. As we have already established, the total area under the curve is set equal to 1.00, and any part of the total is some proportion less than 1.00. By determining the proportion of area between any two values relative to the total area (i.e., 1.00), we have identified the likelihood of drawing a sample whose mean is within some specified range.

Let's suppose that we have a population of ten unique terms. Let's further suppose that the mean of this population is 5.5 and the standard deviation is 1.94. Now let's draw all possible samples of size 2 from this population and compute each sample's mean. These samples and their means are pictured in Figure 15.3.

Graphing these sample means, we obtain the distribution pictured in Figure 15.4. The horizontal axis on this graph represents the values of the sample means. The vertical axis represents the number of times a sample mean of a specified value occurs.

1. The probability of drawing a sample with a mean of 5.5 is 1/9.

$$p = \frac{\text{number of successful outcomes}}{\text{all possible outcomes}} = \frac{5}{45} = \frac{1}{9}$$

2. The probability of drawing a sample with a mean between 4.5 and 6.5 is 21/45.

1,2	2,3	3,4	4,5	5,6	6,7	7,8	8,9	9,10
(1.5)	(2.5)	(3.5)	(4.5)	(5.5)	(6.5)	(7.5)	(8.5)	(9.5)
1,3	2,4	3,5	4,6	5,7	6,8	7,9	8,10	
(2)	(3)	(4)	(5)	(6)	(7)	(8)	(9)	
1,4	2,5	3,6	4,7	5,8	6,9	7,10		
(2.5)	(3.5)	(4.5)	(5.5)	(6.5)	(7.5)	(8.5)		
1,5	2,6	3,7	4,8	5,9	6,10			
(3)	(4)	(5)	(6)	(7)	(8)			
1,6	2,7	3,8	4,9	5,10				
(3.5)	(4.5)	(5.5)	(6.5)	(7.5)				
1,7	2,8	3,9	4,10					
(4)	(5)	(6)	(7)					
1,8	2,9	3,10						
(4.5)	(5.5)	(6.5)						
1,9	2,10							
(5)	(6)							
1,10								
(5.5)								

FIGURE 15.3   Samples of Size 2 Drawn from Population of Ten Unique Terms

$$p = \frac{21}{45} = .4667$$

3. Now suppose we were to view this sampling distribution as a map of all possible outcomes that would occur if samples of size 2 were drawn indefinitely. The area under the curve represents all possible outcomes—1.00. To identify the probability of getting a sample mean between any two identified values (e.g., 4.5 and 6.5), we would simply read the area under the standard normal curve between these two means. In order to read a portion of the area under the standard normal curve, these two identified means must be converted to z form. Using the z-score formula and by substitution, we obtain:

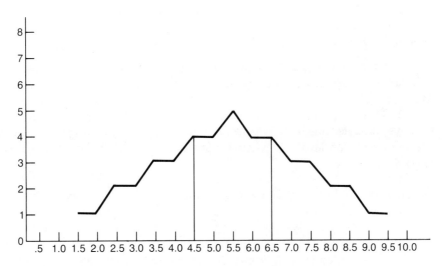

FIGURE 15.4   Sampling Distribution of Sample Means

$$z_{4.5} = \frac{4.5 - 5.5}{1.94} = -.52$$

$$z_{6.5} = \frac{6.5 - 5.5}{1.94} = +.52$$

4. The area between −.52 and +.52 equals .3970. From reading this area, we would conclude that the probability of drawing a sample from the identified population with a mean between 4.5 and 6.5 is approximately .40, or 40 samples out of every 100.

5. Notice how close this probability is to the one calculated from the finite set of discrete outcomes (.4667). If our population were larger and we were drawing samples larger than size 2, the curve of samples means would smooth out and these two probabilities would be even closer in value.

6. Also notice that probability is still the ratio of successful outcomes to all possible outcomes—but now both the numerator and the denominator are expressed as proportions. In essence, this is the way we must proceed when dealing with continuous variables since it is usually not feasible to express all possible outcomes as a finite set.

$$p = \frac{\text{successful outcomes (expressed as a proportion)}}{\text{all possible outcomes (expressed as a proportion)}} = \frac{.40}{1.00} = .40$$

To illustrate the standard normal curve as a probability curve, let's now return to a sampling problem introduced in Chapter 9, that of determining the extent to which a sample mean represents a population mean. Let's assume that the population of housing sales in Memphis, Tennessee, for 1978 is 10,000, with a mean selling price of $36,762.67 and a standard deviation of $15,078.88. Suppose we draw a sample of 100 selling prices and compute the mean for this sample. Although we are working with a sample, our primary concern is not for this sample. What we really want to know is whether this sample mean represents the population mean. Restated, we are really concerned with the probability of drawing a sample whose mean does not deviate *too much* from the population mean.

1. First we must ask, How much is too much? How much deviation from the population mean will we allow and still reason that this sample mean is representative?

2. This question has been answered for us, albeit arbitrarily. From a z-score table we can determine that 95 percent of the area under the sampling distribution curve (or any standard normal curve, for that matter) falls between a z score of ±1.96.

3. Therefore, we know that 95 out of every 100 samples ($p = 95/100$) drawn from the specified population (or any population) will have a mean whose z-score transformation locates them between $z = \pm 1.96$. Only 5 out of every 100 samples drawn randomly from this population will have a mean whose z-score transformation locates them outside this range. These two regions are pictured in Figure 15.5.

4. If our particular sample mean has a z-score transformation that falls within the bounds of ±1.96, we can refer to this outcome as the "expected" outcome since 95 out of every 100 samples will have a mean whose z-score transformation locates

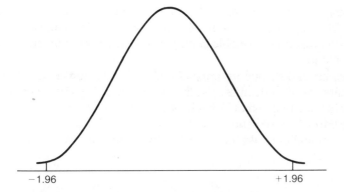

FIGURE 15.5   Boundaries that Separate 95% of the Area under the Curve from the Other 5%

them within this range just by the luck of the draw (i.e., sampling fluctuation). Therefore, we can reason that our sample mean is not really different from the population mean; at least not any different than we would expect by chance, or luck of the draw (i.e., sampling fluctuation).

5. If our sample has a mean whose z-score falls outside of the bounds of ±1.96, we can identify this as an atypical or unusual outcome—one that does not often happen just by the luck of the draw. Thus, we can reason that the difference is not likely one of chance and the sample mean is probably different from the population mean.[1] For our example, the sample mean would have had to be as low as $33,807.21 or as high as $39,718.13 for us to reason that it was probably different from the population mean.

You might be wondering why we go to all this trouble to determine whether a sample's mean is representative of a population's mean when we know the population mean. After all, the z-score formula requires it! Well, most of the time we do not *know* the population mean and/or standard deviation. When we draw one sample from the population, we are actually hypothesizing with respect to the population mean. Suppose, for example, you decided to study a sample of students on your campus. You select a random sample of 200 students. Since campuses usually maintain statistical information on their student bodies, you know that certain pieces of information are available. You should be able to obtain the average age of the student body or the average GPA. Given these population averages, you can check to see if your sample is representative with respect to these variables. While we may not be able to establish representativeness with respect to all variables, establishing it for some variables can make us feel more comfortable about our sample.

Generally speaking, we have little difficulty identifying population values. In

---

[1]In statistical terms, this is known as the .05 level of significance. If the probability of asserting that there is a difference between means is equal to or less than .05, then the difference is said to be significant at the .05 level.

fact, we frequently use published research and/or secondary data sets such as the U.S. Census for obtaining these values. In general, if our sample mean is close to the hypothesized value, we are comfortable in reasoning that our sample represents the population under study.

In sum, theoretical distributions are probability distributions in that they represent a map of all possible outcomes, and the likelihood of any given event can be established by using this map—that is, the likelihood that an event is happening by chance. This procedure is the essence of inferential statistics. And in fact, inferential statistics rests on our ability to use theoretical distributions for evaluating probability.

The t Test for Two Independent Samples

Perhaps the most usual situation that you will face as a researcher is one in which you are interested in drawing two samples from a population instead of one. These samples are generally drawn on the basis of some identifying characteristic. For example, you might draw one sample of males and one sample of females in order to compare males and females with respect to some other variable. Once the samples are drawn, you compute the two means. You then compute the difference between the two sample means ($\bar{X}_1 - \bar{X}_2$). Since both samples come from the same population, you expect this difference to be zero:[2]

$$\bar{X}_1 = \mu$$
$$\bar{X}_2 = \mu$$
Therefore: $\bar{X}_1 = \bar{X}_2$ and $\bar{X}_1 - \bar{X}_2 = 0$

However, in reality, you know that these two $\bar{X}$'s will probably not be exactly the same (due to sampling fluctuations). Our concern, then, is with *just how different* these two means really are. If they are not too different, we can reason they really did come from the same population and are therefore equal. If they are too different, we must reason they did not come from the same population and are therefore not equal. In order to make this evaluation, the difference between these two means, like the single sample mean, must be standardized and located on a standard normal curve of an infinite number of such mean differences. *This standardized difference between sample means is called a t score (instead of a z score), which can vary between zero and infinity.* A *t* score of zero means no difference between $\bar{X}_1$ and $\bar{X}_2$ (although the evaluation is actually based on the sizes of the two samples involved).[3]

If the *t* score is so large that it falls outside the boundary separating 95 percent of the area under the curve from the other 5 percent, we must reason that the two means are different and therefore not equal. If the *t* score falls within these 95 per-

---

[2]The Greek letter μ is the symbol used to represent the population mean.

[3]While *z* is a fixed distribution, the *t* distribution is not. When we do not know the population standard deviation, we must substitute our best guess for this value. Our best guess is the standard deviation of our sample. However, because of sampling fluctuation (sample standard deviation varies from one sample to another), the *t* curve is not a fixed shape. Hence, evaluating a *t* score must take into consideration degrees of freedom—the number of values in a sample that are free to vary.

TABLE 15.1 Exam Scores by Sex

Males	Females
89	92
92	78
76	73
81	81
93	64
68	97
71	83
78	91
73	73
86	83
$\bar{X} = 80.7$	$\bar{X} = 81.4$
$S = 8.945$	$S = 10.035$

cent boundaries (a difference of chance—sampling fluctuation), we can reason that the means are not really different and therefore are equal.

Let's illustrate with an example. Suppose that after your first research methods exam, you wanted to compare the mean exam score for males with the mean score for females. The data for this comparison might appear as in Table 15.1.

The t score for the difference between these two means is .16—a score that easily falls within the 95 percent range (the t score separating the 95 percent area from the other 5 percent for the data is 2.101). Therefore, we can reason that this is a difference that occurs by chance and that the mean test scores for males and females are not really different.

The F Test for Three or More Independent Samples

In our discussion of the t test, recall that the two independent samples were drawn on the basis of some identifying characteristic such as sex. Oftentimes, the identifying characteristic used to draw the random samples is such that more than two independent samples will be drawn. For example, if marital status were the identifying characteristic, we might have three independent samples: (1) married, (2) single, and (3) divorced. When you want to compare simultaneously sample means for more than two samples, the t test can no longer be used since it can compare only two sample means at a time. However, **the F test can make comparisons between more than two sample means** and is an appropriate test for this purpose. This simultaneous comparison between more than two sample means is accomplished by calculating two different estimates of the population variance (σ^2).[4]

1. One estimate of σ^2 is obtained by calculating the variance for each of the independent samples and then taking an average of these estimates. This, in fact, is

---

[4]The symbol σ^2 is used to represent the variance of the population.

our best estimate of the population variance since one way to eliminate variability in a statistic (in this case, variance) from one sample to the next is to draw several samples and take an average of the statistics. Hence, an average of several estimates of the variance provides us with our *best* estimate of the population variance.

2. A second estimate of σ^2 is obtained using the sample means. We begin by treating the same means as a distribution and then calculate the variance for this distribution of sample means. But since this variance is calculated on sample means, it is actually an *estimate of the variance of the sampling distribution of sample means*. Recall, though, from our earlier discussion that there is a relationship between the variance of the population and the variance of the sampling distribution of sample means:

$$\sigma_{\bar{x}}^2 = \frac{\sigma^2}{N}$$

Where: $\sigma_{\bar{x}}^2$ = variance of the sampling distribution of sample means
σ^2 = variance of the population
N = sample size

Since we have an estimate of σ^2 (just calculated from our sample means) and we know the size of the samples drawn, we can obtain our second estimate of the population variance.

The first estimate of the variance is labeled the *within variance,* as it is based on variance *within* samples. The second estimate of the variance is called the *between variance,* as it is based on variance *between* sample means. The F test, then, is simply a comparison of this second estimate to the first estimate. This comparison is accomplished by taking the ratio of the second variance estimate to the first.

$$F = \frac{S_B^2}{S_W^2}$$

If the between-variance estimate is equally as good an estimate as the within-variance estimate, this ratio will be approximately 1.00 (i.e., the two variances will be approximately equal), and we can safely reason that the sample means were computed on samples drawn from the same population. Therefore, all the sample means are equal. If this ratio is considerably larger than 1.00, then we have reason to believe that at least two of the sample means are far apart in value and one or more is probably outside of the actual population spread. Thus, the sample means are not equal. This concept is pictured in Figure 15.6.

To illustrate, let's suppose that we are interested in comparing mean exam scores for married, single, and divorced students. Now we have three independent samples and three means to compare simultaneously. The data for these comparisons appear in Table 15.2.

The within-variance estimate computed from these three samples is 92.45. The between variance computed from these three sample means is 28.67. As with z and t, this F must be evaluated, and it is evaluated on a theoretical distribution known as F. If our F falls within the 95 percent area (easily occurs by chance), then we will reason that the three means are not different. If this F falls outside the 95 percent area (does not often occur by chance), then we will reason that the three means are not

Suggested Spread when the Within and Between Variance are Equal:

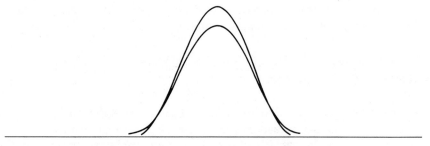

Suggested Spread when the Within and Between Variance are Not Equal:

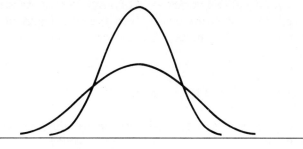

When the Within and Between Variance are NOT Equal, in Reality, Two or Three Populations:

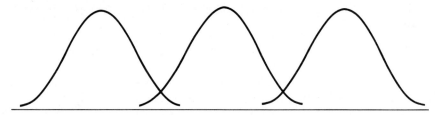

FIGURE 15.6

TABLE 15.2   Exam Scores by Marital Status

Single	Married	Divorced
89	92	73
92	78	81
81	76	71
93	64	83
68	97	78
73	91	86
73	82	
$\bar{X} = 81.29$	$\bar{X} = 82.86$	$\bar{X} = 78.67$

different. As it turns out, this F is well within the 95 percent area. Therefore, we can conclude that the three means are not different—in other words, no different than what we would expect by chance (sampling fluctuation).

Correlation and Regression

Correlation and regression are statistical procedures that make use of bivariate data—that is, pairs of measurements. When using correlation and regression, the essential feature of the data is that one observation can be paired with another observation for each value in the data set. Generally speaking, both variables should be measured at the interval or ratio level of measurement. **As we shall soon see, correlation is primarily concerned with describing the degree of relationship between two variables, whereas regression is concerned with estimating one variable from another.**

Simple Correlation and Regression

Let's begin our discussion of simple correlation and regression with an example. Assume that we have a normally distributed population of achievement test scores with a mean of 75 and a variance of 16. Now suppose we were to draw one test score at random from this population and make a guess as to its value. Although we could conceivably guess any value, realistically our best guess would be the population mean. The reason for this can be stated in terms of the *two* properties of the mean:

1. Our average error will be zero since the sum of our errors will be zero.
2. This guess will produce the smallest error variance. In fact, since μ is our best guess and since σ^2 is the average of the squared deviations from μ, the population variance and the error variance are one and the same.

Realistically, though, we are looking for a procedure whereby we can make predictions with even fewer and smaller errors.

Suppose, for example, we could divide the original population of achievement scores into two subpopulations: one of males and the other of females. Now let us also assume that the mean achievement score is 73 for males and 77 for females. When we draw one achievement score and make a guess as to its value, we now have one additional piece of information: the sex of the individual making the score drawn. Given this additional piece of information, we now have three options with respect to our prediction:

1. We can make a blind prediction (any guess that comes to mind).
2. We can guess the population mean ($\mu = 75$).
3. We can guess the subpopulation mean (if male, 73; if female, 77).

In effect, our best guess is actually the mean of the subpopulation. In other words,

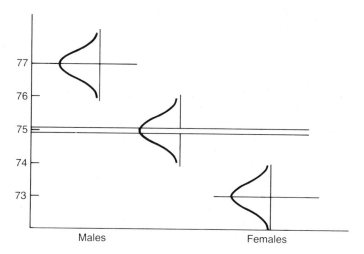

FIGURE 15.7   Logic of Regression Analysis

we use the information we have about sex to make our prediction about test score. In essence, this is the meaning of regression. **Regression can be defined as using one variable (X) to predict another (Y)** (in this case, using sex to predict achievement score) **where the predicted Y (Y′) value is the mean Y (Ȳ) for the designated value of X.** If the score drawn belongs to a male, then a guess of 73 will be closer to the true score than will be a guess of 75, the population mean, since the average male score is 73. In other words, regression is a statistical procedure through which we can analyze the relationship between a dependent or criterion variable and an independent or predictor variable.

In this example, the independent variable is a nominal-level variable. In regression, though, both the independent and dependent variables are usually interval. The independent continuous variable (X) can be thought of in the same way that the independent discrete variable (X, in our example, sex) can be thought of. Each value of X (even though there are an infinite number of X values) can be conceptualized as a category. For every X value (conceptualized as a category), there is a normal distribution of Y's, and each Y distribution has its own mean. When we identify a value (category) of X, our predicted Y value is the mean Y (Ȳ) of the normal distribution of Y's for the designated value (category) of X. Figure 15.7 demonstrates the logic of this procedure.

Let us now draw upon a second example to demonstrate in greater detail the use of interval-level variables. Suppose we are interested in predicting first-year student GPAs from ACT scores. Assume an infinitely large population of GPAs. Now suppose we could divide this population into thirty-six subpopulations—one for each ACT score. For any value of ACT, there is a normal distribution of GPAs with a mean. The predicted GPA for a designated value of ACT is the mean GPA for the normal distribution of ACT at that value of ACT.

Realistically, it is not possible to gain access to an entire population of Y scores.

TABLE 15.3   ACT and GPA Scores

X ACT	Y GPA
15	0.75
24	2.25
30	3.25
34	3.75
18	1.25
20	1.50
26	2.50
28	2.75
16	0.80
31	3.25

Therefore, it is also impossible to identify all the Y values that make up the normally distributed Y subpopulation for a designated value of X. Hence, the predicted Y's for all values of X are determined by using the formula for a straight line:

Predicted Y (Y') = $\alpha + bX$

Where: $\alpha = Y$ intercept – the point where the line crosses the Y axis – the value of Y when $X = 0$

b = slope of the line – rise/run – the increase in Y for a unit increase in X

X = the designated value (category) of X

By using this equation, any predicted Y will be the mean Y of the normal distribution of Y's for the designated value (category) of X. This concept is pictured in Figure 15.7. Each point on this line (and there are an infinite number of points just as there are an infinite number of X values) represents the Y value for the corresponding value of X displayed on the horizontal axis. Using the hypothetical data presented in Table 15.3, we will solve these equations. For this example, the regression equation would be:

$Y' = -1.67 + .16X$

A scatterplot of these data is presented in Figure 15.8. From this scatterplot, you should notice that the points lie almost in a straight line. In fact, most of them are pretty close to the line drawn through the points. In addition, the following observations can be made:

1. The points on the line represent the predicted Y's—the predicted GPAs.
2. The plotted points represent the actual Y values—the actual GPAs.
3. The distance between any plotted point and its corresponding point on the line is a *residual* or error in prediction.
4. Intuitively, you should see that in this example, our error will be small, since the points on the line and the plotted points are quite close.

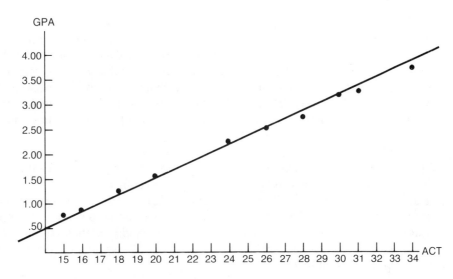

FIGURE 15.8   Scatterplot of Raw Data

The Adequacy of the Fit

Even though we can now look at the actual Y's (GPAs) and the predicted Y's (GPAs) and see that they are indeed close (residuals are small), such a subjective evaluation does not provide sufficient evidence that the equation ($Y' = -1.67 + .16X$) yields a good prediction and therefore is an adequate fit to the data. Consequently, more objective measure of how well an equation "fits" the data should be used. There are several such measures. Let's take a brief look at each.

The Standard Error of the Estimate   One measure of the adequacy of the fit to this regression equation (i.e., closeness of plotted points to the regression line) is the standard error of the estimate, which is really the standard deviation of the residuals. **This statistic provides a measure of the average distance of each residual** (error in predicting $Y - Y'$) **from the mean residual of zero.** If the regression equation were perfect, every prediction would be perfect. Thus, every predicted Y would equal every actual Y. In effect, all residuals would be zero. Thus, the standard deviation of these residuals would be zero. Intuitively, you should recognize that the smaller the standard error (standard deviation of the residuals), the better the predictions and thus the better the regression equation.

The Correlation Coefficient   A second measure of the adequacy of the fit of the data to the regression line (i.e., the closeness of the plotted points to the regression line) is the correlation coefficient. **The correlation coefficient is a measure of the strength of the relationship between two variables, X and Y.** That is, it is a measure of the degree to which these two variables vary together. The correlation coefficient varies between 0 and ±1.00. The extreme values (±1.00) represent perfect correlations. That is, X and Y covary (vary together) perfectly. Stated another way, the plotted points and the predicted points (points on the regression line) are identical, and we will be able to predict perfectly every time. A correlation of +1.00 means the relationship between X and Y is positive. As one variable increases in value, the other variable also increases in value. A correlation of –1.00 means that the relationship between X and Y is negative. As one variable increases in value, the other variable decreases in value. A correlation of zero means no relationship at all. Hence, we have no ability to predict one variable from the other.

Finally, we can test the significance of the correlation coefficient by testing the null hypothesis of no relationship between Y and X in the population—that is, $r = 0$. In effect, the null hypothesis is that the correlation coefficient is zero or nearly zero. This hypothesis is tested with the F statistic. The greater the proportion of variance explained, the larger the value of F. Thus, in a very general sense, the larger the value of F, the greater the likelihood of rejecting the null hypothesis (i.e., the greater the likelihood of a relationship between Y and X and the greater the likelihood of X explaining variation in Y).

The Squared Correlation Coefficient   Another measure of the adequacy of the fit of the data to the regression equation is the squared correlation coefficient, which represents **the proportion of variance in Y (the dependent variable) that is explained by X (the independent variable).** The squared correlation coefficient varies between 0.00 and ±1.00. When the squared correlation coefficient is 0.00 (no ability to predict), 0 percent of the variance in the dependent variable is explained by the independent variable. When the squared correlation coefficient is 1.00 (perfect ability to predict), we know that 100 percent of the variance in the dependent variable is being explained by the independent variable.

A Composite Example

To illustrate simple correlation and regression, let's look at a composite example. Suppose we wanted to predict the selling price of a house from the number of square feet in the house. We will make our prediction from our sample of 100 sales records taken from the population of 10,000 housing sales in Memphis, Tennessee, for 1978. We begin with the following prediction equation:

$$Y' = \alpha + bX$$

Where: Y' = predicted sales price
X = square footage

Now let's examine a scatter diagram of the two variables (X and Y) with price on the vertical axis and square footage on the horizontal axis. This scatter diagram is pictured in Figure 15.9. It is generally a good idea to plot the data before running the regression analysis because this simple visual aid can frequently identify potential problems with the regression analysis. In particular (and this will be discussed at greater length in the next section), we are concerned with the assumption of linearity. As you can see in this scatter diagram, these data form a generally linear pattern from the lower left-hand quadrant of the plot to the upper right-hand quadrant.

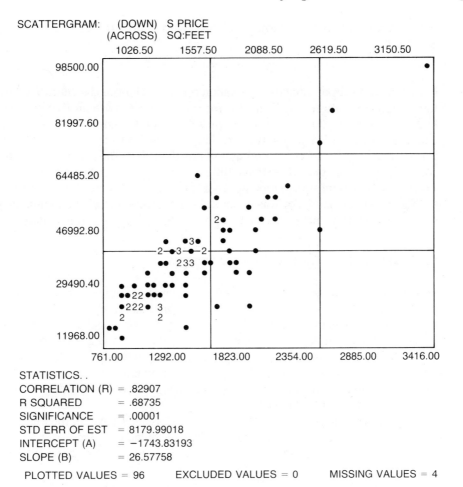

FIGURE 15.9 Scatter Diagram of Square Feet and Selling Price

However, if the plot had indicated a curved or curvilinear relationship, then a straight line (regression line) would not be appropriate for describing this relationship. One of our assumptions in regression is linearity, and even though a curvilinear relation is in a more general sense linear, a straight line is an inappropriate manner in which to describe a curved relationship.

Using the appropriate formulas, suppose we were to obtain the following relationship:

Predicted Y (Y') = –1,743.8 + 26.58 (SQFOOT)

Where: –1,743.8 = Y intercept

26.58 = slope of the line or an increase of $26.58 for each additional square foot

If the square footage of a house is 1,550, we would predict a selling price of $39,455.20.

$$Y' = -1,743.8 + 26.58(1,550) = \$39,455.20$$

Now let's also suppose that the correlation coefficient for our data is .829, which is a fairly high correlation. The F statistic for this r is 206.6. With an F of this size, we know that only one time out of 10,000 would such an F occur by chance. Hence, we can reason that our F is probably not a chance event. This r is significantly different from 0. In short, we reject the null hypothesis that $r = 0$. The correlation coefficient squared (r^2) is .687, indicating that a little over 68 percent of the variance in selling price is explained by square footage. That leaves only 32 percent of the variance in selling price unexplained by this variable. In short, this regression equation is doing an adequate (though not perfect) job of predicting selling price from square footage.

Multiple Correlation and Regression Analysis

Few things in life are perfectly and uniformly related. No single variable is generally the sole predictor of something else. Thus, a more realistic approach to explaining any phenomenon is to look for several variables that work together to explain something else. For example, suppose condition and age of house are also good predictors of selling price, and suppose both of these along with square footage are better predictors than any one is singly. Multiple regression is simply an extension of simple linear regression in that we are now using two or more independent variables to predict the dependent variable.

To understand how multiple regression works, let's consider the following example. Let's assume that we have a normally distributed population of housing selling prices with a mean of $40,000 and a variance of $20,000. Now suppose we could divide this population into four subpopulations: (1) older homes in below-average condition, (2) older homes in above-average condition, (3) newer homes in below-average condition, and (4) newer homes in above-average condition. For this example, let's assume older homes are homes fifteen years old or older and newer homes are homes less than fifteen years old. If we were to draw one sales record from this population and make a guess as to the selling price, we would now have *two* pieces of information to help us with our guess: (1) age (older or newer) and (2) condition (below or above average) of the house sold. And our best guess would be the mean of the subpopulation of the normal distribution of Y's for the designated combination of X's. In other words, we use information that we have about age and condition to make our prediction about selling prices. In essence, this is the meaning of multiple regression. Multiple regression can be defined as using two or more variables ($X_1, X_2, ..., X_k$) to predict another (Y) (in this example, using age of home and condition to predict selling price of a house) where the predicted Y (Y') is the mean Y ($\bar{Y}$) for the designated combination of X values (categories). Restated, **multiple regression is a statistical technique through which we can analyze the relationship between a dependent or criterion variable and a set of independent or predictor variables.**

If, for example, we were to draw a newer home in above-average condition, our predicted selling price would be $65,000 since the average selling price of a new

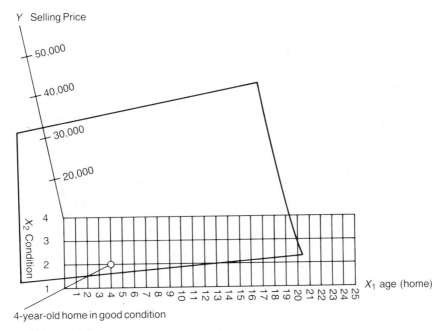

FIGURE 15.10   Predicted Selling Price for Four-Year-Old House in Good Condition (Aerial View)

home in above average condition is $65,000. In other words, a guess of $65,000 every time will be closer to the actual price (i.e., fewer and smaller errors) than will be a guess of $40,000, the population mean. In effect, fewer and smaller errors result from the fact that the sum of the squared deviations from a distribution's mean is a minimum value (smallest sum).

In the example just given, the two independent variables were nominal or at best ordinal. *In regression analysis, both the independent and dependent variables are assumed to be interval.* Independent continuous variables (X_1 and X_2) can be thought of in the same way that the independent discrete variables (age of homes and condition) can be thought of. Each combination of X_1 and X_2 values (even though there are an infinite number of X_1 and X_2 values) can be thought of as a category. For every combination of X_1 and X_2 values (conceptualized as a category), there is a normal distribution of Y's—each of these Y distributions having its own mean. When we identify the desired combination of X_1 and X_2 values, our predicted Y (Y') value becomes the mean Y ($\overline{Y}$) of the normal distribution of Y's for the designated combination of X_1 and X_2 values.

Let's now reexamine our two independent variables—age of home and condition—but this time treated as interval variables. We are still interested in predicting selling price of home from age of home and condition. Now let's suppose we could divide this population into subpopulations—one for each combination of age and condition. Again, for every combination of age and condition, there is a normal distribution of selling prices each with its own mean. And the mean selling price of this normal distribution is the predicted selling price for the designated combination of values on age and condition. This concept is pictured in Figure 15.10. The predicted

Y (selling price) for a four-year-old home in good condition, for example, is the mean Y ($\bar{Y}$) for the normal distribution of Y's (selling price) for this particular combination of X_1 and X_2 (i.e., four-year-old home in good condition).

As in simple linear regression, it is not always possible to gain access to an entire population of Y scores. Similarly, it is not possible to identify all the Y values that make up a normally distributed Y subpopulation for a designated combination of X_1 and X_2. As it turns out, the mean Y's ($\bar{Y}$'s) for all values of X (when there are just two independent variables—X_1 and X_2) are determined by using the formula for a plane:

Predicted Y (Y') $= \alpha_{y.12} + b_{y1.2}X_1 + b_{y2.1}X_2$

Where: $\alpha_{y.12}$ = y intercept or the value of Y when X_1 and X_2 are zero
$b_{y1.2}$ = the increase in Y for a unit increase in X_1 at a constant value of X_2
$b_{y2.1}$ = the increase in Y for a unit increase in X_2 at a constant value of X_1
X_1 = the first independent variable
X_2 = the second independent variable

Multiple regression models can be extended to include k independent variables. When the regression equation contains three or more independent variables, the regression model cannot be pictured geometrically, although it does have a definite algebraic equation. We should also mention that the betas in the multiple regression equation will not ordinarily be the same as those obtained in the two-variable case. In the two-variable case (one independent and one dependent variable), the beta obtained ignores all other independent variables. That is, other variables are not held constant. In contrast, the betas in the multiple regression equation are referred to as partial betas since they represent slopes that are computed controlling for each of the remaining independent variables included in the regression equation.

Finally, we want to introduce you to a standardized beta. *The standardized beta represents the value that would be computed if both the X and Y variables had been entered into the regression equation in z-score form.* Such betas are extremely useful in that they provide a means by which we can compare the relative contributions of each independent variable (i.e., to explain variance in the dependent variable). With the standardized regression equation there is *no* intercept since in standard form this value is always zero.

In Figure 15.11 we present a graphic display of the two-variable multiple regression equation. The points on the plane are the predicted Y's—in our case, the predicted selling prices. The plotted points are the actual Y's—the actual selling prices. The distance between the plotted points and the points on the plane represents our error in predicting.

The Adequacy of the Fit

As with simple linear regression, we can use several objective measures to determine the degree to which the data fit the multiple regression equation.

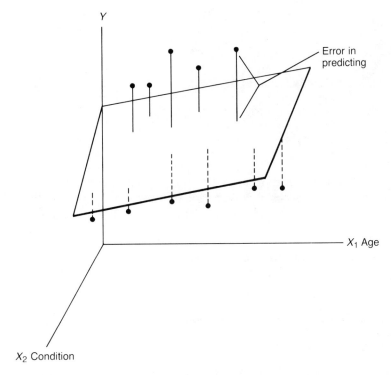

FIGURE 15.11   Graphic Display of Regression Plane

The Standard Error of the Estimate   Like the simple linear regression equation, if the regression equation could predict perfectly, the standard error would be zero. If the regression equation were perfect, every prediction would be perfect. Thus, every predicted Y would equal every actual Y. All residuals $(Y - Y')$ would equal zero. Consequently, the standard deviation of these residuals would be zero. Again, the smaller the standard error (standard deviation of the residuals), the better our ability to predict—hence, the better the regression equation.

The Multiple Correlation Coefficient   A second measure of the adequacy of the fit of the data to the regression plane (i.e., closeness of the plotted points to the regression plane) is the multiple correlation coefficient. It represents the zero-order correlation between the actual Y's and the predicted Y's. Multiple correlation coefficients range between 0 and ±1.00. A correlation of ±1.00 indicates that the regression equation is perfect—that is, it will predict perfectly every time. A correlation coefficient of zero indicates that the regression equation will not be able to predict at all.

The squared multiple correlation coefficient represents the proportion of variance in the dependent variable that is being explained by the regression equation —that is, by the independent variables acting together (in our case, by the two independent variables acting together).

$$R_{y.12}{}^2 = r_{y1}{}^2 + r_{y2.1}{}^2 (1 - r_{y1}{}^2)$$

proportion of variance explained by independent variables 1 and 2

proportion explained by independent variable 1

proportion explained by independent variable 2

proportion left unexplained by independent variable 1

Plotting the Residuals A third measure used for detecting model deficiencies in a multiple regression analysis is examination of the residuals. The *i*th residual is defined as

$$e_i = Y_i - Y_i'$$

These residuals can be standardized as follows:

$$z_e = \frac{e - \bar{e}}{s_e}$$

Since the mean error (*e*) is zero, this equation reduces to

$$z_e = \frac{e}{s_e}$$

These residuals in standard form have a mean of 0 and a standard deviation of 1.00. An appropriate graph of residuals will often expose gross model violations when they are present. Some of the more commonly used plots are those in which the standardized residuals (e_i) are plotted as the *ordinate* (i.e., vertical axis) against:

1. The fitted value, Y'
2. The independent variables, $X_1, X_2, ..., X_k$
3. The time order in which the observations occur

In general, when the model is correct, the standardized residuals tend to fall between –2.00 and +2.00 and are randomly distributed about 0. The residual plot should show no pattern of variation. Residual plots can help to identify several problems including the following:

1. Residual plots can help to identify *outliers*—that is, extreme values.

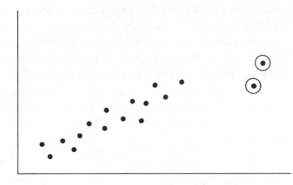

2. Residual plots can help to identify *heteroscedasticity*—that is, fluctuations in variance from one residual to another.

(Can be removed by adding or transforming variables.)

3. Residual plots can detect a *linear relationship between residuals and the variable on the horizontal axis.*

(Can be removed by adding variables.)

4. Residual plots can detect a *curvilinear relationship.*

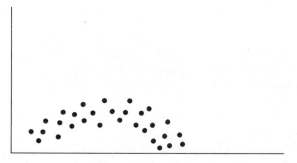

(Can be removed by adding or transforming variables.)

Autocorrelation   One of the standard assumptions in any regression model is that the error terms associated with each of the observations are uncorrelated. Correlation among the error terms suggests that there is additional explanatory information in the data that has not yet been exploited in the current model. *When the observations have a natural sequential order, the correlation is referred to as autocorrelation.* A characteristic pattern that would suggest autocorrelation would be one where several successive residuals would be positive, the next several negative, and so on.

The Durbin–Watson statistic d is a popular test of autocorrelation in regression analysis. There is an approximate relationship between d and r: $d = 2(1 - r)$. The Durbin–Watson statistic d has a range from 0 to 4. When r is close to 0, d is close to 2. Thus, the closer d is to 2.00, the firmer the evidence that there is no autocorrelation.

Colinear Data   Interpretation of the multiple regression equation depends implicitly on the assumption that the explanatory variables are not strongly interrelated. When there is complete absence of linear relationships among the explanatory variables, they are said to be *orthogonal*. In most regression applications, the explanatory variables are not orthogonal. Usually, though, the lack of orthogonality is not serious enough to affect the analysis. However, in some situations the explanatory variables are so strongly interrelated that the regression results are ambiguous. There are several ways to detect multicolinearity:

1. There exist high intercorrelations between the describing variables.
2. There are large variances in the estimates of the regression coefficients.
3. There is a large R^2 coupled with statistically nonsignificant regression coefficients.
4. There are large changes in the values of estimated regression coefficients when new variables are added to the regression.
5. The computer program is unable to compute regression coefficients (because of inability to compute the inverse of the correlation matrix).

There are also several ways to correct for multicolinearity:

1. We can collect additional data.
2. We can remove the variables that are causing trouble from the regression equation.
3. We can combine variables into a summary measure (less often approved).

The sequence of steps in multiple regression analysis can be summarized as follows:

1. Test the null hypothesis of no relationship between all independent variables acting together and Y (i.e., the test of significance for the multiple correlation coefficient).
   a. If there is no relationship, then there is no need to go any further; we do not reject the null hypothesis.
   b. If there is a relationship, then we will also want to test for the influence of each independent variable.
2. Solve for the regression equation, identifying the Y intercept and the unstandardized and standardized betas. The signs of the slopes will tell us the direction of the relationship, and their sizes are an indicator of the amount of change in Y produced by a unit change in X. The F test will tell us whether or not these slopes are significantly different from zero (a horizontal line). The unstandardized slopes, though, should not be used as an indicator of the relative impact of each independent variable on the dependent variable Y. (A change in the units of measurement would change the slopes.) Thus, we calculate the standardized equation where both the "effect" of variable X_1 on Y and the "effect" of variable X_2 on Y are expressed in

the same units of measurement and, thus, can be compared for their "relative" importance in determining Y.

3. Plot the residuals (generally standardized residuals against the standardized predicted Y's) as a measure of the adequacy of the fit.

4. Examine the residuals for autocorrelation.

5. Examine the independent variables for colinearity.

A Composite Example

Now let us return to the example that was presented in the section on simple linear regression. In our discussion of simple linear regression, we used square footage to predict the selling price of a house. As you will recall, this single variable appeared to be a fairly adequate predictor of selling price. However, this model has one problem that we have not yet mentioned—autocorrelation in the residuals. The Durbin–Watson statistic for this equation is 1.58—indicative of autocorrelation for our sample size. This autocorrelation is the result of a definite pattern found among the residuals. In effect, our one independent variable equation tends to overestimate the selling price of low-priced houses and underestimate the selling price of high-priced houses. The presence of autocorrelation suggests that there is probably a better regression equation. In addition, given that only 68 percent of the variance in selling price is explained with this one variable, we might want to examine our options. We could, for example, look for another single variable that performs better than square footage. Or we might try the number of rooms in a house or an amenities index based on the presence or absence of such features as carpet, central air conditioning, and built-in kitchen appliances.

A scatterplot of the amenities index and selling price is pictured in Figure 15.12. As you can see, the pattern is linear. The correlation coefficient is .683, which is lower than the correlation between square footage and selling price. This is our first indicator that this variable will not perform as well as square footage. The squared correlation coefficient is .466, indicating that a little over 46 percent of the variance in selling price is explained by the amenities index. In fact, this variable does not explain as much of the variance in selling price as the first variable, square footage. Additionally, there is still autocorrelation in the residuals (Durbin–Watson $d = 1.67$), and the pattern producing this correlation is essentially the same. The lower-priced houses are overestimated and the higher-priced houses are underestimated.

Looking at these two correlation coefficients and the amount of variance each explains in the dependent variable (68 percent and 46 percent, respectively), you might think that we now have two good variables if taken together. In fact, if you tried to add together the amount of variance each variable explains, you would get over 100 percent (which, of course, is not possible). However, we could only add these two percentages together if there were no relationship between square footage and our amenities index. In other words, these two independent variables would have to correlate at zero. Intuitively, you should know there is a relationship between these two variables. In fact, these two variables correlate with each other at .61. In effect, what this means is that square footage and our amenities index are ex-

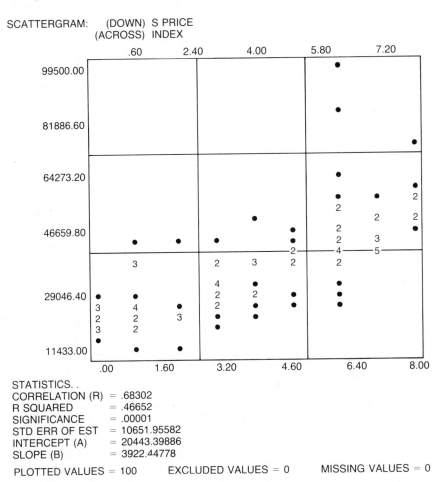

SCATTERGRAM: (DOWN) S PRICE
              (ACROSS) INDEX

STATISTICS. .
CORRELATION (R)   = .68302
R SQUARED   = .46652
SIGNIFICANCE   = .00001
STD ERR OF EST   = 10651.95582
INTERCEPT (A)   = 20443.39886
SLOPE (B)   = 3922.44778

PLOTTED VALUES = 100   EXCLUDED VALUES = 0   MISSING VALUES = 0

FIGURE 15.12   Scatterplot of Amenities Index and Selling Price

plaining some of the same variance in selling price. Hence, we need to identify that portion explained by each. That is, we need to identify that proportion of the variance in selling price left unexplained by square footage that can be explained by the amenities index. In other words, we need to place both of these variables in the regression model at the same time, and that requires a multiple regression model.

We will begin with two independent variables, square footage and our amenities index. The test of this model is displayed in Table 15.4. Our dependent variable is still selling price of a house. The multiple R for this equation is .856. Notice that this correlation indicates a stronger relationship between these two independent variables taken together and selling price than either variable taken singly. However, this relationship is only slightly stronger than the relationship between square footage and selling price. The R^2 is equal to .732, indicating that 73 percent of the variance in selling price is explained by the variables square footage and amenities

TABLE 15.4   Multiple Regression Model

Two Independent Variables

Variable	Unstandardized Beta	Standardized Beta	F
Amenities index	1,545.00	.2705	15.47
Square footage	21.16	.6600	92.06
(alpha)–254.95			

$R^2 = .856$ $F = 126.96$ Standard Error = 7,614.95

Six Independent Variables

Variable	Unstandardized Beta	Standardized Beta	F
Stories–3,014.70	–.006	1.09	
Square footage	24.77	.768	108.09
Car cover	3,324.80	.111	4.18
Condition	–4,734.50	–.169	9.90
Amenities index	1,016.00	.175	4.30
Age of home	–73.86	–.007	
(alpha) 8,578.65			

$R^2 = .805$ $F = 55.13$ Standard Error = 6,618.79

Four Independent Variables

Variable	Unstandardized Beta	Standardized Beta	F
Square footage	23.00	.713	123.84
Car cover	3,218.60	.108	3.97
Condition	–4,692.70	–.168	9.77
Amenities index	1,353.80	.234	12.46

$R^2 = .800$ $F = 81.92$ Standard Error = 6,627.23

index taken together. The test of significance for the multiple R^2 produces an F of 126.96—providing still further evidence that one or both of these variables is explaining variance in the dependent variable, selling price. Both betas produce significant F's, indicating that both variables are significant in the equation. For the amenities index, the unstandardized beta suggests that for each amenity added, we can add $1,545 to the selling price of the house. For square footage, the unstandardized beta suggests that for every square foot added, we can add $21.16.

By comparing the standardized betas, we can also determine the relative importance of each variable in the equation. In effect, square footage has a little over twice the effect of the amenities index on selling price. Additionally, there is no evidence of colinearity even though the two independent variables correlate at .61.

This correlation is not enough to create colinearity. When we compare the standard error of this equation to the standard error of the first, we find it is smaller. However, the Durbin–Watson d statistic still suggests autocorrelation among the residuals (1.577). The pattern creating this autocorrelation remains the same. We are underpredicting the selling price of the higher-priced houses and overpredicting the selling price for lower-priced homes.

To facilitate our search for the best regression equation and to eliminate autocorrelation in the residuals, let's try a six-independent-variable model. The six independent variables being introduced to predict selling price of a house include (1) square footage, (2) amenities index, (3) condition of house, (4) age of house, (5) number of stories, and (6) number of bathrooms. The test of this model appears in Table 15.4.

The multiple correlation coefficient for this equation is .897, and the squared multiple correlation coefficient is .805, indicating that these six variables taken together account for a little over 80 percent of the variance in selling price of a house. Since this model is significant ($F = 55.129$), we will proceed to test each of the independent variables to discern if each is making a significant contribution to the prediction equation. These tests are pictured in Table 15.4. As you can see from the F tests of the beta weights, two variables are not significant—number of stories and age of house. Additionally, although the standard error is smaller (6,618.79) than for our previous model, the Durbin–Watson d statistic still reflects evidence of autocorrelation ($d = 1.64$). To make this model clearer and simpler, the two insignificant variables need to be removed. Consequently, a new model is constructed that includes only four independent variables: (1) square footage, (2) amenities index, (3) condition, and (4) number of bathrooms. The test of this model appears in Table 15.4.

Notice that the multiple R for this equation is .894—a difference of only .003 from the previous six-variable equation. In effect, removing the independent variables "number of stories" and "age of home" has little effect on the fit of the data to this equation. The R^2 is .800, indicating that 80 percent of the variance in selling price is explained by these four variables taken together. A look at the F tests for each of the betas indicates that all four independent variables are significant. Additionally, by examining the standardized betas, we can see the relative importance of these variables: (1) square footage, (2) amenities index, (3) condition of house, and (4) number of bathrooms. The standard error of this equation is also reasonable—6,627.23. There is no evidence of colinearity among the independent variables. In addition, the plot of the standardized residuals against the standardized predicted Y's appears random. However, there still remains the problem of autocorrelation in the residuals (Durbin–Watson $d = 1.58$). This pattern is again such that the low-priced houses are underestimated. In short, it may be that the variables available to us are limited in some way. It may also be that other variables, such as quality of neighborhood, racial mix, and crime rate, need to be included in our model. In any event, it is reasonable to say that we have not yet found the most adequate model.

Chapter 16.

The Interpretation and Consequences of Research Data

Back to paradigms
   The role of theory in the
      interpretation of data
   Modest versus immodest
      interpretations
   The ethical nature of
      interpretation
The consequences of research
   Personal consequences
   Reactions from colleagues

Reactions from the people you
      study
Consequences for the enemies
      of people studied
Inductive and deductive
      interpretations
The logic of interpretation
Telling how the study was done
A final word

In science as in love, concentration on technique is likely to lead to impotence.
—PETER BERGER

Even though it may not seem so, the analysis and the interpretation of data are two quite different things. As you have just seen, the analysis of data collected in a research project involves separating complex material into its constituent parts and showing the relationship between these parts. Interpretation, on the other hand, is the broader task of coming to grips with the meaning of research and is the process by which the research project is finally tied back to the theory from which it evolved.

This is the part of research that we feel is most often neglected both in actual research and in methods texts that discuss how research is done. All one has to do is attend enough dissertation defenses or meetings of researchers who present their work in order to see that the larger question of "What does it mean?" is often lost in the enthusiasm for putting together a "proper" piece of research. This question of meaning is the one laypersons are often most interested in, for methodological slickness does not make up for a research project that people regard as meaningless. In this chapter, we will redress that inadequacy and show how social work research is filled with fascinating meanings and implications, and how best these meanings can be teased out of research findings and presented in a coherent and interesting way.

Back to Paradigms

The Role of Theory in the Interpretation of Data

Research is seldom any better than the theory that guides it. This point we took some pains to make in Chapter 4, and without belaboring it too much, we wish to rejuvenate that notion and discuss it briefly.

You will recall from the discussion in Chapter 4 that a paradigm is

a fundamental image held by members of a professional community about the subject matter of their practice. It serves to define what should be studied, what questions should be asked, how they should be asked, and what rules should be followed in interpreting the answers obtained. The paradigm is the broadest unit of consensus within a profession and serves to differentiate one community (or subcommunity) from another. It subsumes, defines, and interprets the exemplars, theories, methods, and instruments that exist within it.

In other words, theory and method, fact and framework of interpretation are tied together in an inextricable mix. There is no such thing as an independent fact. All pieces of data must be tied to theory or they have no meaning at all. A fact awaiting interpretation is like a windshield wiper waiting to be switched on. Facts are paradigm-dependent, and different paradigms rearrange the criteria for accepting something as "truth." So, if the social work researcher wishes to know something, he or she will have to pay some attention to the body of theory that gives rise to the questions the research will ultimately try to answer.

For example, there has been in sociologically based research in social psychology a continuing preoccupation with questions of the "self." In fact, probably no other single concept has given rise to so much research. On the other hand, while all of this research seems to have a family resemblance, the families can hardly talk to each other when it comes to the question of interpreting the data each derives from its research! This is because the theories and intellectual traditions from which the concept of self arises are so divergent. There are paradigms that see the self as being an indwelling property of the individual that is reflected in that person's behavior.

Such paradigms use paper-and-pencil tests in an effort to reveal who and what people really are [1]. Interpretations of these data then are tied to the basic assumption that a methodological technique is designed to *uncover* something that is already there. There are other paradigms, however, that see the self as a construct that arises out of the interactions one has with others. From the standpoint of this imagery, paper-and-pencil tests could not possibly reveal anything more than the current self the respondent is establishing before the researcher because there is nothing there to be revealed in the first place. Such a paradigm would lead to a very different kind of methodology. Instead of looking for strategies that *reveal*, one develops strategies that *describe* the kind of self that is being constructed and the techniques by which that construction is being accomplished [2]. Interpretive strategies, then, necessarily follow the assumptions of the paradigm, and each researcher would interpret the data from the standpoint of the paradigm guiding the research.

On the other hand, as George Ritzer [3] has pointed out, the greatest pieces of research ever conducted were almost always ones in which the practitioner "bridged paradigms," interpreting findings from the standpoint of several paradigms simultaneously in order to get a better view of findings. This is close to the concept of triangulation, which we have discussed elsewhere in this book—that is, getting at data from several different angles. It is in the interpretation section of a research project that triangulation, in its broadest sense, is most appropriate. Using our example of the self in social psychology, we might note that the creative researcher, even though his or her work is obviously guided by a paradigm that has been carefully elucidated in the project, might wish to examine what his or her finding would be like if interpreted from the standpoint of alternative paradigms. This obviously requires some amount of intellectual honesty and dexterity, for most researchers are tied to the methods of their paradigm so thoroughly that the way of seeing dictated by the underlying assumptions of their paradigm often becomes a set of blinders rather than a set of lenses. (Every set of lenses obscures as well as reveals.)

Nevertheless, social work researchers should always ask themselves how many different ways a given piece of research can be read. In this sense, data are like flights into space: at lift-off a variety of details on the ground are revealed, but as you gain altitude, old perceptions fall away and new ones come into play. Finally, from orbit, one can see a wide variety of features that could not be seen from down low. This example is instructive because it also points out that there is no perspective that does not also conceal, and things begin to look very different when perspectives are switched. Which is the superior perspective depends on what kind of problem you are working on. For example, the view from orbit is terrific for long-term weather forecasting, but not worth a darn if you want to see the features of a flower planted near the launch pad.

In social work research we have a similar problem. Each of the techniques discussed in this book has strengths and weaknesses, long suits and shortcomings. The sensitive researcher overcomes the weaknesses of given methods as much as he or she can, but in the final analysis some weaknesses simply go with the methodological territory one is in, and, as a result, interpretations need to be fairly modest.

Modest versus Immodest Interpretations

For example, trying to make sweeping generalizations from data derived from the technique of participant observation and from its guiding interactionist paradigm is always risky, for the close description, involvement in depth, and firsthand knowledge of a given social world do not usually allow one to generalize too freely to other worlds that were not a part of the researcher's study. Conversely, survey researchers who operate out of a structural–functional paradigm must exercise some restraint in getting too specific about the detail of various social worlds they have not seen firsthand.

These cautions are really caveats about intellectual honesty. Creative interpretation and even a measure of speculation are one thing; arrogance and bluster are quite another. The former are to be cultivated, the latter abhorred.

It is obviously in the researcher's own interests to be relatively modest in the way in which he or she interprets and presents data. Leaps of speculative faith, defined as such, and offered to the reader with appropriate qualifications and cautions are certainly a part of a provocative research project. But throwing caution to the wind in one's enthusiasm to get as much attention as possible for a piece of research to which you have committed a considerable amount of effort can backfire overnight. Unfortunately, social work research in this area is hardly immune to the common tendency in our society for persons (especially the press) to seize upon the weakest statement in a research project and trumpet it as the project's most important finding. This is why modest interpretations are generally better, lest readers wind up making much more out of a finding than the researcher would. On the other hand, risks of being provocative (lots of publicity, making a "name" for yourself, etc.) can be worth it too, and it is up to the individual researcher, in the last analysis, to defend what he or she has done.

The Ethical Nature of Interpretation

Aside from the risks to the researcher in making interpretative leaps that are unwarranted, there are also a number of ethical issues involved in the process of presenting research findings which, in our judgment, need far more attention than they currently get. In this section, we will discuss what we regard as some of the more important ethical issues facing the interpreter of social work research findings. We are dealing here specifically with the ethical nature of *interpretation* as opposed to the many other ethical issues facing researchers as they plan and execute research projects. Those questions we have addressed in Chapter 5.

The first ethical problem in interpretation consists of the dilemma facing every researcher whose research is sponsored by an outside agency. Implicitly or explicitly, the sponsors of research have some kind of agenda in mind, and that is why they funded the research done in the first place. How is the researcher to maintain integrity in the face of the overwhelming power of money or political favor or any number of inducements that might be dangled in front of him or her in order to get the research to say what the sponsoring agency wants it to say? It is the matter of interpretation where such issues may often arise, for as we have said, facts do not speak for themselves and can be arranged in an almost infinite number of ways in order either to contribute to or to demolish various ideologies the sponsor may have in mind. The problem is getting to be so great, in fact, that increasingly researchers are not even funded to do direct research projects, but are merely contracted to do some piece of technical work (e.g., draw a sample, conduct interviews), and the funding agency then completes the research and draws its own conclusions.

On the other hand, sponsoring agencies by and large still fund research projects because part of their ideological interests are best served by being able to give at least the impression of objectivity. In other words, what funders often want is not the truth of a particular bit of the social world but the imprimatur of legitimacy stamped on their policy, product, or agency decision by the social science community. Whether the sponsoring agency is a government body or the manufacturer of a product that comes in an aerosol can, or a social agency providing services to some client population, the dilemmas posed for the researcher trying to keep his or her integrity intact can be enormous. What follows is an example from our not-too-distant past.

An Example: The Effects of Pornography

In 1967, the administration of President Lyndon Johnson decided, after what can safely be called centuries of debate, to fund a blue-ribbon commission to tell the country objectively whether or not exposure to pornographic material causes harm and whether or not access to such materials should be controlled. Commission members included seven university professors (including one social scientist), five lawyers, three clergymen, one nonacademic sociologist, one clinical psychiatrist, and a retired publishing house executive. When approved by Congress, the commission was directed to develop studies and recommendations around four areas. They were:

1. with the aid of leading constitutional law authorities, to analyze the laws pertaining to the control of obscenity and pornography; and to evaluate and recommend definitions of obscenity and pornography;
2. to ascertain the methods employed in the distribution of obscene and pornographic materials and to explore the nature and volume of traffic in such materials;
3. to study the effect of obscenity and pornography upon the public, and particularly minors, and its relationship to crime and other antisocial behavior; and
4. to recommend such legislative, administrative, or other advisable and appropriate action as the Commission deems necessary to regulate effectively the flow of such traffic without in any way interfering with constitutional rights.

Even as the commission began its work, the entire enterprise became embroiled in controversy. As Ray Rist [4] reports in his comprehensive summary of the events that developed around the commission's work, members tried to proceed conscientiously with developing the kind of methodologies, data, and theoretical frameworks that would be appropriate to the questions they were asked to answer, but problems beset them from the outset. Although virtually all of the data and studies they developed pointed to an inescapable conclusion—that pornography has no harmful behavioral effects—by the time the report hit the public arena, both internal and external pressures had built to the point where rational debate no longer prevailed. Two members of the commission, a Catholic priest and the president of Citizens for Decent Literature, who was appointed by President Nixon to replace a member of the original commission who resigned, denounced the findings as degenerate and put out a minority report. Press leaks during the original deliberations about various methodologies used in trying to assess the effects of pornography were seized upon, and various scurrilous interpretations were created. In other words, the commission and its work had come to be a convenient whipping post for politicians who were looking for ways to convince the electorate that they were fighting for public morality and decency.

The Nixon administration, anxious to put distance between itself and the commission's findings, denounced the majority report as the product of "radical liberals" bent on destroying the United States by unleashing a torrent of smut. With the president leading the way, and an election at hand, other members of the Congress introduced various bills to denounce the commission findings. Finally, a week before the election, Nixon himself issued the following statement:

> I have evaluated that report and categorically reject its morally bankrupt conclusions and major recommendations.
>
> So long as I am in the White House, there will be no relaxation of the national effort to control and eliminate smut from our national life.
>
> The Commission contends that the proliferation of filthy books and plays has no lasting harmful effect on a man's character. If that were true, it must also be true that great books, great paintings and great plays have no ennobling effect on man's conduct. Centuries of civilization and ten minutes of common sense tell us otherwise.
>
> The Commission calls for the repeal of laws controlling smut for adults—while recommending continued restrictions on smut for children. In an open society, this proposal is untenable. If the level of filth rises in the adult community, the young people in our society cannot help but also be inundated by the flood. [5]

We have presented this brief example in order to illustrate in as bold relief as possible some of the dilemmas that face social researchers as they interpret their own studies and as others interpret them for themselves. It is apparent from the reaction to the commission's report that the accuracy, validity, generalizability, and other criteria of scientific methodology had precious little to do with the ultimate fate of the report. A variety of interests became party to the commission's work even before it became known exactly what they were doing or what their ultimate findings would be. This is characteristic of social science research on any number of topics, but especially controversial and emotionally charged ones. As Rist has suggested:

Those who bring a social science orientation to commission endeavors, and who seek to address themselves to the issues within such an analytical framework, confront others who do not accept the social science approach as appropriate. Those members of the Obscenity Commission who argued that the debate over sexually explicit material was not one of utility, but one of philosophy and ethics, illustrate this point: from the perspective of an alternative social reality, "mere facts" about the effects of sexually explicit material are irrelevant to the issue. [6]

But, of course, social science does not deal with "mere facts" either, as our discussion of theories and paradigms has shown. So it appears that participation by social scientists in the pornography controversy has the result of presenting "answers" to the questions it was asked from only a limited and partial perspective, which was doomed from the beginning to be unacceptable to a variety of interests. In retrospect, it seems that social scientists on the commission agreed to undertake a series of questions that social science could never really answer. Even though they carefully limited their interpretations of their findings to the data themselves, those data, like most in social science research, were inadequate to the whole range of questions that might be asked of them. For example, the members of the commission who studied the behavioral effects of the exposure of persons to pornographic literature acknowledged that their major finding—that no personal or social harm tended to result from viewing pornography—was subject to a variety of limitations. They noted that their research was on short-term exposure, and that the long-term effects could not be investigated on a commission that worked on that segment of the research for only two years. Furthermore, almost no research was available on the effects of pornography on children, obviously because of the major ethical obstacles to exposing children to pornography for research purposes. Finally, they noted that all of their research on behavioral effects was done with volunteers, and as we have noted repeatedly in this book it is difficult to generalize to nonwilling persons research findings that were obtained from studying willing ones. Nevertheless, even with those limitations, the commission chose to interpret the results of their studies as concluding that "no dangerous effects have been demonstrated on any of the populations which were studied" [7].

The interpretation of the data by commission members was (it seemed to them) relatively modest. But like most interpretations, it really did go beyond the data at hand, even though they carefully couched it in qualified terms. Or, to put the matter another way, persons opposed to pornography could interpret the same data as concluding that social science has *not* proved that pornography is harmless.

Was it worth the effort for social science to get involved in the pornography controversy? The answer is not altogether clear. On the one hand,

the research ... forced a wedge into the political construction of definitions of sexually explicit materials. Although many politicians denounced the Commission's findings and its recommendations, the Report, however briefly, opened a public debate over the issue of "effects' and its relation to the science-vs.-morals debate. [8]

Social science research seems at its best when its findings and tentative conclusions increase the level and quality of discussion in an open society. There is no question that the pornography commission's findings did just that. On the other hand, the commission's work opened far more questions that it was able to answer and seemed to hold social science up to be considerably less than it is often promised to be. In terms of the values of science, opening up more questions is usually a very positive development because it leads to further research, better understanding, and a refinement of both theory and methods. But in terms of the values of society where answers are sought after with an enormous emotional intensity, and decisions have to be made even on the basis of imperfect knowledge, social science seemed to fail to provide the necessary basis for making a decision about such crucial questions.

At the time of this writing (1990), controversy swirls again around the issue of abortion. In 1988 the Reagan administration commissioned Surgeon General Everett Koop to prepare a report about the effects on women who have had an abortion. Strong pro-life political forces wanted the results to give support to their arguments that these women suffer terrible debilitating emotional and psychological effects. The pro-choice forces were convinced that just the opposite effect (i.e., a reduction of emotional and psychological stress resulting from not being forced to carry an unwanted pregnancy) would be supported by a review of the research findings. Surgeon General Koop found himself in an ethical–political "hot seat." The national press has reported that a letter went from Surgeon General Koop to the President indicating that the preponderance of the evidence did not support one view over the other. Several months later, Dr. Koop retired from his position. It will be interesting to see how societal values, political pressures, and individual integrity continue to play out in this political scenario.

The Consequences of Research

We selected the example of the pornography research because we thought it to be a particularly fruitful one for understanding the broader context in which the interpretation of social work research occurs. All actions have consequences, and the research process, no matter how much we may want to make it seem like a neutral scientific enterprise, is fraught with consequential implications for the individual researcher, those whom the research is conducted on or about, and society in general.

Much of the impact of a study is beyond the control of the researcher, but much of it is controllable if we understand the most likely consequences that are to arise from it. The Loflands, whose analysis of the research process we will have occasion to refer to later, have noted that a researcher should anticipate and attempt to shape at least some of the more important consequences of a research project. They list several possible consequences in the following categories [9].

Personal Consequences

Researchers, like other people, have to earn a living and get along with others. For this reason, research often has enormous personal consequences. At its best, the authors of a piece of research will be praised for their efforts, lauded for their interpretive skill, and rewarded in the marketplace of both ideas and money. Unfortunately, not all of the personal consequences may be positive. A piece of research done badly may stalk the authors and their reputations for the rest of their careers. Researchers may feel that they have betrayed the people they were studying in some fundamental way or, like Robert Oppenheimer and his group of physicists who developed the first atomic bomb, that the research was used for negative purposes and had outcomes that were tragic. Social work research is not always so dramatic in its potential for harm, but such potential is there, and many researchers have come to feel that they were guilty of a kind of "treason" [10, 11]. In qualitative research, especially, where close participation with the subjects of your research is both inevitable and generally positive, there can be the sense that the research did not have the consequences that were hoped for or even anticipated.

Consider, for example, the instance where a social worker, an employee of an agency, is directed to conduct a research project aimed at demonstrating to the agency's board of directors the effectiveness of a particular pilot program (and therefore the need for increased financial support). The executive director may not be as interested in "truth" as in having some "objective" support for future planning agendas. The social work researcher can find him- or herself in an ethical dilemma if the resultant findings of the study do not lend support to the agendas as strongly as hoped by the executive director. Subtle or overt pressure could be brought to bear in the interpretation phase of the project for less than a balanced presentation of the findings. In situations like this it is often wise to use outside research consultants to conduct the study or a least to be heavily involved in the initial design, the interpretation, and the report-writing phases.

Reactions from Colleagues

Again, at best, the reactions of colleagues to a published piece of research can be among the most rewarding aspects of all the labor that goes into such an endeavor. One comes to be known as a person who contributed something substantial to the literature within an area or to the continuation of a good service program in the community. Even some measure of fame may come from the authorship of a solid piece of research. Let it be known, however, that even good research (sometimes especially good research) comes under the scrutiny and criticism of colleagues and may be panned, cut up, or even (heaven forbid!) reduced in the pages of some journal or committee meeting room to intellectual rubble. Laud Humphreys's analysis of the homosexual "tearoom" [12] has generated some of the most pointed and acerbic criticism ever aimed at a piece of social research, and Humphreys has had to live with his work, for better or for worse, ever since it was published. Questions of intelligence, credentials, ethics, and prejudices are just a few among many sources of criticism that can be leveled against a researcher. Often the criticism is unfair. No researcher could have anticipated or dealt with all of the contingencies that were raised about a project, a point we saw vividly displayed in the example of the pornography commission. The slings and arrows of outrageous fortune are never more apparent than the fallout from a piece of research that becomes notorious. To engage in research is to put oneself in a position of some vulnerability, and so you might as well get prepared for something other than simply glowing reviews of your work. This point is just as valid for the student in a research methods class doing her first project and hoping to get an A, but ever in danger of getting something less, to the seasoned researcher who is publishing her tenth book.

Agency-based social work research can understandably lead to reactions from one's fellow workers and colleagues in the agency. Reactions can range from being pleased and proud of the fine work you have done, to minor jealousies that you were selected for this special project (with time off from your regular duties), to strong resentments because the program studied eventually was not refunded and job positions were reassigned or terminated. Of course, none of these reactions or resultant agency decisions may have been anticipated by the researcher—but human behavior is often unpredictable!

Reactions from the People You Study

In qualitative research, the people you study will almost always have to be reported back to, and their reaction is likely to be an important factor in your later feelings about the project. There are numerous surprises here, for the people studied rarely respond to a piece of research the way the researcher thinks they will. They may be accepting, but not very impressed with the importance of the work, or they may be downright hostile. Lofland and Lofland have noted the following generalizations about reactions you are likely to get:

○ Most people do not seem to care very much about scholarly analyses that are written about them. Many don't get around to reading them even when they are provided. There are harsh reactions and conflicts only in a minority of cases.

○ Reports dealing with stable communities or ongoing groups are much more likely to generate a response from the participants than studies of more amorphous social situations or fluid groupings.

○ The use of pseudonyms and a scholarly mode of writing tend to minimize the participants' interest in a report.

○ The most interested and reactive participants appear to be members of elite groups in relatively small communities. [13]

In quantitative research it is not always quite so clear just what the impact will be on people you study. First, the actual groups that are interviewed or surveyed may not be identifiable in a statistical summary at all. Second, the impact of the study may be diffused, so that its results are quite subtle. There can be real ethical questions here. For example, to survey people with a fixed-response questionnaire, force them to answer questions in preformed categories, and then use their responses as policy tools often means that a kind of shell game has been played in which social work research is used to imply a consensus about something when no such consensus may have existed at all. This is done all the time and can have enormous consequences on people's lives without very much of an opportunity for them to even know what has happened, much less do anything about it.

If, as in the earlier example of agency-based research, the findings lead to the termination of a program because it is not especially cost-efficient for the agency, those clients who are benefitting from the program services could have some pretty strong feelings about it! On the other hand, if the research findings are supportive of program continuation, or even result in decisions made to expand the program, the researcher is a hero.

Consequences for the Enemies of People Studied

The groups you study in a research project are often asked to reveal aspects of themselves that could be at best embarrassing and at worst the ammunition with which their enemies can launch an attack. Julian Roebuck's study of southern "rednecks" [14], for example, is a sensitive portrayal of a group under considerable pressure from various quarters, and his research, while sympathetic, could be used by a variety of the enemies of that culture to do it harm. Ethical considerations simply mandate that the author of a research project take every available opportunity to anticipate possible harm to subjects and ward it off. The examples are "legion" where research findings have been taken out of context and used to "blame the victims," whether welfare recipients, the unemployed, the homeless, the handicapped, or any identifiable minority group represented in our country. [15]

Inductive and Deductive Interpretations

The Logic of Interpretation

By definition, when we interpret, we move beyond "mere facts" to an arena that is more characterized by art than by science. We want to speculate, but from a base of factual material. We want to move from mere data to the larger plane of human meaning. There are two major ways of interpreting, just as there are two different ways in which the theory game is played, as we put it in Chapter 4. These two basic types of logic are inductive and deductive, and the nature of our interpretive efforts is going to depend in large measure on which of the two ways of analyzing data is used.

Remember that *in deductive logic we move from the general to the specific. It is in this form of theory and research that interpretation seems most tied to the premises of the general theory from which it sprang.* If we have a theory about male–female relationships becoming more problematic in the twentieth century, for example, our data are going to be developed around a rather closely held set of theories and then "plugged into" those theories as they seem to fit. Interpretation is going to be a matter of assessing the fit between facts and theory, perhaps modifying the theory as things move along, or developing new methodologies to test new relationships that seem to be warranted from the emerging facts. Interpretation, in this process, is a matter of seeing the theory in a brighter light or altering it as that light seems to require. Interpretations that are inductively produced are much more difficult because their empirical grounding in a close analysis of a series of cases usually means that their generalizability is not as great. On the other hand, *because* they are empirically grounded, *interpretations that move from an inductive form of logic may be much more powerful levers for interpretation than deductive ones because the facts from which they proceed seem to be so irrevocable.*

One of the most brilliant pieces of research done in the past twenty years proceeds from an inductive base, and its interpretations of social reality are among the most provocative of our time. Daniel Yankelovitch, the head of a survey research polling firm, used a series of interviews and questionnaires in order to assess basic changes occurring in the people's aspirations, goals, and lives. Published in a book called *New Rules*, Yankelovitch's interpretations are by far the most important part of his analysis. He takes mundane pieces of data and weaves them into a mosaic that is insightful, powerful, provocative, stimulating, and useful.

New Rules is a memorable piece of research because it is effective in what the Loflands call the *interpenetration* of data and analysis [16]. The analysis and interpretation have evolved out of the data. Much research seems to consist of a first section and last section that are theoretically and interpretatively interesting, but in between the data consist merely of either low-level descriptions (often characteristics of qualitative research) or reams of numbers (too often found in quantitative research). In this sense, interpretation and analysis are merely tacked onto a research project. It almost seems that the task of collecting and presenting data is so enormous that the researcher has not had time to reflect on, think about, or contemplate the meaning of his or her own work. To merely pile one fact on top of another is not research. Research consists of a full span of activities that includes planning, gathering, writing, reflecting, interpreting, and rewriting.

John and Lyn Lofland have put together one of the most exhaustive analyses of how the practice of social research is accomplished, and while their focus is on qualitative research, many of their suggestions about how to conduct the latter phases of a research project have relevance to *any* kind of research.

Telling How the Study Was Done

Much of the interpretation of a research project can be stimulated by simply describing how the study was done. This includes such things as the origins of the researchers' interest and how and why they undertook the kinds of methods they did. In creating a retrospective about such things, the study becomes situated in both an intellectual as well as a research context. Obviously, the researchers thought that the topic merited investigation, and the exercise of discussing it will make it clearer to both the reader and the investigators why the study was important. As it turns out, this retrospective analysis is usually very revealing if done honestly and leads to a host of interpretations of the problem that might not otherwise be possible. For example, such reflection enables the reader to have access to the process by which the problem became meaningful to the investigators, how it took form and shape in the researchers' minds, how they gained access to the information and settings necessary to do the project, what difficulties they encountered along the way, and how the project changed over time.

In addition, the researchers' own private feelings, doubts, and fears, the kinds of emotions the research generated, and how they were dealt with are extremely revealing and give rise to a host of interpretations not possible by presenting the technical part of a project without such a human dimension.

Describing the data-gathering stage can be equally illuminating. How much time was spent? How did the researchers decide what to look for, whom to talk with, what kind of techniques to use? What kind of techniques did they use to record observations? What barriers did they encounter?

Retrospectives about data analysis are a gold mine of information for the reader as well as the researchers. How were data put together? How did the researchers decide what they meant? How did they reach their conclusions? What were their personal feelings about the research as it unfolded? With the 20/20 vision provided by hindsight, how would they have done it differently?

Giving some thought to the conceptual framework one chose to employ is also a key process in later interpretations of the meaning and import of a piece of research. Obviously, we either invest or borrow concepts, and the arrangement of these concepts is a major part of interpretation. Could different terminologies have been used? What would the research look like if they had been? This is one of the most fertile grounds for stimulating thought, and again, both the researchers and their readers can profit by such an exercise.

Distancing yourself from your work is crucial to the interpretive phase of a research project. After having worked on a piece of research for a long period of time (and this can sometimes mean years), it is wise to put everything aside, and come back to it later. Such a process of distancing can, at its best, create a fresh look at a piece of research that will enable the researcher to gain new insights into a project that was beginning to grow stale from too close a familiarity with it. Even if you don't change a thing, having done this means that everything will be settled in your mind with a certain maturity that grows out of looking at things from several different angles. Part of the distancing process may also involve sharing the research at various times with colleagues who can be depended upon to be constructive and helpful. Some researchers make it a habit never to publish a piece of research without sharing it during its developmental stages with a colleague who over a long period of time has proved his or her dependability for constructive, sensitive criticism. Any number of research projects, at various stages of development, have been improved by doing this. Two heads really are sometimes better than one!

A Final Word

Despite all of our preoccupation with research techniques, it is important to remember that research is, first and foremost, simply a type of scholarship in which a curious mind, intellectual honesty, ethical considerations for subjects, a passion to know the truth, and a desire to communicate it effectively to an audience are all that is really needed. A certain humility about the process will also carry the researcher a long way. In a world where arrogances of all kinds abound, it is well to remember the words of Thomas Edison, one of the foremost minds of any century, who once observed that "the smartest man in the world still only knows 1/1,000,000 about anything."

References

1. T. S. Kuhn, *The Structure of Scientific Revolutions* (Chicago: University of Chicago Press, 1962).
2. E. Goffman, *Presentation of Self in Everyday Life* (New York: Doubleday, 1959).
3. George Ritzer, *Sociology: A Multiple Paradigm Science* (Boston: Allyn and Bacon, 1975).
4. Ray Rist, *The Pornography Controversy* (New Brunswick, NJ: Transaction Books, 1975).
5. Rist, *The Pornography Controversy*, pp. 266–7.
6. Rist, *The Pornography Controversy*, p. 265.
7. J. Q. Wilson, "Violence, Pornography, and Social Science," *Journal of the Public Interest*, 22 (1975): 45–61.
8. Rist, *The Pornography Controversy*, p. 266.
9. John Lofland and Lyn Lofland, *Analyzing Social Settings* (Belmont, CA: Wadsworth, 1984).
10. S. C. Heilman, "Jewish Sociologist: Native-as-Stranger," *American Sociologist* 15 (1980): 100–8.
11. B. Thorne, "Political Activists as Participant Observers: Conflicts of Commitment in a Study of the Draft Resistance Movement of the 1960's," *Symbolic Interactionist* 2 (1979): 73–88.
12. Laud Humphreys, *Tearoom Trade: Impersonal Sex in Public Places* (Chicago: Aldine, 1970).
13. Lofland and Lofland, *Analyzing Social Settings*, p. 158.
14. Julian Roebuck, *Rednecks* (New York: Praeger, 1983).
15. William Ryan, *Blaming the Victim* (New York: Vintage Books, 1971, 1976).
16. Lofland and Lofland, *Analyzing Social Settings*.

Chapter 17

Writing the Research Report

Why write a research report?
Factors to consider when writing
   Aim of the report
   Readership
Characteristics of scientific writing
   Objectivity
   Accuracy
   Clarity
   Economy

Organization of the research report
   Abstract
   Introduction
   Methods
   Presentation of the results
   Discussion section
   References
   Tables
   Appendix
Rewriting the research report

I love being a writer. What I can't stand is the paperwork. —PETER DE VRIES

Why Write a Research Report?

At last, you are near the end of the research process. You have formulated a research question, identified an intriguing theory, chosen a research design, and collected and analyzed data. But this whole process will be in vain if you consider yourself finished. If you stop here, the discoveries you made will go unnoticed and will eventually be forgotten. As a responsible researcher, you owe it to yourself and to other researchers to report your findings. By sharing your research with others, you contribute to the growth of knowledge in the research area. But a research report means writing, and writing is often viewed as a difficult and boring task. The authors of this book, for example, have often heard students say, "The hardest thing about research is writing." Our response to this is, "The hardest thing about writing is knowing." If you are knowledgeable—that is, if you know your subject matter—you will have little difficulty writing. Of course, writing is difficult when you don't know your subject matter. You have nothing to write about!

We think you will find that writing the research report is one of the most exciting, challenging, frustrating, and satisfying tasks in the research process. With this report, you will bring all phases of your research into clear focus, stimulating new insights and new understanding. You will come to know and understand more fully and more clearly your research findings as you seek ways to express them to others. But the path to this expression is not always easy or smooth. It is not always easy to take a large amount of material and condense it into a few sentences or paragraphs. It is not always easy to explain lucidly complicated methodology or statistical analysis. In this chapter we will discuss the rudiments of the research report. This discussion is not designed to teach you to write. We believe the best teacher for this task is experience. Instead, we hope to sharpen and improve your present writing skills. Read and reread this chapter very carefully, and as you read, remember two things: *Don't be afraid to try,* and *there's always room for improvement.*

Factors to Consider When Writing

Aim of the Report

In general, the research report is written for other people. It is written to inform someone else of the research project and its results. For the student, it informs the professor and is the basis for a grade. For the young researcher seeking recognition and support, it is a chance to publish for professional credit. For the established professional, it is an opportunity to add to scientific knowledge and to communicate with colleagues and sometimes the public. Ideally, your writing should carry your readers through the research process as if they were personally experiencing each of the steps. In fact, the successful research report creates an air of sharing the research question and the search for meaningful answers. Above all, the research report should aim to convince your readers, by the combined weight of evidence and logic, of the credibility of your research. The report should move each reader to believe the results and to respect the procedure by which they were obtained.

Readership

Perhaps is goes without saying that the intended reading audience will influence the style and length of your final report. When a report is being written for a general reading audience, you cannot assume an exceptionally high level of specialized knowledge. Therefore, points must be made in more detail and technical terms must be more fully explained. In contrast, when a report is being written for the scientific community, you can generally assume a fair amount of specialized prior knowledge and therefore eliminate much of the explanatory detail and technical information. For either reader, the report must be well organized, well illustrated, and conceptually clear.

Characteristics of Scientific Writing

Before examining the components of the research report, let's take a brief look at some of its more important characteristics. Specifically, we wish to discuss the ways in which a report should reflect the goals of objectivity, accuracy, clarity, and economy.

Objectivity

Objectivity in writing means intellectual honesty in the research report. It means reporting those data that *disconfirm* the research hypothesis as well as those that confirm it. Such an approach ensures that the whole story is told, including acknowledgement of errors, problems in data collection, and conditions or events that may cast doubt on the research. Objectivity also means that you draw only those conclusions that are clearly supported by the data. In effect, when a hypothesis is repeatedly confirmed by well-conducted experiments, a firm conclusion can be made. When the data of just one experiment give support to a hypothesis, conclusions must be tentative with an eye for future testing.

Accuracy

Accuracy in the research report means a thorough checking and rechecking of all source materials. Error, omission, and carelessness will contaminate any report enough to make its value questionable. This surely means failure. You should keep meticulous records on authors, titles, publishers, and page references of relevant literature. And you should make repeated checks to ensure that errors are not generated as this information is moved from source to notebook to draft report to final form. Every person who processes the material is certain to inject some distortion into it. It is important that all such conversions, omissions, and alterations be found and corrected. This will mean checking and double-checking of original data. As a responsible research reporter, you should eliminate as many errors as possible. Only with such care and labor will the research report become error-free.

Clarity

Clarity is the ideal of all writing and is a skill that will sharply improve the chances that your research will have an impact on those who read it. Because research often involves new and unconventional methods, measurement, and theory, it is essential that it be communicated clearly. Although what is new doesn't have to be confusing, it often is, and you can be sure that such confusion will make it all the more difficult for you to persuade the reader of the accuracy and meaningfulness of your work.

How is such clarity achieved? The road to clarity lies in the process of thinking and rethinking the main statement of the problem, the theory, and the methodology. The statement of the research problem should be definitive, short, and declarative. Likewise, the hypothesis that must be tested should also be straightforward and declarative. The numerical data should be presented in simple and well-labeled tables. The written interpretations should address the data in the tables. Finally, you should draw only those conclusions that can be seen in the data presented.

Economy

Economy in report writing means telling the whole story without wasting words, space, or time. In the case of the research report that is published in a national journal, wordiness often means the loss of the article because publishers simply won't publish it! Some of the most influential pieces of research ever published have filled only five or six pages of journal space. Long, turgid, uneconomical writing, even if it is published, not only wastes journal space, but often alienates readers, who simply will not persist in reading to the conclusions.

A word about computers is necessary here, for it is certainly possible to generate, with the aid of a computer, dozens of tables from quantitative sources, and it is sometimes quite difficult to cut it off. Tables and computer-generated data must, like words, be there for a purpose, and the writer must exercise special care not to let them get out of hand. If these matters are not controlled, a long, rambling, overloaded report is produced. Such a strung-out report will generally exhaust the patience and the attention of all who come into contact with it. A short, direct, carefully organized report is much more effective and persuasive because the essential points are more readily identified and understood. Most finished reports can be compressed up to 25 percent with enormous gains in economy and effect.

Organization of the Research Report

Enough said about research report characteristics. What about the organization of the report? While there are a number of different ways to organize the research report, we believe that the organization used by journals for publication is as good as any. Since publication is usually the goal of research, you will have to have experience with the preferred style. In addition, with this organization you have an infinite number of resources (publications) to provide you with examples.

In general, the research report should include the following sections:

1. Abstract (summary of sections 2 through 5)
2. Introduction (includes a statement of the problem, a review of the relevant literature, and the hypotheses to be tested)
3. Methods (includes subjects, measures, and procedures)

4. Results (includes statistical analysis, which provides the basis for the tests of the hypotheses)
5. Discussion (includes interpretation of the results)
6. References (includes an alphabetical list of all references)
7. Tables (presentation of data in table form)
8. Appendix (includes any additional relevant information, such as questionnaire forms, figures, and mathematical formulas)

Abstract

The abstract is a summary of your entire research report and, as such, cannot be completely written until everything else is written. The abstract, which is found at the beginning of your research paper, gives your readers a chance to discover what your research is all about. To give your readers the fullest possible account, your abstract should contain information on all of the following: statement of the research problem, research design, results, and conclusions. *First, your abstract should provide your readers with a brief statement of the research problem.* While you cannot state your entire theory, you should introduce the purpose of your research. *Second, your abstract should briefly establish the basics of your research design.* This means characterizing your subject population (number, age, sex, etc.) and describing your research design, test instruments, research apparatus, or data-gathering procedures. *Third, your abstract should present your primary results.* This means summarizing your data findings in terms of statistical significance. *Finally, your abstract should present any conclusions drawn in your research.* In other words, provide a brief statement of any inferences drawn from your results.

This may seem like a lot of information for an abstract, and you may think you are rewriting your entire paper for this one section. Well, this is not entirely so, because your abstract cannot be quite as long. Rather, it should be between 100 and 200 words. The brevity of the abstract makes it quite a challenge. You may find it difficult to condense what you have done into fewer than 200 words. If you do feel this way, we want you to know that we sympathize. However, we challenge you to write this section as well as you can because many times it is the only section that is read. If you think you disagree with this, try to recall the number of articles that you looked at when doing your research and the number of articles that you actually read. What was the deciding factor?

The following is the abstract from an unpublished manuscript entitled "Assessing Women's Growth in Undergraduate Field Instruction" by Betty Dawson and Rebecca Guy. It is not presented as perfect. Rather, it is presented as a concrete example of what an abstract can look like.

William Perry's theory of intellectual and ethical growth provides the theoretical framework for this pre-test post-test quasi-experimental design, representing a systematic application of this important student development theory in social work education. Female BSW students enrolled in field instruction were tested on the Measure of Intellectual Development (MID).

Demographics also examined include age, race, marital status, and income level. Measures of central tendency, tests of significance, correlation and chi square techniques were used to analyze the data.

Several significant findings are noted. An inverse relationship was found between age of student and change score on the MID, with younger women experiencing significantly more positive change (i.e. growth) than older women. Similarly, an inverse relationship was found between MID pre-scores and positive change, highlighting the importance of the transition from Dualism to Multiplicity on Perry's scheme of development. No significant difference between the growth of black women and white women was found.

Introduction

The task of actually writing the research report begins with the introduction. Here you will want to inform your readers of your research problem, your chosen theoretical position, and the hypotheses you plan to test. While economy is an essential element in any good research report, you should not begin by diving right into your research problem. Begin by setting the stage at some broader level. The following is the introduction from "Assessing Women's Growth in Undergraduate Field Instruction" by Dawson and Guy. Again, this introduction is by no means perfect. If you had written it, you probably would have done some things differently. It is simply offered to you as a concrete example of this part of the research report.

Since the earliest days of social work education teachers have looked for signs of growth and development on the part of individual students. Through the years various theoretical frameworks and research measures have been applied to verify the effectiveness of how we teach and how students learn. The persistent need for sound research into these educational processes remains of particular interest to the profession at this time in order to discover and verify effectiveness.

Traditionally, a major component of the educational process for the social worker has been the intensive and structured experiential learning opportunity of field instruction. Because of many personal and idiosyncratic variations between placement agencies, students, and field instructors, this component has been a particular challenge when attempts have been made to assess its effectiveness. This writer has been interested in and has reflected on the patterns, processes, and evaluation of this element in the curriculum for more than a decade (Dawson, 1975).

William Perry's scheme of cognitive and ethical development (Perry, 1970) is a major theoretical framework which lends itself to assessing growth of social work students. The scheme, although widely applied in other professional educational settings, has not yet been applied in social work in any systematic way.

The original research by William Perry and his associates was done at Harvard in the 1950's, and later at Radcliffe. It arose from a study of students, and although it is primarily a model of student development, many applications can be made beyond this role. The theory is a stage model in the Piagetian tradition (King, 1978; Perry, 1981).

Perry found consistent patterns, not by personality differences, but by *forms* and *structures*, "… evolving ways of seeing the world, knowledge and education, values and oneself" (Perry, 1970, 1981). Knefelkamp, Widick, and Stroad (1976) describe this as a

> sequential and hierarchical development process in which the individual moves from the lower stages characterized by narrow-minded, stereotypic thinking, authoritarianism, and a defensive sense of self, to the upper stages characterized by open-mindedness, an ability to accept responsibility for the consequences of one's actions, and a commitment built on a positive self identity.

These stages can be applied across the span of a lifetime, and have particular significance for university students as they encounter experiences in an academic setting which promotes growth along this continuum.

The nine "positions" of Perry's scheme are generally grouped into four broad categories with clearly identifiable characteristics:

> *Dualism.* (Positions 1 and 2). The student makes meaning of his/her world by recognizing only two realms or polarities. They use discrete, concrete, and absolute categories to understand people, knowledge and values. The legitimacy of alternative perspectives is not yet acknowledged. ("We-Right-Good" vs. "They-Wrong-Bad") "Right answers" exist somewhere and are the domain of the Authority who should tell them.

> *Multiplicity.* (Positions 3 and 4). Diversity of opinion and alternative approaches are recognized as existing. Questions which in dualism had single answers now have multiple answers. Points of view are equally valid until the "Right answer" is discovered. No judgments are made between approaches since "everyone is entitled to his *(or her)* own opinion." By Position 4, students can see the difference between an unconsidered belief and a considered judgment.

> *Relativism.* (Positions 5 and 6). Students realize that knowledge is contextual and relative. Diversity derived from coherent sources allows for analysis and comparison. Students are able to think analytically and can evaluate their own ideas as well as those of others (i.e. think about thinking). The merits of the alternative perspectives are so clear that it becomes difficult to choose among them, fearing that to do so would sacrifice the appreciation for the other views. This significant step is sometimes referred to as the "cognitive flip."

> *Commitment in Relativism.* (Positions 7–9). At these upper stages there is recognition of diverse personal themes in life which must be balanced pro and con. There is the realization that commitments must

be made in the face of uncertainty and relative value. Life decisions such as marriage, religion, career are then made out of a relativistic frame of reference. Positions 8 and 9 represent the setting of priorities among commitments with respect to energy, action, and time (Perry, 1970).

This study is intended to investigate several issues relating to the intellectual and ethical growth of female BSW students which occurs during their field practicum experience, namely: (1) the degree of intellectual/ethical growth as measured on Perry's Scheme; (2) the effect of age on degree of intellectual/ethical growth; (3) and the differences in degree of intellectual/ethical growth experienced by black versus white women students.

The text reproduced here represents approximately two-thirds of the introduction to this article. If you read this part of the introduction closely, you should have noticed several significant things. *First, the opening sentence does not reference a journal.* Instead, it makes a general statement about the need for social work educators to verify the effectiveness of their methods used in social work field educational processes. If we were to characterize the research report from beginning to end, we could liken it to an hourglass. The research report begins at a broad level and becomes more and more specific as you present your own research. Then, as you interpret your own results, the research report broadens again. *Second, notice that the literature review that is incorporated into this part of the introduction summarizes the current state of knowledge.* It informs us of current relevant findings in the research area. *Third, notice that the literature review is composed of a limited number of references.* It doesn't try to cite every article written on the subject.

In general, it is not necessary and usually not possible to cite all journal articles, books, and reports that have an apparent relation to the research being reported. Instead, you should select a limited number of studies that are closely related to your research. A half-dozen relevant references are far more effective than two or three dozen references, including many of only secondary interest. It is important that you have cited the works of researchers who have made recognized contributions to the research area. Be sure you have examined research in related fields. Every serious researcher should dig into related scientific and technical fields as required to support or fortify each research project.

Notice also that the introduction addresses the theoretical framework of the research being reported. This does not mean a detailed description of procedures, which comes later in the methods section. But it does mean a look at the concepts integral to the reported research and the definitions of these concepts. You will also note that this introduction includes a specific listing of the hypotheses to be tested. In this example, three hypotheses are testable using an appropriate research design, and later sections of the research report should reflect evidence for or against each of these hypotheses.

The theory presented may take one of two forms. It may be general theory, historically built up from philosophical and scientific writings. Or it may be specific theory formulated for an individual research project. In this introduction, for example, we see a specific theory reported, and its relevance for the research design discussed.

Methods

As we discussed in an earlier chapter, the research design is the plan by which your research is accomplished. The importance of this plan cannot be overemphasized since another researcher must use it in order to report, test, and prove your theory. Put simply, this plan must be described as simply and in as much detail as possible. The process of repeating research is called *replication* or repetition of the research, and either this procedure will verify the research and increase the support for the theory or it will fail, indicating that the theory is still in doubt. In short, the methods section includes a detailed account of all of the research procedures used to gain evidence for hypothesis testing, including (1) selection of subjects, (2) measurement, (3) data collection, and (4) data processing. Let's take a brief look at each of these important components.

The methods section usually begins by indicating the number of human *subjects* used and describing how these subjects were divided into groups. If your sample is supposed to represent a large theoretical population, the research report must describe fully the random selection process by which the sample was chosen. At the same time, the presumed character of the sampled population should be made explicit. If a table of random numbers is used to select telephone numbers from a city telephone directory, for example, then the population from which this sample is taken is confined to names listed in that directory. It does not include unlisted telephone numbers, new institutions, and individuals not yet listed. If you are a meticulous researcher, you will recognize and estimate the true character of the population that you are sampling. If you decide to use some other method of sample selection, then you must describe this sampling method, together with the number of cases drawn. And the number must be large enough to represent reasonably well a large, heterogeneous population. In instances such as our example when very small numbers are used, great care must be exercised in describing the sample. This will be helpful in enabling the reader to place the research in perspective during the interpretation phase which comes later.

The methods section must also delineate carefully the *measuring instruments* used in your research. Measurements that are so elegant and so definitive in the natural sciences (e.g., mass, energy, velocity, volume, and distance) are scarcely known in social work. This is partly because social work researchers deal with such complicated factors as the effectiveness of clinical interventions, interpersonal relationships, or the efficiency of social agencies. While basic questions have long since been settled by definitive experimentation in the natural sciences, simple questions in social work remain unresolved despite the research efforts of our leading institutions. It is here that the contemporary researcher has the most profound problem but yet the greatest opportunity. Most current measures are implicit in statistical tests, and as the researcher, you must be careful to choose measures that satisfy the requirements of reliable statistical tests.

Finally, *data collection* and *data processing techniques* must be described in sufficient detail that another researcher could repeat them exactly in another research project with the same test objectives. If assistants were used, how were they trained? What was the chronology of the research operations? What was the sequence of contacts with agencies or individuals to be involved or concerned with the project? If instruments were used for measurements, they should be described in enough technical detail that equivalent instrumentation could be developed and applied elsewhere. In addition, relevant environmental conditions such as light, sound, and social conditions should be described in terms of their possible effect on the collection of data.

If instruments such as questionnaires and interviews were used, how were they applied? How did the presence and actions of a researcher seem to affect the respondents? Were gender effects recorded and taken into account? What provisions were made to elicit cooperation and responses from human subjects? What were the intrinsic rewards to human respondents? How and in what direction did these rewards affect subjects' responses? For example, if mailed questionnaires were sent to and intended for employed mothers of school-age children, what steps were taken to identify and exclude questionnaires filled out by unqualified respondents? Finally, what provisions were made to find and eliminate errors in coding the data and in preparing it for statistical analysis?

Let's take a look at the methods section of our research example.

Subjects

The subjects for this study are sixteen (n = 16) female social work majors who were seniors at Memphis State University beginning and completing their required 400 clock hours of field instruction between January of 1985 and May of 1986. This program also calls for the students to be concurrently enrolled in an integrative seminar which meets every two weeks at the university under the direction of the faculty field liaison. Two males were eliminated from the study in order to hold gender constant. Also, two females from foreign countries were not included in order to hold culture constant. The subjects ranged in age from 21 to 36 years, with an average of 26.38. Of the 16 women, seven were black and nine were white. The average age of the black students was 28.86; the average age of the white students was 24.44.

Instrumentation

The instrument used in this study was the Measure of Intellectual Development (MID) developed by Knefelkamp and associates (Knefelkamp, 1974; Widick, 1975; Mentkowski, Moeser, Strait, 1983). Demographic data were also collected.

Measure of Intellectual Development (MID). The women were asked to write a protocol of essays, one within the first two weeks of beginning the first semester of field placement, and the second within the last two weeks of finishing the second semester of field placement. In the first of the two essays (Essay A) they were asked to describe their best high school or college class.

In the second essay (Essay AP), students were asked to describe their ideal learning environment. The essays must be content-analyzed and scored by trained raters. For this study the essays were scored at the Center for Applications of Developmental Instruction. [CADI, 806 High Street, Farmville, VA 23901.]

Scoring. Perry scores are reported in intervals of three per position, such as 222, 223, 233 (scores of 222 through 555 correspond to a particular stage of Dualism, Multiplicity or Relativism). The first digit denotes the dominant stage of a position; the second and third denoting transition. For example, a 223 represents early transition to a new position; 233 represents further movement in that transition. For purposes of this study, each interval is regarded as one step; therefore a student may move two steps within a position and not change positions. For example, a student may have a score on Essay A of 223 and a score on Essay AP of 233. While a score of 223 represents "dominant position 2, opening to position 3" a score of 233 indicates "dominant position 3 with trailing position 2." Thus the ratings reflect an assessment of the cognitive complexity with respect to learning as displayed by the essay (Moore, 1986). There is sufficient evidence to suggest that the Perry Scheme continuum represents an interval scale (Rest, 1980; Moore, 1986; Nunnelly, 1967). Use of the instrument at this measurement level requires only that the ratings be converted to numerical scores. This conversion is based on the assumption that each digit in the Perry score represents one-third of a position. For example, 222 becomes 2.0, 223 becomes 2.33, and 233 becomes 2.67.

Other Variables. Socio-demographic variables were also collected and include race measured as blacks and whites, age measured in years, and income measured in intervals: (1) below $10,000, (2) $11,000–$25,000, (3) $26,000–$35,000, (4) $36,000–$50,000, and (5) above $50,000.

Procedure

The women participating in this study represent three distinct groups with respect to when they began and ended their field placements. Group One (n=3) began field placement in the Spring of 1985 (January), and completed it in the Summer of 1985 (August). Group Two (n=3) began in the Summer of 1985 (May) and completed it in the Fall of 1985 (December). Group Three (n=10) began placement in the Fall of 1985 (September) and ended in the Spring of 1986 (May).

The field instruction component of the Social Work program is standardized with respect to the amount of time spent in the field, the utilization of an agency-based field instructor, time spent in the integrative seminar with the same faculty field liaison, and the written assignments required. Each student also writes a reflective journal entry each week which is reviewed and responded to by the faculty field liaison. Because of this high level of standardization in the field component, these three groups were combined for the purposes of this study.

The data collection procedures utilized with these three groups were identical. Within the first two weeks of each group's field experience, the MID (Essay A) was administered. At the same time the demographic information was collected. Essay AP was administered within the last two weeks of each student's field experience at the end of the second semester.

As earlier noted, the methods section of the research report includes a description of the sample selected, the measurements used, and the data collection and data processing procedures. If you look closely at the methods section presented here, you should find all of these elements. It identifies the number of human subjects used and describes how they were grouped. Since a random sample was not selected, it must be clear how the sample was obtained. It describes the research instrument and how it was applied, and this description is in detail. It describes what was done and in what sequence. Some research reports might also delineate the verbal instructions that subjects received and describe the training and preparation necessary for coding the data. This example shows how the scoring of the instrument was done. In short, this methods section provides the kind of detail that would be necessary if this research were to be replicated.

Presentation of the Results

The fourth section of the research report is the results section. The results that are of primary interest to your readers are the findings that relate immediately to your research hypotheses. As the researcher, you will probably want to search the data for those findings that support your theory and your hypotheses. It is important, though, that you examine the data with objectivity, looking at both the positive and negative findings. While positive findings do suggest the success of your research project and the correctness of the theory, they should be carefully reviewed and verified to establish the actual degree of support. If the evidence is clear and overwhelming, then a claim of success is justified. More often in social research, though, the degree of support is actually limited and marginal. And along with this limited and marginal support, there may be some anomalous findings that call into question the relevance of the theory and the hypotheses. In fact, it is not uncommon for portions of the data to reject the theory by contradicting the hypotheses.

The maximum value of research comes from a thorough and correct evaluation of results in relation to test hypotheses. When the results are inconclusive, no conclusion should be drawn. The theory is not supported, and the research question remains open. If the theory appears to be overturned, you must report this without equivocation. Remember, research "fails" only when you fail to report results that are interpreted honestly and in line with the facts.

To get a more concrete picture of the results section of the research report, let's look at the results section of our ongoing research example.

To test the null hypothesis that female social work students do not experience significant growth during their field practicum experience as measured on the MID, differences between pre- and post-scores were assessed using the t-test for paired samples. The findings support the null hypothesis; specifically the growth experienced does not appear to reach statistical significance (see Table 1). Hence, the null hypothesis is not rejected. However, what change is measured is in the positive direction. That is, the women entered their field practicum experience with an average Perry score of 2.92 (in transition from Dualism to Multiplicity) and completed their field experience with an average Perry score 3.06 (in Early Multiplicity).

The insignificant change statistic is reflective of the disproportionate number of students already in Multiplicity. Table 2 shows the distribution of the pre-scores on the MID for the total group. Of the 16 women, 5 were in transition from Dualism (i.e. "trailing Dualism"), one at position 223 and four at 233. Nine were in Early Multiplicity (all 333's), and two were in transition to Late Multiplicity (334's). Of the five women entering field work in transition from Dualism, all five experienced positive change, with three advancing two-thirds position and two advancing one-third position. This growth advanced four of the five into Multiplicity with one remaining in transition at 233, having advanced from 223.

Table 3 compares the pre- and post-scores of the five students entering field experience in transitional Dualism (positions 223 and 233) using the t-test for paired samples. As demonstrated, significant positive change does occur (tdf = 4 = –6.66; p = .003).

In marked contrast, seven of the nine students entering their field education experience in Early Multiplicity (333) did not advance. One of the remaining two grew one-third position, and one regressed one-third position (see Table 4).

Of the two women entering field experience in position 334, one did not show change on her score and one regressed one-third position to 333. In short, the significant positive change observed among the transition Dualists was not observed with the transition Multiplists.

In summary, while the growth on the MID cannot be evaluated as statistically significant for the total sample, the data does indicate significant positive change (i.e. growth) for students entering field experience at the transitional Dualistic positions. These findings are further substantiated by the correlation coefficient between the pre-score on the MID and change scores for the total sample (r = –.74; p < .01). This correlation suggests an inverse relationship between pre-score and change score. That is, those individuals entering with the lowest MID scores (e.g. 223 and 233) experienced the greatest positive change while those entering with the highest MID scores (e.g. 333 and 334) experienced almost no change.

To test the hypothesis that there is no relationship between age and positive change experienced during the field practicum, a Pearson r Product-Moment correlation coefficient was computed. Findings indicate that age and change are inversely related (r = –.55; p < .05). Hence, the null hypothesis is rejected. The inverse relationship between age and change clearly suggest that the younger women changed more than the older women. To insure that the observed relationship between age and change is not spurious, further analysis was undertaken. Given the significant inverse relationship between pre-score on the MID and change on the MID discussed earlier, a strong positive correlation between pre-score and age might suggest that the relationship between age and change is merely a function of pre-score working though age. If this is the case, once pre-score is controlled for, the relationship between age and change should disappear (Gut, et al., 1986). To test for this possibility, the zero-order correlation between pre-score on the MID and age was computed and found to be insignificant ($r = .31$; $p > .05$).

Additionally, the partial correlation coefficient between age and change was computed controlling for pre-score. This test suggests that the relationship between age and change scores controlling for pre-score on the MID is significant ($r = -.51$; $p < .05$). In fact, the correlation between age and change is barely diminished by the control of pre-scores on the MID. The significant inverse correlation between age and change controlling for pre-scores on the MID supports rejection of the hypothesis of no relationship between age and positive change on the MID experienced during the field practicum. In summary, the statistical evidence demonstrates that younger women experience greater positive change (i.e. growth) on the MID than do older women.

The fourth hypothesis looks at the question of significant difference between the average MID change scores for black women versus white women. The average change scores for blacks and whites is displayed in Table 6. To test the hypothesis a t-test for independent samples was computed. As speculated, no statistical significance was found between average MID change scores for blacks and whites. Hence, the null hypothesis was not rejected.

Congruent with this finding, as shown in Table 7, a comparison of the mean pre-scores on the MID by race produced no significant differences ($tdf = 14 = -1.51$; $p > .05$). Restated, both statistical procedures suggest that blacks and whites do not differ significantly on average pre- and change scores on the MID.

Given the significant inverse relationship between pre-scores on the MID and the MID change scores, the extent to which race influences change scores was further examined controlling for pre-scores on the MID as shown in Table 8.

Specifically, an analysis of covariance (ANOVA) was used to assess the extent to which race influences change on the MID while controlling for pre-score on the MID. Congruent with the earlier findings, the covariance model supports the significant influence of pre-scores on change scores, and fails to support the significant influence of race on change scores. In effect, with pre-score controlled for, race remains an insignificant influence on change scores.

If you have read this results section closely, you should notice at least two significant things. First, it is important to note that this section of the research report focuses on results—that is, research findings. *Each hypothesis and the evidence providing a test of each hypothesis are presented.* This evidence is evaluated statistically and conclusions are drawn. Restated, the evidence either supports or fails to support the hypothesis. Second, notice the absence of interpretations in this section of the research report. This is because *the results section is not concerned with interpretation*. It is concerned with the actual findings. The interpretations applied to these findings are presented in the discussion section of the research report.

Discussion Section

The fifth section of the research report is the discussion section. In this section you must provide a full explanation of your research findings. Remember, the connection of findings with theory is always indirect. The findings relate directly to the test hypotheses, not to the theory. Within this section, at least six specific tasks must be accomplished. Let's take a look at each of these.

Your first task in the discussion section is to explain to what degree the test hypotheses are supported by the data. The weight and direction of the evidence are reported together with reasonable arguments for your conclusions. All test hypotheses must be reviewed, preferably in the same order in which they were originally stated. In rare cases, you will be able to claim strong positive support for each hypothesis. If this is possible, you have taken a major step in convincing your skeptical readers. Such positive support is also likely to motivate some other researchers in the field to replicate your research to test whether the conclusions can be supported with the same kind of source materials and methodology in another setting.

The second task is to show the relationship between your test hypotheses and your theory. As we have already noted, this connection cannot be proved. It can only be made to appear plausible. However, you are now in a better position to support your theoretical statement based on your research procedures, findings, and hypotheses that are logically implied by the theory. Support for your theoretical statement depends on the harmony and mutual implications among all elements of your research operation. It is your responsibility to show care, veracity, and insight in all phases of your project, including the research report. And remember, if support for the test hypotheses is mixed, weak, or missing, you really have no support or confirmation for your theory.

Your third task in the discussion section is to indicate conservatively how the data justify the conclusions. Most good research begins with a reasonable question and ends with a reasonable doubt. Even in the rare cases where there appears to be complete and strong support for the theory, conservatism in making claims is certainly preferable. After all, research represents only one step by one person, presumably on an important and difficult question. The success claimed in the report is really dependent on its credibility when presented to skeptical readers. Further, it must hold up against challenges from many directions because it is the function of the research community to question and to challenge until reasonable doubts have been resolved. (And what is "reasonable" is often in doubt too!) If you are a serious researcher, you will come to expect questions, doubts, and denial from others until repeated tests of the theory can firmly settle the question. If the data support the test hypotheses only in part, then claims for support of the theory come clearly into question. As the research reporter, you should openly acknowledge that the research question remains open because the theory is not well confirmed—though it may not be wrong either.

MID Scores of Subjects

This study of senior female field practicum students has revealed several interesting findings. First, in regard to what one might expect to find in relation to average Perry scores by college classification, this study found that the average Perry position for the senior subjects was 2.92 at the beginning of their field practicum and 3.06 at the end of the experience. This points to the fact that, by comparison, the women in this study came into their senior year field practicum with a slightly lower average score than one might find in other studies; and they finished their senior year at a slightly lower point than that expected from the review of literature (Meyer, 1975, 1977; Blake, 1976; Clinchy, Lief, and Young, 1977; Murrell, 1986). Their Perry positions, however, seem similar to those indicated in other studies (Widick, 1975; Parker, 1978; Mellon and Sass, 1981). Two possible reasons for this finding are offered. The first has to do with the level of educational disadvantage with which many of these women initially enter college. Regions of the South are renowned for the historical and persisting discriminations against minorities and rural populations in their educational systems and institutions. Demographics of the women in this study show that at least nine of the sixteen are from rural areas and/or belong to a minority group. Therefore, the struggle for growth is compounded.

Secondly, the literature points to the importance of Dualists being exposed early in their college careers to multiple perspectives and issues without clearcut answers or solutions (Heath, 1968; Widick, Knefelkamp, and Parker, 1975). It is possible that the general education foundational courses taken previously have not fulfilled this challenge adequately. The overall picture of this study's findings is one of "transition into Multiplicity," which is rather consistent with other research findings which place graduating seniors, male and female, in the Early Multiplistic positions.

In summary of this point, the sixteen BSW field practicum students in this study showed entry Perry scores slightly lower than that found in some other studies, though not markedly lower. Their post-scores likewise placed them slightly lower than where several other studies would indicate, but solidly in Early Multiplicity. Parker (1978) and Widick (1975) have concluded that few students move beyond Multiplicity during their four years of undergraduate education; and this study revealed that no student in the study had achieved Relativism. Since no woman entered field instruction with a score of 4.0 (Late Multiplicity) or higher, there was no opportunity to study any potential change in the higher positions. While the growth achieved did not reach statistical significance, what change was measured was in the positive direction. Significance was achieved, however, when looking at the change scores of those women entering field experience with "trailing Dualism," producing a significant inverse relationship between entry MID and change scores. All five experienced growth, with three of them moving two steps (two-thirds position), and two advancing one step (one-third position). A positive change of two-thirds position is quite impressive within the span of eight months.

The Importance of Transition

The inverse relationship between pre-score and change score also lends support to the findings and literature regarding the importance of transitions between positions (Perry, 1970, 1978; Widick, 1978; Cooper and Lewis, 1983; Goldberger, Marwine, and Paskus, 1978). Piaget has pointed out that it is the "assimilations" of new learning that we tend to remember, rather than the "accommodations" (Perry, 1981). The five women in the study who displayed the greatest growth entered field instruction as "trailing Dualists." This transition signals an opening to cognitive complexity, allowing for multiple perspectives to be seen and pondered. When the lid on this "Pandora's box" is once cracked, it seems that rapid acceleration into Multiplicity can and often does occur. The finding reported here supports previous findings and literature regarding the importance of experiential learning, such as that gleaned in field education, to set the stage for and promote this process.

Age of Subjects

The average age of the women entering field instruction was 26.38 years, with a range of 21 to 36 years. The overall picture, then, is one of women who are considered non-traditional aged students. The findings of this study clearly show an inverse relationship between age and change score on the MID, with younger students demonstrating higher change scores than older students. One possible explanation for this finding is that, since the younger women tended to enter field instruction as "trailing Dualists," while older women tended to have already reached Multiplicity in their development, this age difference was actually a function of lower vs. higher entry MID scores. Statistical analysis, however, demonstrated that this is not the case. This finding is not congruent with at least one other study (Strange, 1978) which found no difference in correlation between age of student and MID score.

Race and Change Scores

This finding indicates that there is no evidence of any differences between black and white women in potential for growth in the field practicum experience. Likewise, there is no evidence that the educational experiences offered to students in the assigned social services agencies were not equally growth-producing for blacks and whites.

Demographics—Annual Income and Marital Status

Demographics indicated that two whites of the nine in the study and three blacks of the seven were in the lowest annual household income category. These five women with annual incomes below $10,000, represent 31 percent of the total group. Likewise, four blacks and no whites were in the income category of $11,000 to $25,000 (25%). The income category of $26,000 to

$35,000 showed six whites and no blacks (38%). There were no subjects in the $36,000 to $50,000 category. The one subject in the highest income category (over $50,000) was white. In short, one hundred percent of the blacks were in the two lowest annual income categories, while seven of the nine whites (78 percent) had an annual income of $26,000 or more. These percentages point to the economic disparity between black and white social work majors in this specific test group. A chi square test of relationship between race and income revealed this to be a significant pattern ($X^2 = 7.87$; $p < .02$). In short, blacks were significantly more likely to be in the lower income categories than whites. Additionally, when marital status was held constant, extreme income disparity between married whites and married blacks was revealed ($p > .05$), with blacks showing significantly less income than whites. This did not hold true, however, for single blacks and single whites in this study.

A fourth task in the discussion section is to identify weaknesses in your research project. One of the primary contributions any researcher can make to an area of study is the presentation of research findings with candor and honesty. In our example study, one obvious weakness to be noted in the discussion section is the small number in the sample, which would definitely influence the study's generalizability. As the research reporter, you must identify and describe the weak elements in your project from beginning to end. Is there any evidence in light of the research experience that the theory was misconceived from the beginning? Certainly, you have made an important discovery if you have determined that a plausible and generally accepted theory is in error.

Robert Merton once began a major research project on the influence of the printed media on readers assuming, as most publishers and advertisers did, that the effect of printed materials is direct on general readers [1]. The media tended to assume an uninformed readership for editorials and advertisements. Merton and his associates started field research with this theory, but soon found that local opinion leaders were the main source of influence in a small circle of acquaintances. In effect, the opinion leaders were the direct consumers of media persuasion. The bulk of the general readers reserved judgment on media appeals until they heard the opinions of an acquaintance who had a special interest and was presumably more knowledgeable about the policy, candidate, or product. Merton changed his theory to the two-step theory of media influence: (1) from publisher to topical opinion leader and (2) from opinion leader to concerned citizen. Merton's study is a good example of how theory is modified in the course of the research process. In short, as research reporter, you should review the main elements of the research process. You should explain areas where problems arose and areas where the information was incomplete, biased, or unknown. Questionnaire responses, for example, do not present facts from the empirical world, but only the claims of the respondent from his or her own viewpoint. It is important to notice such biases and limitations when writing the research report.

A fifth task of the discussion section is to suggest specific questions for further research. A research project is an attempt to learn more about an unknown phenomenon. It usually represents a unique venture and a substantial investment of time, effort, resources, and thought. On concluding a research project, you are in the position of expert. You have a great deal of knowledge on certain aspects of the theory and its relationship to the world. This is the time to outline related questions that require further research. Don't hesitate to recommend what else needs to be done to establish the research theory more completely. Is there some evidence that the research is on the wrong track, whereas the right track is now in view? If so, set forth an improved formulation of the theory. Are there weak areas in the research procedure? If so, identify them and indicate what is needed to avoid such weaknesses in future research.

The sixth task of the discussion section is to indicate new directions for research. The best research is often research that points the way to future study rather than having the last word on a given subject. Research is an ongoing process of discovery, not an attempt to corner the truth so that no one else will ever need study an area again.

Some answered questions were highlighted by our example study: (1) How would the outcomes have been different if the sample had included males as well as females? (2) What differences would have been found if some subjects had tested in the higher positions on the MID pretest? New directions for further research suggested might include comparing the growth process of MSW students with BSW students, or looking at the influence of the agency field instructor's score on the growth process of the student.

References

The sixth section of the research report is the reference section. In this section, you must list every bibliographic reference used in the body of your paper. While the style for references should be consistent throughout your paper, there are several acceptable styles. One of the most widely used reference styles in journals is the author and year notation within the body of the text with references listed alphabetically by author and year at the end of the paper. This is called the *Harvard method* and is used, for example, by the National Association of Social Workers, the American Sociological Association, and the American Psychological Association journals. (This is also the method used in our research example.) To illustrate: Perry found consistent patterns, not by personality differences, but by forms and structures, "... evolving ways of seeing the world, knowledge and education, values and oneself" (Perry, 1970, 1981). The complete reference for this example would appear at the end of the research paper and would list author, year of publication, title, and source.

A second method of identifying references within a research report is the *serial method*. This is the style used in this text. With this method, references are numbered in the order in which they are cited in the text, and they are then listed in that same order at the end of the article. This represents an older journalistic style by which the same references could be listed more than once at the end of the article. It is less convenient for researchers who may be primarily concerned with the references and sources, since they are not listed in standard order, but it provides a ready reference for the reader.

A third method of identifying references is the *alphabet–number system*. With this method, the references are ordered alphabetically by author and then numbered serially. Only the reference number is inserted in the text. This method is slowly gaining favor because it saves space and results in less disruption of the text. With this method, if the Perry reference were the twelfth reference in the alphabetized reference listing, the text would read: "... evolving ways of seeing the world, knowledge and education, values and oneself" (12). Again, regardless of the method you choose, remember to be consistent. The reference section from our ongoing research example is included here to give you once again some concrete examples. You will notice a variety of types of entries, including single author of a book, more than one author of a book, journal articles, chapter in an edited volume, unpublished dissertation or manuscript, and unpublished raw data.

References

Blake, L. (1976). *A measure of developmental change: a cross-sectional study.* Paper presented at the Annual Meeting of the American Psychological Association, Washington, D. C.

Clinchy, Blythe, Lief, Judy, and Young, Pamela. Epistemological and moral development in girls from a traditional and a progressive high school. *Journal of Educational Psychology,* 1977, **69,** 337–343.

Cooper, Terry D., and Lewis, Judith A. The crisis of relativism: helping counselors cope with diversity. *Counselor Education and Supervision,* 1983, **22,** 290-295.

Dawson, Betty G. (1975). Supervising the undergraduate in a psychiatric setting. *The dynamics of field instruction: learning through doing.* New York: Council on Social Work Education.

Goldberger, Nancy, Marwine, Alan, and Paskus, John (1978). *The relationship between intellectual stage and the behavior of college freshmen in the classroom.* Unpublished manuscript, Simon's Rock College.

Guy, Rebecca F., Edgley, Charles K., Arafat, lbtihaj, and Allen, Donald E. (1986). *Social research methods: puzzles and solutions.* Boston: Allyn and Bacon.

Heath, E. H. (1968). *Growing up in college.* San Francisco: Jossey-Bass.

King, Patricia M. (1978). William Perry's theory of intellectual and ethical development. In L. Knefelkamp, C. Widick, and C. A. Parker (Eds.), *New directions for student services: applying new developmental findings* 4. San Francisco: Jossey-Bass.

Knefelkamp, Lee (1974). *Developmental instruction: fostering intellectual and personal growth in college students.* Unpublished doctoral dissertation, University of Minnesota, Minneapolis.

Knefelkamp, Lee, Widick, Carole, and Stroad, Barbara. Cognitive-developmental theory: a guide to counseling women. *The Counseling Psychologist,* 1976, **6,** 15–19.

Mellon, Constance, and Sass, Edmond. Perry and Piaget: theoretical framework for effective college course development. *Educational Technology,* 1981, **21,** 29–33.

Mentkowski, Marcia, Moeser, Mary, and Strait, Michael, J. (1983). *Using the Perry scheme of intellectual development as a college outcomes measure: a process and criteria for assessing student performance.* Milwaukee, WI: Alverno Productions.

Meyer, P. Intellectual development: analysis of religious content. *The Counseling Psychologist*, 1977, **6**, 47–50.

Meyer, P. (1975). *Intellectual development of college students as measured by analysis of religious content.* Unpublished doctoral dissertation, University of Minnesota, Minneapolis.

Moore, William S. (1986). *Interpreting ratings on the measure of intellectual development.* Unpublished manuscript, Center for Applications for Developmental Instruction, Farmville, VA.

Murrell, Patricia H. (1986). [Perry scores of freshmen in a small, sectarian liberal arts college]. Unpublished raw data.

Nunnally, James (1967). *Psychometric theory.* New York: McGraw Hill.

Parker, Clyde A. (1978). *Encouraging development in college students.* Minneapolis: University of Minnesota Press.

Perry, William G., Jr. (1981). Cognitive and ethical growth: the making of meaning. In Arthur W. Chickering (Ed.), *The modern American college,* San Francisco: Jossey-Bass.

Perry, William G., Jr. (1970). *Forms of intellectual and ethical development in the college years: a scheme.* New York: Holt, Rinehart, & Winston.

Rest, James. Development in moral judgment research. *Developmental Psychologist,* 1980, **16**, 251–256.

Strange, C. C. (1978). *Intellectual development, motive for education and learning styles during the college years: a comparison of adult and traditional-age students.* Unpublished doctoral dissertation, University of Iowa.

Widick, Carole C. (1975). *An evaluation of developmental instruction in a university setting.* Unpublished doctoral dissertation, University of Minnesota, Minneapolis.

Widick, Carole C., and Simpson, Deborah (1978). Developmental concepts in college instruction. In Clyde A. Parker (Ed.), *Encouraging development in college students.* Minneapolis: University of Minnesota Press.

Tables

The seventh section of the research report includes all tables that support the results section. Although the tables are really a part of the results section, they are not placed directly in the body of this section. Instead, they are placed at the end of the paper in their own section to avoid disrupting the smooth flow of the text.

Each table in your research report should be typed on a separate sheet of paper. Each should be given a table number and a title. The table number is extremely important since this number is used to reference the table within the body of the text. The title is also important since it gives the reader some idea of what the table is showing. The information included in the table should be labeled with great care to ensure that it can be interpreted on its own without reference to the text. This means that if columns are headed by numbers or letters, there should be a legend with the table that identifies the meaning of those headings. In every case, the headings chosen should reflect relevant, mutually exclusive, and logically exhaustive categories within the context of the table. Generally, independent categories are distributed by column, and the dependent categories are distributed by row. Each table in your research paper must be referenced within the text. The following tables are taken from our research example.

Table 2

Distribution of the pre-Scores on MID
for Total Group

MID Pre-Scores	Frequency	%
223	1	6.3
233	4	25.0
333	9	56.3
334	2	12.5
	16	100.0

Table 3

A Comparison of Pre- and Post-MID Scores
for Students Entering in Transitional Dualism

	N	M	sd	t	p
Pre-MID	5	2.60	.15	−6.66	.003
Post-MID	5	3.13	.30		

Table 8

A Comparison of Mean Change on MID by Race
Controlling for Pre-MID

	SS	df	MS	F	p
Covariates Pre-MID	.828	1	.828	16.47	< .001
Main Effects Race	.040	1	.04	.80	> .050
Residual	.653	13	.05		

Appendix

Although an appendix is rarely called for, it is helpful under certain circumstances. *The criterion for including an appendix should be whether it improves your readers' chances of understanding, evaluating, or replicating your study.* Some examples of suitable materials for an appendix might include (1) a new computer program specifically designed for your research and unavailable elsewhere, (2) an unpublished test and its validation, and (3) a complicated mathematical proof.

Rewriting the Research Report

After completing the written report, you should edit the manuscript with great care, keeping in mind the variety of readers. Does the title correctly suggest the content of your report? Is the ordering of ideas correct, or could it be improved? Do all sentences make sense? Are the spelling and punctuation correct? Can the tables be improved by condensation or more informative titles and subheadings? Is the level of precision reasonable? (Two decimal places are sufficient for correlation and regression values and are usually satisfactory for probability or confidence levels.)

If any portions of the research report are confusing, be sure you take time to rewrite them. Be careful to write all numerals and symbols clearly, with open space around them. Scruffy copy given to your typist delays the typing and invites errors and misreading. The easier the manuscript is for the typist, the better will be the finished product. At this point, then, the report should be typed (or put on a word processor) in clean final form, complete with all sections. But don't breathe a sigh of relief yet. You are not finished! Your printed or typed report is now ready for a preliminary review by several classmates, who can serve as knowledgeable and discriminating critics. Your classmates are in a good position to help you discover and correct defects that would bring negative comments from your instructor. Ask your classmates to be demanding of your text—to mark errors and make critical notes on their copies.

Your classmates' recommendations will represent several viewpoints, some of which may be contradictory. You should survey all comments, correct errors of typing, fact, and reference, and then begin to integrate those recommendations that best present the subject. This is not the time to hurry or save labor. Since your classmates have spent time identifying faults, weak arguments, and oversights, you should thoroughly recast the material so as to meet the criticism as fully as possible. This may require some further analysis of data and a reformulation of tables, discussion, and conclusions. Whatever the cost, it is time and resources well spent in order to bring the research report up to the highest possible standard. By now your paper is in its third or fourth draft and is ready to be retyped or corrected on your computer and printed.

While the procedures described here may seem like a lot of work, they will help to ensure that yours is a worthwhile document. If you follow these steps persistently, you should produce a meaningful research report. Happy research writing, and may all your words be well chosen and wise!

References

1. Robert K. Merton, *Social Theory and Social Structure* (New York: The Free Press, 1949).

__ APPENDIX A _____

Using SPSS X and SPSS PC+

The popularity of SPSS (Statistical Package for the Social Sciences) and its widespread use both in the academic and nonacademic communities have led to numerous revisions of this package—the most recent of which are SPSS X, SPSS PC+, and SPSS MAC. This appendix will deal with only two of these recent versions: SPSS X and SPSS PC+. Since SPSS X and SPSS PC+ are very similar, we will consider both packages in this single appendix.

SPSS (both X and PC versions) is a comprehensive statistical package of considerable magnitude. There is really no way that this chapter can cover all that this package is capable of doing. The *SPSS X User's Guide* and the *SPSS PC+ Base Manual* are each 800 plus pages in length! Instead we will simply attempt to introduce you to the package as it works in both a mainframe and an MS-DOS micro environment. If you wish more information than is provided here or more in-depth information on the mainframe version, consult the *SPSS X User's Guide*. For more information on the microcomputer version, see the *SPSS PC+ Base Manual*.

As with any SPSS program, proper execution requires that you use appropriate computer control commands (sometimes called Job Control Language commands). The control commands that you will need with SPSS depend upon the computer system you are using. Your instructor can provide you with the control commands specific to your school's computer system.

The Language of SPSS X and SPSS PC+

While there are several ways to enter SPSS commands into SPSS PC+ and SPSS X, perhaps the simplest and most economical is through the use of a command file. Very simply, a COMMAND FILE is a file containing all SPSS instructions for a specific computer run.[1] This file can contain every kind of SPSS statement and even raw data. Our presentation of SPSS (both X and PC+) will assume that you are building

---

[1]Many text editors and word processors can be used to build a COMMAND file. You should check with your instructor for the editor and/or word processor to use and for instructions on how to use it.

a command file. If you wish to execute SPSS commands using interactive SPSS on a mainframe, you will need to get specific instructions from your instructor. If you wish to use interactive SPSS PC+, see the *SPSS PC+ Base Manual*.

Every SPSS command (whether X or PC version) begins with a COMMAND keyword (one or more words) and a SPECIFICATION field. While a few commands are complete in themselves, most do require specifications. SPECIFICATIONS, as we shall see, can be comprised of *names, keywords, numbers, literals, arithmetic operators, special delimiters,* and *spacing* needed to separate these various elements. COMMAND keywords *always* begin in column one. In both SPSS X and SSPS PC+, the SPECIFICATION field begins at least one column after the COMMAND keyword (i.e., one column separating the COMMAND and the SPECIFICATION field) and continues for as many lines as required. SPSS X requires that column one be left blank on continuation lines (to indicate to the computer that a line *is* a continuation). Leaving column one blank in SPSS PC+ is not necessary (although not incorrect) as all SPSS PC+ commands *must* end with a period (.). Hence, if a command spans three lines, the period is the last character on the third line. Generally, the maximum length of an input line is 80 characters, but this can vary by type of computer. Again, you should check with your instructor for this maximum line length for your computer. SPSS X and SPSS PC+ accept commands in both upper and lower case—so you may use whichever case you prefer.

SPSS (henceforth, both X and PC+) commands fall basically into four categories: (1) data definition, (2) data transformation, (3) data selection, and (4) procedure commands. In this appendix, we will take a close look at each of these four categories.

Data Definition Commands

Data definition commands tell SPSS how to read and interpret your data. This process involves (1) assigning a name to each variable you want to include in your analysis and (2) specifying the location and format of each variable within the data file (i.e., DATA LIST command). In addition to this information, you must identify any values to be treated as MISSING, and you can provide any VARIABLE LABELS and/or VALUE LABELS you want included with your printout. SPSS uses all of this information to build a dictionary that describes the variables on the active file. Let's take a closer look at the most essential data definition commands.

DATA LIST Command

The keyword command for defining "raw" data in SPSS is DATA LIST. Unlike other versions of this package, in both SPSS X and SPSS PC+, this is the only method for defining "raw" data. The general form for DATA LIST is:

```
DATA LIST FILE='FN'/ VAR1 1 VAR2 2-3 VAR3 4-6(1)
```

where:

DATA LIST	is the keyword for this command
FILE=	is the keyword for identifying the name of the "raw data" file
FN	is the name given to this "raw data" file (must be in single quotes)
VAR1	is the name assigned to the first variable in this "raw data" file
1	is the column(s) used to store variable 1 in the "raw data" file

As we can see, the file storing the raw data is identified in the DATA LIST statement. In the above example, the file name is SOCISTAT. This file name must be placed in single quotes for both SPSS X and SPSS PC+. The slash (/) following the file name serves as a delimiter separating the two types of information housed on the DATA LIST (i.e., file name and variable names). Following the slash, each variable you wish to identify must be given a *unique* name. Each variable name must be between 1 and 8 characters in length and each must begin with an alphabetical character or one of the symbols $, #, or @. Following each variable name, you must list the column or columns used to house the data in the raw data file. If a variable is to be read with a decimal, the number of positions to the right of the decimal is placed within parentheses following the column identifier (see syntax for VAR3 above).

for SPSS X:

```
DATA LIST FILE='SOCISTAT'/ SEX 1 RACE 2 CLASS 3 GPA 7-9(2)
```

for SPSS PC+:

```
DATA LIST FILE='SOCISTAT'/ SEX 1 RACE 2 CLASS 3 GPA 7-9(2).
```

BEGIN DATA and END DATA Commands

SPSS X and SPSS PC+, like all versions of SPSS, offer two options for storing and retrieving raw data. Raw data may be included in the SPSS command file or it may be placed in a separate data file. If raw data are stored in a separate data file, the FILE= keyword is used to identify the name of the data file. If data are included in the SPSS command file (instead of placing the data in a separate data file), the BEGIN DATA and END DATA keywords are used to identify the beginning and ending of the raw data. When the data are included in the SPSS COMMAND file, the BEGIN DATA command precedes the first line of data and the END DATA command follows the last line of data:

for SPSS X:

```
DATA LIST SEX 1 RACE 2 CLASS 3 AGE 4-5 MS 6 GPA 7-9(2)
BEGIN DATA
122211329
214222369
123332218
224252279
114291189
END DATA
```

for SPSS PC+:

```
DATA LIST SEX 1 RACE 2 CLASS 3 AGE 4-5 MS 6 GPA 7-9(2).
BEGIN DATA.
122211329
214222369
123332218
224252279
114291189
END DATA.
```

RECORDS= Command (SPSS X only)

When the data are housed across multiple records, the DATA LIST for SPSS X only is modified to include the RECORDS = command. In addition, records are separated by a slash (/), and the number immediately following the slash identifies the current record. In SPSS PC+, the RECORDS= command is *not* recognized. Instead, the microcomputer version of SPSS recognizes multiple records by use of the slash alone (no numbers immediately follow the slash).

for SPSS X:

```
DATA LIST FILE='FN' RECORDS=2
/1 V1 1 V2 2 V3 3 V4 4-5 V6 6-8(1)
/2 V7 1 V8 2 V9 3 V10 6-9(1)
```

for SPSS PC+:

```
DATA LIST FILE='FN'
/V1 1 V2 2 V3 3 V4 4-5 V6 6-8(1)
/V7 1 V8 2 V9 3 V10 6-9(1).
```

FREE and FIXED Format Commands

The DATA LIST command can be configured to read variables stored in either a FREE or a FIXED format. In a FIXED format, each variable is recorded in the same column(s) on the same record number for each case in the data file. For example, the value for the variable sex might always be stored in column 3 on record 1 for all cases. In a FREE format, each variable is recorded in the same order but not necessarily in the same columns. When the FREE format is used, variables are separated in the data file by blanks or commas. In both SPSS X and SPSS PC+, the default for reading variables is FIXED. Hence, if data are in FIXED columns, there is no need to include this keyword. If data are to be read in FREE format, however, this keyword must be included in the DATA LIST command. Additionally, you should notice that in FREE format, *no* column identifiers are given for the variables defined.

for SPSS X:

```
DATA LIST FILE='FN' FREE/ V1 V2 V3 V4 V5       } one record/case
```

OR

```
DATA LIST FILE='FN' FREE RECORDS=2
/1 V1 V2 V3 V4 V5                                    } two records/case
/2 V6 V7 V8 V9 V10
```

for SPSS PC+:

```
DATA LIST FILE='FN' FREE/ V1 V2 V3 V4 V5.    } one record/case
```

OR

```
DATA LIST FILE='FN' FREE
/ V1 V2 V3 V4 V5                                     } two records/case
/ V6 V7 V8 V9 V10.
```

Alpha Variables

SPSS assumes that all variables are numeric—either integers or nonintegers—unless you tell it otherwise. Consequently, if data have been entered into the data file using alphabetical characters instead of numbers, this information must also be included on the DATA LIST command. In SPSS, alpha variables are identified by placing the letter A in parentheses to the right of the column indicator:

for SPSS X:

```
DATA LIST FILE='FN'/ V1 1 V2 2-3 V3 4-6(1) V5 7(A)
```

for SPSS PC+:

```
DATA LIST FILE='FN'/ V1 1 V2 2-3 V3 4-6(1) V5 7(A).
```

FORTRAN-Like Format

It is permissible to identify the variable definition portion of the DATA LIST using a FORTRAN-LIKE FORMAT. While the column format is more straightforward and probably easier to use, the FORTRAN-LIKE FORMAT may, at times, be more convenient and more economical of space. If you prefer to use this type of format, see the *SPSS X User's Guide* or the *SPSS PC+ Base Manual*.

MISSING VALUES Command

The MISSING VALUES command is used to identify those values in the data file which are to be treated as MISSING. The syntax for this command is:

```
MISSING VALUES V1(9)/V2(8,9)/V3(0,8,9)
```

where:

MISSING VALUES	are the keywords
V1	is the first variable for which a missing value is being defined
(9)	is the missing value for V1

/   is the delimiter separating one variable and its missing values from another variable and its missing values

for SPSS X:

```
MISSING VALUES CLASS (8,9)/GRADSKOL (0,8,9)
```

for SPSS PC+:

```
MISSING VALUES CLASS (8,9)/GRADSKOL (0,8,9).
```

The following rules *always* apply to the MISSING VALUES command:

1. You can specify missing values for any variable identified previous to the introduction of the MISSING VALUES command.
2. You can specify a maximum of three MISSING VALUES per variable.
3. Multiple MISSING VALUES are always enclosed in parentheses and separated by commas or blanks.
4. If the same value is defined as missing for more than one variable, you may list all such variables and separate them with commas:

```
MISSING VALUES V1,V2,V3(9)
```

5. If the same value is defined as missing for ALL variables, you may write:

```
MISSING VALUES ALL(0)
```

6. To specify a missing value for a string, the string missing value must be placed inside parentheses in single quotes:

```
MISSING VALUES STRINGX('?')
```

VARIABLE LABELS Command

It is sometimes difficult to give meaningful names to variables with a maximum of only eight characters. VARIABLE LABELS help us to overcome this limitation. Specifically, the VARIABLE LABELS command is an optional data definition command used to assign an extended descriptive label to a variable. A variable label is always enclosed in single or double quotes and follows the variable name to which the label applies. The syntax for VARIABLE LABELS is:

```
VARIABLE LABELS V1 'SEX'/V2 'MARITAL STATUS'
```

where:

VARIABLE LABELS	are the keywords
V1	is the name of the first variable to which a label is being assigned
'SEX'	is the label for the first variable

is the delimiter separating the first variable and its label from the second variable and its label

for SPSS X:

```
VARIABLE LABELS SEX    'SEX OF STUDENT'/
   CLASS 'CLASSIFICATION IN COLLEGE'
```

for SPSS PC+:

```
VARIABLE LABELS SEX    'SEX OF STUDENT'/
   CLASS 'CLASSSIFICATION IN COLLEGE'
```

The following rules always apply to VARIABLE LABELS:

1. Any previously defined variable can be assigned a VARIABLE LABEL.
2. A VARIABLE LABEL applies to only one variable.
3. A VARIABLE LABEL can be up to 40 characters long and can use any character including blanks.
4. A variable and its label are separated from another variable and its label by a slash(/).

VALUE LABELS Command

The VALUE LABELS command is an optional command used to provide descriptive labels for variable values. The VALUE LABELS command is followed by a variable name or variable list and a list of variable values and their respective labels. A variable and its value labels are separated from another variable and its value labels with a slash (/). The syntax for VALUE LABELS is:

```
DATA LIST SEX 1 RACE 2 CLASS 3 AGE 4-5 MS 6 GPA 7-9(2).
MISSING VALUES ALL(0)
VARIABLE LABELS SEX 'SEX OF STUDENT'/RACE 'RACE OF
STUDENT'/MS 'MARITAL STATUS'
VALUE LABELS SEX 1 'MALE' 2 'FEMALE'/RACE 1 'BLACK' 2 'WHITE'
/MS 1 'MARRIED' 2 'NOT MARRIED'
```

where:

VALUE LABELS	are the keywords
SEX	is the first variable to receive value labels
1 'MALE'	is the first value and its label
2 'FEMALE'	is the second value and its label
/	is the delimiter separating one variable and its values from another variable and its values

for SPSS X:

```
DATA LIST SEX 1 RACE 2 CLASS 3 AGE 4-5 MS 6 GPA 7-9(2)
MISSING VALUES ALL(0)
```

```
VARIABLE LABELS SEX 'SEX OF STUDENT'/RACE 'RACE OF STUDENT'/MS
 'MARITAL STATUS'
VALUE LABELS SEX 1 'MALE' 2 'FEMALE'/RACE 1 'BLACK' 2 'WHITE'
 /MS 1 'MARRIED' 2 'NOT MARRIED'
```

for SPSS PC+:

```
DATA LIST SEX 1 RACE 2 CLASS 3 AGE 4-5 MS 6 GPA 7-9(2).
MISSING VALUES ALL(0).
VARIABLE LABELS SEX 'SEX OF STUDENT'/RACE 'RACE OF STUDENT'/MS
 'MARITAL STATUS'.
VALUE LABELS SEX 1 'MALE' 2 'FEMALE'/RACE 1 'BLACK' 2 'WHITE'
 /MS 1 'MARRIED' 2 'NOT MARRIED'.
```

The following rules always apply to VALUE LABELS:

1. Any previously defined variable can be assigned VALUE LABELS.
2. Each VALUE LABEL is enclosed in apostrophes or quotation marks.
3. VALUE LABELS can contain any character including blanks.
4. VALUE LABELS can contain a maximum of 20 characters.

FINISH Command

The FINISH command tells SPSS that the end of the command file has been reached. The FINISH command has no corresponding specification field. While it is a good practice to include this command in your SPSS command file, omitting it is not fatal to your program. If you do forget it, SPSS will forgivingly generate a FINISH for you:

for SPSS X:

```
DATA LIST FILE='FN'/V1 1 V2 2 V3 3
MISSING VALUES ALL(0)
```

(remainder of command file)

```
FINISH
```

for SPSS PC+:

```
DATA LIST FILE='FN'/V1 1 V2 2 V3 3.
MISSING VALUES ALL(0).
```

(remainder of command file)

```
FINISH.
```

Data Transformations

Data transformation commands can change or manipulate the data in a manner you prescribe. The most commonly used data transformation procedures in SPSS X and SPSS PC+ are the COMPUTE, IF, and RECODE commands.

COMPUTE Command

The COMPUTE command is used to create new variables. All new variables are constructed on a case-by-case basis using the arithmetic or logical transformation you specify in the COMPUTE command. For example, the command:

```
COMPUTE GRADE=THEORY+LAB
```

computes GRADE as the sum of THEORY grade and LAB grade. THEORY and LAB may be variables identified either in the DATA LIST command or variables COMPUTEd prior to computing GRADE.

To create a new variable using the COMPUTE command, specify the Target variable to the left of the equals (=) sign and the expression to the right. SPSS permits the identification of only one Target variable per COMPUTE statement. Additionally, the expression to the right of the equals sign must return a *number* if the Target variable is a numeric variable and a *string* if the Target variable is a string variable.

All legal arithmetic operators are permissible when using the COMPUTE command. Permissible arithmetic operators in SPSS include:

+ addition
− subtraction
* multiplication
/ division
** exponentiation

SPSS also provides a number of arithmetic and statistical functions that can be used in COMPUTE statements including:

ABS(arg[ument])	absolute value
SQRT(arg)	square root
SUM(arg list)	sum of the values across the argument list
MEAN(arg list)	mean of the values across the argument list
SD(arg list)	standard deviation of values across the argument list
VARIANCE(arg list)	variance of the values across the argument list
CFVAR(arg list)	coefficient of variation is the standard deviation divided by the mean
MIN(arg list)	minimum value across the argument list
MAX(arg list)	maximum value across the argument list

for SPSS X:

```
COMPUTE AVEGRADE=MEAN(GRADE1)
COMPUTE ZGRADE1 =(GRADE1-MEAN(GRADE1))/SD(GRADE1)
```

for SPSS PC+:

```
COMPUTE AVEGRADE=MEAN(GRADE1) .
COMPUTE ZGRADE1=(GRADE1-MEAN(GRADE1))/SD(GRADE1) .
```

The first of these two COMPUTE statements computes the arithmetic average for the variable identified as GRADE1. The second and somewhat more complex COMPUTE statement computes the z scores (on a case-by-case basis) for the variable GRADE1.

The order in which arithmetic operations are performed in SPSS is (1) functions; (2) exponentiation; (3) multiplication and division; and (4) addition and subtraction. Arithmetic operations are always performed left to right. If several orders of arithmetic operators are found within an expression, SPSS will make several passes through the expression. Parentheses can be used to override this order if you so choose (e.g., add before you multiply). If parentheses are used, SPSS will work inside the innermost set of parentheses first and move outward. If you are unsure of the order of arithmetic operations, parentheses will help to make the order explicit.

IF Command

The IF command makes COMPUTE-like transformations contingent upon a set of conditions that you specify. The IF command is comprised of a logical expression and an assignment expression. For example, the command:

```
IF (Y EQ 0) X=1
```

assigns the value 1 to X (case by case) only when Y is equal to 0. In this example, the logical expression is **Y EQ 0** and the assignment expression is **X=1**. In this example, the logical expression is placed in parentheses (although parentheses are optional) while the assignment expression maintains the same syntax as that used with the COMPUTE statement. In fact, the assignment expression for the IF command follows all the same rules established for the COMPUTE command.

The assignment portion of the IF statement is only executed if the logical expression is TRUE. In the logical expression of the IF statement, a minimum of two values are compared using relational operators. SPSS allows the following relational operators or the symbolic equivalent of each in logical expressions:

GE	or	>=	greater than or equal to
LE	or	<=	less than or equal to
GT	or	>	greater than
LT	or	<	less than
EQ	or	=	equal to
NE	or	<>	not equal to

For example: or:

```
IF (X LT 0) Y=1        IF (X < 0) Y=1
IF (A GE 0) B=1        IF (A >= 0) B=1
```

It is also permissible to include more complicated arithmetic expressions within the logical expression:

```
IF (X+Y GT A+B) Z=0
```

It is also possible to join two or more relations using the logical operators AND and OR:

```
IF (X EQ 1 AND Y EQ 1) Z=1
```

This command assigns the value 1 to *Z only* if both *X* and *Y* are equal to 1. When logical operators are used, an assignment expression will be executed according to the following rules:

AND   both relations must be true
OR   either relation can be true

You may use only one logical operator to combine two relations. For example, AND/OR is invalid. However it is permissible to combine many relations into a single complex logical expression:

```
IF (X EQ 0 AND Y EQ 0 OR Y EQ 1) A=1
```

Notice also that neither logical operators nor expressions can be implied. For example, in the previous IF statement we could *not* have said **Y EQ 0 OR 1.** We must repeat both the variable name and the relational operator for each comparison in the logical expression.

for SPSS X:

```
IF (THEORY GT 0 AND LAB GT 0) AVEGRADE=MEAN(GRADE1)
IF (SEX =1) ZGRADE1=(GRADE1-MEAN(GRADE1))/SD(GRADE1)
```

for SPSS PC+:

```
IF (THEORY GT 0 AND LAB GT 0) AVEGRADE=MEAN(GRADE1).
IF (SEX =1) ZGRADE1=(GRADE1-MEAN(GRADE1))/SD(GRADE1).
```

RECODE Command

The most direct transformation procedure in SPSS is the RECODE command which instructs SPSS to change the codes for a variable as data are being read. Each value to be recoded is enclosed within its own set of parentheses. The RECODE command is evaluated LEFT to RIGHT, and the values for a case are recoded only once per RECODE command. Input Values not identified in the RECODE command are left unchanged. The syntax for RECODE is:

```
RECODE X (1=2) (2=1)
```

where:

RECODE   is the keyword
X   is the first variable to be recoded
(1=2)   is the recode for the first variable value
(2=1)   is the recode for the second variable value

for SPSS X:

```
RECODE MS (1,2=2) (3,4=2)
```

for SPSS PC+:

```
RECODE MS (1,2=2) (3,4=2).
```

The first four rules apply to all RECODE statements in SPSS X and SPSS PC+. The fifth rule applies only to SPSS X.

1. It is permissible to recode multiple values to a single output value:

```
RECODE Y (0,2=1)(1=2)
```

2. It is permissible to identify multiple variables for the same value specification:

```
RECODE X,Y,Z (1=2) (2=1)
```

3. It is permissible to specify different values for different variables on the same RECODE by separating the RECODE specifications with a slash (/):

```
RECODE V1 (1=2) (2=1)/V2 (1,2=1) (3=2)
```

4. Permissible keywords that can be used with the RECODE command include THRU, LOWEST, HIGHEST, ELSE, and MISSING:

```
RECODE V1 (LOWEST THRU 1=1) (2 THRU HIGHEST=2)
RECODE V2 (0 THRU 1=1) (ELSE=2)
RECODE V3 (MISSING=0)
```

5. In SPSS X only, to RECODE the values of one variable and store them under another variable name leaving the original variable unchanged, use the keyword INTO:

```
RECODE V1 (LOWEST THRU 1=1) (2 THRU HIGHEST=2) INTO V1R
```

This RECODE command would recode the values for variable V1 into variable V1R leaving V1 in its original form. To accomplish this same end with SPSS PC+, you could use the following two commands:

```
COMPUTE V1R=V1.
RECODE V1R (LOWEST THRU1=1) (2 THRU HIGHEST=2).
```

Data Selection Procedures

SPSS permits you to control the number of cases to be used and the characteristics of cases to be included in your statistical analysis. Four commands are used to control the selection of cases to be analyzed by the various statistical procedures: (1) SE-

LECT IF (and PROCESS IF in SPSS PC+ only), (2) N OF CASES, (3) SAMPLE, and
(4) WEIGHT.

SELECT IF Command

The SELECT IF command permanently selects cases based on logical criteria. For example, the command:

for SPSS X:

```
SELECT IF (AGE GT 30)
```

for SPSS PC+:

```
SELECT IF (AGE GT 30).
```

selects cases for which the variable AGE has a value greater than 30. These are the
only cases that will be used in computing the desired statistics. The syntax for the
SELECT IF statement is identical to that for the IF statement. While the logical expression does not have to be enclosed in parentheses, you will probably find the use
of parentheses syntactically helpful.

The specification field for the SELECT IF command is a logical expression that
can be evaluated as true, false, or missing. All arithmetic operators, functions, relational operators, and logical operators are permissible with the SELECT IF.

```
SELECT IF (SEX EQ 1)
SELECT IF (SEX EQ 1 AND MS EQ 1)
SELECT IF (ABS(X) GT 5)
```

PROCESS IF Command (SPSS PC+ only)

The PROCESS IF command, like the SELECT IF command, selects cases based on
logical criteria. However, the selection process is *not* permanent. The selection criteria established in the PROCESS IF command remain in effect *only* for the procedure
immediately following the PROCESS IF command. For example, the command:

```
PROCESS IF (AGE GT 30)
FREQUENCIES VARIABLES=RACE,CLASS/STATISTICS=ALL.
FREQUENCIES VARIABLES=AGE/STATISTICS=ALL.
```

selects cases for which the variable AGE has a value greater than 30 and uses the selected cases for computing FREQUENCIES for the variables RACE and CLASS
since this is the command immediately following the PROCESS IF command. However, when SPSS computes the FREQUENCIES for age, it returns to using the entire
sample.

The syntax for the PROCESS IF statement is identical to that for the SELECT IF
statement. While the logical expression does not have to be enclosed in parentheses,
you will probably find the use of parentheses syntactically helpful.

The specification field for the PROCESS IF command is a logical expression that can be evaluated as true, false, or missing. As with the SELECT IF command, all arithmetic operators, functions, relational operators, and logical operators are permissible with the PROCESS IF command.

```
PROCESS IF (SEX EQ 1)
PROCESS IF (SEX EQ 1 AND MS EQ 1)
PROCESS IF (ABS(X) GT 5)
```

While the PROCESS IF command can be used only with SPSS PC+, there is a command in SPSS X that can function as the PROCESS IF command—the TEMPORARY command (available in SPSS X only).[2] By combining the TEMPORARY command with the SELECT IF command, we accomplish exactly what the PROCESS IF command is designed to accomplish:

for SPSS X:

```
TEMPORARY
SELECT IF (SEX EQ 1).
FREQUENCIES VARIABLES=AGE/STATISTICS=ALL
```

for SPSS PC+:

```
PROCESS IF (SEX EQ 1)
FREQUENCIES VARIABLES=AGE/STATISTICS=ALL.
```

N OF CASES Command

The N OF CASES command in SPSS is used to build a file of the first N cases. In this use of the N OF CASES, the command follows the DATA LIST command. For example, if you have a data file containing 600 cases but you wish to use only the first 300, you can specify:

for SPSS X:

```
DATA LIST SEX 1 RACE 2 CLASS 3 AGE 4-5 MS 6 GPA 7-9(2)
N OF CASES 300
```

for SPSS PC+:

```
DATA LIST SEX 1 RACE 2 CLASS 3 AGE 4-5 MS 6 GPA 7-9(2).
N 300.
```

SAMPLE Command

The SAMPLE command in SPSS X selects a random sample of cases. To select an ap-

---

[2]The TEMPORARY command can be used in ways other than what is discussed here. To learn more about the TEMPORARY command, see the *SPSS X User's Guide*.

proximate percentage of cases, specify a decimal value between 0 and 1. For example, the command

for SPSS X:

```
SAMPLE .50
```

for SPSS PC+:

```
SAMPLE .50.
```

samples approximately 50 percent of the cases on the active file. If you know the exact number of cases on the active file, you can specify an exact sample size:

for SPSS X:

```
SAMPLE 50 FROM 100
```

for SPSS PC+:

```
SAMPLE 50 FROM 100.
```

If you overestimate the number of cases in the file, SPSS will sample proportionately (in this case, sample .5 of some smaller number of actual cases. If you underestimate the number of cases, SPSS will select the sample on the first N cases (in this case, on the first 100 cases).

WEIGHT Command

The WEIGHT command is used to weight cases differently for different analyses. For example, if in your sampling process, you over- or undersampled a group, you can apply the WEIGHT command to obtain population estimates. To illustrate, suppose you sampled males and females in your university and later discovered that you had oversampled the females by a factor of 2. You could compensate when doing your statistical analysis by weighting females by one half:

for SPSS X:

```
IF (SEX EQ 'F') WT=.5
```

for SPSS PC+:

```
IF (SEX EQ 'F') WT=.5.
```

Notice that the WEIGHT command can be abbreviated WT. In SPSS X, weighting factor is considered permanent unless it is preceded by the keyword TEMPORARY. However, a permanent weighting factor can be disabled by including the command:

```
WEIGHT OFF
```

In SPSS PC+, a weighting factor is permanent unless it is changed or turned OFF by using the WEIGHT OFF command.

Procedure Commands

While data definition, data transformation, and data selection commands are used to manage data, procedure commands are used to statistically analyze data. A procedure is defined as any command that actually reads data. Numerous statistical procedures are available in both SPSS X and SPSS PC+. We will not attempt to cover all of these procedures—only the ones we think you are likely to use in a beginning course on research methods. If you have need of a procedure not covered in this appendix, please consult the *SPSS X User's Guide* or *SPSS PC+ Base Manual*.

FREQUENCIES Command

The FREQUENCIES command produces a table of frequency counts and percentages for all specified variables. Additionally, you can request bar charts for the discrete variables, histograms for the continuous variables, univariate summary statistics, and percentiles. These various optional requests are managed through several subcommands. For example, the command

```
FREQUENCIES VARIABLES=AGE
```

would produce a frequency table for the variable AGE using all unique values for age. Conceivably, we might even end up with a frequency distribution of 50 unique ages where many of the ages occur only once.[3]

Subcommands for Procedure FREQUENCIES

FORMAT Subcommand

The FORMAT subcommand of procedure FREQUENCIES provides several formatting options that have an important effect on output. Through the FORMAT subcommand, you can control the formatting of tables and the order in which values are sorted within tables, suppress tables, produce an index of tables, and write the FREQUENCIES display to another file. For example, the command

```
FREQUENCIES VARIABLES=AGE
        FORMAT=NOLABELS DOUBLE/
```

specifies that we do not want variable or value labels printed and that we want the frequencies table to be double-spaced.

SPSS prints frequency tables in ascending order of values unless instructed otherwise. You can override this default with one of three sorting options available on the FORMAT subcommand. For example, the command:

---

[3]The FREQUENCIES command in SPSS X (mainframe version) has a few more features than the same command in SPSS PC+. To avoid confusion, these features are not discussed here. If you are interested in these additional features, please see the *SPSS X User's Guide*.

```
FREQUENCIES VARIABLES=AGE
     FORMAT=DVALUE/
```

will result in a frequency distribution where the ages appear in the frequency table in descending order.

BARCHARTS Subcommand

Bar charts and histograms are graphic representations of frequency distributions. You may request both bar charts and histograms as part of the FREQUENCIES command. For example, the command:

```
FREQUENCIES VARIABLES=SEX/
     BARCHART/
```

would produce a plot of all tabulated values with the horizontal axis scaled in frequencies. Specifically, the scale is determined by the frequency of the largest single category plotted. You can specify minimum and maximum boundaries for plotting and a horizontal scale labeled with percentages or frequency counts by using the options MIN (lower bound), MAX (upper bound), PERCENT (horizontal axis scaled in percentages) and FREQ (horizontal axis scaled in frequencies). For example, the command:

```
FREQUENCIES VARIABLES=AGE/
     BARCHART=FREQ MIN(21) MAX(39)
```

would produce a frequency table for the variable AGE and a bar chart plotting ages 21 through 39 with frequencies on the horizontal axis.

HISTOGRAM Subcommand

The HISTOGRAM subcommand produces histograms. For example, the command

```
FREQUENCIES VARIABLES=AGE
     HISTOGRAM/
```

would produce a frequency table and a histogram of all tabulated values. Once again, the default scale for the horizontal axis is frequencies. The scale is determined by the frequency count of the largest category plotted. The maximum number of values that can be plotted is 21. Subcommand HISTOGRAM permits all of the formatting options available with BARCHART. In addition, optional specifications on subcommand HISTOGRAM include MIN (lower bound), MAX (upper bound), PERCENT (horizontal axis scaled in percentages), FREQ (horizontal axis scaled in frequencies), INCREMENT(n) (interval width), and NORMAL (superimpose the normal curve). For example, the command:

```
FREQUENCIES VARIABLES=AGE/
     HISTOGRAM=INCREMENT(5) FREQ NORMAL
```

would produce a frequency table for the variable age. In addition a histogram would be drawn using frequencies on the horizontal axis with an interval width of 5, and the normal curve would be superimposed on the histogram.

HBAR Subcommand

The HBAR subcommand produces either a bar chart or a histogram depending on the number of values identified in the data. If a bar chart for a variable fits on a single page, HBAR produces a bar chart; otherwise, it produces a histogram. Using a page length of 59 lines, a bar chart will be displayed for any variable with fewer than twelve categories. Histograms will be displayed for variables with twelve or more categories.

PERCENTILE Subcommand

The PERCENTILE subcommand displays the values associated with the requested percentiles for the identified variables. For example, the command:

```
FREQUENCIES VARIABLES=AGE/
    PERCENTILES=25 50 75/
```

would display the values for age associated with the 25th, 50th, and 75th percentiles.

STATISTICS Subcommand

The STATISTICS subcommand is used to display univariate statistics with procedure FREQUENCIES. Statistics that you might use along with their keywords (in parentheses here) include the mean (MEAN), standard error of the mean (SEMEAN), median (MEDIAN), mode (MODE), standard deviation (STDDEV), range (RANGE), minimum (MINIMUM), and maximum (MAXIMUM). DEFAULT, ALL, and NONE are also permissible keywords. The option DEFAULT will produce four statistics: mean, standard deviation, minimum, and maximum. The option ALL will produce all available statistics. The option NONE will suppress all statistics. For example, the command:

```
FREQUENCIES VARIABLES=AGE/
    STATISTICS=MODE DEFAULT
```

will print the four default statistics and the mode for the variable AGE.

One missing values option is available with procedure FREQUENCIES. You may include values previously defined as missing through the MISSING VALUES command with the subcommand MISSING=INCLUDE. For example, the command:

```
MISSING VALUES AGE (0)
FREQUENCIES VARIABLES=AGE/
    MISSING=INCLUDE
```

would serve to include all ages (even those equal to 0) in the frequency table.

for SPSS X:

```
DATA LIST SEX 1 RACE 2 CLASS 3 AGE 4-5 MS 6 GPA 7-9(2)
MISSING VALUES ALL(0)
VARIABLE LABELS SEX 'SEX OF STUDENT'/RACE 'RACE OF STUDENT'/MS
 'MARITAL STATUS'
VALUE LABELS SEX 1 'MALE' 2 'FEMALE'/RACE 1 'BLACK' 2 'WHITE'
 /MS 1 'MARRIED' 2 'NOT MARRIED'
FREQUENCIES VARIABLES=SEX,RACE,CLASS
/FORMAT=NOLABELS DOUBLE
/BARCHART
/PERCENTILES=25 50 75
/STATISTICS=MODE
FREQUENCIES VARIABLES=AGE
/HISTOGRAM=NORMAL INCREMENT (5)
/MISSING=INCLUDE
/STATISTICS=DEFAULT MODE
```

for SPSS PC+:

```
DATA LIST SEX 1 RACE 2 CLASS 3 AGE 4-5 MS 6 GPA 7-9(2).
MISSING VALUES ALL(0).
VARIABLE LABELS SEX 'SEX OF STUDENT'/RACE 'RACE OF STUDENT'/MS
 'MARITAL STATUS'.
VALUE LABELS SEX 1 'MALE' 2 'FEMALE'/RACE 1 'BLACK' 2 'WHITE'
 /MS 1 'MARRIED' 2 'NOT MARRIED'.
FREQUENCIES VARIABLES=SEX,RACE,CLASS
/FORMAT=NOLABELS DOUBLE
/BARCHART
/PERCENTILES=25 50 75
/STATISTICS=MODE.
FREQUENCIES VARIABLES=AGE
/HISTOGRAM=NORMAL INCREMENT (5)
/MISSING=INCLUDE
/STATISTICS=DEFAULT MODE.
```

CROSSTABS Command

Procedure CROSSTABS produces tables that are the joint distribution of two or more variables having a limited number of distinct values. A cell, the basic element of any table, is created by the unique combination of values for two variables.

To compute CROSSTABS, use the keyword TABLES followed by a list of one or more variables, the keyword BY, and another list of one or more variables.[4] For example, the command:

```
CROSSTABS TABLES=SEX BY POLPREF
```

produces a bivariate table with sex as the row variable and political preference as the column variable. The equals sign following the keyword TABLES is optional. A

---

[4]CROSSTABS for SPSS X (mainframe version), when compared to CROSSTABS for SPSS PC+, has several additional features and to avoid confusion we have focused on their similarities. If you are interested in these additional features, please see the *SPSS X User's Guide*.

maximum of 10 dimensions can be specified on a TABLES list. The variable (or list of variables) to the left of the keyword BY is the ROW variable and the variable (or list of variables) to the right of the keyword BY is the COLUMN variable(s). Subsequent variables following a second use of the keyword BY specify the order of control variables. For example, the command:

```
CROSSTABS MS BY POLPREF BY SEX
```

would produce two tables with marital status as the row variable and political preference as the column variable. In each table, sex would be a constant. That is, table 1 would include males only (assuming males are coded as 1) and table 2 would include females only (assuming females are coded as 2).

By default, CROSSTABS prints only the number of cases in each cell. However, you can request a great deal more information through the OPTIONS command. OPTIONS available with procedure CROSSTABS include print row percentages (3), print column percentages (4), print two-way table total percentages (5), and print all cell information (18).

You can also request a number of summary statistics for each subtable with the STATISTICS command. STATISTICS available include chi-square (1), lambda (4), Kendall's tau-b (6), Kendall's tau-c (7), gamma (8), Sommers' d (9), eta (10), and Pearson's r (11), just to name a few. If you are not familiar with all of these statistics, you might want to check a statistics textbook. The following CROSSTABS procedure prints all cell information and the statistic chi-square:

```
CROSSTABS TABLES=SEX BY POLPREF
STATISTICS 1
OPTIONS 18
```

By default, CROSSTABS deletes cases with missing values on a table-by-table basis. A case missing on any of the specified variables is not included in the table nor in the calculation of any requested statistics. If you wish to have missing values reported in the table but excluded from the calculation of percentages and statistics, you should specify OPTION 7. If you wish to have missing cases treated as though they were not missing, you should specify OPTION 1.

for SPSS X:

```
DATA LIST SEX 1 RACE 2 CLASS 3 AGE 4-5 MS 6 GPA 7-9(2)
MISSING VALUES ALL(0)
VARIABLE LABELS SEX 'SEX OF STUDENT'/RACE 'RACE OF STUDENT'/MS
 'MARITAL STATUS'
VALUE LABELS SEX 1 'MALE' 2 'FEMALE'/RACE 1 'BLACK' 2 'WHITE'
 /MS 1 'MARRIED' 2 'NOT MARRIED'
CROSSTABS TABLES=RACE,SEX BY GRADSKOL
STATISTICS=ALL
CROSSTABS TABLES=CLASS BY GRADSKOL/STATISTICS=1
```

for SPSS PC+:

```
DATA LIST SEX 1 RACE 2 CLASS 3 AGE 4-5 MS 6 GPA 7-9(2).
MISSING VALUES ALL(0).
```

```
VARIABLE LABELS SEX 'SEX OF STUDENT'/RACE 'RACE OF STUDENT'/MS
'MARITAL STATUS'.
VALUE LABELS SEX 1 'MALE' 2 'FEMALE'/RACE 1 'BLACK' 2 'WHITE'
/MS 1 'MARRIED' 2 'NOT MARRIED'.
CROSSTABS TABLES=RACE,SEX BY GRADSKOL
/STATISTICS=ALL.
CROSSTABS TABLES=CLASS BY GRADSKOL/STATISTICS=1.
```

TTEST Command

Procedure TTEST tests for the significance of the difference between two sample means. This procedure produces the mean, standard deviation, and standard error for each variable. Even more important, procedure TTEST produces Student's *t*, degrees of freedom, and the two-tailed probability for the comparison between means. In short, this procedure allows the comparison of either independent samples or paired samples.

Independent Samples

An independent-samples test divides cases into two groups and compares the group means on a single variable. This test requires two subcommands: GROUPS and VARIABLES. The GROUPS subcommand followed by an equals sign establishes the criterion for dividing the cases into two groups. Both SPSS X and SPSS PC+ permit three different methods for defining the two groups. First, you may place a single value in parentheses following identification of the grouping variable. SPSS will group all the values equal to or greater than the one specified in one group and all other values will be placed in a second group. For example, the command:

```
TTEST GROUPS=AGE(39)/VARIABLES=GPA
```

would place all cases where age is equal to or greater than 39 in one group and all remaining cases in a second group.

Second, you may place two values in parentheses and the two groups will be comprised of those cases having these values. For example, the command:

```
TTEST GROUPS=MS(1,3)/VARIABLES=GPA
```

would place all cases where marital status equals 1 in one group and all cases where marital status equals 3 in a second group. No other marital status categories would be included in the analysis.

Third, if the grouping variable has only two categories and these two categories are labeled 1 and 2, it is permissible to identify the grouping variable without specifying a value list. For example, the command:

```
TTEST GROUPS=SEX/VARIABLES=GPA
```

would compare the mean GPA for males to that of females—the only two groups.

However, if a two-category grouping variables has categories labeled 0 and 1, you must specify the values in parentheses. For example, if the grouping variable was race and race was coded 0 and one, we would write:

```
TTEST GROUPS=RACE(0,1)/VARIABLES=GPA
```

You should note that the VARIABLES= subcommand always follows the GROUPS= subcommand and that the two commands are separated by a slash.

Paired Samples

A paired-samples *t* test compares two variables with each other—for example, comparing pre- and posttest scores for students in a class. The PAIRS subcommand identifies the variables being compared. For example, the command:

```
TTEST PAIRS TEST1 TEST2
```

compares students' TEST1 scores with the same students' TEST2 scores. If you specify a list of variables with the PAIRS subcommand, SPSS will compare every variable with every other variable. For example, PAIRS=TEST1 TEST2 TEST3 would compare TEST1 with TEST2, TEST1 with TEST3, and TEST2 with TEST3. SPSS X permits up to 400 variables on the PAIRS subcommand while SPSS PC+ permits only 50.

Treatment of Missing Values By default, procedure TTEST deletes cases with missing values on an analysis-by-analysis basis. For independent-samples tests, cases missing on either the GROUPing variable or the analysis variable are excluded from computations. For paired-samples tests, a case missing on either of the variables in a given pair will result in the exclusion of that case from analysis. If you wish to include missing values, you may request OPTION 1. Other OPTIONS available are: exclude missing values listwise (2); suppress variable labels (3); and print with an 80-character width (4).

for SPSS X:

```
DATA LIST SEX 1 RACE 2 CLASS 3 AGE 4-5 MS 6 GPA 7-9(2)
MISSING VALUES ALL(0)
VARIABLE LABELS SEX 'SEX OF STUDENT'/RACE 'RACE OF STUDENT'/MS
 'MARITAL STATUS'
VALUE LABELS SEX 1 'MALE' 2 'FEMALE'/RACE 1 'BLACK' 2 'WHITE'
 /MS 1 'MARRIED' 2 'NOT MARRIED'
TTEST GROUPS=AGE(30)/VARIABLES=MATH
TTEST GROUPS=CLASS(0,1)/VARIABLES=AGE
TTEST GROUPS=SEX/VARIABLES=TEST1
TTEST PAIRS=TEST1,TEST2
TTEST PAIRS=ATTITUD1,ATTITUD2
```

for SPSS PC+:

```
DATA LIST SEX 1 RACE 2 CLASS 3 AGE 4-5 MS 6 GPA 7-9(2).
MISSING VALUES ALL(0).
```

```
VARIABLE LABELS SEX 'SEX OF STUDENT'/RACE 'RACE OF STUDENT'/MS
  'MARITAL STATUS'.
VALUE LABELS SEX 1 'MALE' 2 'FEMALE'/RACE 1 'BLACK' 2 'WHITE'
  /MS1 'MARRIED' 2 'NOT MARRIED'.
TTEST GROUPS=AGE(30)/VARIABLES=MATH.
TTEST GROUPS=CLASS(0,1)/VARIABLES=AGE.
TTEST GROUPS=SEX/VARIABLES=TEST1.
TTEST PAIRS=TEST1,TEST2.
TTEST PAIRS=ATTITUD1,ATTITUD2.
```

ONEWAY Command

Procedure ONEWAY produces a one-way analysis of variance—comparing means for two or more groups. Like procedure TTEST, procedure ONEWAY operates by means of subcommands and associated OPTIONS and STATISTICS commands.

A ONEWAY analysis list is comprised of a list of dependent variables and one independent (grouping) variable with its minimum and maximum values. For example, the command:

```
ONEWAY GPA BY MS(1,4)
```

specifies a one-way analysis of variance of GPA, the dependent variable, by MS (marital status), the independent variable, having a minimum value of 1 and a maximum value of 4. While you can name up to 100 dependent variables per analysis list, only one independent variable is permissible. Additionally, while you can specify any number of groups for the independent variable, contrasts and multiple comparisons are not available for more than 50 groups.

CONTRAST and RANGES Subcommand

The CONTRAST subcommand specifies a priori contrasts to be tested by the t statistic. The RANGES subcommand specifies any of seven different tests appropriate for multiple comparisons between means. Each RANGES subcommand specifies one test. Tests available through the RANGES subcommand include LSD, DUNCAN, SNK, TUKEY B, TUKEY, LSDMOD, and SCHEFFE. For more information on these subcommands, check the *SPSS X User's Guide* or the *SPSS PC+ Base Manual*.

STATISTICS Subcommand

Three optional statistics are also available with procedure ONEWAY: (1) group descriptive statistics, (2) fixed- and random-effects measures, and (3) homogeneity-of-variance tests. You may specify any one or all of these statistics with the STATISTICS command. To specify all of these statistics, use the keyword ALL.

OPTIONS Subcommand

By default, ONEWAY deletes cases with missing values on an analysis-by-analysis basis. If you wish to include missing cases, request OPTION 1.

for SPSS X:

```
DATA LIST SEX 1 RACE 2 CLASS 3 AGE 4-5 MS 6 GPA 7-9(2)
MISSING VALUES ALL(0)
VARIABLE LABELS SEX 'SEX OF STUDENT'/RACE 'RACE OF STUDENT'/MS
 'MARITAL STATUS'
VALUE LABELS SEX 1 'MALE' 2 'FEMALE'/RACE 1 'BLACK' 2 'WHITE'
 /MS 1 'MARRIED' 2 'NOT MARRIED'
ONEWAY AGE BY GRADSKOL(1,3)
/RANGES=SCHEFFE (.01)
OPTIONS 1
STATISTICS ALL
```

for SPSS PC+:

```
DATA LIST SEX 1 RACE 2 CLASS 3 AGE 4-5 MS 6 GPA 7-9(2).
MISSING VALUES ALL(0).
VARIABLE LABELS SEX 'SEX OF STUDENT'/RACE 'RACE OF STUDENT'/MS
 'MARITAL STATUS'.
VALUE LABELS SEX 1 'MALE' 2 'FEMALE'/RACE 1 'BLACK' 2 'WHITE'
 /MS 1 'MARRIED' 2 'NOT MARRIED'.
ONEWAY AGE BY GRADSKOL(1,3)
/RANGES=SCHEFFE (.01)
/OPTIONS 1
/STATISTICS=ALL.
```

ANOVA Command

Procedure ANOVA produces an *n*-way analysis of variance with up to ten factors or independent variables per procedure. In addition to the analysis of variance table, ANOVA prints cell means and sample sizes. The simplest ANOVA command contains one analysis list—that is, a dependent variable list and a factor list. For example, the command:

```
ANOVA GPA BY MS(1,4)
```

produces a one-way analysis of variance where grade point average is the dependent variable and marital status is the independent (i.e., grouping) variable. In the ANOVA procedure, the dependent variables are separated from the independent variables with the word BY. The dependent variable list is to the left of the word BY and the independent variable list is to the right of this keyword. Additionally, multiple designs can be placed on the same ANOVA procedure by separating the analysis lists with a slash (/):

```
ANOVA GPA BY MS(1,4) SEX(1,2)
/INC BY MS(1,4) SEX,RACE(1,2)
```

for SPSS X:

```
DATA LIST SEX 1 RACE 2 CLASS 3 AGE 4-5 MS 6 GPA 7-9(2)
MISSING VALUES ALL(0)
VARIABLE LABELS SEX 'SEX OF STUDENT'/RACE 'RACE OF STUDENT'/MS
```

```
    'MARITAL STATUS'
    VALUE LABELS SEX 1 'MALE' 2 'FEMALE'/RACE 1 'BLACK' 2 'WHITE'
    /MS 1 'MARRIED' 2 'NOT MARRIED'
    ANOVA AGE BY GRADSKOL(1,3) SEX(1,2) CLASS(0,1)
    STATISTICS=ALL
```

for SPSS PC+:

```
    DATA LIST SEX 1 RACE 2 CLASS 3 AGE 4-5 MS 6 GPA 7-9(2).
    MISSING VALUES ALL(0).
    VARIABLE LABELS SEX 'SEX OF STUDENT'/RACE 'RACE OF STUDENT'/MS
    'MARITAL STATUS'.
    VALUE LABELS SEX 1 'MALE' 2 'FEMALE'/RACE 1 'BLACK' 2 'WHITE'
    /MS 1 'MARRIED' 2 'NOT MARRIED'.
    ANOVA AGE BY GRADSKOL(1,3) SEX(1,2) CLASS(0,1)
    /STATISTICS=ALL
```

PLOT Command (SPSS PC+ only)

Procedure PLOT (SPSS PC+ only) produces bivariate plots in which one variable defines the horizontal axis and a second variable defines the vertical axis. With procedure PLOT you can control scaling of the axes, obtain regression statistics, alter the handling of missing values and the printing of grid lines, and take a random sample when your file contains too many cases for a plot.

To obtain a scatterplot of each variable with each other variable, specify a simple variable list where variables are separated with spaces or commas:

```
PLOT AGE GPA INC
```

By default, procedure PLOT uses the observed minimum and maximum values for each variable to establish the upper and lower endpoints of the scale. You can set the scale by specifying the upper and lower bounds for each variable to be plotted. Upper and lower boundaries are placed in parentheses following the variable name:

```
PLOT INC(10000,50000) WITH AGE
```

Values falling outside of the specified range are excluded from the plot.

STATISTICS Subcommand

Statistics available for procedure PLOT include (1) Pearson's r, (2) r2, (3) significance of r, (4) standard error of the estimate, (5) intercept with the vertical axis, and (6) slope. If you wish all statistics, the keyword ALL is permissible.

for SPSS PC+:

```
    DATA LIST SEX 1 RACE 2 CLASS 3 AGE 4-5 MS 6 GPA 7-9(2) ACT 10-12.
    MISSING VALUES ALL(0).
    VARIABLE LABELS SEX 'SEX OF STUDENT'/RACE 'RACE OF STUDENT'/MS
    'MARITAL STATUS'.
    VALUE LABELS SEX 1 'MALE' 2 'FEMALE'/RACE 1 'BLACK' 2 'WHITE'
```

```
/MS 1 'MARRIED' 2 'NOT MARRIED'.
PLOT GPA WITH AGE,ACT
/STATISTICS=ALL.
PLOT GPA WITH ACT BY AGE.
```

CORRELATION Command

The CORRELATION procedure produces Pearson product–moment correlation co-efficients with significant levels. The following command will produce a correlation matrix in which each variable is correlated with each other variable:

```
CORRELATION AGE, INC, GPA
```

It is also appropriate to write:

```
CORRELATION AGE WITH INC,GPA
```

The two examples given here are not the same. The first example will produce a cor-relation matrix where AGE is correlated with INC, AGE with GPA, and INC with GPA. The second example will produce a correlation matrix where AGE is correlat-ed with INC and AGE with GPA. The second example will not produce the correla-tion between INC and GPA.

The correlation coefficient, number of cases, and significance level are auto-matically printed for every combination of variable pairs. Additional statistics can be obtained with the STATISTICS subcommand. Statistics available with procedure CORRELATION include (1) mean, standard deviation, and number of nonmissing cases for each variable, and (2) cross-product deviations and covariance for each pair of variables. For example, the command:

```
CORRELATION AGE INC
STATISTICS 1
```

would produce the correlation coefficient for age and income as well as the statistics mean, standard deviation and number of missing cases.

In addition to the STATISTICS subcommand, the OPTIONS subcommand is also available. For example, adding the command:

```
OPTIONS 1
```

to the above procedure would result in the inclusion of missing values.

for SPSS X:

```
DATA LIST SEX 1 RACE 2 CLASS 3 AGE 4-5 MS 6 GPA 7-9(2)
MISSING VALUES ALL(0)
VARIABLE LABELS SEX 'SEX OF STUDENT'/RACE 'RACE OF STUDENT'/MS
 'MARITAL STATUS'
VALUE LABELS SEX 1 'MALE' 2 'FEMALE'/RACE 1 'BLACK' 2 'WHITE'
```

```
      /MS 1 'MARRIED' 2 'NOT MARRIED'
      CORRELATION VARIABLES=AGE ATTITUD1 ATTITUD2 TEST1 TEST2
      /VARIABLES=AGE WITH ATTITUD1 ATTITUD2 TEST1 TEST2
      /STATISTICS=ALL
```

for SPSS PC+:

```
      DATA LIST SEX 1 RACE 2 CLASS 3 AGE 4-5 MS 6 GPA 7-9(2).
      MISSING VALUES ALL(0).
      VARIABLE LABELS SEX 'SEX OF STUDENT'/RACE 'RACE OF STUDENT'/MS
      'MARITAL STATUS'.
      VALUE LABELS SEX 1 'MALE' 2 'FEMALE'/RACE 1 'BLACK' 2 'WHITE'
      /MS 1 'MARRIED' 2 'NOT MARRIED'.
      CORRELATION AGE ATTITUD1 ATTITUD2 TEST1 TEST2
      CORRELATION AGE WITH ATTITUD1 ATTITUD2 TEST1 TEST2
      STATISTICS 1.
```

REGRESSION Command

Procedure REGRESSION calculates a multiple regression equation with associated statistics and plots. The REGRESSION procedure in SPSS uses the REGRESSION command and its associated subcommands. There are no STATISTICS and OPTIONS commands available with procedure REGRESSION. However, three subcommands are required. The VARIABLES subcommand lists the variables to be used in the regression analysis. The DEPENDENT subcommand identifies the variables to be treated as dependent. The method (i.e., ENTER, FORWARD, BACKWARD, STEP, REMOVE, TEST) subcommand specifies the method of variable selection. For example, the command:

```
      REGRESSION    VARIABLES=AGE,INC,GPA/
                    DEPENDENT=INC/
                    ENTER AGE GPA
```

identifies three variables to be used in this regression analysis. The variable INC is to be the dependent variable. The variables AGE and GPA are to be the independent variables. The subcommand ENTER indicates that both independent variables are to be placed in the regression equation at the same time.

DEPENDENT Subcommand

The DEPENDENT subcommand identifies the dependent variable in the regression analysis. Any variables listed as dependent must be previously named in the VARIABLES subcommand. There are two ways to specify multiple dependent variables in the same REGRESSION command. First, you can list more than one variable on a DEPENDENT subcommand. Second, you can use multiple DEPENDENT subcommands. For example, these two program segments will produce the same results:

```
      REGRESSION    VARIABLES=AGE,INC,GPA/
                    DEPENDENT=INC GPA/
                    ENTER AGE/
```

```
REGRESSION    VARIABLES=AGE,INC,GPA/
              DEPENDENT=INC/ENTER AGE/
              DEPENDENT=GPA/ENTER AGE/
```

In both of these examples, AGE is the independent variable and INC and GPA are the dependent variables. Both examples will run two regression analyses. The first will include AGE (independent variable) and INC (dependent variable), and the second will include AGE (independent variable) and GPA (dependent variable).

Method Subcommand

The method subcommand identifies the procedure used to include the independent variables in the regression model. Six equation-building methods are available in procedure REGRESSION: FORWARD, BACKWARD, STEPWISE, ENTER, REMOVE, and TEST.

The FORWARD method enters the variables into the regression equation one at a time. At each step those variables not yet in the model are examined and the one with the smallest F probability is entered—provided that this probability is smaller than the criterion set for entry.

The BACKWARD method begins by placing all variables in the regression model. Variables are then removed from the equation one at a time. At each step the variable with the largest F probability is removed—provided that the F probability is larger than the criterion set for removal.

The STEPWISE method enters variables, possibly removes them, and possibly enters them again. Specifically, if variables are already in the equation, the variable with the largest F probability is examined for removal. If the probability of F is larger than the removal criterion, the variable is removed. This process continues until no more variables need to be removed. When no more variables need to be removed, all removed variables are then examined for entry. The variable with the smallest F probability is entered if the value is smaller than the entry criterion. Once a variable has been entered, all variables are again examined for removal. This process continues until no variable in the equation needs to be removed and no variable outside of the equation needs to be entered.

The ENTER method enters all variables whose F probability is smaller than the entry criterion. While variables are entered one at a time in order of decreasing tolerance, they are treated as a single block for statistics computed on the equation. The use of ENTER without a variable list will result in the entry of all variables that pass the tolerance criterion.

The REMOVE method removes all specified variables from the equation as a single block. The REMOVE subcommand must be accompanied by a variable list.

The TEST method provides an easy way to test a variety of models using R^2 change and its test of significance as the criterion for the "best" model.

The following REGRESSION commands illustrate each of the available methods:

```
REGRESSION    VARIABLES=AGE,INC,GPA ACT/
              DEPENDENT=INC/FORWARD=AGE GPA/
```

```
                DEPENDENT=INC/BACKWARD=AGE GPA/
                DEPENDENT=INC/STEP=AGE GPA/
                DEPENDENT=INC/ENTER=AGE GPA/
                DEPENDENT=INC/REMOVE=GPA/
                DEPENDENT=INC/TEST(AGE,GPA) (AGE,ACT)
                    (GPA,ACT)/
```

MISSING Subcommand

Procedure REGRESSION has four methods of handling missing data. You may (1) omit a case if it has a missing value on any variable in the model (LISTWISE); (2) delete cases if there are missing data for the pair of variables correlated (PAIRWISE); (3) replace any missing values with the mean for that variable (MEANS); and (4) include cases with missing values (INCLUDE). The MISSING subcommand should precede the VARIABLES subcommand to which it applies. If you do not specify a missing values method, procedure REGRESSION will use the LISTWISE method (i.e., default).

```
REGRESSION      MISSING=MEANS/
                VARIABLES=AGE INC GPA ACT/
                DEPENDENT=INC/
                STEP/
```

DESCRIPTIVE Subcommand

The DESCRIPTIVE subcommand is used to request descriptive statistics with a regression analysis. Statistics available include mean, standard deviation, variance, correlation, and number of cases used to compute the correlation coefficient. If you wish only the mean, standard deviation, and the correlation coefficient, you may specify DEFAULTS. The DESCRIPTIVES subcommand must precede the VARIABLES subcommand to which it applies and it remains in effect until overridden by a new DESCRIPTIVES subcommand or until the subcommand DESCRIPTIVES= NONE is encountered.

```
REGRESSION      DESCRIPTIVES=DEFAULTS/
                VARIABLES=AGE INC GPA ACT/
                DEPENDENT=INC/ENTER/
```

SELECT Subcommand

The SELECT subcommand is used for selecting a subset of cases for computing the regression equation. Only those cases matching the select criteria will be used in computing the regression equation. However, residuals and predicted values are calculated and reported for both selected and unselected cases. The general form for the SELECT subcommand is:

```
SELECT varname relation value/
```

where:

```
SELECT     is the keyword
varname    is the variable name
relation   is the relational operator
value      is the value to be matched
/          is the delimiter
```

For example:

```
REGRESSION    SELECT AGE GT 21/
              VARIABLES=INC GPA ACT/
              DEPENDENT=INC/STEP/
```

In this example, only those cases where age is greater than 21 would be included in the regression equation. You should note that the SELECT subcommand does not override the SELECT IF and SAMPLE commands placed before the REGRESSION command. Additionally, no residuals or predictors are computed for cases deleted with the SELECT IF and SAMPLE commands.

CRITERIA Subcommand

Procedure REGRESSION tests all variables for tolerance prior to entry into an equation. The tolerance of a variable is the proportion of its variance not accounted for by other independent variables in the equation. The minimum tolerance of a variable is the smallest tolerance any variable already in the analysis would have if that variable were included in the analysis. A variable must pass both tolerance and minimum tolerance tests in order to enter a regression equation.

STATISTICS Subcommand

The STATISTICS subcommand is used to produce a number of statistics for the regression equation. There are three types of STATISTICS keywords: (1) controls for the volume of output; (2) summary statistics for the equation; and (3) statistics for the independent variables. The STATISTICS subcommand must appear before the DEPENDENT subcommand. It remains in effect for all new equations until overridden by another STATISTICS subcommand. If you wish all statistics, the keyword ALL is permissible.

for SPSS X:

```
DATA LIST SEX 1 RACE 2 CLASS 3 AGE 4-5 MS 6 GPA 7-9(2) ACT 10-12
MISSING VALUES ALL(0)
VARIABLE LABELS SEX 'SEX OF STUDENT'/RACE 'RACE OF STUDENT'/MS
  'MARITAL STATUS'
VALUE LABELS SEX 1 'MALE' 2 'FEMALE'/RACE 1 'BLACK' 2 'WHITE'
  /MS 1 'MARRIED' 2 'NOT MARRIED'
REGRESSION VARIABLES=GPA,ACT,AGE
/DEPENDENT=GPA
/ENTER
/DEPENDENT=GPA
```

```
/STEP
/DEPENDENT=GPA
/FORWARD
/DEPENDENT=GPA
/BACKWARD
/DEPENDENT=GPA
/TEST (ACT,AGE)
```

for SPSS PC+:

```
DATA LIST SEX 1 RACE 2 CLASS 3 AGE 4-5 MS 6 GPA 7-9(2).ACT 10-12
MISSING VALUES ALL(0).
VARIABLE LABELS SEX 'SEX OF STUDENT'/RACE 'RACE OF STUDENT'/MS
'MARITAL STATUS'.
VALUE LABELS SEX 1 'MALE' 2 'FEMALE'/RACE 1 'BLACK' 2 'WHITE'
/MS 1 'MARRIED' 2 'NOT MARRIED'.
REGRESSION VARIABLES=GPA,ACT,AGE
/DEPENDENT=GPA
/METHOD=ENTER
/DEPENDENT=GPA
/METHOD=STEP
/DEPENDENT=GPA
/METHOD=FORWARD
/DEPENDENT=GPA
/METHOD=BACKWARD
/DEPENDENT=GPA
/METHOD=TEST (ACT,AGE).
```

Figures 1 and 2 provide you with a complete and somewhat complex SPSS program. Figure 1 is a display of this program as it should be written for SPSS PC+. Figure 2 represents the same program written for SPSS X. Figure 3 is a small data set that can be used with either version of this program. As a practice exercise, you might try entering this program (Figure 1 or Figure 2, depending upon the system you are using) and this data set into your computer system and getting it to execute successfully. Once you have accomplished this feat, you will be ready to try your hand at writing your own SPSS program. Don't feel as though you must memorize all commands. Instead, use this appendix (as well as the original SPSS manuals) as a reference for locating the commands you need. In time and with some practice, you should find your skills improving in this important dimension of social work research.

FIGURE 1   SPSS PC+ Program Listing

```
DATA LIST FILE='SWRK3000.DAT' FREE/ID,RACE,CLASS,HOK,MS,
    CHILD,INC,WRKHR,AGE,CESD,HSYM,NORC.
COMPUTE DNORC1=NORC.
COMPUTE DNORC2=NORC.
COMPUTE DNORC3=NORC.
RECODE DNORC1  (1 THRU 52=1)  (ELSE=2).
RECODE DNORC2  (1 THRU 51=1)  (ELSE=2).
```

```
RECODE DNORC3  (1 THRU 51=1)  (53 THRU 999=2).
VARIABLE LABELS
  CLASS 'SOCIAL CLASS'/
  HOK 'HEALTH OK'/
  MS 'MARITAL STATUS'/
  CHILD 'DO YOU HAVE CHILDREN'/
  INC 'INCOME'/
  WRKHR 'WORK HOURS PER WEEK'/
  CESD 'DEPRESSION SCORE'/
  HSYM 'NUMBER OF HEALTH SYMPTOMS'/
  NORC 'OCCUPATIONAL PRESTIGE SCORE'.
VALUE LABELS
  RACE 0 'BLACK' 1 'WHITE'/CLASS 0 'WORKING' 1 'MIDDLE'/
  HOK 1 'NO' 2 'YES'/
  MS 1 'SINGLE' 2 'MARRIED'/
  CHILD 0 'NO CHILDREN' 1 'CHILDREN'.
MISSING VALUES RACE, CLASS, HOK, MS, CHILD (9)/
  INC (9999)/
  WRKHR,AGE,CESD,HSYM,NORC (999).
FREQUENCIES VARIABLES=RACE,CLASS,HOK,MS,CHILD
/FORMAT=NOLABELS DOUBLE
/BARGRAPH
/STATISTICS=MODE.
FREQUENCIES VARIABLES=INC,WRKHR,AGE,CESD,HSYM,NORC
/HISTOGRAM=NORMAL INCREMENT (5)
/PERCENTILES=25 50 75
/STATISTICS=DEFAULT
/MISSING=INCLUDE.
CROSSTABS TABLES=MS BY CHILD/STATISTICS=1.
CROSSTABS TABLES=HOK BY MS BY CHILD/STATISTICS=1.
TTEST GROUPS=MS/VARIABLES=CESD.
TTEST GROUPS=RACE(0,1)/VARIABLES=CESD.
TTEST GROUPS=CHILD(0,1)/VARIABLES=CESD.
ONEWAY CESD BY CLASS(0,1)/STATISTICS=ALL.
ONEWAY INC BY DNORC1(1,2)/STATISTICS=ALL.
ONEWAY INC BY DNORC2(1,2)/STATISTICS=ALL.
ONEWAY INC BY DNORC3(1,2)/STATISTICS=ALL.
ONEWAY INC BY RACE(0,1)/STATISTICS=ALL.
ONEWAY CESD,HSYM BY HOK(1,2)/STATISTICS=ALL.
ANOVA CESD BY RACE(0,1) CLASS(0,1)
/STATISTICS=ALL.
CORRELATION CESD,INC,HSYM,NORC,AGE.
REGRESSION VARIABLES=INC,CESD,NORC,AGE,HSYM
/DEPENDENT=CESD
/METHOD=ENTER HSYM
/DEPENDENT=CESD
/METHOD=ENTER INC
/DEPENDENT=INC
/METHOD=ENTER NORC
/DEPENDENT=HSYM
/METHOD=ENTER AGE
/DEPENDENT=CESD
/METHOD=ENTER AGE.
FINISH.
```

FIGURE 2   SPSS X Program Listing

```
DATA LIST FILE='SWRK3000.DAT' FREE/ID,RACE,CLASS,HOK,MS,
   CHILD,INC,WRKHR,AGE,CESD,HSYM,NORC
COMPUTE DNORC1=NORC
COMPUTE DNORC2=NORC
COMPUTE DNORC3=NORC
RECODE DNORC1    (1 THRU 52=1)   (ELSE=2)
RECODE DNORC2   (1 THRU 51)   (ELSE=2)
RECODE DNORC3   (1 THRU 51)   (53 THRU 999=2)
VARIABLE LABELS
  CLASS 'SOCIAL CLASS'/
  HOK 'HEALTH OK'/
  MS 'MARITAL STATUS'/
  CHILD 'DO YOU HAVE CHILDREN'/
  INC 'INCOME'/
  WRKHR 'WORK HOURS PER WEEK'/
  CESD 'DEPRESSION SCORE'/
  HSYM 'NUMBER OF HEALTH SYMPTOMS'/
  NORC 'OCCUPATIONAL PRESTIGE SCORE'
VALUE LABELS
  RACE 0 'BLACK' 1 'WHITE'/
  CLASS 0 'WORKING' 1 'MIDDLE'/
  HOK 1 'NO' 2 'YES'/
  MS 1 'SINGLE' 2 'MARRIED'/
  CHILD 0 'NO CHILDREN' 1 'CHILDREN'
MISSING VALUES RACE,CLASS,HOK,MS,CHILD (9)/
  INC (9999)/
  WRKHR,AGE,CESD,HSYM,NORC (999)
FREQUENCIES VARIABLES=RACE,CLASS,HOK,MS,CHILD
 /FORMAT=NOLABELS DOUBLE
 /BARGRAPH
 /STATISTICS=MODE
FREQUENCIES VARIABLES=INC,WRKHR,AGE,CESD,HSYM,NORC
 /HISTOGRAM=NORMAL INCREMENT (5)
 /PERCENTILES=25 50 75
 /STATISTICS=DEFAULT
 /MISSING=INCLUDE
CROSSTABS TABLES=MS BY CHILD/STATISTICS=ALL
CROSSTABS TABLES=HOK BY MS BY CHILD/STATISTICS=ALL
TTEST GROUPS=MS/VARIABLES=CESD
TTEST GROUPS=RACE(0,1)/VARIABLES=CESD
TTEST GROUPS=CHILD(0,1)/VARIABLES=CESD
ONEWAY CESD BY CLASS(0,1)/STATISTICS ALL
ONEWAY INC BY DNORC1(1,2)/STATISTICS ALL
ONEWAY INC BY DNORC2(1,2)/STATISTICS ALL
ONEWAY INC BY DNORC3(1,2)/STATISTICS ALL
ONEWAY INC BY RACE(0,1)/STATISTICS ALL
ONEWAY CESD,HSYM BY HOK(1,2)/STATISTICS ALL
ANOVA CESD BY RACE(0,1) CLASS(0,1)
STATISTICS ALL
CORRELATION CESD,INC,HSYM,NORC,AGE
REGRESSION VARIABLES=INC,CESD,NORC,AGE,HSYM
 /DEPENDENT=CESD
```

```
/ENTER HSYM
/DEPENDENT=CESD
/ENTER INC
/DEPENDENT=INC
/ENTER NORC
/DEPENDENT=HSYM
/ENTER AGE
/DEPENDENT=CESD
/ENTER AGE
FINISH
```

FIGURE 3   Data File SWRK3000
to be Used with SPSS X or SPSS
PC+ Program

```
1 1 1 2 2 0 26.5 46 33 32 4 51
2 1 1 1 2 0 33.0 40 39 00 1 53
3 1 1 2 1 1 21.5 40 34 11 6 52
4 1 1 2 1 1 18.0 35 38 22 2 60
5 1 0 1 1 1 19.5 43 35 03 2 59
6 1 0 2 1 1 18.0 40 37 04 5 59
7 1 0 2 1 0 13.5 43 58 24 2 51
8 1 0 1 1 0 23.5 40 40 17 0 51
9 0 1 1 1 1 37.5 50 36 04 2 50
0 0 1 1 2 0 18.0 40 39 10 2 54
1 0 1 1 2 0 37.5 38 39 10 1 60
2 0 1 1 1 1 22.5 50 35 01 1 50
3 0 0 2 1 1 18.0 40 31 09 3 52
4 0 0 1 1 1 25.5 40 38 05 2 51
5 0 0 2 1 1 18.0 65 33 20 3 51
6 0 0 1 1 0 42.5 45 39 05 1 71
7 1 1 2 2 0 26.5 46 33 32 4 51
8 1 1 1 2 0 33.0 40 39 00 1 53
9 1 1 2 1 1 21.5 40 34 11 6 52
0 1 1 2 1 1 18.0 35 38 22 2 60
1 1 0 1 2 0 33.0 40 39 00 1 53
2 1 0 2 1 1 21.5 40 34 11 6 52
3 1 0 2 1 1 18.0 35 38 22 2 60
4 1 0 1 1 1 25.5 40 38 05 2 51
5 0 1 2 1 1 18.0 65 33 20 3 51
6 0 1 2 1 1 18.0 40 31 09 3 52
7 0 1 1 1 1 25.5 40 38 05 2 51
8 0 1 1 1 0 42.5 45 39 05 1 71
9 0 0 2 1 1 18.0 40 31 09 3 52
0 0 0 1 1 1 25.5 40 38 05 2 51
1 0 0 2 1 1 18.0 65 33 20 3 51
2 0 0 1 1 0 42.5 45 39 05 1 71
```

APPENDIX B
Tables

TABLE 1   Random Numbers

92929	15600	47125	66114	36023
89373	91337	92426	31386	56246
60805	25733	85108	77001	76969
60279	26239	58524	91657	14523
99195	93206	14418	80796	89861
60779	19430	68981	86159	75930
53561	54945	96092	78712	60155
87174	15137	82290	92459	13838
77297	14940	94581	40548	25463
61646	75236	92790	16142	10150
49474	75428	88081	36963	91928
32907	58424	29973	60010	62546
32758	91999	84033	91978	50464
93456	55106	21961	40342	81763
88033	12221	37898	42689	94522
54717	37209	51185	87909	98281
89772	24190	62050	25482	89724
62832	64539	28856	94172	22638
71908	67947	13161	33984	61968
22329	86013	13937	39058	35790
26636	38236	90550	13019	21914
87573	87707	72224	47197	52249
18028	25459	75119	74378	93428
10580	56235	41636	53859	34927
55524	14591	59830	45678	92490
61518	45040	99841	29999	65050
78843	26464	19800	30146	27027
51683	87027	43478	15812	16911
71721	91292	30123	40799	29768
99626	10170	25845	78943	93990
79926	14150	12381	17114	24688
63149	49043	29354	93195	48952
62688	19963	22036	13792	16394

(Continued)

TABLE 1   (*Continued*)

22807	63726	91175	52574	70916
81982	78025	75916	55872	50455
30260	37838	28284	64386	80085
36602	97668	74560	55286	87311
20398	67853	46743	16786	35876
37668	16313	28010	56729	54577
30237	53763	73534	18289	89792
50504	11382	57077	64531	54026
38483	99366	46523	20320	13099
11793	70920	94363	29053	84174
54959	11820	71461	10070	95809
59459	71275	78490	60000	32466
13067	66309	30922	30028	62222
61292	93246	90171	78574	63431
32552	23301	76843	51800	67577
46725	47466	29637	72710	65828
88968	31630	71612	95515	90464
75183	53849	61322	52084	19335
49143	70942	76073	38949	41414
51269	85389	91081	68848	49366
64317	29681	42767	43590	19565
78585	98979	44680	99096	25090
47861	52732	95173	58255	40826
28561	65516	65818	58448	43041
32686	57180	25507	97600	30012
39915	36550	85080	75798	33875
57620	37034	23199	17863	29498
75732	88318	80553	43770	89998
56586	84521	59836	27534	75715
33946	97218	13399	66647	12002
43766	52407	73242	88110	32177
92607	83165	56006	88570	90881
16283	18727	51393	24325	75282
63523	61250	17375	92533	42315
11677	86526	53940	29721	72499
53925	84563	49999	75652	98587
95305	26643	94546	89264	97919
83663	57822	56985	30711	89165
19329	28799	99606	78572	56085
76931	37686	79787	15870	27576
36967	80111	41910	43528	65182
58700	31042	94954	67413	40435
17885	11383	55525	55876	37354
81610	25967	21104	41815	57849
55008	82253	60686	50306	69394
79915	48943	90998	68411	31417
21993	99060	49763	32188	55085
62494	20407	26348	62259	89562
75427	84058	80960	83999	69312
81882	40990	22141	69736	41294
20681	16590	30053	70305	73777
36385	84479	52963	66233	58234
17934	74903	90968	60063	55034

TABLE 1   (*Continued*)

75604	34421	83353	27106	38662
10329	63945	85237	17361	16734
46860	38364	29958	48665	69832
63655	22164	83356	17032	28309
75700	74318	78809	13271	38485
91052	65090	35268	38908	65321
61548	36214	98154	27439	41103
28341	60309	17322	85748	88945
15694	71824	65535	29563	18633
13465	32053	20116	85871	25854
13079	39199	46838	54094	74716
41524	50230	18332	25888	34166
53170	42409	46768	58316	20028
54262	70069	39569	76463	28015

TABLE 2 Area under the Normal Curve for Values of Z

Column 1. Values of Z (+ or –). Only positive values of Z are shown. Because the normal distribution is symmetrical, areas for negative Z-values (–Z) are the same as areas for positive Z-values.

Column 2. Proportion of the area under the normal curve between the mean and any value of Z (+ or –).

Column 3. Proportion of the area under the normal curve beyond any value of Z (+ or –).

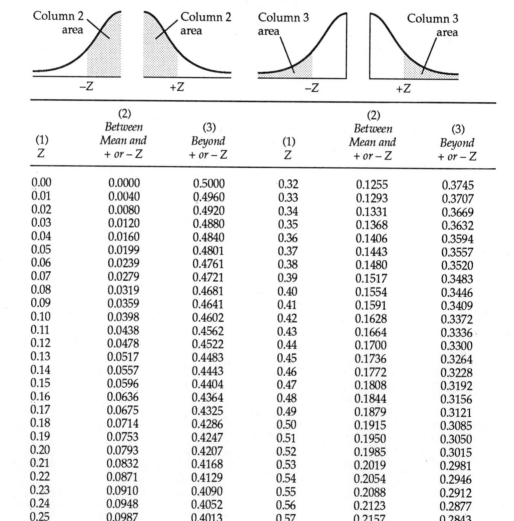

(1) Z	(2) Between Mean and + or – Z	(3) Beyond + or – Z	(1) Z	(2) Between Mean and + or – Z	(3) Beyond + or – Z
0.00	0.0000	0.5000	0.32	0.1255	0.3745
0.01	0.0040	0.4960	0.33	0.1293	0.3707
0.02	0.0080	0.4920	0.34	0.1331	0.3669
0.03	0.0120	0.4880	0.35	0.1368	0.3632
0.04	0.0160	0.4840	0.36	0.1406	0.3594
0.05	0.0199	0.4801	0.37	0.1443	0.3557
0.06	0.0239	0.4761	0.38	0.1480	0.3520
0.07	0.0279	0.4721	0.39	0.1517	0.3483
0.08	0.0319	0.4681	0.40	0.1554	0.3446
0.09	0.0359	0.4641	0.41	0.1591	0.3409
0.10	0.0398	0.4602	0.42	0.1628	0.3372
0.11	0.0438	0.4562	0.43	0.1664	0.3336
0.12	0.0478	0.4522	0.44	0.1700	0.3300
0.13	0.0517	0.4483	0.45	0.1736	0.3264
0.14	0.0557	0.4443	0.46	0.1772	0.3228
0.15	0.0596	0.4404	0.47	0.1808	0.3192
0.16	0.0636	0.4364	0.48	0.1844	0.3156
0.17	0.0675	0.4325	0.49	0.1879	0.3121
0.18	0.0714	0.4286	0.50	0.1915	0.3085
0.19	0.0753	0.4247	0.51	0.1950	0.3050
0.20	0.0793	0.4207	0.52	0.1985	0.3015
0.21	0.0832	0.4168	0.53	0.2019	0.2981
0.22	0.0871	0.4129	0.54	0.2054	0.2946
0.23	0.0910	0.4090	0.55	0.2088	0.2912
0.24	0.0948	0.4052	0.56	0.2123	0.2877
0.25	0.0987	0.4013	0.57	0.2157	0.2843
0.26	0.1026	0.3974	0.58	0.2190	0.2810
0.27	0.1064	0.3936	0.59	0.2224	0.2776
0.28	0.1103	0.3897	0.60	0.2257	0.2743
0.29	0.1141	0.3859	0.61	0.2291	0.2709
0.30	0.1179	0.3821	0.62	0.2324	0.2676
0.31	0.1217	0.3783	0.63	0.2357	0.2643

TABLE 2 *(Continued)*

(1) Z	(2) Between Mean and + or − Z	(3) Beyond + or − Z	(1) Z	(2) Between Mean and + or − Z	(3) Beyond + or − Z
0.64	0.2389	0.2611	1.11	0.3665	0.1335
0.65	0.2422	0.2578	1.12	0.3686	0.1314
0.66	0.2454	0.2546	1.13	0.3708	0.1292
0.67	0.2486	0.2514	1.14	0.3729	0.1271
0.68	0.2517	0.2483	1.15	0.3749	0.1251
0.69	0.2549	0.2451	1.16	0.3770	0.1230
0.70	0.2580	0.2420	1.17	0.3790	0.1210
0.71	0.2611	0.2389	1.18	0.3810	0.1190
0.72	0.2642	0.2358	1.19	0.3830	0.1170
0.73	0.2673	0.2327	1.20	0.3849	0.1151
0.74	0.2704	0.2296	1.21	0.3869	0.1131
0.75	0.2734	0.2266	1.22	0.3888	0.1112
0.76	0.2764	0.2236	1.23	0.3907	0.1093
0.77	0.2794	0.2206	1.24	0.3925	0.1075
0.78	0.2823	0.2177	1.25	0.3944	0.1056
0.79	0.2852	0.2148	1.26	0.3962	0.1038
0.80	0.2881	0.2119	1.27	0.3980	0.1020
0.81	0.2910	0.2090	1.28	0.3997	0.1003
0.82	0.2939	0.2061	1.29	0.4015	0.0985
0.83	0.2967	0.2033	1.30	0.4032	0.0968
0.84	0.2995	0.2005	1.31	0.4049	0.0951
0.85	0.3023	0.1977	1.32	0.4066	0.0934
0.86	0.3051	0.1949	1.33	0.4082	0.0918
0.87	0.3078	0.1922	1.34	0.4099	0.0901
0.88	0.3106	0.1894	1.35	0.4115	0.0885
0.89	0.3133	0.1867	1.36	0.4131	0.0869
0.90	0.3159	0.1841	1.37	0.4147	0.0853
0.91	0.3186	0.1814	1.38	0.4162	0.0838
0.92	0.3212	0.1788	1.39	0.4177	0.0823
0.93	0.3238	0.1762	1.40	0.4192	0.0808
0.94	0.3264	0.1736	1.41	0.4207	0.0793
0.95	0.3289	0.1711	1.42	0.4222	0.0778
0.96	0.3315	0.1685	1.43	0.4236	0.0764
0.97	0.3340	0.1660	1.44	0.4251	0.0749
0.98	0.3365	0.1635	1.45	0.4265	0.0735
0.99	0.3389	0.1611	1.46	0.4279	0.0721
1.00	0.3413	0.1587	1.47	0.4292	0.0708
1.01	0.3438	0.1562	1.48	0.4306	0.0694
1.02	0.3461	0.1539	1.49	0.4319	0.0681
1.03	0.3485	0.1515	1.50	0.4332	0.0668
1.04	0.3508	0.1492	1.51	0.4345	0.0655
1.05	0.3531	0.1469	1.52	0.4357	0.0643
1.06	0.3554	0.1446	1.53	0.4370	0.0630
1.07	0.3577	0.1423	1.54	0.4382	0.0618
1.08	0.3599	0.1401	1.55	0.4394	0.0606
1.09	0.3621	0.1379	1.56	0.4406	0.0594
1.10	0.3643	0.1357	1.57	0.4418	0.0582

TABLE 2   (*Continued*)

(1) Z	(2) Between Mean and + or − Z	(3) Beyond + or − Z	(1) Z	(2) Between Mean and + or − Z	(3) Beyond + or − Z
1.58	0.4429	0.0571	2.05	0.4798	0.0202
1.59	0.4441	0.0559	2.06	0.4803	0.0197
1.60	0.4452	0.0548	2.07	0.4808	0.0192
1.61	0.4463	0.0537	2.08	0.4812	0.0188
1.62	0.4474	0.0526	2.09	0.4817	0.0183
1.63	0.4484	0.0516	2.10	0.4821	0.0179
1.64	0.4495	0.0505	2.11	0.4826	0.0174
1.65	0.4505	0.0495	2.12	0.4830	0.0170
1.66	0.4515	0.0485	2.13	0.4834	0.0166
1.67	0.4525	0.0475	2.14	0.4838	0.0162
1.68	0.4535	0.0465	2.15	0.4842	0.0158
1.69	0.4545	0.0455	2.16	0.4846	0.0154
1.70	0.4554	0.0446	2.17	0.4850	0.0150
1.71	0.4564	0.0436	2.18	0.4854	0.0146
1.72	0.4573	0.0427	2.19	0.4857	0.0143
1.73	0.4582	0.0418	2.20	0.4861	0.0139
1.74	0.4591	0.0409	2.21	0.4864	0.0136
1.75	0.4599	0.0401	2.22	0.4868	0.0132
1.76	0.4608	0.0392	2.23	0.4871	0.0129
1.77	0.4616	0.0384	2.24	0.4875	0.0125
1.78	0.4625	0.0375	2.25	0.4878	0.0122
1.79	0.4633	0.0367	2.26	0.4881	0.0119
1.80	0.4641	0.0359	2.27	0.4884	0.0116
1.81	0.4649	0.0351	2.28	0.4887	0.0113
1.82	0.4656	0.0344	2.29	0.4890	0.0110
1.83	0.4664	0.0336	2.30	0.4893	0.0107
1.84	0.4671	0.0329	2.31	0.4896	0.0104
1.85	0.4678	0.0322	2.32	0.4898	0.0102
1.86	0.4686	0.0314	2.33	0.4901	0.0099
1.87	0.4693	0.0307	2.34	0.4904	0.0096
1.88	0.4699	0.0301	2.35	0.4906	0.0094
1.89	0.4706	0.0294	2.36	0.4909	0.0091
1.90	0.4713	0.0287	2.37	0.4911	0.0089
1.91	0.4719	0.0281	2.38	0.4913	0.0087
1.92	0.4726	0.0274	2.39	0.4916	0.0084
1.93	0.4732	0.0268	2.40	0.4918	0.0082
1.94	0.4738	0.0262	2.41	0.4920	0.0080
1.95	0.4744	0.0256	2.42	0.4922	0.0078
1.96	0.4750	0.0250	2.43	0.4925	0.0075
1.97	0.4756	0.0244	2.44	0.4927	0.0073
1.98	0.4761	0.0239	2.45	0.4929	0.0071
1.99	0.4767	0.0233	2.46	0.4931	0.0069
2.00	0.4772	0.0228	2.47	0.4932	0.0068
2.01	0.4778	0.0222	2.48	0.4934	0.0066
2.02	0.4783	0.0217	2.49	0.4936	0.0064
2.03	0.4788	0.0212	2.50	0.4938	0.0062
2.04	0.4793	0.0207	2.51	0.4940	0.0060

TABLE 2   *(Continued)*

(1) Z	(2) Between Mean and + or − Z	(3) Beyond + or − Z	(1) Z	(2) Between Mean and + or − Z	(3) Beyond + or − Z
2.52	0.4941	0.0059	2.81	0.4975	0.0025
2.53	0.4943	0.0057	2.82	0.4976	0.0024
2.54	0.4945	0.0055	2.83	0.4977	0.0023
2.55	0.4946	0.0054	2.84	0.4977	0.0023
2.56	0.4948	0.0052	2.85	0.4978	0.0022
2.57	0.4949	0.0051	2.86	0.4979	0.0021
2.58	0.4951	0.0049	2.87	0.4979	0.0021
2.59	0.4952	0.0048	2.88	0.4980	0.0020
2.60	0.4953	0.0047	2.89	0.4981	0.0019
2.61	0.4955	0.0045	2.90	0.4981	0.0019
2.62	0.4956	0.0044	2.91	0.4982	0.0018
2.63	0.4957	0.0043	2.92	0.4982	0.0018
2.64	0.4959	0.0041	2.93	0.4983	0.0017
2.65	0.4960	0.0040	2.94	0.4984	0.0016
2.66	0.4961	0.0039	2.95	0.4984	0.0016
2.67	0.4962	0.0038	2.96	0.4985	0.0015
2.68	0.4963	0.0037	2.97	0.4985	0.0015
2.69	0.4964	0.0036	2.98	0.4986	0.0014
2.70	0.4965	0.0035	2.99	0.4986	0.0014
2.71	0.4966	0.0034	3.00	0.4987	0.0013
2.72	0.4967	0.0033	3.10	0.4990	0.0010
2.73	0.4968	0.0032	3.20	0.4993	0.0007
2.74	0.4969	0.0031	3.30	0.4995	0.0005
2.75	0.4970	0.0030	3.40	0.4997	0.0003
2.76	0.4971	0.0029	3.50	0.4998	0.0002
2.77	0.4972	0.0028	3.60	0.4998	0.0002
2.78	0.4973	0.0027	3.70	0.4999	0.0001
2.79	0.4974	0.0026	3.80	0.4999	0.0001
2.80	0.4974	0.0026	3.90 +	>0.4999	<0.0001

Source: Elementary Statistics for the Social Sciences by J. Anthony Capon © 1988 by Wadsworth, Inc. Reprinted by permission of the publisher.
Note: Table values generated by a GWBASIC program on an AT&T 6300 microprocessor.

TABLE 3   Distribution of t

df	Level of significance for one-tailed test					
	.10	.05	.025	.01	.005	.0005
	Level of significance for two-tailed test					
	.20	.10	.05	.02	.01	.001
1	3.078	6.314	12.706	31.821	63.657	636.619
2	1.886	2.920	4.303	6.965	9.925	31.598
3	1.638	2.353	3.182	4.541	5.841	12.941
4	1.533	2.132	2.776	3.747	4.604	8.610
5	1.476	2.015	2.571	3.365	4.032	6.859
6	1.440	1.943	2.447	3.143	3.707	5.959
7	1.415	1.895	2.365	2.998	3.499	5.405
8	1.397	1.860	2.306	2.896	3.355	5.041
9	1.383	1.833	2.262	2.821	3.250	4.781
10	1.372	1.812	2.228	2.764	3.169	4.587
11	1.363	1.796	2.201	2.718	3.106	4.437
12	1.356	1.782	2.179	2.681	3.055	4.318
13	1.350	1.771	2.160	2.650	3.012	4.221
14	1.345	1.761	2.145	2.624	2.977	4.140
15	1.341	1.753	2.131	2.602	2.947	4.073
16	1.337	1.746	2.120	2.583	2.921	4.015
17	1.333	1.740	2.110	2.567	2.898	3.965
18	1.330	1.734	2.101	2.552	2.878	3.922
19	1.328	1.729	2.093	2.539	2.861	3.883
20	1.325	1.725	2.086	2.528	2.845	3.850
21	1.323	1.721	2.080	2.518	2.831	3.819
22	1.321	1.717	2.074	2.508	2.819	3.792
23	1.319	1.714	2.069	2.500	2.807	3.767
24	1.318	1.711	2.064	2.492	2.797	3.745
25	1.316	1.708	2.060	2.485	2.787	3.725
26	1.315	1.706	2.056	2.479	2.779	3.707
27	1.314	1.703	2.052	2.473	2.771	3.690
28	1.313	1.701	2.048	2.467	2.763	3.674
29	1.311	1.699	2.045	2.462	2.756	3.659
30	1.310	1.697	2.042	2.457	2.750	3.646
40	1.303	1.684	2.021	2.423	2.704	3.551
60	1.296	1.671	2.000	2.390	2.660	3.460
120	1.289	1.658	1.980	2.358	2.617	3.373
∞	1.282	1.645	1.960	2.326	2.576	3.291

Source: Table 3 is abridged from Table III of R. A. Fisher and F. Yates, *Statistical Tables for Biological, Agricultural and Medical Research* published by Longman Group UK Ltd., London (previously published by Oliver and Boyd Ltd., Edinburgh) and by permission of the authors and publishers.

TABLE 4 Distribution of F

$p = .05$

n_2 \ n_1	1	2	3	4	5	6	8	12	24	∞
1	161.4	199.5	215.7	224.6	230.2	234.0	238.9	243.9	249.0	254.3
2	18.51	19.00	19.16	19.25	19.30	19.33	19.37	19.41	19.45	19.50
3	10.13	9.55	9.28	9.12	9.01	8.94	8.84	8.74	8.64	8.53
4	7.71	6.94	6.59	6.39	6.26	6.16	6.04	5.91	5.77	5.63
5	6.61	5.79	5.41	5.19	5.05	4.95	4.82	4.68	4.53	4.36
6	5.99	5.14	4.76	4.53	4.39	4.28	4.15	4.00	3.84	3.67
7	5.59	4.74	4.35	4.12	3.97	3.87	3.73	3.57	3.41	3.23
8	5.32	4.46	4.07	3.84	3.69	3.58	3.44	3.28	3.12	2.93
9	5.12	4.26	3.86	3.63	3.48	3.37	3.23	3.07	2.90	2.71
10	4.96	4.10	3.71	3.48	3.33	3.22	3.07	2.91	2.74	2.54
11	4.84	3.98	3.59	3.36	3.20	3.09	2.95	2.79	2.61	2.40
12	4.75	3.88	3.49	3.26	3.11	3.00	2.85	2.69	2.50	2.30
13	4.67	3.80	3.41	3.18	3.02	2.92	2.77	2.60	2.42	2.21
14	4.60	3.74	3.34	3.11	2.96	2.85	2.70	2.53	2.35	2.13
15	4.54	3.68	3.29	3.06	2.90	2.79	2.64	2.48	2.29	2.07
16	4.49	3.63	3.24	3.01	2.85	2.74	2.59	2.42	2.24	2.01
17	4.45	3.59	3.20	2.96	2.81	2.70	2.55	2.38	2.19	1.96
18	4.41	3.55	3.16	2.93	2.77	2.66	2.51	2.34	2.15	1.92
19	4.38	3.52	3.13	2.90	2.74	2.63	2.48	2.31	2.11	1.88
20	4.35	3.49	3.10	2.87	2.71	2.60	2.45	2.28	2.08	1.84
21	4.32	3.47	3.07	2.84	2.68	2.57	2.42	2.25	2.05	1.81
22	4.30	3.44	3.05	2.82	2.66	2.55	2.40	2.23	2.03	1.78
23	4.28	3.42	3.03	2.80	2.64	2.53	2.38	2.20	2.00	1.76
24	4.26	3.40	3.01	2.78	2.62	2.51	2.36	2.18	1.98	1.73
25	4.24	3.38	2.99	2.76	2.60	2.49	2.34	2.16	1.96	1.71
26	4.22	3.37	2.98	2.74	2.59	2.47	2.32	2.15	1.95	1.69
27	4.21	3.35	2.96	2.73	2.57	2.46	2.30	2.13	1.93	1.67
28	4.20	3.34	2.95	2.71	2.56	2.44	2.29	2.12	1.91	1.65
29	4.18	3.33	2.93	2.70	2.54	2.43	2.28	2.10	1.90	1.64
30	4.17	3.32	2.92	2.69	2.53	2.42	2.27	2.09	1.89	1.62
40	4.08	3.23	2.84	2.61	2.45	2.34	2.18	2.00	1.79	1.51
60	4.00	3.15	2.76	2.52	2.37	2.25	2.10	1.92	1.70	1.39
120	3.92	3.07	2.68	2.45	2.29	2.17	2.02	1.83	1.61	1.25
∞	3.84	2.99	2.60	2.37	2.21	2.09	1.94	1.75	1.52	1.00

Values of n_1 and n_2 represent the degrees of freedom associated with the larger and smaller estimates of variance respectively.

(continued)

TABLE 4 *(Continued)*

n_2 \ n_1	1	2	3	4	5	6	8	12	24	∞
					$p = .01$					
1	4052	4999	5403	5625	5764	5859	5981	6106	6234	6366
2	98.49	99.01	99.17	99.25	99.30	99.33	99.36	99.42	99.46	99.50
3	34.12	30.81	29.46	28.71	28.24	27.91	27.49	27.05	26.60	26.12
4	21.20	18.00	16.69	15.98	15.52	15.21	14.80	14.37	13.93	13.46
5	16.26	13.27	12.06	11.39	10.97	10.67	10.27	9.89	9.47	9.02
6	13.74	10.92	9.78	9.15	8.75	8.47	8.10	7.72	7.31	6.88
7	12.25	9.55	8.45	7.85	7.46	7.19	6.84	6.47	6.07	5.65
8	11.26	8.65	7.59	7.01	6.63	6.37	6.03	5.67	5.28	4.86
9	10.56	8.02	6.99	6.42	6.06	5.80	5.47	5.11	4.73	4.31
10	10.04	7.56	6.55	5.99	5.64	5.39	5.06	4.71	4.33	3.91
11	9.65	7.20	6.22	5.67	5.32	5.07	4.74	4.40	4.02	3.60
12	9.33	6.93	5.95	5.41	5.06	4.82	4.50	4.16	3.78	3.36
13	9.07	6.70	5.74	5.20	4.86	4.62	4.30	3.96	3.59	3.16
14	8.86	6.51	5.56	5.03	4.69	4.46	4.14	3.80	3.43	3.00
15	8.68	6.36	5.42	4.89	4.56	4.32	4.00	3.67	3.29	2.87
16	8.53	6.23	5.29	4.77	4.44	4.20	3.89	3.55	3.18	2.75
17	8.40	6.11	5.18	4.67	4.34	4.10	3.79	3.45	3.08	2.65
18	8.28	6.01	5.09	4.58	4.25	4.01	3.71	3.37	3.00	2.57
19	8.18	5.93	5.01	4.50	4.17	3.94	3.63	3.30	2.92	2.49
20	8.10	5.85	4.94	4.43	4.10	3.87	3.56	3.23	2.86	2.42
21	8.02	5.78	4.87	4.37	4.04	3.81	3.51	3.17	2.80	2.36
22	7.94	5.72	4.82	4.31	3.99	3.76	3.45	3.12	2.75	2.31
23	7.88	5.66	4.76	4.26	3.94	3.71	3.41	3.07	2.70	2.26
24	7.82	5.61	4.72	4.22	3.90	3.67	3.36	3.03	2.66	2.21
25	7.77	5.57	4.68	4.18	3.86	3.63	3.32	2.99	2.62	2.17
26	7.72	5.53	4.64	4.14	3.82	3.59	3.29	2.96	2.58	2.13
27	7.68	5.49	4.60	4.11	3.78	3.56	3.26	2.93	2.55	2.10
28	7.64	5.45	4.57	4.07	3.75	3.53	3.23	2.90	2.52	2.06
29	7.60	5.42	4.54	4.04	3.73	3.50	3.20	2.87	2.49	2.03
30	7.56	5.39	4.51	4.02	3.70	3.47	3.17	2.84	2.47	2.01
40	7.31	5.18	4.31	3.83	3.51	3.29	2.99	2.66	2.29	1.80
60	7.08	4.98	4.13	3.65	3.34	3.12	2.82	2.50	2.12	1.60
120	6.85	4.79	3.95	3.48	3.17	2.96	2.66	2.34	1.95	1.38
∞	6.64	4.60	3.78	3.32	3.02	2.80	2.51	2.18	1.79	1.00

Values of n_1 and n_2 represent the degrees of freedom associated with the larger and smaller estimates of variance respectively.

(continued)

TABLE 4 (*Continued*)

$p = .001$

n_2 \ n_1	1	2	3	4	5	6	8	12	24	∞
1	405284	500000	540379	562500	576405	585937	598144	610667	623497	636619
2	998.5	999.0	999.2	999.2	999.3	999.3	999.4	999.4	999.5	999.5
3	167.5	148.5	141.1	137.1	134.6	132.8	130.6	128.3	125.9	123.5
4	74.14	61.25	56.18	53.44	51.71	50.53	49.00	47.41	45.77	44.05
5	47.04	36.61	33.20	31.09	29.75	28.84	27.64	26.42	25.14	23.78
6	35.51	27.00	23.70	21.90	20.81	20.03	19.03	17.99	16.89	15.75
7	29.22	21.69	18.77	17.19	16.21	15.52	14.63	13.71	12.73	11.69
8	25.42	18.49	15.83	14.39	13.49	12.86	12.04	11.19	10.30	9.34
9	22.86	16.39	13.90	12.56	11.71	11.13	10.37	9.57	8.72	7.81
10	21.04	14.91	12.55	11.28	10.48	9.92	9.20	8.45	7.64	6.76
11	19.69	13.81	11.56	10.35	9.58	9.05	8.35	7.63	6.85	6.00
12	18.64	12.97	10.80	9.63	8.89	8.38	7.71	7.00	6.25	5.42
13	17.81	12.31	10.21	9.07	8.35	7.86	7.21	6.52	5.78	4.97
14	17.14	11.78	9.73	8.62	7.92	7.43	6.80	6.13	5.41	4.60
15	16.59	11.34	9.34	8.25	7.57	7.09	6.47	5.81	5.10	4.31
16	16.12	10.97	9.00	7.94	7.27	6.81	6.19	5.55	4.85	4.06
17	15.72	10.66	8.73	7.68	7.02	6.56	5.96	5.32	4.63	3.85
18	15.38	10.39	8.49	7.46	6.81	6.35	5.76	5.13	4.45	3.67
19	15.08	10.16	8.28	7.26	6.61	6.18	5.59	4.97	4.29	3.52
20	14.82	9.95	8.10	7.10	6.46	6.02	5.44	4.82	4.15	3.38
21	14.59	9.77	7.94	6.95	6.32	5.88	5.31	4.70	4.03	3.26
22	14.38	9.61	7.80	6.81	6.19	5.76	5.19	4.58	3.92	3.15
23	14.19	9.47	7.67	6.69	6.08	5.65	5.09	4.48	3.82	3.05
24	14.03	9.34	7.55	6.59	5.98	5.55	4.99	4.39	3.74	2.97
25	13.88	9.22	7.45	6.49	5.88	5.46	4.91	4.31	3.66	2.89
26	13.74	9.12	7.36	6.41	5.80	5.38	4.83	4.24	3.59	2.82
27	13.61	9.02	7.27	6.33	5.73	5.31	4.76	4.17	3.52	2.75
28	13.50	8.93	7.19	6.25	5.66	5.24	4.69	4.11	3.46	2.70
29	13.39	8.85	7.12	6.19	5.59	5.18	4.64	4.05	3.41	2.64
30	13.29	8.77	7.05	6.12	5.53	5.12	4.58	4.00	3.36	2.59
40	12.61	8.25	6.60	5.70	5.13	4.73	4.21	3.64	3.01	2.23
60	11.97	7.76	6.17	5.31	4.76	4.37	3.87	3.31	2.69	1.90
120	11.38	7.31	5.79	4.95	4.42	4.04	3.55	3.02	2.40	1.56
∞	10.83	6.91	5.42	4.62	4.10	3.74	3.27	2.74	2.13	1.00

Source: Table 4 is abridged from Table V of R. A. Fisher and F. Yates, *Statistical Tables for Biological, Agricultural and Medical Research* published by Longman Group UK Ltd., London (previously published by Oliver and Boyd Ltd., Edinburgh) and by permission of the authors and publishers.

Values of n_1 and n_2 represent the degrees of freedom associated with the larger and smaller estimates of variance respectively.

TABLE 5 Distribution of x^2

Probability

df	.99	.98	.95	.90	.80	.70	.50	.30	.20	.10	.05	.02	.01	.001
1	$.0^3157$	$.0^3628$	.00393	.0158	.0642	.148	.455	1.074	1.642	2.706	3.841	5.412	6.635	10.827
2	.0201	.0404	.103	.211	.446	.713	1.386	2.408	3.219	4.605	5.991	7.824	9.210	13.815
3	.115	.185	.352	.584	1.005	1.424	2.366	3.665	4.642	6.251	7.815	9.837	11.341	16.268
4	.297	.429	.711	1.064	1.649	2.195	3.357	4.878	5.989	7.779	9.488	11.668	13.277	18.465
5	.554	.752	1.145	1.610	2.343	3.000	4.351	6.064	7.289	9.236	11.070	13.388	15.086	20.517
6	.872	1.134	1.635	2.204	3.070	3.828	5.348	7.231	8.558	10.645	12.592	15.033	16.812	22.457
7	1.239	1.564	2.167	2.833	3.822	4.671	6.346	8.383	9.803	12.017	14.067	16.622	18.475	24.322
8	1.646	2.032	2.733	3.490	4.594	5.527	7.344	9.524	11.030	13.362	15.507	18.168	20.090	26.125
9	2.088	2.532	3.325	4.168	5.380	6.393	8.343	10.656	12.242	14.684	16.919	19.679	21.666	27.877
10	2.558	3.059	3.940	4.865	6.179	7.267	9.342	11.781	13.442	15.987	18.307	21.161	23.209	29.588
11	3.053	3.609	4.575	5.578	6.989	8.148	10.341	12.899	14.631	17.275	19.675	22.618	24.725	31.264
12	3.571	4.178	5.226	6.304	7.807	9.034	11.340	14.011	15.812	18.549	21.026	24.054	26.217	32.909
13	4.107	4.765	5.892	7.042	8.634	9.926	12.340	15.119	16.985	19.812	22.362	25.472	27.688	34.528
14	4.660	5.368	6.571	7.790	9.467	10.821	13.339	16.222	18.151	21.064	23.685	26.873	29.141	36.123
15	5.229	5.985	7.261	8.547	10.307	11.721	14.339	17.322	19.311	22.307	24.996	28.259	30.578	37.697
16	5.812	6.614	7.962	9.312	11.152	12.624	15.338	18.418	20.465	23.542	26.296	29.633	32.000	39.252
17	6.408	7.255	8.672	10.085	12.002	13.531	16.338	19.511	21.615	24.769	27.587	30.995	33.409	40.790
18	7.015	7.906	9.390	10.865	12.857	14.440	17.338	20.601	22.760	25.989	28.869	32.346	34.805	42.312
19	7.633	8.567	10.117	11.651	13.716	15.352	18.338	21.689	23.900	27.204	30.144	33.687	36.191	43.820
20	8.260	9.237	10.851	12.443	14.578	16.266	19.337	22.775	25.038	28.412	31.410	35.020	37.566	45.315

df														
21	8.897	9.915	11.591	13.240	15.445	17.182	20.337	23.858	26.171	29.615	32.671	36.343	38.932	46.797
22	9.542	10.600	12.338	14.041	16.314	18.101	21.337	24.939	27.301	30.813	33.924	37.659	40.289	48.268
23	10.196	11.293	13.091	14.848	17.187	19.021	22.337	26.018	28.429	32.007	35.172	38.968	41.638	49.728
24	10.856	11.992	13.848	15.659	18.062	19.943	23.337	27.096	29.553	33.196	36.415	40.270	42.980	51.179
25	11.524	12.697	14.611	16.473	18.940	20.867	24.337	28.172	30.675	34.382	37.652	41.566	44.314	52.620
26	12.198	13.409	15.379	17.292	19.820	21.792	25.336	29.246	31.795	35.563	38.885	42.856	45.642	54.052
27	12.879	14.125	16.151	18.114	20.703	22.719	26.336	30.319	32.912	36.741	40.113	44.140	46.963	55.476
28	13.565	14.847	16.928	18.939	21.588	23.647	27.336	31.391	34.027	37.916	41.337	45.419	48.278	56.893
29	14.256	15.574	17.708	19.768	22.475	24.577	28.336	32.461	35.139	39.087	42.557	46.693	49.588	58.302
30	14.953	16.306	18.493	20.599	23.364	25.508	29.336	33.530	36.250	40.256	43.773	47.962	50.892	59.703

For larger values of df, the expression $\sqrt{2x^2} - \sqrt{2df - 1}$ may be used as a normal deviate with unit variance, remembering that the probability for x^2 corresponds with that of a single tail of the normal curve. A slightly more complex transformation, which gives far better approximations for relatively small values of v, is

$$Z = [\sqrt[3]{x^2} - \sqrt[3]{v}(1 - 2/9v)] / \sqrt[3]{v}\sqrt{2/9v}$$

(See A. C. Acock and G. R. Stavig: "Normal Deviate Approximations of x^2," *Perceptual and Motor Skills*, vol. 42, p. 220, 1976.)

Source: Table 5 is reprinted from Table IV of R. A. Fisher and F. Yates, *Statistical Tables for Biological, Agricultural and Medical Research* published by Longman Group UK Ltd., London (previously published by Oliver & Boyd Ltd., Edinburgh) and by permission of the authors and publishers.

GLOSSARY

A-B Design　A form of single-subject qualitative design in which there is a comparison between the baseline condition (A) and a treatment condition (B).

A-B-A Design　A form of single-subject qualitative design in which the baseline (A) is reinstituted after the treatment phase.

A-B-A-C-A Design　Also called successive treatments design. A form of single-subject qualitative design in which the baseline condition (A) is reintroduced several times separating each of several different treatment strategies.

A-B-C-D Design　A form of single-subject qualitative design in which the baseline (A) is established, then several different treatments are instituted successively (B-C-D, etc.).

Abstract　A short summary of the method, data, and primary findings reported in a book or journal article, together with full bibliographic identification of the source.

Anonymity　Maintaining a condition among participants in research in which the identity of individuals is not known.

Arithmetic–Logic Unit　The section of a computer that actually processes the data.

B Design　A form of single-subject qualitative design that is essentially a trial-and-error approach which lacks control of any variables.

Bar graph　One of several forms of graphic displays for research data. A pictorial presentation of a discrete variable.

Behaviorist Paradigm　The patterning of theory definition and research questions on the assumption that social behavior and social relations result from conditioning stimuli that are either rewarding or nonrewarding outcomes for individuals.

Bibliographic Reference　A listing of author(s), title, date, and place of issue of a book or periodical, sufficiently complete that any reader could correctly identify it in a research library.

Central Processing Unit (CPU)　Pertaining to a computer. A term which refers to the control unit and the arithmetic–logic unit combined.

Closed-Ended Question　A question in which a series of response alternatives are provided; also a forced-choice question.

Cluster Sample　The units are grouped by clusters instead of homogeneous strata within the population. Cluster units such as cities, neighborhoods, or census tracts are randomly selected for a sample. Cannot be truly random, since large parts of the population are excluded.

Coder Reliability　The degree to which different coders code the same data with similar results.

Coding　The assignment of numbers or category names to data determined either arbitrarily or by research design.

Cohort Analysis　The study of population characteristics by a uniform series of temporal strata such as single years, five-year strata, or ten-year strata.

Colinearity　Refers to correlations among explanatory or independent variables in multiple correlation analysis. So far as these variables are uncorrelated or weakly correlated among themselves, the multiple correlation coefficient is meaningful. If they are correlated, the multiple correlation coefficient very well may be spurious.

Comparative Analysis　Seeks parallelism and/

or contrast between two or more entirely separated cross-sections of time, or compares consistent variables across two or more cultures.

Computer Publication Search   A library service to scan a large registry of subjects, titles, and authors by accessing a central computer library, usually for a service charge.

Concept   Symbols, labels, or agreed-upon terms that describe a phenomenon. An understanding or idea or mental image; it includes a way of viewing and categorizing objects, processes, relations, and events.

Concurrent Validity   A measure is said to have concurrent validity if it has accurately measured what we already know, and can therefore be trusted in the testing of other populations.

Confidence Interval   The cases of a population distribution, typically 95 percent, included between the limits of tolerable error, typically 5 percent.

Conflict Paradigm   A patterning of theory, definition, and research questions on the assumption that competition and conflict over shares of scarce resources dominate all social relations.

Construct Validity   A measure is said to have construct validity if, at the real-world level, it varies with other measures in ways suggested by the theory.

Content Analysis   The objective and systematic accounting of selected aspects of communication (written records, verbal accounts, media forms, patterns of behavior) for purposes of comparison and assessment.

Contingency Data Cleaning   Elimination of inappropriately coded responses that depend on responses assigned to another variable.

Contingency Question   A question that depends on the response to a previous question.

Continuous Data   Data that can be indefinitely subdivided and normally arise from ratio scale of measurement. Examples include grade-point ratios and unemployment rates. Continuous variables can assume an unlimited number of possible values.

Control   The researcher's ability to manipulate an independent variable to test for predicted effects on a dependent variable.

Control Group   The set of persons or social objects randomly taken from the same population as the experimental group to test for comparative effects of the experimental treatment.

Control Unit   The part of a computer that is responsible for a program's being executed automatically without outside help.

Convenience Sample   The selection of cases that are already grouped by some other influence, such as being students in a classroom, and readily available to the researcher.

Correlation   The ratio of the covariance of two measures paired, case by case, in a sample distribution to the pooled variances of the two measures taken separately. As this ratio approaches +1.00 or –1.00, predictability from one measure to the other becomes high, as measured by the squared correlation. As the correlation approaches zero, the two measures are unrelated.

Correlation Coefficient   A measure of the strength of the relationship between two variables, X and Y.

Cross-Sectional Research   A static study that uses a sample of cases responding to a research instrument at a single point in time.

Data   A collection of measurements systematically collected in strict compliance with a research design.

Data Reduction   The ordering and simplifying of a mass of relevant research data to reveal patterns, relations, and outcomes in relatively simple, concise statements. Examples include means, standard deviation, variance, and correlation.

Deduction   A conclusion about specific cases based on the assumption that they share a characteristic with an entire class of similar cases. Deductive reasoning moves from the general to the specific.

Definition   A precise, short statement that describes and delimits a social object or relation in exact terms suitable to a research operation.

Dependent Variable   The variable expected to show "effect" resulting from manipulation of the independent or causal variable.

Descriptive Research   Research undertaken to increase precision of definition of knowledge in an area where basic parameters are not known.

Discrete Data   Data counted by integers as whole units such as age in years and number of children in the family. Discrete variables can assume only a limited or finite number of values (e.g., gender can have only two values—male and female).

Discriminant Validity   A measure is said to have discriminant validity if the measure consistently identifies or differentiates the construct being measured from other constructs.

Disproportionate Stratified Sampling   Sampling in which the researcher may oversample strata that are too small to yield sufficient numbers for statistical analysis. The sample size of each stratum is not proportionate to the size of each stratum within the population.

Empirical   Grounded in experience and fact, as observed responses, behavior, and events.

Ethics in Research   The requirement that data be collected and treated experimentally with careful attention to accuracy of measurement, fidelity to logic, and respect for the feelings and rights of respondents.

Evaluation Research   Research conducted to test for the effects of purposeful social programs, often with government support.

Evidence   Factual data and integrated reasoning that are persuasive and compelling to skeptical and well-informed judges.

Experiment   A research situation in which a controlled treatment is applied differently to two or more groups of research objects to determine the difference of effects.

Experimental Design   A pattern or system for conducting a research project, including a plan for measurement, recording, analysis, and a decision about the outcome.

Experimental Group   The set of persons or social objects, randomly selected from a population, to which an experimental treatment is applied.

Experimental Mortality   Loss of subjects through normal attrition over time when experimental design requires retesting the same subjects. Compensated for by enlarging the initial sample. (See Mortality)

Exploratory Research   Research undertaken to establish basic conditions in an area of inquiry where very little is already known.

External (Construct) Validity   Correct correspondence between the terms and findings of a research operation and the real world to which it is presumed to apply. (See Construct validity)

F Test   A statistical test to evaluate the differences among three or more sample means: ratio of larger to smaller variance.

Face Validity   The apparent reasonableness of the measure from the observer's point of view.

Facts   In scientific inquiry, refers to that which can be empirically verified.

Feasibility of a Research Question   A consideration of accessibility of data and the probable cost in time, resources, and funds in terms of the potential value of the outcome. The dedicated researcher often accepts considerable risk of expended cost and reduced payoff.

Field Experiment   Application of differential treatments to experimental and control groups in social settings that the researcher does not restrict or control.

Field Research   Studies grounded in the field of their natural occurrence. Most often, an exploratory study undertaken in a natural social setting that is not controlled and only minimally influenced by the presence of the researcher.

Formulation   Act of putting a research question into a precise statement in words, generally into a form that can be tested statistically.

Frequency Distribution   A listing of all variable values and a count of the number of times each value occurs.

Functional Paradigm   A patterning of theory, definition, and research questions on the assumption that all components of a social situation are generated and sustained by a practical need for them. Whatever is there must serve some purpose.

Generalization   A universal statement concerning an entire class of objects or events based on an observation of limited number of objects or events.

Government Documents   Official publications and records of major government agencies such as those issued by the U.S. Government Printing Office or Her Majesty's Stationer's Office in Great Britain.

Grounded Theory   Theory generated from empirical data and from extensive practical experience, as opposed to abstract speculation on convoluted semantic exercises and unfounded suppositions.

Guttman Scale   A scale developed from a series of questions ordered so as to reflect increasing acceptance or approval of an underlying social dimension.

Halo Effect   The tendency of a rater to create a generalized impression of a person (research subject) and to carry this over from one rating to the next.

Hawthorne Effect   A possible research outcome based upon the subject's positive reaction to being in a research situation. The outcomes are less affected by the control variables and more affected by uncontrolled variables (e.g., enhanced social status, positive emotional relationship with researcher, etc.).

Heterogeneity   A condition of rather wide variation and differences in kind within a population aggregate.

Historical Research   Research designed to discover and interpret the wisdom of the past, and thereby reveal something of value for the future. Common approaches are the biography, the case study, and the analysis of evolutionary trends.

History   Having to do with internal validity; specifically refers to the specific events or changes occurring between the first and second measurement of the dependent variable in addition to the manipulated independent variable.

Homogeneity   A condition of relatively similar units predominant within a population, usually characterized by relatively small variance.

Hypothesis   A statement of an unknown but expected outcome in a research operation based on a theory of the relation between variables and capable of rejection. A statement of what we ought to find if our theory is correct. A nonobvious statement that makes an assertion.

Hypothesis Cycle   Each hypothesis is a segment in a series of hypotheses that raise new and more precise questions about a research objective and that, when answered, afford the basis for a modified and more precise hypothesis.

Hypothesis Test   Looking at all evidence, both positive and negative, as a criterion for affirming or disaffirming the hypothesis. Either outcome is valuable for quality research.

Independent Variable   The variable that the researcher controls ("cause") to test for associat-

ed variation or change in another (dependent) variable.

Indexes   Differ from abstracts in that they provide only bibliographic information—no brief summary.

Induction   A conclusion about a class of objects or events based on observation of a small sample taken to represent the entire class. Inductive reasoning moves from the specific to the general.

Inferential Research   Aimed at being able to generalize sample characteristics to a total population.

Instrumentation   Development and application of a device or system for measuring differences in social behavior and response.

Internal Validity   Agreement or consistency among terms, definitions, measurements, and findings within a research report.

Interval Measurement   Assignment of cases to categories by a known dimension along an ordered scale made up of equal intervals. The placement of zero on this scale is arbitrary. Time in years, decades, or centuries is an example.

Interval Width   The number of unique values in each measurement. The highest value in a distribution minus the lowest value, plus one. Relates to range.

Intuition   A way of "knowing." Learning by direct awareness without conscious reasoning or inquiry.

Judgmental Sample   Cases selected because they manifest a property of research interest for investigation of that property, such as recidivist and nonrecidivist offenders in a limited locale.

Laboratory Experiment   Application of differential treatments to experimental and control groups under controlled conditions designed to exclude extraneous effects.

Likert Scale   A set of ranked categories, usually an odd number totaling 3 to 11, permitting a graded series of alternative responses from negative to positive, to represent the strength of a position on a question.

Literature Search   A scanning of books and journals for basic and up-to-date information on a research area, directed at original sources, and sufficiently thorough to minimize the chance of missing a relevant source.

Logic   The rules by which relations between classes of objects must be stated.

Longitudinal Research   A plan applying an instrument to samples of respondents repetitively at two or more points over a span of time. It is used to detect dynamic processes such as opinion change through time.

Matching   A system of selecting experimental subjects so as to eliminate relevant differences except the experimental treatment.

Matrix Questions   A group of related items densely packed and including response alternatives in a minimal space.

Mean   The authentic balance point of a distribution of values obtained by dividing the total of all scores by the number of scores. The mean is changed by a change in one score, and is by far the most sensitive and most precise of the measures of central tendency.

Measurement   The assignment of numerals to objects according to rule.

Measures of Central Tendency   Statistical means used to determine how a distribution of scores "bunch up" in the middle of the distribution, and how widely the scores vary above and below the center of the distribution. Three measures are the mode, median, and mean.

Median   The value that divides the ordered number of values of a distribution exactly in half. An especially important measure when there are a few extreme scores in a distribution.

Memory   The part of a computer in which data are stored.

Methodology   Processes, procedures, and principles used in approaching a research project. Method is influenced by the assumptions and interests of the researcher. Also, the study and description of research methods.

Micro   Reduced in scale, as a small-scale computer, or a small-scale dimension of social action, as in moment-by-moment analysis of behavior or response.

Mode   The most frequent value, usually occurring near the center of a distribution.

Model   A research plan or design describing the system of data collection, the presumed relations among research variables and the statistical test on which the decision will be based.

Modest Interpretation   An interpretation that recognizes the need to be very conservative in making claims from a single research operation, whatever the measured analytical outcomes.

Mortality   Refers to the dropout rate in a study; has to do with internal validity.

Multiple Baseline Design   A rather sophisticated form of qualitative research design in which the A-B logic is employed, but examines simultaneously two or more actions, subject, or situations, or some combination of these.

Multiple Regression   A measure of the change in a dependent variable associated with the combined effect of two or more independent variables. (See Regression)

Multistage Samples   Samples drawn at a series of points in time to identify the dynamics of a social property over time.

Naturalness   A state in which social action is unaltered and unaffected by the intrusion of research instruments and research personnel. There is no effort on the part of the researcher to manipulate or control subjects' behavior.

Nominal Measurement   Assignment of cases to one of a set of named categories that are mutually exclusive and logically exhaustive of the set. The names and numbers of the categories have no mathematical meaning.

Nonparticipant Observation   Nonintrusive direct observation by the researcher so as not to influence the action as it would normally occur without the observer.

Nonprobability Sample   A sample drawn from a population in which the chance of inclusion is not known. Used for those research situations in which probability samples would be extremely expensive and/or when precise representativeness is not essential.

Nonreactive Measures   Assessments of the physical impact of social action in the environment, such as the effect of vandalism on school buildings.

Null Hypothesis   An assertion that the difference between the statistics of two comparison samples is zero and that they may be from the same population. It may be rejected if the difference is large enough to assume a small error risk. It is written in an unambiguous form that negates or nullifies the descriptions or relations specified in the research hypothesis.

Open-Ended Question   A question that calls for

any words by which the respondent chooses to answer.

Operational Definition The presumption that the research outcome is defined in the way it is measured, such as the assumption that tension is whatever the tension test measures.

Ordinal Measure Assignment of cases to one of a set of rank-ordered categories based on an underlying dimension such as preferment or importance.

Panel Study A type of trend study in which the same persons making up the interview "panel" are questioned at selected times after or before a major event to identify a rate of change in public opinion.

Paradigm A pattern of beliefs, values, techniques, and theories shared by members of a scientific community as a fundamental image of subject matter within a science. Also, an illustrative or conventional pattern, model, or arrangement of physical or mental social objects.

Participant Observation Observation in which the researcher is involved in some recognized role as a part of the social process being investigated. Being a part of the action permits more accurate appraisal and analysis.

Phenomenon That which appears to the senses, including events and objects that are observed.

Pie Chart A form of graphic display for research data. A circular graph usually used to show the relative proportions of a conceptual whole.

Pilot Study Essentially a pretest of the research instrument(s) with subjects who seem to be similar to the intended research sample. Changes are sometimes made in the research design as a result of the pilot study results.

Polygon Graph A form of graphic display for research data. The polygon assumes interval data, plots the midpoints above each interval, then connects them with line segments.

Population Distribution A map or plot of all of the unique values for the variable under study and the frequency of occurrence of each value.

Posttest A reexamination of subjects after a test has been applied to measure the effect since the pretest.

Practice Wisdom An element of the professional social work knowledge base that has derived from service information and professional experience accumulated over the years.

Pragmatic Validity The utility or practicality of a research conclusion in terms of research objectives.

Predictive Validity The tendency of a research finding to support successful prediction of similar outcomes using other samples of the same population. When a measure consistently predicts correctly the quality or property that it is constructed to measure.

Pretest Pretrial of a questionnaire or other research instrument on a group of respondents similar to those of the target population. It reveals ambiguous items and flaws.

Primary Source The testimony of an eye witness, or of a witness by any other of the senses, or of a mechanical device like the dictaphone—that is, of one who was present at the events of which she or he tells. A primary source must thus have been produced by a contemporary of the events it narrates.

Principle A general truth or law basic to other truths; that which determines the nature or essence of a thing.

Probability The proportion of successes to total trials in drawing cases in a chance process.

Probability Distribution A list or map of all the possible outcomes that can occur for a designated phenomenon and the likelihood of occurrence for each outcome.

Probability Sample A sample in which the probability of selection from the total population is known.

Procedural Error Inconsistent procedures among interviewers and analysis and erroneous entry of digital data in the recording and analysis. Errors from careless data gathering, coding, and recording invalidate research findings.

Program Pertains to a computer. A sequence of instructions that causes data to be processed in some unique way.

Program Evaluation The application of one or more research skills and techniques to social service agencies, programs, or provisions to accomplish stated purposes.

Proportional Stratified Sample The number of items selected from each stratum will be proportional to the size of the stratum in the population.

Public Records   Records originated and maintained by national, state, and local agencies and usually made available for research purposes.

Publication Index   A voluminous listing by author, subject, and title of all materials published for a given year in a large collection of periodicals or books, and usually devoted to a specific area, such as social science, engineering, or medicine.

Purposive (Judgmental) Sample   Selection of a subgroup that, on the basis of information available to the researcher, can be judged to be representative of the total population.

Qualitative Research   Research that depends mainly on direct observation and descriptive analysis of social interaction and outcomes in specific social settings, sometimes relying on the intuitive skills of the researcher. It tries to describe fully and comprehend the subjective meanings events have to individuals and groups.

Quantitative Research   In social science, research that depends mainly on statistical measures to evaluate differences in variance and means in a variable presumed to have been measured. Scores are often rather arbitrarily developed from cumulative intensity of response scores to groups of items. It attempts to make generalizations to a population based on precisely measured quantities.

Quasi-Experiment   May incorporate aspects of both quantitative and qualitative research. Differs from a true experiment primarily because it lacks the randomness and control characteristic of a true experiment.

Questionnaire   An organized listing of relevant questions to elicit responses to one or more research variables in a social science survey. Questions are chosen because of their relevance, carefully worded for clarity, and carefully formulated for printed copy.

Quota Sample   A nonprobability sample with a controlled number of cases drawn by research category.

Random Assignment   Selection of individual subjects for experimental or control treatment based on a chance event, such as flipping a coin.

Random Error   Error in statistical measures that arises solely from the variability due to random selection of cases. Distortions in the measurement process resulting in fluctuations on either side of the true quantity.

Random Sample   A drawing of sample cases in which each unit and each combination of units has the same probability of being included.

Range   The range of a distribution is measured by the difference between the highest and lowest values of a distribution, plus one, and indicates the scope of breadth of the distribution.

Ratio Measurement   Application of a scale made of ordered equal intervals originating from a mathematical (natural or absolute) zero. Financial assets are scaled positively and negatively from a mathematical zero.

Regression   A measure of the change in the dependent variable of two associated measures relative to a given change in the independent variable. It is determined by the ratio of the covariance of both measures to the variance of the independent variable.

Regression Effect   The tendency for those scoring at the extremes to shift toward the middle or average position on a second test.

Reliability   The actual or presumed characteristic of data sets drawn from the same population to manifest the same measurement properties in repeated drawings. A measuring device is said to be reliable if it gives the same or almost exactly the same results on repeated measures of the same object, assuming that the object itself is stable.

Replication   Repetition of a previous research operation in all essentials to determine the consistency of results when using other samples from the same population as the original study.

Representativeness   The appearance of nearly the same statistical properties in the sample as in the population from which it is drawn. Representativeness implies "generalizability"; the ability to make inferences about the population from knowledge about the sample.

Research   A systematic process of collecting data to represent classes of objects, together with a plan to measure properties relevant to a hypothesis.

Research Design   The plan of procedures to collect data and to analyze them with reference to the research hypothesis.

Research Hypothesis   A statement that predicts a relation between two or more variables in such form that it may be put to test in a research operation.

Research Question   A question that can be answered by using research procedures and techniques.

Research Setting   The social environment in which data collection is carried out.

Rhetoric   Verbal communication including statements and value judgments intended to persuade recipients to an opinion or action.

Rival Hypothesis   A hypothesis that is a plausible alternative to the researcher's main hypothesis and that might explain the research result as well or better.

Sample   A relatively small set of cases drawn randomly from a larger population so as to represent the large population in measurable characteristics and properties.

Sample Distribution   Refers to the way in which the variable as measured is distributed in the sample. The ordered sequence of measures of a statistical sample ranging from least to greatest, generally with high frequencies in the middle of the range, and very low to vanishing frequencies at the extreme values.

Sample Size   The number of cases included in a statistical sample taken to represent a population.

Sampling Error   Variation in the measured statistical properties of samples drawn from the same population that results from chance variation of individuals.

Sampling Theory   A mathematical approach to the form of the distribution of measures for various kinds of populations. The normal curve formula is an application of sampling theory and is called a sampling distribution.

Scale   A standard of measurement providing a basis for common treatment of measured properties of social elements.

Scholarly Journal   A periodic publication by a scientific society or institution devoted to the highest standards of objectivity, evidence, and reasoning in a research field.

Secondary Source   Offers indirect or hearsay evidence by other than eyewitness, and is often an analysis and synthesis of primary sources.

Semantic-Differential Scale   Use of a series of opposed adjectives and adverbs with seven to eleven scale points between each set of extremes, such as "good–bad." An accumulation of such scale-point values permits assignment of a positional measure.

Semi-Interquartile Range   One-half of the difference between the 25th and 75th percentile scores.

Serendipitous Findings   Unexpected research outcomes that lead to new insights about a social relation, fact, or social object. Such findings may reveal widespread misconception.

Single-Subject Design   Examination of the planned change processes of one individual (can also be a family, group or organization) usually involving the establishment of a baseline condition and making comparison to it using one or more controlled treatment procedures.

Snowball Sample   Respondents are used as informants to identify other potential respondents.

Split-Half Reliability   A technique in which the items on a long measure may be divided into two halves and the responses comprising each half compared to give a measure of validity.

Standard Deviation   The square root of the mean of all squared differences between each case and the distribution mean. It measures dispersion. For any distribution, the sum of the deviations from the mean is always zero.

Standardization   The conversion of frequencies to percentages to make data sets of different sizes directly statistically comparable.

Statistical Inference   The process of inferring a population characteristic from a sample characteristic.

Stratified Random Sample   The population is divided into layers or strata. Random selection of cases made within strata of the population proportional to the size of these strata as part of the population. In this case, randomness is permitted only within strata.

Successive Treatments Design   See A-B-A-C-A Design.

Survey   A research process, usually by questionnaire or interview schedule, applied to randomly selected sample groups to determine whether the sample groups could be from the same population.

Symbolic Interactionist Paradigm   The patterning of theory, definition, and research questions on the assumption that social relations and social events arise from individuals' use and application of symbols in interpreting and sustaining the social environment.

Systematic Error   A form of bias in measurement that usually distorts data and findings in one direction (i.e., the respondent's scores will be consistently either too high or too low).

Systematic Random Sample   Selection of every nth unit, starting from a randomly selected source unit from a listing of the whole population.

t Test   A statistical test to evaluate the difference between two sample means measured by the pooled estimates of population variance calculated from the two sample variances.

Tabulation   The art of organizing and condensing data and findings into tables.

Test–Retest Reliability   A measure of agreement between the results of a test when it is administered a first and a second time to the same respondents, perhaps by different testers and/or separated by a lengthy period of time.

Theory   A reasoned set of propositions, derived from and supported by established evidence, which serves to explain a group of phenomena. It is at first conjectural and may or may not be supported by research data. If not supported, the theory may be discredited.

Theory-Research Design Relation   Theory guides the answer to the research question; research design guides the test to this answer.

Thurstone scale   A scale of equal-appearing intervals based on average rankings placed by a large group of judges on a stated social dimension.

Treatment   A controlled condition applied to an experimental group that is withheld or much reduced with a control group.

Trend Study   A form of longitudinal study wherein several cross-sectional studies are conducted successively over some designated period of time; administered to a different sample of respondents.

Triangulation   The practice of developing more than two measures of the same phenomenon to serve as a check on accuracy in the measurement.

Unit of Analysis   A concrete research case used to address the research question.

Validity   A particular research measure does indeed measure what it is purported to measure. The actual or presumed characteristic of a research outcome to be true and factual with regard to the class of objects treated.

Value-Aware Research   Scientific inquiry based on the understanding that the human condition does not allow for totally value-free inquiry, but rather strives to understand and control for value aspects in a research design.

Value-Free Research   Scientific inquiry on a problem open to doubt in which the researcher freely follows the implications of the data and the hypothesis. Researchers who falsify data or the reasoning process to favor a hypothesis are invalidating the research operation.

Variable   A measure of a social property or condition that varies from case to case in a sample set of cases.

Variance   The sum of the squared deviations from the mean divided by the number of squared deviations. The concept of variance also applies to the population distribution but generally is not attainable.

z Score   A deviation of a score from the sample mean, measured in units of the sample standard deviation.

Index

Abstraction, ladder of, 21
Abstracts, 45–51, *table*, 49
  in research report, 363–364
  Sociological Abstracts, 45, *figure*, 46
Accidental samples (*see* Convenience samples)
Accreditation, 3–4
Adequacy of the fit, 331, 336
American Dilemma, An, 126
American Psychological Association, 96
Analysis of evolutionary trends (*see* Historical research)
Analytic research (*see* Historical research)
Appendix, in research report, 381
Area under the normal curve for values of Z, *table*, 420–423
Arithmetic-logic unit, computer, 281
Authority, as source of knowledge, 15
Autocorrelation, 339–340
Availability sample (*see* Convenience samples)

Bar graph, 299–300, *figure*, 300
Becker, Howard, 252
Behaviorism, 77–79
Belmont Report: Ethical Principles and Guidelines for the Protection of Human Subjects of Research, The, 87
Berelson, Bernard, 261
Bias, 101, 216
Biographical Dictionary of Social Welfare in America, 254
Biography, 115, 254
Bridgeman, Percy, 27

Card catalogs, 38, 42–43
Card, computer, 285–288, *figure*, 286
Case study, 115, 254
Central processing unit (CPU), 281
Change scores, 244–245
Chicago School, 252
Citation indexing, 50
Classical theory, 124–125
Clinical care evaluation study, 270
Closed-ended questions, 223, 226, 284
Cluster samples, 185–186
Codebook, computer, 283, *figure*, 288
Coding
  categories, 262
  computer data, 282–285
Coefficient of reproducibility, 156–157
Cohen, Morris, 30
Cohort analysis, 221–222
Colinear data, 340–341
Common sense, as source of knowledge, 13–14
Comparative analysis, 117, 263–264
Computers, 280–281
  block diagram, *figure*, 281
  in report writing, 362
  searches, 51, 257
Concepts, 70–71
Concurrent validity, 167
Confidence interval estimate, 190–191
Consistency (*see* Reliability)
Construct validity, 29, 168
Contamination, 206
Content analysis, 104, 117, 160–161, 260–262

Content validity, 167
Contingency cleaning, data, 292
Contingency questions, 226
Continued stay utilization review, 270
Continuous frequency distribution:
  definition of, 302–303
  graphing, 304–306
Continuous variables, 297
Contrast error, 150
Control, in evaluation research, 110
Control unit, computer, 280–281
Convenience samples, 187
Correlation coefficient, 331
Correlation and regression, 328–344
Cost analysis, 270, *figure*, 271
Council on Social Work Education
      (CSWE), 3–4, 9, 251
Crisis intervention, 79–81
Cronbach's alpha, 169–170
Cross-cultural studies, 263–264
Cross-sectional surveys, 105, 219–220
Current Population Survey, 215–216

Data:
  collection, 119, 259
  editing, 291–293
  formatting for computer input, 285–288
  interpretation and consequences of in-
      ductive and deductive reasoning,
      355–358
    ethical nature of, 348
    paradigms, 346–352
    research consequences, 352–355
  keypunching, 288–291
  meaning of, 276
  organizing and reducing
    reasons for, 276–277
    role of computer in, 277–281
  preparing for computer input, 282–285
  storing, 293–294
Data analysis:
  descriptive statistics
    continuous frequency distribution,
      302–306
    descriptive summary measures,
      306–315
    discrete and continuous data, 297
    discrete frequency distributions,
      298–302

role of statistical methods in re-
      search, 296–297
  inferential statistics
    correlation and regression, 328–344
    description of, 316–317
    F test for three or more independent
      samples, 325–328
    normal curve, 317–318, *figure*, 318
    standard normal curve, 319–324
    t test for two independent samples,
      324–325
de Moivre, Abraham, 317–318
Deception, 91–94
Decision-oriented evaluation, 271–272
Deductive reasoning, 21, 248–249, 355–358
Definitions, in theories, 71
Description, as a research purpose, 109
Descriptive statistics, 295–315
Descriptive summary measures:
  measures of central tendency, 306–309
  measures of variability, 309–315
Design (*see* Research design)
Direct keyboard entry, data, 291
Discrete frequency distributions:
  definition of, 298
  graphing, 299–300
  grouping discrete data, 301
  handling missing data, 299
Discrete variables, 297
Discriminant validity, 168
Discussion section, in research report,
      373–377
Distribution of *F*, *table*, 425–427
Distribution of *t*, *table*, 424
Distribution of x^2, *table*, 428–429
Documentary analysis (*see* Historical re-
      search)
Double Helix, The, 26
Durkheim, Emil, 126–127, 136

Edge coding, data, 290
Editing:
  data, 291–293
  research report, 381
Encyclopedia of Social Work, 37–38
Epistemology, 247–248
Equivalence, 199–200
Errors:
  coding, 284
  measurement, 163–166

Ethics :
    current considerations, 88–89
    federal influences on research, 90–91
    interpretation, 348
    issues in, 91–96
    NASW Code of Ethics, 3, 6, 89–90
    research questions, 61
    resolutions to dilemmas in, 96–97
    in social research, 3, 6
    in social work and social science re-
        search, 89–90
    as an urgent issue, 86–88
Evaluation (*see* Program evaluation)
Evaluation research, 110–112, 206–207
Evidence, 131–136
Ex-post facto experiment (*see* Quasi-exper-
    iment)
*Experimental and Quasi-Experimental De-
    signs for Research*, 207
Experimental design, 104
Experiments:
    control group, 197
    creating equal groups, 198–200
    experimental group, 197
    external validity, 210
    field, 112–113, 205–207
    independent variable, 200–202
    internal validity, 207–210
    laboratory, 112
    laboratory versus field, 204
    posttest-only control group design,
        203–204
    pretest/posttest design, 202–203
    true versus quasi-, 211–212
    variables, 197
Explanation, as a research purpose,
    108–109
Exploration, as a research purpose, 109
External validity (*see* Construct validity)

F-Test for three or more independent sam-
    ples, 325–328
Face validity, 167
Facts, 70–71
Field experiments:
    control in, 206–207
    versus laboratory experiments, 204
Field research, 115, *figure*, 116, 251–252
Field studies, 105
Flexner, Abraham, 246

Format, data, 285–286
Frequency distributions:
    continuous, 302–306
    discrete, 298–301
Functionalism, 75–76

Generalizability, 210, 262 (*see also* Validity)
Generosity error, 150
Genuineness, 29
Goldberg, Phillip, 35
Grounded theory, 125–126, 249
Groups, 104
    control, 197–198
    equal
        matching, 198–200
        random assignment, 199–200
    experimental, 197
Guttman scales, 156–158, *figure*, 158

Halo effect, 149–150
Hammond, Phillip, 26
Haphazard samples, 216
Health and Social Work, 44
Histogram, 304–305
Historical analysis (*see* Historical research)
Historical and public records, as nonreac-
    tive measures, 160
Historical research, 115, 117
    comparative analysis, 263–264
    content analysis, 260–262
    locating sources and retrieving informa-
        tion, 257–258
    primary and secondary sources,
        256–257
    process of, *figure*, 255
    report writing, 259–260
    single-subject design, 264–268
    synthesizing information, 258–259
    types of, 254–255
History, and internal validity, 207–208
Humphreys, Laud, 92–93, 252
Hypotheses, 21, 70, 72, 201–202
    characteristics of, 127–131
    construction, related to theory, 124–126
    definition of, 123–124
    and hypothesis cycle, 136–139
    null, 127
    research, 126–127
    testing, 131–132
    testing typology, 126–127

Hypotheses (*Contd.*)
   triangulation, 132
   use of evidence in testing, 133–136

Independent variable, 200–202
Indexes, 45–51
Induction, 21
Inductive reasoning, 248–249, 355–358
Inferential statistics, 316–344
Input/output (I/O), computer, 281
Instrumentation, 209
Internal consistency, 169–170
Internal validity, 28–29
Interval level of measurement, 145
Interviews, 235–238
Introduction, in research report, 364–367

Joint Commission on Accreditation of
   Hospitals, 269

Keypunching, data, 288–291
Knowledge, everyday sources of, 13–15
Kuhn, Thomas, 16

Laboratory experiments, 204
Ladder of abstraction, 21
Lakoff, Robin, 35
Likert scales, 107, 153–156, *figure,* 153
Literature search, 37–51
Logical positivism, 247
Longitudinal studies, 105, 220
Lundberg, George, 27
Lynd, Robert, 30

Marketing surveys, 217
Maslow, Abraham, 26
Matching, 198–199
Matrix form, 277, *figure,* 278, *figure,* 282
Matrix questions, 226, *figure,* 227
Matrix, data, *figure,* 289
Maturation, 208–209
Mean, 307–309
Measurement:
   comparison of scaling techniques, 159
   evaluating adequacy of, 166–170
   levels of, 143–146
   meaning of, 141
   nonreactive measures, 159
   reasons for, 141–142
   scales as measures, 147–158
   single indicators as measures, 146

sources of error, 163–166
   theory of, 161–162
   types of errors in, 162–163
Median, 307–309
Memory, computer, 280
Merton, Robert, 376
Methodology, 18–19
Methods section, in research report,
   367–370
Milgram, Stanley, 95–96
Mitroff, Ian, 23–24, 34
Mode, 307–309
Models of practice:
   behavioral, 77–79
   crisis intervention, 79–81
   functionalist, 75–76
   problem-solving, 76–77
   psychosocial, 73–75
   task-centered, 81
Mortality, 210
Multiple baseline designs, 118, 267–268
Multiple correlation and regression analy-
   sis, 334–344
Multistage samples, 186, 215
Myrdal, Gunnar, 125–126

National Association of Social Workers
   (NASW), 3, 6, 9, 89–90
National Commission for the Protection of
   Human Subjects of Biomedical and
   Behavioral Research, 87
Naturalness, in evaluation research,
   111–112
New Rules, 356
Nominal level of measurement, 143
Nonrandom sampling, 216
Nonreactive measures:
   content analysis, 160–161
   historical and public records, 160
   physical traces, 159
   social artifacts, 103–104
Normal curve, 317–318, *figure,* 318
Null hypotheses, 127
Nuremberg Code, 4

Obedience to Authority, 94
Objectivity, 101, 261
Observation, participant, 252–253
Open-ended questions, 223, 284
Operational definitions, 26–28
Operationalization, 27

Optical scanning sheets, 290
Ordinal level of measurement, 143–144

Panel studies, 221
Paradigms, 16–17, 23, 72–73, *figure*, 83, 346–352
Park, Robert, 252
Participant observation, 252–253
Peer review program evaluation, 270
Performance objectives, 270
Permuterm indexing, 50
Physical traces, as nonreactive measures, 160
Pie chart, 300, *figure*, 301
Pilot study, 228
Polling, 175–177
Polygon, 305–306
Population, 172, 175, 177
Postcoding, 284
Practice wisdom, 4–5
Pragmatic validity, 28
Precoding, 284
Predictive validity, 28, 167
Pretesting, 228
Primary sources, 256–257
Probability distribution, 317, 320–324
Problem-solving practice model, 76–77
Process analysis, 271
Professional Standards Review Organization, 269
Profile analysis, 270
Program, computer, 280
Program evaluation, 268–272
Proportional stratified samples, 184–185
Psychological Abstracts, 45–51
Psychology of Science, The, 26
Psychosocial practice model, 73–75
Public opinion polling, 216
Punch cleaning, data, 291–292
Purposive or judgmental samples, 187
Pygmalion effect, 92

Qualitative research:
    comparative analysis, 263–264
    compared with quantitative research, 247–251
    content analysis, 260–262
    field research, 251–253
    historical perspective on, 245–247
    historical research, 253–260
    and program evaluation, 268–272
    single-subject design, 264–268
Quality assurance, 269
Quantitative measurement, 161–162
Quantitative research, 141
Quasi-experiment, 211–212, 244
Questionnaires:
    content, 224–225
    cover letter and introduction, 227–228
    face-to-face interviews, 235–238
    format, 225–226
    mailed, 234–235
    pretesting, 228
    reviewing and revising, 227
    sample, *figure*, 228–233
    self-administered, 233
    types of questions in, 222–223
Quota sampling, 188, 216

Random assignment, 199–200
Random numbers, *table*, 417–419
Random sampling, 216
Range, 309
Ratio level of measurement, 145–146
Real group, 104
References, in research report, 377–379
Regression effect, 209–210
Reid, William, 30
Reliability, 29, 168–170
Repeatability (*see* Reliability)
Replication, 102, 135–136
Report writing:
    chronological, 259–260
    and editing and revising, 381
    factors to consider in, 360–361
    organization in, 362–381
    reasons for, 359–360
    scientific, 361–362
    thematic, 259–260
Representativeness, 111, 174, 189
Research:
    applied, 30
    consequences of, 352–355
    deceptive, 91–94
    design
        choosing, 102–112, 118
        definition of, 100–101
        importance of, 101–102
        qualitative, 115–118
        quantitative, 112, 115
        theory related to, 101

Research (*Contd.*)
field, 251–252
historical (*see* Historical research)
human activity, 12
hypotheses, 126–127
journals, *figure*, 6
manipulation, 94–95
objectives, 218
process, 11–19
pure, 30
qualitative (*see* Qualitative research)
questions
    choosing, 35–37
    definitions, 33
    ethics in, 61
    evaluating, 58–61
    formulating, 37–58
    literature search, 37–51
    role of values in choosing and for-
        mulating, 34
relevance of, 1–2
report writing, 359–382
role of statistical methods in, 296–297
and social work education, 2–10
subject, 33
terminology, 28–29
theory, 346–347
use of surveys in, 217–218
Researchers, 248
Responsive evaluation, 272
Results section, in research report, 370–373
Richmond, Mary, 246
Risk-benefit analysis, 96
Rival hypotheses, 201–202

Sample distribution, 179–180
Samples:
nonprobability
    cluster samples, 185–186
    convenience samples, 187
    purposive or judgmental samples,
        187
    quota samples, 188
    snowball samples, 187
probability
    disproportionate stratified samples,
        185
    multistage samples, 186
    proportional stratified samples,
        184–185
    simple random samples, 183

stratified random samples, 184
systematic random samples, 183–184
size
    determining, 191–194
    z-score transformation, 189
Sampling:
definitions, 172
distribution of the sample means, 180
error, 193
frame, 174, 184
multistage, 215
nonrandom, 216
plans, 182–189
quota, 216
random, 216
reasons for, 173–174
representativeness, 174–177
theory, 177–182
Scales:
comparison of, 159–161
definition of, 147
questionnaire-based, 150–151
    Guttman, 156–158
    semantic-differential, 157–158
    Thurstone, *figure*, 151
rating, 147–150
    comparative, 149
    errors in, 149–150
    graphic, 147, *figure*, 148
    itemized, 148–149
Science:
definition of, 19
elements of, 19–22
goal of, 20
language and rhetoric of, 26–29
practice of, 23–29
promise and limitations of, 29–31
social work and, 63–65
traditional models of, 19–22
Scientific attitude, 19–31
Secondary data, 240–242
Secondary sources, 256–257
Selective perception, 101–102
Semi-interquartile range, 309–310
Serendipity, 55–56, 138–139
Settlement House Movement, 245
Simple random samples, 183
Single-measure indicator, 146–147
Single-subject design:
characteristics of, 264–265
types of, 265–268

Single-subject research, 117
Single-variable rule, 265
Smith, Norman J., 26
Snowball samples, 187
Social Diagnosis, 246
Social Science Citation Index, 45–51, 257
Social service interventions, 2–3
Social Work, 44
Social Work Dictionary, 38
Social Work in Education, 44
Social Work Research and Abstracts, 44
Social workers, 2–8
Sociological Abstracts, 45–51
Sociologists at Work, 26
Split-half reliability, 169
SPSS (Statistical Package for the Social Sciences):
    data definition commands, 384–390
    data transformations, 390–398
    language of SPSS X and SPSS PC+, 383–384
    procedure commands, 398–413
Squared correlation coefficient, 332
Standard deviation, 181, 310–315
Standard error of the estimate, 331, 337
Standard normal curve, 319–324
Statistical groups, 104–105
Statistical inference, 177, 317
Statistical methods, 296–297
Stephens, William, 123
Storage, data, 293–294
Stratified random samples, 184
Structure of Scientific Revolutions, The, 16
Successive treatment research, 118
Surveys:
    and constructing a questionnaire, 222–233
    definition of, 214–218
    design of, 105, 115
    face-to-face interviews, 235–238, 239
    mailed questionnaires, 234–235
    planning, 218–222
    self-administered questionnaires, 233, 239
    strengths and weaknesses of, 239–240
    telephone interviews, 238–239
    and use of secondary data, 240–242
Systematic random samples, 183–184
Systems analysis, 270–271

t-Test for two independent samples, 324–325

Tables, in research report, 379–380
Task-centered model of practice, 81–82
Tearoom Trade, 92–93, 252
Testing, 209
Test-retest reliability, 169
Theory:
    classical, 124–125
    definitions of, 70–72
    development of social work theory, 68–70
    dominant models of practice, 73–82
    grounded, 125–126
    paradigms, 72–73
    purpose of, 70
    relationship between theory and practice, 65–68
    science and social work and, 63–65
Thurstone scales, 151–152
Time order, variables, 201
Tradition, source of knowledge, 14–15
Transfer sheet, 288–289
Treatment group, 104
Trend studies, 220–221
Triangulation, 119–120, 132
True experiment, 211–212

Unit of analysis, 102–105, 262
United States Census, 215–216

Validity, 28–29, 166–168, 170
    external, 210
    internal
        experimental mortality, 210
        history, 207–208
        instrumentation, 209
        maturation, 208–209
        regression effect, 209–210
        testing, 209
Values, 34–58, 128, 248
Variables, 108, 197
    continuous, 297
    discrete, 297
    manipulation of, 201–202
Variance, 310–315

Wallin, Paul, 157
Warner, Lloyd, 131–132
Watson, James, 26
Weber, Max, 124–125

z-Score transformation, *figure*, 319

This constitutes an extension of the copyright page.

pp. 167, 169, 193, 255, 256, 258, 262, and 263 from Williamson, Karp, Dalphin, and Gray, *The Research Craft: An Introduction to Social Research Methods,* 2nd ed., © 1982. Reprinted by permission of Scott, Foresman and Company.

pp. 27, 183–84, 185, 187, 193–94, 244, 247, 248, 249, 254, 255, 259, and 271 reproduced by permission of the publisher, F. E. Peacock Publishers, Inc., Itasca, Illinois. From Richard M. Grinnell, Jr., *Social Work Research and Evaluation,* 3rd ed., 1988, copyright © 1988 by F. E. Peacock Publishers, Inc.

pp. 244, 245, 246, 248, and 250 from Rodwell, Mary, "Naturalistic Inquiry: An Alternative Model for Social Work Assessment," *Social Service Review* (June 1987), pp. 241–246. Copyright © 1987 by The University of Chicago. All rights reserved.

pp. 269 and 270 from "Single-Subject Evaluation: A Tool for Quality Assurance," *Social Work,* Vol. 31(5), September 1986, pp. 359, 360, and 363 by Elaine M. Nuehring and Anne B. Pascone. Reprinted with permission. Copyright 1986, National Association of Social Workers, Inc.

pp. 23 through 25 from "Norms and Counternorms in a Select Group of the Apollo Moon Scientists: A Case Study of the Ambivalence of Scientists," by Ian I. Mitroff, *American Sociological Review,* Vol. 39, August 1974, pp. 579–94.

pp. 59–60, 92–93, and 252 adapted with permission from Laud Humphreys, *Tearoom Trade: Impersonal Sex in Public Places* (New York: Aldine de Gruyter). Copyright 1970, 1975 by R. A. Laud Humphreys.

pp. 117, 160, 260, 261, and 262 from *Content Analysis in Communication Research* by Bernard Berelson (Hafner Press, Macmillan Publishing Company, N.Y., 1971). Copyright, 1952, by Bernard Berelson. Reprinted by arrangement with The Free Press, A Division of The Macmillan Company, 1971.